MW01634266

Educational Communications and Technology: Issues and Innovations

Series Editors
J. Michael Spector
M. J. Bishop
Dirk Ifenthaler

More information about this series at http://www.springer.com/series/11824

Xun Ge • Dirk Ifenthaler • J. Michael Spector
Editors

Emerging Technologies for STEAM Education

Full STEAM Ahead

 Springer

Editors
Xun Ge
University of Oklahoma
Norman
Oklahoma
USA

J. Michael Spector
College of Information
University of North Texas
Denton
Texas
USA

Dirk Ifenthaler
University of Mannheim
Mannheim
Germany

Educational Communications and Technology: Issues and Innovations
ISBN 978-3-319-02572-8   ISBN 978-3-319-02573-5 (eBook)
DOI 10.1007/978-3-319-02573-5

Library of Congress Control Number: 2015945813

Springer Cham Heidelberg New York Dordrecht London

Preface

There has been a great deal written about the need for addressing the 21st century digital literacy in curricula at all levels and the particular concerns about failing to prepare college graduates for careers in science, technology, engineering, the arts, and humanities (STEAM), as well as other career areas. However, there is not much scholarly work existing to address those concerns. It is commonly accepted that there is a need to reconceptualise and reform curricula at all levels, from K-12 to college and graduate level in order to successfully prepare college graduates for the STEAM professions. The field needs theoretical and practical works to guide educational researchers and practitioners in efforts to prepare future generations to meet the challenges of the 21st century and be creative and productive problem solvers.

This volume places emphasis on reconceptualising curricula for K12 and higher education in various domains. It includes invited chapters from a symposium on Emerging Technologies and STEAM Education that was held at the University of Oklahoma in Spring 2013 as well as contributions from an open call which was disseminated in Fall 2013.

We organised the chapters included in this edited volume into five major thematic parts (excluding Part I - Prologue and Part VII - Epilogue): (1) Science, (2) Technology and Technology Integration, (3) Engineering, (4) Arts, and (5) Mathematics. Our intention is not to isolate these subjects in the context of STEAM education, but rather to examine how the Arts (i.e., language, arts, design disciplines, and the humanities) can be integrated into STEM disciplines, or vice versa, to promote learners' 21st century skills.

The first chapter of this volume focuses on technology-enhanced learning informed by the arts and humanities as a way to balance tensions between individual and societal interests (J. Michael Spector, Chapter "Education, Training, Competencies, Curricula and Technology").

In Part II, chapters place emphasis on the science domain. Chapter "Active Learning Approaches to Integrating Technology into a Middle School Science Curriculum Based on 21st Century Skills" describes active learning strategies that are not currently widely adopted but have been shown to be effective in enhancing middle school deep learning of content, as well as fostering positive dispositions toward science and related fields (Rhonda Christensen and Gerald Knezek, Chapter "Active Learning Approaches to Integrating Technology into a Middle School Science Curriculum Based on 21st Century Skills"). The next chapter examines how to prepare students with critical skills to succeed in the 21st century (Jiangyue Gu and Brian R. Belland, Chapter "Preparing Students with 21st Century Skills: Integrating Scientific Knowledge, Skills, and Epistemic Beliefs in Middle School Science Curricula"). In Chapter "Reconceptualizing a College Science Learning Experience in the New Digital Era: A Review of Literature", three interrelated core principles that can help design coherent science instruction, curriculum, and assessments at the college level that meet the needs of the new digital era are proposed (Ji Shen, Ou Lydia Liu, and Shiyan Jiang, Chapter "Reconceptualizing a College Science Learning Experience in the New Digital Era: A Review of Literature"). In the final chapter of this part, the history behind teaching science, such as its impact on the workforce today, the inclusion of STEAM and 21st century skills, and its influence on teaching and learning in the middle school classrooms are examined (October Smith, Chapter "There is an Art to Teaching Science in the 21st Century").

In Part III, chapters focus on technology and technology integration. Chapter "An Indigenous Learning Approach to Computer Science Education" focuses on the ANCESTOR (AborigiNal Computer Education through Storytelling) program that was developed to explore computer science as a career option through digital storytelling and to address cultural literacy with Aboriginal youth in British Columbia, Canada (Dianne Biin and Marla Weston, Chapter "An Indigenous Learning Approach to Computer Science Education"). In Chapter "The Potential of Embodied Cognition to Improve STEAM Instructional Dynamic Visualizations", a diverse number of studies that show the instructional benefits of embodied cognition, manipulations, and gestures are reviewed. Specifically, the authors address how these evolved skills can be employed to effectively learn from STEAM dynamic visualizations (Juan C. Castro-Alonso, Paul Ayres, Fred Paas, Chapter "The Potential of Embodied Cognition to Improve STEAM Instructional Dynamic Visualizations"). The next chapter attempts to re-conceptualize the engagement of STEAM teacher-candidates with technology during their formative years in order to help them meet these rapidly changing goals (Marina Milner-Bolotin, Chapter "Technology-Enhanced Teacher Education for 21st Century: Challenges and Possibilities"). Chapter "Using Mobile Devices to Support Formal, Informal and Semi-formal Learning" explains how individuals learn using mobile devices during their daily lives—within K-12 schools, higher education, and outside of educational institutions altogether—with specific attention to STEAM disciplines (Michael M. Grant, Chapter "Using Mobile Devices to Support Formal, Informal and Semi-formal Learning"). In the final chapter of this part, factors to drive the explosive growth of mobile devices in STEAM are discussed (Hong Lin, Chapter "Implementing Large-Scale Mobile Device Initiatives in Schools and Institutions").

In Part IV, chapters report issues facing the field of Engineering education. The first chapter of this part documents findings focusing on the students' change of attitudes, self-concept, and team dynamics while taking the re-designed graduate course *Designing for Open Innovation* (Dirk Ifenthaler, Zahed Siddique and Farrokh Mistree, Chapter "Designing for Open Innovation: Change of Attitudes,

Self-Concept, and Team Dynamics in Engineering Education"). The next chapter discusses the implementation of "pillar" courses, particularly with regards to meta-cognitive awareness, critical and creative thinking, while emphasizing the potential of Tablet PCs and associated technologies (Enrique Palou, Silvia Husted, Gladis Chávez-Torrejón, Zaira Ramírez Apud, Lourdes Gazca, Judith Virginia Gutiérrez Cuba, Nelly Ramírez-Corona, and Aurelio López-Malo, Chapter "Critical Support Systems to Enhance the Development and Assessment of 21st Century Expertise in Engineering Students").

In Part V, chapters place emphasis on the arts domain. The first chapter of this part questions to what extent are the language arts relevant, useful, and self-sustaining in an era of rapid technological and scientific innovation (Lawrence Baines, Chapter "The Language Arts as Foundational for Science, Technology, Engineering, Art, and Mathematics"). The next chapter seeks to connect current debates about the value of traditional liberal arts education to emerging trends in the learning sciences that promote metacognition, active learning, and other 21st century skills (Armanda L. Lewis, Chapter "Putting the "H" in STEAM: Paradigms for Modern Liberal Arts Education"). Chapter "Reconceptualizing Liberal Education in the 21st Century" reviews the essential learning outcomes that students develop through a 21st Century liberal education, along with principal themes in the literature about higher education and shows examples of high impact liberal education practices in both European and American colleges and universities (Aytac Gogus, Chapter "Reconceptualizing Liberal Education in the 21st Century"). The final chapter of this part makes the assertion that the addition of STEAM will prepare liberal arts graduates with the skills required for a 21st century knowledge based economy (Michael Marmon, Chapter "Predicting The Future: Altering the Course of Future Liberal Arts Curriculum through an Examination of the Discipline and the Addition of Steam Elements").

In Part VI, chapters focus on issues in the mathematics curriculum. Chapter "The 21st Century Mathematics Curriculum: A Technology-enhanced Experience" focuses on the 21st Century Skills, students' problem posing, and technology integration as vehicles to change classroom mathematics (David A. Coffland and Ying Xie, Chapter "The 21st Century Mathematics Curriculum: A Technology-enhanced Experience"). The next chapter inspects how logic is expected to be taught according to the USA K-12 Common Core State Standards and how it is compared with the Singapore curriculum (Hong Liu, Maria Ludu, and Douglas Holton, Chapter "Can K-12 Math Teachers Train Students to Make Valid Logical Reasoning?"). The last chapter of this part reviews the theoretical foundation of model-centered learning and instruction and elaborates a model-centered prospective on the teaching and learning of middle and high school mathematics (Lingguo Bu and Markus Hohenwarter, Chapter "Modeling for Dynamic Mathematics: Toward Technology-Integrated Aesthetic Experiences in School Mathematics").

The final chapter of this edited volume revisits the concept of STEAM and reflects on the future of STEAM as a research and pedagogical concept (Xun Ge, Dirk Ifenthaler, and J. Michael Spector, Chapter "Moving Forward with STEAM Education Research").

The editors acknowledge the generous funding of the symposium on Emerging Technologies and STEAM Education by the University of Oklahoma under the Faculty Investment Program and the Jeannine Rainbolt College of Education. Without the assistance of experts in the field of STEAM education, the editors would have been unable to prepare this volume for publication. We wish to thank our board of reviewers for its tremendous help with both reviewing the chapters and linguistic editing. We must also thank the series editors and Springer for believing in the potentials of this book project and agreeing to publish it.

Norman, OK, USA
Mannheim, Germany
Denton, TX, USA

Xun Ge
Dirk Ifenthaler
J. Michael Spector

Contents

Part VI   Mathematics

Part VII   Epilogue

About the Editors

Xun Ge is Professor of Instructional Psychology and Technology and Chair of the Department of Educational Psychology, Jeannine Rainbolt College of Education, the University of Oklahoma. She holds a Ph.D. in Instructional Systems from the Pennsylvania State University. Dr. Ge's primary research interest involves scaffolding students' complex and ill-structured problem solving and self-regulated learning through designing instructional scaffolds, cognitive tools, learning technologies, and open learning environments (including virtual learning community, game-based learning, inquiry-based learning, and problem-based learning). Over the past years, her scholarly works has evolved to link cognition to motivation. Dr. Ge is also interested in studying the impact and assessment of game-based learning in supporting complex, ill-structured problem solving. Dr. Ge has extensive research experience in STEM education, and she has collaborated with scholars from diverse disciplines around the world. Dr. Ge's research has been published in a co-edited book published by Springer, multiple book chapters in some highly regarded books, and numerous articles in many leading journals of the field, not to mention many other conference proceeding papers. Dr. Ge has been recognized for three prestigious awards she has received—*2012 Outstanding Journal Article, 2004 Outstanding Journal Article 2003,* and *Young Scholar awarded by Educational Technology Research & Development* and the American Educational Communications and Technology.

Dirk Ifenthaler is Professor for Instructional Design and Technology at the University of Mannheim, Germany as well as an Adjunct Professor at Deakin University, Australia. His previous roles include Professor and Director, Centre for Research in Digital Learning at Deakin University, Australia, Manager of Applied Research and Learning Analytics at Open Universities Australia, and Professor for Applied Teaching and Learning Research at the University of Potsdam, Germany. Dirk was a 2012 Fulbright Scholar-in-Residence at the Jeannine Rainbolt College of Education, at the University of Oklahoma, USA. Professor Ifenthaler's research focuses on the intersection of cognitive psychology, educational technology, learning science, data analytics, and computer science. He developed automated and computer-based methodologies for the assessment, analysis, and feedback of graphical and natural language representations, as well as simulation and game environments for teacher education. His research outcomes include numerous co-authored books, book series, book chapters, journal articles, and international conference papers, as well as successful grant funding in Australia, Germany, and USA—see Dirk's website for a full list of scholarly outcomes at www.ifenthaler. info. Professor Ifenthaler is the Editor-in-Chief of the Springer journal *Technology, Knowledge and Learning* (www.springer.com/10758). Dirk is the Past-President for the AECT Design and Development Division, 2013–2015 Chair for the AERA Special Interest Group Technology, Instruction, Cognition and Learning and Co-Program Chair for the international conference on Cognition and Exploratory Learning in the Digital Age (CELDA).

J. Michael Spector is a Professor of Learning Technologies at the University of North Texas. Previously he was a Professor of Educational Psychology and Instructional Technology at the Learning and Performance Support Laboratory at the University of Georgia, Associate Director of the Learning Systems Institute at Florida State University, and Chair of Instructional Design, Development and Evaluation at Syracuse University. Prior to that, he was Director of the Educational Information Science and Technology Research Program at the University of Bergen, and the Senior Scientist for Instructional Systems Research at Armstrong Laboratory. He earned a Ph.D. in Philosophy from The University of Texas at Austin. His research focuses on intelligent support for instructional design, assessing learning in complex domains, and technology integration in education. Dr. Spector served on the International Board of Standards for Training, Performance and Instruction (*ibstpi*). He is a Past-President of the Association for Educational and Communications Technology and a Past-Chair of the Technology, Instruction, Cognition and Learning Special Interest Group of AERA. He is editor of *Educational Technology Research & Development* and edited the third and fourth editions of the *Handbook of Research on Educational Communications and Technology,* as well as the *Encyclopedia of Educational Technology*.

Contributors

Paul Ayres University of New South Wales, Sydney, Australia

Lawrence Baines The University of Oklahoma, Norman, USA

Brian R. Belland Utah State University, Logan, USA

Dianne Biin Camosun College, Victoria, Canada

Lingguo Bu Southern Illinois University, Carbondale, USA

Juan C. Castro-Alonso University of New South Wales, Sydney, Australia

Gladis Chávez-Torrejón Center for Science, Engineering, and Technology Education, Universidad de las Americas Puebla, Puebla, Mexico

Rhonda Christensen University of North Texas, Denton, USA

David A. Coffland Idaho State University, Pocatello, USA

Lourdes Gazca Center for Science, Engineering, and Technology Education, Universidad de las Americas Puebla, Puebla, Mexico

Xun Ge University of Oklahoma, Norman, USA

Aytac Gogus Okan University, Istanbul, Turkey

Michael M. Grant University of South Carolina, Columbia, USA

Jiangyue Gu Utah State University, Logan, USA

Judith Virginia Gutiérrez Cuba Center for Science, Engineering, and Technology Education, Universidad de las Americas Puebla, Puebla, Mexico

Markus Hohenwarter Johannes Kepler University, Linz, Austria

Douglas Holton Embry-Riddle Aeronautical University, Daytona Beach, FL, USA

Silvia Husted Center for Science, Engineering, and Technology Education, Universidad de las Americas Puebla, Puebla, Mexico

Dirk Ifenthaler University of Mannheim, Mannheim, Germany
Deakin University, Melbourne, Australia

Shiyan Jiang University of Miami, Coral Gables, USA

Gerald Knezek University of North Texas, Denton, USA

Armanda L. Lewis New York University, New York, USA

Hong Lin University of Oklahoma, Norman, USA

Hong Liu Embry-Riddle Aeronautical University, Daytona Beach, FL, USA

Ou Lydia Liu Educational Testing Service, Princeton, USA

Aurelio López-Malo Chemical, Environmental, and Food Engineering,
Universidad de las Americas Puebla, Puebla, Mexico

Maria Ludu Embry-Riddle Aeronautical University, Daytona Beach, FL, USA

Michael Marmon University of North Texas, Denton, USA

Marina Milner-Bolotin University of British Columbia, Vancouver, Canada

Farrokh Mistree University of Oklahoma, Norman, USA

Fred Paas University of New South Wales, Sydney, Australia; Erasmus University
Rotterdam, Rotterdam, Netherlands

Enrique Palou Center for Science, Engineering, and Technology Education,
Universidad de las Americas Puebla, Puebla, Mexico

Zaira Ramírez Apud Center for Science, Engineering, and Technology
Education, Universidad de las Americas Puebla, Puebla, Mexico

Nelly Ramírez-Corona Chemical, Environmental, and Food Engineering,
Universidad de las Americas Puebla, Puebla, Mexico

Ji Shen University of Miami, Coral Gables, USA

Zahed Siddique University of Oklahoma, Norman, USA

October Smith University of North Texas, Denton, USA

J. Michael Spector University of North Texas, Denton, USA

Marla L Weston Camosun College, Victoria, Canada

Ying Xie Northern Illinois University, DeKalb, USA

Part I
Prologue

Education, Training, Competencies, Curricula and Technology

Full STEAM Ahead

J. Michael Spector

Abstract Educational goals are relatively stable with shifting emphases among such large aims as developing critical thinkers, effective problem-solvers, productive workers, responsible citizens and lifelong learners. Nations strive to develop and maintain thriving economies with opportunities for citizens. Companies focus on gaining a secure place in the market and increasing profits and returns on investments. Technologies, however, are changing rapidly and, as a result, changing how people work and interact in nearly every sector, including education. One consequence of this convergence of situations is a tension in training and education. On one hand, new technologies provide the ability to support highly personalized and learner-centered education. On the other hand, there is pressure to focus on knowledge and skill development in the areas of science, technology, engineering and mathematics, in large part to serve economic growth and expansion in a highly competitive world. This chapter focuses on technology-enhanced learning informed by the arts and humanities as a way to balance tensions between individual and societal interests.

Keywords Competency-based instruction · Curriculum design · Educational goals · Training design · Technology integration

Introduction

The history of education dates back thousands of years. In one form or another, education has generally involved training people how to succeed in life. Such training might have emphasized the development of hunting and fishing skills or knowledge about soils and plants in earlier times. In modern times, educational goals are more often associated with the development of problem solving and critical thinking skills. In addition, education aims at the development of responsible citizens and lifelong learners (Spector, Johnson, & Young, 2014).

J. M. Spector (✉)
University of North Texas, Denton, USA
e-mail: Mike.Spector@unt.edu

© Springer International Publishing Switzerland 2015
X. Ge et al. (eds.), *Emerging Technologies for STEAM Education,*
Educational Communications and Technology: Issues and Innovations,
DOI 10.1007/978-3-319-02573-5_1

Broad educational goals can be deconstructed into things that can be learned and supported with instruction and performance support. These can be further categorized in terms of a particular task domain or cluster of related knowledge and skill sets, which might then become parts of a curriculum. For example, a critical thinking goal might be decomposed into sub-goals, such as analyzing arguments, identifying assumptions, evaluating evidence, formulating implications, and so on (Fisher & Scriven, 1997). At a certain level of decomposition in many cases, it is possible to specify measures and assessments that can be associated with competent or masterful performance. This line of thinking from goals to clustered objectives with associated assessments is the basis of competency-based curricula that one finds implemented in many training situations. Such thinking has been more or less loosely used to structure primary, secondary and tertiary educational curricula in many subject areas as well.

There is an increasing emphasis on competence-based curricula as societies strive to increase the ability to create and sustain globally competitive economies (Rust, Portnoi, & Bagley, 2010; see also http://tencompetence-project.bolton. ac.uk/). The pressure to create a workforce educated to be competitive in the 21st century has led to an emphasis on STEM (science, technology, engineering, and mathematics) education. While new technologies make it possible to design, develop and deploy powerful STEM learning environments, many of these technologies can also support learning that is not tightly linked to competence development, such as open-ended, informal, technology-enhanced environments such as San Francisco's Exploratorium (see http://www.exploratorium.edu/).

As it happens, education in the liberal arts and humanities has not been easily or readily adapted to a competency-based model. In many liberal arts subjects, emphasis is on creativity and personal expressions which are not so easily measured or assessed. As it happens, there is evidence to support the notion that a liberal arts education with a rich infusion of the humanities can prepare a person for success in many occupations requiring creative and flexible thinking (Ferrall, 2011). In this chapter, a competency-based, technology-enhanced framework that is appropriate for STEAM (science, technology, engineering, arts, and mathematics) is developed, along with a discussion of associated issues and controversies. An elaboration of the framework in the domain of advanced learning technologies is then presented. The chapter concludes with implications for further research and development.

STEAM is a movement championed by the Rhode Island School of Design to integrate art and design into STEM curricula (see http://stemtosteam.org/). This effort has been adopted as a central focus of the National Technology Leadership Coalition (NTLC; see http://www.ntlcoalition.org/) and its 11 member associations and journal editors who meet annually for a National Technology Leadership Summit (NTLS; see http://www.ntls.info/index.htm). The research in terms of impact on learning for STEAM curricula is basically qualitative (e.g., case studies) as the effort is relatively young without large-scale empirical studies. However, one indicator of the impact of STEAM can be seen in many transmedia books that have emerged from NTLS, the University of Virginia, MIT and other institutions around the world (Bernardo, 2011; Phillips, 2012; Pratten, 2011). A transmedia book is essential a story told using digital technologies as an integral part of the story. Often there are activities for learners aimed at developing their critical thinking and problem solving skills. As a consequence, excellent examples of STEAM can be found in those transmedia books now available that illustrate how art, design, storytelling, and collaborative problem solving activities can be effectively integrated into a STEM curriculum.

Definitions and Rationale

In the course of developing a framework for integrating the arts and humanities into curricula for STEM disciplines, it is necessary to define key terms and provide a rationale. First, the following definitions inform this framework:

- Competence: an observable set of related skills, knowledge and attitudes that enable a person to effectively and consistently perform a task or job or achieve a desired outcome.
- Education: systematic efforts to develop critical thinkers (those who think critically and engage in higher order reasoning), effective problem solvers, productive workers, responsible citizens and lifelong learners; encompasses both formal and informal learning as well as apprenticeship, training and professional development.
- STEM: academic and professional disciplines associated with science, technology, engineering and mathematics; typically conceived of separately with sub-disciplines, although new pedagogical approaches encourage cross-disciplinary learning in areas.
- STEAM: the inclusion of the liberal arts and humanities in STEM education; some STEAM conceptions simply use the 'A' to indicate a fifth discipline area—namely, arts and humanities, with sub-disciplines as have historically existed for STEM areas; however, an alternative conception is to integrate liberal arts and humanities into STEM education as an expansion of an expanded cross-disciplinary approach being advocated for STEM education; some refer to this approach as *trans-disciplinary* and it is the approach advocated in this chapter (Nicolescu, 2008; Spector & Anderson, 2000; see also http://www.steamedu.com/ and http://stemtosteam.org/).

The rationale for integrating arts and humanities into and throughout STEM disciplines is multi-dimensional. One dimension concerns career progression. As has been demonstrated by the International Board of Standards for Training, Performance and Instruction (*ibstpi*) and many other organizations, advancement within a career area is highly correlated with communication skills, typically developed in courses offered within a liberal arts college (e.g., composition, debating, rhetoric, technical writing, etc.) or a business college (e.g., advertisement, leadership, persuasion, etc.). Communication skills are part and parcel of most jobs in the information age, but they are rarely emphasized in college courses in a STEM area. Those who can speak clearly naturally migrate to leadership and management positions.

I recall from my own experience with formal preparation in philosophy that when computers became commonplace in the workplace and in universities that new programs had to be developed for computer science teachers and those who would be working with computers after graduation. As there was a shortage of college faculty to teach computer science, initially mathematicians and engineers were recruited and cross-trained, but that effort did not meet the demand, so musicians and philosophers were then recruited and cross-trained, in part because those professionals also had experience with formal systems and symbolic notation. In short, there is historical evidence that preparation in the liberal arts and humanities can serve some people well in professional STEM areas.

Another dimension concerns ethics and values, which are normally taught in a philosophy department and which are not very popular with students majoring in STEM areas. However, many professional organizations have ethical standards that apply to everyone in that organization. While many do not regard professional ethics as a high priority personally, their professional associations do place emphasis on ethics. Evidence of this exists in the many large-scale surveys of professionals by the International Board of Standards for Training, Performance and Instruction (*ibstpi*; see www.ibstpi.org). That board establishes competencies and professional standards in a number of areas, and does so based on what practicing professionals regard as critical skills. When asked about the criticality of ethical practice in performing their various tasks, the respondents rank ethical competence as not critical. The Board has chosen in the case of ethics to base its standards on the Board's own view as opposed to the survey data; thankfully, that Board emphasizes ethics and recognizes the role of values in job performance.

In the 21st century with an explosion of information on the Internet, the responsibilities for respecting individual privacy and intellectual property rights is of increasing significance. It is all too easy to violate such rights, and the consequences can be personally and professionally devastating. There are recent examples in the area of ship, airplane and vehicular accidents that illustrate how poorly designed products as well as poorly designed training can result in the loss of life. Currently, the treatment of ethics and values in many STEM courses preparing those who develop complex systems and train professionals using those systems is minimal or non-existent. However, such issues are frequently discussed in philosophy and sociology courses, and relevant lessons could be usefully integrated into STEM courses.

Perhaps the strongest argument for integrating the liberal arts and humanities into STEM education is to emphasize the development of abilities associated with esthetics, innovation, and creativity (see the elaboration of a sample curriculum below). There are multiple strands to such an argument. First, many of the things associated with STEM careers involved the creation of products. Often, the success of a new product involves non-technical aspects of that product—notably, its esthetic appeal to targeted users. Some experience and familiarity with the design arts, can add significantly to the creation of various products that engineers and technologists develop.

Additionally, there is clearly value in having a sense of history. Understanding the past, including situations and developments that might be directly relevant to the present as well as those that might appear quite different, provides a basis for thinking about alternatives. For example, the success in war of a small army over a larger one might be understood in terms of a particular technology, and that understanding could lead to an innovative application of a derivative of that technology to serve a peacetime engineering need. While it is not well understood how discoveries occur, there does seem to be value in a liberal arts education in terms of creativity and innovation (Chopp, Frost, & Weiss, 2014; Jobs, 2013).

Finally, to create roughly equal emphasis on the common educational goals mentioned earlier and advocated by so many educators, it is essential to include some emphasis on developing an understanding of individuals, groups, cultures, nations, and such enterprises as design and public service (Dewey, 1916; see also http://www.aacu.org/leap/what_is_liberal_education.cfm).

A Competency Framework for STEAM

Based on the argument that a balanced STEM curriculum can be designed to integrate the liberal arts and the humanities, a preliminary and provisional framework for doing so is presented in this section. First, it should be noted that there is an active effort to integrate various STEM disciplines and subjects in curricula at different levels, especially in the USA. For example, the recently updated standards for teaching high school mathematics in Georgia dropped traditional courses dedicated to geometry, algebra, statistics and trigonometry in favor of integrated mathematics courses that covered related mathematical topics. In Mathematics I, algebra geometry and statistics are woven together in one course (for an elaboration see https://www.georgiastandards.org/Standards/Pages/BrowseStandards/MathStandards9-12.aspx). The Next Generation Science Standards (NGS) promoted by the National Research Council in the USA (see http://www.nextgenscience.org/). The NGS standards are a systematic effort to integrate science, technology, mathematics and engineering at the level of specific standards to be taught in various courses in K-12 settings in the USA. An example of a middle school standard in the area of forces and interaction is 3-PS2-3, which says that students who meet this standard will be able to ask questions to determine cause and effect relationships of electric or magnetic interactions between two objects not in contact with each other. For each NGS standard, a clarification statement is provided along with relevant science and engineering practices, core ideas and crosscutting concepts. This ambitious program to reform STEM education in public education is meeting resistance from teachers who have the task of supporting new standards. Nonetheless, there is widespread recognition that teaching separate subjects divorced from practical problems and real world practice is not meeting the needs of the 21st century.

Based on the assumption that industrial/manufacturing age curricula will eventually give way to dramatic curricular reformulations that are more interdisciplinary, integrative and holistic in nature, a provisional framework for such a STEAM curriculum reformation is presented next. First, it is worth noting developmental differences in a number of dimensions (see Fig. 1).

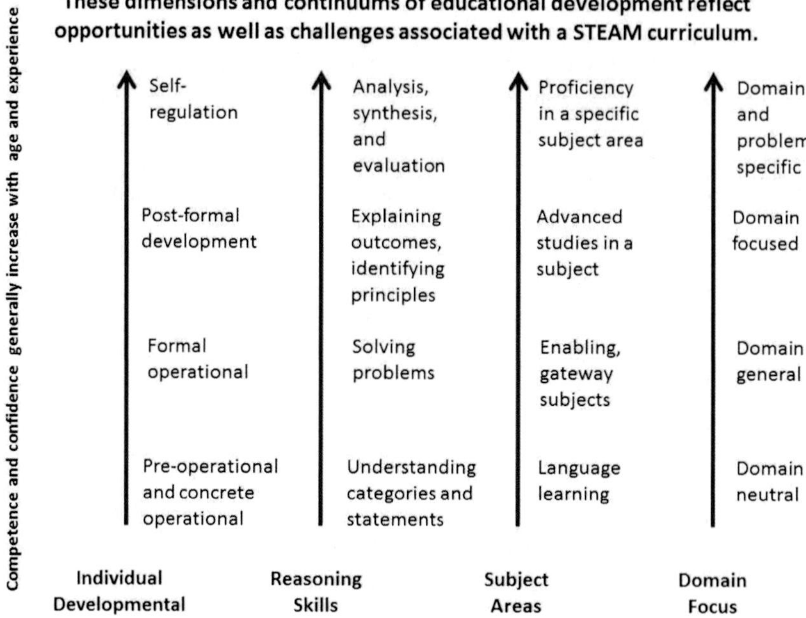

Fig. 1 Developmental dimensions

One way to elaborate a curriculum for a STEM subject involving systems (e.g., astronomy, biology, computer systems, ecology, engineering, etc.), especially for the middle parts of the developmental dimensions in Fig. 1, is in terms of graduated complexity (Milrad, Spector, & Davidsen, 2003). In terms of learner development, the progression would be from problem orientation (becoming familiar with representative problems and their dimensions) to inquiry exploration (engaging in hypothesis formulation and simple experimentation) and then to policy development (formulating decision making rules and guides appropriate for further inquiry and investigation). A holistic and systematic view would be supported throughout the curriculum. Specific challenges for learners (not unlike the challenges associated with NGS) could be sequenced from simpler to more complex as follows: (a) challenge learners to characterize the standard behavior of the complex system or document how system components changes over time; (b) challenge learners to identify key variables that affect the system; (c) challenge learners to explain how and why the system appears to change as it does, including those aspects of the system that might be amenable to control; (d) challenge learners to reflect and represent the dynamic aspects of a system in the form of white papers, decision guides, images, and dynamic models; (e) challenge learners to encapsulate a system in the form of a model or simulation including provisions for interaction and hypothesis testing; and (f) challenge learners to refine the model based on the results of hypothesis testing and the analysis and synthesis of related findings.

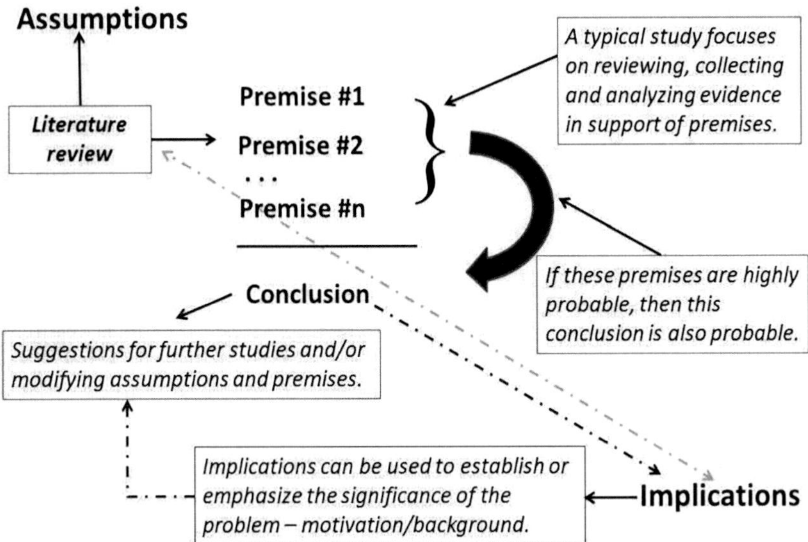

Fig. 2 Argumentation skills

Such a curriculum progression helps a learner develop increasingly sophisticated reasoning skills and includes skills that are typically developed outside a particular subject area focus (e.g., argumentation skills, mathematical modeling skills, visual representation skills, writing skills, etc.). Another way to frame a STEAM curriculum is with respect to a specific set of reasoning skills, such as argumentation. Figure 2 presents a framework focused specifically on the nature of argumentation skills, which might be associated with various parts of the dimensions in Fig. 1, depending on which argumentation aspects are emphasized.

Figure 2 depicts the general structure of an argument as consisting of some statements (premises) proposed as evidence or support for another statement (the conclusion). As it happens, this framework is appropriately applied to research as well as the development of critical reasoning skills. In a curriculum progression, early language training is typically focused on understanding statements. Gradually, comprehension is extended to paragraphs that might have a topical sentence or claim being supported. At that level of language developed, a curriculum informed by logic might challenge learners to distinguish the statements offered as evidence from those offered as the main point. A higher level of reasoning might then challenge learners to determine type of support being offered for the conclusion—probabilistic or certain (as in a mathematical proof). Then a learner could be challenged to examine additional literature to find support for the premises or conflicting evidence suggesting that the premises are not as strong as represented. Having learners identify unstated assumptions and the implications of a conclusion are again representative of higher order reasoning skills. In other words, applying lessons learned in a logic sequence typically taught in a philosophy curriculum could easily be infused throughout a STEM curriculum. Arguably, logic should be taught at the secondary level prior to college, although that is not standard practice in the USA.

An Elaboration for Advanced Learning Technology (ALT)

An example of a curriculum that integrates arts and humanities into a technology domain is one developed by the IEEE (Institute for Electrical and Electronic Engineers) Technical Committee on Advanced Learning Technologies (ALT) as part of a 3-year project ending in 2010 (Hartley, Kinshuk, Koper, Okamoto, & Spector, 2010). The domain was advanced learning technology. The IEEE Computer Society charged the committee with the task of developing a model curriculum for the preparation of the next generation of educational technologists that accounted for the dramatic changes occurring with regard to technology and scientific approaches to learning.

The five persons on the committee represented multiple disciplines (computer science, educational computing, educational psychology, educational technology, and philosophy) as well as having experience in academia as well as in business and governmental agencies in different countries and with a wide variety of institutions. The committee developed initial ideas based on their experience and preliminary research, and then held separate focus groups to expand those ideas. Eventually surveys of large groups of representative professional practitioners and academics were circulated and data analyzed and refined over a number of iterations and with the assistance of additional experts.

The initial perspective that resulted from the experience of two significant efforts—TEN-Competence in Europe (see http://tencompetence-project.bolton.ac.uk/) and the International Board of Standards for Training, Performance and Instruction (*ibstpi*), both of which had made extensive use of a competency approach with obvious success. A competence can be defined as a related set of skills, knowledge and attitudes that enable a person to consistently and successfully perform a particular task or job. Competences are by nature decomposable into sub-sets that lend themselves to measurements and assessments. As a result, competences are often associated with credentials and accreditation. Here is an example of an *ibstpi* competence for instructional designers (see www.ibstpi.org):

"Communicate effectively in visual, oral, and written form."

This competency statement is considered essential (required of all instructional designers) and elaborated in terms of ten performance indicators, with the following four considered essential:

a) Write and edit messages that are clear, concise, and grammatically correct.
b) Deliver presentations that effectively engage audiences and communicate clear messages.

c) Use active listening skills.
d) Solicit, accept, and provide constructive feedback.

Once a competence approach is adopted, the task is then to determine which competencies comprise a competency set and what the indicators of those competencies are. This is not a trivial undertaking and typically takes a significant period of time working with a large number of professionals in different contexts and locations.

The ALT committee took a year to develop the competency approach and about 2 years to determine a set of competencies appropriate for preparing advanced learning technologists. Working with the messy data collected, the committee arrived at 13 sets of related skills, knowledge and attitudes in terms of 13 topic areas:

1. Familiarity with advanced learning technologies;
2. Familiarity with human learning;
3. Prominent developments and how ALT has evolved;
4. Typologies and approaches for integrating technologies into learning;
5. User perspectives of learning and technology;
6. Learner perspectives of learning and technology;
7. Systems perspectives and systems thinking;
8. Social perspectives, including collaboration;
9. Design requirements, including needs assessment;
10. Design processes and the development lifecycle;
11. Instructional design, including alternative models;
12. Evaluation models and practices; and
13. Emerging issues in ALT.

These 13 topical areas were not necessarily intended to become separate courses; rather, they represent one way that the knowledge, skills and attitudes could be clustered into what might become units of instruction or parts of various courses. Here is how the committee elaborated topic area #2 in the above list (Hartley et al., 2010):
"The themes, issues and sub-competencies in this section include:

• Understanding and explaining human learning;
• Behaviourist and reinforcement views of human learning;
• Cognitive interpretations of learning;
• Socio-constructivist and emotive aspects of learning;
• Collaborative and cooperative learning;
• Distributed and distance learning;
• Instructional design perspectives, and
• Systems and Information processing approaches to learning." (p. 208)

This elaboration also demonstrates that the committee believes that a competent technologist should have a basic understanding of human psychology. Another way the committee looked at the data was in terms of competence domains; this perspective further highlights how the arts and humanities might be infused into a technology or engineering oriented curriculum. The committee identified these five domains that accounted for all of the competencies collected in the study:

- Knowledge competence—for example, the ability to synthesize research and theory pertaining to various aspects of advanced learning technologies.
- Process competence—for example, understanding how a particular system architecture creates some affordances as well as some limitations.
- Application competence—for example, the ability to transform a design specification into a prototype.
- Personal and social competence—for example, awareness of group dynamics and ethical issues.
- Innovative and creative competence—for example, understanding limitations and investigating alternative approaches.

The competence domains as well as the elaboration of the 13 topic areas lend themselves to implementation with a Four Component Instructional Design model (4C/ID; see van Merriënboer, 1997) or other instructional design framework that takes a holistic approach to learning and instruction (Spector, 2000).

These competence domains reflect a commitment to all of the educational goals mentioned at the beginning of this article—developing critical thinkers, effective problem solvers, productive workers, responsible citizens, and lifelong learners. Unlike many curricula, which target only one or two of the goals, the IEEE ALT curriculum addresses and integrates all of those goals. What does this demonstrate? This example can only suggest that it is possible to conceptualize a curriculum in a STEM area that integrates the arts and humanities, making it what could be considered a STEAM curriculum. It does not demonstrate the efficacy of such a curriculum, as that is a task yet to be undertaken.

Concluding Remarks

The message underlying the framework and example presented in this chapter is not simply that the arts and humanities should not be left out of a discussion about education in the 21st century. On the contrary, the message is that education in the arts and humanities should be part and parcel of education in every domain. There is empirical evidence that those with a strong background in the liberal arts are likely to be successful in attaining the education goals mentioned at the outset—namely, becoming critical thinkers, effective problem solvers, productive workers, responsible citizens and lifelong learners. Moreover, there is value in instilling the values associated with the arts and humanities into education—namely, the value of appreciating the complexities of life and the rich diversity of the world. Whether this is good for everyone at every level in an educational progression can be debated. The argument here is that a STEAM curriculum can inform both secondary and tertiary education, and help promote the value of inquiry in any discipline.

After all, inquiry involves a commitment to finding answers and explanations and an openness to alternative approaches and perspectives. As Perkins and Salomon (1989) have argued, a combination of domain-specific and general knowledge can function well in developing cognitive skills and expertise. Moreover, in becoming a critical thinker, effective problem solver, responsible citizen and life-long learner, there are also non-cognitive factors that can help or hinder those developments. Those non-cognitive factors are all often ignored in STEM courses. Addressing non-cognitive factors (e.g., cultural predispositions, deep-seated biases, emotional states, habits, motivation, etc.) can enhance learning outcomes. In addition, integrating aspects emphasized in the arts and humanities (argumentation, discourse analysis, esthetics, ethics, logic, etc.) can transform the current emphasis on STEM jobs and domain specific skills to inquiry-centered knowledge development appropriate for STEAM-based curricula (e.g., broad inquiry-based educational goals).

Acknowledgements The ideas expressed in this chapter are my own, as are any misconceptions and misleading comments. However, whatever stands the test of time, I owe to my parents, my siblings, my children, my teachers, my students and my friends from whom I have learned that becoming educated is learning to have questions, to pursue answers, and to admit limitations.

References

Bernardo, N. (2011). *The producers guide to transmedia: How to develop, fund, produce and distribute compelling stories across multiple platforms*. London: beActive Books.

Chopp, R., Frost, S., & Weiss, D. H. (Eds.). (2014). *Remaking college: Innovation and the liberal arts*. Baltimore: John Hopkins Press.

Dewey, J. (1916). *Democracy and education: An introduction to the philosophy of education*. New York: Macmillan.

Ferrall, V. E. (2011). *Liberal arts at the brink*. Cambridge: Harvard University Press.

Fisher, A., & Scriven, M. (1997). *Critical thinking: Its definition and assessment*. Norwich: Centre for Research in Critical Thinking.

Hartley, R., Kinshuk, Koper, R., Okamoto, T., & Spector, J. M. (2010). The education and training of learning technologists: A competences approach. *Educational Technology & Society, 13*(2), 206–216.

Jobs, S. (22 October 2013). Liberal arts essential for innovation. *The Daily RIFF.* http://www.thedailyriff.com/articles/steve-says-technology-liberal-arts-innovation-648.php. Accessed 31 March 2014.

Milrad, M., Spector, J. M., & Davidsen, P. I. (2003). Model facilitated learning. In S. Naidu (Ed.), *Learning and teaching with technology: Principles and practices* (pp. 13–27). London: Kogan Page.

Nicolescu, B. (Ed.). (2008). *Transdisciplinarity: Theory and practice*. Cresskill: Hampton Press.

Perkins, D. NI., & Salomon, G. (1989). Are cognitive skills context bound? *Eduational Researcher, 18*(1), 16–25.

Phillips, A. (2012). *A creator's guide to transmedia storytelling: How to captivate and engage audiences across multiple platforms*. New York: McGraw-Hill.

Pratten, R. (2011). *Getting started in transmedia storytelling: A practical guide for beginners*. London: CreateSpace.

Rust, V. D., Portnoi, L., & Bagley, S. S. (Eds.). (2010). *Higher education, policy, and the global competition phenomenon*. New York: Palgrave Macmillan.

Spector, J. M. (2000). Building theory into practice in learning and instruction. In J. M. Spector & T. M. Anderson (Eds.), *Integrated & holistic perspectives on learning, instruction & technology: Understanding complexity* (pp. 79–90). Dordrecht: Kluwer Academic Publishers.

Spector, J. M., & Anderson, T. M. (Eds.). (2000). *Integrated and holistic perspectives on learning, instruction and technology: Understanding complexity*. Dordrecht: Kluwer Academic Publishers.
Spector, J. M., Johnson, T. E., & Young, P. A. (2014). An editorial on research and development in and with educational technology. *Educational Technology Research & Development, 62*(1), 1–12.
van Merriënboer, J. J. G. (1997). *Training complex cognitive skills: A four-component instructional design model for technical training*. Englewood Cliffs: Educational Technology Publications.

J. Michael Spector is a Professor of Learning Technologies at the University of North Texas. Previously he was a Professor of Educational Psychology and Instructional Technology at the Learning and Performance Support Laboratory at the University of Georgia, Associate Director of the Learning Systems Institute at Florida State University, and Chair of Instructional Design, Development and Evaluation at Syracuse University. Prior to that, he was Director of the Educational Information Science and Technology Research Program at the University of Bergen, and the Senior Scientist for Instructional Systems Research at Armstrong Laboratory. He earned a Ph.D. in Philosophy from The University of Texas at Austin. His research focuses on intelligent support for instructional design, assessing learning in complex domains, and technology integration in education. Dr. Spector served on the International Board of Standards for Training, Performance and Instruction (*ibstpi*). He is a Past-President of the Association for Educational and Communications Technology and a Past-Chair of the Technology, Instruction, Cognition and Learning Special Interest Group of AERA. He is editor of *Educational Technology Research & Development* and edited the third and fourth editions of the *Handbook of Research on Educational Communications and Technology*, as well as the *Encyclopedia of Educational Technology*.

Part II
Science

Active Learning Approaches to Integrating Technology into a Middle School Science Curriculum Based on 21st Century Skills

Rhonda Christensen and Gerald Knezek

Abstract In order to prepare our next generation of scientists, continual improvements in the curriculum are required to capture students' interest in the sciences early in their developmental years. Improving students' conceptual understanding, perceived value and enjoyment of science is critical in creating the scientific literacy that is necessary for the 21st century. This chapter describes active learning strategies that are not currently widely adopted but have been shown to be effective in enhancing middle school deep learning of content, as well as fostering positive dispositions toward science and related fields. The authors propose that mechanisms such as these can be institutionalized in the middle school science curriculum. Reasons for why these more innovative strategies are not currently employed by a wider community and steps conducive to wide scale adoption are discussed. Examples of successful programs that use the strategies of active, engaged learning are described as well as ways in which these innovative approaches can be implemented into the classroom.

Keywords Active learning · Twenty-first century skills · Deep learning · Middle school

Introduction

This chapter focuses on using active, deep learning strategies to foster middle school student interest in science and future careers in science. The integration of technology is an integral part of any future career. Student-centered active learning has been shown to improve long-term knowledge retention and deep understanding (Akinoglu & Tandogan, 2007; Bonwell & Eison, 1991; Gallagher, 1997). The strategies used for active learning closely align with guidelines employed by the National Research Council to develop the next generation science standards

R. Christensen (✉) · G. Knezek
University of North Texas, Denton, USA
e-mail: rhonda.christensen@gmail.com

G. Knezek
e-mail: gknezek@gmail.com

© Springer International Publishing Switzerland 2015
X. Ge et al. (eds.), *Emerging Technologies for STEAM Education,*
Educational Communications and Technology: Issues and Innovations,
DOI 10.1007/978-3-319-02573-5_2

(NGSS). For example, one goal is to have students understand concepts as opposed to memorizing facts. The NGSS standards are intended to teach the application of concepts to real world contexts.

In addition, the focus of these new standards is the integration of core concepts and coherent progression of knowledge. To prepare students for college and for science careers, these standards focus on deeper understanding of content (depth rather than breadth), and it is expected that the outcomes will be measured using performance-based expectations. An additional emphasis of the new standards is on raising engineering design to the same level of respectable activity as scientific inquiry.

In a report about engineering education published by the National Research Council, (2009), the committee summarized the benefits of teaching engineering principles to K-12 students. The committee found:

> K-12 engineering education may improve student learning and achievement in science and mathematics; increase awareness of engineering and the work of engineers; boost youth interest in pursuing engineering as a career; and increase the technological literacy of all students. The committee believes engineering education may even act as a catalyst for a more interconnected and effective K-12 STEM education system in the United States. (National Research Council, 2009, p. 1)

Conceptual Framework

Several theories of learning and models of instructional best practices provide the rationale for approaches supported in this chapter. These theories are briefly introduced as individual sub-topics in the initial portions of the section, then they are interwoven toward specific implications for curricular innovation in the later portions of the section narrative.

Active and Deep Learning

When using the active learning approach, education becomes more personally meaningful and takes advantage of students' natural curiosity. This approach prepares students for the future by having students communicate, collaborate, and try new approaches in finding solutions to real world problems.

Middle school is an appropriate age to develop an interest in science that will persist through secondary school, into college and beyond into a career. Providing authentic, active learning experiences contributes to the internalization of learning about science.

Active learning principles are rooted in Dewey's "learning by doing and experiencing" principle (Dewey, 1938). Dewey advocated that a child's schoolwork should have meaning and be engaging as well as have connections to other disciplines and life experiences. In an active learning model, the learner takes more responsibility for his/her own learning under the guidance of a teacher. Characteristics that are included in active learning include:

- relevance to real world applications
- authentic solving of real world problems
- application of prior knowledge and/or experiences to solve new problems
- collaboration with others
- integration of subject matters (interdisciplinary) and
- self-directed learning.

Within this context, it is proposed that strategies promoting active learning be defined as instructional activities "involving students in doing things and thinking about what they are doing" (Bonwell & Eison, 1991).

Jonassen, Howland, Moore, and Marra (2003) defined meaningful learning as "occurring when students were actively engaged in making meaning. They broke down this definition into five *interrelated, interactive, and interdependent attributes* with the most meaningful learning activities supporting combinations of these attributes".

Collectively these researchers have established the importance of active, engaged learning in creating learning that is deep and meaningful.

The Four Cs: Super Skills for the 21st Century

The Partnership for 21st Century Skills (Partnership for 21st Century, 2011) has consolidated components of numerous theories, models, and studies of 21st century workforce needs to produce the following list of four essential skills for students in the 21st Century. These skills along with brief explanations of each skill set are:

- Communication (sharing thoughts, questions, ideas and solutions)
- Collaboration (working together to reach a goal—putting talent, expertise and smarts to work)
- Critical Thinking (looking at problems in a new way, linking learning across subjects and disciplines), and
- Creativity (trying new approaches to get things done equals innovation & invention) (Partnership for 21st Century, 2011)

These four C's align well with the active and meaningful learning principles and, provide a conceptual foundation for targeting the types of activities needed in a middle school science curriculum for the 21st Century.

Theoretical Support for the Four C's as a Means for Learning Science

Learning science in a more active, discovery-learning style that incorporates relevance and authenticity leads to a deeper understanding and retention of scientific concepts. Piaget (1983) laid the foundation for our understanding of how children construct their own understanding of the world, working from concrete to abstract, while Vygotsky (1978) showed how children's skills and understanding grow through social interaction within the zone of proximal development. Piaget's ideas directly support the Critical Thinking component of the four C's in that critical thinking often involves beginning with a concrete instance and generalizing across many instances to the level of abstraction. Vygotsky's reported contention that "all meaningful learning occurs in a social context" supports both Communication and Collaboration as two of the four C's.

Jerome Bruner is credited for furthering the concept of discovery-based learning in the 1960s. In his words, "Practice in discovering for oneself teaches one to acquire information in a way that makes that information more readily viable in problem solving" *(Bruner,* 1961*)*. Bruner's views on discovery learning directly support Creativity as being worthy of status as one of the four C's.

Engaging Students in Science

Two longitudinal studies conducted by Aschbacher, Ing, and Tsai (2013) concluded that many students believe science is too hard, uninteresting, and irrelevant and that their school experiences play a significant role in whether students want to learn science or will be prepared for science, engineering or medical-related jobs. These researchers surveyed 7th through 12th grade students and found one characteristic that set apart the high school students who persisted in science, engineering or medical aspirations, compared to those who dropped out of the pipeline, was the opportunity to experience compelling, authentic STEM experiences *outside* of school. They concluded that more students might be interested in learning science if learning opportunities were more personally relevant and provided more space to explore and develop who they might want to be (Aschbacher et al., 2013). These findings imply that school curriculum developers should consider adopting strategies of authentic, hands-on learning activities that have been shown to work in settings outside of school.

Given that STEM knowledge is constantly changing, it is critical that everyone, STEM professionals as well as common citizens alike, is able to update their STEM understanding. Fortunately, we now appreciate that the public acquires science information continuously across their day and throughout their lives.

Dierking and Falk (2003) identified the following free-choice learning goals for older children and youth, designed to complement the goals of schooling and work place learning for that age group:

1. To develop and practice lifelong learning skills in real world contexts.
2. To engage in more in-depth study of topics or areas of interest than typical schooling experiences offer.
3. To learn and interact with family and other adults in increasingly meaningful ways, modeling adult thinking and social problem-solving including acceptance, self-confidence, self-monitoring and team play.
4. To explore and experiment with efforts to be increasingly independent and responsible.

5. To begin to master skills and interests, make initial decisions about the kind of life they hope to pursue, and to develop a sense of self.
6. To find supportive mentors who can provide guidance and supervision as youth practice and experiment with lifelong learning skills.

These free-choice learning goals are consistent with the conceptual framework for preparing students for the 21st century (Partnership for 21st Century, 2011). They closely align with the active, deep, learning approach proposed by the authors of this chapter for a middle school science curriculum.

Challenges of Teaching Science at the Middle School Level

There are distinctive challenges in teaching science to middle school students. Middle school students are unique in that they desire to become more independent in their thoughts and actions while at the same time being consumed with physical challenges such as puberty and social issues such as acceptance by peers. Researchers who have studied middle school students seeking an optimal learning environment have found that students' motivation, meaningful curriculum and students' choice are important factors in engaging these students in learning (Maday, 2008).

In addition to social and physical awkwardness, middle school students are the most likely group of K-12 students to doubt their academic ability (Heller, Calderon, & Medrich, 2003). Students may not have had elementary teachers who were enthusiastic or qualified to teach science. When these students enter middle school, there may be some expectation that the students have some prior learning of science concepts that were never attained.

Embedding Twenty-First Century Skills in Science Teaching and Learning

The *P21 Framework* represents a holistic view of 21st century teaching and learning that combines a discrete focus on 21st century student outcomes (a blending of specific skills, content knowledge, expertise and literacies) with innovative support systems to help students master the multi-dimensional abilities required of them in the 21st century and beyond. According to this framework, a focus on creativity, critical thinking, communication and collaboration is essential to prepare students for the future.

Technology readiness involves more than just technology literacy skills. It involves the ability to choose the appropriate tools for the task at hand in order to be productive citizens. Technology plays a major role in the definition of 21st Century skills, critical thinking, problem-solving, communication, and collaboration. As observed by Resta, Searson, Patru, Knezek, and Voogt (2011), "An important change has occurred in the way new digital tools and collaborative environments have enhanced learning, moving from an emphasis on reproducing information to content creation and sharing in virtual environments." This set of skills is commonly referred to as digital literacy.

Digital literacy is a broad concept that has several aspects: technological literacy, Information and Communication Technology (ICT) literacy and information literacy (Resta et al., 2011). "Digital literacy includes the confident use of ICT for work, learning, communication, and leisure and is considered one of the eight essential skills for lifelong learning" (Resta et al., 2011). According to the New Media Consortium (NMC) Horizon Report (2012), digital media literacy is a key skill in every discipline and profession (Johnson, Adams, & Cummins, 2012). To compete in the global knowledge economy, successful workers will need to have multiple literacies. According to Spector (2012) these include digital literacy, information literacy, visual literacy, and technology literacy. "In addition, successful knowledge workers will need to be creative and critical thinkers, and have good communication and self-regulation skills" (Spector, 2012, p. 134).

Critical thinking is an essential skill both in school and beyond the classroom. With the massive amount of information and human connections available via the Internet, today's learners must have the capacity to critically judge which parts are trustworthy. "Today's citizens must be active critical thinkers in order to compare evidence, evaluate competing claims, and make sensible decisions" (P21, 2007, p. 13). According to a survey of 431 human resource officials, critical thinking is the most important among a dozen valuable 21st Century skills (Casner-Lotto & Barrington, 2006).

Problem solving involves collaboration and communication. According to a report by the Partnership for 21st Century Skills, "Communication skills are especially critical in the expanding service economy—estimated to be 81 % of jobs by 2014" (P21, 2007, p. 17). Preparing the future workforce to work with colleagues who are not in the same location or in the same time zone means they must learn to collaborate regardless of time and space. This type of working environment requires problem solving, collaboration and communication to work effectively with vast amounts of information and with people from varying cultures.

As a result of the projected needs of our society, many national and international groups have created lists and descriptions of 21st Century skills that address the needs of preparing students to contribute to a global, collaborative workforce. These groups have found overlapping commonalities in their list of skills. All of these lists involve a very different set of skills than were required just a decade ago. What does not appear in any of the skill sets is rote memorization. What does appear directly or indirectly is the need for critical thinking, problem solving and effective communication. The facts-based knowledge and skills of the previous generation of schooling are no longer sufficient for today's students. Students need to become lifelong learners. Therefore, it is important that they learn how to learn so they can adapt to an ever-changing technological society and economy.

Spector (2012) suggested that the P21 framework shown in Table 1 places a premium on independent, higher-order reasoning skills necessary for productive citizens in the 21st Century. These higher-order reasoning skills span three major categories of: (1) learning and innovation skills; (2) information, media and

Table 1 Framework for skills necessary for productive citizens in the 21st century. (Source: Spector, 2012)

Learning and innovation skills	Creativity and innovation
	Critical thinking and problem solving
	Communication and collaboration
Information, media and technology skills	Information literacy
	Media literacy
	ICT literacy
Life and career skills	Flexibility and adaptability
	Initiative and self-direction
	Social and cross-cultural skills
	Productivity and accountability
	Leadership and responsibility

technology skills; and (3) life and career skills. Both the P21 framework and the ISTE National Educational Technology Standards (NETS) emphasize critical thinking, problem-solving, communication, collaboration and digital literacy.

Examples of Middle School Science Curriculum

The Next Generation Science Standards for Today's Students and Tomorrow's Workforce (Quinn, Schweingruber, & Keller, 2013) are composed of the three dimensions adopted from the Framework for K-12 Science Education developed by the National Research Council (2012). Twenty-six states and their broad-based teams worked together with a 41-member writing team and partners throughout the country to develop the standards. Dimension 1 recommendations regarding next generation practices is particularly relevant to the ideas presented in this chapter:

> ... Practices describe behaviors that scientists engage in as they investigate and build models and theories about the natural world and the key set of engineering practices that engineers use as they design and build models and systems. The NRC uses the term practices instead of a term like "skills" to emphasize that engaging in scientific investigation requires not only skill but also knowledge that is specific to each practice. Part of the NRC's intent is to better explain and extend what is meant by "inquiry" in science and the range of cognitive, social, and physical practices that it requires.
>
> Scientific inquiry involves the formulation of a question that can be answered through investigation, while engineering design involves the formulation of a problem that can be solved through design. Strengthening the engineering aspects of the Next Generation Science Standards will clarify for students the relevance of science, technology, engineering and mathematics (the four STEM fields) to everyday life. (Quinn, Schweingruber, & Keller, 2013, np)

Engagement in scientific inquiry is a key component of NGSS, where scientific inquiry is perceived as sufficiently broad to include engineering design. Scholars such as Savage, Chen, and Vanasupa (2009) have suggested American institutions and students must evolve and become equipped to be "global engineers" who are: (a) technically versatile (multi-disciplinary), (b) able to solve problems from a system-level perspective, (c) capable of effective communication, (d) able to function on diverse ethnic teams, and (e) demonstrably aware of social responsibility. K-12 education will have to produce the beginning of a path that results in university graduates capable of meeting these needs. The technology integration examples provided in this section all have in common active engagement in engineering design or traditional scientific inquiry as a means of learning in a classroom environment.

Example One: Monitoring Energy Usage, Reducing Global Warming

In response to projected deficiencies in the STEM and Information and Communications Technologies (ICT) workforce, the National Science Foundation (NSF) created the Innovative Technology Experiences for Students and Teachers (ITEST) program. Founded in 2003, ITEST supports the development, implementation, evaluation, and scale-up of student-centered curriculum in any NSF-supported content area for the purpose of building K-12 students' capacity to participate in the important STEM and ICT workforce.

Middle Schoolers Out to Save the World (MSOSW) is a multi-year National Science Foundation (NSF) Innovative Technology Experiences for Students and Teachers (ITEST) project that focuses pre-teen interest in activities to foster learning about energy consumption in students' homes and communities. Middle Schoolers Out to Save the World (MSOSW) project activities match the criteria for fostering active, deep learning.

The overarching goal of MSOSW is to incubate interests and knowledge about STEM majors and careers by using a problem-based active learning approach. The project activities were developed using the multiple theory basis formed from the theories of constructivist learning (Bentley, Ebert, & Ebert, 2007; Lave & Wenger, 1991; Means, 2003) as well as theories that bear on the intersection of technology and real-world scientific inquiry in K-8 classrooms (Bentley et al., 2007; Bevan & Semper, 2006; Crane, Nicholson, Chen & Bitgood, 1994; Douglas, 2006; Glock, Meyer & Wertz, 1999).

Inquiry-based learning has been strongly encouraged by most science educators because students are provided with opportunities to ask questions, explore, plan, and most importantly, construct new knowledge and reflect on their learning (Chen & Howard, 2010). When activities like the one mentioned integrate technology with science and mathematics concepts, it helps develop interest in both content areas (Sherrod, Dwyer, & Narayan, 2009). Such hands-on activities cannot only improve achievement but also develop communication, critical thinking and problem-solving (Verma, Dickerson, & McKinney, 2011).

During the MSOSW project, with the help of their teachers who received professional development training through a summer institute, sixth and seventh grade students learn to measure the vampire power used by various appliances in the students' homes. After measuring standby power, students combine their data together with their classmates to explore energy conservation plans that could lower a family's monthly electric bill and reduce the greenhouse gas emissions that contribute to global climate change. Students share their results with other middle school students from across the U.S. Current sites served by the project are located in Texas, Louisiana, Vermont, Maine, North Carolina and Hawaii.

A U.S. government study conducted in the early 21st century (Ross & Meir, 2000) estimated that between 5 and 26% of all electricity consumed by households in the U.S. is wasted in standby power that trickles away 24 hours per day, 365 days per year. This loss is roughly equivalent to the electricity produced by 17 power plants in the U.S. More recently the Environmental Protection Agency (EPA) has estimated that 75 percent of the electricity used during the lifetime of a typical electronic device is consumed while the unit is powered off (Gray, 2007). This wasted power costs money and has a negative impact on the environment. If students become aware of their energy usage at a young age, this awareness might influence their energy usage throughout life. Knowledgeable middle schoolers can positively impact their homes and communities and become adults who prioritize environmental stewardship.

The activities in the energy-based curriculum enhance existing curriculum but uses engaging activities that support active learning. The project incorporates principles of relevance, authentic solving of real world problems, collaboration, integration of subject matters as well as choices in the learning environment.

Example Two: Digital Design and Fabrication

Digital Fabrication is being used to promote higher order thinking and problem solving skills in middle school students. Digital fabrication involves automated conversion of a digital design into a physical object through a computer-controlled fabrication system. The Society of Manufacturing Engineering concludes that personal digital fabrication will offer "revolutionary changes for both manufacturers and the everyday consumer." The Society lists personal fabrication as one of the key *Innovations that Could Change Engineering*, noting that the U.S. Department of Education has identified this kind of innovation as a key to future prosperity.

The Fab@School digital fabrication project began in September 2010. This 4-year project implemented digital design and fabrication activities at the upper elementary school level in order to increase student interest and skills in science, mathematics, and engineering. Major goals of this project were:

- To increase elementary children's attitudes toward and competence in science and mathematics while simultaneously increasing their interest in STEM careers, and
- To develop a comprehensive system for introducing digital fabrication in the elementary grades that integrates hardware, software, a curriculum, and a collaborative space.

Fab@School makes digital fabrication in the elementary and middle-school grades scalable and allowing students to learn skills and concepts such as 3D visualization that are equally applicable to larger industrial systems. The classroom Fab@School project is used to enhance technology, mathematics, and engineering (STEM) instruction while preparing students for the STEM workforce. A non-profit/for-profit collaborative team was assembled to develop the necessary infrastructure for introduction of digital fabrication in schools, including four essential components: hardware, software, an online collaborative space, and a curriculum.

Learning modules for students consisted of hands-on activities where students created virtual 3D models, constructed those models into physical objects with cardstock and other materials, and re-designed their models based on initial testing (Alexander, Knezek, Christensen, & Tyler-Wood, 2014). Students were allowed choices in their designs and the curriculum included collaboration with others, application of prior knowledge and problem solving in addition to the integration of multiple content areas.

Example Three: STEM to STEAM Initiatives

STEAM activities that incorporate the arts into science, technology, engineering, and mathematics (STEM) projects have emerged in many K-12 environments in recent years. Many educational innovators feel that although "… innovation remains tightly coupled with Science, Technology, Engineering and Math—the STEM subjects. Arts + Design are poised to transform our economy in the 21st century just as science and technology did in the last century" (STEM to STEAM, 2014, np). Educational improvement organizations such as Edutopia (Maeda, 2012) contend that including the arts in K-12 education is key to building a strong economy.

Grass-roots movements at the school district level in conjunction with agencies such as NASA, enable classrooms to be engaged by current scientific activities such as "Students […] participating in NASA's MMS 2014 Challenge [… to be] learning about solar weather, the sun, applications of the scientific method, and NASA's MMS 2014 mission. STEAM is allowing for students and teachers to be more creative with approaches used in the classroom" (Miller, 2014, p. 1424). For example, Miller (2013) observed:

> … integrating STEAM content throughout the K-12 curriculum highly engages students and develops systemic learning communities. STEAM programs stimulate students' curiosity and motivation to Bloom's higher-order thinking skills to include problem solving, teamwork, self-directed learning, project-based learning, challenge-based learning, research, and solutions (Bloom, 1984). STEAM programs allow students to become contributors of knowledge and often engage students with real-world scenarios encountered by professionals in the career field of STEAM. As a result, STEAM programs produce a higher percentage of students interested in pursuing careers to support the fields of math and science. Producing a workforce skilled in the fields of math and science is essential to the economic growth of any community and the nation at large. (Miller, 2013, p. 3290)

Miller (2013) reported that students involved in STEAM learning activities researched topics, produced artistic reflections, built structures, conducted hands-on science experiments, and created a variety of multimedia videos on STEAM content related to space weather and NASA's Magnetospheric Multi-Scale (MMS) 2014 mission studying the effects of peak sunspot activity on the Earth's magnetosphere. Anecdotal reports indicated the STEAM curriculum was a professional development activity for the entire rural community, resulting in family discussions about topics such as the sun, the Earth's magnetosphere, and solar storms. Participating teachers reported it made them more aware of connections between science and other content areas across the curriculum. One student indicated he wished to be an astronomer after going through the STEAM camp and received a telescope for his birthday (Miller, 2013).

In analyzing effects of a STEAM camp emphasizing space weather, green energy, and green cities, Miller and Phillips (2014) used quantitative measures to demonstrate positive pre-post trends in perceptions of technology, engineering, and STEM as a career for students participating in STEAM activities related to the NASA's MMS mission and local sustainability. This STEM to STEAM project incorporated the characteristics of active learning with emphasis on authentic solving of real world problems, integration of subject matters including the arts and collaboration with others.

Research Findings from Curriculum Projects that Succeed in These Active and Deep Learning Approaches

Research studies aimed at comparing active, problem-based learning strategies to traditional teaching methods have shown positive impacts on student conceptual development as well as student attitudes when using the more active learning models.

An experimental study was conducted comparing a treatment group of 7th grade students in Istanbul to a control group studying the same science content. The treatment group used problem-based learning strategies while the control group learned with the standard science curriculum. The *Force and Motion Energy Unit* was taught for 30 class periods over 10 weeks. Content, attitudinal and open-ended data were collected pre and post to the intervention. It was determined that the implementation of the problem-based active learning model positively affected the students' academic achievement as well as their attitudes toward science. In addition, the problem-based active learning model impacted the students' conceptual development in a positive way while keeping their misconceptions of science concepts at a lower level than the control group (Akinoglu & Tandogan, 2007).

Middle school students participating in a project that included many components of active learning, such as hands-on activities as well as real world applications showed changes in students' dispositions toward STEM. Pre-post test items were adapted from the National Center for Education Statistics Longitudinal Study (NELS) and the American Women in Engineering item banks (Nolte & Harris, 2010). These were used to measure career aspirations and demographics on identical pre and post tests. Among the primary findings, a 15.8 % increase was found for project students who say they will obtain a Ph.D., M.D., or other advanced degree

(Nolte & Harris, 2010). Project researchers have confirmed through an 8-year longitudinal follow-up study that similar projects can indeed have an impact on STEM dispositions as students advance from elementary school to college. Specifically, Tyler-Wood, Ellison, Lim, and Periathiruvadi (2011) used Facebook to follow up with fourth grade girls (and their contrast group participants) who took part in the NSF-funded Bringing Up Girls in Science (BUGS) during 2001–2002. In the BUGS project, girls participated in hands-on, environmental science activities solving real world problems. During the follow-up study, first year BUGS participants were freshmen in college. Former BUGS participants retained positive STEM dispositions as they advanced to college age. These dispositions were roughly equivalent to those of a comparison group of junior and senior college women who were enrolled in STEM majors. These dispositions were significantly higher than those of the BUGS contrast group, who were matched at the fourth grade level to BUGS participants using science achievement scores obtained on the Iowa Test of Basic Skills (ITBS). These projects provide credible evidence that STEM-related active learning projects for students in grades 4–8 can make an impact on their interest in STEM-related aspirations.

School curriculum involving digital fabrication activities is becoming more common. These activities typically include problem-based, active learning attributes to teach science, mathematics and design-based engineering concepts. One study employed digital fabrication activities to teach a *Waves and Sounds* science unit to 8th graders. Learning modules for this project consisted of hands-on activities where students created virtual 3-D models using a computer or tablet, constructed those models into physical objects utilizing digital fabrication machines, and re-designed their models based on initial testing. This method is known as the Engineering Design Process. The students participating in this project were found to have measurably large content gains (Christensen, Knezek, Standish, Kjellstrom, & Tyler-Wood, 2014). Findings from this study are consistent with previous research that found that fabrication coupled with engineering design projects may reduce the achievement gap among students while boosting standardized test scores in science subjects (Cantrell, Pekcan, Itani, & Velasquez-Bryant, 2006). Fortus, Dershimer, Krajcik, Marx, and Mamlok-Naaman (2004) demonstrated significant gains in students who engaged in design based learning in science classrooms. These students constructed scientific knowledge through hands-on activities that encouraged them to problem solve and demonstrate their knowledge gains. Other findings showed that by fabricating models of a scientific concept, students demonstrated a deeper understanding of the science being studied (Hmelo, Holton, & Kolodner, 2000). For high-risk urban classrooms implementing the engineering design process significant gains were reported in the science classroom (Silk, Schunn, & Strand Cary (2009).

Strobel and van Barneveld (2009) did a meta-synthesis of meta-analyses regarding problem-based learning (PBL) to create a generalizable statement about PBL. The results of their synthesis favored traditional instruction for short-term knowledge retention. However, the results for longer-term retention and skill development favored PBL, which was received more favorably by both students and teachers.

What Changes can be Made to the Current Educational System to Create Deep, Active Learning in the Middle School Science Classroom?

Changing the current educational system from traditional teaching models is not an easy task. It involves many variables at multiple school levels. Studying innovations that work and provide positive findings for change are necessary for modifications to occur.

Christensen, Knezek, & Tyler-Wood (2015) gathered attitudinal data from 364 high school students participating in a residential mathematics and science academy on a university campus in which they complete their last 2 years of high school in conjunction with their first 2 years in college. Surveys were completed by 204 first-year students (11th graders) and 160 second-year (12th graders). These students were asked to provide their perspective looking back to what made a difference in their interest in science and to provide recommendations for making changes in the education system. One question asked of these students focused on ways to improve STEM education in the U.S. When asked for suggestions for improving STEM education in the United States, there were many ideas that were frequently mentioned. These suggestions included more hands-on and engaging lessons, more STEM-related (including engineering) courses offered, career education at an earlier age, making classes more relevant to the real world, and more passionate and qualified teachers. Many of these suggestions are consistent with the research showing that younger students are thought to benefit most from exposure to scientific inquiry during the naturally curious stages of development, in which they display a natural inclination to the fundamentals of engineering design processes; designing and building things; and taking things apart to see how they work (Lachapelle & Cunningham, 2007). Participant suggestions could be easily translated into research agendas to be tested regarding measurable impact, in a traditional experimental paradigm.

Overcoming Challenges of Science Education in Middle School Classrooms

Previous science reform efforts have found an inability to maintain effective change when the efforts were organized from the top down (Cuban, 1990). This is often because change in practice occurs at the classroom level and may need to address the influential nature of the teachers' attitudes and beliefs about necessary changes to teaching the science curriculum (Jones & Eick, 2007). As one component of acknowledging that teachers are the most important element in how science is taught in the classroom, effective training and support must be provided to the classroom teacher. Teachers need to have the opportunity to deepen and expand their subject matter knowledge (Borko & Putnam, 1996) as well as learn the content and the pedagogy by engaging in models of teaching that engage active and meaningful learning in science. Research indicates that teacher learning should be provided within the classroom setting making stronger links from training to practice (Davis, 2002). Most importantly, teachers require time and support to reflect on what they are teaching as well as interactions with other teachers and mentors (Davis, 2002). In summary, effective change is a step-by-step process that first requires a change in belief that the innovation will improve learning. Once a teacher accepts that the new innovation could improve learning for his/her students, assessment of where each teacher is in their level of comfort and competence in the innovative change is important for targeting effective professional development.

Engaging middle school students in learning is quite a challenge due to the complex changes that are already occurring within the student. Because this is the age in which students often set the course for their career goals, there is an urgency in creating an interest in science. Active learning practices can create an environment to be effective for middle school students. Allowing students to have some input into their learning environment by creating an environment of choice is one strategy that supports the growing need of independence for middle school students. By choosing learning activities that infuse relevance, authenticity and choice into the curriculum, educators can make learning more focused (Caskey & Anfara, 2007). "Young adolescents are more likely to engage in the classroom when they connect content and learning tasks with life beyond the classroom walls" (Maday, 2008, p. 3).

Diffusion of Innovation

Evidence has accumulated in recent decades that the revision of an established curriculum and wide diffusion into classroom practice cannot be accomplished overnight. In the words of Surry and Ely (1999), "… the adoption of an innovation is not a single act, but a process that occurs over time." Christensen and Knezek (Knezek & Christensen, 2000; Christensen & Knezek, 2001) have shown through a series of studies that the most optimistic expectation for bringing a technology-infused curricular innovation into standard classroom practice, across a large school, district or statewide level, is approximately one stage of adoption per year. This is on a continuum of six stages as shown in Fig. 1.

If one substitutes the phrase "active learning science curriculum" for "technology" then a similar step by step development process can be envisioned for any curricular innovation, and, in fact this model has been shown to be congruent with the Concerns-Based Adoption Model (CBAM) Levels of Use sequence developed by Hall, Loucks, Rutherford, and Newlove (1975) for removing concerns in educators arising from new educational innovations. Hall et al.'s work was built on conceptual foundations for models of educational change by Fullan (1982) and others. These models are still widely respected into the 21st Century.

The Stages of Adoption sequence shown in Fig. 1 has its primary roots in the general concept of Diffusion of Innovations (Rogers, 1995), first introduced by Everett Rogers in the 1960s. Rogers' ideas on the acceptance rate of an innovation by

Stages of Adoption

Instructions: Please read the descriptions of each of the six stages related to adoption of technology. Choose the ONE stage that best describes where you are in the adoption of technology.

(	**Stage 1: Awareness** I am aware that technology exists but have not used it - perhaps I'm even avoiding it. I am anxious about the prospect of using computers
(	**Stage 2: Learning the process** I am currently trying to learn the basics. I am sometimes frustrated using computers. I lack confidence when using computers.
(	**Stage 3: Understanding and application of the process** I am beginning to understand the process of using technology and can think of specific tasks in which it might be useful.
(	**Stage 4: Familiarity and confidence** I am gaining a sense of confidence in using the computer for specific tasks. I am starting to feel comfortable using the computer.
(	**Stage 5: Adaptation to other contexts** I think about the computer as a tool to help me and am no longer concerned about it as technology. I can use it in many applications and as an instructional aid.
(	**Stage 6: Creative application to new contexts** I can apply what I know about technology in the classroom. I am able to use it as an instructional tool and integrate it into the curriculum.

Fig. 1 Christensen's (2002) six stages of adoption of technology based on Russell (1995)

teachers at the classroom level has been shown to be reasonably accurate over a wide range of educational innovations, including recently emerging areas such as distance learning (Alajmi, 2010). The basic concept is that a small proportion (3%) of any typical large collection of teachers (perhaps at the school-wide level) will be innovators, adopting a new educational innovation immediately, while a larger but still small proportion (14%) will be early adopters and enthusiastically embrace the change. Must larger proportions (34%) will be Early Majority in following the Early Adopters, and approximately an equal proportion will be Late Majority, that is, will follow the majority. A sizeable proportion (16%) will be Laggards, those who only reluctantly adopt an innovation after the innovation has been put into regular classroom practice by everyone else. Rogers' Model is shown in Fig. 2.

Alajmi (2010) has shown that educators' self reported Stages of Adoption (Fig. 1) correlate highly with the same educators' ratings of their Diffusion of Innovation level. A major difference is that Stages of Adoption adopts the lens of one teacher or a group of teachers advancing through various stages of development, while Diffusion of Innovations (Fig. 2) is focused on the portion of the total group that has adopted an innovation at any point in time. As Surry and Ely (1999) pointed out, the process that is necessary for wide adoption of an innovation within a population is sometimes lengthy but also natural and predictable. One major calibration of expectations to be derived from these models and scholarly observations is that a 5-year plan for having most teachers adopt a new curricular innovation might be a realistic expectation.

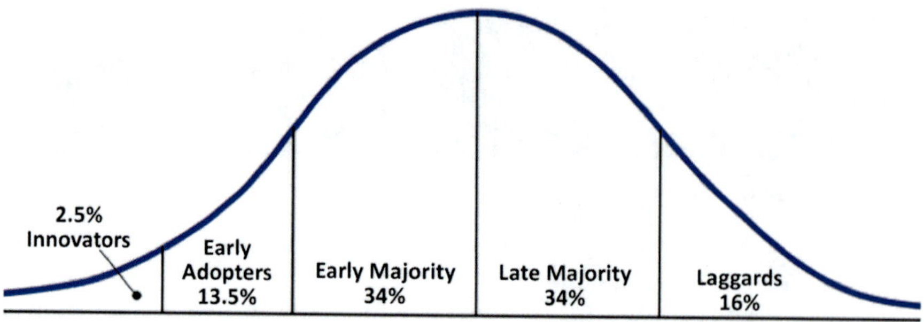

Fig. 2 Roger's Diffusion of Innovations Model, Hypothesized distribution of adopter categories within a typical population

The authors have developed a model of technology integration consistent with Rogers's model of diffusions of innovation and aimed at relating teacher development to student achievement. The Will, Skill, Tool Model of Technology Integration includes the educator's desire to use technology (will), training in pedagogically sound infusion of technology (skill) and access to hardware, software and support structures (tool) as necessary components for full integration of technology into the classroom environment (Knezek, Christensen, Hancock, & Shoho, 2000). Research has shown that teacher proficiency in technology integration accounts for 8–12% of student achievement (Morales, 2007).

Implementation of Innovation

From an educational systems perspective, there are other considerations such as implementation and institutionalization that are important in addition to diffusion and adoption at the classroom level. Fullan (1996) defined implementation as "…the actual use of an innovation in practice," while Surry and Ely (1999) have pointed out that in general each product, procedure, and practice has to maintain a high fidelity to the original (with some local adaptation) for implementation to be successful. This is analogous to what Dede (2010) has referred to as the need to pay attention to frequency, intensity, and duration for a new innovation to be successful. Ely (1999) has provided factors commonly associated with successful curricular implementations. These include: dissatisfaction with the status quo, a focus on meaningful training, shared decision-making, and leadership support of innovation.

According to Dede (2006), "Scaling up" involves adapting an innovation successful in some local setting to effective usage in a wide range of contexts. Scalable designs for educational transformation must avoid what Wiske and Perkins (2005) term the "replica trap": the erroneous strategy of trying to repeat everywhere what worked locally, without taking account of local variations in needs and environments. In the context of innovations in teaching/curriculum, scale encompasses four interrelated dimensions: depth, sustainability, spread, and shift in reform ownership (Dede & Rockman, 2007).

Professional development can be targeted using a model such as the Will, Skill, Tool Model so that educational leaders can assess baseline proficiencies of teachers and track progress due to targeted initiatives. Since research has shown that teachers can advance one level/stage per year on average with targeted professional development, it is important that a school district plan for a sustained effort over several years in order to be able to verify positive outcomes. Gathering data from teachers on their willingness to integrate the innovation, whether it be technology or other science-based active learning curriculum, can be accomplished with selected attitudinal measures. The skill or self-efficacy can be measured using indicators of confidence in using the innovation—and the necessary tools should be included in the implementation of the innovation. Many states and professional associations have recommended that 30% of funding for an innovation be used for the very important area of training.

Institutionalization

Institutionalization is sometimes referred to as "routinization" or "continuation"; where the innovation is routinely used in the settings for which it was designed (Surry & Ely, 1999). Six common indicators of institutionalization have been identified by Eiseman, Fleming, and Roody (1990):

1. The innovation has been accepted by relevant participants
2. The innovation is stable and routinized
3. The innovation is widely used throughout the institution or organization
4. There is a firm expectation by the stakeholders that the practice will continue
5. Continuation does not depend on specific individuals but upon organizational culture, structure or procedures, and
6. There are routine allocations of time and money to the innovation.

When all of these steps are successfully completed, the case can be made that the new curriculum is no longer an innovation but an embedded and essential part of the 21st century classroom.

References

Akinoglu, O., & Tandogan, R. O. (2007). The effects of problem-based active learning in science education on students' academic achievement, attitude and concept learning. *Eurasia Journal of Mathematics, Science & Technology Education, 3*(1), 71–81.

Alajmi, M. (2010). *Faculty members' readiness for e-learning in the college of basic education in Kuwait*. Doctoral dissertation, University of North Texas, August, 2010. http://digital.library. unt.edu/ark:/67531/metadc31523/?q=Kuwait. Accessed 5 March 2014.

Alexander, C., Knezek, G., Christensen, R., & Tyler-Wood, T. (2014). (Unpublished manuscript submitted for review). *Piloting Innovative Learning Experiences: Measuring Outcomes of Digital Fabrication Activities across Five Classrooms.*

Aschbacher, P. R., Ing, M., & Tsai, S. M. (2013). Boosting student interest in science. *Kappan Magazine, 95*(2), 47–51.

Bentley, M., Ebert, E., & Ebert, S. (2007). *Teaching constructivist science, K-8: Nurturing natural investigators in the standards-based classroom.* Thousand Oaks: Corwin Press.

Bevan, B., & Semper, R. (2006). *Mapping informal science institutions onto the science education landscape.* http://www.exploratorium.edu/CILS/documents/RTsystemsBB.pdf.

Bloom, B. (1984). *Taxonomy of educational objectives: The classification of educational goals. Book I: Cognitive domain.* New York: Longman.

Bonwell, C., & Eison, J. (1991). *Active learning: Creating excitement in the classroom. AEHE-ERIC Higher Education Report No. 1.* Washington, D. C.: Jossey-Bass.

Borko, H., & Putnam, R. T. (1996). Learning to teach. In R. C. Calfee & D. Berliner (Eds.), *Handbook on educational psychology* (pp. 673–708). New York: Macmillan.

Bruner, J. S. (1961). The act of discovery. *Harvard Educational Review, 31,* 21–32.

Cantrell, P., Pekcan, G., Itani, A., & Velasquez-Bryant, N. (2006). The effects of engineering modules on student learning in middle school science classrooms. *Journal of Engineering Education, 95,* 301–309. doi:10.1002/j.2168-9830.2006.tb00905.x.

Caskey, M. M., & Anfara, V. A., Jr. (2007). *Research summary: Young adolescents' developmental characteristics.* Westerville: National Middle School Association.

Casner-Lotto, J., & Barrington, L. (2006). *Are they really ready to work? Employers' perspectives on the basic knowledge and applied skills of new entrants to the 21st century U.S.* Washington, D. C.: The Conference Board, Inc., the Partnership for 21st Century Skills, Corporate Voices for Working Families, and the Society for Human Resource Management.

Chen, C.-H., & Howard, B. (2010). Effect of live simulation on middle school students' attitudes and learning toward science. *Educational Technology & Society, 13,* 133–139.

Christensen, R. (2002). Impact of technology integration education on the attitudes of teachers and students. *Journal of Research on Technology in Education, 34*(4), 411–434.

Christensen, R., & Knezek, G. (2001). *Equity and diversity in K-12 applications of information technology: Key instructional design strategies (KIDS) project findings for 2000–2001, Year Two Report.* Denton, TX: Institute for the Integration of Technology into Teaching and Learning (IITTL).

Christensen, R., Knezek, G., Standish, N., Kjellstrom, W., & Tyler-Wood, T. (Unpublished manuscript submitted for review, 2014). *Gains in content knowledge from middle school students participating in digital fabrication activities.*

Christensen, R., Knezek, G., & Tyler-Wood, T. (2015). A retrospective analysis of STEM career interest among mathematics and science academy students. *International Journal of Learning, Teaching and Educational Research, 10*(1), 45–58.

Crane, V., Nicholson, H., Chen, M., & Bitgood, S. (Eds.). (1994). *Informal science learning: What the research says about television, science museums, and community-based projects.* Dedham: Research Communications Ltd.

Cuban, L. (1990). Reforming again, again, and again. *Educational Researcher, 19*(1), 3–14.

Davis, K. S. (2002). Change is hard: What science teachers are telling us about reform and teacher learning of innovative practices. *Science Education, 87*(1), 3–30.

Dede, C. (2006). Scaling up: Evolving innovations beyond ideal settings to challenging contexts of practice. In R. K. Sawyer (Ed.), *Cambridge handbook of the learning sciences* (pp. 551–556). New York: Cambridge University Press.

Dede, C. (2010). Technological supports for acquiring 21st century skills. In E. Baker, B. McGaw & P. Peterson (Eds.), *International encyclopedia of education* (3rd ed.). Oxford: Elsevier. http://learningcenter.nsta.org/products/symposia_seminars/iste/files/Technological_Support_for_21stCentury_Encyclo_dede.pdf.

Dede, C., & Rockman, S. (2007). Lessons learned from studying how innovations can achieve scale. *Threshold: Exploring the Future of Education, 5*(1), 4–10.

Dewey, J. (1938). *Experience and education. A touchstone book.* New York: Kappa Delta Pi.

Dierking, L. D., & Falk, J. H. (2003). Optimizing youth's out-of-school time: The role of free choice learning. *New Directions for Youth Development, 97,* 75–89.

Douglas, R. (2006). *Linking science & literacy in the K-8 classroom*. Arlington: NSTA Press.

Eiseman, J. W., Fleming, D. S., & Roody, D. S. (1990). *Making sure it sticks: The school improvement leader's role in institutionalizing change*. Andover: The Regional Laboratory.

Ely, D. P. (1999) *New perspectives on the implementation of educational technology innovations*. Paper presented at the Association for Educational Communications and Technology Annual Conference, Houston, TX. ED427775.

Fortus, D., Dershimer, R. C., Marx, R. W., Krajcik, J., & Mamlok-Naaman, R. (2004). Design-based science (DBS) and student learning. *Journal of Research in Science Teaching, 41*(10), 1081–1110.

Fullan, M. (1982). *The meaning of educational change*. New York: Teachers College Press.

Fullan, M. (1996). Curriculum implementation. In D. P. Ely & T. Plomp (Eds.), *International encyclopedia of educational technology* (2nd ed.) (pp. 273–281). New York: Pergamon Press.

Gallagher, S. (1997). Problem-based learning: Where did it come from, what does it do and where is it going? *Journal for Education of the Gifted, 29*(4), 332–362.

Glock, J., Meyer, M., & Wertz, S. (1999). *Discovering the naturalist intelligence: Science in the school yard*. Tucson: Zephyr Press.

Gray, K. (2007). Watt-waster phantom loads steal electricity, pour carbons into air. *Emory Report, 60*(8), n.p. http://www.emory.edu/EMORY_REPORT/erarchive/2007/October/Oct22/WattWasterPhantom.htm.

Hall, G. E., Loucks, S. F., Rutherford, W. L., & Newlove, B. W. (1975). Levels of use of the innovation: A framework for analyzing innovation adoption. *Journal of Teacher Education, 26*(1), 52–56. doi:10.1177/002248717502600114.

Heller, R., Calderon, S., & Medrich, E. (2003). *Academic achievement in the middle grades: What does research tell us? A review of literature*. Atlanta: Southern Regional Education Board.

Hmelo, C. E., Holton, D. L., & Kolodner, J. L. (2000). Designing to learn about complex systems. *Journal of the Learning Sciences, 9*(3), 247–298.

Johnson, L., Adams, S., & Cummins, S. (2012). *The NMC horizon report: 2012 higher education edition*. Austin: The New Media Consortium.

Jonassen, D. H., Howland, J. L., Moore, J. L., & Marra, R. M. (2003). *Learning to solve problems with technology: A constructivist perspective*. Upper Saddle River: Merrill Prentice Hall.

Jones, M. T., & Eick, C. J. (2007). Implementing inquiry kit curriculum: Obstacles, adaptations, and practical knowledge development in two middle school science teachers. *Science Education, 91*(3), 492–513.

Knezek, G., & Christensen, R. (2000). *Refining best teaching practices for technology integration: KIDS project findings for 1999–2000*. Denton: Institute for the Integration of Technology into Teaching and Learning (IITTL).

Knezek, G., Christensen, R., Hancock, R., & Shoho, A. (2000). *Toward a structural model of technology integration*. Paper presented at the American Educational Research Association (AERA), Chicago, IL.

Lachapelle, C. P., & Cunningham, C. M. (2007). *Engineering is elementary: Children's changing understandings of science and engineering*. Presented at the ASEE Annual Conference and Exposition, Honolulu, HI.

Lave, J., & Wenger, E. (1991). *Situated learning—legitimate peripheral participation*. New York: Cambridge University Press.

Maday, T. (2008). *Stuck in the middle: Strategies to engage middle-level learners*. Washington, D. C.: The Center for Comprehensive School Reform and Improvement.

Maeda, J. (2. October 2012). STEM to STEAM: Art in K-12 is key to building a strong economy. *Edutopia: What works in education*. http://www.edutopia.org/blog/stem-to-steam-strengthens-economy-john-maeda.

Means, B. (2003). Technology and constructivist learning. http://www.ncrel.org/cscd/pubs/lead51/51means.htm.

Miller, J. (2013). STEAM for student engagement. In R. McBride & M. Searson (Eds.), *Proceedings of society for information technology & teacher education international conference 2013* (pp. 3288–3298). Chesapeake: AACE.

Miller. J. (2014). *Dublin independent school district STEAM camp overview*. Dublin Independent School District (ISD), TX. http://www.dublin.k12.tx.us/Page/1424. Accessed 2 March 2014.

Miller, J., & Phillips. L. (2014). Middle school STEAM camp perspectives and attitudes towards STEM. In M. Ocha & M. Searson (Eds.), *Proceedings of society for information technology & teacher education international conference 2014* (pp. in press). Chesapeake: AACE.

Morales, C. (2007). Testing predictive models of technology integration in Mexico and the United States. *Computers in the Schools, 24*(3/4), 153–173.

National Research Council. (2009). *Engineering in K-12 education: Understanding the status and improving the prospects committee on K-12 engineering education*. Washington, D. C.: The National Academies Press (L. Katechi, G. Pearson, & M. Feder. (Eds.)).

National Research Council. (2012). *A framework for K-12 science education: Practices, crosscutting concepts, and core ideas*. Washington, D. C.: The National Academies Press.

Nolte, P., & Harris, D. (June 2010). Middle schoolers out to save the world, June 30, 2010 Evaluation Report. The University of North Texas, Institute for the Integration of Technology into Teaching and Learning, website: http://iittl.unt.edu/IITTL/itest/msosw_web/evaluations/MSOSW_External_Evaluators_Report_2010.pdf.

Partnership for 21st Century Skills (P21). (2007). *The international ICT literacy panel, digital*. Washington, D. C.: Partnership for 21st Century Skills. http://www.p21.org.

Partnership for 21st Century Skills (P21). (2011). *P21 common core toolkit: A guide to aligning the common core state standards with the framework for 21st century skills*. The partnership for 21st Century Skills, Washington, D. C.: Partnership for 21st Century Skills

Piaget, J. (1983). Piaget's theory. In P. Mussen (Ed.), *Handbook of child psychology* (4th ed. Vol. 1). New York: Wiley.

Quinn, H., Schweingruber, H., & Keller, T. (Eds.). (2013). *The next generation science standards for today's students and tomorrow's workforce*. Washington, D. C.: Committee on Conceptual Framework for the New K-12 Science Education Standards; Board on Science Education (BOSE); Division of Behavioral and Social Sciences and Education (DBASSE); National Research Council.

Resta, P., Searson, M., Patru, M., Knezek, G., & Voogt, J. (Eds.). (8–10 June 2011). Summary report of the EDUsummIT 2011. Invitational summit held at UNESCO, Paris. edusummit.nl/results2011.

Rogers, E. M. (1995). *Diffusion of innovations* (4th ed.). New York: Free Press.

Ross, J. P., & Meier, A. (2000, September). *Whole-house measurements of standby power consumption*. In Proceedings of the Second International Conference on Energy Efficiency in Household Appliances, Naples, Italy.

Russell, A. L. (1995). Stages in learning new technology: Naive adult email users. *Computers in Education, 25*(4), 173–178.

Savage, R. N., Chen, K. C., & Vanasupa, L. (2009). Integrating project-based learning throughout the undergraduate engineering curriculum. *Engineering Management Review, 37*(1), 15–28.

Sherrod, S. E., Dwyer, J., & Narayan, R. (2009). Developing science and math integrated activities for middle school students. *International Journal of Mathematical Education in Science and Technology, 40*, 247–257.

Silk, E. M., Schunn, C. D., & Strand Cary, M. (2009). The impact of an engineering design curriculum on science reasoning in an urban setting. *Journal of Science Education and Technology, 18*(3), 209–223. doi:10.1007/s10956-009-9144-8.

Spector, J. M. (2012). *Foundations of educational technology*. New York: Routledge.

STEM to STEAM (2014). What is STEAM? Rhode island independent school district: STEM to STEAM initiative. http://stemtosteam.org.

Strobel, J., & van Barneveld, A. (2009). When is PBL more effective? A meta-synthesis of meta-analyses comparing PBL to conventional classrooms. *Interdisciplinary Journal of Problem-Based Learning, 3*(1). http://docs.lib.purdue.edu/ijpbl/vol3/iss1/4/.

Surry, D. W., & Ely, D. P. (1999). *Adoption, diffusion, implementation, and institutionalization of educational technology*. http://www.usouthal.edu/coe/bset/surry/papers/adoption/chap.htm.

Tyler-Wood, T. L., Ellison, A., Lim, O., & Periathiruvadi, S. (2011). Bringing up girls in science (BUGS): The effectiveness of an afterschool environmental science program for increasing female student's interest in science careers. *Journal of Science Education Technology, 21*(1), 46–55.

Verma, A. K., Dickerson, D., & McKinney, S. (2011). Engaging students in STEM careers with project-based learning—marine tech project. *Technology & Engineering Teacher, 71*(1), 25–31.

Vygotsky, L. (1978). *Mind and society*. Cambridge: Harvard University Press.

Wiske, M. S., & Perkins, D. (2005). Dewey goes digital: Scaling up constructivist pedagogies and the promise of new technologies. In C. Dede, J. Honan, & L. Peters (Eds.), *Scaling up success: Lessons learned from technology- based educational innovation* (pp. 27–47). San Francisco: Jossey-Bass.

Rhonda Christensen is a research scientist in the Learning Technologies Department in the College of Information at the University of North Texas. She is an associate director of the Institute for the Integration of Technology into Teaching and Learning at UNT. She is a Co-PI and project manager for the Going Green! Middle Schoolers Out to Save the World (MSOSW) project funded by the U.S. National Science Foundation (NSF). She serves as the Information Technology Council Chair for the Society for Information Technology in Teacher Education (SITE) international organization. She was a classroom teacher for 7 years and a technology coordinator for 4 years. In the coordinator role she provided professional development to teachers and also worked with middle school teachers and students in integrating technology into hands-on science activities. She has co-authored and taught a pre-service technology integration course for more than 15 years. She also teaches doctoral courses on research design and analysis. Her research interests include the impact of technology integration in education, enhancing STEM education in middle schools and mobile learning in education.

Gerald Knezek is Regents Professor of Learning Technologies at the University of North Texas and Director of the Institute for the Integration of Technology into Teaching & Learning (IITTL) at UNT. He is Past President (2008–2011) of the Society for Information Technology & Teacher Education (SITE). He is currently Lead Principal Investigator for the US National Science Foundation Innovative Technologies Project Going Green! Middle Schoolers Out to Save the World. He was a Fulbright Scholar at the Tokyo Institute of Technology during 1993–1994 and shared time between Texas and Ecuador on a Fulbright Senior Specialist appointment during 2006–2007. He held a second Fulbright Senior Specialist appointment to The Netherlands during 2011–2012. His research interests include measuring attitudes toward information technology, assessing the impact of technology integration, bridging formal and informal learning through ubiquitous learning environments, enhancing creativity and fostering innovative STEM education.

Preparing Students with 21st Century Skills: Integrating Scientific Knowledge, Skills, and Epistemic Beliefs in Middle School Science Curricula

Jiangyue Gu and Brian R. Belland

Abstract In the 21st century, every citizen needs to acquire adequate scientific knowledge and skills to be competitive in the job market, and be scientific literate in everyday contexts. The recent push for STEAM education calls for integrating science, technology, engineering, art, and mathematic components together to prepare students for 21th century challenges. To address these concerns, in this chapter we discuss how to prepare students with critical skills to succeed in the 21st century. Our discussion of reconceptualizing science curriculum in middle school level is based on three major perspectives. To prepare students to face the challenges in the 21st century, educators need to help students (1) acquire sufficient core scientific knowledge, (2) gain skills needed to engage in scientific practice, and (3) develop sophisticated epistemic beliefs to understand the nature of scientific knowledge and the methods of making it. We discuss the importance of each perspective in science education in light of the current literature, and address some remaining issues for future directions.

Keywords Science curriculum · 21st century skills · Argumentation · Epistemology · Middle school

Introduction

Overarching Goal of Science Education in the 21st Century

In the 21st century, as modern society has been reshaped by technological advancement, scientific innovation, and globalization, workforce development demands

J. Gu (✉) · B. R. Belland
Utah State University, Logan, USA
e-mail: jiangyue.gu@aggiemail.usu.edu

B. R. Belland
e-mail: brian.belland@usu.edu

© Springer International Publishing Switzerland 2015
X. Ge et al. (eds.), *Emerging Technologies for STEAM Education,*
Educational Communications and Technology: Issues and Innovations,
DOI 10.1007/978-3-319-02573-5_3

have shifted (NSTA, 2011). In science education, rather than being expected to know a list of science topics, American high school graduates are expected to "(1) appreciate the beauty and wonder of science, (2) have adequate knowledge to engage in public discussion on socio-scientific issues, (3) become careful consumers of scientific and technology information in their daily lives, (4) be capable of and continue to learn science outside of school, and (5) acquire adequate skills of science to enter the career of their choice" (NRC, 2012, p. 1). Core to strong performance in science is the integration of technology, engineering, arts, and mathematics into science education, as these complementary disciplines provide tools and processes by which people can investigate natural phenomena and design solutions to scientific problems (Bequette & Bequette, 2012; NGSS Lead States, 2013; Platz, 2007).

Challenges for Students in the 21st Century

Compared to non-STEM careers, STEM-related employment will increase greatly in the next few decades (Ashby, 2006; BLS, 2013). However, too few American middle school students are proficient in mathematics and science, which makes it difficult for them to enter STEM fields (PCAST, 2010). Fewer than one in five twelfth graders are proficient in mathematics and interested in STEM subjects (BHEF, 2010). Besides mathematics, students need to have sufficient scientific knowledge and critical skills to engage scientific practices (NSTA, 2011). Although not every student will choose to work in STEM fields, as citizens in the 21st century, they all need to be well prepared to address authentic scientific problems.

In the 21st century, the continuing expansion of human knowledge demands that everyone gain the skills to acquire, select, evaluate, and use information appropriately and effectively (AASL, 2007). In a society where the Internet is the defining technology for literacy and learning (Leu et al., 2011), students need to be able to read, write, learn, and communicate using the Internet and other information technology (Drew, 2013).

Modern society also requires that people be able to solve increasingly complex problems in everyday and professional contexts (Jonassen, 2011). Every student needs to be able to use modern technology and tools such as computers and information and communications technology (ICT) as an aid to construct and communicate new information to solve problems (Kim & Lee, 2013).

With the development of modern society, a growing number of socio-scientific issues have been presented in society. Every individual, as a citizen, needs to be equipped with decision making skills and scientific literate to make well-informed decisions and take active roles in society (Saunders & Rennie, 2013; Walker & Zeidler, 2007).

Potential Solutions

To help students meet 21st century challenges, there is an urgent need to reconceptualize and reform current science curriculum at K-12 level. In this chapter, we focus on core scientific knowledge, critical skills for scientific practices, and so-phisticated epistemic beliefs as three major perspectives to reconceptualize science education in middle school level. To prepare students to face 21st century challeng-es, educators need to help students (1) acquire sufficient core scientific knowledge, (2) gain skills needed to engage in scientific practice, and (3) develop sophisticated epistemic beliefs to understand the nature of scientific knowledge and the methods of constructing it. We discuss each perspective in the following sections.

How to Teach Scientific Knowledge in the 21st Century

In an age of knowledge explosion, the purpose of K-12 science education is not to teach students all the scientific knowledge they need in their everyday and pro-fessional contexts, but rather to focus on a limited number of disciplinary core ideas and crosscutting concepts (NRC, 2007, 2012; NGSS Lead States, 2013). These core ideas and crosscutting concepts are fundamental to the development of science understanding so that students can continually build on and connect with many related scientific concepts (NRC, 2007). Helping students gain core scientific knowledge and improve their information literacy will enable students to continue to learn scientific knowledge in and out of school (Kereluik, Mishra, Fahnoe, & Terry, 2013).

Integration of Core Scientific Knowledge

Crosscutting Concepts and Disciplinary Core Ideas

The National Research Council proposed that K-12 science education should be centered on three major dimensions: scientific and engineering practices, cross-cutting concepts, and disciplinary core ideas (NRC, 2012). This framework forms the foundation of K-12 science curriculum by outlining what to teach (crosscutting concepts and disciplinary core ideas) and how to teach (through scientific and en-gineering practices). Crosscutting concepts are concepts that bridge and unify vari-ous fields in science and engineering as they present a common way of knowing in science (Duschl, 2012). Learning these crosscutting concepts can enable students to connect knowledge from various disciplines to form a coherent understanding of scientific methods. For instance, by learning the first two crosscutting concepts—*patterns* and *cause and effect*—students can understand that scientists observe and explore patterns and use scientific methods to investigate cause and effect relation-ships to explain and interpret patterns (NRC, 2012).

There are several core ideas (e.g., Newton's laws of motion and the theory of biological evolution) in the physics, life sciences, earth and space sciences, and engineering, technology and application of science (NRC, 2012). The disciplinary core ideas are foundational and central concepts and theories that help students build conceptual understanding in natural sciences. In engineering, there are certain core ideas that are different from those of science. Besides core ideas in the field of natural sciences, students should also learn core ideas of engineering, technology, and art design processes, such as delimiting engineering problems, and optimizing design solutions, and balancing aesthetic and utility concerns.

Integration of Core Scientific Knowledge Through Scientific and Engineering Practice

In the past few decades, teaching science through a process of inquiry has long been advocated in several policy documents (e.g., AAAS, 1990; NRC, 1996). However, research has consistently shown that simply engaging in scientific inquiry is insufficient to help students acquire disciplinary core ideas and understanding of the nature of science (Khishfe & Abd-El-Khalick, 2002; Sandoval, 2005; Schwarz & White, 2005). Many school scientific inquiry tasks do not incorporate the epistemic aspect of real science and engineering practices (Chinn & Malhotra, 2002; Prins, Bulte, & Pilot, 2011). Moreover, a narrow focus on the performance of inquiry skills may cause the understanding of the nature of science and disciplinary core ideas in science education to be deemphasized (Abd-El-Khalick et al., 2004).

To be clear, we do not mean that students should not engage in scientific inquiry; as one form of scientific practice, scientific inquiry certainly involves most scientific practices. In the framework for K-12 science education (NRC, 2012), eight science and engineering practices (such as developing and using models, using mathematics and computational thinking, constructing explanations) were emphasized. However, it is not likely that inquiry-based learning tasks can cover all of these practices. Therefore, teachers can use crosscutting concepts and disciplinary core ideas as the foundational content onto which particular scientific or engineering practices can build. As such, certain scientific and engineering practices can focus on a few particular types of practices to emphasize relevant core scientific knowledge. In this way, by engaging in science practice, students can perceive how core scientific knowledge is constructed and developed, which will help them to develop understandings of the nature of science as well as relevant inquiry skills (Abd-El-Khalick et al., 2004; Ford, 2008). Engaging in engineering practice can also help students understand how engineers apply various knowledge, modern tools, scientific methods to solve practical problems (Sneider, 2012). By integrating core scientific knowledge with scientific and engineering practices, students will have opportunities to deepen their understanding of core ideas in each disciplinary and apply crosscutting concepts across disciplines (NRC, 2012). In addition, science and engineering practices are often applied in design process for inventing and innovating artifacts and products to address functional, aesthetic, environmental, and economic concerns. As one way to connect science, engineering, and art practices, teaching design process holds potential to integrate STEM education and art education in K-12 curriculum (Vande Zande, 2010).

Integration of Core Scientific Knowledge Through Addressing Socio-Scientific Issues

In the past few decades, a growing number of complex, controversial, and problematic issues such as global warming, alternative fuels, and genetically modified food have been presented in our society. Such issues are often referred to as socio-scientific issues—issues "based on scientific concepts or problems, controversial in nature, discussed in public outlets and frequently subject to political and social influences" (Sadler & Zeidler, 2005, p. 113). All citizens need to be equipped with decision making skills and scientific literacy to make well-informed decisions and take active roles in society (Saunders & Rennie, 2013; Walker & Zeidler, 2007).

In recent years, researchers have encouraged the incorporation of socio-scientific issues (SSI) in science curricula (Sadler & Donnelly, 2006; Saunders & Rennie, 2013). Socio-scientific issues, by definition, have political and social implications for everyone in society (Sadler & Zeidler, 2005). By integrating SSIs with a focus on scientific content knowledge in science instruction, students may perceive the importance and value of scientific knowledge and see how scientific practices issues are related to their daily lives, which in turn may motivate students' interests in science (Dawson & Venville, 2010; Dolan, Nichols, & Zeidler, 2009). More importantly, SSIs can provide meaningful contexts for science instruction, which can potentially support students' learning of content knowledge (Sadler, Barab, & Scott, 2007). By engaging in learning with SSIs, students can significantly improve their understanding of relevant content knowledge (Applebaum, Barker, & Pinzino, 2006; Barab, Sadler, Heiselt, Hickey, & Zuiker, 2010) As SSIs often involve interdisciplinary knowledge, they can provide contexts for students to see how crosscutting concepts apply across different fields. Moreover, SSIs are often found in areas of science in which there are disagreements among experts and few simple and clear solutions (Kolstø et al., 2006). By addressing SSIs, students' understanding of the nature of science can be promoted (Eastwood et al., 2012; Khishfe & Lederman, 2006).

Development of Skills to Engage in Scientific Practice in the 21st Century

21st Century Skills

To ensure that students are well prepared to face 21st century challenges, researchers and educators have started to identify the essential skills needed in 21st century. Proposed by National Research Council (2010), there are five skills that are essential for every student to acquire in a fast-paced, rapidly changed world: adaptability, complex communication/social skills, non-routine problem solving, self-management/self-development, and systems thinking. According to the Partnership for 21st century skills (P21, 2009), 21st century skills consist of:

- Learning and innovation skills, which include (1) creativity and innovation, (2) critical thinking and problem solving, (3) communication and (4) collaboration.
- Information, media and technology literacy skills, which include (1) information literacy, (2) media literacy, and (3) information and communication technology literacy.
- Life and career skills, which include: (1) adaptability and, flexibility (2) initiative and self-direction, (3) cross-cultural and social skills, (4) accountability and productivity, and (5) responsibility and leadership.

The two definitions of 21st century skills proposed by both P21 and NRC together reflect the requirements and expectations for students as workers and citizens in the 21st century. Science education cannot and should not take full responsibility to develop all 21st century skills, but science education can offer a rich context for developing many 21st century skills (Bybee, 2010). Twenty-first century skills also provide new perspectives to frame essential skills in science that have long been valued, and new skills that are required for future generations (P21, 2009). Based on the 21st century skills proposed by NRC (2010) and P21 (2009), we identified a few essential skills that are critical for students to succeed in science education in middle school level.

Essential Skills to be Developed in Science Education

Effectively Acquiring and Evaluating Information

The continuing expansion of human knowledge demands that every student be able to acquire, evaluate, use, and integrate information appropriately and effectively (AASL, 2007). Especially with the increasing use of the Internet in and out of school, students need to be information literate to be able to read, write, learn, and communicate using the Internet and other information technology (Drew, 2013). In the context of science education, information literacy involves evaluating the credibility, validity, and reliability of information to interpret data, critically integrating information from multiple sources, and constructing scientific arguments to effectively engage in science learning (P21, 2009). During problem solving, students often need to search for or connect to relevant knowledge, propose solutions, and evaluate potential solutions against certain criteria (Jonassen, 2003). To be effectively engaged in scientific practices and complex problem solving, especially in online learning environments, students need to have sufficient skills to identify information needs, locate information sources, evaluate, and synthesize information from a variety of sources (Brand-Gruwel, Wopereis, & Walraven, 2009).

In the 21st century, computers and the Internet have been widely used in K-12 schools. In fall 2008, the ratio of students to instructional computers with Internet access was 3.1–1 in the U.S. public school (Gray, Thomas, & Lewis, 2010).

Although provided with easy access to an abundance of online resources, students often do not have sufficient skills to critically acquire, use and evaluate online information (Kuiper, Volman, & Terwel, 2009). Much web-based information combines varied text structures and formats, which poses unique challenges for young students to read and comprehend. Moreover, since online information is easy to create and distribute, determining the credibility of online information can be difficult (Baildon & Damico, 2011). In the context of science education, middle school students often struggle to use the Internet effectively to acquire relevant information during their scientific practices (Raes, Schellens, & De Wever, 2010). First, middle school students tend to use the Internet to search for quick answers rather than take time to understand and make sense of the online information (Kim, Hannafin, & Bryan, 2007). Second, middle school students' online learning is often disoriented and inefficient as students do not have sufficient searching skills and they are easily distracted by irrelevant online information (Zhang & Quintana, 2012). Third, online inquiry requires strong self-regulation ability and metacognitive awareness to monitor learning process (Brand-Gruwel et al., 2009); however, middle school students often lack such skills to plan or monitor their online learning process (Kuiper et al., 2009).

Constructing Scientific Arguments

Engaging in argumentation is a critical scientific process, as scientists often construct evidence-based arguments to interpret results and make conclusions (Bricker & Bell, 2008; Ford, 2012; Osborne, Erduran, & Simon, 2004). Therefore, argumentation skill, defined as the skill to support claims with evidence and premises through critical thinking and social interaction (Golanics & Nussbaum, 2007; Perelman & Olbrechts-Tyteca, 1958), is an essential skill in science learning. For instance, to engage in problem solving or scientific discussion, students need to gain sufficient argumentation ability to weigh the risks and benefits of alternative solutions, pose questions, evaluate evidence and counter evidence to make well informed decisions and engage in debate and discussion about problem solutions (Dawson & Venville, 2010). Central to argumentation is design of an argument and consideration of an audience, and such design can be informed by design processes and client interaction processes in engineering (Dym, Agogino, Eris, Frey, & Leifer, 2005) and the arts (Swanson, 1994). Unfortunately, engaging in argumentation is challenging for middle school students (Yoon, 2011). Middle school students often find it difficult to identify and gather relevant evidence (Pedersen & Liu, 2002), and struggle to back up claims with evidence (Glassner, Weinstock, & Neuman, 2005). Students' difficulties might be due to two reasons: middle school students' often lack sufficient cognitive ability (Kuhn & Udell, 2007) to engage in argumentation, and they often do not have sophisticated epistemological understanding of the meaning of justification and how to use evidence to justify something (Mason & Boscolo, 2004). Effective integration of engineering and art design processes into science curricula may also enhance middle school students' argumentation abilities (Dym et al., 2005; Swanson, 1994).

Using Modern Tools to Solve Problems Collaboratively

As Popper (1999)noted, all life is problem solving. As problems people face in their daily and professional contexts become increasingly complex, people use various modern tools to solve problems instead of their bare hands (Jonassen, 2003). Therefore, students not only need to be able to search for and use online information, but also need to use information and communications technology (ICT) as an aid to construct, communicate new information to solve problems (Kim & Lee, 2013). ICT innovations provide students with new tools for doing science including gathering, interpreting and analyzing data and communicating results (P21, 2009). As such, ICT literacy (the ability to use "digital technology, communications tools, and/or networks to access, manage, integrate, evaluate and create information" (International ICT Literacy Panel, 2002, p. 2) is an essential ability for students to solve real-world problems (Casner-Lotto, Barrington, Barrington, & Barrington, 2006; EU Communities, 2007). Moreover, to solve problems in a computer-based learning environment, students need to cope with technological complexity so that the joint cognitive system (human and computer) can perform its intended functions (Angeli, 2013; Hollnagel & Woods, 2005).

In the 21st century, most scientific investigations are conducted by groups of researchers rather than individuals, which requires researchers to effectively communicate and collaborate with their team members to solve problems (Hung, 2013). Only if research is appropriately presented and described, it can be understood, confirmed, and advanced by other researchers. In the context of science education, students also need to be able to communicate effectively about science through written and oral communication (Anderman, Sinatra, & Gray, 2012). Communication and collaboration skills, defined by the abilities to understand and respond appropriately to both verbal and nonverbal information (such as mathematical and graphical representation of ideas and observation) from others, are critical for students to succeed in the 21st century (NRC, 2010; P21, 2009). In K-12 science education, students often conduct group projects or assignments, so adequate communication and collaboration skills are essential for them to build shared understandings various communication needs.

Technologies to Support Students

Technology to Support Online Inquiry

To help students overcome these difficulties, computer-based scaffolds have been used in K-12 classroom in recent years. Scaffolding is interactive support provided by a more capable person or technological tools to enable students perform a task that they cannot do without help (Belland, 2014; Puntambekar & Hubscher, 2002; Wood, Bruner, & Ross, 1976). For example, Zhang and Quintana (2012) designed a computer-based scaffold called the *Digital IdeaKeeper* to help students search for, analyze, and synthesize online information and regulate their inquiry process. First, *IdeaKeeper* provides an integrated learning environment for students to conduct online inquiry. By embedding the Google search engine and other tools in it, *IdeaKeeper* keeps online inquiry activities in one space to make it more efficient. Second, it helps students plan their online inquiry by articulating the driving questions and sub-questions as the objects of online inquiry. Students can monitor their progress by referring to the driving questions, which in turn help them to manage their inquiry process. Third, by outlining four activity spaces (planning, searching, analyzing, and synthesizing), *IdeaKeeper* makes the structure of online inquiry more explicit to students to foster deep engagement with learning content. It contains several prompts for students to evaluate the trustworthiness and usefulness of online information. Last, *IdeaKeeper* can automatically record URLs, search term and results, and browsing history for students; therefore, students can focus on more meaningful learning tasks such as note taking, sense making, and synthesizing. The affordances of *IdeaKeeper* enable students to engage in more efficient and deep learning during online inquiry through two mechanisms of computer-based scaffolds, structuring and problematizing (Reiser, 2004). It provides needed structures for students to engage in online inquiry by making the learning objects and process more explicit, and also problematizes the meaningful learning tasks by guiding students to critically evaluate and synthesize online information.

Tools to Construct Scientific Arguments

The technology-based argument construction tools can potentially help middle school students overcome the challenges of constructing arguments and build more coherent and cohesive arguments (Linn, 2003). For instance, a context-specific computer-based scaffold called *ExplanationConstructor* is designed to help students construct and evaluate scientific explanations for natural phenomena (Sandoval & Reiser, 2004). *ExplanationConstructor* is an electronic journal to record students' investigations. It embeds several prompts for students to set up investigation goals, construct scientific explanation, and use evidence to support causal claims. *ExplanationConstructor* provides domain-specific prompts for students to guide students use evidence to construct and evaluate their scientific explanations. It makes epistemic criteria more explicit to help students evaluate evidence, which in turn can help them understand what counts as explanations and evidence. The guides in *ExplanationConstructor* make the scientific way of knowing more explicit for students by helping them understand how to construct coherent scientific explanation and framing students' inquiry process in epistemically important ways (Sandoval & Reiser, 2004).

The key feature of domain-general scaffolds is to support students' development of more generic concepts and skills that can be applied across domains (Davis, 2003). For instance, as an example of domain-general computer-based scaffolds, the *Connection Log* (Belland, Glazewski, & Richardson, 2010) provides domain-general scaffolds for students to construct evidence-based arguments. To support students' development of argumentation skills in a domain-generic way, the *Connection Log* divides construction of arguments into five common stages: define the problem, determine needed information, find and organize needed information, develop claim, link evidence to claim (Belland, Glazewski, & Richardson, 2008). Within each stage, students follow the prompts to engage in different components of argumentation such as search for evidence, link evidence to claims, and back claims with evidence.

Designers who wish to promote generic skills that can be applied across domains may choose to develop domain-general scaffolds (McNeill, Lizotte, Krajcik, & Marx, 2006). However, meta-analysis indicates no significant difference between domain-general and domain specific scaffolds on cognitive outcomes (Belland, Walker, Olsen, & Leary, 2015). Thus, designers can make the additional considerations of whether target students need the additional content knowledge support that might be provided with context-specific scaffolds, or whether developing a scaffold that can be used more widely with units of varying content is desired.

Technology to Support Collaborative Learning

Collaborative learning, defined as two or more individuals working together to complete certain learning tasks, has been documented to be an effective way to support learning (Chiu & Khoo, 2003; Fawcett & Garton, 2005). In collaborative learning, students need to interact with their peers, to acquire deep understandings of the content knowledge, and establish and maintain share understandings of the learning tasks (Janssen & Bodemer, 2013). To help students effectively engage in collaborative learning, computer-supported collaborative learning (CSCL) environments have been developed to help students share ideas and construct knowledge and scientific explanations (Noroozi, Weinberger, Biemans, Mulder, & Chizari, 2012). For instance, Linn, Davis and Bell (2004) developed an online learning environment called Web-based Inquiry Science Environment (WISE) to support students to engage in collaborative learning in scientific inquiry. Within the WISE platform, Clark, D'Angelo and Menekse (2009) developed an online discussion tool called *personally-seeded scripts* that demonstrated effective to help ninth grade students engage in online argumentative discussion. In the *personally-seeded scripts*, students need to articulate and select their initial scientific explanations of certain concepts, such as heat and thermal equilibrium, from a set of pre-scripted phrases. To help students engage in a more meaningful argumentative discussion from different perspectives, students who select different explanations will be assigned into a discussion group. Then, students with different perspectives can elaborate their scientific explanations in their own words and engage in asynchronous online discussion to co-construct, revise, and evaluate their scientific explanations (Clark et al., 2009). The *personally-seeded scripts* enable students with different perspectives to work together to increase diversity of perspective in the discussion, which adopts a critical pedagogical strategy to engage students in argumentation (Osborne et al., 2004). In addition, in the *personally-seeded scripts*, rather than simply dividing up the labor to accomplish learning tasks efficiently, students collaborate together in a more meaningful way by providing their unique insights and knowledge to construct their shared understandings of scientific concepts.

With the development of information and communication technology, the collaborative learning can also be supported in mobile learning environments. In a recent study, Laru, Järvelä and Clariana (2012) developed a mobile message application called *Flyer to* help middle school students engage in collaborative learning in a context of outdoor field trip. During field trips, students are presented with relevant scientific problems composed by scientists on the storyboard messages in the *Flyer*. Each student can use *Flyer* to develop scientific claims to answer the questions by using the embedded template that requires students to fill out their claims, evidence, and warrant. Students can send out and receive "flyers" of their scientific claims to each other, and engage in small group discussion to compare their knowledge claims with their group members (Laru et al., 2012). With the embedded procedural and metacognitive scaffolds in the *Flyer*, students can engage in scientific inquiry in authentic settings, which in turn can promote their science learning (Anderson, Thomas, & Nashon, 2009).

Prompting Sophisticated Epistemic Beliefs

It has long been a goal of science education that students develop an understanding of the nature of science (Abd-El-Khalick, 2012). Middle school students who are proficient in science should understand the nature and development of scientific knowledge (NRC, 2007). In fact, students do not automatically develop sophisticated understandings of science by experiencing inquiry tasks in school (Abd-El-Khalick et al., 2004). Research on epistemic beliefs in the context of science education can help educators understand how and why students understand the nature of science in certain ways and how to promote their understandings of the nature of science (Sandoval, 2005; Wu & Wu, 2010).

Middle School Students' Epistemic Beliefs

In the current literature, researchers adopt different ways to conceptualize individuals' epistemic beliefs. According to the developmental approach, individuals' epistemic beliefs develop from a naïve position to a more sophisticated position through a stage-like, developmental sequence (Greene, Azevedo, & Torney-Purta, 2008; Hofer & Pintrich, 1997). Among developmental frameworks of epistemic beliefs, the sequenced levels in these models can be commonly labeled as: (1) absolutism/objectivism in which individuals believe that knowledge is either right or wrong and can be known with certainty, (2) multiplism/subjectivism, in which individuals believe knowledge consists of subjective, uncertain opinions which can be equally right (Buehl & Alexander, 2001), and (3) evaluativism/objectivism-subjectivism, which views knowledge as evolving and needing to be critically judged based on criteria such as critical thinking and evidence (Kuhn, Cheney, & Weinstock, 2000). Although some research suggested that students' epistemological beliefs do not develop much prior to high school age due to inadequate cognitive and metacognitive ability to monitor and control their thinking process (Kitchener, 2002), more recent studies showed that early adolescents can hold relatively sophisticated beliefs (Muis, Bendixen, & Haerle, 2006). For instance, some middle school students can hold evaluativist epistemic beliefs and these relatively sophisticated epistemic beliefs influenced the process and strategies they use during internet-based learning (Barzilai & Zohar, 2012).

As a multidimensional approach, Hofer and Pintrich (1997) proposed that epistemic beliefs include four independent dimensions: (1) the certainty of knowledge, (2) the simplicity of knowledge, (3) the source of knowledge, and (4) the justification of knowledge (Hofer, 2000). Research based on the multidimensional approach (e.g., Mason, Boldrin, & Ariasi, 2009) indicated that middle school students can express reflections about the nature of knowledge and the knowing process on the four factors of epistemic beliefs proposed by Hofer and Pintrich (1997). In other words, in each dimension, certain (not all) middle school students can hold relatively sophisticated epistemic beliefs. Generally speaking, the current literature showed that middle school students to some extend can perceive their active role in knowledge construction and hold suboptimal understanding of the complex, uncertain, changing nature of the scientific knowledge (Ricco, Schuyten Pierce, & Medinilla, 2009).

Critical Epistemic Beliefs to Engage in Scientific Practices

The epistemic beliefs frameworks mentioned above often were developed or verified by interviews, questionnaire, and assessments which focus on students' self-reported beliefs about the professional science or formal scientific practices (Wu & Wu, 2010). To be distinguished from this type of epistemic beliefs, Sandoval (2005) proposed a term 'practical epistemologies', which refers to four critical practical epistemological notions that are essential for students to effectively engage in scientific inquiry and evaluate scientific claims. The first practical epistemology is that *scientific knowledge is constructed*, which means students need to understand that scientific knowledge is socially constructed, so people do not simply accept knowledge because it is true. Rather, the authority of knowledge is evaluated based on whether it provides value (such as provide an explanation to a phenomenon) for certain social, historical communities (Sandoval, 2005). The second notion of Sandoval's practical epistemologies is *diversity of scientific methods*, which posits that there is no universal scientific method. In reality, scientists adopt a broad range of methods as they explore different kinds of phenomena in various domains (Windschitl, 2004). By understanding the diversity of scientific methods, students are expected to be able to evaluate the appropriateness of the scientific method of a particular practice (Sandoval, 2005). The third notion of Sandoval's practical epistemologies is *forms of scientific knowledge*, which varied in their explanatory or predictive power and in their ways to interpret and describe the nature world (Sandoval, 2005). Scientific inquiry involves different types of practices for different purposes such as proposing hypotheses, verifying explanation, applying theories to interpret certain patterns. By perceiving the difference between various types of knowledge, students can deepen their understanding of the purposes of scientific practices, which in turn can support their inquiry practices. The last practical epistemology is *scientific knowledge varies in certainty* (Sandoval, 2005). This notion is similar to the dimension of uncertain, tentative nature of science presented in the frameworks of epistemic beliefs discussed earlier. The tentativeness of knowledge does not mean that no knowledge is worth believe, rather, it reflect an evaluativism point of view: knowledge varied in its tentativeness and need to be critically evaluated based on certain criteria such as reasoning or evidence-based argumentation (Kuhn et al., 2000). To sum up, these four notions of practical epistemologies complement the conceptualization of formal epistemic beliefs. Practical epistemologies represent several important epistemological goals for students to engage in scientific practices: understand the nature of scientific knowledge, the process of constructing scientific knowledge, and the criteria of evaluating scientific knowledge during their own inquiry practices.

Promoting Sophisticated Epistemic Beliefs

Promoting students' understanding of the nature of science and inquiry is not an easy task. Since epistemic beliefs are innate characteristics of students, one cannot simply teach students to hold sophisticated beliefs. Although few studies in the current literature examined in what way students' epistemic beliefs can be promoted (Ferguson & Bråten, 2013; Knight & Mattick, 2006), the current literature can still shed some light on the strategies to promote students' epistemic beliefs.

Challenging Students' Current Beliefs—Prompt Epistemic Doubt

Cognitive disequilibrium is a driving force for individuals to progress through stages of cognitive development (Piaget, 1985). Likewise, the development of epistemic beliefs may be driven by cognitive disequilibrium (Hofer & Pintrich, 1997). Bendixen and Rule (2004) proposed a mechanism of change of epistemic beliefs in which epistemic doubt is the driving force of epistemic beliefs development. As an impetus for epistemic change, epistemic doubt involves weighing evidence and discerning the truthfulness of conflicting beliefs (Bendixen & Rule, 2004). Advancing epistemic beliefs also require epistemic volition that can protect one's concentration on solving epistemic doubt and avoid distractions (Bendixen &

Rule, 2004). By using resolution strategies such as reflection and social interaction (e.g., engaging in argumentation with other individuals), epistemic beliefs can be advanced, or at least changed. Epistemic beliefs develop in a dynamic process influenced by many contextual and social factors; as such, one's epistemic beliefs can develop in fits and starts, and can thus become more primitive before it becomes more sophisticated (Bendixen & Rule, 2004). The components of this mechanism of epistemic change (epistemic doubt and resolution strategies) have been identified while college students read multiple documents containing conflicting scientific evidence (Ferguson, Bråten, & Strømsø, 2012). Middle school students can reflect on and develop their epistemic beliefs by reading conflicting online sources (Barzilai & Zohar, 2012). As such, one strategy to prompt epistemic beliefs is to enable students to challenge their current naïve epistemic beliefs. For example, engaging in online inquiry may help students be exposed to multiple sources of knowledge during their knowledge construction process. Therefore, students may perceive the uncertain, subjective nature of scientific knowledge, which can in turn promote a reassessment of their current epistemic beliefs such as scientific knowledge is certain and unchanging.

Prompting Students to Set High Level Epistemic Aims and Epistemic Values

Epistemic aims are goals of finding, understanding, and explaining things, and forming beliefs, which refers to what type of epistemic achievement (e.g., true beliefs, minimally justified beliefs) an individual pursues (Chinn, Buckland, & Samarapungavan, 2011). Epistemic values refer to the value system people have toward different types of epistemic achievement (Alfano, 2012; Chinn et al., 2011). For example, one may hold the epistemic value that the pursuit of truth is the ultimate goal. Such an epistemic value would lead one to strive to find truth through consultation of multiple, high quality sources (Alfano, 2012; Chinn et al., 2011), an approach that tends to reliably lead to truth (Goldman, 1993). An individual whose epistemic aim is to acquire minimally justified beliefs might accept a knowledge claim even if its justification is weak (Chinn et al., 2011). Individuals who value theoretical knowledge over practical knowledge (such as how to conduct an experiment) will more likely set sophisticated epistemic aims to acquire theoretical knowledge than practical knowledge.

As one component of epistemic cognition, individual's epistemic beliefs and epistemic aims and value are interrelated. Helping students to set up sophisticated epistemic aims will motivate them to perceive the complex nature of scientific knowledge and enable them to conduct personal justification of scientific knowledge. In the context of science education, teachers can help students set up high level epistemic aims during knowledge acquisition and perceive values of scientific knowledge, which in turn will help students develop their epistemic beliefs.

Establishing a Positive Epistemic Climate

To help students develop sophisticated epistemic beliefs, educators need to establish an environment or climate in which such sophisticated epistemic beliefs are encouraged. The epistemic climate—"how the nature of knowledge and knowing is portrayed and perceived" (Muis & Duffy, 2013, p. 124) —is critical to students' development of epistemic beliefs. Research showed that epistemic climate can be established through teaching and modeling of critical thinking, evaluation of problem solving approach, and making connections to students' prior knowledge, which in turn can help graduate students reflect on and challenge their current epistemic beliefs, and promote their epistemic beliefs and use of critical thinking strategies (Muis & Duffy, 2013). In the context of middle school, the epistemic climate is even more important as students are at critical age to form their beliefs system.

Another important aspect to establishing a positive epistemic climate is the cultivation of students' epistemic virtues. Individual's dispositions such as truth-seeking, systematicity, and maturity correlated with their epistemic beliefs (Valanides & Angeli, 2008). In Chinn et al.'s framework (2011), epistemic virtues such as intellectual carefulness, intellectual courage, and open-mindedness, are dispositions that can effectively help people achieve epistemic aims. To establish an epistemic climate that supports the development of epistemic beliefs, teachers need to cultivate epistemic virtues such as intellectual carefulness and intellectual courage to encourage students to set up higher epistemic aims and pursue them. By using strategies such as rewarding students who display epistemic virtues, establish or preset role models, teacher can set up a learning culture that value epistemic virtues.

Remaining Issues

Are Middle School Students Ready to Develop Sophisticated Epistemic Beliefs?

As discussed earlier, a few studies showed that some middle school students can perceive the complex, uncertain nature of scientific knowledge and acknowledge their active role in knowledge construction (Ricco et al., 2009). However, applying these beliefs during their scientific practices requires epistemic monitoring and judgment (Hofer, 2004). For example, during online searching, metacognitive thinking processes might guide students to spontaneously monitor and judge online information during their searching. However, such metacognitive processes might be too advanced for middle school students to acquire (Mason & Boldrin, 2008). Even first-year college students hold strong beliefs that scientific knowledge comes from external authorities and recognized expertise rather than themselves (Hofer, 2000).

Students often hold strong beliefs that justification needs to be provided by authorities until they reach college age (Greene et al., 2008). The fact that many middle school students tend to rely external authority as the source of knowledge and justification may simply be because they do not have the abilities or resources to conduct personal justification. Students may consider textbooks as credible sources of knowledge because they believe that knowledge claims in textbooks are supported by a large body of empirical evidence (Chinn et al., 2011). In certain contexts of science learning, such as doing a simple calculation, relying on authorities might be an effective way for learning as this type of knowledge is considered fixed and certain (Muis & Duffy, 2013). As a result, students' epistemic beliefs should be considered and evaluated within certain learning contexts. Future research is needed to address the influence of contextual factors on students' epistemic beliefs, and explore how to design instructions to promote students' epistemic beliefs in various learning contexts.

How can One Help Students Transfer Learned Knowledge and Skills in the Future?

The purpose of science education is to prepare students with adequate knowledge and skills, and the ability to apply such in future. Although computer-based scaffolds can provide substantial supports for students to engage in scientific practices in various ways, in the current literature few studies examine transfer of scaffolded skills. It remains unknown whether students can apply the knowledge and skills they learn after receiving scaffolding. The notion of scaffolding is to provide temporary support for students and help them eventually accomplish tasks on their own (Puntambekar & Hubscher, 2002). Hence, it is necessary to uncover what students have learned in a computer-based scaffolding learning environment, as well as whether and how they can transfer learned knowledge and skills in future. As studies consistently showed that students fail to transfer learned knowledge and skills, researchers started to reconceptualize transfer from an abstract, highly conceptual process to a perceptual processes (Day & Goldstone, 2012). For instance, in a recent conceptual framework of transfer of learning, Nokes-Malach and Mestre (2013) conceptualized transfer of learning as a sense-making and satisficing process in which individuals keep constructing representations of context and generating and making sense of solutions so that different types of transfer mechanisms can be triggered when individual is dealing with complex cognitive tasks. Therefore, one instructional implication is to engage students in complex, integrated learning tasks so that application of multiple mechanisms might be promoted (Nokes-Malach & Mestre, 2013). However, future research is needed to explore how to design instructions with specific aims to promote students' transfer of learning.

References

AASL. (2007). Standards for the 21st-century learner. http://www.ala.org/aasl/standards-guide-lines/learning-standards. Accessed 24 April 2014.

Abd-El-Khalick, F. (2012). Examining the sources for our understandings about science: Enduring conflations and critical issues in research on nature of science in science education. *International Journal of Science Education, 34*(3), 353–374. doi:10.1080/09500693.2011.629013.

Abd-El-Khalick, F., BouJaoude, S., Duschl, R., Lederman, N. G., Mamlok-Naaman, R., Hofstein, A., et al. (2004). Inquiry in science education: International perspectives. *Science Education, 88*(3), 397–419. doi:10.1002/sce.10118.

Alfano, M. (2012). Expanding the situationist challenge to responsibilist virtue epistemology. *The Philosophical Quarterly, 62*(247), 223–249. doi:10.1111/j.1467-9213.2011.00016.x.

American Association for the Advancement of Science. (1990). *Science for all Americans*. New York: Oxford University Press.

Anderman, E. M., Sinatra, G. M., & Gray, D. L. (2012). The challenges of teaching and learning about science in the twenty-first century: Exploring the abilities and constraints of adolescent learners. *Studies in Science Education, 48*(1), 89–117.

Anderson, D., Thomas, G. P., & Nashon, S. M. (2009). Social barriers to meaningful engagement in biology field trip group work. *Science Education, 93*(3), 511–534. doi:10.1002/sce.20304.

Angeli, C. (2013). Examining the effects of field dependence–independence on learners' problem-solving performance and interaction with a computer modeling tool: Implications for the design of joint cognitive systems. *Computers & Education, 62,* 221–230. doi:10.1016/j.compedu.2012.11.002.

Applebaum, S., Barker, B., & Pinzino, D. (2006). *Socioscientific issues as context for conceptual understanding of content*. San Francisco: Paper presented at the National Association for Research in Science Teaching.

Ashby, C. M. (2006). *Higher education: Science technology engineering mathematics trends and the role of federal programs*. United States Government Accountability Office, GAO-06-702T.

Baildon, M., & Damico, J. (2011). Judging the credibility of Internet sources: Developing critical and reflexive readers of complex digital texts. *Social Education, 75*(5), 269–273.

Barab, S. A., Sadler, T. D., Heiselt, C., Hickey, D., & Zuiker, S. (2010). Erratum to: Relating narrative, inquiry, and inscriptions: Supporting consequential play. *Journal of Science Education and Technology, 19*(4), 387–407. doi:10.1007/s10956-010-9220-0.

Barzilai, S., & Zohar, A. (2012). Epistemic thinking in action: Evaluating and integrating online sources. *Cognition and Instruction, 30*(1), 39–85. doi:10.1080/07370008.2011.636495.

Belland, B. R. (2014). Scaffolding: Definition, current debates, and future directions. In J. M. Spector, M. D. Merrill, J. Elen, & M. J. Bishop (Eds.), *Handbook of research on educational communications and technology* (4th edn., pp. 505–518). New York: Springer.

Belland, B. R., Glazewski, K. D., & Richardson, J. C. (2008). A scaffolding framework to support the construction of evidence-based arguments among middle school students. *Educational Technology Research and Development, 56*(4), 401–422.

Belland, B. R., Glazewski, K. D., & Richardson, J. C. (2010). Problem-based learning and argumentation: Testing a scaffolding framework to support middle school students' creation of evidence-based arguments. *Instructional Science, 39*(5), 667–694. doi:10.1007/s11251-010-9148-z.

Belland, B. R., Walker, A., Olsen, M. W., & Leary, H. (2015). Influence of computer-based scaffolding characteristics and methodological quality on cognitive outcomes in STEM education: A meta-analysis. *Educational Technology and Society, 18*(1), 183–197.

Bendixen, L. D., & Rule, D. C. (2004). An integrative approach to personal epistemology: A guiding model. *Educational Psychologist, 39*(1), 69–80. doi:10.1207/s15326985ep3901_7.

Bequette, J. W., & Bequette, M. B. (2012). A Place for art and design education in the STEM conversation. *Art Education, 65*(2), 40–47.

Brand-Gruwel, S., Wopereis, I., & Walraven, A. (2009). A descriptive model of information problem solving while using internet. *Computers & Education, 53*(4), 1207–1217. doi:10.1016/j.compedu.2009.06.004.

Bricker, L. A., & Bell, P. (2008). Conceptualizations of argumentation from science studies and the learning sciences and their implications for the practices of science education. *Science Education, 92*(3), 473–498. doi:10.1002/sce.20278.

Buehl, M. M., & Alexander, P. A. (2001). Beliefs about academic knowledge. *Educational Psychology Review, 13*(4), 385–418.

Bureau of Labor Statistics. (2013). *Employment projections: 2012–2022 summary*, http://www.bls.gov/news.release/ecopro.toc.htm.

Business-Higher Education Forum. (2010). *Increasing the number of U.S. STEM graduates: Insights from the STEM education modeling project*. Washington, D. C.: Business-Higher Education Forum. http://www.ncci-cu.org/downloads/BHEF_STEM.pdf.

Bybee, R. (2010). A new challenge for science education leaders: Developing 21st century workforce skills. In J. Rhoton (Ed.), *Science education leadership: Best practices for a new century* (pp. 33–49). Arlington: NSTA Press.

Casner-Lotto, J., Barrington, L., Barrington, L., & Barrington, L. (2006). Are they really ready to work?: Employers' perspectives on the basic knowledge and applied skills of new entrants to the 21st century U.S. workforce. United States: Conference Board: Partnership for 21st Century Skills: Corporate Voices for Working Families: Society for Human Resource Management. http://www.p21.org/storage/documents/FINAL_REPORT_PDF09-29-06.pdf.

Chinn, C. A., & Malhotra, B. A. (2002). Epistemologically authentic inquiry in schools: A theoretical framework for evaluating inquiry tasks. *Science Education, 86*(2), 175–218. doi:10.1002/sce.10001.

Chinn, C. A., Buckland, L. A., & Samarapungavan, A. (2011). Expanding the dimensions of epistemic cognition: Arguments from philosophy and psychology. *Educational Psychologist, 46*(3), 141–167. doi:10.1080/00461520.2011.587722.

Chiu, M. M., & Khoo, L. (2003). Rudeness and status effects during group problem solving: Do they bias evaluations and reduce the likelihood of correct solutions? *Journal of Educational Psychology, 95*(3), 506–523. doi:10.1037/0022-0663.95.3.506.

Clark, D. B., D'Angelo, C. M., & Menekse, M. (2009). Initial structuring of online discussions to improve learning and argumentation: Incorporating students' own explanations as seed comments versus an augmented-preset approach to seeding discussions. *Journal of Science Education and Technology, 18*(4), 321–333. doi:10.1007/s10956-009-9159-1.

Davis, E. A. (2003). Prompting middle school science students for productive reflection: Generic and directed prompts. *The Journal of the Learning Sciences, 12*(1), 91–142.

Dawson, V. M., & Venville, G. (2010). Teaching strategies for developing students' argumentation skills about socioscientific issues in high school genetics. *Research in Science Education, 40*(2), 133–148. doi:10.1007/s11165-008-9104-y.

Day, S. B., & Goldstone, R. L. (2012). The import of knowledge export: Connecting findings and theories of transfer of learning. *Educational Psychologist, 47*(3), 153–176. doi:10.1080/00461520.2012.696438.

Dolan, T. J., Nichols, B. H., & Zeidler, D. L. (2009). Using socioscientific issues in primary classrooms. *Journal of Elementary Science Education, 21*(3), 1–12.

Drew, S. V. (2013). Open up the ceiling on the common core state standards: Preparing students for 21st-century literacy—now. *Journal of Adolescent & Adult Literacy, 56*(4), 321–330.

Duschl, R. A. (2012). The second dimension—Crosscutting concepts. *The Science Teacher, 9*(2), 34–38.

Dym, C. L., Agogino, A. M., Eris, O., Frey, D. D., & Leifer, L. J. (2005). Engineering design thinking, teaching, and learning. *Journal of Engineering Education, 94*(1), 103–120. doi:10.1002/j.2168-9830.2005.tb00832.x.

Eastwood, J. L., Sadler, T. D., Zeidler, D. L., Lewis, A., Amiri, L., & Applebaum, S. (2012). Contextualizing nature of science instruction in socioscientific issues. *International Journal of Science Education, 34*(15), 2289–2315. doi:10.1080/09500693.2012.667582.

European Communities. (2007). *Key competences for lifelong learning: European reference framework*. Luxembourg: Office for Official Publications of the European Communities. http://www.britishcouncil.org/sites/britishcouncil.uk2/files/youth-in-action-keycomp-en.pdf.

Fawcett, L. M., & Garton, A. F. (2005). The effect of peer collaboration on children's problem-solving ability. *British Journal of Educational Psychology, 75*(2), 157–169. doi:10.1348/000709904X23411.

Ferguson, L. E., & Bråten, I. (2013). Student profiles of knowledge and epistemic beliefs: Changes and relations to multiple-text comprehension. *Learning and Instruction, 25,* 49–61. doi:10.1016/j.learninstruc.2012.11.003.

Ferguson, L. E., Bråten, I., & Strømsø, H. I. (2012). Epistemic cognition when students read multiple documents containing conflicting scientific evidence: A think-aloud study. *Learning and Instruction, 22*(2), 103–120. doi:10.1016/j.learninstruc.2011.08.002.

Ford, M. (2008). Disciplinary authority and accountability in scientific practice and learning. *Science Education, 92*(3), 404–423. doi:10.1002/sce.20263.

Ford, M. J. (2012). A dialogic account of sense-making in scientific argumentation and reasoning. *Cognition and Instruction, 30*(3), 207–245. doi:10.1080/07370008.2012.689383.

Glassner, A., Weinstock, M., & Neuman, Y. (2005). Pupils' evaluation and generation of evidence and explanation in argumentation. *British Journal of Educational Psychology, 75*(1), 105–118. doi:10.1348/000709904X22278.

Golanics, J. D., & Nussbaum, E. M. (2007). Enhancing online collaborative argumentation through question elaboration and goal instructions. *Journal of Computer Assisted Learning, 24*(3), 167–180. doi:10.1111/j.1365-2729.2007.00251.x.

Goldman, A. I. (1993). Epistemic folkways and scientific epistemology. *Philosophical Issues, 3,* 271–285. doi:10.2307/1522948.

Gray, L., Thomas, N., & Lewis, L. (2010). *Educational technology in U.S. public schools: Fall 2008 (NCES 2010-034). U.S. Department of Education, National Center for Education Statistics*. Washington, D. C.: U.S. Government Printing Office.

Greene, J. A., Azevedo, R., & Torney-Purta, J. (2008). Modeling epistemic and ontological cognition: Philosophical perspectives and methodological directions. *Educational Psychologist, 43*(3), 142–160. doi:10.1080/00461520802178458.

Hofer, B. K. (2000). Dimensionality and disciplinary differences in personal epistemology. *Contemporary Educational Psychology, 25*(4), 378–405. doi:10.1006/ceps.1999.1026.

Hofer, B. K. (2004). Epistemological understanding as a metacognitive process: Thinking aloud during online searching. *Educational Psychologist, 39*(1), 43–55. doi:10.1207/s15326985ep3901_5.

Hofer, B. K., & Pintrich, P. R. (1997). The development of epistemological theories: Beliefs about knowledge and knowing and their relation to learning. *Review of Educational Research, 67*(1), 88–140.

Hollnagel, E., & Woods, D. D. (2005). *Joint cognitive systems: Foundations of cognitive systems engineering*. CRC Press.

Hung, W. (2013). Team-based complex problem solving: A collective cognition perspective. *Educational Technology Research and Development, 61*(3), 365–384. doi:10.1007/s11423-013-9296-3.

International ICT Literacy Panel. (2002). *Digital transformation: A framework for ICT literacy*. Princeton: Educational Testing Services http://www.ets.org/Media/Research/pdf/ICTREPORT.pdf.

Janssen, J., & Bodemer, D. (2013). Coordinated computer-supported collaborative learning: Awareness and awareness Tools. *Educational Psychologist, 48*(1), 40–55. doi:10.1080/0046 1520.2012.749153.

Jonassen, D. H. (2003). Using cognitive tools to represent problems. *Journal of Research on Technology in Education, 35*(3), 362–381.

Jonassen, D. H. (2011). *Learning to solve problems: A handbook for designing problem-solving learning environments*. New York: Routledge.

Kereluik, K., Mishra, P., Fahnoe, C., & Terry, L. (2013). What knowledge is of most worth: Teacher knowledge for 21st century learning. *Journal of Digital Learning in Teacher Education, 29*(4), 127–140.

Khishfe, R., & Abd-El-Khalick, F. (2002). Influence of explicit and reflective versus implicit inquiry-oriented instruction on sixth graders' views of nature of science. *Journal of Research in Science Teaching, 39*(7), 551–578. doi:10.1002/tea.10036.

Khishfe, R., & Lederman, N. (2006). Teaching nature of science within a controversial topic: Integrated versus nonintegrated. *Journal of Research in Science Teaching, 43*(4), 395–418. doi:10.1002/tea.20137.

Kim, J., & Lee, W. (2013). Meanings of criteria and norms: Analyses and comparisons of ICT literacy competencies of middle school students. *Computers & Education, 64,* 81–94.

Kim, M. C., Hannafin, M. J., & Bryan, L. A. (2007). Technology-enhanced inquiry tools in science education: An emerging pedagogical framework for classroom practice. *Science Education, 91*(6), 1010–1030. doi:10.1002/sce.20219.

Kitchener, R. F. (2002). Folk epistemology: An introduction. *New Ideas in Psychology, 20*(2), 89–105.

Knight, L. V., & Mattick, K. (2006). "When I first came here, I thought medicine was black and white": Making sense of medical students' ways of knowing. *Social Science & Medicine, 63*(4), 1084–1096.

Kolstø, S. D., Bungum, B., Arnesen, E., Isnes, A., Kristensen, T., Mathiassen, K., et al. (2006). Science students' critical examination of scientific information related to socioscientific issues. *Science Education, 90*(4), 632–655. doi:10.1002/sce.20133.

Kuhn, D., & Udell, W. (2007). Coordinating own and other perspectives in argument. *Thinking & Reasoning, 13*(2), 90–104.

Kuhn, D., Cheney, R., & Weinstock, M. (2000). The development of epistemological understanding. *Cognitive Development, 15*(3), 309–328.

Kuiper, E., Volman, M., & Terwel, J. (2009). Developing Web literacy in collaborative inquiry activities. *Computers & Education, 52*(3), 668–680. doi:10.1016/j.compedu.2008.11.010.

Laru, J., Järvelä, S., & Clariana, R. B. (2012). Supporting collaborative inquiry during a biology field trip with mobile peer-to-peer tools for learning: A case study with K-12 learners. *Interactive Learning Environments, 20*(2), 103–117. doi:10.1080/10494821003771350.

Leu, D. J., McVerry, J., Ian O'Byrne, W., Kiili, C., Zawilinski, L., Everett-Cacopardo, H., et al. (2011). The new literacies of online reading comprehension: Expanding the literacy and learning curriculum. *Journal of Adolescent & Adult Literacy, 55*(1), 5–14.

Linn, M. (2003). Technology and science education: Starting points, research programs, and trends. *International Journal of Science Education, 25*(6), 727–758. doi:10.1080/09500690305017.

Linn, M. C., Davis, E. A., & Bell, P. (2004). *Internet environments for science education.* Mahwah: Routledge.

Mason, L., & Boldrin, A. (2008). Epistemic metacognition in the context of information searching on the Web. In M. S. Khine (Ed.), *Knowing, knowledge and beliefs* (pp. 377–404). Dordrecht: Springer. http://link.springer.com/chapter/10.1007/978-1-4020-6596-518.

Mason, L., & Boscolo, P. (2004). Role of epistemological understanding and interest in interpreting a controversy and in topic-specific belief change. *Contemporary Educational Psychology, 29*(2), 103–128. doi:10.1016/j.cedpsych.2004.01.001.

Mason, L., Boldrin, A., & Ariasi, N. (2009). Epistemic metacognition in context: Evaluating and learning online information. *Metacognition and Learning, 5*(1), 67–90. doi:10.1007/s11409-009-9048-2.

McNeill, K. L., Lizotte, D. J., Krajcik, J., & Marx, R. W. (2006). Supporting students' construction of scientific explanations by fading scaffolds in instructional materials. *The Journal of the Learning Sciences, 15*(2), 153–191.

Muis, K. R., & Duffy, M. C. (2013). Epistemic climate and epistemic change: Instruction designed to change students' beliefs and learning strategies and improve achievement. *Journal of Educational Psychology, 105*(1), 213–225. doi:10.1037/a0029690.

Muis, K. R., Bendixen, L. D., & Haerle, F. C. (2006). Domain-generality and domain-specificity in personal epistemology research: Philosophical and empirical reflections in the development of a theoretical framework. *Educational Psychology Review, 18*(1), 3–54. doi:10.1007/s10648-006-9003-6.

National Research Council. (1996). *National science education standards*. Washington, D. C.: National Academy Press.

National Research Council. (2007). *Taking science to school: Learning and teaching science in grades K-8*. Washington, D. C.: The National Academies Press.

National Research Council. (2010). *Exploring the intersection of science education and 21st century skills: A workshop summary*. Washington, D. C.: National Academies Press.

National Research Council. (2012). *A framework for K-12 science education: Practices, crosscutting concepts, and core ideas*. Washington, D. C.: The National Academies Press.

National Science Teachers Association. (2011). NSTA Position statement: Quality science education and 21st-century skills. http://www.nsta.org/about/positions/21stcentury.aspx

NGSS Lead States. (2013). *Next generation science standards: For states, by states*. Washington, D. C.: The National Academies Press.

Nokes-Malach, T. J., & Mestre, J. P. (2013). Toward a model of transfer as sense-making. *Educational Psychologist, 48*(3), 184–207. doi:10.1080/00461520.2013.807556.

Noroozi, O., Weinberger, A., Biemans, H. J. A., Mulder, M., & Chizari, M. (2012). Argumentation-based computer supported collaborative learning (ABCSCL): A synthesis of 15 years of research. *Educational Research Review, 7*(2), 79–106. doi:10.1016/j.edurev.2011.11.006.

Osborne, J., Erduran, S., & Simon, S. (2004). Enhancing the quality of argumentation in school science. *Journal of Research in Science Teaching, 41*(10), 994–1020. doi:10.1002/tea.20035.

Partnership for 21st Century Skills (P21). (2009). Framework for 21st Century Learning. http://www.p21.org/storage/documents/1.__p21_framework_2-pager.pdf.

Pedersen, S., & Liu, M. (2002). The transfer of problem-solving skills from a problem-based learning environment: The effect of modeling an expert's cognitive processes. *Journal of Research on Technology in Education, 35*(2), 303–320.

Perelman, C., & Olbrechts-Tyteca, L. (1958). *La nouvelle rhétorique: Traité de l'argumentation* [The new rhetoric: Treatise on argumentation] (Vols. 1–2). Paris: Presses Universitaires de France.

Piaget, J. (1985). *The equilibration of cognitive structures*. Chicago: University of Chicago Press.

Platz, J. (2007). How do you turn STEM into STEAM? Add the arts! http://www.oaae.net/en/resources/educator/stem-to-steam.

Popper, K. (1999). *All life is problem solving*. London: Routledge.

President's Council of Advisors on Science and Technology (PCAST). (2010). Prepare and inspire: K-12 education in science, technology, engineering, and math (STEM) for America's future. http://www.whitehouse.gov/sites/default/files/microsites/ostp/pcast-stemed-report.pdf.

Prins, G. T., Bulte, A. M. W., & Pilot, A. (2011). Evaluation of a design principle for fostering students' epistemological views on models and modelling using authentic practices as contexts for learning in chemistry education. *International Journal of Science Education, 33*(11), 1539–1569. doi:10.1080/09500693.2010.519405.

Puntambekar, S., & Hubscher, R. (2002). Scaffolding in complex learning environments: What we have gained and what we have missed. *Educational Psychologist, 40*, 1–12.

Raes, A., Schellens, T., & De Wever, B. (2010). The impact of web-based collaborative inquiry for science learning in secondary education. In *Proceedings of the 9th International Conference of the Learning Sciences* (Vol. 1, pp. 736–741). Chicago: International Society of the Learning Sciences. http://dl.acm.org/citation.cfm?id=1854360.1854454.

Reiser, B. J. (2004). Scaffolding complex learning: The mechanisms of structuring and problematizing student work. *The Journal of the Learning Sciences, 13*(3), 273–304.

Ricco, R., Schuyten Pierce, S., & Medinilla, C. (2009). Epistemic beliefs and achievement motivation in early adolescence. *The Journal of Early Adolescence, 30*(2), 305–340. doi:10.1177/0272431609333299.

Sadler, T. D., & Donnelly, L. A. (2006). Socioscientific argumentation: The effects of content knowledge and morality. *International Journal of Science Education, 28*(12), 1463–1488.

Sadler, T. D., & Zeidler, D. L. (2005). Patterns of informal reasoning in the context of socioscientific decision making. *Journal of Research in Science Teaching, 42*(1), 112–138. doi:10.1002/tea.20042.

Sadler, T. D., Barab, S. A., & Scott, B. (2007). What do students gain by engaging in socioscientific inquiry? *Research in Science Education, 37*(4), 371–391. doi:10.1007/s11165-006-9030-9.

Sandoval, W. A. (2005). Understanding students' practical epistemologies and their influence on learning through inquiry. *Science Education, 89*(4), 634–656. doi:10.1002/sce.20065.

Sandoval, W. A., & Reiser, B. J. (2004). Explanation-driven inquiry: Integrating conceptual and epistemic scaffolds for scientific inquiry. *Science Education, 88*(3), 345–372. doi:10.1002/sce.10130.

Saunders, K. J., & Rennie, L. J. (2013). A pedagogical model for ethical inquiry into socioscientific issues in science. *Research in Science Education, 43*(1), 253–274.

Schwarz, C. V., & White, B. Y. (2005). Metamodeling knowledge: Developing students' understanding of scientific modeling. *Cognition and Instruction, 23*(2), 165–205. doi:10.1207/s1532690xci2302_1.

Sneider, C. (2012). Core ideas of engineering and technology. *Science Teacher, 79*(1), 32–36.

Swanson, G. (1994). Graphic design education as a liberal art: Design and knowledge in the university and the "real world.". *Design Issues, 10*(1), 53–63. doi:10.2307/1511656.

Valanides, N., & Angeli, C. (2008). An exploratory study about the role of epistemological beliefs and dispositions on learners' thinking about an ill-defined issue in solo and duo problem-solving contexts. In M. S. Khine (Ed.), *Knowing, knowledge and beliefs* (pp. 197–218). Springer. http://link.springer.com/chapter/10.1007/978-1-4020-6596-59.

Vande Zande, R. (2010). Teaching design education for cultural, pedagogical, and economic aims. *Studies in Art Education, 51*(3), 248–261.

Walker, K. A., & Zeidler, D. L. (2007). Promoting discourse about socioscientific issues through scaffolded inquiry. *International Journal of Science Education, 29*(11), 1387–1410. doi:10.1080/09500690601068095.

Windschitl, M. (2004). Folk theories of "inquiry:" How preservice teachers reproduce the discourse and practices of an atheoretical scientific method. *Journal of Research in Science Teaching, 41*(5), 481–512. doi:10.1002/tea.20010.

Wood, D., Bruner, J. S., & Ross, G. (1976). The role of tutoring in problem solving. *Journal of Child Psychology and Psychiatry, 17*(2), 89–100.

Wu, H.-K., & Wu, C.-L. (2010). Exploring the development of fifth graders' practical epistemologies and explanation skills in inquiry-based learning classrooms. *Research in Science Education, 41*(3), 319–340. doi:10.1007/s11165-010-9167-4.

Yoon, S. A. (2011). Using social network graphs as visualization tools to influence peer selection decision-making strategies to access information about complex socioscientific issues. *Journal of the Learning Sciences, 20*(4), 549–588. doi:10.1080/10508406.2011.563655.

Zhang, M., & Quintana, C. (2012). Scaffolding strategies for supporting middle school students' online inquiry processes. *Computers & Education, 58*(1), 181–196.

Jiangyue Gu is a PhD Candidate in the Department of Instructional Technology and Learning Sciences at Utah State University. Her research interests focus on using instructional technology to promote students' argumentation skills and epistemic beliefs in the context of K-12 science education.

Brian R. Belland is an Associate Professor of Instructional Technology and Learning Sciences at Utah State University. His research interests center on scaffolding in STEM education, including that to support argumentation in middle school science.

Reconceptualizing a College Science Learning Experience in the New Digital Era: A Review of Literature

Ji Shen, Shiyan Jiang and Ou Lydia Liu

Abstract Despite all the exciting new digital forms of living, our college science education remains relatively unchanged. Students sit quietly in large classrooms listening to lectures (or not), complete individual labs following cookbook instruction, and take exams only to solve problems of no practical importance. It is the time to reconceptualize a college science learning experience for all students. In this chapter, we review research on technology-enriched instruction and assessments for science education at the college level that target students' 21st century skills such as problem solving, critical thinking, and collaboration. We propose three interrelated core principles that can help design coherent science instruction, curriculum, and assessments at the college level that meet the needs of the new digital era: (1) Set the development of lifelong learning skills for students as a top priority; (2) incorporate multi-layered instructional supports using technologies; and (3) design new assessments for individual students that demonstrate and facilitate their growth of the lifelong learning capacity.

Keywords College science education · Learning objectives · Instructional support · Automated scoring

Introduction

One of the most important societal advancements of the 21st century is the rise of information and communication technology (ICT), which has fundamentally transformed our daily lives. We find dining places via smart phones, chat with

J. Shen (✉) · S. Jiang
University of Miami, Coral Gables, USA
e-mail: j.shen@miami.edu

S. Jiang
e-mail: s.jiang@umiami.edu

O. L. Liu
Educational Testing Service, Princeton, USA
e-mail: lliu@ets.org

© Springer International Publishing Switzerland 2015
X. Ge et al. (eds.), *Emerging Technologies for STEAM Education,*
Educational Communications and Technology: Issues and Innovations,
DOI 10.1007/978-3-319-02573-5_4

strangers in a virtual world, and seek information through a large collection of social networks. Despite all the exciting new forms of living, our college science education remains relatively unchanged (Deslauriers, Schelew, & Wieman, 2011; Mazur, 2009). Students sit quietly in large classrooms listening to lectures, complete individual labs following cookbook instruction, and take exams only to solve problems of no practical importance. It is the time to reconceptualize a new college science experience for all students (Mervis, 2013). In this chapter, we propose a guiding framework that can help design coherent science instruction, curriculum, and assessments at the college level that meet the needs of the new digital era. The framework considers three interrelated core principles: (1) Set the development of lifelong learning skills (e.g., critical thinking, scientific reasoning, collaborative problem solving) for all students as a top priority; (2) incorporate multi-layered instructional supports using technologies; and (3) design new assessments for individual students that demonstrate and facilitate their growth of the lifelong learning capacity.

Reseting Learning Objectives

Learning objectives including content standards have been a common topic in any educational reform. This is more so in K-12 public education than in higher education. Many modern ideas on learning objectives can be traced back to Bloom's taxonomy (Bloom et al., 1956), which sets learning objectives for students in three domains: cognitive, affective, and psychomotor. For instance, within the cognitive domain, the learning objectives are placed along a hierarchy that includes (from the lower level to the higher level) knowledge, comprehension, application, analysis, synthesis, and evaluation. The higher-level objectives are often referred as higher-order thinking or higher-level skills.

More recently the 21st century skills have been proposed in various policy documents and reports (e.g., http://www.p21.org/). In order to synthesize the abundant and multifaceted works related to the 21st century skills, the committee of the recent NRC, (2012) report, *Education for Life and Work: Developing Transferable Knowledge and Skills in the 21st Century*, identified three broad domains of competence: cognitive, intrapersonal, and interpersonal. These are summarized in Table 1. These skills relevant to science learning may take various forms such as problem solving (Hodges, 2012), scientific reasoning (e.g., Bao et al., 2009), and critical and collaborative argumentation (e.g., Osborne, 2010).

The essence of these new learning objectives, we believe, is to prepare students as adaptive, lifelong learners. Therefore, the first principle we propose to reform college science education is *setting the development of lifelong learning skills for all students as a top priority*. This first principle is particularly relevant for college science education in the 21st century because of the knowledge expansion dilemma. On the one hand, there is a large body of basic (textbook) scientific knowledge

Table 1 The three domains of the 21st century competencies proposed in NRC, (2012)

Domain	Clusters of competencies	Examples
Cognitive domain	Knowledge, Creativity, Cognitive processes and strategies	Critical thinking, information literacy, reasoning and argumentation, and innovation
Intrapersonal domain	Intellectual openness, Work ethic and conscientiousness, Positive core self-evaluation	Flexibility, initiative, appreciation for diversity, and metacognition (the ability to reflect on one's own learning and make adjustments accordingly)
Interpersonal domain	Teamwork and collaboration, Leadership	Communication, collaboration, responsibility, and conflict resolution

distilled through a long human history for students to learn. Without mastering this body of basic knowledge, students can hardly move on to their next level of education or work and eventually (for some of them) contribute to the frontier scientific research and development. On the other hand, new knowledge advances faster than ever. It appears that students are never able to catch up with the knowledge expansion if the focus is on assimilating existing knowledge. Therefore, if students develop lifelong learning skills in schooling, they can continue their own learning after graduation.

These 21st century skills or higher-level learning objectives are often enduring and do not change rapidly. They serve to prepare students for future learning (Bransford & Schwartz, 1999) in the ever-changing world. They should not be decorative additives appearing in course syllabi. Instead, they should be infused in every single activity of the courses students take. These objectives may differ over time because of "society's desire that all students attain levels of mastery—across multiple areas of skill and knowledge—that were previously unnecessary for individual success in education and the workplace" (NRC, 2012, p. 3). One particular new demand of the 21st century is the development of digital literacy (Lei, Shen, & Johnson, 2013). In the next sections, we highlight technological resources for college science education including new forms of assessment that take advantages of technology.

Maximizing Instructional Support Through Technology

Instructional Practices Promoting Lifelong Learning

Froyd (2008) listed eight promising instructional practices in undergraduate STEM education. Based on these, we propose the following four instructional practices that may promote students' lifelong learning skills:

1. *Designing activities to engage and motivate students in active learning.* The essence of this practice is to develop strategies to help students take more ownership and responsibility of their learning through making the classrooms more student-centered environments. These activities range from demonstrating interesting science phenomena, making science content relevant to students' personal lives, extending learning to outside class realms, and linking science to other interesting academic disciplines or even entertainment.
2. *Using scenario-based content organization.* Scenario-based approaches refer to the wide range of instructional practices that organize learning materials for a longer period of time around one or more scenarios. These practices are often labeled as problem-based, project-based, case-based, inquiry-based, or challenge-based learning.
3. *Organizing students in collaborative work.* This practice is combined from the two separate practices proposed by Froyd (2008), organizing students in small groups and organizing students in learning communities. Collaborative work can happen in many forms including within a course or across multiple courses, in or after class, and through face-to-face or virtual interaction.
4. *Conducting research.* This practice aims to involve undergraduate students, typically advanced ones, in science research either in an established lab or under the supervision of a faculty member.

These practices are closely related with each other and have overlaps (Fig. 1). For instance, scenario-based approaches and collaboration are often considered as important ingredients in active student learning environments. Nonetheless, active

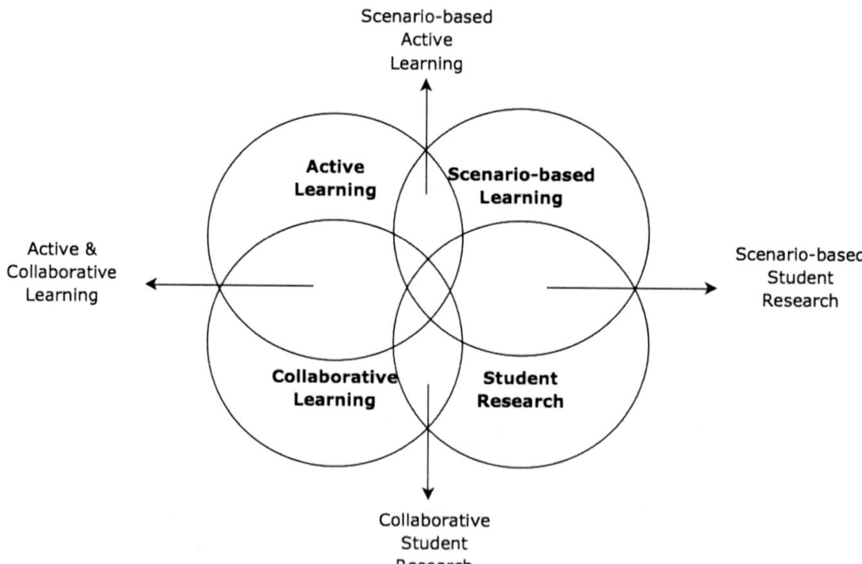

Fig. 1 The interrelated instructional practices that promote lifelong learning

learning can be individual-based and can occur in classes with more traditional ways of content organization. Interested readers can fill out the inner overlapping areas depicted in Fig. 1.

Technological Resources

Advanced technologies have made significant impacts on how students learn and how teachers teach (Lei et al., 2013; NSF Task Force on CyberLearning, 2008). In this section we highlight a few technology resources that can augment the afore-mentioned instructional practices to prepare college students to be lifelong learners in the 21st century.

Personal Response Systems Personal response systems, or clickers, have become a popular tool for large lectures in college science classrooms. The use of clickers is often accompanied with the instructional practice called Peer Instruction (Crouch & Mazur, 2001; Mazur, 1997), a pedagogy developed to engage all students in large classrooms in college science courses. Peer Instruction uses conceptually challeng-ing questions to engage students in scientific reasoning and argumentation. In a Peer Instruction session, students are typically presented with a conceptual ques-tion in multiple-choice format. After they spend a minute or two to think about the problem, they use clickers (or other alternatives such as flashcards) to submit their individual answers. The instructor then provides corresponding feedback or follow-up questions based on the distribution of students' responses. For instance, if a large amount of students respond incorrectly, then the instructor can ask the students to discuss the problem with their neighbors (especially one with a different answer). The students then answer the question again before the instructor finally reveals and explains the answer.

Peer Instruction has shown success in improving college students' conceptual learning and problem solving, and retaining students in STEM majors (Kalman, Milner-Bolotin, & Antimirova, 2010; Mazur, 2009; Watkins & Mazur, 2013). Deslauriers et al. (2011) described a comparison study in which they measured the impact of deliberate practice (Ericsson, Krampe, & Tesch-Römer, 1993) in a large-enrollment introductory physics course. In the constructivism-based deliber-ate practice approach, students solve a series of challenging questions, make and test predictions, and critique their own and peers' arguments during class time that require them to practice physicist-like habit of mind and receive frequent feedback from peers and the instructor. Clickers were used to aid students' problem solving activities during class. Compared with a traditional lecture session taught by an experienced and highly rated instructor, in the 3-h intervention session taught by a trained but inexperienced instructor the students exhibited increased attendance, higher engagement, and much more conceptual learning.

Despite all the documented success, a major constraint of using clickers is that the instructor needs to develop a set of high quality and challenging questions for the students, similar to traditional approaches. This may drive students into thinking deeply about the subject matter on the one hand, but may inhibit students from developing the essential skill of raising critical questions, an inherent trait of a lifelong learner, on the other hand.

Computer Visualizations and Simulations Computer visualizations and simulations (CVS) including computer-based modeling environments and virtual experiments have become popular instructional tools in science education at all levels (NRC, 2011; Scalise, Timms, Moorjani, Clark, & Holtermann, 2011; Shen, Lei, Chang, & Namdar, 2014). One well-known example is the PhET Interactive Simulations developed at the University of Colorado, Boulder (http://phet.colorado.edu/). PhET simulations include various science (and math) topics covering elementary, secondary, and university levels. They not only visualize abstract and complex scientific phenomena, but also provide opportunities for students to interact with the simulations and therefore, practice inquiry learning (e.g., Lancaster, Moore, Parson, & Perkins, 2013; Wieman, Adams, & Perkins, 2008). For example, Podolefsky, Perkins, and Adams (2010) examined how college students interacted with PhET simulations with minimal explicit guidance. They documented two cases on how students worked with a particular simulation – Wave Interference. Using this simulation, students may choose different objects to show, different measurement tools to use, and different variables to manipulate to make progress towards developing a scientific model of wave interference. Given the flexibility of the PhET simulation, the students followed different exploration paths, similar to how scientists investigate natural phenomena. Another good example is the ChemCollective (www. chemcollective.org) developed at Carnegie Mellon University. It is a collection of online activities including virtual labs, tutorials, and tests for general chemistry instruction. These virtual labs are designed to engage students in authentic chemistry problem-solving and complement algebraic computations for better conceptual understanding. Students' engagement in ChemCollective has been shown to help identify misconceptions, facilitate deeper conceptual understanding, and predict posttest performance (Yaron, Karabinos, Lange, Greeno, & Leinhardt, 2010). Taking a community approach, ChemCollective allows instructors from other institutions to contribute to the development of instructional materials.

With a workforce orientation, Stephens and Richey (2013) cautioned us that it is unlikely that computers and simulations will fully substitute for real world experiences. They observed that the new employees recently hired by the Boeing Company were generally good at using digital tools. However, many of them had rarely been put in situations where they had to create a product of value, and after training, were still weak in skills needed to manipulate materials effectively. Finkelstein et al. (2005) showed that well-designed computer simulations could be used productively in lieu of real laboratory equipment when they were used in proper contexts. The key factor that led to the success of their project was that the circuit simulation they used provided a variety of visual representations to make invisible physics concepts visible to students. de Jong, Linn, and Zacharia, (2013) reviewed the affordances and constraints of physical and virtual laboratories in science and engineering education, and recommended that:

…Combinations of virtual and physical laboratories offer advantages that neither one can fully achieve by itself…. Research on virtual and physical laboratories calls for nuanced decision-making…. Designers of instruction can improve outcomes by taking advantage of the affordances of each type of laboratory…. To design laboratories that take advantage of powerful guidance requires interdisciplinary teams involving domain experts, technologists, and learning scientists. (p. 308)

Computer-Supported Collaborative Learning The works on computer-supported collaborative learning (CSCL) rise with information, network, and Web technologies (for a conceptual review, see Goodyear, Jones, & Thompson, 2014; Stahl, Koschmann, & Suthers, 2006). This instructional approach focuses on developing computer-based learning environments that are built on a deep understanding of social structure, interaction, and dynamics with a relatively broader learning outcome in mind. Frisch, Jackson, and Murray (2013) described the WIKIed Biology course in which they infused Web 2.0 tools (del.i.cious, CiteULike, and Google docs and sites) to help college students collaborate with each other and learn biology knowledge. Using these tools, students worked together to find, create, and disseminate information and knowledge related to the course topics. Results showed that the students increased their understanding of certain biology topics as well as critical thinking skills. In order to understand how students collectively organize information in multiple modes and argue about social scientific issues accordingly, Namdar and Shen (2014) documented a study where they developed a science learning unit on nuclear energy for preservice science teachers. The learning unit incorporated a newly developed knowledge building and sharing platform (ikos.miami.edu) that offers three distinctive types of representational modes: pictorial, textual, and concept maps. The study indicated that the group of learners were able to generate a relatively dense knowledge network. Moreover, concept maps and wiki entries were more connected than the pictorial mode. The findings also suggested that students' knowledge organization and their argumentation practices informed each other in a complex way.

One challenge to incorporate CSCL in college settings is the grading part since in most college classes students are graded individually. How to balance individual accountability and productive collaboration in CSCL still needs more empirical research.

Educational Video and Computer Games Video and computer games have become a popular entertainment means for people of all ages. Gee (2007) asserted that in game playing, players are learning actively and critically to experience the world in a new way and developing resources for future learning. However, evidence for effectiveness of games for science learning is still contested and science learning with games rarely occurs in college settings (NRC, 2011). One major challenge to adopt gaming in college science education is to make game playing really educative and meaningful. A well-known example is Foldit (https://fold.it/portal), an online puzzle video game about protein folding. It takes a citizen science approach that allows users to contribute to actual scientific research related to protein structure and unfolding, which is critical in bioinformatics, molecular biology, and medicine research. The highest scored solutions submitted by players are analyzed by researchers to evaluate their scientific values in solving real world problems. Notable accomplishments through FoldIt playing include deciphering the crystal structure of the Mason-Pfizer monkey virus retroviral protease (Khatib et al., 2011), and achieving the first crowd-sourced redesign of a protein (Eiben et al., 2012). A similar game is EteRNA (http://eterna.cmu.edu/web/) that enables players to solve puzzles related to the folding of RNA molecules. However, it is still an open question that how these games can be embedded in formal curricula.

OpenCourseWare With the goal of enhancing human learning worldwide through the Internet, OpenCourseWare (OCW) became a popular source for knowledge dissemination for many world's top universities during the first decade of the 21st century. For instance, a well-known physics series is offered by MIT professor Walter Lewin, including Newtonian Mechanics, Electricity & Magnetism, and Vibration and Waves (http://ocw.mit.edu/courses/). Recently, OCW has evolved into Massive Open Online Courses (MOOCs), web-based and large-scale free courses that have no restrictions on enrollment (Adamopoulos, 2013; Balfour, 2013). Overcoming geographic and financial restrictions, a massive number of learners can pursue their individual learning in MOOCs. Popular MOOCs platforms include edX, Coursera, and Udacity.

Hollands and Tirthali (2014) interviewed 83 individuals who were knowledgeable about MOOCs, including administrators, faculty members, researchers and other roles. The authors identified six major goals for MOOCs: (1) extending reach and access (the most stated goal), (2) building and maintaining brand, (3) improving economics, (4) improving educational outcomes, (5) innovation, and (6) research on teaching and learning. The authors suggested that institutions have achieved success to a certain degree regarding these goals except improving economics. Many interviewees agreed that MOOCs can improve educational outcomes. For instance, integrating MOOCs with on-campus courses has shown some signs of success – in this approach students can spent more class time in problem-solving instead of listening to lectures.

A major criticism of MOOCs is that the retention rate is quite low. Only 50–60% of the students enrolled in an MOOC return after the first course and only about 5% earned a credential after completing a course (Koller, Ng, Do, & Chen, 2013). Recent studies have explored students' engagement patterns and associated causes. Since videos are a central element in all MOOCs, Guo, Kim, and Rubin (2009) examined student engagement with videos. They obtained data from 6.9 million video watching sessions from four edX courses: Intro to CS and Programming (MIT, $n=59,126$), Statistics for Public Health (Harvard, $n=30,742$), Artificial Intelligence (Berkeley, $n=22,690$), and Solid State Chemistry (MIT, $n=15,281$). Students' engagement was assessed in terms of how long they watched the video and whether they attempted to answer post-video assessment problems. Video property was measured by the length, type, presentation style, quality, and speaking rate of instructors. The results showed that shorter videos, videos that combine instructors' "talking head" with slides, videos where instructors show their personal feeling, and videos with Khan-style drawing (see https://www.khanacademy.org/) are more engaging than longer videos, videos only with slides, videos with high-fidelity studio recordings, and videos with still screencasts. Using the same courses, Kim et al. (2014) investigated within-video engagement behaviors. In order to understand the causes that lead to video interaction peaks that indicate points of interest or confusion within the video, the study combined peak profile analysis (log) with visual content analysis (image similarity metric). The results showed that the interaction peaks can be explained by five student activity patterns: starting from the beginning of a new material, returning to missed content, following a tutorial step, replaying a brief segment, and repeating a non-visual explanation.

Connection to Arts Efforts have been made to connect science education with art education because arts practices can promote inspiration and interests. Here we highlight a few examples that take advantage of technologies. A common approach is to develop a course or program that integrates arts and sciences. Jennifer Burg at Wake Forest University initiated a project that aimed to develop curricular materials that integrate mathematics, science, computer science, and digital sound production (http://csweb.cs.wfu.edu/~burg/CCLI/Templates/ home.php). The project brought college-level teachers and students from science and art disciplines to carry out, refine, and disseminate the curricular materials. Sciences and arts can support each other for students to learn science concepts. For example, Bopegedera (2005) conducted a light-related program in which students participated in both art workshops and science labs in order to help students to use scientific understanding of light to create artistic products. In the art workshops students could draw and paint products by hand or using graphing software (e.g., constructing light waves with yarn), while in the science labs students could learn concepts related to light (e.g., the relationships among frequency, wavelength, and the speed of light). Another approach to think about linking arts and sciences is to exploit the power of visualization. A good piece of software that can help practicing scientists to create and animate 3-D molecules is Molecular Flipbook (http://molecularflipbook.org). With the powerful visual aid of molecular graphs, scientists can communicate their findings to others aesthetically and informatively (Atwood & Barbour, 2003). Other creative ways to visualize and disseminate science ideas to the public have also been promoted. For example, Science Magazine hosted a competition named "Dance Your PhD" to encourage college students' using art to communicate scientific ideas and fuel creative thinking. The 2014 Dance Your PhD was awarded to a UGA plant biology student who danced out how forests regenerate after tornado (UGA Today, 2014). Despite these innovative approaches, however, research on connecting arts and science at the college level still needs much empirical work.

Summary In this section, we described a few notable examples of technologies that can be used to promote college students' lifelong learning competencies. We note that a number of important technologies have been left out in this review due to space limit. These may include physical sensors (e.g., Milner-Bolotin & Moll, 2008), virtual or mixed realities (e.g., Cheng & Tsai, 2013), mobile devices

Table 2 Technological resources that can be used to facilitate promising college science education instructional practices

	Designing activities to engage students in active learning	Using scenario-based content organization for complex problem solving and integrated learning	Organizing students in collaborative learning	Involve students in conducting scientific research for independent and critical thinking
Personal response system (i.e., Clickers)	Clicker questions engage students in critical thinking, reflection, and argumentation with peers	N/A	Students discuss and argue with their neighbors about their responses to clicker questions	N/A
Computer visualizations and simulations (CVS), including virtual labs	CVS can draw students' attention and increase students' active interaction	CVS can provide vivid depiction of specific scenarios	CVS renders collective artifacts for collaborative learning	CVS may be involved in research
Computer-supported collaborative learning (CSCL), including online discussion and social networks	CSCL may facilitate the development of a learning community and promote students' active learning	CSCL can be used in a scenario-based approach	CSCL by definition incorporates features to facilitate students' collaborative learning	CSCL can facilitate collaborative research
Educational video & computer games (VCG)	VCG requires users' active participation and learning	VCG is typically built on well designed storylines and scenarios	Multiplayer VCG including MUVE involves collaboration among players; game playing involves game-based learning community	Games can be developed to facilitate scientific research
OpenCourseWare (OCW) & MOOCs	OCW can engage motivated students, but still need improvement to engage all students	Exemplar scenario-based OCW is yet to be developed	OCW provides students with online collaboration opportunities	N/A

(e.g., Hwang, Yang, Tsai, & Yang, 2009), and artificial intelligence (e.g., Koedinger & Corbett, 2006), to name a few. We want to echo the position that it is not just the technology but how the technology is being used that matters (Mazur, 2009; Mishra & Koehler, 2006). Each individual instructor needs to consider the available resources and student needs to incorporate these technological resources. Table 2 summarizes the relevant features of these technological resources with respect to the instructional practices that promote life long learning.

Technology-Enriched Assessment for Learning

Without appropriate assessments, a pedagogical innovation will be incomplete (Pellegrino, 2013). Technological advancements have great potential to expand how science assessment can be designed and utilized. In this section, we describe a few assessment approaches that draw heavily on technology to nurture students' lifelong learning capacity.

Embedded Formative Assessment

Formative assessment has been increasingly used in science instruction. Black and Wiliam's seminal paper (1998) emphasized on the various ways that formative assessment can be practiced in classrooms and the ways evidence can be gathered to evaluate the effectiveness of the practices. A characteristic that distinguishes formative assessment from summative assessment is that formative assessment is *for* learning, not *of* learning (Black, 1993). Driven by this distinction, formative assessment offers opportunities for students to understand their misconceptions and improve understanding based on timely feedback.

Although formative assessment has great potential to complement instruction and enhance learning, a few prerequisites need to be satisfied for it to benefit students. First, sufficient professional development needs to be provided to teachers for them to fully understand formative assessment strategies and know when and under what circumstances each strategy should be practiced (Furtak et al., 2008). Second, formative assessment needs to meet quality standards for the assessment to elicit valid information from students. Last, mechanisms need to be developed for teachers to make use of the results from formative assessment. It is not uncommon that assessment results are left sitting on the shelf after a substantial amount of effort has been spent on collecting the results (Ruiz-Primo & Furtak, 2007). After a decade of research on formative assessment, Bennett (2011) provided a comprehensive review of formative assessment, and called for a more critical view of how formative assessment should be implemented and how its effectiveness should be assessed.

Formative assessment can take a variety of forms. For instance, in a college-level medical science course, Riffat, Quadri, Waseem, Mahmud, and Iqbal (2010) practiced a variety of learning and formative assessment tools such as small group discussion, self-direct learning and quizzes. The authors reported improved critical thinking skills and course understanding through the integrated learning and assessment methods. Lancor (2013) described an approach that used student-generated analogies as a formative assessment tool to elicit students' ideas about energy in biology, chemistry, and physics. Computer technology provides an efficient way to embed formative assessment in lesson sequences (Liu, Ryoo, Sato, Svihla, & Linn, 2013). Kibble (2007) reported a program using online quizzes as formative assessment. The study found that the students who participated in the formative quizzes received higher scores on summative assessments and self-reported that the quizzes were useful in providing quality feedback.

A key component of formative assessment is the mechanism of providing informative feedback for students to improve their learning. For instance, the aforementioned Peer Instruction method (Mazur, 1997; Crouch & Mazur, 2001) is a form of formative assessment. In this method, students receive instant feedback from the automated response distribution of the whole class, from their peers through discussion and argumentation, and from their instructor for clarification and explanation. One constraint of this approach is that students have to attend the class, which they should, to receive the feedback. In contrast, Doige (2012) described an informal, email-based formative assessment program employed to encourage freshmen to constantly revisit their first-year general chemistry materials in a low-stake environment. The students would receive a formative assessment question through email twice a week and, if participating in the program, respond to the question through email. The instructor then would provide timely and personalized feedback to the participating students. The study revealed certain patterns of student participation in this voluntary-based program, and showed that students who participated regularly in the program were more likely to be successful in the summative assessments. One drawback of this approach is that if a large number of students participate in such a program, the responses and feedback for individual students would be extremely time-consuming.

In general, formative assessment should be practiced more frequently in college science classrooms given its potential to provide helpful feedback and improve learning. Formative assessment strategies are particularly needed for large-scale courses including MOOCs as they may be able to help increase student engagement and retention.

Automated Scoring

Automated scoring of constructed-response items is one of the most prominent technologies developed for assessing students' deep understanding (Bennett & Sebrechts, 1996; Dzikovska, Nielsen, & Brew, 2012; Leacock & Chodorow, 2003; Mitchell, Russell, Broomhead, & Aldridge, 2002; Nielsen, Ward, & Martin, 2008; Sandene, Horkay, Bennett, Braswell, & Oranje, 2005). Science educators call for the use of constructed-response items in measuring deep understanding and eliciting reasoning (e.g., Lane, 2004; Shepard, 2000). However, the use of constructed-response items has been limited due to the cumbersome scoring and long turn-around time. Automated scoring, if accurate, can shorten the time between test administration and score report, reduce the number of human raters, and avoid bias typically introduced by human raters (Burstein, Marcu, & Knight, 2003; Liu, Brew, Blackmore, Gerard, Madhok, & Linn, In Press; Williamson, Xi, & Breyer, 2012).

A number of studies have employed automated scoring to score college students' responses to science assessments. Attali, Powers, Freedman, Harrison, and Obetz (2008) applied c-rater®, an automated scoring tool developed by the Educational

Testing Service for content scoring, to score college-level science items in biology and psychology. The responses to the items were typically 1–3 sentences long. The average kappa indicating the agreement between automated and human scores was.62 for biology and.83 for psychology items. Dzikovska et al. (2012) used the content scoring engine BEETLE II to score college-level physics and the responses were 1–2 sentences long. The kappa value was around.69 for the items tested.

Nehm and colleagues have applied machine-learning techniques to automatically score college students' written responses related to evolutionary biology (Ha, Nehm, Urban-Lurain, & Merrill, 2011; Nehm, Ha, & Mayfield, 2011). Nehm et al. (2011) evaluated the scoring performance of the machine-learning software Summarization Integrated Development Environment (SIDE; http://www.cs.cmu.edu/~cprose/SIDE.html) program against that of human experts, using a corpus of 2,260 student explanations on evolutionary change written by 565 college students. The study found that overall the SIDE software performed very well (i.e., kappa >0.80) and excellent for the natural selection understanding in terms of Key Concept Diversity. Similarly, Ha et al. (2011) applied SIDE to score biology major and nonmajor students' written responses (number of responses >1000) related to evolutionary change in introductory biology courses from two institutions. The results indicated that the automated scoring software did perform well in most cases, accurately evaluating students' understanding of evolutionary change. The authors also identified several common types of students' responses that led to poor performance of computer scoring. These include responses using many key terms but missing important aspects, responses using key terms that are scattered throughout a response, responses using uncommonly used or complex expression, and responses containing spelling and spacing errors.

Going forward, automated scoring has great potential to facilitate immediate feedback to students' written responses to open ended items. In a formative assessment setting, if students can receive instant feedback on their answers to a question and be pointed to relevant instructional steps, learning can be facilitated in a much direct and engaging way. Linn et al. (2014) provided empirical evidence that machine-generated automated feedback is as effective as the feedback provided by an expert teacher in terms of prompting students to revisit instruction and revise answer.

Automated scoring and feedback can be particular helpful for large classrooms including MOOCs in which students are unlikely to receive adequate feedback from the instructor given the mass number of students enrolled in these classes. Automated scoring and feedback offer the possibility for these students to receive meaningful and timely feedback, therefore, increasing their engagement and performance.

Learning Analytics

Since science learning involves complex processes such as inquiry, modeling, argumentation, and collaboration, new forms of assessments need to address the dynamic nature of these processes in order to better capture and facilitate student learning (Gobert, Sao Pedro, Raziuddin, & Baker, 2013). Learning analytics is an emerging method in educational application that focuses on "developing tools and techniques for capturing, storing, and finding patterns in large amounts of electronic data; representing them in generative and useful ways; and integrating them into intelligent tools that personalize and optimize learning environments" (Martin & Sherin, 2013, p. 12).

There has not been much work conducted in applying learning analytics in college science education. Baker, Hershkovitz, Rossi, Goldstein, and Gowda (2013) presented a supervised method for analyzing student's moment-by-moment learning over time. In the study, participating students used an intelligent tutoring system for college level genetics called Genetics Cognitive Tutor. The researchers then applied a program to create graphs of student moment-by-moment learning. The graph is based on the probability a student knows a concept or skill at a particular time point (the BKT model, Corbett & Anderson, 1995) and learned the concept or skill at a particular step (e.g, a specific step during a problem-solving process; Baker, Goldstein, and Heffernan 2011). The study found that these graphs are correlated with different learning outcomes.

Learning analytics has also been applied in understanding students' engagement patterns in MOOCs. For instance, Kizilcec, Piech and Schneide (2013) proposed a mechanism to identify students' engagement trajectories in MOOCs based on patterns of learners' interaction with video lectures and assessments. Using k-means clustering analysis, they classified learners in three computer science MOOCs into four major patterns: auditing, completing, disengaging, and sampling. Based on learners' self-report, "completing" learners had a significantly better learning experience than the other three groups. They also compared clusters based on learner characteristics and behaviors. They found out two major factors motivated a learner's enrollment: (a) the course is challenging and (b) the learner is interested in the content of the course.

Apparently, more empirical studies need to be conducted in extracting information from learning analytics to facilitate college students' science learning. One possible direction is to utilize these fine-grained data to build more informative digital profiles of learners. In this way, students as well as instructors can better reflect on their learning experience and therefore, take appropriate actions to improve learning as needed.

Conclusion

In this chapter we propose that college science education needs to prioritize the goal of developing students' lifelong learning skills. We reviewed a set of promising pedagogies and new forms of assessments that exploit innovative technologies in college science instruction that can facilitate this goal. We applaud that some of the technology-infused approaches, rare in their kinds, make connections between science and arts instruction at the college level. We stress that it is not about technology per se, but how it is integrated in instruction in different contexts that matters. To make this happen, we need to engineer creative ways to support faculty in using these innovative methods and technologies. A good example of a University-level imitative is the Science Teaching and Learning Fellows through the Carl Wieman Science Education Initiative at University of British Columbia (http://www.cwsei.ubc.ca). We believe that a large-scale implementation of these new forms of technologies, either through a bottom-up or top-down approach, has potential to bring about transformative changes to reach the goal of college science education in the 21st century.

References

Adamopoulos, P. (2013, December). *What makes a great MOOC? An interdisciplinary analysis of student retention in online courses.* Proceedings of the 34th International Conference on Information Systems (ICIS), Milan, Italy.

Attali, Y., Powers, D., Freedman, M., Harrison, M., & Obetz, S. (2008). *Automated scoring of short-answer open-ended GRE Subject Test items (ETS GRE Board Research Report No. 04-02).* Princeton: Educational Testing Service.

Atwood, J. L., & Barbour, L. J. (2003). Molecular graphics: From science to art. *Crystal Growth & Design, 3*(1), 3–8.

Balfour, S. P. (2013). Assessing writing in MOOCs: Automated essay scoring and calibrated peer review. *Research & Practice in Assessment, 8*(1), 40–48.

Baker, R. S. J. d., Goldstein, A. B., & Heffernan, N. T. (2011). Detecting learning moment-by-moment. *International Journal of Artificial Intelligence in Education, 21*(1–2), 5–25.

Baker, R. S., Hershkovitz, A., Rossi, L. M., Goldstein, A. B., & Gowda, S. M. (2013). Predicting robust learning with the visual form of the moment-by-moment learning curve. *Journal of the Learning Sciences, 22*(4), 639–666.

Bao, L., Cai, T., Koenig, K., Fang, K., Han, J., Wang, J., et al. (2009). Learning and scientific reasoning. *Science, 323*(5914), 586–587.

Bennett, R. E. (2011). Formative assessment: A critical review. *Assessment in Education: Principles, Policy & Practice, 18*(1), 5–25. doi:10.1080/0969594X.2010.513678.

Bennett, R. E., & Sebrechts, M. M. (1996). The accuracy of expert-system diagnoses of mathematical problem solutions. *Applied Measurement in Education, 9*(2), 133–150. doi:10.1207/s15324818ame0902_3.

Black, P. (1993). Formative and summative assessment by teachers. *Studies in Science Education, 21*(1), 49–97. doi:10.1080/03057269308560014.

Black, P., & Wiliam, D. (1998). Assessment and classroom learning. *Assessment in Education, 5*(1), 7–74. doi:10.1080/0969595980050102.

Bloom, B. S. (Ed.). (1956). *Taxonomy of educational objectives: The classification of educational goals, Handbook 1: Cognitive domain.* New York: David McKay.

Bopegedera, A. M. R. P. (2005). The art and science of light: An interdisciplinary teaching and learning experience. Journal of Chemical Education, 82(1), 55.

Bransford, J. D., & Schwartz, D. L. (1999). Rethinking transfer: A simple proposal with multiple implications. In A. Iran-Nejad & P. D. Pearson (Eds.), *Review of research in education* (Vol. 24, pp. 61–199). Washington, D. C.: American Educational Research Association.

Burstein, J., Marcu, D., & Knight, K. (2003). Finding the WRITE stuff: Automatic identification of discourse structure in student essays. *IEEE Intelligent Systems: Special Issue on Advances in Natural Language Processing, 18*(1), 32–39. doi:0.1109/MIS.2003.1179191.

Cheng, K., & Tsai, C. (2013). Affordances of augmented reality in science learning: Suggestions for future research. *Journal of Science Education and Technology, 22,* 449–462. doi:10.1007/s10956-012-9405-9.

Corbett, A. T., & Anderson, J. R. (1995). Knowledge tracing: Modeling the acquisition of procedural knowledge. *User Modeling and User-Adapted Interaction, 4,* 253–278.

Crouch, C., & Mazur, E. (2001). Peer instruction: Ten years of experience and results. *American Journal of Physics, 69*(9), 970–977.

de Jong, T., Linn, M. C., & Zacharia, Z. (2013). Physical and virtual laboratories in science and engineering education. *Science, 340*(6130), 305–308.

Deslauriers, L., Schelew, E., & Wieman, C. (2011). Improved learning in a large-enrollment physics class. *Science, 332*(6031), 862–864.

Doige, C. A. (2012). E-mail-based formative assessment: A chronicle of research-inspired practice. *Journal of College Science Teaching, 41*(6), 32–39.

Dzikovska, M. O., Nielsen, R. D., & Brew, C. (2012). *Towards effective tutorial feedback for explanation questions: A dataset and baselines.* In Proceedings of the 2012 Conference of the North American Chapter of the Association for Computational Linguistics: Human Language Technologies (pp. 200–201). Montreal, Canada.

Eiben, C., Siegel, J., Bale, J., Cooper, S., Khatib, F., Shen, B., & Baker, D. (2012). Increased diels-Alderase activity through backbone remodeling guided by Foldit players. *Nature Biotechnology, 30*(2), 190–192. doi:10.1038/nbt.2109.

Ericsson, K. A., Krampe, R. Th., & Tesch-Römer, C. (1993). The role of deliberate practice in the acquisition of expert performance. *Psychological Review, 100*(3), 363–406.

Finkelstein, N. D., Adams, W. K., Keller, C. J., Kohl, P. B., Perkins, K. K., Podolefsky, N. S., et al. (2005). When learning about the real world is better done virtually: A study of substituting computer simulations for laboratory equipment. *Physical Review Special Topics-Physics Education Research, 1,* 010103–010110.

Frisch, J. K., Jackson, P. C., & Murray, M. C. (2013). WikiED: Using Web2.0 tools to teach content and critical thinking. *Journal of College Science Teaching, 43*(1), 71–80.

Froyd, J. (2008, June). *White paper on promising practices in undergraduate STEM education.* Paper presented at the National Research Council's Workshop Linking Evidence to Promising Practices in STEM Undergraduate Education, Washington, D. C.

Furtak, E. M., Ruiz-Primo, M. A., Shemwell, J. T., Ayala, C. C., Brandon, P., Shavelson, R. J., et al. (2008). On the fidelity of implementing embedded formative assessments and its relation to student learning. *Applied Measurement in Education, 21*(4), 360–389. doi:10.1080/08957340802347852.

Gee, J. P. (2007). *What video games have to teach us about learning and literacy* (2nd edn.). New York: Palgrave Macmillan.

Gobert, J. D., Sao Pedro, M., Raziuddin, J., & Baker, R. (2013). From log files to assessment metrics: Measuring students' science inquiry skills using educational data mining. *Journal of the Learning Sciences, 22*(4), 521–563.

Goodyear, P., Jones, C., & Thompson, K. (2014). Computer-supported collaborative learning: Instructional approaches, group processes and educational designs. In J. M. Spector, M. D. Merrill, J. Elen, & M. J. Bishop (Eds.), *Handbook of research on educational communications and technology* (4th ed., pp. 439–451). New York: Springer.

Guo, P. J., Kim, J., & Rubin, R. (2014, March). *How video production affects student engagement: An empirical study of MOOC videos.* In Proceedings of the first ACM conference on Learning@ scale conference (pp. 41–50). New York: ACM Press.

Ha, M., Nehm, R. H., Urban-Lurain, M., & Merrill, J. E. (2011). Applying computerized-scoring models of written biological explanations across courses and colleges: Prospects and limitations. *CBE-Life Sciences Education, 10,* 379–393.

Hodges, K. V. (2012). Solving complex problems. *Science, 338*(6111), 1164–1165.

Hollands, F. M., & Tirthali, D. (2014, April). *MOOCs: Expectations and reality.* Paper presented at the 2014 American Educational Research Association annual conference, Philadelphia, PA.

Hwang, G. J., Yang, T. C., Tsai, C. C., & Yang, S. J. (2009). A context-aware ubiquitous learning environment for conducting complex science experiments. *Computers & Education, 53*(2), 402–413.

Kalman, C. S., Milner-Bolotin, M., & Antimirova, T. (2010). Comparison of the effectiveness of collaborative groups and Peer instruction in a large introductory physics course for science majors. *Canadian Journal of Physics, 88*(5), 325–332.

Khatib, F., DiMaio, F., Foldit Contenders Group, Foldit Void Crushers Group, Cooper, S., Kazmierczyk, M., Gilski M., Krzywda S., Zabranska H., Pichova I., Thompson J., Popović Z., Jaskolski M., Baker D. (2011). Crystal structure of a monomeric retroviral protease solved by protein folding game players. *Nature Structural & Molecular Biology, 18,* 1175–1177. doi:10.1038/nsmb.2119.

Kibble, J. D. (2007). Use of unsupervised online quizzes as formative assessment in medical physiology course: Effects of incentives on student participation and performance. *Advances in Physiology Education, 31,* 253–260.

Kim, J., Guo, P. J., Seaton, D. T., Mitros, P., Gajos, K. Z., & Miller, R. C. (2014, March). *Understanding in-video dropouts and interaction peaks inonline lecture videos.* Proceedings of the first ACM conference on Learning@ scale conference (pp. 31–40). ACM.

Kizilcec, R. F., Piech, C., & Schneider, E. (2013, April). Deconstructing disengagement: Analyzing learner subpopulations in massive open online courses. In D. Suthers, K. Verbert, E. Duval, & X. Ochoa (Eds.), *Proceedings of the Third International Conference on learning analytics and knowledge.* New York: ACM.

Koedinger, K., & Corbett, A. (2006). Cognitive tutors: Technology bringing learning science to the classroom. In K. Sawyer (Ed.), *The Cambridge handbook of the learning sciences* (pp. 61–78). Cambridge: Cambridge University Press.

Koller, D., Ng, A., Do, C., & Chen, Z. (2013). Retention and intention in massive open online courses. *EDUCAUSE Review,* May/June, 62–63.

Lancaster, K. V., Moore, E. B., Parson, R., & Perkins, K. (2013). Insights from using PhET's design principles for interactive chemistry simulations. In J. Suits & M. Sanger (Eds.), *Pedagogic roles of animations and simulations in chemistry courses* (pp. 97–126), ACS Symposium Series, 2013. American Chemical Society.

Lancor, R. A. (2013). The many metaphors of energy: Using analogies as a formative assessment tool. *Journal of College Science Teaching, 42*(3), 38–45.

Leacock, C., & Chodorow, M. (2003). C-rater: Automated scoring of short-answer questions. *Computers and the Humanities, 37*(4), 389–405. doi:10.1023/a:1025779619903.

Lane, S. (2004). Validity of high-stakes assessment: Are students engaged in complex thinking? *Educational Measurement: Issues and Practice, 23*(3), 6–14. doi:10.1111/j.1745-3992.2004. tb00160.x.

Lei, J., Shen, J., & Johnson, L. (2013). Digital technologies and assessment in 21st century schooling. In M. P. Mueller, D. J. Tippins, & A. J. Stewart (Eds.), *Assessing schools for generation R (Responsibility): A guide to legislation and school policy in science education* (pp. 185–200). New York: Springer.

Linn, M. C., Gerard, L., Kihyun, R., McElhaney, K., Liu, O. L., & Rafferty, A. N. (2014). Computer-guided inquiry to improve science learning. *Science, 344*(6180), 155–156. doi:10.1126/science.1245980.

Liu, O. L., Ryoo, K., Sato, E., Svihla, V., & Linn, M. C. (2013, April). *Designing assessment to measure cumulative learning of energy topics.* Paper presented at the 2013 Annual Conference of the American Educational Research Association, San Francisco.

Liu, O. L., Brew, C., Blackmore, J., Gerard, L., & Madhok, J. (In Press, early view). Automated scoring for inquiry science assessment: Prospects and obstacles. *Educational Measurement: Issues and Practice.* doi:10.1111/emip.12028.

Martin, T., & Sherin, B. (2013). Learning analytics and computational techniques for detecting and evaluating patterns in learning: An introduction to the special issue. *Journal of the Learning Sciences, 22*(4), 511–520.

Mazur, E. (1997). *Peer instruction: A user's manual.* Upper Saddle River: Prentice Hall.

Mazur, E. (2009). Farewell, lecture? *Science, 323*(5910), 50–51.

Mervis, J. (2013). Transformation is possible if a university really cares. *Science, 340*(6130), 292–296.

Milner-Bolotin, M., & Moll, R. F. (2008). Physics exam problems reconsidered: Using Logger Pro technology to evaluate student understanding of physics. *The Physics Teacher, 46*(8), 494–500.

Mishra, P., & Koehler, M. J. (2006). Technological pedagogical content knowledge: A framework for teacher knowledge. *Teachers College Record, 108*(6), 1017–1054.

Mitchell, T., Russell, T., Broomhead, P., & Aldridge, N. (2002). Towards robust computerized marking of free-text responses. In *Proceedings of the Sixth International Computer Assisted Assessment Conference* (pp. 233–249). Loughborough: Loughborough University.

Namdar, B., & Shen, J. (2014, June). *Knowledge organization with multiple external representations for socioscientific argumentation: A case on nuclear energy.* Proceedings of the 11th International Conference of the Learning Sciences (ICLS), Boulder, CO.

National Research Council. (2011). Learning science through computer games and simulations. Committee on science learning: Computer games, simulations, and education. In M. A. Honey & M. L. Hilton (Eds.), *Board on science education, division of behavioral and social sciences and education.* Washington, D. C.: The National Academies Press.

National Research Council. (2012). Education for life and work: Developing transferable knowledge and skills in the 21st century. Committee on Defining Deeper Learning and 21st Century Skills, J.W. Pellegrino and M.L. Hilton, Editors. Board on Testing and Assessment and Board on Science Education, Division of Behavioral and Social Sciences and Education. Washington, D. C.: The National Academies Press.

Nehm, R. H., Ha, M., & Mayfield, E. (2011). Transforming biology assessment with machine learning: Automated scoring of written evolutionary explanations. *Journal of Science Education and Technology, 21*(1), 183–196.

Nielsen, R. D., Ward, W., & Martin. J. H. (2008). *Classification errors in a domain-independent assessment system.* Proceedings of the Third Workshop on Innovative Use of NLP for Building Educational Applications (pp. 10–18), Columbus, OH.

NSF Task Force on CyberLearning. (2008). *Fostering learning in the networked world: The cyberlearning opportunity and challenge.* Washington, D. C.: NSF.

Osborne, J. (2010). Arguing to learn in science: The role of collaborative, critical discourse. *Science, 328*(5977), 463–466.

Pellegrino, J. W. (2013). Proficiency in science: Assessment challenges and opportunities. *Science, 340*(6130), 320–323.

Podolefsky, N. S., Perkins, K. K., & Adams, W. K. (2010). Factors promoting engaged exploration with computer simulations. *Physical Review Special Topics-Physics Education Research, 6,* 020117–020127.

Riffat, S., Quadri, K. H. M., Waseem, A., Mahmud, S. N., & Iqbal, M. (2010). Experience with a theme-based integrated renal module for a second-year MBBS class. *Advances in Physiology Education, 34*(1), 15–19.

Ruiz-Primo, M. A., & Furtak, E. M. (2007). Exploring teachers' informal formative assessment practices and students' understanding in the context of scientific inquiry. *Journal of Research in Science Teaching, 44*(1), 57–84. doi:10.1002/tea.20163.

Sandene, B., Horkay, N., Bennett, R., Braswell, J., & Oranje, A. (2005). *Online assessment in mathematics and writing: Reports from the NAEP Technology-Based Assessment Project, research and development series (NCES 2005-457).* Washington, D. C.: U.S. Government Printing Office.

Scalise, K., Timms, M., Moorjani, A., Clark, L., & Holtermann, K. (2011). Student learning in science simulations. Design futures that promote learning gains. *Journal of Research in Science Teaching, 48*(9), 1050–1078.

Shen, J., Lei, J., Chang, H., & Namdar, B. (2014). Technology-enhanced, modeling-based instruction (TMBI) in science education. In J. M. Spector, M. D. Merrill & J. Elen, & M. J. Bishop (Eds.), *Handbook of research on educational communication and technology* (4th ed., pp. 529–540). New York: Springer.

Shepard, L. A. (2000). The role of assessment in a learning culture. *Educational Researcher, 29*(7), 4–14. doi:10.3102/0013189X029007004.

Stahl, G., Koschmann, T., & Suthers, D. (2006). Computer-supported collaborative learning: An historical perspective. In R. K. Sawyer (Ed.), *Cambridge handbook of the learning sciences* (pp. 409–426). Cambridge: Cambridge University Press.

Stephens, R., & Richey, M. (2013). A business view on U.S. education. *Science, 340*(6130), 313–314.

UGA Today (2014). UGA plant biology student wins international 'Dance Your Ph.D.' contest. http://news.uga.edu/releases/article/plant-biology-student-wins-international-dance-your-phd-contest-1114/. Accessed 23 Nov 2014.

Watkins, J., & Mazur, E. (2013). Retaining students in science, technology, engineering, and mathematics (STEM) majors. *Journal of College Science Teaching, 42,* 36–41.

Wieman, C., Adams, W. K., & Perkins, K. K. (2008). PhET: Simulations that enhance learning. *Science, 322*(5902), 682–683.

Williamson, D., Xi, X., & Breyer, J. (2012). A framework for evaluation and use of automated scoring. *Educational Measurement: Issues and Practice, 31*(1), 2–13. doi:10.1111/j.1745-3992.2011.00223.x.

Yaron, D., Karabinos, M., Lange, D., Greeno, J. G., & Leinhardt, G. (2010). The ChemCollective-virtual labs for introductory chemistry courses. *Science, 328*(5978), 584–585.

Ji Shen is Associate Professor in the Department of Teaching and Learning at the University of Miami (UM). Dr. Shen's scholarly work focuses on interdisciplinary science learning and assessment, technology-enhanced learning environments in STEM education, modeling-based teaching and learning, and preservice science teacher education. His work has been funded by the National Science Foundation. Dr. Shen holds a bachelor's degree in Geophysics from Peking University and doctoral degree in Physics from Washington University in St. Louis.

Shiyan Jiang is a third-year doctoral student in the program of STEM (Science, Technology, Engineering and Mathematics) education in the Department of Teaching and Learning at the University of Miami. Her research interests include visualizations of learning process, technology-enhanced learning, emerging technologies for teaching and learning, Computer Supported Collaborative Learning (CSCL), and instructional design. Ms. Jiang holds a bachelor's degree in educational technology from East China Normal University.

Ou Lydia Liu is Managing Senior Research Scientist at the Educational Testing Service (ETS). Her main research areas include assessment of student learning outcomes in higher education and innovative science assessment in K-12. She is currently leading a NSF funded project and Co-PI for three other NSF funded projects on science assessment. Dr. Liu served on the advisory panel for the OECD's AHELO (Assessment of Higher Education Learning Outcomes) project. Dr. Liu has published widely in applied measurement, higher education, and science education journals. She was the recipient of the NCME Jason Millman Promising Measurement Scholar Award in 2011. Dr. Liu holds a bachelor's degree in Science & English from the University of Science and Technology of China and a doctoral degree in Quantitative Methods and Evaluation from the University of California, Berkeley.

There is an Art to Teaching Science in the 21st Century

October Smith

Abstract For the last decade, there has been a push to integrate science, technology, engineering and math (STEM) in education. Recently, the inclusion of the arts into STEM has made a push for STEAM in the classroom. This integration of these subjects does not mean offering the individual classes at school, but rather blending all five subjects together for a topic of study. The importance of STEAM integration is having an impact on the workforce which is looking for graduates that are prepared by knowing how to collaborate, communicate, create and problem solve. These "21st century skills" are not something that can be taught overnight; instead, and they must be developed throughout a student's schooling. Because of the natural integration of the STEAM subjects and 21st century skills, they often go hand-in-hand when discussing best practices for teaching science. This chapter examines the history behind teaching science, such as its impact on the workforce today, the inclusion of STEAM and 21st century skills, and its influence on teaching and learning in the middle school classrooms.

Keywords STEM · 21st century skills · PBL · Creativity · Collaboration

Introduction

> Murray Gell-Mann, Nobel laureate in physics and avowed multidisciplinarian, made an intriguing claim about our time: In the 21st century, the most valued mind will be the synthesizing mind—the mind that can survey a wide range of sources, decide what is important and worth paying attention to, and then put this information together in ways that make sense to oneself and ultimately, to other persons as well. (Gardner, 2006)

We no longer live in a world where memorizing facts is the key to a career path. The ability to process information, determine what is valuable, and then use that valuable information accordingly will be what sets each person apart from another. The synthesizing minds will be the ones that continue to advance our knowledge

O. Smith (✉)
University of North Texas, Denton, USA
e-mail: OctoberSmith@my.unt.edu

© Springer International Publishing Switzerland 2015
X. Ge et al. (eds.), *Emerging Technologies for STEAM Education,*
Educational Communications and Technology: Issues and Innovations,
DOI 10.1007/978-3-319-02573-5_5

"

base and technology growth. But how do we teach young students to effectively synthesize information? This chapter will examine the history behind teaching science, why it has an impact on the workforce today, the inclusion of STEAM and 21st century skills, and the role middle school plays in all of this.

Science Education

Science and art, theory and practice are often taught in isolated instances. Schools focus on each subject independently, each teacher with their expert knowledge in a particular area. Ultimately, this is not how the real world works. Jobs today are no longer routine factory jobs, and they encompass a wide range of skills. New employees are expected to enter the workforce knowing how to communicate, collaborate and generate creative ideas. This is a far cry from the factual knowledge-based curriculum that once proliferated the curriculum in the United States. Not only are educators responsible for the factual knowledge of all subject areas, but now they must also attempt to integrate subject areas, such as math and science, in a meaningful, applicable way, while encouraging collaborative skills among students.

Learning- A Timeline of Events

How people learn has been a topic of interest dating back to ancient Greek philosophers such as Socrates (470-399BC), Plato (427-347BC) and Aristotle (384-322BC). Philosophers and educators continued to study the topic of learning every century thereafter. Nonetheless, this section will start with a newly formed nation, just after the American Revolution. Thomas Jefferson (1743–1826), proposed a radical idea that children should have the right to at least 3 years of a public school education (Mondale, 2001). Although Jefferson did not get very far in his quest for improving education during his time in office, it did allow for others such as Horace Mann (1796–1859), to begin leading a reform in education. Mann's focus was on the physical conditions of the school buildings, citing things such as light, heat, and ventilation (Mondale, 2001), but he also noticed the lack of standardized textbooks. He encouraged a new system of "common schools" where children would receive an "equal chance in life" (Mondale, 2001). Public education continued to become more systemic and regulated as the years went by, and around the turn of the 20th century, learning theories became part of educational pedagogy. John Dewey (1859–1952) constructed a philosophy of education that compared to that of Plato's ideas (Cahn, 1997). Dewey believed that the scientific method was the basis of how all education should be taught.

Following WWII, the United States became a leader in industry and technology. Veterans were attending college on the G.I. Bill and the interest in science and math careers increased. Russia launched Sputnik and the US responded by putting a man on the moon. The 1960's saw another turning point in education, as many of the nation's youths were disenchanted with the Vietnam War, leading to high social turmoil and a move away from established educational importance (Lederman, 2008). The value of education steadily declined until the early 1980's when "A Nation at Risk" was published. The message was harsh, citing declining SAT scores and indicating that schools were doing a poor job of preparing students for the workforce. This prompted supporters (and non-supporters) of the report to recognize that major changes to the education system were desperately needed. New reform efforts were launched, such as No Child Left Behind and Race to the Top, in an attempt to improve the quality of education. The beginning of the 21st century saw rapid changes and advancements in technology, bringing about new ideas for learning theories.

These new reform efforts needed to be analysed to ensure that the quality of education in America was actually improving from these educational changes. Thus, standard curriculum and standardized tests were implemented in every public school classroom. These standardized tests were criticized for narrowing the curriculum to a very specific knowledge set (Silva, 2009). If it could not be answered with a multiple-choice test, then it would not be asked—this was an idea that often eliminated higher-level thinking and creative thought. With the emphasis on standardized tests today, teachers need to find a way to teach the necessary subject content while infusing skills that will be needed for the future workforce.

Educational reform is a very slow process. To some, this may be a good thing as it allows educators to rely on tried-and-true methods and discourages the latest fads (Gardner, 2006). Others might enjoy the challenges that come with trying something new. Either way, we are doing our children a disservice by not moving quickly to facilitate acquisition of the skills they need to enter the workforce. Restructuring schools takes time and experimentation, allowing the culture of the schools to evolve and adapt, but it must be at a rate comparable to that of our society (Bassett, 2005). It is imperative that teachers design a curriculum that reinforces basic knowledge, while developing skills that encourages critical thinking among students (Bassett, 2005).

A STEM/STEAM Push

Concerns over declining STEM fields (science, technology, engineering, and math) launched the creation of the Perkins Career and Technical Act of Education in 2006. The Perkins Act provided funding for schools to improve STEM classes. In 2008, there was a big push to include the arts into the STEM fields, moving the term to STEAM. The integration of STEAM into education attempted to "balance technical expertise with artistic vision" (Peppler, 2013). STEAM integration is important because it provides students with real-life challenges rather than learning each part separately and having to put them together at the end (Wang & Moore, 2011). For the purpose of this writing, the term STEAM will be used with the understanding that the creative aspects of art integration are just as important as science, technology, engineering, and math.

Science and math are core subject areas that have customarily been taught in isolation since the early 1900's. The typical elementary class has one teacher that teaches all of the subjects to the students throughout the day. Larger elementary schools, with multiple sections per grade level, will often divide the courses based on teacher ability and comfort level. In one grade there might be a math, science, social studies teacher, and then the students will switch classes and have a different reading, language, writing teacher. This design allows for better integration among subject areas, but it does not always happen.

As students get older and move on to the secondary level, the subject area division becomes more defined. The structure of the secondary (middle and high school) education system puts students in a specific class, at a specific time during the day. It is a common practice in the US to hire teachers based on their expertise in a particular subject area. The push for STEAM integration becomes more complicated as teachers are used to being silos, teaching their content in their classroom, and now they are being asked to integrate multiple subjects including art.

Although content standards are set forth on the national or state level, educators continue to struggle with how to teach those standards (Bassett, 2005). This is one of the biggest challenges for STEAM, because there is no prescribed way of integrating STEAM subjects in the classroom (Wang & Moore, 2011). Currently, the STEAM subjects are taught independently, making curriculum integration challenging. It is not easy to integrate different subject areas together into one, especially at the secondary level.

When STEAM integration does happen, there is usually a primary subject area, and small tasks involving other subject areas are added to the activity. An example of this can be found in science, where students discuss simple machines, force, and motion using mousetrap cars. The primary subject is science, but students could easily design and engineer their own car. Alternatively, there might be a focus on two subjects, such as math and science, and the subject areas of engineering and technology can be added as the teacher finds appropriate (Roehrig, Moore, Wang & Park, 2012). In order to have the greatest impact with STEAM integration, major changes to the current curriculum need to be implemented. The Next Generation Science Standards (NGSS) is an attempt to address this issue by incorporating the engineering and cross-cutting concepts into the standards.

Teachers and Implementation

The educators in the classroom are the ones that are ultimately responsible for blending science, technology, engineering, art and mathematics to create a seamlessly integrated STEAM curriculum. With the engineering aspect built into the NGSS and technology being a part of our everyday lives, it would seem that integration should come easily in the classroom; but surprisingly that is not the case. Contributing factors to the lack of STEAM integration includes lack of training for teachers, little time to collaborate with other teachers, teachers sometimes having a difficult time grasping processes in their own field of study, and difficult to make connections among core disciplines in general (Lederman, 2008).

Pre-service teachers spend a large amount of time learning the best practices for teaching students and the content knowledge comes second to this. During teacher education training, usually in college or an alternative teacher certification program, teachers focus on lesson planning, classroom management, and professional development. The best practices are broad and the intention is that teachers will be trained on specific aspects once they are on the job. However, with standardized testing, data analysis, and general campus procedure information, things like good pedagogy and STEAM integration get pushed to the side when it comes to in-service teacher training. It takes a dedicated teacher to seek out the training needed to learn what it takes to master STEAM integration.

STEAM integration relies heavily on teacher collaboration. Teachers must work together to come up with sound activities that stretch across the subject areas. Lack of time is a major reason why teacher collaboration is not very common (Gorder, 2008; Wang & Moore, 2011). Unless an administrator makes time for teachers to meet and plan together as a group, the collaboration does not happen as often as it should.

All educators have specific content in their area that they prefer to teach. It is a passion or love that extends outside of the classroom, making it easy to teach to the students. Content outside of a teacher's preferred subject area becomes more of a challenge and the students may not receive information at the depth necessary to fully grasp the concept.

Authentically assessing STEAM integration is a difficult task. It requires teachers to be more subjective, which is difficult since grades are typically derived objectively from worksheets and tests. Once again, teachers need time to collaborate and make tests that will accurately reflect STEAM integration and higher order thinking skills.

One thing to note is the theme that runs through this section. There is discussion about communication, collaboration, creation of materials and problem solving among teachers. Teachers no longer open up a textbook, have the students take notes, do the section questions at the end, and then give the pre-made test. While there may be books available to help with STEAM subjects, there is not a set of resources that give prescribed instructions on STEAM integration. These are skills that are not taught on the job, but expected. This begs the question, how are these skills learned?

21st Century Skills

Each part of STEAM is critical for the success of the other parts, as the subjects are intertwined. An emphasis should be placed on creativity, critical thinking, problem solving, communication and collaboration. These skills are important for students as they leave school and enter their careers. A growing trend of holding multiple careers has emerged since the late twentieth century, and early twenty-first century. Considering the current trends in workforce training which indicates that people no longer hold life-long careers, but instead will change positions every 3–5 years, these career-readiness skills take on even more importance in preparing our youth for careers. "People can expect to have many jobs in multiple fields during their careers. Learning critical thinking leads students to develop other skills, such as higher level of concentration, deeper analytical abilities, and improved thought processing" (National Education Association, 2010).

The Workforce Then and Now

In 1940, most jobs were blue-collar jobs and the skills needed were learned at the job site. Three-fourths of all workers had never finished high school (Potter, 2002). In contrast, jobs today require a range of skills, such as organization and interpersonal skills that were not as essential several decades ago.

> Workforce skills and demands have changed dramatically in the last 20 years. The rapid decline in 'routine' work has been well documented by many researchers and organizations. There has been a rapid increase in jobs involving non-routine, analytic and interactive communication skills. (National Education Association, 2010)

All workers today need to be able to analyze information from a variety of sources and use the information to make informed decisions and create new ideas (Silva, 2009). These creative design skills are the most valuable within the job market today. Let's use a teacher's job for example. Educators are given numerous resources to use in the classroom, but it is up to the teacher to pull these resources together to best fit the needs of the students. This idea of pulling of resources and creating something new is becoming more prevalent; there is even a website called Teacher-PayTeachers.com where teachers can buy other teachers' materials.

Critics argue that teaching 21st century skills is meaningless and that educators should focus on core content knowledge rather than watering down the curriculum (Kereluik, Fahnoe, & Karr, 2013; Silva, 2009). What these critics fail to recognize is that without encouraging students to develop the 21st century skills at an earlier age, they would not be well prepared as they enter the workforce with communication and creative skills. It is hard to find a job that does not expect the employee to have communication and creative skills when they enter the job. Common interview questions are, "What project have you created from scratch and seen through to the finish? Who helped you with this project? How did you delegate the tasks for the project?" These skills can and should be taught in school so that the students are well prepared.

"In today's world of global competition and task automation, innovative capacity and creative spirit are fast becoming requirements for personal and professional success" (National Education Association, 2010). This creative spirit is embedded in the open-source community. Open-source is the availability of a programs code to be freely used, changed and/or shared. Small groups of programmers have developed a wide range of software that falls under the open-source category. Linux is an operating system that is open-source and free. If Microsoft Office is out of your price range, LibreOffice is a production suit that includes a word processor, spreadsheet application, presentation program and more.

Similar to open-source code, the creative commons licenses allow for sharing of other types of content. Wikipedia is an example of content that carries a creative commons license. Several collaborators work together to put out the most up-to-date free encyclopedia out there. This all takes communication, collaboration and a creative spirit to develop these ideas.

Outlining 21st Century Skills

In 2002, the NEA partnered with the Partnership for 21st Century Skills and created what has become known as the "Framework for 21st Century Learning" (National Education Association, 2010). The learning and innovation skills of the P21 Framework focus on creativity, critical thinking, communication and collaboration, all of which are essential for preparing students for the future. People today live in a technology rich world and have access to an abundance of information, rapid changes in technology tools, and the ability to collaborate and make personal contributions on a global scale. Students will need to be able to navigate an increasingly complex life and work experience in this globally competitive information age. In order to better prepare students for these life experiences, schools need to examine how they structure learning environments.

The typical elementary classroom today is set up in groups. Students work together and play together, especially in the lower grades. Enter a secondary classroom and you will see desks in rows. Students work quietly and individually. Generally speaking, this kind of structure with desks in a row and students working individually is typically not something done in the current workforce. Once students leave school, they will once again be working in groups to come up with creative new ideas. As schools reform to meet the 21st century skills, middle and high schools will look more like thematic based elementary schools, posing real-world challenges to students (Bassett, 2005).

Middle School is the Right Time

The objective of a middle school education should be focused on teaching students 21st century skills as well as gaining deep content knowledge (Kay, 2009). Middle school aged children (between 11–14 years old) are in a unique position. It is a time during those years that students become engaged and motivated to achieve in school (Kay, 2009). However, it is also during these years that students can begin to fall academically behind and no longer feel like achievement is possible, becoming unmotivated and disinterested in school. It becomes imperative that the teachers recognize the students that might end up in this situation, and work with them to provide a successful academic path.

One way to keep students interested and motivated in school is to find activities that engage them. There is a trend right now to incorporate a "genius hour" or "20% time" where students are given the freedom to work on a project/problem that they come up with. Depending on the parameters the teacher sets, students are free to choose anything they are interested in. Projects can range from designing a new type of foosball table to investigating the best types of grass for producing biofuel. If the teacher is cognizant of these "passion projects," they have the potential to successfully model what STEAM integration is about. Take the example of a foosball table mentioned above, the student must design (art, technology and engineering) and build (science, math and engineering) the game table.

Middle school is a time when students need to begin taking responsibility for their own learning. Middle school students should be ready for deeper inquiry, abstract thinking and exploration of the world around them. They have the foundational knowledge of learning, are enthusiastic, energetic and love working in groups (Kay, 2009). "As a result of students working collaboratively, the group can generate more knowledge, making collaboration a key ingredient to student success in today's global society" (National Education Association, 2010). The social and academic connections that students experience make middle school an ideal time for STEAM integration.

The Science Classroom Today

Science is the first part of STEAM, so let's spend some time examining middle school science. There is an art to teaching science in today's classroom. Story telling is an integral part of processing science, being able to tell who did what, why and how we know (Lederman, 2008). Education is no longer a sit-and-get environment as it was 50 years ago. The now, learner-focused classroom encourages students to problem solve and research through practical, real world applications. Challenges such as eCybermission, Siemens- We Can Change the World and Toshiba's- ExploraVision invite students to pose solutions to problems their communities face.

In keeping with this shift of pedagogical thinking, science instruction has moved from the teacher demonstrating in front of the class, to the students doing the demonstration themselves or in small groups. As part of this process, it is important that students understand that failure is part of the learning process, especially when learning something new. Focusing on real-world examples of problem solving encourages learners to have depth along with breadth. This gives them a genuine understanding of the problem solving process for similar problems and the skills they will need in order to face the career challenges ahead of them.

Middle School Students are not Experts…Yet

In traditional classrooms, the teacher stands in the front of the room lecturing. Students are given problems to complete outside of class for homework and then come back and take tests that correspond to the work they did out of the textbook. If a person is only able to hold seven chunks of information at a time in short term memory, then the retention of the vast amount of information given during a lecture is questionable at best. "Traditional science instruction concentrates on teaching factual knowledge, with the implicit assumption that expert-like ways of thinking about the subject come along naturally or are already present" (Weiman, 2008).

The following lab scenario is common when thinking about a typical middle school science classroom. After the teacher has given lecture notes, a structured lab gives students hands-on experience. Students are asked to follow a set of instructions to complete the lab, and it is expected that the intended outcome of the lab would yield the same results for all the students if the lab is completed correctly according to the instructions. However, the fact is that science experimenting in everyday life is not a list of prescribed instructions, rarely are the students able to understand what they are testing. These "cookbook" labs increase student frustration when the results are not typical.

The more quality time is spent on practicing a skill, the more likely that skill will be mastered. This can be done through formal education, apprenticeship or self-directed learning. Once that mastery has been achieved, it is important to continue practicing that skill or it will be lost. Expert scientists have a vast amount of tacit knowledge to draw from. Middle school students do not have that vast knowledge…yet. Educators must be aware that while building that knowledge that will be stored in long term-memory, "we need to transform how students think so that they can understand and use science like scientists do" (Weiman, 2008). Middle school students should therefore not be treated like expert scientists.

Defining the Curriculum

The elementary curriculum is easy; students are learning how to learn. They are taught the foundations of reading, math, and writing. The high school curriculum is also defined, preparing students for college, digging deep into subject material. Middle school has no "galvanizing vision or goal around which to organize standards, curriculum, instruction, assessments and learning environments" (Kay, 2009). To complicate matters, the US education system is decentralized, so each state is responsible for the education of its students.

In April 2013, the NGSS was publically released and was developed by the states to provide science standards for K-12 that will include core content information, science and engineering practices, and crosscutting concept ideas. This is moving the curriculum in the direction of STEAM integration. However, since every state is responsible for its own standards, some states will choose not to adopt the NGSS. That means those states will be responsible for an alternative way to integrate STEAM into their educational curriculum.

One way to address STEAM integration and 21st century skills is through problem-based learning (PBL). Problem-based learning gives students the opportunity to work with a real problem and analyze it to come up with a solution for the problem.

Teachers are thought of as guides, leading the students down a path for a solution to the problem. Students typically work in groups and new knowledge is formed through self-directed learning as the problem is solved. Science is a particularly easy subject to incorporate PBL lessons since it is naturally conducive to solving problems. PBL is grounded in a constructivist philosophy where students learn by doing. "Every 21st Century skills implementation requires the development of core academic subject knowledge and understanding among all students. Those who can think critically and communicate effectively must build on a base of core academic knowledge" ("P21 Framework Definitions," 2009).

Activities that Engage

The most important aspect of engaging students in STEAM integration and 21st century skills is creating a learning environment that encourages students to explore and take risks. Students must feel comfortable enough in their learning environments in order to try different approaches to a problem that they previously attempted but failed to solve. Integrating a PBL environment can facilitate this type of learning. Although students may not correctly solve the problem on the first try, they will be practicing the process of problem solving and using different methods. The process is more important than the outcome.

Games From Word with Friends, to Angry Birds, games have become a standard app on electronic devices. The easy access to games provides an excellent way to incorporate STEAM activities into the class. *Minecraft* is an excellent free-play game that can be used in any subject area. The lego-type blocks in Minecraft can be used to create scenes and objects. Students may be asked in a physical science class to develop a car that prevents pollution and uses kinetic and potential energy in an innovative and efficient way. After using additional resources for research, the students, working in groups might come up with a car that uses magnets and wind for power. They can build the car in *Minecraft* while incorporating the concepts they have learned in class in order to explain their choice of design of the car. Math skills can be used to scale the car to size and an artist can render the final design.

Programming When surveyed, students unfamiliar with programming responded that programming was "hard and boring" (Repenning, 2013). By developing an avenue for students to be creative and take ownership in computer programming, teachers can get students excited about the process of learning programming. Programs such as Scratch and Alice have been developed to guide students through understanding the concepts of coding/programming. Scratch is a game coding program that was developed by researchers at MIT Media Lab. Students use a simple drag-and-drop interface to organize instruction bubbles that fit together like puzzle pieces to create a game. The Scratch website (scratch.mit.edu) has pre-made games and games that other users have made, and anyone can use the existing games to create new ones with similar coding. Similar to Scratch, Alice is another program that allows users to drag instructions to create a 3D animation or game. Whereas upper elementary students easily use Scratch, Alice is a bit more complicated and is better suited for middle school students. Once students are comfortable with basic programming, they can begin to integrate the subject content into a project. For example, students can use Scratch to teach the carbon cycle by developing a drag and drop game that completes a "cycle" with the appropriate vocabulary game.

eTextiles A fairly new approach to programming is the avenue of e-textiles or wearable computing technology. E-textiles often require the knowledge of programming using math and science skills, as well as an artistic mind to create new designs. Users are able to design elaborate costumes that have embedded micro-controller boards, such as the Lily Pad Arduino (http://lillypadarduino.org), which is sewn into place with special conductive thread that connects to mini LED lights. The board is then programmed to turn the LED lights on and off, ultimately producing a wearable light show.

Conclusion

The education system in the United States has gone through many changes since its foundation in the 1700's, but there are still some things that remain the same. Commonalities include a board at the front, chairs with backs and standardized textbooks. These are just some of the physical things that Horace Mann so desperately wanted for his "common schools." Yet over the 250 + years, the educational pedagogy has changed. The beginnings were rooted in just getting children to learn to read. Today we expect children to read, write, solve problems, think creatively, communicate effectively, collaborate with one another, and more.

The 21st century is an exciting time to be living and working in! A strong educational foundation is important for all students to be successful in life. By providing students with collaborative experiences in science, technology, engineering, art and math, they are better equipped with the skill sets they may need for their future careers. In-service teachers must have the training and allotted time to effectively integrate STEAM collaborative experiences in their classrooms. Teacher and principal preparation programs must actively incorporate this STEAM integration training in their curriculum.

The goal of an education is to prepare students to be able to successfully navigate whatever career choice they might make. The workforce today is expecting to see employees that have excellent skills in communication, collaboration, creative thinking, and problem solving. By embedding these skills into content areas in the K-12 classroom, teachers can better prepare their students with these skills when they leave school.

Teachers must step out of the rigors of the standardized curriculum and tests in order to give students the opportunity to explore projects and interests beyond what is required. Passion projects have the ability to integrate, not only STEAM concepts, but also 21st century skills. Middle school is the ideal time to include "genius hour" and PBL activities because students are at the age where they are engaged, involved and feel personally responsible for their education. Other avenues to explore beyond the curriculum to successfully integrate STEAM activities include games, programming, and e-textiles. Through all of this, science becomes an art to teach in the 21st century.

References

Bassett, P. F. (2005). Reengineering schools for the 21st century. *Phi Delta Kappan, 87*(1), 76–83.

Cahn, S. (1997). *Classic and contemporary readings in the philosophy of education* (p. 144). New York: McGraw-Hill.

Gardner, H. (2006). *Five minds for the future*. Boston: Harvard Business Review Press.

Gorder, L. (2008). A study of teacher perceptions of instructional technology integration in the classroom. *Delta Pi Epsilon Journal, 50*(2), 63–76.

Kay, K. (2009). Middle schools preparing young people for 21st century life and work. *Middle School Journal, 40*(5), 41–50.

Kereluik, K., Fahnoe, C., & Karr, J. A. (2013). What knowledge is of most worth: Teacher knowledge for 21st century learning. *Journal of Digital Learning in Teacher Education, 29*(4), 127–140.

Lederman, L. M. (2008). Scientists and 21st century science education. *Technology in Society, 30*(3–4), 397–400.

Mondale, S. (2001). *School: The story of American public education*. Boston: Beacon Press.

National Education Association. (2010). Preparing 21st century students for a global society: An educator's guide to the "Four Cs." http://www.nea.org/assets/docs/A-Guide-to-Four-Cs.pdf. Accessed 10 March 2014.

Peppler, K. (2013). STEAM-Powered computing education: Using e-textiles to integrate the arts and STEM. *Computer, 46*(9), 38–43.

Potter, E. E. (2002). Improving skills and employability in the 21st century. *Industrial and Labor Relations Review, 55*(4), 739–745.

Repenning, A. (2013). Making programming accessible and exciting. *Computer, 46*(6), 78–81.

Roehrig, G. H., Moore, T. J., Wang, H.-H., & Park, M. S. (2012). Is Adding the E enough? Investigating the impact of K-12 engineering standards on the implementation of STEM integration. *School Science and Mathematics, 112*(1), 31–44.

Silva, E. (2009). Measuring skills for 21st-century learning. *Phi Delta Kappan, 90*(9), 630–634.

Wang, H., & Moore, T. (2011). STEM integration: Teacher perceptions and practice. *Journal of Pre-College Engineering Education Research, 1*(2), 1–13.

Weiman, C. (2008). Science education in the 21st century—Using the tools of science to teach science. *Forum for the Future of Higher Education*, 61–64. https://net.educause.edu/forum/ff08.asp.

October Smith has embraced a career in education with a deep passion for learning. Ms. Smith has a Master's Degree in Curriculum and Instruction with an emphasis on technology integration. She has worked as a teacher in elementary and high school before becoming a district instructional technologist. Her latest career journey has her back in the classroom as a science teacher for grades 6–12 at a small private school. Ms. Smith has enjoyed training others (mainly teachers) on various aspects of incorporating technology into the classroom as well as best practices using Marzano's Instructional Strategies. She also has a strong background in online learning and has worked as a trainer for a Moodle partner. Ms. Smith is a Google Certified Teacher and Moodle Course Creator Certified. She has presented at numerous local, state and national conferences such as TCEA (Texas Computer Education Association), TxDLA (Texas Distance Learning Association) and ISTE (International Society for Technology in Education). Ms. Smith is currently pursuing a doctorate in Educational Computing at the University of North Texas.

Part III
Technology and Technology Integration

An Indigenous Learning Approach to Computer Science Education

21st Century Skills for Middle and High School Aboriginal Children on British Columbia's West Coast

Dianne Biin and Marla L Weston

Abstract The ANCESTOR (AborigiNal Computer Education through Storytelling) program was developed to explore computer science as a career option through digital storytelling and address cultural literacy with Aboriginal youth in British Columbia, Canada. A team of educators from Camosun College collaborated with post-secondary students, secondary school educators, and First Nation communities to build and deliver a culturally responsive program. Indigenous knowledge, pedagogy and holistic learning practice guided the delivery of the program in First Nation communities, middle and secondary schools and First Nation operated secondary schools on the West Coast. The program success can be attributed to the Indigenous values and principles of reciprocity, relationship, ritual, respect, relevance, reverence, and repetition.

Keywords Storytelling · Literacy · Holistic lifelong learning · Indigenous · Pedagogy

The Need for a New Approach

This chapter refers to a distinct group of peoples and knowledge. For many people, the term "Aboriginal" refers to indigenous "Aborigines" peoples of Australia. However, in Canada, the term "Aboriginal" includes people who are descendants of the Indigenous peoples of North America and are identified as either status or non-status Indians, First Nations, Métis and Inuit. The term "Indigenous" is then used

D. Biin (✉) · M. L. Weston
Camosun College, Victoria, Canada
e-mail: biind@camosun.bc.ca

M. L. Weston
e-mail: weston@cs.camosun.bc.ca

© Springer International Publishing Switzerland 2015
X. Ge et al. (eds.), *Emerging Technologies for STEAM Education,*
Educational Communications and Technology: Issues and Innovations,
DOI 10.1007/978-3-319-02573-5_6

to refer to traditional knowledge, cultural practices and laws and protocols of First Nation, Métis and Inuit peoples (IECC, 2013).

Within British Columbia, the Aboriginal population accounts for 5.4% of the general population and it is a young, with over 45% under the age of 25 years. Compared to the general population, youth under the age of 25 account for only 28% (BC Stats, 2013). However, graduation rates from high school and pursuit of higher education are lower (almost half) among Aboriginal peoples than the general population.

This disconnect of Aboriginal youth in mainstream education has a historical and political context in Canada. The multi-generational effects of colonization practices, assimilation legislation and marginalizing of Indigenous knowledge have significantly impacted educational success. The first unified voice for inclusive Aboriginal education began in the 1970's in response to further assimilation legislation. The *Indian Control of Indian Education* policy paper, produced by the Native Indian Brotherhood in 1972, provided the pathways for where, how, when, and who could provide Indigenous education and has shaped Aboriginal peoples participation in education for the past 40 years. Active resistance and resilience from Indigenous scholars and Aboriginal communities for inclusive education has led to "important pedagogical shifts in colleges and university, K-12 settings, and formal and non-formal learning contexts" (Friedel, Archibald, Big Head, Martin, & Muñoz, 2012, p. 2).

When asked what helped contribute to success at the secondary and post-secondary level, Aboriginal learners confirmed that culturally relevant curricula, inclusion activities in and out of the classroom, and support systems (cultural and academic) enabled an environment to succeed. For instance, in the Sooke School District in southern Vancouver Island, they raised their Aboriginal graduation rates from 38% to over 73% within the span of 4 years due to aggressive cultural engagement and literacy competency support within the district (Huber, 2011).

Building Educational Participation

Camosun College serves southern Vancouver Island and Gulf Islands within the traditional territories of the Lk'wungen (Esquimalt and Songhees), W̱SÁNEĆ (Malahat, Pauquachin, Tsartlip, Tsawout, Tseycum), Scia'new and T'sou-ke peoples of the Coast Salish First Nation, and Paachedaht peoples of the Nuu Chah Nulth First Nation. The college offers both Indigenous courses and programs on campus and in urban First Nation communities. Enrollment has steadily increased over the past decade with now over 1000 Aboriginal students taking part in various certificate, diploma and degree programs. Since 2004, the College has actively supported the incorporation of "Indigenous ways of knowing, being, doing and relating…into educational, organization, cultural and social structures" (Camosun College, 2013, p. 6).

While there has been steady representation of Aboriginal learners in academic and health science programs at the College, the technologies and engineering programs have had historically low Aboriginal participation and success. This can be partly attributed to the cultural disconnect between western and Indigenous knowledge, values and principles, and limited opportunities to Indigenize practice and content in these disciplines. A report from Canadian Council on Learning (CCL) highlights the importance of providing culturally relevant curriculum that stands alongside western science; yet guards against incorporating a pan-cultural approach as curriculum needs to be relevant to place. The report also shares how introducing early college activities with secondary students helps build awareness of science education past graduation (CCL, 2007).

As shown in Fig. 1, which is a portion of a larger provincial map, there are over 27 distinct First Nations in British Columbia that have unique languages, traditions, laws and protocols. Generalization of Indigenous knowledge is not possible when developing Indigenous curriculum in the province nor is it desired. Land-based education is a common approach to Indigenizing curriculum at the secondary and higher learning levels. For instance, the provincial Ministry of Education recently completed an Aboriginal Curriculum Integration Project with a local school district to incorporate Indigenous knowledge into Grade 7 and 9 curricula so as to "be authentically reflective of the knowledge, culture, and history of Aboriginal people." (http://abed.sd79.bc.ca/acip/indexfiles/acip_intropage.html). From whom and from where cultural knowledge comes is acknowledged at the beginning, and Aboriginal and non-aboriginal learners are encouraged to explore their cultural backgrounds when discussing concepts and current issues. As Battiste (2002) states "learning through authentic experiences and individualized instruction" (p. 18) engages Aboriginal learners on multiple levels. First Nation and Métis communities are

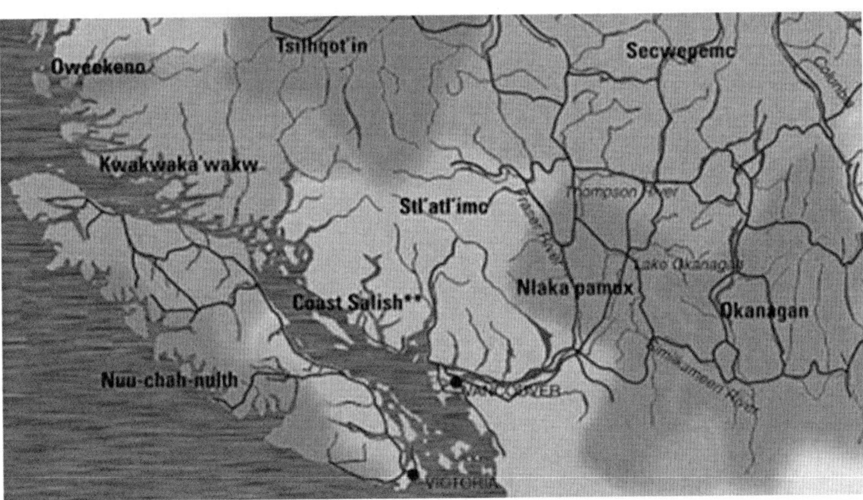

Fig. 1 Portion of the "Map of First Nation Peoples of British Columbia". (Retrieved from http://www.bced.gov.bc.ca/abed/map.htm)

recognized as key contributors to local curriculum and help foster welcoming and supportive learning spaces.

The ANCESTOR Program

As a way to encourage educational participation and increase digital and cultural literacy, we developed the ANCESTOR (AborigiNal Computer Education through STORytelling) program. The program would use digital storytelling as a means of promoting an interest in computer science for Aboriginal youth and adult learners, and it would also foster an understanding of natural environments.

Carnegie Mellon University's Alice 3D programming environment was the tool of choice for students to use in creating their animations. WebWire in 2007 reported that Alice was being used by approximately 10% of U.S. colleges and universities, as well as in many high schools around the world. The percentage has grown significantly since that time (Wanda Dann, personal communication, December 13, 2013). Alice has also been used successfully to incorporate cultural perspectives into the teaching of computer programming by the University of Hawai'i at Hilo (Edwards, Gersting, & Tangaro, 2007). Based on past experience, students seem to enjoy using Alice as a storytelling medium and it is freely available to download from the Alice website (http://www.alice.org).

For Aboriginal youth, Alice has an additional advantage in that the programming environment is expressed in terms of a "world", which provides an effective parallel to an interconnected Indigenous world view. Storytelling as an Indigenous pedagogy was incorporated into the ANCESTOR program as a way to bridge the mainstream curriculum (Burk, 2000). An important outcome of storytelling is personal empowerment as youth incorporate traditional knowledge and current realities into their learning environment rather than being passive recipients of knowledge. Telling or sharing a story gives value and significance to events in a student's life (Brown, 1995). Traditional cultural expressions through storytelling and transference of history (Young-In, 2008) are done in a protected and respected manner to ensure relevance of place to peoples.

It is this detail to creating an effective, interconnected world that matches the logic of the Alice environment. Courses and/or workshops with such a focus, along with lesson plans, encouraged Aboriginal learners to build computer games or animated stories that relate to their culture, connections to the land, and current realities. Throughout the program we enlisted the aid of computer science capstone students, fine art graduates, and secondary educators to help refine the curriculum as a distance education resource and build character assets in Alice that would resonate with Aboriginal learners. It was through these numerous collaborations in various environments that enable the team to create Indigenized materials and practices to a primer for computer science education.

Building a Culturally Responsive Approach

Our work on this program was initiated as needs-based and community driven rather than experimental and research-based. We worked with small numbers of students rather than large groups so we could be more flexible and responsive to immediate needs. When we approached communities and educators with the program, we acknowledged the importance of communal knowledge and ensured that anything the students created stayed with students in their communities. We also sought appropriate permissions to build Indigenous scenarios and tales within the Alice platform. One of the strengths of Indigenous pedagogy, in relation to our program, is the ability to have curriculum that is adaptive and dynamic, based on skills, abilities and problem solving techniques (Battiste, 2002). It was with this in mind that our curriculum was developed in different formats and styles of delivery.

Some of the differences in our delivery were a result of the age ranges involved, but we also had to be mindful of literacy levels. As noted by the Canadian Council on Learning, literacy levels of Aboriginal youth in BC are statistically lower than the general population. One of the conclusions of the Canadian Council on Learning report (2008), regarding literacy levels among Aboriginal Canadians, is the need for schools to be more culturally inclusive of Aboriginal students and Aboriginal approaches to learning. They specifically state:

> A number of studies have demonstrated that, in different cultures, different aspects of learning are emphasized and valued. For example, researchers have observed that many Aboriginal students prefer co-operative rather competitive learning, and that many learn through imitation, observation, and trial and error rather than direct instruction. Given that learning style factors can contribute to the alienation of Aboriginal students within classrooms, attending to these factors should contribute to more successful outcomes among Aboriginal students. (p. 6)

Hence, our delivery style changed from delivering a lecture to modelling sequences and providing hands-on guidance. As noted by Battiste (2002), "Indigenous pedagogy values a person's ability to learn independently by observing, listening, and participating with a minimum of intervention or instruction. This pattern of direct learning by seeing and doing, without asking questions, makes Aboriginal children diverse learners" (p. 15).

The First Nations Holistic Lifelong Learning Model

To develop culturally relevant curricula, it required us to incorporate an Indigenous life-long learning approach to build competencies and inclusion for the delivery team, teachers, communities and students. A model, which identifies many aspects of life-long learning contributing to success for First Nations, is the "The First Nations Holistic Lifelong Learning Model" (Fig. 2). This model is the outcome of a February 2007 workshop that brought together First Nations learning professionals, community practitioners, researchers and governments and is seen as a living draft (AFN, 2009).

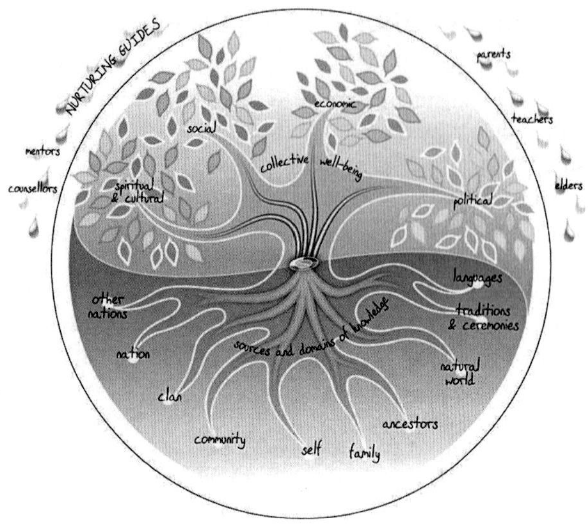

Fig. 2 First Nations Holistic Lifelong Learning Model. (Canadian Council on Learning, 2007)

The Holistic Lifelong Learning Model emphasizes the interconnectedness of life and learning. There is not a single, linear approach to learning but rather it encompasses learning experiences at all stages of life in both traditional and non-traditional settings.

This model acknowledges the impact of informal and formal learning and literacy in a cultural context (family, language, the natural world and ceremony). It illustrates the purpose of different sources and domains of knowledge; articulates the process of how learning and personal development (emotional, physical, spiritual and intellectual) occurs in a cyclical manner; and recognizes that the outcomes of life-long learning support community wellness. Learning is experiential as it occurs through observation and imitation. Learning is reinforced through storytelling and ceremony, and it is an adaptive process as First Nation learners integrate two realms of knowledge—traditional and western (Cappon, 2008). Building success based on local terms is the foundation for the lifelong learning model as the learner "dwells in a world of continual re-formation, where interactive cycles, rather than disconnected events, occur" (CCL, 2007, p. 2).

The model, as depicted in Fig. 2, has four main components:

1. The sources and domains of knowledge or the roots. "The roots emphasize the importance of relationships with the land, family, community, ancestors, nation and one's language, traditions and ceremonies" (Cappon, 2008, p. 63).
2. The internal rings of the tree (not viewable in this figure) is the individual's lifelong learning cycle in Western and Indigenous knowledge. Cappon (2008) states that the rings of the tree give "… equal importance to formal and informal and experiential learning" (p. 63). Individual learning grows just as a tree grows as learners develop new rings.
3. The individual's personal development is shown in the branches of the living tree. "Personal harmony comes when an individual learns to balance the spiri-

tual, physical, mental (includes critical thinking and analytical skills, the practice of visioning or dreaming and First Nations language ability), and emotional (such as self-esteem, awareness of personal gifts) aspects of their being" (Cappon, 2008, p. 64).

4. The leaves of the branches represent how a community supports life-long learning. "The fact that leaves, grow, decay and grow again reflects the cyclical, regenerative learning process that influences community well-being. A community's well-being nourishes its roots and, in turn, the individual's learning cycle" (Cappon, 2008, p. 64).

The model resonated with the team as it is a strength-based approach rather than "focus[ing] on learning deficits relative to non-Aboriginal standards. [The model] underlines the critical connections between community generation and well-being and individual learning." (Cappon, 2008, p. 64). The model provided a framework for us on who needed to be involved and how one could be involved in the program. It provided a check on what could realistically be learnt in a short time frame—experiential rather than transformative and that success would vary from learner to learner.

Theoretical Model of Storywork

Another model that influenced our work was developed by Jo-ann Archibald. She worked with Coast Salish and Stó:lō elders to develop methodological principles for conducting research in First Nation communities, based on the strengths of storytelling. By exploring the nuances of traditional stories, shared meaning or cultural literacies could emerge. The focus changes from finding the record of traditional knowledge to learning the ways of knowing. (Archibald, 2008) In an editorial, Archibald states:

> …when I think about how these two Elders [late Dr. Vincent Stogan and late Chief Dr. Simon Baker] 'lived'…In their elder years, they took on the responsibility of teaching others through example, through their interactions with individuals, leading ceremonies and cultural events, giving public talks, and guiding many community organizations…they both taught me about the importance of understanding and living the cultural values of respect, responsibility, reciprocity and reverence. Through example, they also taught me about the importance of developing and using ritual, repetition, and relationships in order to know and live these values and to appreciate Aboriginal knowledge. (2001, p. 1)

Archibald explains the storywork pedagogy as a process-oriented approach "where the learner engages in the story to find answers and meaning. The subjective meaning is often not evident until the learner engages in and works through the story process". (2001, p. 5)

Storytelling traditions in Aboriginal communities are intrinsic to the intergenerational transmission of Indigenous knowledge. Borrows (2005) notes "…oral history in numerous Aboriginal groups is conveyed through interwoven layers of culture that entwine to sustain national memories over the lifetime of many generations. The transmission of oral tradition in these societies is bound up with the configuration of language, political structures, economic systems, social relations, intellectual methodologies, morality, ideology and their physical world" (p. 191). The British Columbia Ministry of Education's guide on integrating Aboriginal content recognizes that "storytelling is an important cultural expression" and provides a framework on how schools can integrate this 'shared learning' into curricula (p. 94). For our program, Aboriginal learners would find their own meaning and expression by creating digital stories.

There are many definitions for the term "digital storytelling". It can be as simple as "using digital media to tell stories", to the more detailed. "At its core, a digital story is a narrative expressed in digital form for a variety of purposes, with applications ranging from education to personal expression, record keeping to movement promotion and everything in between" (Sussex, 2012). Barrett (2006) feels that digital storytelling facilitates the convergence of four, student-centered learning strategies: student engagement, reflection for deep learning, project based learning, and the effective integration of technology into instruction. Many of these strategies fit in with the skills deemed by the "21st Century Literacy Summit" (2005) as key elements to developing essential digital literacy skills for the future. The Literacy Summit report states that "access to tools that empower expression in these new forms must be as ubiquitous as word processing software or spreadsheets. In schools, tools for creating new media should be available as early as possible, even in primary grades, and more advanced tools provided as students' progress and gain facility using them" (p. 14).

Applying the Holistic Model

Both the First Nations Holistic Lifelong Learning and Storywork models greatly affected how we built curriculum and engaged schools and communities in the ANCESTOR program. When working with Aboriginal learners with limited voice in the secondary school learning system, we had to be aware of emotional and spiritual vulnerabilities youth would experience while finding their voice. As has been seen in other realms of Indigenous scholarship, "…stories as Indigenous knowledge work not only to regenerate Indigenous traditions and knowledge production, but also work against the colonial epistemic frame to subvert and recreate possibilities and spaces for resistance." (Sium & Ritskes, 2013, p. III). In building interest in digital storytelling, we wanted to ensure Aboriginal learners could have the opportunity to begin building their voice through their own story or retelling their cultural stories in a modern context. Positive reinforcements and a fun environment (laughing at our mistakes and at the weird gravity defying postures of Alice characters) sustained a healthy learning environment. If a student was quiet or having a bad day, we provided emotional support and simply sat beside them. Confidence-building was present in all stages of our educational practice.

Shifting away from the typical STEM silo approach to a holistic life-long learning approach enabled both educators and Aboriginal students the ability to transfer knowledge across different subjects, create an environment where one could construct their own meaning and build 21st century literacies. These are confirmed in the principles of STEAM (science, technology, engineering, mathematics, arts) education (Yakman, 2010). Yakman (2014) indicates that a STEAM approach "help[s] make good education better...[as] it delivers high quality team-based education to all students." (p. 3) Our holistic approach and STEAM principles parallel one another in that the program was culturally responsive, adaptable to learning situations, and engaged, in a positive way, with non-traditional learners.

We varied our teaching situations so as to gather the most amount of experience with the Indigenized computer science curriculum and practice. The lack of empirical information on how to build culturally responsive technology education made it necessary to build and test throughout the project. A curriculum was developed and first tested with Aboriginal students at the ŁÁU,WELNEW Tribal School near Victoria, British Columbia, Canada. Based on feedback from both teachers and students, we updated the curriculum, developed video tutorials (posted on YouTube) to support the curriculum and then tested it with non-Aboriginal 'digital natives' (21st Century Literacy Summit, 2005, p. 2) students. Based on the results with the non-aboriginal students, we further refined the curriculum and then delivered it to Aboriginal learners using several different approaches depending on local needs. One was a summer camp that took place within a First Nations community over 3 weeks, and another a special elective for grade 6 Aboriginal students at Shoreline Middle School in Victoria. Our final test situation occurred in three remote communities on British Columbia's west coast. The first two included a community high school in Bella Bella located on Campbell Island and an elementary school in Shearwater located on Denny Island. The third was a band operated K-7 school on Cormorant Island. 2 and 3 day workshops with about 6 hours of instruction and collaboration were delivered at each site to different aged learners.

The core values and practices from the storywork pedagogy and the First Nations Holistic Lifelong Learning Model guided our practice—relevance, repetition, responsibility, respect, reciprocity, ritual, reverence and relationship. We used these values and practices to remain true to local Indigenous realms of knowing and doing.

Relevance

We observed that two areas needed to be developed to make the programming and content relevant to Aboriginal learners. The assets within Alice needed to be consolidated and include Aboriginal specific characters, animals, and infrastructure. To that end, an ANCESTOR gallery was created within Alice 2.4 to house these assets. What couldn't be easily adapted to reflect west coast structures and animals had to be created. We worked with fine art students from the University of Pittsburgh and fine art graduates from Emily Carr University of Art and Design over the years to begin building culturally appropriate assets such as martin, raccoon, bluejay, ocean going canoe, deer, fishing gaff hooks and otter. There is an exhaustive list of assets to create to develop a fully rich library, but for the purposes of our program, we asked for assets for our sample sequences. Many of the secondary teachers we worked with in the program commented that as soon as the Aboriginal students saw the culturally relevant gallery elements, they were very excited and encouraged to try to create traditional stories. (Weston & Biin, 2011).

Secondly, we developed our curricula for each unique teaching situation and timeframe. A team consisting of Camosun College Computer Science, School of Business and Indigenous Education and Community Connections faculty, plus two Computer Science students initially worked together to build a test curriculum. These curricula included a one-day workshop to encourage learners to want to know more by having them create a fun, simple animation. A 1 week workshop plus a semester long course were also developed. The curriculum was largely derived from the extensive online resources available for teaching Alice.

Where possible, to further make the curricula relevant, local oral tales and age-appropriate published Aboriginal stories were used for the programming sequences. For instance, the ANCESTOR YouTube tutorials incorporated two local SENĆOŦEN legends—the great flood creation story and the origin of lightning. Both stories have been adapted into published works by the Saanich Heritage Society (a group of elders from the WSÁNEĆ communities) in Brentwood Bay and we secured permission to use the tales in the educational tutorials.

An age appropriate published work used in our curricula with middle school learners was the Haida story called "Dog Days" (Raven Tales, 2012). This story is available both as an animated video and graphic novel, and readily available in many secondary schools. Students were referred to the part of the story where the giant dog rescues the children of the story from a distant island. In the story the children ride the dog as he swims them back to safety. Having reviewed the story with the students, they were then provided with an Alice "world" (Fig. 3) to start their animation.

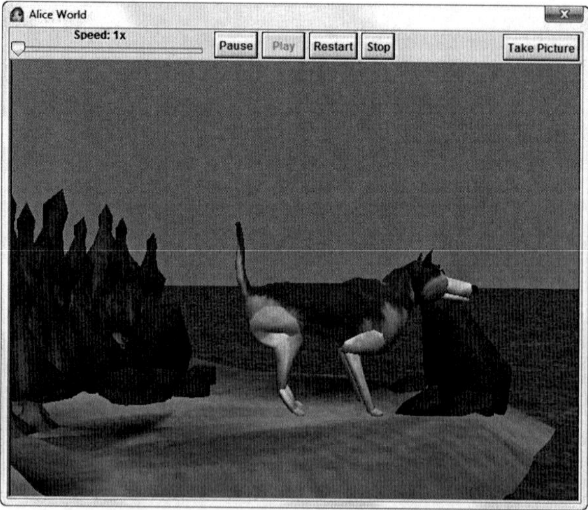

Fig. 3 The starting Alice world for the "Dog Days" animation

Repetition

Since the Alice environment is so rich, students would often get lost and thus frustrated. Many of the students in our first teaching situation at the ŁÁU,WELNEW Tribal School had limited exposure to computers, and thus the curriculum had to find the right balance to accommodate disparate skill sets. The backgrounds of the students (ranging from grades 7–10) varied enormously. Also, the 1 hour per week class time meant the students forgot what they had learned the week before and had to review before continuing. It was clear that more repetition was needed which led to the development of the online video tutorials.

Our second situation involved "technology savvy" access students who represented a distinct contrast to the tribal school students. For one, these students were generally older; most were grade 12 students. For another, all were very comfortable with technology as evidenced by the wealth of smart phones and tablets that arrived with the students. On the whole, learners were enthusiastic about the online video tutorials and teachers appreciated the straight forward lesson material. Students liked that they could proceed at their own pace through a lesson, replaying tutorials as needed. After a brief, introductory lecture at the start of each lesson, the teacher was then free to provide one-on-one help and encouragement.

Responsibility

As mentioned previously, our initial goal in the ANCESTOR program was to be community focused rather than research based, and we knew it was essential to respect and honour ownership of stories in building our curriculum. We acknowledged and reaffirmed in all of our teaching situations that the stories and sequences would remain with community. The richness of the program comes from the realities of the students as reflected in their created animated sequences and games, along with the stories and tales that shape cultural traditions. Proper permissions were secured for online tutorials and knowledge keepers were involved in the animation process for traditional stories.

In building our curriculum, we were mindful that just under half (46%) of all Aboriginal Peoples in Canada live in non-urban areas (Statistics Canada, 2008). The Canadian Council on Learning report (2010), notes that Aboriginal adults living in rural communities and smaller towns and cities were more likely to participate in distance learning than Aboriginal people living in cities, where the majority of post-secondary institutions are located. To meet this reality, the curriculum and tutorials were loaded into the open-source content management system 'Moodle' (https://moodle.org/). The Moodle server and curriculum (Fig. 4) were installed on a virtual machine that could then be ghosted onto any number of servers, local or remote.

Fig. 4 Sample screen from Moodle course site

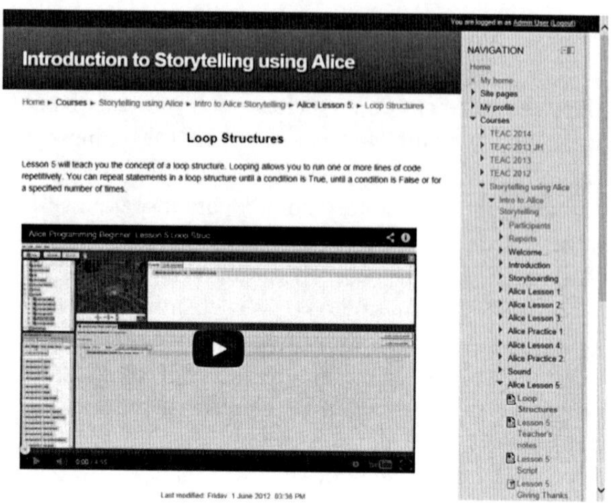

Respect

Respect, as used by our team, revolved around the learner and community. For instance, care was taken to not make the handouts too complex. Minimal text and the use of screen shots of the sequence and programming code ensured that we did not experience literacy barriers and thus we respected the student realities. Hence, the materials used different modalities of learning to ensure youth were engaged. One of the most important roles for the facilitator, beyond helping with the actual animation, was to laugh alongside students when their animated characters spiralled out of control. Students quickly realized that what they did was not 'wrong' but only a programming quirk that could be easily altered.

Involvement of elders and parents was welcomed in all teaching situations. Acknowledging that Aboriginal students come from extensive families, we included community connections whenever we could in the delivery of curricula. For instance, in the first week of the summer camp at Songhees First Nation, parents and relatives dropped in throughout the day to check in on their children or niece/nephew and engage us as the teachers to learn more about our family and cultural backgrounds. After we developed a rapport with community members, the children came back for the second week and subsequently completed the summer camp. Our willingness and comfort to incorporate community in the classroom built a respectful place of shared learning.

Reciprocity

At some points in delivery, teachers became learners and learners became teachers. Two instances of reciprocity, or giving back occurred with students and the delivery team. The technology Access students were quick to provide feedback on any part of the curriculum they felt did not meet their needs. As a result, topics and/or video tutorials that were too complex were quickly identified and corrected for the next offering. Where carefully prepared animated scenarios were presented to students so they could be walked through the solution we saw Aboriginal students immediately work with each other. This was true in all situations. When one student found a solution, he or she happily shared it with the others. This was second nature to the students in our remote delivery situations.

Shearwater Elementary is on Denny Island and has a multi-age classroom that works with students from kindergarten to grade seven. With one teacher and aide, higher grades are covered through distance education and out of class learning through field trips are common. We did not use the Alice platform with the learners in Shearwater due the young ages, instead we used MIT's Scratch program (http:// scratch.mit.edu/) which is more accessible to younger audience. Collaborative learning came naturally to the Shearwater elementary students due to their classroom environment. Once older students grasped the concept of program re-mixing, they would assist younger students.

For those who wanted to play online games, the facilitators asked that a series of games be critiqued. Students would play the series and provide feedback on what they liked and didn't like about the games. They were then walked through a re-mixing of a game, experimenting with the drag and drop coding features. Many of the students spent the next few days re-mixing games or revising animated greeting cards which made for very noisy classrooms. On the last day, the facilitators debriefed with the group. For many, this was the first time they had been exposed to programming, so it was a steep learning curve; yet, concepts were easily grasped and then manipulated and shared.

Ritual

When we look at this practice, we are not attempting to address this in a secular manner but "rather as a cultural pattern of activity used to establish an environment conducive to listening and learning." (Archibald, 2001, p. 5). To build a learning environment, we provided numerous prizes to acknowledge accomplishments and contributions. Camosun College swag and small gifts were always present when we worked with students. Students would earn prizes for either the first three who completed a sequence or the daily 'hard luck prize'. If students showed their animations to others, they earned a prize. Usually by the end of the sessions everyone had a prize, so the competitive aspect was not apparent; it was now fun making up categories each time we were with students. We realized that students were engaged when we had fun with the content and they would complete the course or workshop. Students paid attention to the programming sequences we shared at the beginning of class, replicated and then augmented. As time progressed, the students were sufficiently engaged so the prizes became secondary.

Another ritual in the program was having a formal closing to our activities in schools and communities. There was always a space created in our teaching situations to showcase accomplishments. Inviting others into our learning space was encouraged, and when appropriate, students were invited to the College to showcase their animations.

Actively modelling the learning process was another ritual we practiced in the program. Our delivery team consisted of a programming expert (Weston) and a cultural facilitator (Biin) who had minimal programming background. The programming expert would first demonstrate the sequence, and then the cultural facilitator would attempt it, actively asking questions and seeking clarification on the programming tasks. By watching our interactions with each other on how to do the animated sequences, the students in the classroom realized it was acceptable that they did not know how to accomplish the programming immediately. They then felt comfortable and safe to ask questions and seek assistance.

Reverence

Reverence is knowing there are concepts and processes that are not in our realm of understanding but are recognized as important. For the youth it was building a storyboard and sharing traditional stories. In the beginning of the summer camp, a cultural storytelling exercise was done with the youth. A brief explanation of storyboarding was provided and with a series of sticky notes, youth were asked to create a scene they heard from the cultural story. Storyboarding was a difficult exercise, as the youth had no experience recording a sequence. When we agreed upon a common scene from one of the stories, it was re-read and youth attempted to create the scene. After this exercise, we debriefed and realized that listening to a story, building a character and creating a scene from the story required different skills.

When we created this segment, we sought guidance from the animation department of Emily Carr University of Art and Design in Vancouver. In our discussions, we knew that participants would have problems adapting an oral tale to 3-D environment so we needed to guide this segment carefully so as to not discourage participants. Various animated movies were brought in and the bonus features on the DVD's were explored so students could see how complex and detailed storyboards guide the creative process. In the camp, the traditional tale was developed by adults, while the younger students made their own story. Building worlds in Alice was easy, yet it was still hard to build the story in advance. Spontaneous creation and group discussions guided the summer camp animated sequences. Youth realized the importance of storyboarding, but it was beyond their comprehension and ability at that time to master the process.

Relationship

As demonstrated throughout our narrative, relationships at all levels were important to the program, not only relationships between individuals and communities, but also relationships in the delivery environment. As much as possible we tried to create an inclusive atmosphere in our classes, camps and workshops. One way to build relationships is by coming together over a meal. Where appropriate, we would take breaks and have snacks where we could all sit together and get to know each other. The fear and shyness would always disappear after a plate of cookies or sandwich and juice were finished. It was usually over our snack period that debriefing and future planning occurred with students.

Conclusion

The results of our curriculum trials fully support the conclusions of the Canadian Council on Learning. Students in the tribal school, summer camp, the middle school elective and the remote community workshops worked well together and were keen to share new skills with each other. Walking through initial examples with the students allowed them to build the confidence to move forward on their own. It was important to distinguish learning the tool (in this case Alice), from learning how to create a story. We found that the students first needed to see what the tool could do before they could see how it applied to a story. Students were enthused to see the relevance in the curriculum before them, and were appreciative of reciprocal relationships fostered in the classroom. They supported each other and we learned from each other. These students were immersed in using Alice to create their own stories.

As we discovered in the summer camp, creating or listening to a story, building a character, and creating a scene from the story required different skills. This was borne out at the middle school. Although the students had seen many movies, and had heard and read stories, it was clear that starting with creating a storyboard and script was not going to work for this group of learners. They first needed to build a comfort level with the computer and the animation tool before they were ready to let their imaginations loose.

The students also gained new perspectives from their classmates, which led them to push their skills to new levels. Living in remote communities requires active problem-solving using limited resources and quick adaptation and understanding of one's environment. It was readily apparent that these skills transferred to their academic learning in Bella Bella, Shearwater and Alert Bay.

Although this work has been focused on Aboriginal peoples within Canada, other Indigenous peoples around the world face similar challenges and have similar needs. This also applies to at risk, non-Indigenous student populations, and any students who do not feel connected to the school system. The core principles and values of relevance, repetition, responsibility, respect, reciprocity, ritual, reverence and relationship enable all of us to become a community of lifelong learners.

Acknowledgements The work with Aboriginal youth, schools and communities was supported by a PromoScience grant from the Natural Sciences and Engineering Research Council (NSERC) awarded to Dr. Marla Weston. A BC Campus grant supported work with adult learners and the development of video tutorials. The BC Campus grant was awarded to both authors in partnership with Emily Carr University of Art & Design, Carnegie-Mellon University, the University of Hawai'i at Hilo and the WSÁNEĆ School Board.

We also want to acknowledge and thank all the capstone computer science students and fine arts graduates who have worked with us on this program to build relevant curriculum and assets. The elders, community educators and First Nation communities that have invited us into their learning spaces are much appreciated and this chapter is dedicated to their graciousness and willingness to contribute to this program.

We all support and serve Aboriginal students in their lifelong learning journeys.

References

21st Century Literacy Summit. (2005). *A global imperative. The report of the 21st Century Literacy Summit*. Austin: The New Media Consortium.

Archibald, J. (2001). Editorial: Sharing Aboriginal knowledge and Aboriginal ways of knowing. *Canadian Journal of Native Education, 25*(1), 1–5.

Archibald, J. (2008). *Indigenous storywork: Educating the heart, mind, body and spirit*. Vancouver: University of British Columbia Press.

Assembly of First Nations (AFN). (2009). Community dialogues on First Nations holistic lifelong learning. Learning as a community for renewal and growth. http://www.afn.ca/uploads/files/education2/community_dialogues_on_first_nations_holistic_lifelong_learning,_2009.pdf.

Barrett, H. (2006). Researching and evaluating digital storytelling as a deep learning tool. In C. Crawford, et al. (Eds.), *Proceedings of society for information technology & teacher education International Conference 2006* (pp. 647–654). Chesapeake,: AACE.

Battiste, M. (2000). Maintaining Aboriginal identity, language, and culture in modern society. In M. Battiste (Ed.), *Reclaiming indigenous voice and vision* (pp. 192–208). Toronto: University of British Columbia Press.

Battiste, M. (2002). Indigenous knowledge and pedagogy in First Nations education. A literature review with recommendations. Prepared for the National Working Group on Education and the Minister of Indian Affairs. Indian and Northern Affairs Canada. p. 1–69. http://www.usask.ca/education/profiles/battiste/assets/ikp_e.pdf.

BC Stats. (2013). 2011 Census fast facts. Issue 2011-3. http://www.bcstats.gov.bc.ca/StatisticsBySubject/Census/2011Census.aspx.

Borrows, J. (2005). Indigenous legal traditions in Canada. *Washington University Journal of Law and Policy, 19*, 167–223.

British Columbia Ministry of Education. (2006). Shared learnings: Integrating BC Aboriginal content K-10. http://www.bced.gov.bc.ca/abed/shared.pdf.

British Columbia Ministry of Education. (2014). Aboriginal education resources. http://www.bced.gov.bc.ca/abed/documents.htm.

Brown, C. (1995). *The light that kindles their eyes: Improving cultural awareness through storytelling*. Indianapolis, Indiana: Paper presented at the Central States Communication Association Conference, Indianapolis, Indiana. (As reported by Burk, 2000).

Burk, N. (2000). *Empowering at-risk students: Storytelling as a pedagogic tool.* 86th Annual Meeting of the National Communication Association, Seattle. November. ERIC#: ED447497.

Camosun College. (2013). Inspiring relationships: Indigenization plan 2013-14. http://camosun. ca/learn/school/indigenous-education-community-connections/about/publications/indigenization-plan13.pdf..

Canadian Council on Learning (CCL). (2007). Lessons in learning: The cultural divide in science education for Aboriginal learners. http://www.ccl-cca.ca/pdfs/LessonsInLearning/Feb-01-07-The-cultural-divide-in-science.pdf.

Canadian Council on Learning. (2007). First Nations holistic lifelong learning model. Living Draft. http://www.ccl-cca.ca/pdfs/RedefiningSuccess/CCL_Learning_Model_FN.pdf.

Canadian Council on Learning. (2008). Improving literacy levels among Aboriginal Canadians. http://www.ccl-cca.ca/pdfs/LessonsInLearning/Sep-04-08-Improving-literacy-levels.pdf.

Canadian Council on Learning. (2010). State of learning in Canada: A year in review, Ottawa. http://www.ccl-cca.ca/pdfs/SOLR/2010/SOLR-2010-Report-FINAL-E.pdf.

Cappon, P. (2008). Measuring success in First Nations, Inuit and Métis learning. *Policy Options,* 60–66.

Edwards, H. K., Gersting, J. L., & Tangaro, T. (2007). Teaching Alice in Hawai'i: Cultural perspectives. Frontiers in Education Conference—Global Engineering: Knowledge Without Borders, Opportunities Without Passports, FIE, 07. 37th Annual. October 10–13, 2007 (p. T3A-1–T3A-5). Milwaukee, WI.: IEEE.

Friedel, T., Archibald, J., Big Head, R., Martin, G., & Muñoz, M. (2012). Editorial—Indigenous pedagogies: Resurgence and restoration. *Canadian Journal of Native Education, 35*(1), 1–6.

Huber, C. (2011). First Nations grad rates up in SD62. Goldstreamgazette.com. http://www.sd62. bc.ca/News/tabid/136/EntryId/151/High-Graduation-Rate-of-Aboriginal-Students-in-SD62. aspx (cited by J. Cambridge).

Indigenous Education and Community Connections (IECC). (2013). http://intranet.camosun. bc.ca/aecc/Terms.php.

National Indian Brotherhood. (1972). Indian control of Indian education. http://64.26.129.156/ calltoaction/Documents/ICOIE.pdf.

Raven Tales. (2012). *Dog days. Episode 15. Adapted by Chris Kientz.* Ontario: Rubicon Publishing Inc.

School District 49. (2014). Aboriginal curriculum integration project introduction. http://abed. sd79.bc.ca/acip/indexfiles/acip_intropage.html.

Sium, A., & Ritskes, E. (2013). Speaking truth to power: Indigenous storytelling as an act of living resistance. *Decolonization: Indigeneity, Education & Society, 2*(1), I–X.

Statistics Canada. (2008). Aboriginal peoples in Canada in 2006: Inuit, Metis and First Nations, 2006 Census. Catalogue no. 97-558-XIE. http://www12.statcan.ca/census-recensement/2006/ as-sa/97-558/pdf/97-558-XIE2006001.pdf.

Sussex, J. (2012). Digital storytelling: Literature review. http://teamlab.usc.edu/Digital%20Storytelling%20FINAL%202012.pdf.

WebWire. (2007 December, 10). Professor developed Alice animation tool to teach computer programming. http://www.webwire.com/ViewPressRel.asp?aId=54742.

Weston, M., & Biin, D. (2011). The ANCESTOR (AborigiNal Computer Education through STORytelling) project: Aboriginal youth engagement in alternative careers. In T. Bastiaens & M. Ebner (Eds.), *Proceedings of World Conference on Educational Multimedia, Hypermedia and Telecommunications 2011* (pp. 1698–1702). Chesapeake: AACE.

Yakman, G. (2010). What is the point of STE@M? A brief overview. http://www.academia. edu/8113832/What_is_the_Point_of_STEAM_A_Brief_Overview_of_STEAM_Education.

Yakman, G. (2014). STE@M education program description. http://www.steamedu.com/wp-content/uploads/2014/12/STEAM-Education-Program-Description-29Dec14.pdf.

Young-In, G. (2008). Conflicts, discourse, negotiations and proposed solutions regarding transformations of traditional knowledge. In R. Hulan & R. Eigenbrod (Eds.), *Aboriginal oral tradition: Theory, practice, ethics* (pp. 61–78). Halifax: Fernwood Publishing.

Dianne Biin is currently an Indigenous Faculty Developer in the Centre for Excellence in Teaching and Learning (CETL) at Camosun College and she also works with the Centre of Centre for Indigenous Education and Community Connections (IECC). Dianne teaches in various Indigenous courses and programs across the college. She has worked for provincial and First Nation governments, and has operated her consultant business for over 15 years in the fields of Indigenous relations research, event management and enterpreneurship. She is of Tsilhqot'in descent and her traditional territory is located in BC's interior. Her Bachelor of Arts degree is in Sociology and Archaeology and was earned within a First Nation controlled program in partnership with Simon Fraser University.

Marla L Weston has focused on innovative applications of computer technology throughout her years. Dr. Weston obtained her PhD in 1982 in vertebrate paleontology from the University of British Columbia (Vancouver, Canada), and subsequently pursued a post-doctoral fellowship at the University of Cambridge (England) supported by the National Museums of Canada. At Cambridge, she also worked for a not-for-profit organization where she applied spatial and temporal data management, and heterogeneous data integration to a variety of data sets, including paleontological and geological, and examined the alignment of these data with emerging international standards. Dr. Weston continued this work upon returning to Canada, consulting for both the public and private sectors. For the past 25 years, Dr. Weston has also taught in the Computer Science department at Camosun College where she served as Department Chair for several years. The ANCESTOR program evolved from a desire to combine the power and innovations in computer technology with the needs of the local community.

The Potential of Embodied Cognition to Improve STEAM Instructional Dynamic Visualizations

Juan C. Castro-Alonso, Paul Ayres and Fred Paas

Abstract An embodied cognition perspective recognizes that the evolution of the human mind has been shaped by the evolution of the species' whole body in its interaction with the environment. For example, hand actions—such as object manipulations and gestures—have been fundamental for human survival, and thus they continue to trigger different areas of the evolved mind. One of these areas is the mirror neuron system, a major processor of bodily movement, which allows humans to learn manipulations and gestures with relative ease. A clear implication for instruction, across many Science, Technology, Engineering, Arts and Mathematics (STEAM) topics, is to profit from the effortlessness of hand actions in order to enhance the learning of difficult concepts or challenging educational materials. One example of demanding instructional materials is dynamic visualizations (e.g., animation, video), which can be too transient to follow, understand and learn from. However, we argue that dynamic visualizations may overcome the transiency problem by including embodied activity. In this chapter, we will review a diverse number of studies that show the instructional benefits of embodied cognition, manipulations, and gestures. Specifically, we will address how these evolved skills can be employed to effectively learn from STEAM dynamic visualizations.

Keywords Embodied cognition · Biologically primary ability · Manipulation · Gesture · Static versus dynamic visualization · Spatial ability

J. C. Castro-Alonso (✉) · P. Ayres · F. Paas
University of New South Wales, Sydney, Australia
e-mail: j.c.castroalonso@unsw.edu.au

P. Ayres
e-mail: p.ayres@unsw.edu.au

F. Paas
Erasmus University Rotterdam, Rotterdam, Netherlands
e-mail: paas@fsw.eur.nl

© Springer International Publishing Switzerland 2015
X. Ge et al. (eds.), *Emerging Technologies for STEAM Education,*
Educational Communications and Technology: Issues and Innovations,
DOI 10.1007/978-3-319-02573-5_7

113

Dynamic Visualizations and Instruction

A visualization can show static or moving elements. In the latter case, it is referred to as a *dynamic picture* or *dynamic visualization*, where *animation* and *video* are the most popular examples, intersecting with many facets of a modern student's life. To mention one example of the popularity of these dynamic visualizations, Tang and Austin (2009) observed that, among five instructional methods (video, PowerPoint, projector, Internet, and lecture), the strongest association reported by students with the variable *enjoyment* was with video. Given this outcome, this enjoyment of animation and video should be aligned with the educational potential of dynamic visualizations.

Learning Opportunities Fostered by Dynamic Visualizations

Arguably, the fascination triggered by dynamic visualizations is due to the basic fact that they show elements in motion. As a consequence, instructional materials that use animation or video can include rich temporal and spatial information that is generally absent in static images or textual resources. For example, the following learning opportunities can be provided with instruction aided by dynamic visualizations:

- To change the pace of real-time phenomena whose speed/duration is impractical to study live. For example, very slow processes can be speeded up, and very fast processes can be slowed down (Tosi, 1993).
- To analyze the same dynamic event repeatedly, or to preserve permanently a rare live phenomenon (Tosi, 1993).
- To study dynamic processes in unapproachable places, such as inside a living organism, in outer space, in extreme habitat conditions (Tosi, 1993), or in rather avoidable situations (Dowrick, 1991).
- To perceive movement or details that in real-life motion would be overlooked. For example, the video technique of reverse motion (e.g., Dowrick, 1991) can help to study bodily processes. In addition, different video editing methods can be employed to study *movement* in art disciplines (e.g., Nadaner, 2008).
- To watch otherwise invisible events, by using X-rays, infrared, gamma, ultraviolet techniques, and many others (Tosi, 1993). Similarly, dynamic visualizations can assist in explaining not inherently visible phenomena, such as electrical circulation or energy (Bétrancourt, 2005).
- To compare simultaneously two or more dynamic processes by splitting the screen accordingly. This can be a valuable tool in science learning, where a concrete video can be juxtaposed to an abstract molecular animation (e.g., Nugteren, Tabbers, Scheiter, & Paas, 2014), and also to study performing arts, such as dance (e.g., Harris & Fenner, 1995), where different parts of the dancer can be analyzed simultaneously.

Table 1 Examples of STEAM contents depicted in studies about dynamic visualizations

Study	Discipline					Content
	S	T	E	A	M	
Dorethy, 1973				x		Visual analysis of space
Shipley, Butt, Horwitz, & Farbry, 1978	x					Patient getting an endoscopy
Rieber, 1990	x					Newton's laws of motion
Mayer & Sims, 1994	x					Human respiratory apparatus
Harris & Fenner, 1995				x		Choreographic dancing
Williamson & Abraham, 1995	x					Chemistry reactions
Lowe, 2003	x					Weather map sequences
Yang, Andre, Greenbowe, & Tibell, 2003	x					Electrochemistry in a flashlight
Stith, 2004	x					Cell apoptosis
Mayer, Hegarty, Mayer, & Campbell, 2005			x			Brakes and flushing systems
Cooley, 2007				x		Audiovisual poetry
Boucheix, 2008			x			Gear systems
Kalyuga, 2008					x	Linear and quadratic functions
Fischer, Lowe, & Schwan, 2008			x			Mechanism of pendulum clock
Marbach-Ad, Rotbain, & Stavy, 2008	x					Protein synthesis
Nadaner, 2008				x		Perception of movement
Boucheix & Lowe, 2010			x			Piano elements kinematics
Huk, Steinke, & Floto, 2010	x					Enzyme ATP-synthase
Linek, Gerjets, & Scheiter, 2010					x	Probability calculations
Meyer, Rasch, & Schnotz, 2010			x			Internal combustion engine
Scheiter, Gerjets, & Schuh, 2010					x	Algebraic worked-out examples
Yarden & Yarden, 2010	x					PCR method in biotechnology
Höffler & Schwartz, 2011	x					Surfactants and washing
Lin & Atkinson, 2011	x					The rock cycle
Ryoo & Linn, 2012	x					Energy flow in photosynthesis
Brucker, Scheiter, & Gerjets, 2014	x					Fish swimming patterns
Sánchez & Wiley, 2014	x					Plate tectonics

These instructional opportunities have been applied to teach various concepts of Science, Technology, Engineering, Arts and Mathematics (STEAM) disciplines. Significant research has been conducted into dynamic images and a wide variety of STEAM topics to provide evidence for the effectiveness of such instructional visualizations. Table 1 provides a sample of this research, where the studies are listed chronologically.

In addition to the learning opportunities and the interest that dynamic visualizations can trigger, these depictions are increasingly easier to produce, replicate and disseminate for instructional purposes. However, despite potential educational advantages, dynamic pictures can be very problematic learning materials if they are heavily reliant on *transient information*. The negative effect of transient information has been observed in experiments that show poorer learning outcomes after receiving long verbal passages in auditory rather than in textual forms (e.g., Leahy & Sweller, 2011; Singh, Marcus, & Ayres, 2012). As discussed by Leahy and Sweller

(2011), students cannot easily review transient information (auditory passages), but permanent information (textual passages) can be re-read at convenience. An analogous phenomenon has been described for dynamic versus static visualizations.

Transiency of Dynamic Visualizations

A dynamic visualization is composed of a number of different static images (frames) that are played at a sufficient speed to give the illusion of dynamism (Roncarrelli, 1989). The illusion of movement can generally be achieved with approximately 12 frames per second. As a consequence, a dynamic visualization can generate transient effects as information can change rapidly from frame to frame. This problematic phenomenon has been termed as the *transient information effect of animations* (see Ayres & Paas, 2007a, b). As a result, dynamic pictures may impose extra processing burdens on students' working memory; what Lowe (2003) described as an *overwhelming* effect. Particularly, as discussed by Ayres and Paas (2007b) and van Gog, Paas, Marcus, Ayres, & Sweller (2009), students may have to perform three mental activities in order to learn from a dynamic visualization: (a) observing the current information depicted, (b) memorizing the important depictions no longer shown, and (c) combining these two streams of information. By contrast, a static visualization, which is permanent and thus can be reexamined repeatedly if necessary, is much less cognitive demanding, and consequently more working memory resources are available for learning (see *cognitive load theory* in Sweller, Ayres, & Kalyuga, 2011).

Consequently, static visualizations often show better learning outcomes than comparable dynamic pictures. This trend has been observed with many STEAM concepts. For example, when Koroghlanian and Klein (2004) studied learning outcomes for the concepts of mitosis and meiosis in high-school biology students, they observed that the animation conditions required more time to learn than the statics groups, without an increase in performance. Similarly, Mayer et al., (2005) compared *static images plus text* versus *narrated animations* as learning tools for the mechanisms of toilet tanks, lightning formation, cars brakes and ocean waves, and observed that the participants studying static pictures outperformed those given dynamic visualizations. Also, Scheiter, Gerjets, and Catrambone (2006) compared the effects of appending static versus dynamic visualizations to texts about probability theory, and found that, compared to the text-only materials, adding statics improved performance but adding dynamic pictures hindered learning outcomes. In contrast, there is research showing better outcomes from dynamic rather than static pictures, with STEAM disciplines such as physics (e.g., Rieber, 1990), cellular biology (e.g., Stith, 2004), chemistry (e.g., Ardac & Akaygun, 2005), and visual arts (e.g., Dorethy, 1973).

Nevertheless, some questions have been raised about the validity of the controls in experiments comparing statics with animated materials. Tversky, Morrison, and Betrancourt (2002) argue that the animation advantage found in some studies could be due to additional information contained within the dynamic images, which is not replicated in the static resources. In spite of the often conflicting results when dynamic visualizations are compared to static images, and the different theories proposed in support of this research, evidence is accumulating that transient information is a major impediment to learning from dynamic pictures (see Ayres & Paas, 2007a; Sweller et al., 2011; see also Castro-Alonso, Ayres, & Paas, 2014b). Hence, much recent research has focused on finding strategies to deal with transient information contained within dynamic visualizations (see Castro-Alonso, Ayres, & Paas, 2014a).

Overcoming the Transiency of Dynamic Visualizations

One straightforward strategy to manage the transient information of some dynamic images is to include in these resources a pause facility, which makes the animation/video more permanent by stopping it, thus giving the learner extra time to memorize the important depictions if necessary. This strategy is often referred to as *pace-control*—also known as *stepwise, self-pacing,* or *learner-controlled*— where learners can manage the transitory nature of the dynamic depiction by simply pausing the presentation. Researchers have predicted that pace-controlled animations should be better instructional materials than *continuous* or *system-controlled* versions (see Ayres & Paas, 2007a; Mayer, 2008; Schnotz & Rasch, 2008). Supporting evidence comes from Höffler and Schwartz (2011), who found that pace-controlled groups outperformed and reported less working memory demands than system-controlled conditions in a study where university students had to learn about chemical dirt removal. Similarly, Mayer and Chandler (2001) observed that learners who studied the formation of lightning from a self-pacing animation presented higher transfer scores than those studying from the continuous version of the visualization. Also, Hasler, Kersten, and Sweller (2007) found a learner-controlled advantage in a study with primary school students learning about the causes of day and night. As these studies show, the pace-control strategy gives the learners opportunities to interact with the depictions. However, further discussion of the additional advantages of interactivity (e.g., in simulations and virtual models; see Moreno & Mayer, 2007) is beyond the main focus of this chapter.

Another strategy to deal with transitory visualizations is *segmenting*. This method consists of segmenting whole animations into shorter parts that are not as cognitive demanding as the total block (Moreno, 2007). A prediction that follows this strategy is that segmented dynamic visualizations should be better instructional resources than whole dynamic visualizations (Ayres & Paas, 2007a). A supporting example is the previously mentioned experiment by Hasler et al. (2007) that compared learner- versus system-controlled animations, which also included a segmented version in the comparison. The study found that learner-controlled and segmented animations were equally effective, and that both outperformed the system-controlled whole version. Similar findings supporting both pace-control and segmenting strategies were reported by Spanjers, van Gog, Wouters, and van Merriënboer (2012) with animations depicting probability calculation tasks.

Finally, a third strategy is signaling—also named *attention-guiding* (e.g., Bétrancourt, 2005) or *attention cueing* (e.g., de Koning, Tabbers, Rikers, & Paas, 2009). It is predicted that a student will learn better if cues are added to the dynamic visualizations, which signals the relevant information and thus avoids disorientation (for a review, see Mayer, 2008). Although this technique does not prevent a negative transitory effect directly, it prevents learners' disorientation when depictions are showing multiple elements continuously changing. Examples of this technique include arrows and texts, which have been employed effectively as signals in scientific animations that depict (a) the rock cycle (Lin & Atkinson, 2011), (b) gear systems (Boucheix, 2008), or (c) an enzyme's structure and function (Huk et al., 2010). Similarly, signals such as giving more luminance or color to the important elements have been added to animations that show the cardiovascular system (e.g., de Koning, Tabbers, Rikers, & Paas, 2010).

In contrast to these encouraging results that support strategies to overcome the transiency of dynamic pictures, there are also conflicting findings or inconclusive outcomes, which are mainly found in the pace-control strategy (e.g., Boucheix, 2008; Kriz & Hegarty, 2007; Tabbers & de Koeijer, 2010). Boucheix (2008) provides an explanation, which especially applies for low spatial ability learners self-controlling a dynamic image: When these students are constantly observing the controls to pause/play the dynamic visualizations, they are diverting their attention away from the important elements shown in the depictions.

Although identification of the transient information effect on dynamic visualizations has made—and continues to make—a contribution to the field, the complex nature of computer-based learning means that more than one category of strategies is required to create optimum learning environments. Hence, researchers must explore new directions. One promising direction outlined in this chapter is *embodied cognition*, which entails a relatively new approach to the study of cognitive processes.

The Embodied Cognition Perspective

Even though the traditional views of cognition (e.g., Atkinson & Shiffrin, 1968; Simon & Gilmartin, 1973) tend to describe mental processes as centralized and independent of the peripheral body, a more current embodied, or grounded cognition perspective (see Barsalou, 2010) acknowledges the connection between the mind to the rest of the body and to their common natural habitat. As suggested by Wilson (2002), humans have evolved an embodied cognition because they originally had to persist in continuous interactions between their mind, bodies and environment, in order to avoid death. Wilson refers to this cognition as *on-line*, because it is a mental activity connected always to its inputs and outputs. Then, after many millennia, civilization reduced the survival threats, so human mental processes were able to further employ *off-line* abstract cognition, which was more independent of the perceptual and motoric (related to muscle movement) elements that allow interactions between the mind, body, and the environment. However, even the most abstract process of contemporary human cognition can profit from embodied experiences, since cognition has evolved a foundation in sensorimotor processing that connects the mind's perception and action streams (Wilson, 2002).

The embodied nature of cognition has been observed in studies that show how visual perception interacts with the motor system, particularly during object manipulation (e.g., Chao & Martin, 2000; Witt, Kemmerer, Linkenauger, & Culham, 2010). Moreover, attention and memory for abstract depictions can be enhanced by showing hands reaching these elements (see Brockmole, Davoli, Abrams, & Witt, 2013; see also Weidler & Abrams, 2014). Extending these findings, some of the abstract STEAM concepts could be facilitated by showing hand movements, such as *manipulations* and *gesturing*. This endorsement of using on-line evolved skills (in this case, manipulations and gesturing) to teach off-line skills (in this case, STEAM concepts) is arguably the main goal of *evolutionary educational psychology*.

Evolutionary Educational Psychology

Recognizing facial expressions, employing physical materials as tools, inferring the intention of other individuals, and understanding gestures can all be considered rather uncomplicated tasks for humans, as we have evolved those skills over countless generations (Geary, 2002). The *Homo sapiens* species has had several millennia, and thus opportunities, to evolve or refine, for example, the skill of gesturing. This implies that we evolved an embodied cognition, appropriate to process the particular information that is involved in making and observing gestures (Geary, 2007). Therefore, gesturing is an ability that evolved because it helped us to establish advantageous relationships to access essential supplies for our species (Geary, 2002). Similarly, every other skill that was beneficial for the survival of our ancestors, such as object manipulation, should have evolved to be a relatively effortless ability today (Geary, 2007). Thus, these skills have been termed by evolutionary educational psychology researchers as *biologically primary abilities* (Geary, 1995).

In contrast to the skills shaped by evolution, there are *biologically secondary abilities*, which are shaped by a more current force: human culture (Geary, 1995). Examples of these abilities are reading, solving mathematical problems, learning to use novel instruments, and studying various science concepts (e.g., energy, force, and mitosis). Moreover, most of the school syllabi and STEAM instruction concerns biologically secondary abilities. The acquisition of this secondary knowledge is slower and more effortful than the attainment of the evolved skills (Geary, 1995). However, both are equally required to "survive" in a civilized society where primary knowledge is no longer sufficient (Geary, 2002). In consequence, the schooling system emerged to teach these necessary but effortful abilities.

Considering the greater difficulty to learn secondary abilities, Geary (2002) claims that primary knowledge should be used as a vehicle for learning secondary knowledge. In support of this view, for example, Paas and Sweller (2012) argue that the relatively easy acquisition of two primary abilities, object manipulation and gesturing, can assist the learning of the more difficult secondary skills of formal instruction. In addition, when dealing with secondary abilities that are even more challenging because they are presented with transient visualizations, the rationale to use primary skills in this case becomes more apparent (see *the human movement effect* in Paas & Sweller, 2012). As described in Section "Embodied Dynamic Visualizations for STEAM Instruction", research around the human movement effect shows a relatively new embodied strategy to facilitate learning of STEAM topics via dynamic visualizations.

In conclusion, evolution shaped the human brain to learn certain biologically primary abilities more easily than the non-evolved secondary knowledge. In other words, there are cognitive systems evolved to deal with primary abilities. For example, the *mirror neuron system* (for a review, see Rizzolatti & Craighero, 2004) is arguably the most important cognitive processor that has evolved to deal with the imitation of human manipulation and gesturing.

The Mirror Neuron System

Mirror neurons were firstly described by di Pellegrino, Fadiga, Fogassi, Gallese, & Rizzolatti (1992), who observed these nerve cells in the brain's premotor cortex of macaques (*Macaca nemestrina*). The authors named these cells as *mirror neurons* because they were triggered (a) when the animals directly performed certain hand actions, such as grasping and manipulating objects; and also (b) when the macaques observed the same actions being performed by the human experimenters. Fadiga, Fogassi, Pavesi, and Rizzolatti (1995) extended the mirror neuron phenomenon to humans by recording responses from a number of forearm and hand muscles. The pattern of muscle contraction observed in the participants when they performed certain arm and hand actions was very similar to the pattern recorded when they observed the same movements executed by the experimenter.

In humans, the mirror neurons constitute a system that has an extensive brain distribution over the premotor, parietal, and subcortical areas (Cross, Hamilton, & Grafton, 2006). In other words, the mirror neuron system is connected to brain areas that participate in embodied activities of perception and action for hand tasks. These systems have evolved to help humans manage the information associated with manipulation and gesturing, and it is believed that these processors are mainly triggered during natural manipulation and gesturing conditions. In contrast, phenomena not associated with human evolution are less likely to activate the mirror neurons and related action–recognition systems. This rationale has been supported by findings where the observation of robotic hand or arm actions has led to smaller (e.g., Press, Bird, Flach, & Heyes, 2005) or non-significant effects (e.g., Kilner, Paulignan, & Blakemore, 2003) on the observer's motoric system, as compared to the observation of human limbs performing the movements. Analogously, Järveläinen, Schürmann, Avikainen, & Hari (2001) reported that the motor cortex of their participants was more strongly triggered when they watched live human hand movements as compared to the same video recorded actions. Finally, Shimada and Oki (2012) showed that an area of the mirror neuron system was activated more when the participants watched an animated character's arm doing natural continuous movements rather than jerky and paused motions. Thus, because *biological, live*, and *continuous* hand actions coevolved with embodied systems, these actions may activate the mirror neuron system more strongly than *artificial, recorded*, and *jerky* hand movements.

Nevertheless, the previous findings do not imply that any non-natural phenomenon will be ineffective in triggering cognition. Such a radically embodied approach would lead to the erroneous rejection of all technological (non-natural) solutions in instruction. For example, animated or video recorded hand actions could be regarded as futile approaches to deal with problematic STEAM concepts. However, although artificially (video) observed hand actions may trigger brain processors to a smaller extent than live actions (e.g., Järveläinen et al., 2001), Rohbanfard and Proteau (2013) showed that such artificial methods were still productive for learning a sequential timing hand task. In addition, there is accumulating research showing that object manipulations and gestures are important in learning from complex dynamic visualizations, as described next.

Embodied Dynamic Visualizations for STEAM Instruction

Characterizing the human movement effect, Paas and Sweller (2012) predicted that evolved embodied systems could help to manage problematic learning materials, in particular instructional animations and videos conveying transient information. Moreover, because evolved mechanisms such as the mirror neuron system are triggered more with fluent movement (e.g., Shimada & Oki, 2012), it could be expected that dynamic visualizations of manipulations and gesturing would show better learning outcomes than their static equivalents. Hence, the problem of transiency in these specific dynamic visualizations could be overcome by the greater activation of evolved cognitive systems. This has huge potential for STEAM instruction, where human manipulations and gestures could be used as part of the dynamic visualizations in these disciplines.

It is worth noting that both a dynamic visualization of an object manipulation and that of a gesture share the property of showing human hand actions. The main contrast between manipulations and gestures is their different dependency on manipulable objects (cf. Ping, Goldin-Meadow, & Beilock, 2014). Manipulations need to show the manipulatives, which is less mandatory with gesturing. For example, it has been reported that the effectiveness of showing gestures is not hampered when the corresponding objects are not depicted (Ping & Goldin-Meadow, 2010). Conversely, gestures need to show the hands, which is less compulsory with manipulations. For example, the effectiveness of showing a manipulation may not be hindered when the corresponding hands are not depicted, provided that the objects are manipulative enough to trigger by themselves the positive embodied effects (e.g., Wong et al., 2009). This difference among visualizations of human hand actions is shown in Fig. 1 (top).

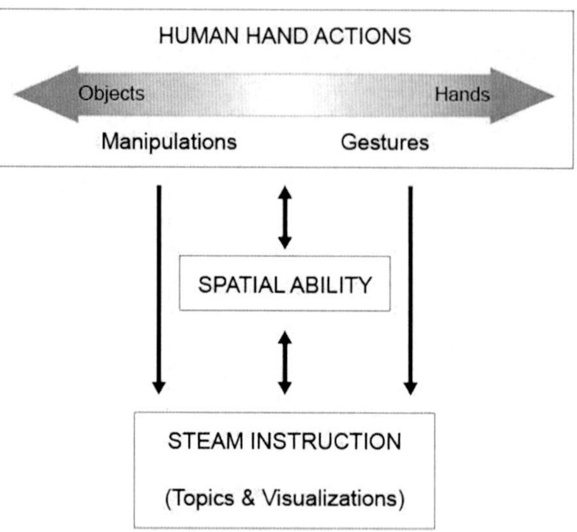

Fig. 1 Interrelationship between human hand actions (manipulations and gestures), spatial ability, and STEAM instruction (STEAM topics and STEAM visualizations). The arrows show beneficial relationships

The depiction of hand actions—manipulations and gestures—can be effectively employed in any kind of dynamic visualization of STEAM topics, such as movies, animations, simulations, and videos. One example of video and object manipulation concerns the biological concept that the cell membrane is a fluid mosaic, which can be illustrated with a video that shows the teacher manipulating different balls (representing proteins and lipids) in a tray with water (Miller, 1998). One example of animation and gesture is about the meteorological concept of lightning formation, which can be instructed with an animation that includes a dynamic pointing hand that constantly signals the relevant elements (de Koning & Tabbers, 2013).

Manipulations and gestures will be described separately in this section, focusing on their use in STEAM dynamic visualizations. Subsequently, spatial ability, important to understanding manipulations and gestures, is described at the end of this section. Note that the focus on this chapter is not in the beneficial effects of performing hand actions, but on observing them as manipulations and gestures. Accordingly, the execution of hand actions, whether directly or via interactive simulations, will only be briefly addressed.

Manipulations in Dynamic Visualizations

It was mentioned previously that, as compared to static pictures, dynamic visualizations show more promise as learning tools for human motor skills (for a review, see Castro-Alonso et al., 2014a). For example, the review by Park and Hopkins (1992) that searched for instructional purposes for animations concluded that dynamic visualizations were most effectively employed for human actions that followed a procedure. Similarly, Höffler and Leutner (2007) reported that the largest differences favoring dynamic over static images were observed when the depictions showed procedural skills.

Moreover, growing research suggests that manipulative–procedural tasks are better portrayed in animation or video rather than in static images. A classical study was conducted by Spangenberg (1973), in which the task of disassembling a machine gun was compared between a group that watched the steps though video versus the conditions that studied the steps though equivalent static images. The procedure was better executed by the video conditions. Note that, as it is fundamental for this dynamic versus statics comparisons, Spangenberg used the same medium (television) to deliver both video and still images. Similarly, Michas and Berry (2000) compared equivalent video versus video stills conditions in learning to apply a bandage to a wounded hand. Here, the video condition outperformed the still group in bandaging performance and test retention scores. Also in controlled between-subjects experimental conditions, Ayres, Marcus, Chan, and Qian (2009) observed that the animation groups presented higher cognitive and transfer results than the statics, where the manipulations involved solving hand-puzzle rings and replicating knots. In addition, for other knot tying tasks, research has shown better performance associated to animated rather than to static learning presentations (Garland & Sánchez, 2013; Marcus, Cleary, Wong & Ayres, 2013). Interestingly, Garland and Sánchez (2013) also compared performance between two dynamic conditions that differed in viewing angles. The video with the perspective that supposedly elicited more of the mirror neuron system (over-the-shoulder, first person view) was a better learning tool than the video with the angle that activated less of this embodied system (face-to-face, third person view). A further example of animation outscoring static images was reported in a study using paper-folding tasks by Wong et al. (2009). Also notable in this study was that when the manipulative folding task was replaced by a non-manipulative task, dynamic images were no longer superior to statics, indicating that the human movement effect may had disappeared and transiency could not be handled as efficiently. Altogether, these findings support the human movement effect due to embodied mechanisms (such as the mirron neuron system, see van Gog et al., 2009), and suggest that dynamic images should be favored over statics when learning procedural and manipulative tasks.

Although the previous studies about dynamic visualizations of manipulatives could be easily applied to the Technology or Arts disciplines, the literature is scarce for the other branches of STEAM. For example, in Science and Mathematics, manipulative learning rarely entails observation of the manipulations through visualizations, but rather the direct manipulation of real objects or virtual models. Thus, research of manipulations to instruct a wide range of STEAM concepts through visualizations is not abundant. However, we argue here that, due to the embodied mirror mechanisms, some of the effects of direct manipulations could also apply when observing others (e.g., teachers) doing the manipulations in video or animation. Consequently, the gathered evidence about direct manipulations to learn STEAM concepts (e.g., Manches, O'Malley & Benford, 2010; Miller, 1998; Zacharia & Olympiou, 2011) could be applied to instructional dynamic visualizations depicting manipulations. Likewise, the remaining discussion of this subsection, which focuses on manipulations performed by the learners, could be applied in future research about visualizations that show manipulations.

Because, as commented above, the main depiction of a manipulation is the manipulative object, research has focused on the *type of object* used, for example, whether the element is rather *concrete* or *abstract*. Since STEAM concepts are largely based on underlying mechanisms, as opposed to readily visual relations, objects that imply these mechanisms—abstract—instead of showing much visual information—concrete—tend to be preferred (e.g., Brown, McNeil & Glenberg, 2009; Kaminski, Sloutsky & Heckler, 2009; but see Sowell, 1989), as the rich information of concrete elements may distract attention from the more relevant but underlying STEAM principles. Although this seems to suggest that concrete type of objects should be discarded, Fyfe, McNeil, Son, and Goldstone (2014) proposed a less radical mixed strategy of three connected steps, from concrete to abstract manipulatives, which benefits both from the concrete object (embodied perceptual and motoric experiences) and from the abstract model (without distracting features, better to understand and transfer the concept). Altogether, it seems that mixed dynamic visualizations that include both concrete and abstract objects should be fostered to understand STEAM concepts.

In addition to the type of object, there is also another differentiation of manipulatives. This new dimension respects the *type of environment* for the manipulation, which distinguishes between *physical* (real objects moved by physical hands) versus *virtual* (virtual replicas of the objects being moved by the mouse, keyboard, etc.). In a review of controlled experiments, de Jong, Linn, and Zacharia (2013) concluded that both physical and virtual manipulatives were equally successful for acquiring different science concepts. However, a promising new approach instead of comparing both type of environments, is to mix these scenarios (see de Jong et al., 2013), similarly to the blended method with type of manipulative. Furthermore, recent technologies of *mixed reality* (see Lindgren & Johnson-Glenberg, 2013), which allow real hands to manipulate virtual objects, are blurring the boundaries between physical and virtual environments.

In short, when designing manipulative tasks for dynamic visualizations, mixed approaches of the type of manipulative (concrete and abstract) and the type of environment (physical and virtual) are advisable. Arguably, other instructional methods that use embodied visualizations could benefit from mixed approaches, such as showing both physical and virtual hands in depictions of gestures.

Gestures in Dynamic Visualizations

Because gesturing is an evolved primary skill, diverse evidence illustrate how easily or pervasively it is acquired by humans: (a) children can gesture before speaking, and they gesture to convey information not already in a verbal state (e.g., Goldin-Meadow & Wagner, 2005); (b) gestures get so integrated to the concurrent speech, that it is difficult to determine whether the information was given verbally or by gestures (e.g., Kelly & Church, 1998; McNeill, Cassell & McCullough, 1994); and (c) when doing motoric actions while observing gestures, the speed in responding to the message is hampered, suggesting that the motor system of the observant is activated to understand gestures (Ping et al., 2014). Thus, gestures are embodied and evolved human communicative skills that, as human manipulations, can be effective educational means to learn new concepts.

Evidence is accumulating that gesturing may be very important in STEAM instruction. For example, it has been shown that when students are allowed to gesture while explaining their solutions to mathematical problems, this embodied activity frees cognitive capacity to deal with secondary memory tasks (Goldin-Meadow, Nusbaum, Kelly & Wagner, 2001). Also, in addition to performing gestures, direct observation of these hand signals has also proven effective in mathematics instruction. For instance, Richland, Zur, and Holyoak (2007) analyzed use of analogies by mathematics eighth-grade teachers in USA, Hong Kong and Japan. One of the findings that the authors linked to better standardized-test performances in both Asian countries was that Hong Kong and Japan teachers used significantly more hand or arm gestures than USA instructors in connecting source analogs with their targets.

However, more pertinent to the focus of this chapter is the effect that the observation of gestures via dynamic visualizations has on instruction. A classic study on this topic was conducted by Riseborough (1981), who reported the benefits of including gestures when presenting verbal information via video. In the tasks of guessing an object that was described, recalling different verbs from an oral list, or remembering important words from a short story, Riseborough (1981) found better outcomes in the participants in the gesture conditions, as compared to no movements or vague movements conditions. Similarly, Church, Ayman-Nolley, and Mahootian (2004) reported that the concept of Piagetian conservation was better understood by elementary grade children who learnt from a video with speech plus gestures as compared to children that watched the speech only video. Interestingly, the main objective of this study was to find the effects that the observation of gestures on video could have in students with a poor English knowledge. In other words, Church et al. investigated how gestures would affect learning a mathematical concept when the capacity to verbally understand the concept was diminished. The authors found that the number of non-English speakers who understood the concept of conservation via speech and gestures was more than double the number of those who learnt without gestures. Another study about the benefits of dynamic visualizations depicting gestures was conducted by Valenzeno, Alibali, and Klatzky (2003) on preschool children studying a video about the concept of bilateral symmetry. The authors observed that the participants in the speech with gestures video condition gave more advanced and frequent explanations about symmetry than the children in the speech only condition. Kang, Hallman, Son, and Black (2013) showed that, for adults learning the biological concept of mitosis, the participants who studied a video with the instructor providing spoken explanations and meaningful gestures gained a deeper understanding of mitosis than those who observed a video with the instructor giving spoken explanations without showing the hands (non-gesturing condition). Hence, several examples with diverse students and STEAM contents show more positive learning outcomes after studying from audiovisuals with gestures than from equivalent depictions with only speech and not gestures.

Regarding the underlying causes for these favorable effects of dynamic images with gestures, there are three non-mutually exclusive mechanisms to consider (cf. Valenzeno et al., 2003). Firstly, as discussed above, videos and animations with gestures activate embodied mechanisms, and also relate abstract concepts to the real physical environment. Secondly, dynamic depictions showing gestures capture students' attention better than those without these motions, as Valenzeno et al. (2003) found with preschool students. And thirdly, gestures provide an additional informational channel, simultaneous to the verbal channel being used in speech, thus conveying supplementary data to the learner.

However, this same advantage of providing more information could result in the unfavorable effect of providing unnecessary redundant information (see *the redundancy principle* in Sweller, 2005). In other words, showing hands performing gestures adds more depictions than are needed to learn a task, which might distract instead of foster learning (e.g., Castro-Alonso et al., 2014b). This is particularly evident when gestures are not *representational*, thus, they do not convey meaning. For example, Riseborough (1981) measured word recall from a verb list or a short story delivered through videos. In contrast to the significant positive effects of showing meaningful gestures when narrating the words, only a slight benefit was found for vague movements compared to no movement at all. Similarly, Kang et al. (2013) reported no advantages of *beat gestures*—which only stress speech elements but do not convey meaning—when learning the concept of mitosis, in contrast to representational gestures. Thus, as Kang et al. suggested, gestures in dynamic visualizations should mean something, rather than being just hand movements with no clear representation, as this latter scenario may even hamper learning.

Embodied Spatial Ability

We have described above the potential for using manipulations and gestures in dynamic visualizations. However, the capability to understand both is aided by *spatial ability*. In a meta-analysis, Linn and Petersen (1985) defined spatial ability as a skill to represent, transform and generate non-verbal information. In addition to helping learn human hand actions, spatial ability is very important for learning STEAM topics (see this central role of spatial ability in Fig. 1). For example, after analyzing a dataset of approximately 400,000 high-school students in their progress through Bachelors, Masters and Doctorates degrees, Wai, Lubinski, and Benbow (2009) reported that spatial ability was always higher than verbal ability (but lower than mathematical ability) for those in the disciplines of Math/Computer Science, Physical Science, and Engineering.

Moreover, spatial ability is fundamental to studying from video and animation. For example, Höffler (2010) showed in his meta-analysis that spatial ability was an essential capacity in learning from dynamic and static visualizations. In other words, spatial ability not only can aid the learning of STEAM topics, but also of STEAM visualizations, what implies that it is very beneficial for understanding STEAM instruction. Also, as shown in Fig. 1, the opposite applies and STEM instruction is very advantageous to boost spatial ability (e.g., Lord, 1990; Pallrand & Seeber, 1984; Stransky, Wilcox, & Dubrowski, 2010). In consequence, increasing spatial abilities in students (e.g., Baenninger & Newcombe, 1989; Yang & Chen, 2010) could be an effective instructional approach.

Spatial ability is a construct that can be divided into subfactors, one of which is *mental rotation* (e.g., Linn & Petersen, 1985)—sometimes referred to as *spatial relations* (e.g., Höffler, 2010). In arguably the seminal study of mental rotation, Shepard and Metzler (1971) asked participants to compare pairs of three-dimensional figures made with cubes, in order to determine if each pair showed either (a) the same figures, but rotated differently; or (b) different figures, meaning that they were not only rotated but also reflected. Shepard and Metzler observed that the reaction times to determine the correct answer (*same* or *different* configuration) were linearly correlated with the angular differences between the pair of figures.

The fact that smaller angles implied faster mental rotations has been proposed as a connection between mental and actual physical rotation (see Cooper, 1976; Janczyk, Pfister, Crognale & Kunde, 2012). In other words, spatial ability, and particularly mental rotation, can also be regarded as an embodied cognitive process. For example, a number of findings have shown a link between mental rotation and embodied mechanisms (see Krüger, Amorim & Ebersbach, 2014). Furthermore, the extent of the embodiment of mental rotation has been observed with both manipulation and gesturing tasks. For instance, Wexler, Kosslyn, and Berthoz (1998) reported a strong link between mental and simultaneous manual rotation of two-dimensional figures. Interestingly, the interaction between the mental and motoric turning of the figures was affected by the direction, speed and final position of both the mental and the manipulative rotation. Similarly, Janczyk et al. (2012) showed that a mental rotation task positively influenced a following manual rotation task in the same gyratory direction. Regarding gestures, Chu and Kita (2011) observed that students who were encouraged to gesture in order to solve difficult three-dimensional rotation tasks outperformed the participants restrained from gesturing. Moreover, this gesturing effect was transferred to subsequent spatial ability tasks where gesturing was no longer allowed, showing that the positive effects of these hand movements extended over time. A last noteworthy finding in this study was that, as expertise to solve the mental rotations increased, gesturing frequency decreased, arguably because the spatial processes supported by embodiment had become internalized. These embodied effects of spatial ability suggest that this ability is not only important to learn human hand actions, but that the reverse is also true: Human hand actions, such as manipulations and gestures, are helpful in tasks that demand spatial ability (see Fig. 1). In addition—as the research reported in this chapter suggests—these human hand actions are very relevant for STEAM instruction.

Implications for Instruction

From the wide variety of STEAM topics that could benefit from instructional dynamic visualization showing manipulations, we provide two specific examples. For the concept of photosynthesis in biology, all the agents involved (sun, energy, water, etc.) and their relationships could be written or drawn on different pieces of paper, and these paper notes could be manipulated in a video with auditory explanations. So, for example, the teacher could be video-recorded manipulating a piece of paper with the word *energy* written on it, and moving it toward another piece representing *leaf*, while explaining that the *energy of the sun is received by the leaf.* For arithmetic concepts in mathematics, animations of virtual fingers moving squares from one group to another could help understand the computations involved. For example, a simple addition such as *1 + 1 = 2*, could be represented by two animated fingers moving a square each with the number *1* written on it, and placing them together to form a combination labeled as *2*. In general, when designing manipulations for a dynamic visualization, consider also that blended methods, which mix type of objects (concrete vs. abstract) and/or type of environments (physical vs. virtual), may be more effective.

For dynamic visualizations of gestures, we also provide two examples. To solve linear equations, a video of a moving hand can be very effective in showing that certain operations can be represented by moving the various variables from one side of the equation to the other. In music education, animations of static hands in different states (open, fist, etc.) can represent the different duration of musical notes. When designing gestures for a dynamic visualization, it is important to note that gestures should convey meaning and not include meaningless hand movements.

A number of additional implications for the design of STEAM animated or static visualizations follow:

- Due to transiency conveyed in dynamic visualizations, static images may sometimes be better resources for learning. Similarly, due to the transient information effect, dynamic visualizations that include methods to overcome the transiency (e.g., pace-control, segmenting, or signaling) may be more effective than animations and videos that do not use these strategies.
- Because spatial ability plays such a critical role, it is also highly recommended that learners' spatial ability should be developed independently or as part of STEAM instruction.

Future Directions for Research

We consider four interesting directions for further research about embodied dynamic visualizations for STEAM instruction. Firstly, provided that both manipulation and gestures are similar mechanisms that depict hand actions, their differential dependency to either manipulative objects or hands could be further investigated. That is, one direction for future research is to continue investigating the impact of object manipulations when the hands are depicted or not shown in the visualizations. Similarly, another future direction is to compare the effectiveness of gesturing when the corresponding objects are shown or not shown.

Secondly, the majority of research on manipulative tasks involves direct manipulations by the learners, either physically or virtually. Future studies could investigate the more indirect effect of observing STEAM dynamic visualizations depicting real or virtual manipulations. These studies could benefit from the effective instructional applications that have been reported for direct manipulations. Also, this direction could widen the research on the mirror neuron system by comparing performing hand actions versus only observing these actions.

Thirdly, the studies on visualizations of manipulative tasks and gestures need to broaden their scope to include concepts from more diverse disciplines. Indeed, much of the reported manipulative dynamic visualizations could be connected to Technology or Arts; similarly, gesturing visualizations tend to focus on Mathematics. Thus, the Science and Engineering branches of STEAM seem to be underrepresented in these investigations. Similarly, other educational areas, such as Language, could be equally benefited by the visualization of human hand actions.

Finally, the human movement effect and its impact on dynamic versus static images have been shown for many manipulative tasks, but not many for gesturing. In that sense, a step forward would be to compare the learning effectiveness of static or dynamic STEAM visualizations that include gestures.

Conclusion

Although dynamic visualizations are increasingly more appealing and easier to produce, and can be linked to gaming applications and high motivation, their benefits may be counterbalanced by the problematic transient information that they can convey. Beyond three popular methods to manage this transient information, we recommend a relatively newer approach from the embodied cognition research: the use of the embodied evolved skills of manipulation and gesturing. The new research reported in this chapter provides more evidence that the embodied cognition perspective, in the form of manipulations and gestures, has a great potential to enhance the use of both dynamic and static visualizations for STEAM topics. However, it is important to note that spatial ability is a factor that must be considered. Not only does it moderate the effectiveness of learning from dynamic and static representations, but it is also a crucial factor in the capacity to learn many STEAM concepts.

Acknowledgements This research was partially supported by an UIPA scholarship from University of New South Wales to the first author, and by an Australian Research Council grant (DP140103307) to the second and third authors.

References

Ardac, D., & Akaygun, S. (2005). Using static and dynamic visuals to represent chemical change at molecular level. *International Journal of Science Education, 27*(11), 1269–1298. doi:10.1080/09500690500102284.

Atkinson, R. C., & Shiffrin, R. M. (1968). Human memory: A proposed system and its control processes. In K. W. Spence & J. T. Spence (Eds.), *Psychology of learning and motivation* (Vol. 2, pp. 89–195). New York: Academic Press. doi:10.1016/S0079-7421(08)60422-3.

Ayres, P., & Paas, F. (2007a). Can the cognitive load approach make instructional animations more effective? *Applied Cognitive Psychology, 21*(6), 811–820. doi:10.1002/acp.1351.

Ayres, P., & Paas, F. (2007b). Making instructional animations more effective: A cognitive load approach. *Applied Cognitive Psychology, 21*(6), 695–700. doi:10.1002/acp.1343.

Ayres, P., Marcus, N., Chan, C., & Qian, N. (2009). Learning hand manipulative tasks: When instructional animations are superior to equivalent static representations. *Computers in Human Behavior, 25*(2), 348–353. doi:10.1016/j.chb.2008.12.013.

Baenninger, M., & Newcombe, N. S. (1989). The role of experience in spatial test performance: A meta-analysis. *Sex Roles, 20*(5–6), 327–344. doi:10.1007/BF00287729.

Barsalou, L. W. (2010). Grounded cognition: Past, present, and future. *Topics in Cognitive Science, 2*(4), 716–724. doi:10.1111/j.1756-8765.2010.01115.x.

Bétrancourt, M. (2005). The animation and interactivity principles in multimedia learning. In R. E. Mayer (Ed.), *The Cambridge handbook of multimedia learning* (pp. 287–296). New York: Cambridge University Press.

Boucheix, J.-M. (2008). Young learners' control of technical animations. In R. K. Lowe & W. Schnotz (Eds.), *Learning with animation: Research implications for design* (pp. 208–234). New York: Cambridge University Press.

Boucheix, J.-M., & Lowe, R. K. (2010). An eye tracking comparison of external pointing cues and internal continuous cues in learning with complex animations. *Learning and Instruction, 20*(2), 123–135. doi:10.1016/j.learninstruc.2009.02.015.

Brockmole, J. R., Davoli, C. C., Abrams, R. A., & Witt, J. K. (2013). The world within reach: Effects of hand posture and tool use on visual cognition. *Current Directions in Psychological Science, 22*(1), 38–44. doi:10.1177/0963721412465065.

Brown, M. C., McNeil, N. M., & Glenberg, A. M. (2009). Using concreteness in education: Real problems, potential solutions. *Child Development Perspectives, 3*(3), 160–164. doi:10.1111/j.1750-8606.2009.00098.x.

Brucker, B., Scheiter, K., & Gerjets, P. (2014). Learning with dynamic and static visualizations: Realistic details only benefit learners with high visuospatial abilities. *Computers in Human Behavior, 36*, 330–339. doi:10.1016/j.chb.2014.03.077.

Castro-Alonso, J. C., Ayres, P., & Paas, F. (2014a). Dynamic visualisations and motor skills. In W. Huang (Ed.), *Handbook of human centric visualization* (pp. 551–580). New York: Springer. doi:10.1007/978-1-4614-7485-222.

Castro-Alonso, J. C., Ayres, P., & Paas, F. (2014b). Learning from observing hands in static and animated versions of non-manipulative tasks. *Learning and Instruction, 34*, 11–21. doi:10.1016/j.learninstruc.2014.07.005.

Chao, L. L., & Martin, A. (2000). Representation of manipulable man-made objects in the dorsal stream. *NeuroImage, 12*(4), 478–484. doi:10.1006/nimg.2000.0635.

Chu, M., & Kita, S. (2011). The nature of gestures' beneficial role in spatial problem solving. *Journal of Experimental Psychology: General, 140*(1), 102–116. doi:10.1037/a0021790.

Church, R. B., Ayman-Nolley, S., & Mahootian, S. (2004). The role of gesture in bilingual education: Does gesture enhance learning? *International Journal of Bilingual Education and Bilingualism, 7*(4), 303–319. doi:10.1080/13670050408667815.

Cooley, M. (2007). Video poems seeking insight. *Canadian Review of Art Education: Research & Issues, 34*, 88–98.

Cooper, L. A. (1976). Demonstration of a mental analog of an external rotation. *Perception & Psychophysics, 19*(4), 296–302. doi:10.3758/BF03204234.

Cross, E. S., Hamilton, A. F. d. C., & Grafton, S. T. (2006). Building a motor simulation de novo: Observation of dance by dancers. *NeuroImage, 31*(3), 1257–1267. doi:10.1016/j.neuroimage.2006.01.033.

de Jong, T., Linn, M. C., & Zacharia, Z. C. (2013). Physical and virtual laboratories in science and engineering education. *Science, 340*(6130), 305–308. doi:10.1126/science.1230579.

de Koning, B. B., & Tabbers, H. K. (2013). Gestures in instructional animations: A helping hand to understanding non-human movements? *Applied Cognitive Psychology, 27*(5), 683–689. doi:10.1002/acp.2937.

de Koning, B. B., Tabbers, H. K., Rikers, R. M. J. P., & Paas, F. (2009). Towards a framework for attention cueing in instructional animations: Guidelines for research and design. *Educational Psychology Review, 21*(2), 113–140. doi:10.1007/s10648-009-9098-7.

de Koning, B. B., Tabbers, H. K., Rikers, R. M. J. P., & Paas, F. (2010). Learning by generating vs. receiving instructional explanations: Two approaches to enhance attention cueing in animations. *Computers & Education, 55*(2), 681–691. doi:10.1016/j.compedu.2010.02.027.

di Pellegrino, G., Fadiga, L., Fogassi, L., Gallese, V., & Rizzolatti, G. (1992). Understanding motor events: A neurophysiological study. *Experimental Brain Research, 91*(1), 176–180. doi:10.1007/bf00230027.

Dorethy, R. E. (1973). Motion parallax as a factor in the differential spatial abilities of young children. *Studies in Art Education, 14*(2), 15–27. doi:10.2307/1319874.

Dowrick, P. W. (Ed.). (1991). *Practical guide to using video in the behavioral sciences.* New York: Wiley.

Fadiga, L., Fogassi, L., Pavesi, G., & Rizzolatti, G. (1995). Motor facilitation during action observation: A magnetic stimulation study. *Journal of Neurophysiology, 73*(6), 2608–2611.

Fischer, S., Lowe, R. K., & Schwan, S. (2008). Effects of presentation speed of a dynamic visualization on the understanding of a mechanical system. *Applied Cognitive Psychology, 22*(8), 1126–1141. doi:10.1002/acp.1426.

Fyfe, E. R., McNeil, N. M., Son, J. Y., & Goldstone, R. L. (2014). Concreteness fading in mathematics and science instruction: A systematic review. *Educational Psychology Review, 26*(1), 9–25. doi:10.1007/s10648-014-9249-3.

Garland, T. B., & Sánchez, C. A. (2013). Rotational perspective and learning procedural tasks from dynamic media. *Computers & Education, 69*, 31–37. doi:10.1016/j.compedu.2013.06.014.

Geary, D. C. (1995). Reflections of evolution and culture in children's cognition: Implications for mathematical development and instruction. *American Psychologist, 50*(1), 24–37.

Geary, D. C. (2002). Principles of evolutionary educational psychology. *Learning and Individual Differences, 12*(4), 317–345. doi:10.1016/s1041-6080(02)00046-8.

Geary, D. C. (2007). Educating the evolved mind: Conceptual foundations for an evolutionary educational psychology. In J. S. Carlson & J. R. Levin (Eds.), *Psychological perspectives on contemporary educational issues* (pp. 1–99). Charlotte: Information Age Publishing.

Goldin-Meadow, S., & Wagner, S. M. (2005). How our hands help us learn. *Trends in Cognitive Sciences, 9*(5), 234–241. doi:10.1016/j.tics.2005.03.006.

Goldin-Meadow, S., Nusbaum, H., Kelly, S. D., & Wagner, S. (2001). Explaining math: Gesturing lightens the load. *Psychological Science, 12*(6), 516–522.

Harris, K., & Fenner, D. E. W. (1995). Video-preservation of dance. *Journal of Aesthetic Education, 29*(1), 69–78. doi:10.2307/3333518.

Hasler, B. S., Kersten, B., & Sweller, J. (2007). Learner control, cognitive load and instructional animation. *Applied Cognitive Psychology, 21*(6), 713–729. doi:10.1002/acp.1345.

Höffler, T. N. (2010). Spatial ability: Its influence on learning with visualizations—A meta-analytic review. *Educational Psychology Review, 22*(3), 245–269. doi:10.1007/s10648-010-9126-7.

Höffler, T. N., & Leutner, D. (2007). Instructional animation versus static pictures: A meta-analysis. *Learning and Instruction, 17*(6), 722–738. doi:10.1016/j.learninstruc.2007.09.013.

Höffler, T. N., & Schwartz, R. N. (2011). Effects of pacing and cognitive style across dynamic and non-dynamic representations. *Computers & Education, 57*(2), 1716–1726. doi:10.1016/j.compedu.2011.03.012.

Huk, T., Steinke, M., & Floto, C. (2010). The educational value of visual cues and 3D-representational format in a computer animation under restricted and realistic conditions. *Instructional Science, 38*(5), 455–469. doi:10.1007/s11251-009-9116-7.

Janczyk, M., Pfister, R., Crognale, M. A., & Kunde, W. (2012). Effective rotations: Action effects determine the interplay of mental and manual rotations. *Journal of Experimental Psychology: General, 141*(3), 489–501. doi:10.1037/a0026997.

Järveläinen, J., Schürmann, M., Avikainen, S., & Hari, R. (2001). Stronger reactivity of the human primary motor cortex during observation of live rather than video motor acts. *Neuroreport, 12*(16), 3493–3495. doi:10.1016/j.neuroimage.2004.06.010.

Kalyuga, S. (2008). Relative effectiveness of animated and static diagrams: An effect of learner prior knowledge. *Computers in Human Behavior, 24*(3), 852–861. doi:10.1016/j.chb.2007.02.018.

Kaminski, J. A., Sloutsky, V. M., & Heckler, A. (2009). Transfer of mathematical knowledge: The portability of generic instantiations. *Child Development Perspectives, 3*(3), 151–155. doi:10.1111/j.1750-8606.2009.00096.x.

Kang, S., Hallman, G. L., Son, L. K., & Black, J. B. (2013). The different benefits from different gestures in understanding a concept. *Journal of Science Education and Technology, 22*(6), 825–837. doi:10.1007/s10956-012-9433-5.

Kelly, S. D., & Church, R. B. (1998). A comparison between children's and adults' ability to detect conceptual information conveyed through representational gestures. *Child Development, 69*(1), 85–93. doi:10.1111/j.1467-8624.1998.tb06135.x.

Kilner, J. M., Paulignan, Y., & Blakemore, S.-J. (2003). An interference effect of observed biological movement on action. *Current Biology, 13*(6), 522–525. doi:10.1016/s0960-9822(03)00165-9.

Koroghlanian, C., & Klein, J. D. (2004). The effect of audio and animation in multimedia instruction. *Journal of Educational Multimedia and Hypermedia, 13*(1), 23–46.

Kriz, S., & Hegarty, M. (2007). Top-down and bottom-up influences on learning from animations. *International Journal of Human-Computer Studies, 65*(11), 911–930. doi:10.1016/j.ijhcs.2007.06.005.

Krüger, M., Amorim, M.-A., & Ebersbach, M. (2014). Mental rotation and the motor system: Embodiment head over heels. *Acta Psychologica, 145*, 104–110. doi:10.1016/j.actpsy.2013.11.004.

Leahy, W., & Sweller, J. (2011). Cognitive load theory, modality of presentation and the transient information effect. *Applied Cognitive Psychology, 25*(6), 943–951. doi:10.1002/acp.1787.

Lin, L., & Atkinson, R. K. (2011). Using animations and visual cueing to support learning of scientific concepts and processes. *Computers & Education, 56*(3), 650–658. doi:10.1016/j.compedu.2010.10.007.

Lindgren, R., & Johnson-Glenberg, M. (2013). Emboldened by embodiment: Six precepts for research on embodied learning and mixed reality. *Educational Researcher, 42*(8), 445–452. doi:10.3102/0013189×13511661.

Linek, S. B., Gerjets, P., & Scheiter, K. (2010). The speaker/gender effect: Does the speaker's gender matter when presenting auditory text in multimedia messages? *Instructional Science, 38*(5), 503–521. doi:10.1007/s11251-009-9115-8.

Linn, M. C., & Petersen, A. C. (1985). Emergence and characterization of sex differences in spatial ability: A meta-analysis. *Child Development, 56*(6), 1479–1498. doi:10.2307/1130467.

Lord, T. (1990). Enhancing learning in the life sciences through spatial perception. *Innovative Higher Education, 15*(1), 5–16. doi:10.1007/BF00889733.

Lowe, R. K. (2003). Animation and learning: Selective processing of information in dynamic graphics. *Learning and Instruction, 13*(2), 157–176. doi:10.1016/S0959-4752(02)00018-X.

Manches, A., O'Malley, C., & Benford, S. (2010). The role of physical representations in solving number problems: A comparison of young children's use of physical and virtual materials. *Computers & Education, 54*(3), 622–640. doi:10.1016/j.compedu.2009.09.023.

Marbach-Ad, G., Rotbain, Y., & Stavy, R. (2008). Using computer animation and illustration activities to improve high school students' achievement in molecular genetics. *Journal of Research in Science Teaching, 45*(3), 273–292. doi:10.1002/tea.20222.

Marcus, N., Cleary, B., Wong, A., & Ayres, P. (2013). Should hand actions be observed when learning hand motor skills from instructional animations? *Computers in Human Behavior, 29*(6), 2172–2178. doi:10.1016/j.chb.2013.04.035.

Mayer, R. E. (2008). Research-based principles for learning with animation. In R. K. Lowe & W. Schnotz (Eds.), *Learning with animation: Research implications for design* (pp. 30–48). New York: Cambridge University Press.

Mayer, R. E., & Chandler, P. (2001). When learning is just a click away: Does simple user interaction foster deeper understanding of multimedia messages? *Journal of Educational Psychology, 93*(2), 390–397. doi:10.1037/0022-0663.93.2.390.

Mayer, R. E., & Sims, V. K. (1994). For whom is a picture worth a thousand words? Extensions of a dual-coding theory of multimedia learning. *Journal of Educational Psychology, 86*(3), 389–401. doi:10.1037/0022-0663.86.3.389.

Mayer, R. E., Hegarty, M., Mayer, S., & Campbell, J. (2005). When static media promote active learning: Annotated illustrations versus narrated animations in multimedia instruction. *Journal of Experimental Psychology: Applied, 11*(4), 256–265. doi:10.1037/1076-898x.11.4.256.

McNeill, D., Cassell, J., & McCullough, K.-E. (1994). Communicative effects of speech-mismatched gestures. *Research on Language and Social Interaction, 27*(3), 223–237. doi:10.1207/s15327973rlsi2703_4.

Meyer, K., Rasch, T., & Schnotz, W. (2010). Effects of animation's speed of presentation on perceptual processing and learning. *Learning and Instruction, 20*(2), 136–145. doi:10.1016/j.learninstruc.2009.02.016.

Michas, I. C., & Berry, D. C. (2000). Learning a procedural task: Effectiveness of multimedia presentations. *Applied Cognitive Psychology, 14*(6), 555–575. doi:10.1002/1099-0720(200011/12)14:6<555::aid-acp677>3.0.co;2-4.

Miller, J. E. (1998). Three big hands-on noncomputer models for the biology classroom. *The American Biology Teacher, 60*(1), 52–53. doi:10.2307/4450413.

Moreno, R. (2007). Optimising learning from animations by minimising cognitive load: Cognitive and affective consequences of signalling and segmentation methods. *Applied Cognitive Psychology, 21*(6), 765–781. doi:10.1002/acp.1348.

Moreno, R., & Mayer, R. (2007). Interactive multimodal learning environments. *Educational Psychology Review, 19*(3), 309–326. doi:10.1007/s10648-007-9047-2.

Nadaner, D. (2008). Teaching perception through video art. *Art Education, 61*(1), 19–24.

Nugteren, M. L., Tabbers, H. K., Scheiter, K., & Paas, F. (2014). Simultaneous and sequential presentation of realistic and schematic intructional dynamic visualizations. In W. Huang (Ed.), *Handbook of human centric visualization* (pp. 605–622). New York: Springer. doi:10.1007/978-1-4614-7485-224.

Paas, F., & Sweller, J. (2012). An evolutionary upgrade of cognitive load theory: Using the human motor system and collaboration to support the learning of complex cognitive tasks. *Educational Psychology Review, 24*(1), 27–45. doi:10.1007/s10648-011-9179-2.

Pallrand, G. J., & Seeber, F. (1984). Spatial ability and achievement in introductory physics. *Journal of Research in Science Teaching, 21*(5), 507–516. doi:10.1002/tea.3660210508.

Park, O.-C., & Hopkins, R. (1992). Instructional conditions for using dynamic visual displays: A review. *Instructional Science, 21*(6), 427–449. doi:10.1007/BF00118557.

Ping, R. M., & Goldin-Meadow, S. (2010). Gesturing saves cognitive resources when talking about nonpresent objects. *Cognitive Science, 34*(4), 602–619. doi:10.1111/j.1551-6709.2010.01102.x.

Ping, R. M., Goldin-Meadow, S., & Beilock, S. L. (2014). Understanding gesture: Is the listener's motor system involved? *Journal of Experimental Psychology: General, 143*(1), 195–204. doi:10.1037/a0032246.

Press, C., Bird, G., Flach, R., & Heyes, C. (2005). Robotic movement elicits automatic imitation. *Cognitive Brain Research, 25*(3), 632–640. doi:10.1016/j.cogbrainres.2005.08.020.

Richland, L. E., Zur, O., & Holyoak, K. J. (2007). Cognitive supports for analogies in the mathematics classroom. *Science, 316*(5828), 1128–1129. doi:10.1126/science.1142103.

Rieber, L. P. (1990). Using computer animated graphics in science instruction with children. *Journal of Educational Psychology, 82*(1), 135–140. doi:10.1037/0022-0663.82.1.135.

Riseborough, M. G. (1981). Physiographic gestures as decoding facilitators: Three experiments exploring a neglected facet of communication. *Journal of Nonverbal Behavior, 5*(3), 172–183. doi:10.1007/BF00986134.

Rizzolatti, G., & Craighero, L. (2004). The mirror-neuron system. *Annual Review of Neuroscience, 27*, 169–192. doi:10.1146/annurev.neuro.27.070203.144230.

Rohbanfard, H., & Proteau, L. (2013). Live vs. video presentation techniques in the observational learning of motor skills. *Trends in Neuroscience and Education, 2*(1), 27–32. doi:10.1016/j.tine.2012.11.001.

Roncarrelli, R. (1989). *The computer animation dictionary: Including related terms used in computer graphics, film and video, production, and desktop publishing.* New York: Springer.

Ryoo, K., & Linn, M. C. (2012). Can dynamic visualizations improve middle school students' understanding of energy in photosynthesis? *Journal of Research in Science Teaching, 49*(2), 218–243. doi:10.1002/tea.21003.

Sánchez, C. A., & Wiley, J. (2014). The role of dynamic spatial ability in geoscience text comprehension. *Learning and Instruction, 31*, 33–45. doi:10.1016/j.learninstruc.2013.12.007.

Scheiter, K., Gerjets, P., & Catrambone, R. (2006). Making the abstract concrete: Visualizing mathematical solution procedures. *Computers in Human Behavior, 22*(1), 9–25. doi:10.1016/j.chb.2005.01.009.

Scheiter, K., Gerjets, P., & Schuh, J. (2010). The acquisition of problem-solving skills in mathematics: How animations can aid understanding of structural problem features and solution procedures. *Instructional Science, 38*(5), 487–502. doi:10.1007/s11251-009-9114-9.

Schnotz, W., & Rasch, T. (2008). Functions of animations in comprehension and learning. In R. K. Lowe & W. Schnotz (Eds.), *Learning with animation: Research implications for design* (pp. 92–113). New York: Cambridge University Press.

Shepard, R. N., & Metzler, J. (1971). Mental rotation of three-dimensional objects. *Science, 171*(3972), 701–703. doi:10.2307/1731476.

Shimada, S., & Oki, K. (2012). Modulation of motor area activity during observation of unnatural body movements. *Brain and Cognition, 80*(1), 1–6. doi:10.1016/j.bandc.2012.04.006.

Shipley, R. H., Butt, J. H., Horwitz, B., & Farbry, J. E. (1978). Preparation for a stressful medical procedure: Effect of amount of stimulus preexposure and coping style. *Journal of Consulting and Clinical Psychology, 46*(3), 499–507.

Simon, H. A., & Gilmartin, K. (1973). A simulation of memory for chess positions. *Cognitive Psychology, 5*(1), 29–46. doi:10.1016/0010-0285(73)90024-8.

Singh, A.-M., Marcus, N., & Ayres, P. (2012). The transient information effect: Investigating the impact of segmentation on spoken and written text. *Applied Cognitive Psychology, 26*(6), 848–853. doi:10.1002/acp.2885.

Sowell, E. J. (1989). Effects of manipulative materials in mathematics instruction. *Journal for Research in Mathematics Education, 20*(5), 498–505. doi:10.2307/749423.

Spangenberg, R. W. (1973). The motion variable in procedural learning. *Educational Technology Research and Development, 21*(4), 419–436.

Spanjers, I. A. E., van Gog, T., Wouters, P., & van Merriënboer, J. J. G. (2012). Explaining the segmentation effect in learning from animations: The role of pausing and temporal cueing. *Computers & Education, 59*(2), 274–280. doi:10.1016/j.compedu.2011.12.024.

Stith, B. J. (2004). Use of animation in teaching cell biology. *Cell Biology Education, 3*(3), 181–188. doi:10.1187/cbe.03-10-0018.

Stransky, D., Wilcox, L. M., & Dubrowski, A. (2010). Mental rotation: Cross-task training and generalization. *Journal of Experimental Psychology: Applied, 16*(4), 349–360. doi:10.1037/a0021702.

Sweller, J. (2005). The redundancy principle in multimedia learning. In R. E. Mayer (Ed.), *The Cambridge handbook of multimedia learning* (pp. 159–167). New York: Cambridge University Press.

Sweller, J., Ayres, P., & Kalyuga, S. (2011). *Cognitive load theory*. New York: Springer.

Tabbers, H. K., & de Koeijer, B. (2010). Learner control in animated multimedia instructions. *Instructional Science, 38*(5), 441–453. doi:10.1007/s11251-009-9119-4.

Tang, T. L.-P., & Austin, M. J. (2009). Students' perceptions of teaching technologies, application of technologies, and academic performance. *Computers & Education, 53*(4),), 1241–1255. doi: 10.1016/j.compedu.2009.06.007.

Tosi, V. (1993). *El lenguaje de las imágenes en movimiento*. English edition: How to make scientific audio-visuals for research (2nd Ed.) (trans: M. Broissin). México: Grijalbo.

Tversky, B., Morrison, J. B., & Betrancourt, M. (2002). Animation: Can it facilitate? *International Journal of Human-Computer Studies, 57*(4), 247–262. doi:10.1006/ijhc.2002.1017.

Valenzeno, L., Alibali, M. W., & Klatzky, R. (2003). Teachers' gestures facilitate students' learning: A lesson in symmetry. *Contemporary Educational Psychology, 28*(2), 187–204. doi:10.1016/S0361-476×(02)00007-3.

van Gog, T., Paas, F., Marcus, N., Ayres, P., & Sweller, J. (2009). The mirror neuron system and observational learning: Implications for the effectiveness of dynamic visualizations. *Educational Psychology Review, 21*(1), 21–30. doi:10.1007/s10648-008-9094-3.

Wai, J., Lubinski, D., & Benbow, C. P. (2009). Spatial ability for STEM domains: Aligning over 50 years of cumulative psychological knowledge solidifies its importance. *Journal of Educational Psychology, 101*(4), 817–835. doi:10.1037/a0016127.

Weidler, B. J., & Abrams, R. A. (2014). Enhanced cognitive control near the hands. *Psychonomic Bulletin & Review, 21*(2), 462–469. doi:10.3758/s13423-013-0514-0.

Wexler, M., Kosslyn, S. M., & Berthoz, A. (1998). Motor processes in mental rotation. *Cognition, 68*(1), 77–94. doi:10.1016/S0010-0277(98)00032-8.

Williamson, V. M., & Abraham, M. R. (1995). The effects of computer animation on the particulate mental models of college chemistry students. *Journal of Research in Science Teaching, 32*(5), 521–534. doi:10.1002/tea.3660320508.

Wilson, M. (2002). Six views of embodied cognition. *Psychonomic Bulletin & Review, 9*(4), 625–636. doi:10.3758/bf03196322.

Witt, J. K., Kemmerer, D., Linkenauger, S. A., & Culham, J. (2010). A functional role for motor simulation in identifying tools. *Psychological Science, 21*(9), 1215–1219. doi:10.1177/0956797610378307.

Wong, A., Marcus, N., Ayres, P., Smith, L., Cooper, G. A., Paas, F., et al. (2009). Instructional animations can be superior to statics when learning human motor skills. *Computers in Human Behavior, 25*(2), 339–347. doi:10.1016/j.chb.2008.12.012.

Yang, J. C., & Chen, S. Y. (2010). Effects of gender differences and spatial abilities within a digital pentominoes game. *Computers & Education, 55*(3), 1220–1233. doi:10.1016/j.compedu.2010.05.019.

Yang, E.-m., Andre, T., Greenbowe, T. J., & Tibell, L. (2003). Spatial ability and the impact of visualization/animation on learning electrochemistry. *International Journal of Science Education, 25*(3), 329–349. doi:10.1080/09500690210126784.

Yarden, H., & Yarden, A. (2010). Learning using dynamic and static visualizations: Students' comprehension, prior knowledge and conceptual status of a biotechnological method. *Research in Science Education, 40*(3), 375–402. doi:10.1007/s11165-009-9126-0.

Zacharia, Z. C., & Olympiou, G. (2011). Physical versus virtual manipulative experimentation in physics learning. *Learning and Instruction, 21*(3), 317–331. doi:10.1016/j.learninstruc.2010.03.001.

Juan C. Castro-Alonso is a Postdoctoral Research Fellow in the School of Education, University of New South Wales, Australia. His current research fields are Multimedia Learning, Dynamic Visualizations, Biology and Chemistry Instruction, Embodied Cognition, Educational Psychology, and Cognitive Load Theory. Before being granted a PhD in Education, Cris had been awarded a Bachelor of Biochemistry, a Postgraduate Diploma in Audiovisual Documentary Writing, and a Masters in Communication and Education. Previous to his current educational researcher role, Cris' endeavor was as producer and designer of instructional multimedia for the Faculty of Biological Sciences, Pontificia Universidad Católica de Chile.

Paul Ayres is an emeritus professor in Educational Psychology at the University of New South Wales, Sydney, Australia. His research focus is in the field of learning and instruction, particularly cognitive load theory (CLT), a theory that originated at UNSW. Much of his recent research has been into multimedia design and E-learning, specifically into the effectiveness of instructional animations, for which he has received a number of Australian Research Council grants in partnership with Professor Fred Paas (Erasmus University). He is on the Editorial board of several international journals and is an Associate Editor of Applied Cognitive Psychology.

Fred Paas a Professor of Educational Psychology at Erasmus University Rotterdam in the Netherlands and a Visiting Professorial Fellow at the University of New South Wales and the University of Wollongong in Australia. His main research interest is in interdisciplinary approaches to the instructional control of cognitive load in the training of complex cognitive tasks. He has (co-) authored over 150 publications in (S)SCI listed journals, which have been cited over 12,000 times.

Technology-Enhanced Teacher Education for 21st Century: Challenges and Possibilities

Marina Milner-Bolotin

Abstract Science, Technology, Engineering, Art and Mathematics (STEAM) education goals have transformed dramatically during the last half of the century. Presently, they include developing an appreciation of the beauty and wonder of science; possessing sufficient knowledge to engage in public discussions; becoming careful consumers of information; learning about STEAM inside and outside school; and having the skills to enter careers of their choice, including, but not limited to STEAM. Unlike their 20th century predecessors who were exploring if and how technology might enter the public education realm, modern educators focus on how technology can address these goals. At the same time, the preparation of future STEAM teachers hasn't always kept pace with the changing technology-rich educational landscape. Teachers can barely keep up with technological innovations and often end up placing the pedagogical aspects of technology engagement on the back burner. New educational goals coupled with new educational technologies should be reflected in how we prepare STEAM teachers. This chapter attempts to re-conceptualize the engagement of STEAM teachercandidates with technology during their formative years in order to help them meet these rapidly changing goals. To make the argument more meaningful, we use an example of a physics methods course in which an instructor modeled technology-enhanced active engagement pedagogy and teacher-candidates were able to experience this learning environment both as students and as future teachers. The chapter also discusses the impact of this course on teacher-candidates' Technological Pedagogical Content Knowledge (TPCK), their attitudes about science teaching and learning, and their pedagogical decision-making during the practicum.

Keywords Active engagement · Conceptual understanding · Educational technology · Peer Instruction · STEAM teacher education · STEM education · Technological Pedagogical Content Knowledge (TPCK)

M. Milner-Bolotin (✉)
University of British Columbia, Departmentn of Curriculum and Pedagogy,
UBC Faculty of Education 2125 Main Mall Vancouver, Canada V6T 1Z4
e-mail: marina.milner-bolotin@ubc.ca

© Springer International Publishing Switzerland 2015
X. Ge et al. (eds.), *Emerging Technologies for STEAM Education,*
Educational Communications and Technology: Issues and Innovations,
DOI 10.1007/978-3-319-02573-5_8

Introduction

In his introduction to the edited book "The Emperor's New Computer: ICT, Teachers and Teaching", Di Petta (2008) challenged us to look beyond the "hype and fashion" of information and communications technology (ICT) through a thorough examination of what ICT can do for improving student learning (p. 2). In particular, he called on "pragmatic re-visioning of the fable of the Emperor's New Clothes, looking behind the fashionable masks and costumes of ICT and examining how information and communication technologies affect the complex process of human interconnection known as teaching and learning" (p. 2). The ideas suggested in the book have significant ramifications for examining the current state of educational technologies' implementation in Science, Technology, Engineering, and Mathematics (STEM) education.

Almost half a century has passed since computers first began entering North American public schools and educational technology visionaries and thinkers like Alan Kay (1987) and Seymour Papert (1980) began exploring computer-assisted STEM learning. Their focus was on how people learn *with* technology and what technology can do that cannot be achieved otherwise. Nevertheless, powerful political, corporate, and educational forces, coupled with the endless barrage of new educational gadgets, devices, and software, propel many educators to continue looking for *the perfect technological solution* to the old educational problems, while ignoring the importance of pedagogically-driven implementation of these technologies. The focus on purely technological solutions divorced from solid educational research that will identify the pedagogical problems to be solved and then drive the development of technologies to solve these problems significantly diminishes the pedagogical effects of these innovations. Kay (1987) referred to this issue as "a technological tail wagging a pedagogical dog". In this chapter we raise and examine the *what, why,* and *how* questions in the context of technology-enhanced STEM teacher education. These are key pedagogical questions that we need to ask and answer again and again in order to understand how technology can be used to improve how students learn STEM disciplines (Hofer & Swan, 2008; Konold & Lehrer, 2008; Sfard, 2012). Focusing on the implementation of educational technologies, without questioning the reasons for *why* these technologies are being used and *what* pedagogical problems they are attempting to address, is doing a disservice to our teachers and students. This chapter, thus, emphasizes the importance of what we call a *deliberate technology-enhanced pedagogical practice* in STEM teacher education.

Now is the perfect time to re-examine STEM teachers' engagement with technology, while considering how technology can help teachers to reunite the arts and the sciences, thus turning STEM into STEAM (Science, Technology, Engineering, Arts, and Mathematics) education. This examination is a 1000-mile journey and we begin it with a single step: an investigation of STEM teacher-candidates' engagement with technology during their teacher education program. This engagement has a profound effect on forming their teaching philosophy, which will have a significant impact on their teaching careers. It is also very timely, as unlike their predecessors, most contemporary teacher-candidates are digital natives (Prensky, 2001a, 2001b): they were born into the "age of computers". However, as we shall see below, being digital natives does not guarantee that teacher-candidates know how to use educational technologies to promote meaningful STEM learning (Milner-Bolotin, 2014a). We focus our discussion on exploring the following question:

> *Why* and *how* should educational technologies be incorporated into STEM teacher education in order to nurture the next generation of teachers capable of designing and implementing *deliberate technology-enhanced pedagogies* in their classrooms?

This is a big question that might have many answers. It is also complicated by the fact that digital technologies are "*protean* (usable in many different ways) (Papert, 1980), *unstable* (rapidly changing), and *opaque* (their inner-workings are hidden from users) (Turkle, 1995)" (Mishra & Koehler, 2007, p. 2215).

Therefore, we will unpack this big question through answering more specific sub-questions, such as:

1. *What* are the key goals of 21st century STEM education?
2. *Why* is educational technology a valuable tool to help address these goals?
3. *How* might STEM teacher-educators implement *deliberate technology-enhanced pedagogies* in order to engage teacher-candidates in meaningful learning?

To answer these questions we need to adopt a theoretical framework that will help us critically examine available research evidence. The Technological Pedagogical Content Knowledge (TPCK) framework will serve the theoretical lens for this chapter (Koehler & Mishra, 2009; Mishra & Koehler, 2007). It is discussed in detail in the following section.

Theoretical Framework: TPCK

STEM teacher education in the 21st century is even more important and challenging than it was a century ago. Computers and new technologies haven't replaced teachers, but they have profoundly affected the roles teachers play in our schools. Unlike the STEM teachers of the 20th century, modern teachers cannot continue assuming the role of authoritative dispensers of information, as their students have an unprecedented access to it. Moreover, as these digital savvy students are very different from the students we taught in the past (Levin & Arafeh, 2002) and as STEM standards are continuously evolving (National Research Council, 2013), 21st century teachers have to learn how to use rapidly evolving technologies to address the educational challenges of the new millennium (Crippen, Biesenger, & Ebert, 2010; Gerard, Varma, Corliss, & Lin, 2011; Harris & Hofer, 2011; Krajcik & Mun, 2014).

Therefore, it is the right time to break away from the educational technology pendulum mentality that swings educators back and forth between two pedagogical extremes: from the incurable technophilia (the "unconditional love" for all technological innovations without paying attention to their potential pedagogical impact) to the unyielding educational technophobia expressed through the unabating fear and skepticism towards novel educational technologies and their potential pedagogical impact (Cuban, 2001; Cuban, Kirkpatrick, & Peck, 2001; Kirkpatrick & Cuban, 1998; Krajcik & Mun, 2014). As Cuban warned educators more than two decades ago, if we do not carefully examine the pedagogical implications of computer-based instruction and how educational technologies can help address the issues of teaching and learning, we are bound to keep reforming our educational system again, again, and again with little significant results (Cuban, 1990).

Cuban's admonition resonates with the concerns expressed by Shulman in his seminal 1986 American Educational Research Association Presidential Address (Shulman, 1986). In his paper, he traced the knowledge growth in the teaching profession in the United States over the last century and emphasized that teacher-educators should focus on helping teacher-candidates develop their Pedagogical Content Knowledge (PCK) that comprises both the content knowledge (i.e. mathematics, science, art, history) and the knowledge of pedagogical approaches relevant to teaching the content and the practices of the subject to a particular group of students. Shulman called the lack of focus on PCK in teacher education programs the "missing paradigm" problem. He emphasized that teacher-educators should not limit themselves to discussing general context-free pedagogical practices (today we can compare it with discussing general context-free educational technologies), but should embed these pedagogical practices in a subject-specific context. In Shulman's own words:

> My colleagues and I refer to the absence of focus on subject matter among the various research paradigms for the study of teaching as the "missing paradigm" problem. The consequences of this missing paradigm are serious, both for policy and for research… Research programs that arose in response to the dominance of process-product work accepted its definition of the problem and continued to *treat teaching more or less generically or at least as if the content of instruction were relatively unimportant.* (Shulman, 1986, p. 6) (italics added)

Thus, PCK for teaching physics, mathematics, art or history will undoubtedly have common elements, yet there will also be many essential subject-specific aspects. Moreover, Shulman's address clearly highlighted the difference between the knowledge of the subject matter, Content Knowledge, (the fundamental content knowledge needed for future educators, researchers, engineers, etc.) and the knowledge of the content-driven pedagogies required to be able to teach this subject (PCK).

With the development of educational technologies, Shulman's PCK framework was expanded to include the technological component. The Technological Pedagogical Content Knowledge (TPCK) framework was proposed by Koehler and Mishra (2009) to emphasize the role of educational technologies in this process. Teachers should learn how specific educational technologies can be utilized in order to promote student understanding of both the subject content and its practices. Thus, the "T" (Technological) in TPCK refers to both the mastery of the technological tools and their pedagogical implications. According to this framework, in order to help teachers acquire TPCK, they have to actively engage in designing *authentic pedagogical tasks* that use educational technologies to serve specific pedagogical purposes. This active and deliberate engagement with technology should begin early in teachers' careers. In this chapter, we argue that this process should start during the teacher education program in order to allow teacher-candidates to experience educational technologies both as learners and as future teachers (Milner-Bolotin, 2014a; Milner-Bolotin, Fisher, & MacDonald, 2013). In addition, educational technologies are tools that shape teacher-candidates' views and attitudes about teaching and learning (Milner-Bolotin, 2014a). This active pedagogically-driven engagement with educational technologies will support teacher-candidates in becoming active designers of pedagogically-driven technology-enhanced educational materials (Milner-Bolotin, 2014b).

In examining the process of engagement of STEM teacher-candidates with educational technologies, we will be guided by the techno-pragmatic approach suggested by Di Petta (2008) that focuses on technology serving specific pedagogical goals and by the TPCK framework discussed above.

Exploring STEM Teacher-Candidates' Engagement with Technology

This section explores STEM teacher-candidates' engagement with technology. We begin by identifying the key questions faced by modern STEM educators. Then we discuss how they can be addressed through pedagogically-driven use of educational technologies. We finish with the discussion of a possible model for technology-enhanced STEM teacher education and its pedagogical implications.

What are the Key Goals of 21st Century STEM Education?

STEM education has been profoundly affected by the rapid technological advances occurring in our society (Krajcik & Mun, 2014). For example, ubiquitous access to information and the availability of real life data collection tools deemphasize the importance of factual memorization, while placing a renewed emphasis on authentic problem solving and critical thinking (Eijck & Roth, 2009; Milner-Bolotin, 2012; Milner-Bolotin & Moll, 2008; Schwartz, Lederman, & Crawford, 2004). Ever increasing computing and visualization power of modern computers requires students to be able to model real life physical phenomena rather than solve highly simplified "plug-and-chug" problems (Finkelstein et al., 2005; Milner-Bolotin & Nashon, 2012). The availability of computer simulations has opened unprecedented opportunities for student-driven scientific investigations that were unimaginable before, thus requiring very different skills from the students (Perkins et al., 2006; Wieman, Adams, Loeblein, & Perkins, 2010). Lastly, the low level of scientific literacy and interest in STEM in the general population stresses the importance of improving student interest in and attitudes about STEM (Let's Talk Science, 2012, 2013; Wieman & Perkins, 2005).

These changes prompted many countries to reconsider their STEM education goals. For example, the Next Generation Science Framework (recently released U.S. Science Standards) expressed the desired science outcomes for the 21st century through five distinct STEM learning goals:

> The overarching goal of our framework for K-12 science education is to ensure that by the end of 12th grade, *all* students (1) have some appreciation of the beauty and wonder of science; (2) possess sufficient knowledge of science and engineering to engage in public discussions on related issues; (3) are careful consumers of scientific and technological information related to their everyday lives; (4) are able to continue to learn about science outside school; and (5) have the skills to enter careers of their choice, including (but not limited to) careers in science, engineering, and technology. (Committee on a Conceptual Framework for New K-12 Science Education Standards, 2013, p. 14) (numbering added)

The five STEM education goals outlined above emphasize the importance of engaging students in inquiry-based authentic problem-solving which extends beyond the traditional classroom science. For example, modern art, architecture and design require deep STEM knowledge, while "the appreciation of the beauty of science" highlights the reciprocity of arts and sciences. Technology is viewed as a vehicle for exploration of science and mathematics ideas permeating the world we live in, a tool for engineering design, artistic expression, as well as a field of inquiry within itself.

> Engineering and technology are featured alongside the physical sciences, life sciences, and earth and space sciences for two critical reasons: to reflect the importance of understanding the human-built world and to recognize the value of better integrating the teaching and learning of science, engineering, and technology. (Committee on a Conceptual Framework for New K-12 Science Education Standards, 2013, p. 18)

The successful implementation of these Standards will require STEM teachers to reconsider the role of technology in their classrooms. This, in turn, will necessiatate teachers to acquire a STEM-specific TPCK. The following section uses three subject-specific examples to illustrate how educational technology can help address these 21st century STEM education goals.

How Can Technology Help Address 21st Century STEM Goals?

This section briefly outlines three examples of technology-enhanced pedagogies that help address the STEM education goals mentioned above. The first example illustrates the use of live acquisition systems to conduct authentic investigations. The second one focuses on the use of computer simulations and visualizations. The last example illustrates how electronic response systems (clickers) can be used to engage students in conceptual science learning in order to promote their critical thinking skills.

Using Data Acquisition Systems to Promote Authentic STEM Learning

In order to help students develop appreciation of STEM, it is important to engage them in authentic investigations that are rooted in everyday life phenomena (Eijck

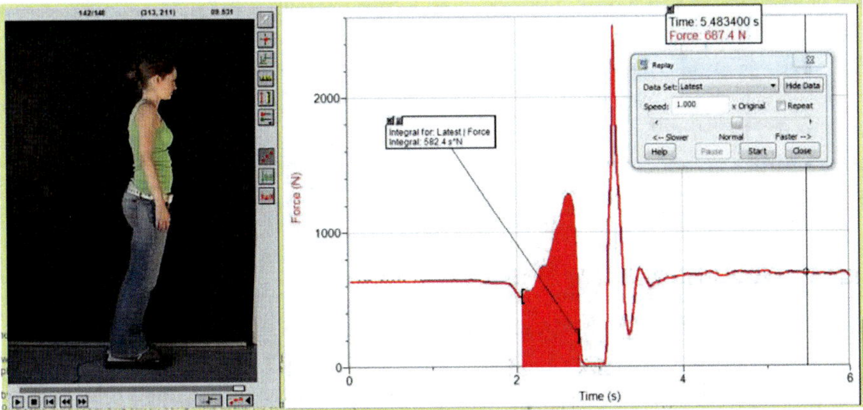

Fig. 1 An analysis of a student's jump off a scale performed using a Logger Pro data acquisition system. The student is standing on a digital scale that records the force exerted by the student (which is often incorrectly interpreted as student's weight) and sends it to a computer

& Roth, 2009; Milner-Bolotin, 2012). This also helps students become critical consumers of STEM-related information. These inquiry activities rely on students' ability to collect and analyze real-life data using data acquisition systems, such as Logger Pro (Vernier-Technology, 2015). These data acquisition systems include various sensors (hardware) and software available for data analysis that allow synchronous or asynchronous data acquisition and analysis. In addition, sensor-driven data acquisition can be combined with video recording of the experiment to help students connect multiple representations of the same phenomenon, such as graphs, video recording, equations, etc. For example, data of a student jumping off a force plate can be collected in class, such as shown in Fig. 1. The students can then perform an analysis of this data, connecting theoretical knowledge (learning about Newton's laws) with practical applications and kinesthetic experiences (Milner-Bolotin, Kotlicki, & Rieger, 2007). Moreover, the students can video record experiments or everyday life phenomena outside of class, such as water coming out of a water hose, various moving objects, collisions, launch of a water rocket, etc. Then these files can be imported into video analysis software to conduct a frame-by-frame investigation (Antimirova & Milner-Bolotin, 2009). This is especially valuable as many scientific phenomena happen at very short time scales and slowing them down can reveal a lot of interesting and often hidden information. In addition, students can analyze video files posted by others on the internet, for example, short-lived phenomena, such as collisions and objects' deformations recorded with very expensive equipment (for example, a fast speed camera) that might not be available to the students (Brown, 2010).

Data acquisition systems can also be used to engage students in authentic inquiry-based learning that is akin to a scientific process through asking students to make predictions based on scientific concepts they studied earlier and then test these predictions in real time (Milner-Bolotin, 2012; Sokoloff & Thornton, 2004). This helps students to transform scientific facts into scientific ideas and explore their implications in classroom science and everyday life. This is crucial for helping students develop critical thinking capacities and become critical consumers of science-related information. Henri Poincare once said "Science is built up with facts, as a house is with stones. But a collection of facts is no more a science than a heap of stones is a house". To help students realize that the power of scientific ideas is their ability to predict the results of new experiments and new phenomena, the students have to have an opportunity to experience this first hand and not just to read about it in textbooks (Etkina et al., 2010).

Use of Computer Simulations and Modeling Software to Promote Scientific Mind Set and Critical Thinking Skills

While data collection and analysis are crucial components of authentic scientific inquiry, not every experiment can be performed under "real-life" conditions. And even if an experiment can be performed, the scientific mechanism behind it might be invisible "to the naked eye". For example, in recent years due to the Fukushima disaster there have been a lot of discussions about the effects of nuclear power plants and radiation in general on our lives. While the topic of radiation prominently featured in public debate, few laypeople possess scientific knowledge to be able to critically participate in such a discussion. Computer simulations, such as the PhET project (Wieman et al., 2010) is an example of a suite of STEM computer simulations built on solid educational research evidence (Figs. 2 and 3). These simulations help students not only to understand scientific concepts, such as radioactive decay shown in Fig. 2, but also conduct scientific investigations in these virtual environments. Since many of these simulations are free, they can be used by the

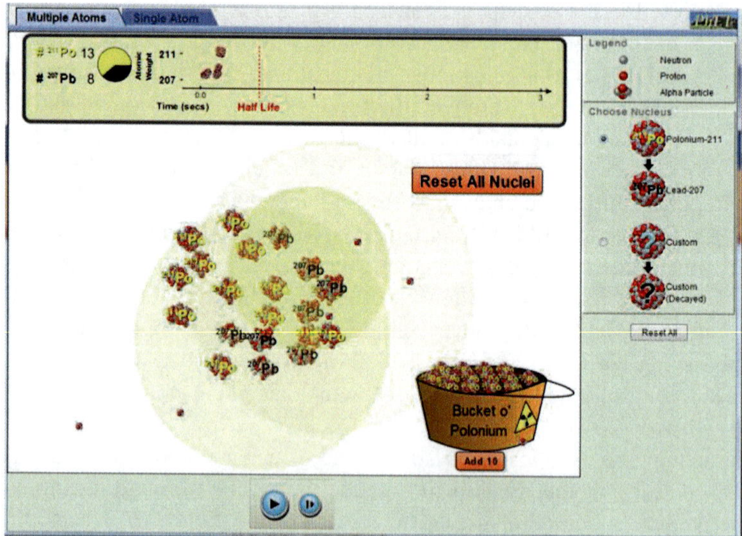

Fig. 2 PhET computer simulation "Alpha Decay"

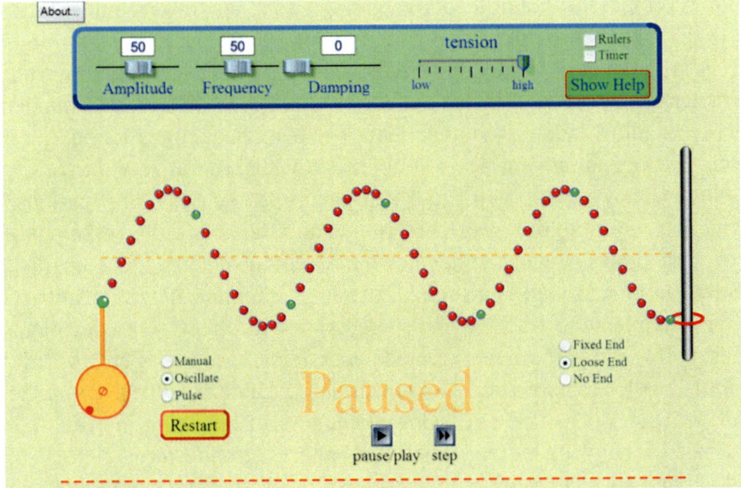

Fig. 3 PhET computer simulation "Waves on a string"

students both in school and at home. Simulations can also help students understand the relationships between the sciences and the arts. For example, through exploring computer simulations of the natural phenomena such as radioactivity, light and sound, the students can understand the workings of musical instruments, and appreciate scientific contributions to the realms of arts, architecture, music, medicine, environment and everyday life (Figs. 2 and 3).

The investigations of the physical properties of waves (Fig. 3) and their applications to the design of musical instruments and the production of sound become especially meaningful when students, many of whom are interested in music, realize these connections (Jeans, 1968). Moreover, many famous scientists, such as Sir James H. Jeans mentioned above were also musicians and artists, making the modern distinction between the arts and the sciences a relatively recent phenomenon. Lastly, the recent symbiosis of the arts and the sciences in the realm of the digital arts, such as visual effects in film, television, and video game production, helps build bridges between the fields, producing very powerful STEAM education opportunities. It enriches students from both the arts and the sciences and opens new creative opportunities in both fields.

As a result of the proliferation of computer simulations, there has been a lot of interest in comparing student learning in virtual and real-life learning environments. Ample research indicates that learning in virtual environments has significant benefits for promoting student conceptual understanding (Finkelstein et al., 2005). Moreover, as indicated earlier, virtual learning environments have an additional benefit: students can test their ideas and receive immediate feedback to guide their investigation. This is not as easy to implement with real-life equipment. Lastly, it has to be noted that as with any technology, the pedagogical effect of computer simulations in STEM classrooms depends on teachers' abilities to implement them effectively in day-to-day instruction and align these activities with the final assessment.

Another prominent example of technology that empowers students to apply STEM to their lives through bridging the arts and the sciences, thus turning STEM into STEAM, is dynamic modeling software, such as GeoGebra (Hohenwarter, 2014) or Geometer's Sketchpad (Sinclair & Yurita, 2008). These dynamic mathematical software tools allow students to experience mathematical construction, the interdependencies between mathematical variables and visual (often very artistically beautiful) objects. Unlike traditional paper and pencil geometrical constructions, where a construction or a graphical representation cannot be changed or manipulated easily, GeoGebra allows students to develop a mathematical language, dynamically test their understanding, as well as visualize abstract mathematical relationships. GeoGebra is freely available to teachers and students, and the GeoGebra educational community is a powerful community-created pedagogical resource (Fenyvesi, Budinski, & Lavicza, 2014; Hohenwarter, Hohenwarter, & Lavicza, 2008). Dynamic mathematical software opens doors to using mathematical modeling in order to explore the relationships between art (e.g. paintings, patterns, architecture, textile, and mosaics) and mathematics. The dynamic features of GeoGebra or Geometer's Sketchpad allow students to manipulate geometrical shapes, visualize abstract mathematical concepts and search for mathematical patterns and relationships behind everyday life phenomena, artistic artifacts, or natural phenomena. For example, students can use GeoGebra to explore regular and semi-regular tessellations, mosaics and geometrical patterns, and their use in art and architecture (many of these activities can be found on GeoGebraTube—www.geogebratube.org) (Fig. 4).

Fig. 4 An example of a construction of a cycloid bounded by tangent lines using GeoGebra software (http://www.talljerome.com/mathnerd.html)

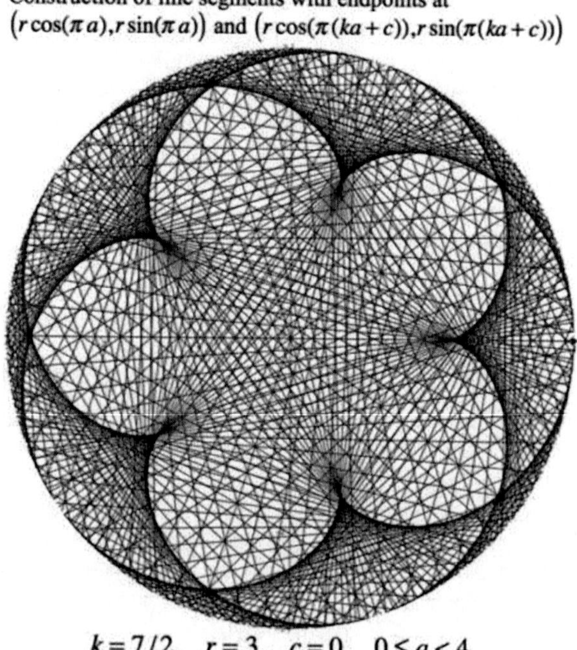

One of the most striking modern examples of the deep interconnections of all elements of STEAM fields is the use of art "powered" by mathematics and science in modern movies and animation films. Recently Tony DeRose—a computer scientist working with artists and animators at Pixar Animation Studios—presented an invited talk "Math in Movies" at the Mathematics Association of America Distinguished Lecture Series. In this talk he noted:

> There is indeed a lot of mathematics behind the scenes… In each of these animated films, constructed entirely on computers, trigonometry helps rotate and move characters, algebra creates the special effects that make images shine and sparkle, and integral calculus helps light the scenes. (http://www.maa.org/news/interview-tony-derose, October 15, 2009)

These are only few examples of powerful interconnections of STEAM disciplines and the growing opportunities for productive and creative collaborations of artists, scientists and mathematicians. In order to help students to see these opportunities we have to educate a new generation of STEAM teachers who are ready to use technology in order to engage their students in meaningful learning.

Use of Electronic Response Systems to Promote Active Student Engagement and Meaningful Learning

In order to help students relate STEM disciplines to their lives and build the knowledge that they can use outside of school, students have to be actively engaged not only during labs and hands-on activities, but also during "traditional" lessons (Hake, 1998).

One of the most common active engagement pedagogies in postsecondary STEM classrooms is Peer Instruction (PI) (Lasry, Mazur, & Watkins, 2008; Mazur, 1997). It utilizes Classroom Response Systems (clickers) to engage students in interactive activities and discussions through conceptual multiple-choice questions that target student difficulties, often referred to as misconceptions (Milner-Bolotin et al., 2013) (Fig. 5).

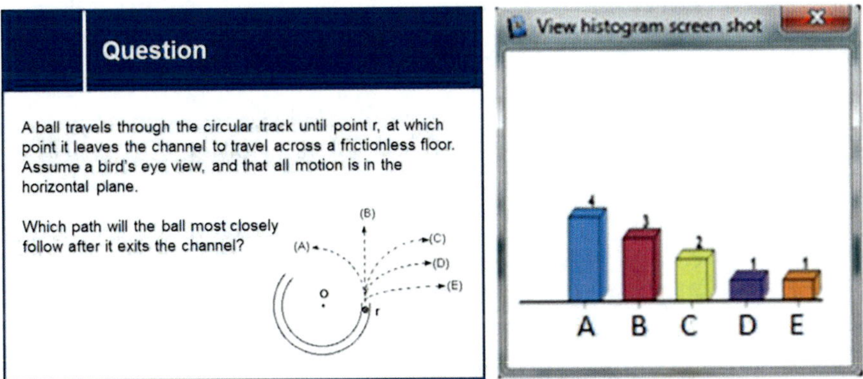

Fig. 5 An example of a conceptual multiple-choice question and the distribution of students' responses. The correct answer B was chosen by 3 out of 11 students

PI has been found to be very effective in college STEM classrooms when students used either clickers (Hake, 1998; Milner-Bolotin, Antimirova, & Petrov, 2010) or flashcards (Lasry, 2008). However, due to its cost (each student has to have a clicker to take part in the voting), PI has not been widely used in K-12 classrooms. With the advent of new cost-effective models for its implementations (such as using smartphones or tablets instead of clickers), it is becoming more popular in secondary schools. We have written about the implementation of this pedagogy (Kalman, Milner-Bolotin, & Antimirova, 2010; Milner-Bolotin, 2004; Milner-Bolotin et al., 2013). There is extensive research evidence that the success of PI or any other clicker-enhanced pedagogy is not in the technology itself, but in the pedagogical skills of the teachers and in the quality of the available resources (Milner-Bolotin et al., 2013). These findings highlight the importance of developing teacher-candidates' TPCK during teacher education programs, so teachers will be ready to utilize this technology when it becomes available in their classrooms (Milner-Bolotin, 2014b).

How Should STEM Teacher-Educators Implement Technology-Enhanced Learning Environments: Exploring Possible Models for Technology-Enhanced STEM Teacher Education

While it is impossible to prepare teacher-candidates for all the technological innovations that are to emerge during their careers, they should begin the acquisition of their TPCK as soon as they enter the teacher education program (Milner-Bolotin et al., 2013). Teacher-candidates should be engaged in thinking about technology as a vehicle to help promote STEM educational goals. Therefore, the main argument of this chapter is that in order to prepare STEM teacher-candidates for a successful teaching career in the 21st century, they have to experience multiple support mechanisms during their teacher education program. In particular, science methods courses have to support teacher-candidates in:

a. Learning how to utilize educational technologies as enablers of big pedagogical ideas;
b. Experiencing active technology-enhanced engagement as learners and as teachers;
c. Adopting pedagogical values congruent with this technology-enhanced active engagement;
d. Designing and implementing technology-enhanced educational materials that serve clear pedagogical purposes.

The following section will expand on what we mean by the four-way support structure through a study situated in the context of physics teacher education at a large research university in Western Canada. The study took place during a semester-long physics methods course and a 13-week school practicum that followed. The goal of the study was to explore how educational technologies can be used to help STEM teacher-candidates acquire subject-specific TPCK and to translate this knowledge into active engagement pedagogical practices during the consequent school practicum and hopefully during their future STEM teaching.

Developing Teacher-Candidates' TPCK Through Modeling Peer Instruction in a Physics Methods Course

As discussed earlier, while Peer Instruction (PI) is very common in large undergraduate courses, it is still rare in K-12 classrooms. It is also seldom found in STEM methods courses. One of the commonly cited reasons for not using this technology in teacher education is the cost of the system and the reluctance of schools to spend money on it. Yet, with the developments of smartphone technologies and the Bring-Your-Own-Device "revolution" in K-12 schools, it is becoming apparent that this technology will soon penetrate the school walls. Two questions remain: (1) Will the teachers with the access to this technology have the TPCK necessary to draw pedagogical benefits from PI and question-driven pedagogy? and (2) What can teacher educators do in order to assure that PI will not become another example of a technological fad that will fade away as soon as it came? Our response to these questions is preparing teacher-candidates through incorporating PI into the physics methods course. We described how we have done it in detail elsewhere (Milner-Bolotin et al., 2013). We briefly outline the study below.

The study was conducted in a Physics Methods course in the Teacher Education Program at a large research university in Western Canada during the 2012–2013 academic year. The course lasted for one term (39 h in total) and included 13 physics teacher-candidates. It took place in a flexible laboratory environment so that different modes of student engagement were able to be implemented during the same class period. PI pedagogy was modeled during every class meeting.

In order to help teacher-candidates see the big pedagogical ideas behind PI and learn how clicker-enhanced pedagogy should be implemented, the course began with a discussion of the importance of active student engagement and how PI helps promote it in a physics teaching context. Research evidence was brought and discussed during the class (Hake, 1998). Then the instructor focused on student conceptual learning and the development of pedagogically effective conceptual questions (Beatty, Gerace, Leonard, & Dufresne, 2006). At the same time, different conceptual multiple-choice questions were modeled and teacher-candidates were invited to participate in PI pedagogy first as students and consequently as teachers. This dual experience of technology-enhanced pedagogy by teacher-candidates (both as students and as future teachers) was central to the course philosophy. Teacher-candidates were also encouraged to use a special resource of STEM conceptual questions designed by our research team that modeled effective conceptual questions (Milner-Bolotin, 2015). This provided pedagogical support and scaffolding required for mastering the necessary TPCK. This brought up many discussions about the value of powerful distractors (incorrect choices in a multiple-choice question) and the ability to test different scientific hypotheses with the students. It also opened doors to the discussion about how various technologies were utilized in order to support active student engagement, conceptual learning, and building bridges between science as experienced in class and as experienced in everyday life. This helped teacher-candidates not only to experience this technology-enhanced pedagogy, but also to slowly uncover and adopt the pedagogical values associated with its pedagogically effective use.

As teacher-candidates' TPCK strengthened, they were asked to start working on designing their own conceptual questions (every teacher-candidate was required to submit five conceptual multiple-choice questions). These questions had to include clear pedagogical purposes and detailed explanations of the distractors. The course instructor and a Teaching Assistant provided detailed formative feedback on these questions. In addition, the questions were shared between the group members so that teacher-candidates had an opportunity to comment on them and exchange ideas. During the following year, the PeerWise system (Denny, 2014) was used to promote effective sharing and collaboration of conceptual multiple-choice questions designed by teacher-candidates (Milner-Bolotin, 2014b). PeerWise is an online collaborative database that allows students to upload their multiple-choice questions (including solutions), respond to the questions designed by their peers, rate these questions, provide comments, and respond to the comments provided by their peers and the course instructor.

This methods course was followed by a 10-week school practicum where teacher-candidates were able to teach physics lessons and implement the pedagogy of their choice, including PI, in practice. During their school practicum teacher-candidates were observed by their school and university advisors, as well as by the physics methods course instructor.

In the following section, we will briefly outline the results of the research study that investigated the effects of this pedagogy on teacher-candidates' TPCK, their attitudes about active engagement, and their views on the nature of science and of science education.

The Effects of PI Modeling on Teacher-Candidates' TPCK and Their Attitudes About Science Teaching and Learning

In order to investigate the effects of modeling PI pedagogy on teacher-candidates' TPCK and their attitudes about science teaching and learning we collected and analyzed conceptual questions contributed by the teacher-candidates. We also conducted multiple individual interviews with teacher-candidates and a focus group during the year and observed their teaching during the practicum that followed the course. In addition, we collected teacher-candidates' reflections and observed their behavior during class. We described this analysis in detail elsewhere (Milner-Bolotin et al., 2013). Here we would like to outline a few of the most important findings.

1. Teacher-candidates acquired PCK necessary for designing pedagogically effective conceptual multiple-choice questions. The questions submitted at the end of the course were rated using Bloom's Taxonomy of Educational objectives

(1956). Their average cognitive level corresponded to the application level on Bloom's taxonomy. Most of the questions targeted specific conceptual difficulties, were scientifically accurate, and had meaningful distractors that were justified by the teacher-candidates.

2. Teacher-candidates used technology, such as computer simulations and data acquisition systems to design inquiry-driven questions that integrated experimental and theoretical knowledge and skills in order to achieve specific pedagogical goals. This required them to possess significant TPCK.

3. Teacher-candidates modeled different ways of PI implementation during the methods course. A number of them also implemented PI during the practicum using clickers, smartphones, or flashcards. This illustrates that they were able to transfer the TPCK they acquired in the methods course to their practicum.

4. The interviews and focus group discussion indicated that teacher-candidates' active engagement during their physics methods course had a significant positive effect on their teaching philosophy and their views on the importance of student engagement in science. Teacher-candidates not only learned about new educational technologies, but also began seeing technology as a powerful tool to promote deeper conceptual understanding and meaningful science learning.

We will finish this section with a few quotes from the teacher-candidates. These teacher-candidates discussed how clicker-enhanced pedagogy can become a mechanism for promoting active student engagement and conceptual science learning. These quotes shed light on the emergence of teacher-candidates' TPCK and their views about the role of technology in STEM education:

> It wasn't just the clickers alone. It was also in…. the presentation of the question. It wasn't a simple plug in the answer-type question. It had to be conceptual, in which you could promote …, the Bloom's taxonomy, the higher learning of students. So, in itself, clickers… is only a tool. But it needs to be complemented with good conceptual questions in order to make it work (Teacher-candidate E).

> … Some of the physics 11 s who are just doing it to do a science, and are just, 'Alright, Physics, I'll try it out.' Some of them were not as engaged, and I think doing the… voting-style questions helped get them more into it and more involved. So I'd say… it's helpful to get those students who hide at the back in these 30 person classes (Teacher-candidate C).

The third quote sheds light on the teacher-candidates' views on the nature of science and their science teaching philosophy:

> … physics is…not about applying formulas, and doing math. It is…about gaining an appreciation of the world around us. And, being able to use your understanding and extrapolate … explain what's happening around you… (Teacher-candidate A).

These quotes highlight the importance of active pedagogical engagement of STEM teacher-candidates in their methods courses and the role of technology in this process. As we described in the beginning of this section, in order to promote meaningful teacher-candidates' engagement with technology, teacher educators should model it in the classroom, allow teacher-candidates to experience the effects of technology-enhanced pedagogies on their own learning, support them in adopting the philosophical values congruent with the use of this technology, and provide teacher-candidates with safe opportunities to practice the implementation of these technology-enhanced pedagogies into practice.

While this physics methods course used technology extensively, teacher-candidates realized that technology was a vehicle for promoting active engagement and not the purpose within itself. This pedagogically-driven technology-enhanced engagement had a positive impact on their teaching philosophy and views on the nature of science teaching. This brings us back to the techno-pragmatic approach suggested by Di Petta (2008), as the success of technology-enhanced pedagogy should be judged not by the extent of the technology use, but by the impact of technology that was used in achieving clear pedagogical goals.

Conclusions and Future Directions

This chapter examined the 21st century pedagogical goals that can be addressed through STEM teacher-candidates' engagement with technology. It also discussed the possibilities of using modern technologies in order to bring the "A" into STEAM education, such as computer simulations, dynamic mathematical software, and virtual learning environments. We outlined *why* active technology engagement should become an important part of teacher education programs and *how* technology can be incorporated into STEM methods courses. We also discussed how modern educational technologies can help build bridges between the arts and the sciences, thus engaging teacher-candidates and consequently students involved in STEAM education at a more meaningful level. This active engagement should become the first step in helping teacher-candidates build solid TPCK and positive attitudes about educational technologies. More importantly, technology can provide opportunities for interdisciplinary projects, where students and teachers with different interests, skills and backgrounds can collaborate to create meaningful artefacts, exploring architectural designs, tessellations, the occurrence of special mathematical curves and shapes in art and nature, fractals, animation, visual effects, etc. We focused on three types of educational technologies pertinent to STEM (and possibly STEAM): data acquisition systems, computer simulations and dynamic visualization software, and electronic response systems. We provided examples of how they were used in a physics methods course for secondary physics teachers. We also discussed the effects of these technologies on teacher-candidates' TPCK, their teaching philosophies, and their views on the nature of STEAM teaching.

The main conclusion of this chapter is that in order to help STEAM teachers develop positive attitudes about educational technologies, they have to have an opportunity to start building their TPCK during their formative teacher education years. Teacher-candidates should also have ample opportunities to experience these technologies both as students and as future teachers. STEAM methods courses in teacher education programs are perfect opportunities for teacher-candidates to acquire these experiences in a safe and supportive environment. Moreover, STEAM education research on the effective use of educational technologies should become a theoretical base for these methods courses. Teacher-candidates should also be encouraged to read these papers and incorporate their results in their lesson planning. This will build much needed and often missing bridges between the results of STEAM education research and STEAM education practice.

Technology has the potential to become a very powerful educational tool, yet in order to benefit from it teachers have to be continuously supported in the development of their TPCK. It is not surprising that technology will be as effective as the TPCK of the teachers who are implementing it. We strongly believe that figuring out effective ways of providing this support to teacher-candidates, as well as to practicing teachers will become the focus of extensive STEAM education research in the coming decades.

Acknowledgements I would like to acknowledge the Teaching and Learning Enhancement Fund at the University of British Columbia for their continuous support. I also would like to acknowledge Davor Egersdorfer for his help with editing this chapter.

References

Antimirova, T., & Milner-Bolotin, M. (2009). A brief Introduction to Video Analysis. *Physics in Canada, 65*, 74.

Beatty, I. D., Gerace, W. J., Leonard, W. J., & Dufresne, R. J. (2006). Designing effective questions for classroom response systems teaching. *American Journal of Physics, 74*(1), 31–39.

Bloom, B. S. (1956). *Taxonomy of educational objectives: Cognitive domain* (Vol. 1). New York: Longman.

Brown, D. (2010). Tracker: Open source physics Java Video Analysis. http://www.cabrillo.edu/~dbrown/tracker/. Accessed 25 April 2010.

Committee on a Conceptual Framework for New K-12 Science Education Standards. (2013). *A framework for K-12 science education: Practices, crosscutting concepts, and core ideas.* Washington, D. C.: The National Academies Press.

Crippen, K. J., Biesenger, K. D., & Ebert, E. E. (2010). Using professional development to achieve classroom reform and science proficiency: An urban success story from Southern Nevada. *Professional Development in Education, 36*(4), 637–661.

Cuban, L. (1990). Reforming again, again, and again. *Educational Researcher, 19*(1), 3–13.

Cuban, L. (2001). *Oversold and underused: Computers in the classroom.* Cambridge: Harvard University Press Review.

Cuban, L., Kirkpatrick, H., & Peck, C. (2001). High access and low use of technologies in high school classrooms: Explaining an apparent paradox. *American Educational Research Journal, 38*(4), 813–834.

Denny, P. (2014). PeerWise. http://peerwise.cs.auckland.ac.nz/. Accessed 10 April 2014.

Di Petta, T. (2008). *The emperor's new computer: ICT, teachers and teaching.* Rotterdam: Sense Publishers.

Eijck, M., & Roth, W. M. (2009). Authentic science experiences as a vehicle to change students' orientations towards science and scientific career choices: Learning from the path followed by Brad. *The Culture of Science Education, 4*, 611–638.

Etkina, E., Karelina, A., Ruibal-Villasenor, M., Rosengrant, D., Jordan, R., & Hmelo-Silver, C. E. (2010). Design and reflection help students develop scientific abilities: Learning in introductory physics laboratories. *Journal of the Learning Sciences, 19*(1), 54–98. doi:10.1080/10508400903452876.

Fenyvesi, K., Budinski, N., & Lavicza, Z. (2014). *Two solutions to an unsolvable problem: Connecting origami and GeoGebra in a Serbian high school*. Paper presented at the Bridges 2014: Mathematics, Music, Art, Architecture, Culture, Seoul, South Korea.

Finkelstein, N. D., Adams, W. K., Keller, C. J., Kohl, P. B., Perkins, K. K., Podolefsky, N. S., & LeMaster, R. (2005). When learning about the real world is better done virtually: A study of substituting computer simulations for laboratory equipment. *Physical Review Special Topics— Physics Education Research, 1*(1), 010103.

Gerard, L. F., Varma, K., Corliss, S. B., & Lin, M. C. (2011). Professional development for technology-enhanced inquiry science. *Review of Educational Research, 81*(3), 408–448.

Hake, R. R. (1998). Interactive-engagement versus traditional methods: A six-thousand-student survey of mechanics test data for introductory physics courses. *American Journal of Physics, 66*(1), 64–74.

Harris, J. B., & Hofer, M. J. (2011). Technological Pedagogical Content Knowledge (TPACK) in action: A descriptive study of secondary teachers' curriculum-based, technology-related instructional planning. *Journal of Research on Technology in Education, 43*(3), 211–229.

Hofer, M., & Swan, K. O. (2008). Technological Pedagogical Content Knowledge in action: A case study of a Middle School Digital Documentary Project. *Journal of Research on Technology in Education, 41*(2), 179–200.

Hohenwarter, M. (2014). GeoGebra: www.geogebra.org. Accessed 17 June 2015.

Hohenwarter, J., Hohenwarter, M., & Lavicza, Z. (2008). Introducing dynamic mathematics software to secondary school teachers: The case of GeoGebra. *Journal of Computers in Mathematics and Science Teaching, 28*(2), 135–146.

Jeans, S. J. (1968). *Science & music*. Toronto: General Publishing Company.

Kalman, C. S., Milner-Bolotin, M., & Antimirova, T. (2010). Comparison of the effectiveness of collaborative groups and Peer Instruction in a large introductory physics course for science majors. *Canadian Journal of Physics, 88*(5), 325–332.

Kay, A. (Producer). (1987). Doing with images makes symbols. The Distinguished Lecture Series: Industry leaders in computer science. https://www.youtube.com/watch?v=0oonXT-gYjU. Accessed 17 June 2015.

Kirkpatrick, H., & Cuban, L. (1998). Computers make kids smarter—right? *Technos Quarterly, 7*(2), 26–31.

Koehler, M. J., & Mishra, P. (2009). What is technological pedagogical content knowledge? *Contemporary Issues in Technology and Teacher Education, 9*(1), 60–70.

Konold, C., & Lehrer, R. (2008). Technology and mathematics education: An essay in honor of Jim Kaput. In H. o. I. R. i. M. Education (Ed.), *Handbook of international research in mathematics education* (2nd ed.). New York: Handbook of International Research in Mathematics Education.

Krajcik, J. S., & Mun, K. (2014). Promises and challenges of using learning technologies to promote student learning of science. In L. Norman G & S. K. Abell (Eds.), *Handbook of research on science education* (Vol. II, pp. 337–360). New York: Routledge.

Lasry, N. (2008). Clickers or flashcards: Is there really a difference? *The Physics Teacher, 46*(5), 242–244.

Lasry, N., Mazur, E., & Watkins, J. (2008). Peer instruction: From Harvard to the two-year college. *American Journal of Physics, 76*(11), 1066–1069.

Let's Talk Science. (2012). Spotlight on science learning: A benchmark of Canadian talent (p. 40). Canada: Amgen.

Let's Talk Science. (2013). *Spotlight on science learning: The high cost of dropping science and math*. Toronto: Let's Talk Science.

Levin, D., & Arafeh, S. (2002). The digital disconnect: The widening cap betweem internet savvy students and their schools. In L. Rainie & A. Lenhart (Eds.), *Pew internet & American life project* (p. 37). Washington, D. C.: American Institutes for Research.

Mazur, E. (1997). *Peer instruction: User's manual*. Upper Saddle River: Prentice Hall.

Milner-Bolotin, M. (2004). Tips for using a peer response system in the large introductory Physics classroom. *The Physics Teacher, 42*(8), 47–48.

Milner-Bolotin, M. (2012). Increasing interactivity and authenticity of chemistry instruction through data acquisition systems and other technologies. *Journal of Chemical Education, 89*(4), 477–481.

Milner-Bolotin, M. (2014a). Promoting research-based physics teacher education in Canada: Building bridges between theory and practice. *Physics in Canada, 70*(2), 99–101.

Milner-Bolotin, M. (2014b). Using PeerWise to promote student collaboration on design of conceptual multiple-choice questions. *Physics in Canada, 70*(3), 149–150.

Milner-Bolotin, M. (2015). Mathematics and Science Teaching and Learning through Technologies. 2014, http://scienceres-edcp-educ.sites.olt.ubc.ca/. Accessed 17 June 2015.

Milner-Bolotin, M., & Moll, R. F. (2008). Physics exam problems reconsidered: Using logger pro technology to evaluate student understanding of physics. *The Physics Teacher, 46*(8), 494–500.

Milner-Bolotin, M., & Nashon, S. (2012). The essence of student visual–spatial literacy and higher order thinking skills in undergraduate biology. *Protoplasma, 249*(1), 25–30. doi:10.1007/s00709-011-0346-6.

Milner-Bolotin, M., Kotlicki, A., & Rieger, G. (2007). Can students learn from lecture demonstrations: The role and place of interactive lecture experiments in large introductory science courses. *Journal of College Science Teaching, 36*(4), 45–49.

Milner-Bolotin, M., Antimirova, T., & Petrov, A. (2010). Clickers beyond the first year science classroom. *Journal of College Science Teaching, 40*(2), 18–22.

Milner-Bolotin, M., Fisher, H., & MacDonald, A. (2013). Modeling active engagement pedagogy through classroom response systems in a physics teacher education course. *LUMAT: Research and Practice in Math, Science and Technology Education, 1*(5), 525–544.

Mishra, P., & Koehler, M. J. (26 March 2007). *Technological Pedagogical Content Knowledge (TPCK): Confronting the wicked problems of teaching with technology.* Paper presented at the Society for Information Technology & Teacher Education International Conference, San-Antionio, TX.

National Research Council. (2013). *Next generation science standards: For States, by States* (Committee on Conceptual Framework for the New K-12 Science Education Standards (Ed.)). Washington, D. C.: The National Academies Press.

Papert, S. (1980). *Mindstorms: Children, computers and powerful ideas.* New York: Basic Books, Inc., Publishers.

Perkins, K., Adams, W., Dubson, M., Finkelstein, N., Reid, S., Wieman, C., & LeMaster, R. (2006). PhET: Interactive simulations for teaching and learning physics. *The Physics Teacher, 44,* 18–23.

Prensky, M. (2001a). Digital natives, digital immigrants part I: A new way to look at ourselves and our kids. *On the Horizons, 9*(5), 1–6.

Prensky, M. (2001b). Digital natives, digital immigrants part II: Do they really think differently? *On the Horizons, 9*(6), 1–9.

Schwartz, S., Lederman, G., & Crawford, A. (2004). Developing views of nature of science in an authentic context: An explicit approach to bridging the gap between nature of science and scientific inquiry. *Science Education, 88,* 610–645.

Sfard, A. (2012). New clothes—and no emperor. *For the Learning of Mathematics, 32,* 2–4.

Shulman, L. S. (1986). Those who understand: Knowledge growth in teaching. *Educational Researcher, 15*(2), 4–14.

Sinclair, N., & Yurita, V. (2008). To be or to become: How dynamic geometry changes discourse. *Research in Mathematics Education, 10*(2), 135–150.

Sokoloff, D. R., & Thornton, R. K. (2004). *Interactive lecture demonstrations: Active learning in introductory physics.* Danvers: Wiley.

Turkle, S. (1995). Life on the screen: Identity in the age of the internet. New York: Simon and Schuster.

Vernier-Technology. (2015). *Logger Pro (Version 3.6.1).* Portland: Vernier Technology. www.vernier.com. Accessed 17 June 2015.

Wieman, C., & Perkins, K. (2005). Transforming physics education. *Physics Today, 58*(11), 36–42.

Wieman, C. E., Adams, W. K., Loeblein, P., & Perkins, K. K. (2010). Teaching physics using PhET simulations. *The Physics Teacher, 48,* 225–227.

Marina Milner-Bolotin is an Assistant Professor at the Department of Curriculum and Pedagogy at the University of British Columbia, Vancouver, Canada. She earned her M.Sc. in theoretical physics at Kharkov National University in Ukraine in 1991, and M.A. and Ph.D. in mathematics and science education, at the University of TX at Austin (2000/2001). Her research interests focus on the investigation of the impact of educational technologies on science (physics) teaching and learning and on using educational technologies to promote conceptual understanding and student interest in science. As part of her studies, she investigates how educational technology can be used in STEM teacher education and studies the impact of technology-enhanced methods courses on future teachers' science knowledge, attitudes about active learning, and their pedagogical practices. She leads a team that designs research-based educational materials for K-12 mathematics and science teaching and learning (http://scienceres-edcp-educ.sites.olt.ubc.ca/). Prior to becoming a member of the UBC Faculty of Education, she was a middle and secondary school STEM teacher in Israel (1991–1998) and an instructor in undergraduate introductory physics courses in the United States and in Canada (1998–2009). In 2010, she was awarded a Canadian Associaton of Physicists' Medal for Excellence in Undergraduate Physics Teaching.

Using Mobile Devices to Support Formal, Informal and Semi-formal Learning

Uses and Implications for Teaching & Learning

Michael M. Grant

Abstract Mobile devices are ubiquitous. They are often invisible to accomplish our everyday tasks and learning goals. This chapter explains how individuals learn using mobile devices during their daily lives—within K-12 schools, higher education, and outside of educational institutions altogether—with specific attention to STEAM disciplines. First, brief definitions of mobile devices and mobile learning are presented, then types of learning, i.e. formal, informal, and semiformal, are discussed. Next, seven categories describe how mobile devices have been used for teaching and learning with examples as appropriate from STEAM disciplines: (a) increasing access to student information and campus resources, (b) increasing interaction with learning contents, (c) creating representations of knowledge, (d) augmenting face-to-face instruction, (e) supporting performance and decision-making, (f) enabling personalized learning, and (g) deploying instruction. Finally, five implications for employing mobile devices for teaching and learning are discussed.

Keywords Mobile learning · Formal learning · Informal learning · Semi-formal learning · Social media

Introduction

Mobile devices continue to grow in their numbers, as well as permeate our everyday lives. It is no surprise that these devices are also considered part of our educational landscape. In 2013, the Horizon Report for K-12 (Johnson et al., 2013b) and the Horizon Report for Higher Education (Johnson et al., 2013a) listed mobile learning with smartphones and tablets and tablet computing, respectively, as significant impacts within 1 year or less. Similarly, the annual EDUCAUSE Center for Analysis and Research (ECAR) Study of Undergraduate Students and Information Technology (Dahlstrom, Walker, & Dziuban, 2013) reported that it was equally common for undergraduate students in the U.S. to own two, three, four, or more Internet-capable

M. M. Grant (✉)
University of South Carolina, Columbia, USA
e-mail: michaelmgrant@sc.edu

devices, including laptop computers, smartphones, tablets, and e-readers. Most recently, the 2014 Horizon Report for Higher Education (Johnson, Adams Becker, Estrada, & Freeman, 2014) identified social media for learning as an accelerating trend along with mobile apps, tablet computing, mobile learning, personal learning environments, and location-based services as key emerging technologies.

In parallel, the integration of mobile devices in education also dovetails with the broad goals of STEM (science, technology, engineering, mathematics) education and the more recent STEAM education, which includes the visual and performing arts (Ostler, 2012). The novelty of mobile devices (Ciampa, 2014) and their ubiquitous uses for "communication, collaboration, gathering, and sharing" (Lai, Khaddage, & Knezek, 2013b, p. 2) in and outside of schooling may increase interest in STEM careers and postsecondary study. Plus, there is some evidence to suggest that the use of mobile technologies with appropriate pedagogies can aid retention in postsecondary STEM majors (e.g., Romney, 2011). To the second goal, mobile devices may "improve the proficiency of all students in STEM" (Thomasian, 2011, p. 12) when used meaningfully with teaching and learning. However, there is little empirical evidence of the STEAM interdisciplinarity advocated by Ostler (2012).

The purpose of this practical chapter is to describe how individuals learn during their daily lives—both within school and outside of educational institutions—and how mobile devices are being used to engender this learning, particularly within STEAM disciplines. First, I briefly define mobile computing devices and mobile learning, then types of learning and the purposes for which they occur. Next, I present how mobile devices have been used for teaching and learning, and I offer selected examples of how mobile devices are or could be used, highlighting STEAM disciplines where most appropriate. Finally, implications for employing mobile devices for teaching and learning are discussed.

Mobile Devices and Mobile Learning

Learning with mobile devices has been described and defined in myriad ways. Mobile devices themselves have included technologies that broadly operationalize mobility and transportability, such as cellphones, smartphones, tablet computers, laptop computers, and netbooks (Valk, Rashid, & Elder, 2010). Keegan (2005), however, recognized that mobile learning should focus on the actual mobility of the device, recognizing that some devices in fact are more mobile than others, primarily predicated on their sizes. Therefore, mobile learning should be "restricted to learning on devices which a lady can carry in her handbag or a gentleman can carry in his pocket" (Keegan, 2005, p. 33). Moreover, Traxler (2007) described devices that learners are accustomed to "carrying everywhere with them" and that they "regard as friendly and personal" (p. 129). Some of the definitions for mobile learning found in the literature focus specifically on the technology; others focus on the learner; still others attempt some combination. Most recently, Crompton (2013) as an extension of Sharples' (Sharples, Taylor, & Vavoula, 2007) definition stated that mobile learning is "learning across multiple contexts, through social and content interactions, using personal electronic devices" (p. 4).

Because the field of mobile learning and the technologies of mobile devices are both still rapidly evolving, it seems prudent to offer some compromise to defining mobile learning that respects and reflects the litany of previous work with an eye to future advances and changes. Therefore, in this chapter, mobile teaching and learning is operationalized as (a) learning that is more than delivered and supported by handheld, mobile computing devices (Keegan, 2005; Mobile Learning Network (MoLeNET), 2009) but (b) learning that can be both formal and informal (Quinn, 2000; Sharples et al., 2007; Traxler, 2007, 2010) or learning that incorporates elements of both formal and informal learning, and (c) learning that is context dependent across different settings and authentic for the learner (Sharples et al., 2007; Traxler, 2005, 2007, 2010).

Types of Learning

Barron (2006) describes a learning ecology in terms of contexts for physical and virtual spaces. Lai et al. (2013b) interpreted this to mean that "learning in a physical environment in a classroom setting and can be classified as formal" and virtual learning "occurs outside a formal classroom setting … and can be classified as informal" (p. 2). Hull and Schultz (2001) and Eshach (2006) emphasizes, however, that using physical environment characteristics may be insufficient to distinguish between formal and informal learning environments. Moreover, with the increased uses of online learning and mobile learning, classifying formal learning within a physical space is inadequate. Instead, it is more advantageous and forward thinking to consider types of learning along a continuum (c.f., Lai, Khaddage, & Knezek, 2013a) with respect to their origins and learner motivations. More details are explained below for formal, informal, and semi-formal learning.

Formal Learning

In this chapter, formal learning is considered where learners are engaged with materials developed by a teacher, trainer, or faculty member to be used during a program of instruction in an educational environment (Colley, Hodkinson, & Malcom, 2003; Halliday-Wynes & Beddie, 2009). These are often initiated, led, and evaluated by an instructor and associated with credentials (Jubas, 2010). Certainly courses, coursework, and required activities in K-12 schools and higher education are considered formal learning. Eshach (2006) also depicts formal learning as structured and prearranged in which learners are extrinsically motivated. Within this definition, if a teacher were to require learners to collect or create examples outside of class to be analyzed, reviewed, reflected upon, or evaluated, then this would still be deemed formal learning.

With regard to mobile devices, Zhang et al. (2010) describe elementary-aged students building KWL (i.e., What you know, What you want to know, What you want to learn) charts on mobile devices to document their prior knowledge and learning progress with science content as part of a required science curriculum on fungi. In higher education, Isabwe, Reichert, Carlsen, and Lian (2014) created a computer tablet-based mathematical assessment application. In the application, peers provided formative feedback on mathematical tasks.

Informal Learning

At the other end of the spectrum, Hrimech (2005) describes informal learning as learning "which people do on their own" (p. 310). Informal learning is motivated and initiated by an individual. Activities, such as reading and Internet searches; visiting community resources, such as libraries, museums, nature centers, and zoos; attending local events; gaining expertise in avocational hobbies; and learning on-the-job (e.g., Hull & Schultz, 2001) are considered informal learning activities. This type of learning is sometimes "unanticipated, unorganized, and often unacknowledged, even by the learner" (Jubas, 2010, p. 229). This type of learning can also be referred to as free-choice learning or incidental learning. Barron (2006) acknowledges compulsory formal learning can sometimes lead to informal learning, where an individual's interests are piqued for further investigations.

Much educational research with informal learning has been focused around (a) science education and science centers, such as museums and nature centers (e.g., Yoon & Wang, 2014); (b) out-of-school mathematical experiences (e.g., White, Booker, Ching, & Martin, 2012; White & Martin, 2014); and (c) literacies (e.g., Hull & Schultz, 2001). However, there is considerable interest in leveraging much more informal contexts with learning. Informal learning opportunities can also include what Caron and Caronia (2007) refer to as "non-places" and "non-times" (p. 38), such as waiting in line at a grocery, crossing a street, or waiting at a bus stop. Grant and Hsu (2014) identify mobile devices being used informally for "communications, searching, creation, sharing, curation, and aggregation" (p. 33).

With mobile learning, Cui and Roto (2008) describe how individuals used mobile devices for fact-finding to seek out a specific piece of information and for information gathering, where they collected information from multiple sources to compare or aggregate the information in order to make a decision. These tasks are completed as part of the individuals' daily routines and are not required as part of a curriculum. In addition, Balasubramanian, Thamizoli, Umar, and Kanwar (2010) describe the use of mobile phones by women in rural India to become business women for goat rearing. The women were encouraged to use the phones as tools for discussion among the 320 participants to converse on topics such as business, technologies, and goat rearing, as well as emergent cultural and legal issues.

Semi-Formal Learning

As mentioned previously, many authors (e.g., Impedovo, 2011; Koole, 2009; Roschelle, Patton, & Tatar, 2007) contend that mobile learning blurs the lines of formal and informal learning, or at the very least, links informal learning to formal learning. Along a continuum, this type of learning is referred to here as semi-formal learning to indicate that this type of learning shares characteristics with both formal and informal learning. These contexts and opportunities for learning are also sometimes referred to as non-formal learning (e.g., Colley, Hodkinson, & Malcolm, 2002; Thompson, 2012). White et al. (2012) lament that "few examples exist of school-based attempts to fully integrate formal and informal learning" (p. 8).

Two examples of semi-formal learning in science and medicine are provided below. GeoJourney (see BGSU Monitor, 2007; http://www.geojourney.org) is an undergraduate field-based geography course at Bowling Green State University. In this course, students travel across the United States to geophysically and historically significant geographical sites. Students prepare between stops with iPods packed with slides, videos, and documentaries designed and organized by the faculty member. In addition, Pimmer et al. (2014) describe how nurses and nurse educators in South Africa connect workplace learning with their formal educational experiences. In these rural settings, they mention the use of mobile phones and a Facebook group to share and reflect on on-the-job practice within their formal education coursework. These types of instruction and learning reflect both formal learning and informal learning elements. So, the distinctions between the two types of learning are blurred, and in some instances, the lines among semi-formal, informal, and formal learning may be blurred. Admittedly, it is quite possible for an individual to move among these fluidly, such as through multitasking or personal interests.

Uses of Mobile Devices for Teaching and Learning

Having examined the types of learning that can occur with mobile devices, this section will offer a broad taxonomy for understanding how mobile devices have been used with these types of learning. Specifically, there are seven primary ways in which mobile devices have been used to support teaching and learning. These are to (a) increase access to student information and campus resources, (b) increase interaction with learning contents, (c) create representations of knowledge, (d) augment face-to-face instruction, (e) support performance & decision-making, (f) enable personalized learning, and (g) deploy instruction. These groups are not mutually exclusive, and they are summarized in Table 1. Select examples of these uses are also provided, focusing on STEAM disciplines where most relevant.

Table 1 Uses of mobile devices for teaching and learning

Use	Example
Increase access to student information and campus resources	Students use university app to access library databases (Bushhousen et al., 2013)
Increase interaction with learning contents	Students use commercial or school-specific app to practice engineering vocabulary (Redd, 2011)
Create representations of knowledge	Students create short videos of mathematical concepts (White & Martin, 2014).
Augment face-to-face instruction	Teachers/faculty members encourage students to pose questions using social media during large class lectures (Rankin, 2009)
Support performance & decision-making	Medical practitioners use app to help compare, analyze, and prepare report of diagnosis (Lower, 2010)
Enable personalized learning	Medical students use social media, social networks, and mobile devices to participate in a medical education community Facebook page (Pimmer et al., 2014)
Deploy instruction	Students access interactive content on nuclear science (Chang, Wu, & Hsu, 2013)

Increase Access to Student Information and Campus Resources

As an initial entry, many universities are accommodating mobile devices with dissemination of university information. Universities such as Stanford (http://mobile.stanford.edu), Duke (http://m.duke.edu/), Vanderbilt (http://vanderbilt.edu/apps/), Missouri State (http://missouristate.edu/mobile/), and Texas A&M (http://tamu.edu/mobile/apps/) have developed specific applications for students to access information about campus transportation, athletic events, course directories for registration, university related events and even university resources such as the library database (e.g., Keller, 2011; O'Neill, 2013). For example, at the University of Florida, the Health Science Center Libraries (Bushhousen et al., 2013) used survey data to form a mobile technology committee in order to support and propagate information and resources specific to their patrons with mobile devices. Likewise, there have been a number of these needs analyses and subsequent implementations in higher education, such as the University of Nebraska at Omaha (Wright, 2011), GB Pant University of Agriculture and Technology in India (Goria, 2012), and the Himmelfarb Library at George Washington University's School of Medicine and Health Sciences (Gomes & Abate, 2012). These approaches do not typically have direct impact to learning as it relates to accessing and interacting with course content, fellow students, and instructors. However, the access to resources and information is valuable to students in and outside of class. So, this is a common initial method to implement and integrate the mobile devices that learners are already bringing to campus.

Increase Interaction with Learning Contents

Another way in which mobile devices have been used to support learning is to increase the interactions individuals have with instructional content. From a cognitivist perspective, repetition and practice with new knowledge and skills are successful in improving learning (Cavus & Ibrahim, 2009; Driscoll, 2005). For example in formal learning, an app was developed for a Statistics I course at Abilene Christian University that featured touch screen simulations for experiential and interactive learning, calculators that graphed bell curves for student experimentation, and decision making flowcharts for conceptual understanding (Nihalani & Mayrath, 2010). The students felt they learned more being able to access the software more often on both tablet and smartphone devices. Similarly, the University of North Carolina's Project Numina offered students the opportunity to actively engage in mathematical and science concepts using mobile devices (Heath et al., 2005). Students engaged with charts and graphs, and the results were displayed publicly.

Abrams (2013) presents a number of mobile app games that support engineering concepts. These games are most likely used by individuals to support informal learning, such as Tinkerbox by Autodesk. However, the engineering concepts and content built into Schnittkraftmeister and Fourbar are sophisticated enough to integrate with curricula in higher education for formal and semi-formal learning. The use of games and digital game-based learning can support increased interactions with content, such as through practice and review (Redd, 2011).

Create Representations of Knowledge

Many of the built-in features to mobile devices, such as photo capture, video recording, audio recording, and SMS text messaging, in addition to installed apps, allow the creation of representations of learners' knowledge. These artifacts represent the learner, the learning, and the context in which the learning has occurred (Grant, 2011; Krajcik, Blumenfeld, Marx, & Soloway, 1994; Marx, Blumenfeld, Krajcik, & Soloway, 1997). Impedovo (2011) suggests that mobility in learning and the use of personal mobile devices allows autonomy for learners to produce multimedia artifacts as needed. So, learners can use devices they have on hand, during the stream of their daily lives and across different contexts.

For example, at the University of Reading (UK) (France, Whalley, & Mauchline, 2013), microbiology students conducted fieldwork with tablet computers in Iceland that meshes formal learning and semi-formal learning charateristics. They collected GPS data, photos, videos, and field notes to be aggregated into research presentations and video reflections. In K-12, Soloway and Norris (e.g., Project Tomorrow, 2010; Zhang et al., 2010) have been working with schools with the GoKnow Mobile Learning Environment. Small applications, such as PicoMap for concept mapping and Sketchy for drawing or animations, allow students to create artifacts that reflect their learning. Similarly, students in Scotland made videos to showcase their country, and other students used an "iPad at home to capture and edit their own multimedia compositions, such as short movie trailers, biographical videos of family members" (Burden, Hopkins, Male, Martin, & Trala, 2012, p. 70). So, many built-in functions and downloadable applications make mobile devices powerful tools for learners to generate evidence of their knowledge.

Augment Face-to-Face Instruction

Teachers and university faculty members can also use mobile devices to enhance their face-to-face formal instruction. Rankin (2009) provides a well-known and publicized example of using Twitter in her large class for discussions and backchanneling, which is posting questions and comments during a lecture or event. Havelka (2013), however, has implemented face-to-face courses on information literacy with students using smartphones and tablet computers exclusively. In my own teacher professional development, I have used the web service PollEverywhere.com with mobile devices to demonstrate in-class polling options. With PollEverywhere.com for example, teachers and faculty members can use SMS text messaging or a web page to submit responses for quick knowledge checks with mathematics (see Fig. 1) and to spark discussions with open-ended reactions (see Fig. 2). In these instances, the formal learning may look less like mobile learning. Instead, the learning with mobile computing devices may be a replacement technology, replicating existing or previous practice (White & Martin, 2014). Mobile devices in these cases are smaller and more convenient as compared to larger laptop or desktop computers and classroom response systems (i.e., clickers).

Support Performance & Decision-Making

Instead of relying completely on memory, digital performance supports and decision supports can help individuals at the times of need, particularly indicative of informal learning. These technologies can be used to improve productivity and efficiency delivering information and support just-in-time (Nyugen, 2012). Rossett (2010) describes performance and decision supports as "external resources that can be referred to as they are needed, when they are needed" ("Table 1: Mobile

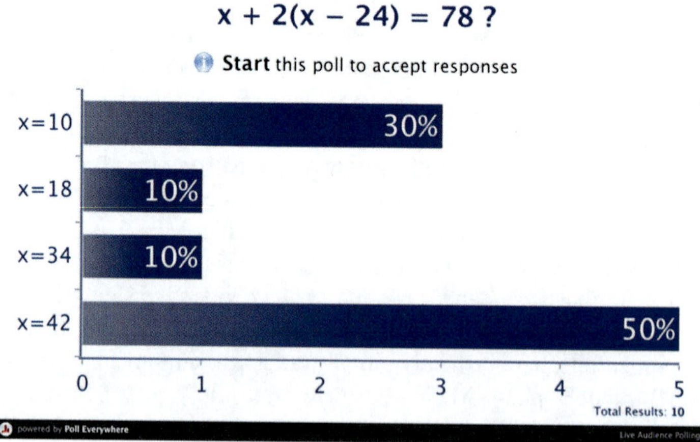

Fig. 1 Using PollEverywhere.com for a quick knowledge check in math class

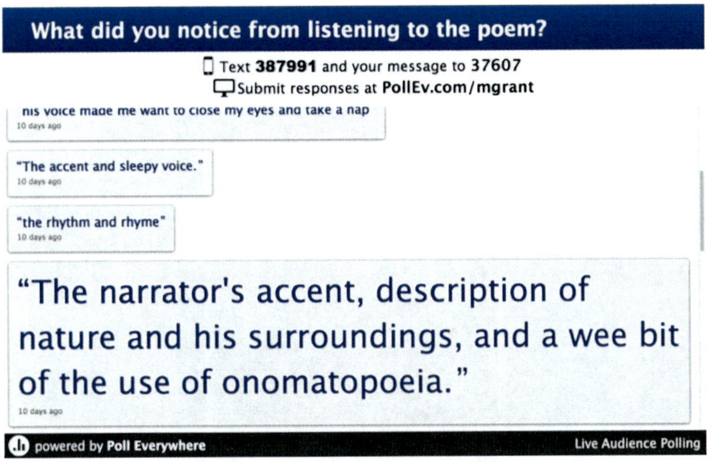

Fig. 2 Using PollEverywhere.com for an open-ended response to an audio reading of a poem

Learning and Mobile Performance Support Compared"). Because mobile devices are often easily accessible, individuals may not need to "break from the work context entirely" in order to use a performance support (Nyugen, 2012, p. 153). Instead, digital performance supports on mobile devices may resemble what Nyugen (2012) identifies as extrinsic and even intrinsic supports, which are more integrated into work systems and user interfaces. One example of a common mobile performance support is QuickCite. QuickCite is a mobile app that allows an individual to scan the bar code from a book, and then the application will email the reference citation in APA or MLA form (see Fig. 3). The individual does not have to remember the formatting rules for a book citation, and an individual does not have to write down the reference information for a book while searching. In both instances, QuickCites helps at the time of need.

Fig. 3 Screen shots of Quick Cite app for reference citation capture. Used with permission QuickCite

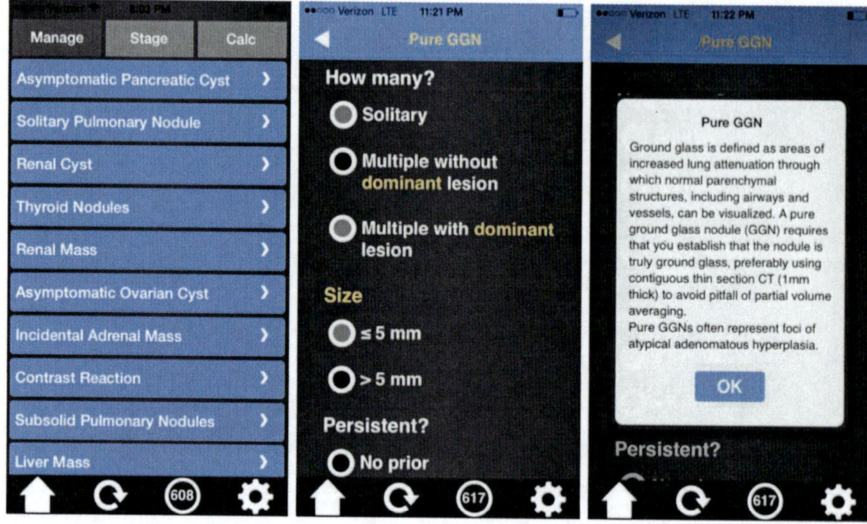

Fig. 4 Screen shots from RadsBest, a clinical decision support app for radiologists. Used with permission RadsBest

In terms of decision support, much has been done in the health and medicine fields. Martínez-Pérez et al. (2014) describe clinical decision support systems as a connection between "health observations with health knowledge to influence health choices by clinicians for improved health care" (Martínez-Pérez et al., 2014, p. 2). For example, RadsBest (see Fig. 4) is a decision support tool, deployed as a mobile app, to aid radiologists. While radiologists have been extensively trained and continue professional education, it can be challenging to be aware and use the most recent medical research and standards. The app integrates "algorithms from published standards into a user-friendly series of questions" (Lower, 2010, para. 3) in order to help radiologists analyze patient data. The app also helps radiologists interpret their findings and make appropriate recommendations to referring physicians for patient care.

Enable Personalized Learning

Informal mobile learning also affords continuous learning and personalized learning. Attwell (2007) depicted the needs of personal learning and, subsequently, personal learning environments. He recognized that (a) an individual identifies his or her learning needs, which extend across informal learning, workplace learning, and formal learning; (b) learning takes place in various circumstances and conditions; and (c) all learning needs cannot be addressed through one program of study or environment. Networked personal learning leverages a collection of devices (e.g., computers, smartphones, tablet computers), software/applications (e.g., mobile applications), and web services/learning resources/objects (e.g., SMS text messaging, video tutorials) that together serve an individual's learning needs (Attwell, 2007; Dabbagh & Kitsantas, 2012; France et al., 2013; Martindale & Dowdy, 2010). For example, personal digital magazines, such as Flipboard, present relevant information or resources based on a learner's previous preferences.

Personalized learning is initiated by an individual. Learning opportunities, such as "unintentional discoveries, events, and various experiences" (Lai et al., 2013b, p. 2), may be opportunistic or spontaneous. In the visual arts, Philadelphia's Museum Without Walls is a city-wide collection of outdoor art, sculptures, and statues (Brady, 2014). Through a cellphone call or smartphone app, individuals can listen to various voices describing the cultural or historical significance of the works. Because the works are public and outside, an individual must be motivated to pursue the learning. But, there continues to be little research on the motivations for individuals to use mobile devices (c.f., Ciampa, 2014).

Personalized learning can also take the form of continuous professional development with personal learning networks and professional learning networks. For example, Pimmer et al. (Pimmer, Linxen, & Gröhbiel, 2012; Pimmer et al., 2014) describe the uses of social networking sites, like Facebook, for individuals to solve problems with their peers while on-the-job. This personalized learning is especially beneficial when individuals are "working in professional isolation," such as in rural settings (Pimmer et al., 2014, p. 1402). Medical professionals use searches on their mobile devices *in situ* to look up unfamiliar terms and cases, as well as provide examples to peers on social networks of unusual or rare cases. Experts within personal learning networks and professional learning networks can tweet or retweet relevant information, resources, and links to their followers. Even for an individual mobile learner, all of these data can be selectively saved into social bookmarking systems (e.g., Diigo, Pinterest) or personal note-taking applications (e.g., Evernote) with relevant metadata (i.e., tags with bookmarking sites, specific boards for Pinterest or Learn.ist) for later retrieval.

Deploy Instruction

Some authors (e.g., Georgiev, Georgieva, & Smrikarov, 2004; Motiwalla, 2007; Quinn, 2000) have related mobile learning to extensions of distance education and elearning. As such, it is possible to use mobile devices to deploy complete formal units of instruction and learning activities. For example, Grant and Barbour (2013) describe a small study with an online advanced placement (AP) European History course. Two of the 26 units in the course were completed through a mobile application *Mobl21*. In my own graduate courses, I have also piloted the deployment of complete units with this mobile application. One online course in graduate teacher education (see Fig. 5) integrated texts, graphics, and videos into the *Mobl21* application delivered by iOS devices or a computer desktop application using Adobe AIR. Another course was a senior-level graduate course in developing interactive

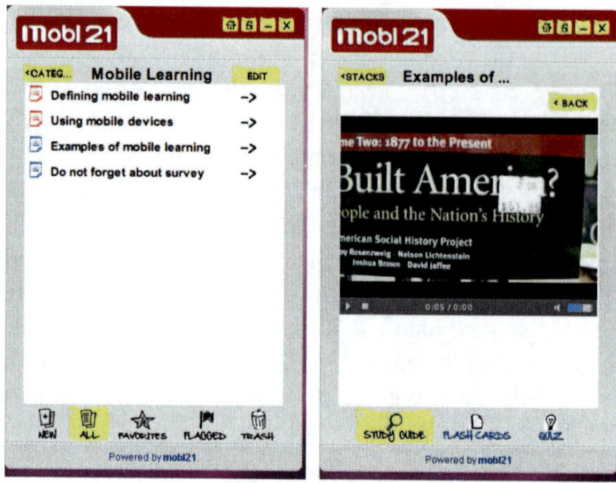

Fig. 5 Screen shots of course unit on mobile learning for a graduate teacher education course built with *Mobl21*

instruction for instructional design majors. Again, texts, graphics, and videos on rapid prototyping and rapid elearning were chunked into small modules.

In science education, Chang et al. (2013) describe the use of augmented reality that superimposed virtual environmental elements, such as radiation levels, indoor conditions, and indoor construction materials, onto geographical locations. Ninth grade students in Taiwan considered nuclear energy and radiation in a simulation of the Fukushima Daiichi Nuclear Power Plant accident in Japan. The students were positive toward the mobile implementation, and there was initial evidence that the instructional strategy was effective. Similarly, Zimmerman and Land (2014) describe the creation of augmented reality elements to accompany an arboretum, where fourth graders and the public "could observe trees like a botanist— understanding the important ecological and biological concepts relevant in their own community" (p. 80). A mobile website and QR codes allowed access to tree-specific scientific information.

Implications for Employing Mobile Devices with Teaching and Learning

Using mobile devices to support teaching and learning within STEAM disciplines is not simple. In the previous section, I presented seven uses for mobile devices to support teaching and learning. Planning formal, informal, and semi-formal learning environments that leverage mobile devices, however, requires attention to pedagogical, technological, content, and contextual characteristics. This section discusses implications for employing mobile devices with teaching and learning. Five broad themes are presented: (a) situatedness and learning mobilely, (b) distinctions between mobile devices and mobile services, (c) mediating interactions in physical and networked environments, (d) mobile learner characteristics to evaluate resources and information, and (e) teaching and learning with mobile devices versus mobile learning.

Situatedness and Learning Mobile-ly

An implication of using mobile devices with teaching and learning is the complexities of ubiquity and situated learning. Because of mobile devices, social media, social networks, and pervasive access to the Internet, individuals are "always on" (Northcliffe, & Middleton, 2013, p. 200). Learning is a social endeavor situated in particular contexts and embedded within a certain environment (Bereiter & Scardamalia, 1985; Lave & Wenger, 1991). Applications on mobile computing devices allow learners to create video/audio, take photographs, geotag, microblog, receive or send SMS text messages, and access social networking sites for communication with classmates, their instructor, and even experts. By using the applications available on mobile devices, a personalized, authentic learning experience can be created by learners and for learners during the course of their everyday lives. Within the STEAM discipline of mathematics, White and Martin (White & Martin, 2014; White et al., 2012) have researched and discussed this in terms of "making the personal mathematical and ... making mathematics personal" (p. 9). This meaning making is an important component of semi-formal and informal learning.

Mobile semi-formal and informal learning may, however, be difficult to achieve. Caron and Caronia (2007) explain that mobile devices can afford active learning during "non-times" and "non-places" (p. 38). Learning in places and times with little meaning may produce fragmented knowledge (Traxler, 2010). While learning *in situ* and across multiple networked communities, there is justifiable concern that this isolated and disconnected knowledge will become inert (Bereiter & Scardamalia, 1985), unable to be generalized or integrated into existing schemata. Knowledge and context-dependent skills must be encouraged to transfer across disciplines or domains. Unfortunately, not all contexts or times are significant, so we must be explicit in emphasizing, or encouraging individual learners to emphasize, when context matters.

Moreover, learning in small episodes of time may make retention problematic. Designing learning contents or encouraging learning that can tolerate disruptions and episodes of discontinuity may be very difficult to achieve. Disconnected pieces of information must be integrated and internalized before they can be considered knowledge (Tella, 2003).

Distinctions Between Mobile Devices and Mobile Services

Little attention has been given to the distinctions between using mobile devices and using mobile services with mobile devices. For example, many mobile devices have cameras that allow photo and video capture. However, to use the text messaging features on mobile devices, subscription to a data plan is required. Admittedly, for many individuals these differences may go unnoticed. Many examples of mobile teaching and learning depict the integration of mobile devices and mobile services (e.g., Ducate & Lomicka, 2013; Herrington, 2009; Northcliffe & Middleton, 2013; Pimmer et al., 2012). However, how the devices and the services are used for mobile learning is significant because many mobile services, such as data plans that afford persistent network access, allow learners to enact characteristics of mobile learning. This includes many of the examples of informal learning with networked communities and access to information and resources.

In addition, the costs associated with mobile devices and data plans should not be dismissed. In some recent research with K-12 online learners (Grant & Barbour, 2013), there were a number of secondary students who did not have access to devices or who chose not to use their devices to the fullest extent because of barriers such as cellular coverage or data plan rates. This differentiation in functionality highlights a concern for the costs associated with data plans and the lack of widespread coverage of cellular networks.

Mediating Interactions in Physical and Networked Environments

Another implication for using mobile devices is recognizing mediated interactions. Based in Activity Theory, human activity is mediated through the use of an artifact, such as mobile computing devices (Impedovo, 2011). Moreover, learners act as agents in their learning environments, transforming them as needed to achieve their individual goals. Human agency is directly linked to the relationship between the learner and the artifacts, or tools he uses. So mobile computing devices and mobile services both mediate the interactions for learning and the interactions with others, bridging the transactional distance between individuals and translating the interactions with the learning environment (Looi & Toh, 2014; Park, 2011). So, the mediation by the mobile devices helps to overcome the distance between networked learners and the course content.

In K-12 mathematics, White and Martin (2014) researched how seventh, eighth, and ninth grade students captured photographs and video of algebraic concepts, and these examples were then anayzed in class. Ryu and Parsons (2012) describe how dyads collaboratively explored a simulated training program with mobile text messaging communications to share observations, photos, and questions. Similarly, France et al. (2013) recount uses of social media by higher education students for reflection of scientific fieldwork. So, the mobile devices mediate, or help interpret, the human activity.

In another example, Pimmer et al. (2012) describe the use of a social networking site with mobile phones to support professional medical education in emerging countries. The "Medical Profession, wow I Love it" Facebook page is an informal learning environment, where participants can choose when and to what extent they will engage. Pimmer et al. suggest that through the discussions and responses to the moderator's questions and posts, practicing professionals and students were grounded in a specialized context. So, in this case, the learner may be mobile but still rooted in a meaningful professional learning network.

Mobile Learner Characteristics to Evaluate Resources & Information

Learning in a variety of places and times requires critical thinking for reflection, monitoring, and metacognition as part of learning autonomously. Tella (2003) and Traxler (2010) warn that learning across various places and in small chunks of time require that a learner combine and internalize small pieces of knowledge together into existing cognitive structures (e.g., assimilation, accommodation, accretion, tuning). For learners to succeed in personalized learning, Dabbagh and Kitsanstas (2012) argue that learners must engage first with personal information management, then social interaction and collaboration, and finally, information aggregation and management. As Sha, Looi, Chen, and Zhang (2012) explain, learners must be willing and capable to determine the "right things ... right time ... right place ...and ...right strategies" (p. 367).

However, mobile learners may be ill prepared for this evaluation of resources and information. Mobile learners may need to distinguish between information and knowledge. While there are not universal definitions discriminating information from knowledge, Wiig (1999) characterizes the generally accepted proposition that information represents facts or data that is situated to a particular context while knowledge embodies an individual's beliefs and has been incorporated into his schemata. So, mobile learners may have autonomy and self-direction for specific learning goals, but they may need increased levels of scaffolding for self-regulation to solve information problems and integrate knowledge (Shih, Chen, Chang, & Kao, 2010).

Distinctions between experts and novice mobile learners may also impact problem solving. Naïve information problem solvers, like mobile learners attempting to search for a solution to a domain-specific problem, are often reactive in information seeking, having difficulties in identifying both what they know and do not know (Hill, 1999; Yang, 1997). They may use random actions with little evaluation and information problem-solving strategies are limited to browsing and exploration. Knowledgeable learners are most self-directed with a higher level of understanding for the problem domain and they tend to use more advanced strategies for problem-solving. The more knowledgeable learners have a well-developed schema in order to integrate new or missing knowledge.

Teaching & Learning with Mobile Devices v. Mobile Learning

As described above, mobile devices have been used to augment formal face-to-face instruction in classroom settings and increase interactions with curricular content. However, it is significant to note that these examples of using mobile devices with teaching and learning may not depict wholly mobile learning. In an earlier section of this chapter, I indicated that mobile learning was more than instruction and learning delivered and supported by handheld, mobile computing devices (e.g., Keegan, 2005; Mobile Learning Network (MoLeNET), 2009). Mobile learning should also be authentic and context dependent (Sharples et al., 2007; Traxler, 2005, 2007, 2010). In some instances of teaching and learning with mobile devices, the learner and the device may neither be mobile. For example, some schools are experimenting with classroom sets of mobile devices, where the teacher determines when the devices will be used and the students are unable to take the devices home or use them with autonomy (e.g., Grant et al., in press; Greenberg, 2010). Kiger (2012) describes the use of iPod Touch devices and math software applications for third grade multiplication practice. The students practiced on the devices with specific applications during class and did not take the devices home. In addition, Rankin's (2009) use of Twitter in class for backchanneling may be limited as mobile learning. In these instances, the formal learning may look less like mobile learning. Instead, learning with mobile devices may be using a technology that is simply smaller, more convenient, or supplied by the student.

Conclusion

In this chapter, I have provided categories for understanding how mobile devices have been used with teaching and learning in K-12 schools, higher education institutions, and even everyday circumstances as they relate to STEAM disciplines. Of particular interest is the lack of empirical research to document and describe the use of mobile devices in technology supported informal learning (Jones, Scanlon, & Clough, 2013). Connecting formal learning and informal learning continues to be a challenge (White et al., 2012) while leveraging the ubiquity of mobile devices so individuals can learn at differing times and spaces (Sha et al., 2012). This, of course, is related to the challenges in capturing meaningful data and measuring learning at potentially non-times and non-places (c.f., Boticki & So, 2010), as well as in instances when learners may be unaware they are even learning (Jubas, 2010). The type of research by Cui and Roto (2008) with extensive data collection into how, where, and under what conditions learners are conducting searches is a beginning to understand informal learning with mobile devices. Additional research with large data sets may help us to understand more about how mobile devices are integrated with everyday lives and how learning is segmented, or chunked, in between events in our everyday lives.

In addition, I presented five broad implications for integrating mobile devices within teaching and learning. These implications highlight the complexities in designing formal, informal, and semi-formal learning environments that exploit mobile devices and mobile learners. Pedagogically, teachers and higher education faculty should consider when mobile devices will be used for practice with specific learning contents and when mobile devices may be used in authentic contexts to interact with peers, experts, or environments. These decisions directly reflect whether learning with mobile devices authentically depicts mobile learning or whether mobile devices are replacement technologies (Traxler, 2007). The examples presented in this chapter that are most authentic, meaning those instances that are most reflective of real world practices (e.g., Balasubramanian et al., 2010; Cui & Roto, 2008; France et al., 2013; Pimmer et al., 2014, 2012; White & Martin, 2014), are also the most representative of mobile learning as defined at the beginning of this chapter.

The potential of teaching and learning with mobile devices in STEAM disciplines is promising. In order to employ this potential, we must recognize the inherent characteristics of formal, informal, and semi-formal learning environments, as well as the affordances and opportunity costs to mobile devices. These include the on-board features of mobile devices in addition to data and network services, social media, social networks, and installed applications.

References

Abrams, M. (2013, July). Learning engineering using game apps. *Mechanical Engineering, 12*–13.

Attwell, G. (2007). Personal learning environments—The future of elearning? *eLearning Papers, 2*(1), 1–8.

Balasubramanian, K., Thamizoli, P., Umar, A., & Kanwar, A. (2010). Using mobile phones to promote lifelong learning among rural women in Southern India. *Distance Education, 31*(2), 193–209. doi:10.1080/01587919.2010.502555.

Barron, B. (2006). Interest and self-sustained learning as catalysts of development: A learning ecology perspective. *Human Development, 49*(4), 193–224. doi:10.1159/000094368.

Bereiter, C., & Scardamalia, M. (1985). Cognitive coping strategies and the problem of inert knowledge. In S. S. Chipman, J. W. Segal, & R. Glaser (Eds.), *Thinking and learning skills: Vol. 2. Current research and open questions* (pp. 65–80). Hillsdale: Erlbaum.

BGSUMonitor. (2007). GeoJourney students use iPods to enhance learning. *BGSU Monitor.* http://www2.bgsu.edu/offices/mc/monitor/01-15-07/page26071.html. Accessed 11 March 2014.

Boticki, I., & So, H. (2010). Quiet captures: A tool for capturing the evidence of seamless learning with mobile devices. In S. R. Goldman, J. Pellegrino, K. Gomez, L. Lyons, & J. Radinsky (Eds.), *Proceedings of the International Conference of the Learning Sciences (ICLS) 2010* (Vol. 2010, Part 1, pp. 500–507). Chicago, IL.

Brady, S. (8. January 2014). This museum has no walls, but it can talk. *The Philadelphia Daily News.*

Burden, K., Hopkins, P., Male, T., Martin, S., & Trala, C. (2012). *iPad Scotland evaluation.* East Yorkshire, England.

Bushhousen, E., Norton, H. F., Butson, L. C., Auten, B., Jesano, R., David, D., & Tennant, M. R. (2013). Smartphone use at a university health science center. *Medical Reference Services Quarterly, 32*(1), 52–72. doi:10.1080/02763869.2013.749134.

Caron, A. H., & Caronia, L. (2007). *Moving cultures: Mobile communication in everyday life.* Montréal: McGill-Queen's University Press.

Cavus, N., & Ibrahim, D. (2009). m-Learning: An experiment in using SMS to support new English language words. *British Journal of Educational Technology, 40*(1), 78–92. doi:10.1111/j.1467-8535.2007.00801.x.

Chang, H.-Y., Wu, H.-K., & Hsu, Y.-S. (2013). Integrating a mobile augmented reality activity to contextualize student learning of a socioscientific issue. *British Journal of Educational Technology, 44*(3), E95–E99. doi:10.1111/j.1467-8535.2012.01379.x.

Ciampa, K. (2014). Learning in a mobile age: An investigation of student motivation. *Journal of Computer Assisted Learning, 30*(1), 82–96. doi:10.1111/jcal.12036.

Colley, H., Hodkinson, P., & Malcolm, J. (2002). *Non-formal learning: Mapping the conceptual terrain.* Leeds, England.

Colley, H., Hodkinson, P., & Malcom, J. (2003). *Informality and formality in learning: A report for the learning and skills research centre.* University of Leeds, United Kingdom.

Crompton, H. (2013). A historical overview of m-learning: Toward learner-centered education. In Z. L. Berge & L. Y. Muilenburg (Eds.), *Handbook of mobile learning* (pp. 3–14). New York: Routledge.

Cui, Y., & Roto, V. (2008). How people use the web on mobile devices. In *Proceeding of the 17th international conference on World Wide Web—WWW '08* (pp. 905–914). New York, ACM Press. doi:10.1145/1367497.1367619.

Dabbagh, N., & Kitsantas, A. (2012). Personal learning environments, social media, and self-regulated learning: A natural formula for connecting formal and informal learning. *The Internet and Higher Education, 15*(1), 3–8. doi:10.1016/j.iheduc.2011.06.002.

Dahlstrom, E., Walker, J. D., & Dziuban, C. (2013). *ECAR study of undergraduate students and information technology.* Louisville, CO, EDUCAUSE Center for Analysis and Research. http://www.educause.edu/library/resources/ecar-study-undergraduate-students-and-information-technology-2013. Accessed 19 June 2015.

Driscoll, M. (2005). *Psychology of learning for instruction.* Boston: Pearson.

Ducate, L., & Lomicka, L. (2013). Going mobile: Language learning with an iPod Touch in intermediate French and German classes. *Foreign Language Annals, 46*(3), 445–468. doi:10.1111/flan.12043.

Eshach, H. (2006). Bridging in-school and out-of-school learning: Formal, non-formal, and informal Education. *Journal of Science Education and Technology, 16*(2), 171–190. doi:10.1007/s10956-006-9027-1.

France, D., Whalley, W. B., & Mauchline, A. L. (2013). The international desk. *Council on Undergraduate Research Quarterly, 34*(2), 38–43.

Georgiev, T., Georgieva, E., & Smrikarov, A. (2004). *M-learning—A new stage of e-learning.* Paper presented at the International Conference on Computer Systems and Technologies—CompSysTech'2004, Rousse, Bulgaria.

Gomes, A., & Abate, L. (2012). Rethinking our mobility: Supporting our patrons where they live. *Medical Reference Services Quarterly, 31*(2), 140–149. doi:10.1080/02763869.2012.670574.

Goria, S. (2012). Building website for mobile phone users of an Indian agriculture university library: A model. *Journal of Library & Information Technology, 32*(4), 358–364.

Grant, M. M. (2011). Learning, beliefs, and products: Students' perspectives with project-based Learning. *Interdisciplinary Journal of Problem-Based Learning, 5*(2), 37–69. doi:http://dx.doi.org/10.7771/1541-5015.1254.

Grant, M. M., & Barbour, M. K. (2013). Mobile teaching and learning in the classroom and on-line: Case studies in K-12. In Z. Berge & L. Muilenburg (Eds.), *Handbook of mobile learning* (pp. 285–292). New York: Routledge.

Grant, M. M., & Hsu, Y.-C. (2014). Making personal and professional learning mobile: Blending mobile devices, social media, social networks, and mobile apps to support PLEs, PLNs, & ProLNs. In A. V. Stavros (Ed.), *Advances in communications and media research* (Vol. 10, pp. 27–46). New York: Nova Science Publisher.

Grant, M. M., Tamim, S. R., Brown, D. B., Ferguson, F. K., Jones, L. B., & Sweeney, J. (in press). *Teaching and learning with mobile computing devices: Case study in K-12 classrooms.* Tech-Trends.

Greenberg, S. (16. December 2010). iPods for kids: Touch-screen devices a helpful resource for learning, fun. *The Commercial Appeal.* Memphis, TN.

Halliday-Wynes, S., & Beddie, F. (2009). *Informal learning at a glance.* Adelaide: National Centre for Vocational Education Research.

Havelka, S. (2013). Mobile information literacy: Supporting students' research and information needs in a mobile world. *Internet Reference Services Quarterly, 18*(3–4), 189–209. doi:10.1080/10875301.2013.856366.

Heath, B. P., Herman, R. L., Lugo, G. G., Reeves, J. H., Vetter, R. J., & Ward, C. R. (2005). Project Numina: Enhancing student learning with handheld computers. *Computer, 38*(6), 46–53. doi:10.1109/MC.2005.199.

Herrington, A. (2009). Incorporating mobile technologies within constructivist-based curriculum resources. In J. Herrington, A. Herrington, J. Mantei, I. Olney, & B. Ferry (Eds.), *New technologies, new pedagogies: Mobile learning in higher education*. Wollongong, Australia: University of Wollongong.

Hill, J. (1999). A conceptual framework for understanding information seeking in open-ended information systems. *Educational Technology Research and Development, 47*(I), 5–27.

Hrimech, M. (2005). Informal learning. In L. M. English (Ed.), *International encyclopedia of adult education* (pp. 310–312). New York: Palgrave Macmillan.

Hull, G., & Schultz, K. (2001). Literacy and learning out of school: A review of theory and research. *Review of Educational Research, 71*(4), 575–611. doi:10.3102/00346543071004575.

Impedovo, M. (2011). Mobile learning and activity theory. *Journal of E-Learning and Knowledge Society, 7*(2), 103–109.

Isabwe, G., Reichert, F., Carlsen, M., & Lian, T. A. (2014). Using assessment for learning mathematics with mobile tablet based solutions. *International Journal of Emerging Technologies in Learning, 9*(2), 29–37.

Johnson, L., Adams Becker, S., Cummins, M., Estrada, V., Freeman, A., & Ludgate, H. (2013a). NMC horizon report: 2013 higher education edition. Austin, Texas: The New Media Consortium.

Johnson, L., Adams Becker, S., Cummins, M., Estrada, V., Freeman, A., & Ludgate, H. (2013b). NMC horizon report: 2013 K-12 edition. Austin, Texas: The New Media Consortium.

Johnson, L., Adams Becker, S., Estrada, V., & Freeman, A. (2014). NMC Horizon report: 2014 higher education edition. Austin, Texas: The New Media Consortium.

Jones, A. C., Scanlon, E., & Clough, G. (2013). Mobile learning: Two case studies of supporting inquiry learning in informal and semiformal settings. *Computers & Education, 61*, 21–32. doi:10.1016/j.compedu.2012.08.008.

Jubas, K. (2010). Everyday scholars: Framing informal learning in terms of academic disciplines and skills. *Adult Education Quarterly, 61*(3), 225–243. doi:10.1177/0741713610380444.

Keegan, D. (2005). The incorporation of mobile learning into mainstream education and training. In *Proceedings of mLearn 2005- 4th World Conference on mLearning* (pp. 1–17). Cape Town, South Africa.

Keller, J. (2011). As the web goes mobile, colleges fail to keep up. *The Chronicle of Higher Education, 57*(21), A1–A14.

Kiger, D. (2012). Examining the influence of a mobile learning intervention on third grade math achievement. *Journal of Research on Technology in Education, 45*(1), 61–82.

Koole, M. (2009). A model for framing mobile learning. In M. Ally (Ed.), *Mobile learning: Transforming the delivery of education and training* (pp. 25–47). Edmonton: Athabasca University Press.

Krajcik, J., Blumenfeld, P. C., Marx, R. W., & Soloway, E. (1994). A collaborative model for helping middle grade science teachers learn instruction. *The Elementary School Journal, 94*(5), 482–497.

Lai, K., Khaddage, F., & Knezek, G. (2013a). Blending student technology experiences in formal and informal learning. *Journal of Computer Assisted Learning, 29*(5), 414–425. doi:10.1111/jcal.12030.

Lai, K., Khaddage, F., & Knezek, G. (2013b). Working group 2: Advancing mobile learning across formal and informal contexts. In *International Summit on ICT in Education* (Vol. 2012, pp. 1–7).

Lave, J., & Wenger, E. (1991). *Situated learning: Legitimate peripheral participation. Learning in doing* (Vol. 95). Cambridge: Cambridge University Press. doi:10.2307/2804509.

Looi, C.-K., & Toh, Y. (2014). Orchestrating the flexible mobile learning classrooms. In M. Ally & A. Tsinakos (Eds.), *Increasing access through mobile learning* (pp. 161–174). Vancouver: Commonwealth of Learning and Athabasca University.

Lower, J. (2010). Management of findings: There's an app for that. Imaging Economics. http://www.imagingeconomics.com/2014/01/management-findings-theres-app/. Accessed 26 March 2014.

Martindale, T., & Dowdy, M. (2010). Personal learning environments. In G. Veletsianos (Ed.), *Emerging technologies in distance education* (pp. 177–194). Edmonton: Athabasca University Press.

Martínez-Pérez, B., de la Torre-Diez, I., López-Coronado, M., Saniz-de-Abajo, B., Robles, M., & Garcia-Gómez, J. M. (2014). Mobile clinical decision support systems and applications: A literature and commercial review. *Journal of Medical Systems, 38*(4), 1–10. doi:10.1007/s10916-013-0004-y.

Marx, R. W., Blumenfeld, P. C., Krajcik, J. S., & Soloway, E. (1997). Enacting project-based science. *The Elementary School Journal, 97*(4), 341. doi:10.1086/461870.

Mobile Learning Network (MoLeNET). (2009). What is mobile learning? http://www.molenet.org.uk. Accessed 30 Dec 2009.

Motiwalla, L. F. (2007). Mobile learning: A framework and evaluation. *Computers & Education, 49*, 581–596. doi:10.1016/j.compedu.2005.10.011.

Nihalani, P., & Mayrath, M. (2010). *Mobile learning : Evidence of increased learning and motivation from using an iPhone app.* Austin, TX: GetYA Learn On. http://gylo.com/WhitePaper_03302010_Stats1.pdf. Accessed 19 June 2015.

Northcliffe, A., & Middleton, A. (2013). The innovative use of personal smart devices by students to support their learning. In L. A. Wankel & P. Blessinger (Eds.), *Increasing student engagement and retention using mobile applications: Smartphones, Skype and texting technologies* (pp. 175–208). Bingley: Emerald Group Publishing Limited.

Nyugen, F. (2012). Performance support. In R. A. Reiser & J. V. Dempsey (Eds.), *Trends and issues in instructional design and technology* (3rd ed., pp. 147–157). Boston: Pearson.

O'Neill, M. (2013, November 4). Once sideshows, colleges' mobile apps move to center stage. *The Chronicle of Higher Education.* http://chronicle.com/article/Once-Sideshows-Colleges/142775/. Accessed 28 March 2014.

Ostler, E. (2012). 21st Century STEM Education: A tactical model for long-range success. *International Journal of Applied Science and Technology, 2*(1), 28–33. (University of N. at O).

Park, Y. (2011). A pedagogical framework for mobile learning: Categorizing educational applications of mobile technologies into four types. *The International Review of Research in Open and Distance Learning, 12*(2), 78–102.

Pimmer, C., Linxen, S., & Gröhbiel, U. (2012). Facebook as a learning tool? A case study on the appropriation of social network sites from mobile phones in developing countries. *British Journal of Educational Technology, 43*(5), 726–738. doi:10.1111/j.1467-8535.2012.01351.x.

Pimmer, C., Brysiewicz, P., Linxen, S., Walters, F., Chipps, J., & Gröhbiel, U. (2014). Informal mobile learning in nurse education and practice in remote areas-A case study from rural South Africa. *Nurse Education Today, 34*(11), 1398–1404. doi:10.1016/j.nedt.2014.03.013.

Project Tomorrow. (2010). *Learning in the 21st century: Taking it mobile! Executive summary.* Irvine: Project Tomorrow.

Quinn, C. (2000). mLearning: Mobile, wireless, in-your-pocket learning. *LineZine.* http://www.linezine.com/2.1/features/cqmmwiyp.htm. Accessed 18 Dec 2012.

Rankin, M. (2009). Some general comments on the "Twitter Experiment." *elua.net.* http://www.elsua.net/2009/06/01/the-twitter-experiment-by-dr-monica-rankin/. Accessed 11 March 2014.

Redd, J. B. (2011). Using mobile devices and gaming as a means of building vocabulary. *International Journal of Interactive Mobile, 5*(4), 30–39.

Romney, C. A. (2011). Tablet PC use in freshman mathematics classes promotes STEM retention. In *2011 Frontiers in Education Conference (FIE)* (pp. F1J–1–F1J–7). Rapid City, SD, IEEE. doi:10.1109/FIE.2011.6142773.

Roschelle, J., Patton, C., & Tatar, D. (2007). Designing networked handheld devices to enhance school learning. *Advances in Computers, 70*, 1–60.

Rossett, A. (2010). Ode to mobile performance support. *Learning Solutions Magazine.*

Ryu, H., & Parsons, D. (2012). Risky business or sharing the load?—Social flow in collaborative mobile learning. *Computers & Education, 58*(2), 707–720. doi:10.1016/j.compedu.2011.09.019.

Sha, L., Looi, C.-K., Chen, W., & Zhang, B. H. (2012). Understanding mobile learning from the perspective of self-regulated learning. *Journal of Computer Assisted Learning, 28*(4), 366–378. doi:10.1111/j.1365-2729.2011.00461.x.

Sharples, M., Taylor, J., & Vavoula, G. (2007). A theory of learning for the mobile age. In R. Andrews & C. Haythornthwaite (Eds.), *The Sage handbook of elearning research* (pp. 221–247). London: Sage.

Shih, K.-P., Chen, H.-C., Chang, C.-Y., & Kao, T.-C. (2010). The development and implementation of scaffolding-based self-regulated learning system for e/m-learning. *Educational Technology & Society, 13*(1), 80–93.

Tella, S. (2003). M-learning—Cybertextual travelling or a herald of post-modern education? In H. Iahti & P. Seppälä (Eds.), *Mobile learning* (pp. 7–21). Helsinki: IT Press.

Thomasian, J. (2011). *Building a science, technology, engineering, and math education agenda.* Washington, D.C.: National Governors Association Center for Best Practices. http://files.eric.ed.gov/fulltext/ED496324.pdf. Accessed 1 Oct 2014.

Thompson, C. (2012). The lessons of non-formal learning for urban youth. *Educational Forum, 76*(1), 58068.

Traxler, J. (2005). *Defining mobile learning.* Paper presented at ADIS International Conference Mobile Learning, Qawra, Malta. http://www.iadis.net/dl/final_uploads/200506C018.pdf. Accessed 18 Dec 2012.

Traxler, J. (2007). Defining, discussing and evaluating mobile learning: The moving finger writes and having writ... *The International Review of Research in Open and Distance Learning, 8*(2). http://www.irrodl.org/index.php/irrodl/article/view/346/875. Accessed 18 Dec 2012.

Traxler, J. (2010). Distance education and mobile learning: Catching up, taking stock. *Distance Education, 31*(2), 129–138. doi:10.1080/01587919.2010.503362.

Valk, J., Rashid, A. T., & Elder, L. (2010). Using mobile phones to improve educational outcomes: An analysis of evidence from Asia. *International Review of Research in Open and Distance Learning, 11*(1), 13–14.

White, T., & Martin, L. (2014). Mathematics and mobile learning. *TechTrends, 58*(1), 64–70.

White, T., Booker, A., Ching, C. C., & Martin, L. (2012). Integrating digital and mathematical practices across contexts: A manifesto for mobile learning. *International Journal of Learning and Media, 3*(3), 7–13. doi:10.1162/IJLM_a_00076.

Wiig, K. M. (1999). Introducing knowledge management into the enterprise. In J. Liebowitz (Ed.), *Knowledge management handbook* (pp. 3.1–3.41). Boca Raton: CRC Press.

Wright, T. A. (2011). *The University of Nebraska at Omaha's Criss Library mobile resources: A study of user's preferences* (unpublished thesis). University of Nebraska, Lincoln. USA.

Yang, S. (1997). Information seeking as problem-solving using a qualitative approach to uncover the novice learners' information-seeking processes in a Perseus hypertext system. *Library & Information Science Research, 19*(1), 71–94. doi:10.1016/S0740-8188(97)90006-2.

Yoon, S. A., & Wang, J. (2014). Making the invisible visible in science museums through augmented reality devices. *TechTrends, 58*(1), 49–55.

Zhang, B., Looi, C.-K., Seow, P., Chia, G., Wong, L.-H., Chen, W., & Norris, C. (2010). Deconstructing and reconstructing: Transforming primary science learning via a mobilized curriculum. *Computers & Education, 55*(4), 1504–1523. doi:10.1016/j.compedu.2010.06.016.

Zimmerman, H. T., & Land, S. M. (2014). Facilitating place-based learning in outdoor informal environments with mobile computers. *TechTrends, 58*(1), 77–83.

Michael M. Grant is an Assistant Professor in the Educational Technology program at the University of South Carolina. His research considers three complementary areas: the design and development of technology-enhanced learning environments, graphic and instructional designs to support learning, and key learner characteristics. His most recent scholarship has focused on how to design, develop, and implement mobile teaching and learning in K-12 and higher education. Dr. Grant earned his Ph.D. from The University of Georgia in Instructional Technology. He is currently the Editor of the *Interdisciplinary Journal of Problem-based Learning,* and he can be contacted via his website Viral-Notebook.com or through Twitter @michaemgrant.

Implementing Large-Scale Mobile Device Initiatives in Schools and Institutions

Hong Lin

Abstract This chapter discusses factors to drive the explosive growth of mobile devices in Science, Technology, Engineering, Arts, and Mathematics (STEAM). Drawing upon these factors, the chapter examines the innovations of mobile devices adopted in the STEAM classroom and barriers experienced by educators in the process of mobile technology integration. Built on the innovations and barriers of the use of mobile devices, the chapter continues to discuss what essential conditions are needed to ensure successful implementation of large-scale mobile device initiatives in STEAM. These factors, innovations, barriers, and conditions also position academic leaders and educators to rethink domain-related curriculum in STEAM and harness increasingly ubiquitous mobile technology in order to meet the needs of the 21st century.

Keywords Mobile devices · Mobile learning · Large-scale initiatives · Bring Your Own Device (BYOD) · Technology trends

Introduction—Mobile Device Trends in Schools and Institutions

The recent evolution of handheld mobile devices and wireless technology has led to large-scale implementation of mobile devices, such as tablets and smartphones, in educational settings. Anderson University in South Carolina launched The Mobile Learning Initiative, providing iPads to all biology students with apps for in-class and collaborative research projects (Anderson University, 2014). Jackson State University (JSU) provided iPads to all full-time freshmen, enabling them to access eBooks and dozens of apps that allow them to take notes, collaborate on content, communicate with instructors and peers, tap into math references, learn a foreign language, listen to thousands of audiobooks, and much more (Jackson State University News Room, 2013). Similarly, the Jeannine Rainbolt College of Education

H. Lin (✉)
University of Oklahoma, Norman, USA
e-mail: honglin@ou.edu

© Springer International Publishing Switzerland 2015
X. Ge et al. (eds.), *Emerging Technologies for STEAM Education,*
Educational Communications and Technology: Issues and Innovations,
DOI 10.1007/978-3-319-02573-5_10

(JRCoE) at the University of Oklahoma provided iPads to all its full-time under-graduate students. The goal is not just to transform students' learning experiences, but also to prepare pre-service teachers to incorporate technology in their future classrooms, and to cultivate their long-term use of tablets as professional educators (JRCoE, 2013). K-12 schools are not left behind. After a brief pause and reflection, the Miami-Dade County Public School District (M-DCPS) resumed their plan to give digital devices to all 354,000 students. This initiative is one of the largest one-to-one digital computing initiatives in the country (Blazer, 2014).

There are three distinct trends that have been driving the exponential adoption of mobile devices in educational settings during the 2000s. First, unlike the late 1980s and 1990s when portable devices were primarily laptops and notebooks, the implementation of portable devices in the millennium is focusing more on small-er, handheld devices such as tablets and smartphones (Zaranis, Kalogiannakis, & Papadakis, 2013). For this reason, another trend in the 2000s is the increasing adop-tion of mobile learning to enhance students' experience. Researchers have indicated that mobile learning, through the use of tablets and smartphones, presents new op-portunities for learning and strengthens the learning experience in ways other devic-es simply cannot achieve (Lam & Duan, 2012; Zaranis et al., 2013). In other words, mobile learning takes into account the mobility of technology, students, and learn-ing (Sharples, Taylor, & Vavoula, 2007). The third trend, it follows, is that more and more schools and institutions are launching large-scale mobile device initiatives and taking a systematic approach to embrace the advantages of mobile learning (The Technology Outlook for STEM + Education 2013–2018 Report, 2013; UNES-CO, 2012). The systematic approach is crucial to ensure that stakeholders such as leaders, educators, students, technicians, vendors communicate and collaborate ef-fectively (Blazer, 2014; Herold, 2014; The Technology Outlook for STEM + Educa-tion 2013–2018 Report, 2013).

As a result of these trends, some unaddressed questions naturally come to our attention. What drives the explosive growth of mobile devices in educational set-tings? What happens when mobile devices are introduced and integrated in the STEAM classroom? What infrastructure should be in place to ensure a large-scale mobile device initiative succeeds and scales up? The following sections address these questions in the context of how mobile devices are implemented and adminis-tered in Science, Technology, Engineering, Art, and Math (STEAM). It will review emerging empirical studies on various aspects of research on mobile learning in STEAM education and discuss essential conditions for successful mobile device initiatives in STEAM.

Factors Influencing the Growth of Mobile Device Usage in Educational Settings

What drives the explosive growth of mobile devices in STEAM? This section will summarize three organizing factors identified in the literature regarding the mobil-ity of technology, students, and learning.

The Mobility of Technology

The mobile market consisted of more than 6.8 billion users by 2013, and the market continues to grow (MobiThinking, 2014). A 2014 survey showed that nearly 160 million people in the U.S. owned smartphones, which is 66.8% of the total phone market penetration in the U.S. (ComScore Report, 2014). In addition to smartphones, over 70 million of 285 million tablet owners worldwide at the end of 2013 were in the U.S. (TabTimes, 2013). The widespread use of smartphones and tablets has pushed developers to further explore ways to optimize the hardware and software inside cell phones and tablets. The goal is to make mobile devices more capable, user interfaces more natural and apps more educationally friendly (Matthews, 2011; The Technology Outlook for STEM+Education 2013–2018 Report, 2013). With this understanding, a factor to drive the explosive growth of mobile devices in STEAM is the rapid development in mobile technologies that provide new possibilities for STEAM educators and students to accomplish what they otherwise could not (O'Shea, Gabriel, & Prabhu, 2010; Vogel, Spikol, Jurti, & Milrad, 2010).

A review of literature identified three major mobile advancements that enable augmented teaching and learning experience in STEAM. The first mobile advancement involves the concept of cloud computing. Cloud computing has five essential characteristics: (1) On-demand self-service, which means users can obtain computing capabilities automatically without requiring human interaction and assistance; (2) Broad network access, which enables the provision of processing, storage, remote networks, and other computing resources in mobile phones, tablets, laptops, and workstations; (3) Resource pooling, where computing resources are dynamically assigned and reassigned according to user demand; (4) Rapid elasticity, which allows hardware and software capabilities to be elastically provided and released in response to user demands; (5). Measured service, which means users and providers of the services can both monitor and control resource usage to ensure transparency of resource usage (Koutsopoulos & Kotsanis, 2014). Empowered by cloud computing capabilities, the hardware and software capabilities in mobile devices have unveiled a new era in STEAM.

In conjunction, the second advancement is the hardware capabilities in a variety of mobile platforms, which include, but are not limited to, smart phones, tablets, pocket PCs, personal audio players, personal digital assistants, e-readers, and Global Positioning Systems (GPS). The hardware in these mobile platforms usually support WiFi networking which allows the mobile device to connect to the Internet. They also support Bluetooth networking to support and increase the use of headphones, microphones, keyboards, and other peripheral devices (Koutsopoulous & Kotsanis, 2014; Minaie, Sanati-Mehrizy, Sanati-Mehrizy, & Sanati-Mehrizy, 2011; Murray & Olcese, 2011). Additionally, these platforms have hardware systems that integrate the capabilities of GPS such as depicting a map of stars and planet that are either above the horizon or below, day or night (Murray & Olcese, 2011). Moreover, a majority of tablets have a touch screen interface that not only allows various gestures such as pinch, flick, stretch, and rotate, but also allows multi-touch display. As such, a piano student, for instance, can pinch the screen to the size of his or her wish, handle more than one touch simultaneously, play multiple keys, and hear multiple notes (Murray & Olcese, 2011).

Arguably, researchers indicated that the hardware capabilities in various mobile platforms have reshaped the ways in which information is created, accessed, and disseminated in STEAM (Avraamidou, 2008; Cantrell & Knudson, 2006; STEM Education Coalition, 2014; UNESCO, 2012). For example, students can work on real-world scientific questions and solutions individually and collaboratively by using various digitally-mediated tools, such as podcasting, remote monitoring, digital recording, digital storytelling board, desktop sharing, and videoconferencing. Researchers pointed out that while students can assess these cloud-based computing tools via their desktop computers as well, mobile devices allow students to leverage the ease of access to information related to scientific questions and observations at their fingertips (Chew-Hung et al., 2012; Evagorou, 2008; Peffer, Bodzin, & Smith, 2013).

To couple with the hardware specifications in various mobile platforms, the third mobile advancement is the software applications used by mobile devices. After all, what makes a difference in how mobile devices are adopted is what applications are developed to take the advantages of the hardware. The mobile apps in Apple and Android, two of the most popular mobile operating systems, have skyrocketed during the past few years. By July 2014, more than 1.3 million apps including 10,000 education apps were created for the Android hardware, and more than 1.2 million apps including 8000 education apps were on the Apple hardware (AppBrain, 2014; iPad in Education, 2014a; The Statistics Portal, 2014). Researchers pointed out that "we are in the era of the mobile platform now, and apps is reigning as king" (Norris & Soloway, 2011, p. 5).

These educational apps cover a wide range of subjects, accommodate different learning styles, and are ambitious to change the landscape of education. For instance, the iTunes U app on the Apple platform can allow educators of all levels to create their courses featuring audio, video, books, and other content. Students can access their assignments, materials, study notes, and discussions all together in iTunes U. This app touts the ability to keep students prepared for class and engaged in learning for free and at their fingertips (iPad in Education, 2014b). Some apps such as Dropbox and Box connect to web-based services and enable efficient file sharing and archiving (Murray & Olcese, 2011). Some apps support students organizing their calendar, worksheets, homework, learning notes, tests, and projects (Novello, 2012). In the context of STEAM, a variety of apps can be leveraged to enhance teaching and learning. Some apps help STEM teachers deliver digital content such as lectures, online multimedia materials, and reference materials to students (White & Martin, 2012). Some apps allow both STEAM teachers and students to create content such as voice recordings, video and images, photo slideshows, and concept map (White & Martin, 2012). Additionally, some other apps introduce STEAM concepts, enable students to use interactive rubrics to receive immediate feedback on quizzes in preschool classrooms (Aronin & Floyd, 2013; Novello, 2012).

The Mobility of Students

Along with the mobility of technology discussed above is the second factor to drive the explosive growth of mobile devices —the mobility of students. Students today desire to move freely and easily and still be productive anywhere and anytime (Aronin & Floyd, 2013; Avraamindou, 2008; El-Hussein & Cronje, 2010; O'Shea et al., 2010). In other words, students do not want to "sit in a small space for 5 h a day while a teacher talks about the past and present" (Wiles, 2007, p. 2). Instead, they increasingly desire to access, create, and share information wherever and whenever they want (Sharples et al., 2007; The Technology Outlook for STEM + Education 2013-2018 Report (2013). For this reason, mobile devices with powerful hardware and software capabilities in cloud computing, as discussed in the previous section, meet students' desire of mobility.

Although the desktop computer still plays an important role in the classroom and student learning, its use drops every year compared with that of mobile devices (Norris & Soloway, 2011). The first reason is that desktop computing is place-bound for students while mobile devices are wireless and portable (Chew-Hung et al., 2012; El-Hussein & Cronje, 2010; Evagorou, 2008). The wireless and portable functionalities allow users to interact and collaborate more freely and easily while on the move (Chew-Hung et al., 2012; El-Hussein & Cronje, 2010; Evagorou, 2008). The second reason is that the use of mobile devices represents a shift from a teacher-driven approach to a student-centered learning environment where students are encouraged to interact and collaborate when they are on move (Koutsopoulos & Kotsanis, 2014; Serio, Ibáñez, & Kloos, 2013). Specifically, in a student-centered learning environment, the availability of mobile devices to students is inevitable because students nowadays "do more than reproduce knowledge; they question and challenge the ideas of others and forward their own opinions and ideas" (Koutso-poulos & Kotsanis, 2014, p. 50). Such an observation aligned with the results of a recent study of 2350 K-12 students who valued a student-centered learning environ-ment with mobile devices. According to the survey, 92 % of the surveyed students in elementary, middle, and high school in the U.S. believed that mobile devices will change the way they learn in the future and make learning more fun. More-over, 69 % of them would like to see more mobile device integration in their class-rooms (Booker, 2013). "It is inevitable that all computing will be mobile" (Norris & Soloway, 2011, p. 5).

To scale up the use of mobile devices in the classroom, some K-12 schools which usually prefer to provide mobile devices to students now allow their students to bring their own devices to the classrooms including tablets, phones, and laptops (CISCO, 2012; George, 2014). Bring Your Own Device (BYOD) allows students access to the same mobile devices at school and at home without switching among devices, thus making students work with technology with which they are already comfort-able and familiar (CISCO, 2012; Horizon Project, 2013). Researchers and educators stated that Bring Your Own Device (BYOD) is a great approach to engage students in that the devices are integral to the world in which students live, therefore, BYOD will make learning part of their lives and enable a personalized learning experience (El-Hussein & Cronje, 2010; George, 2014; Horizon Project, 2013; Walling, 2012). Instead of banning BYOD, researchers argued that schools should teach students how to use their own devices properly (CISCO, 2012; DeWitt, 2012).

In the context of STEAM, the mobility of students ensures that learning activities turn quickly from concept to reality. For example, STEAM freshmen at Jackson State University enjoyed carrying their iPads provided by the university to do graphing calculation and access math reference formulas in class and outside of the classroom (Jackson State University, 2013). Students at Instituto Technologicoy de Estudios Superiores de Monterrey were engaged in a Mobile Intelligent Laboratory, in which students collaborated on the move in a physics experiment. In the same fashion, art students adopted a BYOD approach to create and leverage a mobile blogging site to bridge meaning making across school and various art museum settings (Pierroux, Krange, & Sem, 2011).

The Mobility of Learning

The third factor to drive the explosive growth of mobile devices in STEAM is that online learning has become mainstream and is optimized for mobile learning. A survey supported by the Sloan Foundation found that senior executives in higher education—presidents, provosts, deans, campus leaders—increasingly considered online learning as a strategic element in policy making. The survey also reported that 66 % of the senior academic officers from 2500 colleges and universities agreed that online learning was a critical element in their institutional strategic goals (Allen & Seaman, 2013). As a result, schools and institutions are adding new online courses and programs, adopting apps into their curriculum, and modifying websites, educational materials, resources, and tools to optimize learning for mobile devices (The Technology Outlook for STEM+Education 2013–2018 Report, 2012). For instance, Brown University launched a free online engineering course to teach high school students about the merits and challenges of the field (The New York Times, 2013). Florence-Darlington Technical College created the online physics course "Power Up: High Tech Online" to train the next generation of nuclear engineers by virtually connecting students with nuclear professionals (The Huffington Post, 2013).

Mobile learning is at the intersection of online learning and mobile computing (El-Hussein & Cronje, 2010). Schools and universities are involved in pioneering experiments for transmitting all instructional online materials to students by means of mobile devices (El-Hussein & Cronje, 2010; Walker, 2007). One noticeable trend is that schools and universities are employing mobile apps in their learning management systems (LMS). Schoology, a LMS adopted by K-12 teachers, recently released a mobile app that helps teachers streamline student submissions and the grading workflow with a simple gesture: swiping left or right in a mobile device (STEMblog, 2014). Blackboard, the most widely adopted LMS in higher education in the U.S., offers a mobile platform to allow students access to all content and assignments virtually anywhere with any types of mobile devices including smartphones (Blackboard Mobile Learn, 2014). Desire2Learn, another big player of LMS in higher education, touts to let students take charge of their learning experience when they can easily work with course materials, cloud drives, and mobiles apps all in one place—at the students' fingertips (Desire@Learn Binder, 2014). Together with the mobility of technology and students, mobile LMS save students' and faculty's valuable time spent in going through the regular LMS processes in the desktop computing, which can now be done while they are on the move (University of Central Oklahoma, 2014).

All things considered, the three key factors—the mobility of technology, students, and learning—drive the widespread growth of mobile devices in schools, universities and the STEAM sector. The following section discusses what happens when mobile applications are integrated into the curriculum.

Mobile Applications and Technology Integration Barriers in STEAM

As discussed in the previous section, advanced mobile communication, hardware, and software capabilities have enabled augmented teaching and learning experiences in STEAM that otherwise could not be accomplished. Educators now are challenged to develop innovative ways to integrate mobile devices into their curricula. What happens when mobile devices are introduced and integrated in the STEAM classroom?

Mobile Applications in the STEAM Classroom

The use of mobile devices is playing an increasingly pivotal role in transforming the landscape of teaching and learning in STEAM (Ahmed & Parsons, 2012; Lutz, Schäfer, & Diehl, 2012; STEM Education Coalition, 2014; UNESCO, 2012). Research in STEAM has explored many aspects of integrating mobile devices into curricula to support and augment a variety of learning activities.

In science settings, mobile devices were used in a variety of contexts and for different purposes. Some educators used mobile devices to promote inquiry-based science learning (Ahmed & Parsons, 2012; Vogel et al., 2010). In an ecology course, mobile devices were used to support flexible ecology learning contexts in various locations across school and home contexts (Luckin et al., 2005). Additionally, educators used mobile devices to support student learning in informal science settings as a continuum from formal science settings (Scanlon, Jones, & Waycott, 2005). Mobile devices were also used to connect to a local wireless network so as to document and share information quickly during professional field trips (Cantrell & Knudson, 2006).

Mobile computing is becoming widely integrated in the undergraduate and graduate curricula within computer science and computer engineering settings. A survey of 33 universities, from Carnegie Melon University to Utah State University, indicated that the majority of these surveyed universities were offering graduate courses on mobile computing (Minaie et al., 2011). Meanwhile, many programs in these surveyed universities had lined up to change their curricula to offer mobile computing courses for their undergraduate students, too. As such, computer science educators are implementing mobile devices to serve a variety of purposes. One educator integrated handheld devices into a programming course and had students deploy mobile applications to support lab-intensive courses (Mahmoud, 2008). Similarly, some educators used mobile devices to create collaborative learning activities during lecture to scale up lecture-based courses. A majority of the students in the study found the redesigned courses with mobile devices more motivating and engaging (Simon, Anderson, Hoyer, & Hu 2004).

In engineering classrooms, team-based learning is a key aspect of any student's academic success (Lutz et al., 2012). For this reason, the use of mobile devices focused on creating collaborative learning environments for students. In higher education, students used mobile apps to create remote labs so that they could collaborate and help each other in those rote labs (Barcia-Zubia, López-de-Ipiña, & Orduña, 2010). Another study reported that engineering students used mobile devices consistently to build a collaborative environment in the classroom, in which teamwork is a required component in engineering education (Lutz et al., 2012). In K-12 environments, elementary school girls used mobile devices in a *Simple Machine in Your Life* project to collaboratively learn about the simple machines in their surroundings. Moreover, elementary students in the *GreenHat* project used a GPS-enabled Smartphone to explore the natural environment through expert's perspectives in their group assignments (Ryokai, Agogino, & Oehlberg, 2012).

In mathematics settings, the use of mobile devices usually focuses on helping students solve authentic math questions. A study showed that middle school students worked as mathematicians by carrying out authentic math activities using mobile phones collaboratively. The study filled a literature gap that few research studies had examined middle school students' building of mathematical knowledge using mobile phones (Daher, 2010). Educators also used mobile devices to teach realistic mathematics to kindergarten students (Zaranis et al., 2013). Moreover, educators developed an application to support families in real-life situations where problem solving involved mathematics (Alexander et al., 2010).

In art settings, mobile devices are also widely used in order to design authentic opportunities for learning where students "do" arts, therefore, motivating heretofore unmotivated students. First, augmented reality (AR), which integrated 3-D virtual objects into a 3-D real environment in real time, is a great way to motivate students by connecting to real or simulated 3-D environments (O'Shea et al., 2010; Serio et al., 2013). In an art course, students used an AR system and incorporated location-aware mobile technologies to trigger digital characters, objects, and events on Asian arts. Eventually, the mobile technologies helped these art students create, implement, and evaluate their augmented reality experience for the San Diego Museum of Arts (O'Shea et al., 2010). Similarly, an augmented reality system was deployed in mobile devices to motivate middle school students learning in a visual art course. Results found that students' attention and motivation in a learning environment based on augmented-reality were much better than those obtained in a PowerPoint-slides-based learning environment (Serio et al., 2013). Moreover, AR was also integrated into a mobile guide system in a painting course to teach students painting appreciation (Change et al., 2014). Second, in addition to AR, mobile devices were also used creatively to enhance traditional ways of learning arts. One study showed that educators used digital media and tools on tablets to prepare all arts majors to enhance traditional drawing and design media (Moore College, 2014). In the same fashion, art students created and leveraged a mobile blogging site with their mobile devices to bridge meaning making across school and various art museum settings (Pierroux et al., 2011).

The examination of the above-mentioned studies indicated various ways of using mobile devices to support innovative learning environments in domain-related curriculum in STEAM. Now powered by mobile devices, do STEAM educators transition well from traditional instruction to mobile-device-enhanced instruction? What barriers have they experienced in the process of mobile technology integration in their curricula?

Barriers to Effective Mobile Technology Integration in STEAM Curricula

Compared with the exciting capabilities of mobile technologies, less exciting news is that many STEAM educators also reported barriers to effectively integrating mobile devices into their curricula. Some barriers of mobile technologies were related to what Ertmer (1999, 2005) called first-order or external barriers, such as access to technology, time, training of technology use, and support (Bannon, Martin, & Nunes-Bufford, 2012; Hechter & Vermette, 2013). National data consistently showed increasing improvement in the access of mobile devices, bandwidth, technical support, and training on the mechanical use of mobile devices in the K-12 and university classrooms (O'Shea et al., 2010; The Technology Outlook for STEM+Education 2013–2018 Report, 2013; Vogel et al., 2010). In particular, the Federal Communications Commission made available more than $ 2 billion in 2014 and $ 1 billion annually afterwards to significantly expand Wi-Fi networks to all schools and libraries (Federal Communications Commission, 2014).

Another barrier to the use of mobile devices is related to the digital divide. The notion of digital divide is that not everyone has access to technology and Internet. The unbalanced access to technology and Internet could further divide a growing gap between the underprivileged members of society and the wealthy, middle-class people in terms of their access to, use of, or knowledge of information and communication technologies (Dewan & Riggins, 2005; Warschauer, 2004). The digital divide could pose new concerns in the age of social networking and mobile devices as well (Bauerlein, 2011). A few schools experienced the concern of digital divide in their mobile device initiatives when some economically disadvantaged K-12 students and parents complained not having Wi-Fi at home when mobile devices were allowed to bring home (Herold, 2014; Iasevoli, 2013). Although literature is lacking to examine how digital divide could affect mobile teaching and learning in the STEAM settings, it could shed lights to STEAM leaders and educators during planning.

Beyond access, bandwidth, technical support, and the digital device—the first order of effective mobile technology integration, the literature documented a prevalent barrier to hinder mobile technology integration in STEAM—the second-order or internal barriers of effective pedagogy of technology integration (Ertmer, 1999, 2005). Studies reported that STEAM teachers experienced great barriers in using effective pedagogy to integrate mobile technology into their classrooms. In a recent survey of 430 in-service science educators, 80 % of them indicated that various technologies, including mobile devices are available to them. However, about one quarter of respondents stated that they did not receive effective pedagogical training of technology integration (Hechter & Vermette, 2013). In a survey of urban school mathematics teachers, researchers also found that while mobile technologies were widely accessible to students and teachers, a decline of the use and integration of computer technology, including mobile devices, was apparent among the surveyed mathematics teachers (Wachira & Keengwe, 2011).

Clearly, when STEAM educators passed the initial phase of the mechanical use of mobile devices, they experienced more barriers in pedagogically integrating mobile technologies. In other words, it is critical for STEAM educators to understand that mobile devices are not just about the availability of tools and apps, but more about a new way of thinking and teaching (The Technology Outlook for STEM + Education 2013–2018 Report, 2013; Windschitl, 2009). In particular, the effective pedagogy of technology integration means "incorporating technology and technology practices into all aspects of teaching and learning, specifically, incorporating appropriate technology in objectives, lessons, and assessment of learning outcomes" (Wachira & Keengwe, 2011, p. 17). Researchers identified that teachers' fundamental beliefs about teacher-student roles, curricular emphases, and assessment practices had significant impact on their effective technology integration (Ertmer, 1999, 2005; Hew & Brush, 2007). In relation to technology integration in science, it is suggested to use constructivist pedagogies that encourage hands-on applications with science-based technologies and that allow students to interact with their peers (Harris, 2005). As for mobile technology integration in mathematics, it is recommended focusing on student-centered active learning strategies and also aligning appropriate mobile applications with learning activities (Bannon et al., 2012).

A question naturally arises whether STEAM educators receive necessary professional training on mobile technology integration into their curricula. Unfortunately, despite the widespread recognition of the importance of mobile learning in STEAM, many STEAM educators have not had training or professional development opportunities equipping them to effectively adopt best pedagogies of mobile technology (Meyer, 2013). Researchers called for systematic teacher preparation and professional development for STEAM educators (Bannon et al., 2012; Hechter & Vermette, 2013; Meyer, 2013; The Technology Outlook for STEM + Education 2013–2018 Report, 2013; Windschitl, 2009). Arguably, it is critical for schools and institutions to provide initial technical support along with ongoing professional development opportunities to address STEAM educators' external and internal barriers. Such support and opportunities are part of the essential conditions for successful mobile device initiatives that will be discussed in the following section.

Essential Conditions for Successful Mobile Device Initiatives in STEAM

What infrastructure should be in place to ensure a large-scale mobile device initiative to succeed and scale up? The following section answers this question in the context of STEAM.

Visionary Leadership and Commitment

As in any large-scale initiative, visionary leadership and commitment are central to spearheading innovation and change in STEAM (Abdul-Alim, 2012). Visionary leaders should position mobile device initiatives as part of the overall institutional goals and efforts to get broader support from educators, students, and departments (MindShift, 2012). Anderson University (AU) launched their Mobile Learning Initiative in 2011. The initiative particularly enabled biology and art students to benefit huge gains in student understanding of materials. The leadership of the University touts their commitment to be a pioneer of mobile technology in STEAM and overall undergraduate education (Anderson University, 2014). Similarly, the Moore iPad Initiative at the Moore College of Art was strongly supported by its top administration. Their Academic Dean, Dona Lantz stated that: "Faculty at Moore are committed to educating students for contemporary careers in art and design. The iPad is a pivotal learning tool in the new Foundation curriculum where the integration of digital media and tools are taught and used in tandem with traditional drawing and design media" (The Moore iPad Initiative, 2014, p. 1).

In the same fashion, some institutions have established a center, office, or committee at the state, or institutional level to support the use of mobile devices in STEAM education. The Carnegie Science Center, which is one of the four Carnegie Museums of Pittsburgh, partnered with the Army National Guard's Mobile Learning Center Programs to promote a cutting-edge mobile teaching and learning lab (Hohenbrink, 2011). The State of North Carolina has a STEM Center that serves as a catalyst for innovation and change. They collaborated with institutions and schools to provide educational services, grants for mobile device initiatives, and professional development opportunities on mobile technology (SMT, 2014).

In contrast, weak leadership can sink a well-intentioned large-scale mobile initiative. In particular, weak leaders would see mobile device initiatives as a technology project, rush to roll out the mobile devices, and not communicate or collaborate effectively across different departments (Roscorla, 2014). A case in point is Los Angeles Unified School District's (LAUSD) iPad initiative in 2013. As the nation's second-largest school district, LAUSD planned to distribute iPads to all of its 651,000 students by the end of 2014. Soon after, the LAUSD had to dramatically scale back its initiative. One of the biggest complaints was that district leaders had rushed the deployment of the mobile devices without planning strategically, setting realistic timelines, and getting buy-in from educators (Herold, 2014).

Clearly, strategic leadership is critical to communicate and harmonize the coordination of access of mobile devices, bandwidth, technical support, the digital divide, and professional development, among other issues (Herold, 2014; O'Shea et al., 2010; Roscorla, 2014; The Technology Outlook for STEM + Education 2013–2018 Report, 2013; Vogel et al., 2010). Putting strong leadership in the context of mobile device initiatives in STEAM, it is clear that strong leaders draw capable people to cultivate a unified vision across the board so that the vision of large-scale mobile device initiatives can be implemented as a cautionary tale (MindShift, 2012).

Strategic Education Goals

Mobile device initiatives should work in harmony with strategic educational goals such as making learning mobile, supporting different learning needs, leveraging advanced technologies and online resources, and reaching students who would not otherwise have the opportunity to participate (Kukulska-Hulme & Sharpe, 2007). These educational goals should be aligned with curriculum redesign, technology integration, and assessment when mobile device initiatives are mapped out. It is critical that people involved in implementing the initiatives have a clear understanding of the goals, intended outcomes, and risks (UNESCO, 2012). A case in point: the Miami-Dade County Public Schools (M-DCPS) in Florida paused their one-to-one computing initiative to give digital devices to all of its 354,000 students. Learning from Los Angeles Unified School District's (LAUSD) mistakes, M-DCPS reviewed their educational goals and assessment plans before they resumed the initiative in 2015 (Blazer, 2014)

One mistake from LAUSD and M-DCPS's large-scale rollout of mobile devices that these initiatives were promoted as a technology initiative (Herold, 2014; Iasevoli, 2013). In fact, if that happens, educators and students may perceive the tool as a fad or passing trend. Instead, a mobile device initiative should be purposed and positioned as an educational initiative to support or transform pedagogy and curriculum (MindShift, 2012). As discussed in Section "Mobile Applications in the STEAM classroom", a large body of studies in mobile applications across STEAM-related curricula focused on leveraging mobile devices to support and augment learning activities that could not be done traditionally (Ahmed & Parsons, 2012; Lutz et al., 2012; STEM Education Coalition, 2014; UNESCO, 2012). The ultimate educational goals in these learning activities with mobile devices are to promote critical thinking, problem solving, and collaboration (Ahmed & Parsons, 2012; Barcia-Zubia et al., 2010; O'Shea et al., 2010; Zaranis et al., 2013).

Overall, any mobile device initiative should not be a stand-alone component just about the availability of tools; rather, it should be aligned with strategic educational goals and objectives. In doing so, the mobile device initiative is more likely to get broader support from educators, students, and departments (MindShift, 2012).

Educational Scalability

When mobile devices are introduced in schools and institutions on a large scale, *start small, think big* is the guiding principle many schools and institutions employ when implementing and managing their initiatives (MindShift, 2012; UNESCO, 2012). The reason is two-fold. First, the initial small-scale implementation can decrease risk tremendously, help diagnose problems quickly, and revise strategic planning accordingly (Blazer, 2014; Herold, 2014). Second, the experience gained from a small-scale mobile device project can help lay out the foundation for expansion, so that large-scale implementation across the campus can have a better chance to succeed.

A few schools and institutions have started their mobile device initiative small and scaled it up. Canby School District in Oregon began with iPod touches and iPads in just a few classrooms. On the basis of those experiences, they expanded to more classrooms in the next year (Dungca, 2011). Saddleback Valley Unified School District, Rockdale Independent School District, and Kathy Independent School District all started their "Bring Your Own Device" (BYOD) pilot programs first. They reflected on implementation and lessons learned and continued to expand their success to more classrooms (MindShift, 2012). Similarly, Anderson University started their Mobile Learning Initiatives with a few biology courses. Building on their experiences, their officials expected that nearly one third of all courses would be redesigned for mobile learning in the coming years (Anderson University, 2014).

Sufficient Professional Development

To help STEAM educators better understand the process of integrating technology into their curricula in a way that adds the most value to learning from mobile devices, it is critical to develop a comprehensive approach to engage educators in professional development opportunities. These opportunities should include not just how to use the devices, which is a common pitfall in incorporating new technology (MindShift, 2012), but also how to integrate mobile devices into STEAM teachers' pedagogical repertoire and promote critical thinking, problem solving, and collaboration, as discussed in Section "Mobile Applications in the STEAM Classroom" (Ahmed & Parsons, 2012; Barcia-Zubia et al., 2010; O'Shea et al., 2010; Zaranis et al., 2013). In other words, transforming the role of educators by using effective mobile technology pedagogy will tailor students' needs in their learning experience and improve student engagement and interest in STEAM subjects (Koutsopoulos

& Kotsanis, 2014; Meyer, 2013; The Technology Outlook for STEM+Education 2013–2018 Report, 2013; Windschitl, 2009).

To address the mobile technology integration issue effectively, some institutions have implemented collective and collaborative training programs. One effective strategy is to put STEAM teachers in professional learning communities (PLCs) so that they can learn, share, and support each other (Fulton & Britton, 2011; Mindshift, 2012). For instance, the UTeach Institute, launched by the University of Texas at Austin, aims to model a variety of pedagogical methods to aspiring teachers in PLCs to use mobile devices in STEM (Bolkan, 2013). With 35 participating universities across the country, the UTeach Institute trains pre-service teachers to incorporate mobile technologies into inquiry-based lessons. Additionally, a math teacher education program had pre-service teachers use iPads to facilitate collaborative and authentic professional learning experiences (Kearney & Maher, 2013).

Robust Technology Capacity

Wireless networks must now routinely host a wide range of mobile devices running bandwidth-intensive applications such as videos and music. As such, a successful mobile device initiative requires a thorough analysis of existing technological infrastructure such as wireless connectivity throughout the campus, broadband requirements, hardware and software, data storage, off-campus access, security and privacy, technical support, accepted use policies, among other infrastructural features (MindShift, 2012; Scott, 2012; UNESCO, 2012). In fact, a careful analysis of existing technological infrastructure should be the first step in ensuring that a mobile device initiative can and will support educational goals (Scott, 2012). Without robust technology capacity, it is likely that a mobile device initiative would not reach its potential technically, pedagogically, or logistically (MindShift, 2012).

Additionally, it is suggested that more wireless access points be installed across campuses, especially in high density environments, where users can carry two or three mobile devices generating significant increases in the amount of traffic (Netgear, 2014). Meanwhile, maintenance issues, such as Wi-Fi connectivity, access points, upgrades, and various application support for different operating systems and hardware, must be taken into consideration (JISC Digital Media, 2014; Netgear, 2014). It is suggested that schools and institutions start by accommodating whichever the most commonly used mobile platform and trying to reach as many devices as possible (JISC Digital Media, 2014).

Supporting Policies

To support their mobile device initiatives, many schools and institutions may need to revise their existing policies or create new policies. On the one hand, some existing policies may need to be reviewed to determine whether mobile learning disrupts or fits into traditional education approaches. Any policy that prohibits students from using portable devices in learning should be eliminated (UNESCO, 2012). For instance, some schools and institutions have changed wording from *acceptable use* to *responsible use* in their rules and guidance documents (Scott, 2012; UNESCO, 2012). The shift indicated a change in mindset. Instead of simply policing whether students' use of mobile devices, especially the use of their own devices (BYOD), is acceptable or not, the goal is to move toward making students responsible for their behavior when using their devices (CISCO, 2012; DeWitt, 2012).

On the other hand, schools and institutions may need to create new policies to guide a collection of users for various purposes. For example, new policy for mobile devices can be created to ensure that all e-mail communication about patient care and non-public matters in a smartphone or tablet is secure and confidential (Research Information Services & Computing, 2014). Another example is that more than 300 high school students at LAUSD skirted the tablets' security to surf social-networking sites during learning (Iasevoli, 2013). For this reason, a new security policy will ensure that mobile devices will not be left out of a common set of security settings as well (Microsoft, 2014; Research Information Services & Computing, 2014). Meanwhile, the process of creating new policies must be triangulated with evidence of students' learning experience and performance with mobile devices (UNESCO, 2012). In doing so, the new policies can better support initiatives in terms of scaling up or being broad enough to allow for different contexts (Scott, 2012; UNESCO, 2012).

Conclusion

In summary, this chapter discusses factors to drive explosive growth of mobile devices in STEAM. Drawing upon these factors, the chapter provides ample evidence that mobile devices have transformed how STEAM is learned and taught within and outside of the classrooms. In the meanwhile, educators also have experienced barriers in the process of mobile device integration into their curricula. Built on the innovations of the use of mobile devices in the STEAM classroom, the chapter proceeds to discuss essential conditions that ensure the successful implementation of large-scale mobile device initiatives in schools and institutions.

Building on this chapter and looking forward, more empirical studies are needed to provide evidence on the following major areas to help scale up the initial usage of mobile devices in the STEAM classroom (Ahmed & Parsons, 2012; Avraamidou, 2008; Bauerlein, 2011; Luckin et al., 2005; Lutz et al., 2012; O'Shea et al., 2010; Serio et al., 2013; STEM Education Coalition, 2014).

- Innovations and details of the processes by which students come to understand STEAM subjects through mobile devices
- Best pedagogical practices and barriers of technology integration in domain-related curriculum for STEAM educators
- Evidence of student learning gains through mobile devices

- Best practices of professional development model to support STEAM educators
- Interactions and collaborations of stakeholders and support system
- Impact of mobile devices on digital divide
- Support system and new policies necessary for large-scale mobile device initiatives

The evidence of empirical studies will help educators pedagogically, technically, and administratively respond to the increasingly ubiquitous mobile learning in order to meet the needs of the 21st century (Bolkan, 2013; Fulton & Britton, 2011; Meyer, 2013; Windschitl, 2009). Equally important is that the evidence of empirical studies will help academic leaders rethink school and institutional goals and resources in order to support STEAM-curriculum innovations on a large-scale level (Horizon Project, 2013; Lam & Duan, 2012; UNESCO, 2012; Zaranis et al., 2013).

References

Abdul-Alim, J. (2012). Academic leaders share STEM education ideas. http://diverseeducation.com/article/17141/.

Ahmed, S., & Parsons, D. (2012). Adductive science inquiry using mobile devices in the classroom. *Computer and Education, 63,* 62–72.

Alexander, A., Blair, K. P., Goldman, S., Jimenez, O., Nakaue, M., Pea, R., & Russell, A. (2010). *Go math! How research anchors new mobile learnings environments. Proceedings of the 6th IEEE international conference on wireless, mobile, and ubiquitous technologies in education* (pp. 57–64). Taiwan: Institute of Electrical and lectronics Engineers.

Allen, E., & Seaman, J. (2011). Going the distance—Online education in the United States. *Babson Survey Research Group.* http://www.onlinelearningsurvey.com/reports/goingthedistance.pdf.

Anderson University. (2014). The mobile learning initiative. http://www.andersonuniversity.edu/mobile-learning-initiative.

AppBrain (2014). Number of Android applications. http://www.appbrain.com/stats/number-of-android-apps.

Aronin, S., & Floyd, K. K. (2013). Using an iPad in inclusive preschool classrooms to introduce STEM concepts. *Council for Exceptional Children, 45*(4), 34–39.

Avraamidou, L. (2008). Prospects for the use of mobile technologies in science education. *AACE Journal, 16*(3), 347–365.

Bannon, S., Martin, G., & Nunes-Bufford, K. (2012). Integrating iPads into mathematics education. In P. Resta (Ed.), *Proceedings of society for information technology & teacher education international conference 2012* (pp. 3519–3522).

Barcia-Zubia, J., López-de-Ipiña, D., & Orduña, P. (2010). Mobile devices and remote labs in engineering education. Proceedings of the 6th IEEE international conference on wireless, mobile, and ubiquitous technologies in education (pp. 620–622). Taiwan: Institute of Electrical and Electronics Engineers.

Bauerlein, M. (2011). *The digital divide: Arguments for and against facebook, google, texting, and the age of social networking.* New York: Jeremy P. Tarcher/Penguin.

Blackboard Mobile Learn. (2014). What can you do with blackboard mobile learn? http://www.blackboard.com/resources/mobile/mobile_learn_splash/desktop/portal-nonsprint.html#android.

Blazer, C. (2014). School district experience with one-to-one and BYOD. http://drs.dadeschools.net/AdditionalReports/OnetoOne_BYOD.pdf.

Bolkan, J. (2013). UTeach initiative aims to improve STEM Ed with mobile tech. http://campustechnology.com/articles/2013/12/10/uteachlaunches-initiative-to-improve-stem-ed-with-mobile-technology.aspx.

Booker, E. (2013). Students want more mobile devices in classroom. http://www.informationweek.com/mobile/students-want-more-mobile-devices-in-classroom/d/d-id/1109825?

Cantrell, P., & Knudson, M. S. (2006). Using technology to enhance science inquiry in an outdoor classroom. *Computers in the Schools, 23*(1–2), 7–18.

Change, K., Change, C., Hou, H., Sung, Y., Chao, H., & Lee, C. (2014). Development and behavioral pattern analysis of a mobile guide system with augmented reality for painting appreciation instruction in an art museum. *Computers & Education, 71,* 185–197.

Chew-Hung, C., Kalyani, C., Dion Hoe-Lian, G., Yin Leng, T., Ec-Peng, L., Aixin, S., Khasfariyati, R., Thi Nhu Quynh, K., & Quang Minh, N. (2012). Lessons from learner experiences in a field-based inquiry in geography using mobile devices. *International Research in Geographical & Environmental Education, 21*(1), 41–58.

CISCO. (2012). *Schools plug into BYOD: Mobile devices transform learning at Katy ISD.* San Jose: CISCO.

ComScore Reports. (2014). ComSore reports January 2014 U.S. smartphone subscribers market share. https://www.comscore.com/Insights/Press-Releases/2014/3/comScore-Reports-January-2014-US-Smartphone-Subscriber-Market-Share.

Daher, W. (2010). Building mathematical knowledge in an authentic mobile phone environment. *Australasian Journal of Educational Technology, 26*(1), 85–104.

Desire@Learn Binder. (2014). A better way to LEARN. http://binder.desire2learn.com/.

Dewan, S., & Riggins, F. J. (2005). The digital divide: Current and future research directions. *Journal of the Association for Information Systems, 6*(12), 298–337.

DeWitt, P. (2012). Are schools prepared to let students BYOD? *Education Week.* http://www.hewlett-woodmere.net/cms/lib03/NY01000519/Centricity/Domain/30/Prepare%20for%20BYOD%20Attachment%202.1.pdf.

Dungca, N. (2011). With high hopes for test scores, Canby School District invests in iPod touches and iPads. *The Oregonian.* http://www.oregonlive.com/clackamascounty/index.ssf/2011/01/canby_school_district_invests.html.

El-Hussein, M. O. M., & Cronje, J. C. (2010). Defining mobile learning in the higher education landscape. *Educational Technology & Society, 13*(3), 12–21.

Ertmer, P. A. (1999). Addressing first-and second-order barriers to change: Strategies for technology integration. *Educational Technology Research and Development, 47*(4), 47–61.

Ertmer, P. A. (2005). Teacher and pedagogical beliefs: The final frontier in our quest for technology integration? *Educational Technology Research and Development, 53*(4), 25–39.

Evagorou, M. (2008). Using online technologies and handhelds to scaffold students' argumentation in science. ED-MEDIA—World Conference on educational multimedia, hypermedia & telecommunications, pp. 5212–5218.

Federal Communications Commission. (2014). FCC modernizes e-rate to expand robust Wi-Fi in schools and libraries. http://www.fcc.gov/document/fcc-modernizes-e-rate-expand-robust-wi-fi-schools-libraries.

Fulton, K., & Britton, T. (2011). STEM teachers in professional learning communities: From good teachers to great teaching. National Commission of Teaching and American's Future. http://www.brokersofexpertise.net/cognoti/content/file/resources/documents/34/34069d8d/34069d8d1ab1b33b095ff40826876c26ad18f293/downloadedfile_1479378601675970318_NCTAFreportSTEMTeachersinPLCsFromGoodTeacherstoGreatTeaching.pdf.

George, D. S. (2014). Schools move forward 'Bring Your Own Device' to boost student tech use. http://www.washingtonpost.com/local/education/stem/schools-move-toward-bring-your-own-device-practices-to-boost-student-tech-use/2014/09/14/4d1e3232-393e-11e4-9c9f-ebb47272e40e_story.html.

Harris, J. (2005). Our agenda for technology integration: It's time to choose. *Contemporary Issues in Technology and Teacher Education, 5*(2), 116–122.

Hechter, R. P., & Vermette, L. A. (2013). Technology integration in K-12 science classrooms: An analysis of barriers and implications. *Themes in Science & Technology Education, 6*(2), 73–90.

Herold, B. (September 2014). Hard lesson learned in ambitious L.A. iPad initiative. http://www.edweek.org/ew/articles/2014/09/10/03lausd.h34.html.

Hew, K. F., & Brush, T. (2007). Integrating technology and learning: Current knowledge gaps and recommendations for future research. *Educational technology research and Development, 55*(3), 223–252.

Hohenbrink, M. (2011). Mobile learning center promotes STEM, energy awareness. http://thejournal.com/articles/2011/08/22/mobile-learning-center-promotes-stem-energy-awareness.aspx.

Horizon Project. (2013). *NMC horizon project—Project short list 2013 K-12 edition. New media consortium.* Austin: New Media Consortium.

Iasevoli, B. (2013). After bungled iPad rollout, lessons from LA put tablet technology in a timeout. http://www.edweek.org/ew/articles/2014/09/10/03lausd.h34.html.

iPad in Education. (2014a). Everything you need to teach anything. http://www.apple.com/education/ipad/apps-books-and-more/?cid=wwa-us-kwg-features-com.

iPad in Education. (2014b). iTunes U courses. http://www.apple.com/education/ipad/itunes-u/.

Jackson State University News Room. (2013). JSU freshmen start groundbreaking iPad project. http://jacksonstate.wordpress.com/2012/09/05/jsu-freshmen-start-groundbreaking-ipad-project/.

JISC Digital Media. (2014). Mobile learning for education. http://www.jiscdigitalmedia.ac.uk/guide/mobile-learning-for-education.

JRCoE—The Jeannine Rainbolt College of Education (JRCoE). (2013). College of Education iPad one University digital initiative. http://www.ou.edu/education/ipad/.

Kearney, M., & Maher, D. (2013). Mobile learning in math's teacher education: Using ipads to support pre-service teachers' professional development. *Australian Educational Computing, 24*(3), 76–84.

Koutsopoulos, K. C., & Kotsanis, Y. C. (2014). School on cloud: Towards a paradigm shift. *Themes in Science & Technology Education, 7*(1), 47–62.

Kukulska-Hulme, A., & Sharpe, R. (2007). *Rethinking pedagogy for a digital age: Designing and delivering e-learning.* London: Routledge.

Lam, J., & Duan, G. (2012). A review of mobile learning environment in higher education sector of Hong Kong: Technological and social perspectives. In S. K. S. Cheung, J. Fong, L. Kwok, D. Li, & R. Kwa (Eds.), *ICHL* (pp. 165–173). Guangzhou, Springer.

Luckin, R., Boulay, B. D., Smith, H., Underwood, J., Pitzpatrick, G., Holmber, J., Kerawalla, L., Tunley, H., Brewster, D., & Pearch, D. (2005). Using mobile technology to create flexible learning contexts. *Journal of Interactive Media in Education, 22,* 1–22.

Lutz, R., Schäfer, S., & Diehl, S. (2012). Using mobile devices for collaborative requirements engineering. Proceedings of the 27th IEEE/ACM international conference on automated software engineering (ASE).

Mahmoud, Q. H. (2008). Integrating mobile devices into the computer science curriculum. Proceedings of 38th ASEE/IEEE frontiers in education conference. http://ieeexplore.ieee.org/stamp/stamp.jsp?tp=&arnumber=4720686&tag=1.

Matthews, J. N. A. (2011). Harnessing consumer mobile devices for science. *Physics Today, 64*(8), 24–25.

Meyer, L. (2013). Report: Professional development for mobile learning improves student engagement and interest in STEM subjects. http://thejournal.com/articles/2013/06/27/report-professional-development-for-mobile-learning-improves.aspx.

Microsoft. (2014). Mobile device mailbox polices. http://technet.microsoft.com/en-us/library/bb124315%28v=exchg.150%29.aspx.

Minaie, A., Sanati-Mehrizy, R., Sanati-Mehrizy, A., & Sanati-Mehrizy, R. (2011). Integration of mobile devices into computer science and engineering curriculum. *American Society for Engineering Education.* http://www.asee.org/public/conferences/1/papers/2161/view.

MindShift. (2012). What it takes to launch a mobile learning program in schools. http://blogs.kqed.org/mindshift/2012/07/what-it-takes-to-launch-a-mobile-learning-program-in-schools/.

MobiThinking. (2014). Global mobile statistics 2013 part A. http://mobithinking.com/mobile-marketing-tools/latest-mobile-stats/a.

Moore College. (2014). The iPad initiative. http://moore.edu/admissions/bfa-admissions/moore-ipad-initiative.

Murray, O., & Olcese, N. (2011). Teaching and learning with iPads, ready or not? *TechTrends, 55*(6), 42–48.

Netgear. (2014). Best practices for high density wireless network design in education and small/medium businesses. http://www.netgear.com/images/pdf/High_Density_Best_Practices.pdf.

Norris, C. A., & Soloway, E. (2011). Learning and schooling in the age of mobilism. *Educational Technology, 51*(6), 1–8.

Novello, J. M. (2012). Using technology in the classrooms: An interview with Pam Varnado. *Educational Technology, 78*(4)12–15.

O'Shea, P., Gabriel, K., & Prabhu, V. (2010). The crane: Creating, implementing, and evaluating an augmented reality art curriculum. In D. Gibson & B. Dodge (Eds.), *Proceedings of society for information technology & teacher education international conference 2010* (pp. 2013–2019). Chesapeake: AACE.

Peffer, T. E., Bodzin, A. M., & Smith. J. D. (2013). The use of technology by nonformal environmental educators. *The Journal of Environmental Education, 44*(1), 16–37.

Pierroux, P., Krange, I., & Sem, I. (2011). Bridging contexts and interpretations: Mobile blogging on art museum field trips. *Journal of Media and Communication, 50,* 30–47.

Research Information Services and Computing. (2014). New policy for mobile devices at partners. http://rc.partners.org/node/570.

Roscorla, T. (2014). 5 ways to run a successful mobile device initiative. Center for Digital Education. http://www.centerdigitaled.com/news/5-Ways-to-Run-a-Successful-Mobile-Device-Initiative.html.

Ryokai, K., Agogino, A., & Oehlberg, L. (2012). Mobile learning with the engineering pathway digital library. *International Journal of Engineering Education, 28*(5), 119–126.

Scanlon, E., Jones, A., & Waycott, J. (2005). Mobile technologies: Prospects for their use in learning in informal science settings. *Journal of Interactive Media in Education.* http://www-jime.open.ac.uk/jime/article/viewArticle/2005-25/303.

Scott, E. (2012). What it takes to launch a mobile learning program in school. http://blogs.kqed.org/mindshift/2012/07/what-it-takes-to-launch-a-mobile-learning-program-in-schools/.

Serio, A. D., Ibáñez, M. B., & Kloos, C. D. (2013). Impact of an augmented reality system on students' motivation for a visual art course. *Computers & Education, 68,* 586–596.

Sharples, M., Taylor, J., & Vavoula, G. (2007). A theory of learning for the mobile age. In R. Andrews & C. Haythornthwaite (Eds.), *The Sage handbook of e-learning research* (pp. 221–247). London: Sage. doi:10.4135/9781848607859n10.

Simon, B., Anderson, R., Hoyer, C., & Su, J. (2004). Preliminary experiences with a tablet PC based system to support active learning in computer science courses. Proceedings of Annual Conference on innovation and technology in computer science education, pp. 213–217.

SMT—North Carolina Science, Mathematics, and Technology Education Center. (2014). Commitment to STEM. http://ncsmt.org/about/commitment-to-stem/.

STEM Education Coalition. (2014). The case for STEM education as a national priority: Good jobs and American competiveness. http://www.stemedcoalition.org/wp-content/uploads/2013/10/Fact-Sheet-STEM-Education-Good-Jobs-and-American-Competitiveness-June-2013.pdf.

STEMblog. (2014). Schoology releases native mobile annotations and improved grading workflows. http://blog.stemconnector.org/schoology-releases-native-mobile-annotations-and-improved-grading-workflows.

TabTimes. (2013). The state of the tablet market. http://tabtimes.com/resources/the-state-of-the-tablet-market.

The Huffington Post. (2013). Where online education and nuclear science meet. http://www.dailybuzzle.com/en/source/topical/where-online-education-and-nuclear-science-meet-378548539883659264.

The Moore iPad Initiative. (2014). https://moore.edu/stories/student-videos/the-moore-ipad-initiative.

The New York Times. (2013). Brown University creates online course for high school students. http://thechoice.blogs.nytimes.com/2013/04/17/brown-university-creates-a-mooc-for-high-school-students/?_php=true&_type=blogs&_r=0.

The Statistics Portal. (2014). Number of apps available in leading app store as of July 2014. http://www.statista.com/statistics/276623/number-of-apps-available-in-leading-app-stores/.

The Technology Outlook for STEM + Education 2013–2018 Report. (2013). The new media consortium. http://www.nmc.org/pdf/2013-technology-outlook-for-STEM-education.pdf.

UNESCO. (2012). Working paper series on mobile learning. http://www.unesco.org/new/en/unesco/themes/icts/m4ed/mobile-learningresources/unescomobilelearningseries/.

University of Central Oklahoma. (2014). Desire2Learn Mobile Apps. Desire2LearnMobileApps.

Vogel, B., Spikol, D., Jurti, A., & Milrad, M. (2010). Integrating mobile, web and sensory technologies to support inquiry-based science learning. Proceedings in the 6th IEEE International Conference on wireless, mobile, and ubiquitous technologies in education (pp. 65–72). Taiwan: Institute of Electrical and Electronics Engineers.

Wachira, P., & Keengwe, J. (2011). Technology integration barriers: Urban school mathematics teachers' perspectives. *Journal of Science Education and Technology, 20,* 17–25.

Walker, K. (2007). Introduction: Mapping the landscape of mobile learning. In M. Sharples (Ed.), *Big issue in mobile learning: A report of a new workshop by the kaleidoscope network of excellence mobile learning initiative* (pp. 5–6). UK: Learning Science and Research Institution, University of Nottingham.

Walling, D. R. (2012). The Tech-Savvy triangle. *TechTrends: Linking Research & Practice to Improve Learning, 56*(4), 42–46.

Warschauer, M. (2004). *Technology and social inclusion: Rethinking the digital divide.* Cambridge: The MIT Press.

White, T., & Martin, L. (2012). Integrating digital and STEM practices. *Leadership, 42*(2), 22–26.

Wiles, J. W. (2007). *Leading curriculum development.* Thousand Oaks: Corwin Press.

Windschitl, M. (2009). *National academics of science workshop on 21st century skills.* http://sites.nationalacademies.org/xpedio/idcplg?IdcService=GET_FILE&dDocName=DBASSE_072614&RevisionSelectionMethod=Latest.

Zaranis, N., Kalogiannakis, M., & Papadakis, S. (2013). Using mobile devices for teaching realistic mathematics in kindergarten education. *Creative Education, 4*(7), 1–10.

Hong Lin is Associate Director of the Center for Teaching Excellence at the University of Oklahoma (OU). With more than 20 years of professional experience in higher education, she has been a faculty member, instructional designer, and director with expertise in faculty development, instructional design, and educational technology. Before joining OU, she was the Department Head of Faculty Development at Oklahoma State University, where she led faculty development initiatives and served on university committees to enhance teaching effectiveness and technology integration into the curriculum. The 6-week Preparing Online Instructors certificate program that she led and taught won 2010 Oklahoma Distance Learning Association Best Practice Award. Hong teaches undergraduate and graduate courses in instructional design and technology. She publishes in leading academic journals and serves on the editorial board of peer-reviewed journals in teaching and technology. She earned a doctoral degree in Learning and Performance System—Workforce Education from Penn State.

Part IV
Engineering

Designing for Open Innovation: Change of Attitudes, Self-Concept, and Team Dynamics in Engineering Education

Dirk Ifenthaler, Zahed Siddique and Farrokh Mistree

Abstract Within Science, Technology, Engineering, Arts, and Mathematics (STEAM) education initiatives, a learner-centric paradigm that instills in individuals the habit of becoming self-directed and life-long learners is a major objective. The implemented instructional framework presented recognizes that students develop mental models that represent their competencies in Engineering. Findings of a case study report the students' change of attitudes, self-concept, and team dynamics while taking the re-designed graduate course. The findings guide the further instructional design of the course and the development of future research projects.

Keywords Engineering · Self-concept · Attitudes · Team · Scaffolding

Introduction

For the past several years, Science, Technology, Engineering, Arts, and Mathematics (STEAM) education initiatives have addressed the concern that the United States is globally losing its competitive edge. It is further argued that individuals are required to continuously refresh and adapt their competencies. It is also well documented that the changing environment of the 21st century and the diverse learning needs of individuals demand a change in the existing paradigm of engineering education (Mistree et al., 2014). What is needed is a flexible, learner-centric paradigm that,

D. Ifenthaler (✉)
University of Mannheim, Mannheim, Germany
e-mail: dirk@ifenthaler.info

Deakin University, Melbourne, Australia

Z. Siddique
University of Oklahoma, Norman, USA
e-mail: zsiddique@ou.edu

F. Mistree
University of Oklahoma, Norman, USA
e-mail: farrokh.mistree@ou.edu

© Springer International Publishing Switzerland 2015
X. Ge et al. (eds.), *Emerging Technologies for STEAM Education,*
Educational Communications and Technology: Issues and Innovations,
DOI 10.1007/978-3-319-02573-5_11

among other things, instills in individuals the habit of becoming self-directed and life-long learners (Mistree, Panchal, & Schaefer, 2012; Williams & Mistree, 2006).

Over the past few years, at the University of Oklahoma, a graduate course titled AME5303 *Designing for Open Innovation*[1] has been designed, course content and assignments developed, and a learner centric paradigm instantiated. Different facets of this course have been described in several publications—most recently in (Ifenthaler, Mistree, & Siddique, 2014; Mistree, Ifenthaler, & Siddique, 2013; Mistree et al., 2014). In these papers, the authors explore the key question: *How can we foster learning how to learn and develop competencies?*

In this chapter, we document our findings focusing on the students' change of attitudes, self-concept, and team dynamics while taking the re-designed graduate course. Next, we cover the salient features of AME5303 *Designing for Open Innovation.* In the following, we outline the organization of our case study and report and discuss our findings. We end this paper with closing remarks on future developments.

Salient Features—AME5303 Designing for Open Innovation

The orchestration of this course is different to typical graduate courses in engineering. Firstly, the concept of Senge's (1990) Learning Organization was emphasized throughout the lectures and the assignments. This allowed a fluent development of both competencies and learning objectives. Secondly, each lecture was focused on one or more *questions for the day.* These questions provided the rationale for covering the material on a particular day. When viewed at the end of the semester, the questions represented a framework within which the course was orchestrated and a means for the students to frame their *semester learning essay.*

Course Organization

The relationship between the team organization and the course content is displayed in Fig. 1. The course content is centered on deliverables and lectures that are associated with dilemmas involving economy, society, and environment. Each assignment and deliverable which was addressed in the class content was designed to support the team organization. Early in the semester students were given the *question for the semester* in the context of their semester competencies they wished to develop along with their supporting learning objectives. There were lectures focused on higher-level topics related to "learning how to learn" along with content-based lectures

---

[1] From 2009 through 2012 the course was offered using a generic (temporary) temporary course number AME5740.

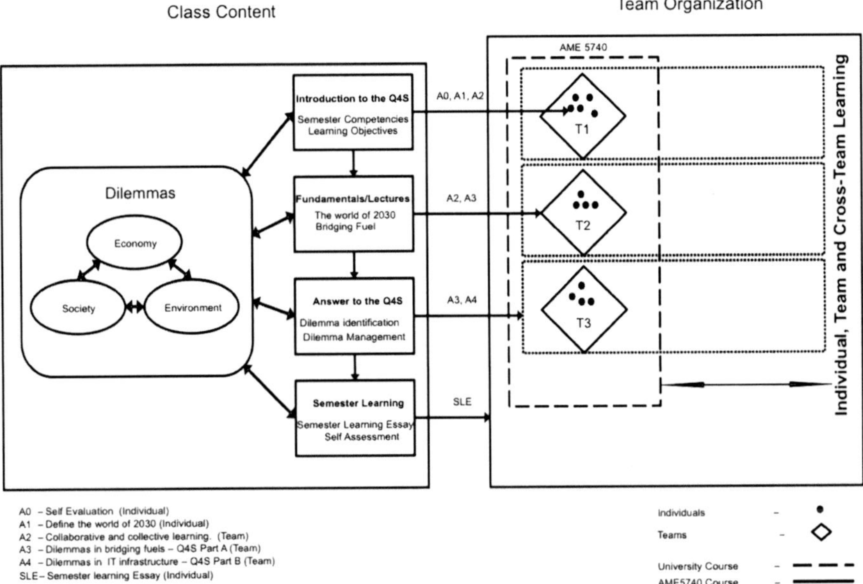

Fig. 1 Overview on the course organization

focusing on bridging fuels and the wired and connected world of 2030. Lectures on tools to help frame and answer the *question for the semester* through dilemma identification and management were also included. Finally, students reflected upon their semester learning through a *semester learning essay*. All of the class content was focused on dilemmas resulting from economical, sociological, and environmental aspects that arise in energy policy and bridging fuels.

The team organization was supported through the class content and the assignments developed around this content. There were several levels of the team organization. Firstly, there were assignments early on in the semester designed for students to identify the competencies that they wished to develop throughout the semester. This allowed for individual learning. Next, there were assignments that allowed students to get experience working in teams. Teams of three formed at the university level. This level of team organization allowed team-based learning. The assignments were designed to support collective learning through the use of technologies to address the possible geographical differences. The *question for the semester* was finally a compilation of two assignments and the answer was compiled and submitted by each team. One of the unique aspects of this course was the collaborative structure in which students worked in team settings in order to answer the *question for the semester*. Students were asked to identify competencies needed to be successful at creating value in a culturally diverse, distributed engineering world. The students developed these competencies by completing various assignments designed to collaboratively answer the *question for the semester.* Students completed these assignments individually and collaboratively in teams.

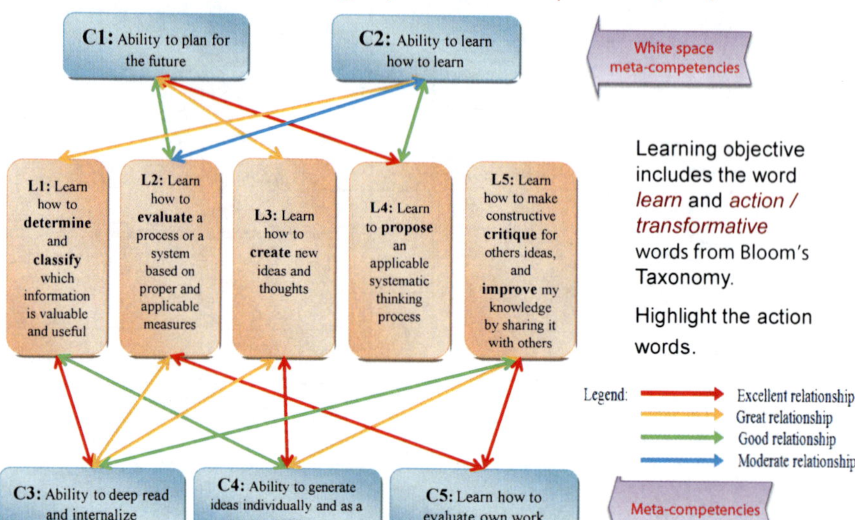

Fig. 2 Examples of student mental models of competencies and learning objectives at the end of the semester

Learning Organization

According to Senge (1990), a Learning Organization is "an organization that facilitates the learning of all its members and consciously transforms itself and its context". A learning organization exhibits five main characteristics: (1) systems thinking, (2) personal mastery, (3) mental models, (4) a shared vision, and (5) team learning. Throughout this course, assignments were framed with these five disciplines.

We used Senge's (1990) framework to create a learning community made up of individuals, teams and, cross-teams within the class. In our approach, systems-thinking is achieved by posing a high-level question (*question for the semester*) for the students to be addressed by scaffolded activities and assignments throughout the semester. Personal mastery is achieved by students defining and striving to achieve personal learning objectives that are tied to the development of competencies. At the start of the course, the students are asked to identify the competencies that they wish to achieve as a result of taking this course. The competencies are classified as white space competencies, meta-competencies, and competencies. The competencies are supported by learning objectives. The learning objectives are anchored in Bloom's Taxonomy (Anderson et al., 2001; Bloom, Engelhardt, Furst, Hill, & Krathwohl, 1956; Krathwohl, 2002). The mental model of one students' perception of the relationship of the competencies that he wishes to achieve and the associated learning objectives is illustrated in Fig. 2.

Competencies are the result of integrative learning experiences in which skills, abilities, and knowledge interact to form bundles that have currency in relation to the task for which they are assembled. On the other hand, learning objectives

Justifications / Introductions	Learning Statements
• Through x (From x, By doing x, ..) • I did not consider x initially • I thought (expected) x before / initially	• I learned y • I realized y • I found out y • I discovered y • I became conscious of y

Fig. 3 Structure of learning statements in keeping with Kolb's model of experiential learning

embody cognitive skills that students wish to attain so that they become competent in performing the task. Learning objectives are defined in terms of the six learning domains in Bloom's taxonomy (knowledge, comprehension, application, analysis, synthesis, and evaluation) (Bloom et al., 1956). In the example of learning objectives (see Fig. 2), the keywords from Bloom's taxonomy are underlined.

The authors are aware of the revision of Bloom's taxonomy and changes (remember, understand, apply, analyze, evaluate, create) (Anderson et al., 2001). After reflection, they have consciously chosen to use the older version for this course in engineering.

The questions that students were asked during the first lecture were: "What competencies do you need to develop to be successful at addressing dilemmas associated with the realization of complex, sustainable, socio-techno-eco system in a distributed engineering world?" and "What competencies do you wish to develop in this course so that you are competitive in the world of 2030?"

This required reflection: What competencies do I have? In the context of the world of 2030 what competencies do I need to develop? Based on the competencies that a student wished to develop, he/she defined the learning objectives and related these objectives to the competencies with appropriate justification.

In keeping with Senge's five main characteristics (disciplines) the team assignments are structured as follows:

1. **System:** Given an assignment.
2. **Personal Mastery:** Internalize the assignment. Develop an approach for tackling it. Post this approach for your colleagues to see.
3. **Mental Model:** Reflect on the progress you have made on your attaining your competencies so far then in the context of your approach for tackling the assignment identify two competencies that you would like to develop by doing this assignment. Post your mental model for review by your teammates.
4. **Team Vision:** Collectively develop a Team Vision that accommodates the proposed Mental Models and includes a plan of action: What needs to be done, by when and who is responsible, etc. Agree on a Team Contract.
5. **Implement Plan of Action:** Be conscious of what you are doing, reflect and identify via *learning statements* what you are taking away and thence achieving your learning objectives and attaining competencies.

Learning statements are anchored in Kolb's Experiential Learning Model, namely that learning is attained through active experimentation-reflective observation and abstract conceptualization-concrete experience. Accordingly, students are required to include in their learning statements justifications/introductions as shown in Fig. 3.

Lecturing with a Purpose

Each lecture started with a *question for the day*. The question for the day was designed to give meaning to each lecture and to frame each lecture with a purpose. In addition, the *question for the day* made students think about one aspect which was designed to help answer the *question for the semester*. These questions were labeled in sequence in order to identify with the flow of information through the lectures. The following list shows examples of the *question for the day* for the foundational lectures.

- What are the key foundational white space competencies that "tool maker" engineers must have to be able to create value in a wired and interconnected, culturally diverse world?
- What competencies do you wish to develop to be successful at addressing dilemmas associated with the realization of complex, sustainable, socio-techno-eco system in the wired, interconnected and culturally diverse world of 2030?
- What are some of the changing business paradigms for the world of 2030?
- How will workforce-employer relationships have to change to be more successful in a G3/Open Innovation/Mass Collaborative environment of the year 2030?
- What exactly does "success" mean and how can it be measured?

Assignments to Scaffold Learning and Team Formation

One of the main differences between this course and that of a traditional nature in engineering is how the assignments were used to scaffold student learning and team formation. In this course, learning was achieved at three levels: individual learning, team learning, and learning from each other in the AME5303 community. This structure was systematically developed using the assignments (see Appendix A for examples). Initially, the assignments were focused on the individual to help each student identify his/her own mental model (Ifenthaler & Seel, 2011, 2013). The teams were core to developing an answer to the *question for the semester* and an important component of the end of semester deliverables. In addition to the team answer to the *question for the semester* at the end of the semester, each student submitted two reports, namely, an *answer to the question for the semester* and a *semester learning essay*. In keeping with the notion of empowering the students to take charge of their learning all students were required to evaluate their own performance in the class and suggest a grade.

Case Study

Research Context

Foundational to our learning-centric paradigm is the notion of mental models. We recognize that students develop mental models that represent their competencies.

These mental models differ from person to person, especially among people from different engineering disciplines and from different universities.

In Fall 2012, we received IRB approval to investigate the impact of individual mental models on the shared (team) mental model (and vice versa), how individual mental models change over the course of a semester and how students with different mental models prepare themselves to learn how to learn in an increasingly wired, interconnected and culturally diverse world. In Fall 2013, based on the initial findings (Ifenthaler et al., 2014), we have modified the course delivery and increased the amount of scaffolding, for example, introduced four exercises that lead into the major assignments, shared past examples of work, provided time for classroom discussion, paused and asked questions, encouraged all students to meet socially and share their work with the entire class.

In this case study we investigate (1) the change of attitudes towards engineering, (2) the student's self-concept, and (3) team dynamics in the course of a semester. Specifically, the following research questions were addressed:

1. How do attitudes towards engineering change over the course of a semester?
2. How does confidence for performing in the course (a) and performing on the first engineering job (b) change over the course of a semester?
3. How do team dynamics change over the course of a semester?

Method

Participants

Nine students who enrolled in Fall 2012 and ten students who enrolled in Fall 2013 in AME5303 *Designing for Open Innovation* were invited to participate voluntarily in this study. Based on the response to Assignment 0 and Assignment 1, the course instructor assigned students to teams to work on Assignment 2. Each team had three students.

The final sample for this study consisted of participants from four teams (nine males and three females). The average age of the participants was 24.8 years ($SD=2.98$). All participants described themselves as non-Hispanic white and six participants declared themselves as international students. Their reported average GPA was 3.44 ($SD=0.36$).

Instruments

Attitudes Towards Engineering

The 44 questions focusing on attitudes towards engineering were answered on a five-point Likert scale (1 = strongly disagree; 2 = disagree; 3 = neutral; 4 = agree; 5 = strongly agree).

Self-Concept

The participant's self-concept was measured with the confidence scale (Bandura, 2006) consisting of eight items which were answered on a five-point Likert sale (1 = strongly disagree; 2 = disagree; 3 = neutral; 4 = agree; 5 = strongly agree; Cronbach's alpha = 0.87). Four items focused on the participant's confidence for performing in the course (CPC) and four items focused on their confidence for performing on their first engineering job after graduation (CPJ).

Team Assessment and Diagnostic Measure

The TADM (team assessment and diagnostic measure) instrument measures team-related knowledge (Johnson, Lee, Lee, & O'Connor, 2007). TADM consists of 17 items forming six factors (team knowledge, communication, attitudes, dynamics and interactions, resources and environment, satisfaction/frustration). The questions were answered on a five-point Likert scale (1 = strongly disagree; 2 = disagree; 3 = not sure; 4 = agree; 5 = strongly agree).

Procedure

At the start of the semester, demographic data (5 min), learner characteristics (beliefs, self-concept; 10 min), and a pre-assessment of attitudes towards engineering (15 min) were collected. During the semester, three waves of data collection were administered as follows: Individual mental model (three paragraphs—350 words—focusing on declarative, procedural, and metacognitive knowledge; 30 min), shared mental model (two paragraphs—350 words—focusing on self and other participant's contribution to the team; 20 min), TADM (team assessment and diagnostic measure; 5 min), self-concept (5 min). The last wave of data collection additionally included a post-assessment of attitudes towards engineering (15 min). The individual and shared mental models are not part of this case study, however, more information can be found related work (Ifenthaler, 2014b; Ifenthaler et al., 2014).

Results

Change of Attitudes Towards Engineering

A Wilcoxon Signed-ranks test indicated that the attitudes towards engineering were significantly higher at the end of the semester ($Mdn = 4.01$) than at the beginning of the semester ($Mdn = 3.84$), $Z = 2.64$, $p = 0.008$, $r = 0.86$.

Overall, participants reported high attitudes towards engineering; however, the integrative learning experiences in which they achieved higher competencies during the semester increased their positive attitudes towards engineering.

Change of Confidence

The change of confidence for performing in the course and on the first engineering job was analyzed using Friedman's test. The change of confidence for performing in the course changed significantly over the course of the semester, $\chi2(4)=9.57$, $p=0.048$. Overall, the confidence for performing in the course significantly increased from the first measurement point ($M=4.08$, $SD=0.64$) to the last measurement point ($M=4.36$, $SD=0.73$).

Additionally, the change of confidence for performing on the first engineering job changed significantly over the course of the semester, $\chi2(4)=13.12$, $p=0.011$. Overall, the confidence for performing in the course significantly increased from the first measurement point ($M=3.73$, $SD=0.81$) to the last measurement point ($M=4.29$, $SD=0.59$).

Change of Team Dynamics

The change of team dynamics was analyzed using Friedman's test indicating a significant change over the course of four measurement points, $\chi2(3)=11.72$, $p=0.008$.

Overall, team dynamics increased positively during the course of the semester from $M=3.82$ ($SD=0.45$) at the first measurement point, $M=4.04$ ($SD=0.51$) at the second measurement point, $M=4.17$ ($SD=0.46$) at the third measurement point, and $M=4.32$ ($SD=0.43$) at the forth measurement point.

Disucssion

Currently, there are many initiatives underway to facilitate STEAM competencies. engineering education research is contributing to these initiatives in many ways (King & Magun-Jackson, 2009). Our approach is focused on students developing competencies needed in diverse and quickly evolving world. We argue that advocating the mass customization of courses will allow students to identify and develop selected competencies (Williams & Mistree, 2006).

The reported case study focused on the students' (1) attitudes towards engineering, their (2) self-concept for performing in engineering, and (3) their team dynamics as a key 21st century competence.

First, the findings of this study revealed that the students already had high attitudes towards engineering at the beginning of the semester. Despite the initial high attitudes, the integrative learning experiences during the semester increased their positive attitudes towards engineering. This finding suggests that the course as conceived and implanted shows promise. Second, the findings revealed that the students gained confidence in their ability to take charge of their learning over the course of the semester. This suggests that the students internalized the Bloom's taxonomy construct used to scaffold their learning and gained confidence in their ability to frame problems and prosecute their solution as they will be called on to do when they enter industry or academia. Third the findings revealed that there was a positive increase in team dynamics. This suggests that the students were in harmony with the learning community construct that was used to scaffold individual and team learning.

Implications and Limitations

There is no simple recipe for designing learning environments (Bransford, Brown, & Cocking, 2000) and the design of learning environments will always change in line with the change of educational goals (Gosper & Ifenthaler, 2014; Ifenthaler & Gosper, 2014). In general, the design of STEAM learning environments includes the three simple questions: What competencies have to be learned? How are they learned? How are they assessed? Yet, the design of STEAM learning environments is not simply asking the above stated three questions. Rather, it includes a systematic analysis, planning, development, implementation, and evaluation phases (Gagné, 1965; Merrill, 2007). Further, Bransford et al. (2000) differentiate four perspectives for the design of learning environments. Learner-centered, knowledge-centered, assessment-centered, and community-centered learning environments. It is of course difficult to predict new developments or trends in the domain of the design of STEAM learning environments with any kind of precision, but one thing is certain: They will continue to be dictated to a great extent by the increasing globalization, 21st century trends, and rapid development of information and communication technology (Ifenthaler, 2012).

Especially within STEAM learning environments, creativity is a core competence. Taking into account that creative inventions are understood as artifacts that are new as well as useful and are created by a divergent way of thinking, this requires an iterative process of model-building (Ifenthaler, 2013; Ifenthaler & Seel, 2013). However, the development and successful application of creative inventions often requires quite a lot of time and mental effort due to basic processes of analogical reasoning or internal simulations (Jonassen & Cho, 2008). Therefore, linking educational technology and STEAM learning environments suggests to implement computer-based modeling tools for externalizing the internal simulation process which might take off the learner's cognitive effort and might highlight specific problems when designing creative invention.

Clearly, the presented case study has limitations. Though the findings may not be generalizable, case studies such as this allow us to theorize relationships that may otherwise remain covert. Additionally, the data from two different cohorts may limit the internal validity of the presented case study. However, controlling for effects between the two cohorts did not show any significant differences.

Closing Remarks

In this chapter, we document our findings focusing on the students' change of attitudes, self-concept, and team dynamics while taking the re-designed graduate course.

While implementing this course, we have developed an automated assessment methodology which enables the process oriented analysis of individual mental models and team mental models (Ifenthaler, 2014b). AKOVIA (Automated Knowledge Visualization and Assessment) (Ifenthaler, 2014a) provides just-in-time scaffolding and feedback on semantic and structural aspects of the learner's or team's learning progression and responses to complex problems at all times during the learning process (Ifenthaler, 2009). Such dynamic and timely scaffolds can promote the learner's self-regulated learning and individual characteristics such as metacognition, motivation, beliefs, and attitudes (Ifenthaler et al., 2014). These analysis results could be further utilized to re-design course content, learning objectives, or curricular elements (Ifenthaler & Widanapathirana, 2014).

Clearly, the principal outcome from taking this course is not the test result attained, but a student's ability to *learn how to learn*, which is illustrated through the development of personal competencies in a collaborative learning framework and environment.

Acknowledgements The authors express their deep appreciation to their colleagues Professors Janet K. Allen, Randa Shehab, and Deniz Eseryel at University of Oklahoma for the framing of the study. Dirk Ifenthaler acknowledges the support from the U.S. Department of State Fulbright Scholarship and the support from the University of Oklahoma, School of Education and School of Aerospace and Mechanical Engineering. Farrokh Mistree acknowledges the support from the L.A. Comp Chair and NSF EAGER grants 1042340 and 1258439.

Appendix A

Examples of assignments graduate course titled AME5303 *Designing for Open Innovation*.

Assignment 1: Define the world of 2030 through Deep Reading, Observe-Reflect-Articulate (ORA) and Critical Thinking.

This assignment was completed individually. In this assignment, the students were asked to deep read and critically evaluate two articles from Friedman. Some of the questions that the students are asked to answer after reading the articles are: (i) what are the key issues facing the world of 2030 as highlighted by the author? (ii) how are the issues related to the three aspects of sustainability (social, economic, and environmental)? (iii) what are the interdependencies between the issues identified by the author? and (iv) what are the relationships between globalization and the issues identified above? The students were also asked to take a first step towards identifying the dilemmas associated with energy policy.

The expected outcomes of this assignment were (a) vision for the engineering world of 2030, (b) a vision of the energy infrastructure in the world of 2030, and (c) refined competencies and learning objectives in the context of the world of 2030.

Assignment 2: Collaborative and collective learning.

This assignment was completed collaboratively within the students own university and had two primary objectives. The first objective was to experience using a virtual environment to collaborate in a globalized mass-collaborative environment. The second objective was to gain an understanding of the efficacy and limitations inherent in Senge's Learning Organization.

This assignment is used to develop a learning organization within the class using Senge's concepts. After the students have formalized their mental models in Assignment 0 by identifying what they know and would they would like to achieve, the next step is to create a team vision. As a part of the team vision, the students are asked to identify (a) the goals they would like to achieve as a team, (b) the tasks that the team needs to carry out, and (c) the assignment of responsibilities for completing the tasks. At the end of this assignment, the students develop a team contract that outlines the tasks, responsibilities and overall team outcomes. Team learning is achieved through the process of collectively completing the assignments and answering the Q4S. The deliverable of this assignment was presented as the following:

In the context of a Learning Organization, you are required to propose a plan of action to develop an outline for a paper titled *Product Realization Processes for Open innovation in the Globalization 3.0 World.*

1. *Personal Mastery:* Introduce yourself. Include the competencies you wish to develop and the supporting learning objectives.
2. *Mental Model:* Review the postings of your team members. Suggest two competencies you wish to develop as a result of doing this assignment.
3. *Team Vision:* Collectively develop a Team Vision that includes a plan of action: What needs to be done, by when and who is responsible, etc. This may involve your having to modify your Mental Model.
4. *Solution:* Propose a solution to the problem, namely, develop an outline for a paper titled *Characteristics, Features and Functionalities of IT Infrastructure for Open Innovation.*
5. *Individual Learning and Evaluation:* Reflect on your performance in this assignment. Please respond to the following questions in full sentences and *write at least 350 words per sub-question.*

a) What are the most significant *theoretical concepts* (e.g., features of Streamz) you used in completing this assignment? Please elaborate in full sentences and write at least 350 words guided by the following matters of detail:

    a. What is the author's (developer's) message?
    b. What is the purpose of Streamz?
    c. What is the utility of StreamZ in helping you develop your competencies and the associated learning objectives?

b) What are the most significant strategies (e.g., search for information) you applied in completing this assignment? Please elaborate in full sentences and write at least 350 words guided by the following matters of detail:

    a. What strategy worked? Justify.
    b. What strategy did not work? Justify.
    c. What strategies do you plan to implement in undertaking the next assignment?

c) What is the state of your overall learning in this course so far? Please elaborate in full sentences and write at least 350 words to include:

    a. The degree to which you attained your competencies and learning objectives. Please justify.
      – What change in strategy is warranted and why.
      – The changes (if any) you propose for your personal competencies and associated learning objectives and why.

The competencies/learning objectives you plan to improve in the next assignment and why.

6. *Team Learning and Evaluation:* We would like to get an idea about the vision of your team. Please respond to the following questions in full sentences and *write at least 350 words per sub-question.*

a) What are the most significant theoretical concepts, strategies, and ideas proposed by you and adopted by the team?

b) What are the most significant theoretical concepts, strategies, and ideas proposed by others that were adopted by the team?

References

Anderson, L. W., Krathwohl, D. R., Airsasian, P. W., Cruikshank, K. A., Mayer, R. E., Pintrich, P. R., & Wittrock, M. C. (Eds.). (2001). *A taxonomy for learning, teaching, and assessing: A revision of Bloom's taxonomy of educational objectives*. New York: Longman.

Bandura, A. (2006). Guide for constructing self-efficacy scales. In F. Pajares & T. C. Urdan (Eds.), *Self-efficacy beliefs of adolescents* (Vol. 5, pp. 307–337). Hershey: Information Age Publishing.

Bloom, B. S., Engelhardt, M. B., Furst, E. J., Hill, W. H., & Krathwohl, D. R. (1956). *Taxonomy of educational objectives: The classification of educational goals. Handbook I: The cognitive domain.* New York: Longman.

Bransford, J. D., Brown, A. L., & Cocking, R. R. (Eds.). (2000). *How people learn: Brain, mind, experience, and school.* Washington, D. C.: National Academies Press.

Gagné, R. M. (1965). *The conditions of learning.* New York: Holt, Rinehart, and Winston.

Gosper, M., & Ifenthaler, D. (2014). Curriculum design for the twenty-first century. In M. Gosper & D. Ifenthaler (Eds.), *Curriculum models for the 21st century. Using learning technologies in higher education* (pp. 1–15). New York: Springer.

Ifenthaler, D. (2009). Model-based feedback for improving expertise and expert performance. *Technology, Instruction, Cognition and Learning, 7*(2), 83–101.

Ifenthaler, D. (2012). Design of learning environments. In N. M. Seel (Ed.), *Encyclopedia of the sciences of learning* (Vol. 4, pp. 929–931). New York: Springer.

Ifenthaler, D. (2013). Models for creative inventions. In E. G. Carayannis (Ed.), *Encyclopedia of creativity, invention, innovation, and entrepreneurship* (pp. 1313–1315). New York: Springer.

Ifenthaler, D. (2014a). AKOVIA: Automated Knowledge Visualization and Assessment. *Technology, Knowledge and Learning, 19*(1–2), 241–248. doi:10.1007/s10758-014-9224-6.

Ifenthaler, D. (2014b). Toward automated computer-based visualization and assessment of team-based performance. *Journal of Educational Psychology, 106*(3), 651–665. doi:10.1037/a0035505.

Ifenthaler, D., & Gosper, M. (2014). Guiding the design of lessons by using the MAPLET framework: Matching aims, processes, learner expertise and technologies. *Instructional Science, 42*(4), 561–578. doi:10.1007/s11251-013-9301-6.

Ifenthaler, D., & Seel, N. M. (2011). A longitudinal perspective on inductive reasoning tasks. Illuminating the probability of change. *Learning and Instruction, 21*(4), 538–549. doi: 10.1016/j.learninstruc.2010.08.004

Ifenthaler, D., & Seel, N. M. (2013). Model-based reasoning. *Computers & Education, 64,* 131–142. doi: 10.1016/j.compedu.2012.11.014

Ifenthaler, D., & Widanapathirana, C. (2014). Development and validation of a learning analytics framework: Two case studies using support vector machines. *Technology, Knowledge and Learning, 19*(1–2), 221–240. doi:10.1007/s10758-014-9226-4.

Ifenthaler, D., Mistree, F., & Siddique, Z. (2014). Learning how to learn in a team-based engineering eduction. *Interactive Technology and Smart Education, 11*(1), 63–82. doi:10.1108/ITSE-10-2013-0025.

Jonassen, D. H., & Cho, Y. H. (2008). Externalizing mental models with mindtools. In D. Ifenthaler, P. Pirnay-Dummer, & J. M. Spector (Eds.), Understanding models for learning and instruction. *Essays in honor of Norbert M. Seel* (pp. 145–160). New York: Springer.

Johnson, T. E., Lee, Y., Lee, M., & O'Connor, D. L. (2007). Measuring sharedness of team-related knowledge: Design and validation of a shared mental model instrument. *Human Resource Development International, 10*(4), 437–454.

King, B. A., & Magun-Jackson, S. (2009). Epistemological beliefs of engineering students. *The Journal of Technology Studies, 35*(2), 56–64.

Krathwohl, D. R. (2002). A revision of Bloom's taxonomy. An overview. *Theory into Practice, 41*(4), 212–237.

Merrill, M. D. (2007). The future of instructional design: The proper study of instructional design. In R. A. Reiser & J. V. Dempsey (Eds.), *Trends and issues in instructional design and technology* (pp. 336–341). Upper Saddle River: Pearson Education, Inc.

Mistree, F., Panchal, J. H., & Schaefer, D. (2012). Mass-customization: From personalized products to personalized engineering education. In A. Crosnik & Y. Xiong (Eds.), *Supply chain management* (pp. 150–174). Croatia: INTECH.

Mistree, F., Ifenthaler, D., & Siddique, Z. (2013). *Empowering engineering students to learn how to learn: A competency-based approach. AC 7324.* Paper presented at the ASEE Annual Conference and Exposition, Atlanta.

Mistree, F., Panchal, J. H., Schaefer, D., Allen, J. K., Haroon, S., & Siddique, Z. (2014). Personalized engineering education for the 21st century: A competency based approach. In M. Gosper & D. Ifenthaler (Eds.), *Curriculum models for the 21st century. Using learning technologies in higher education* (pp. 91–112). New York: Springer.

Senge, P. M. (1990). *The fifth discipline*. New York: Doubleday.

Williams, C., & Mistree, F. (2006). Empowering students to learn how to learn: Mass customization of a graduate engineering design course. *The International Journal of Engineering Education, 22*(6), 1269–1280.

Dirk Ifenthaler is Professor for Instructional Design and Technology at the University of Mannheim, Germany as well as an Adjunct Professor at Deakin University, Melbourne, Australia. His previous roles include Professor and Director, Centre for Research in Digital Learning at Deakin University, Australia, Manager of Applied Research and Learning Analytics at Open Universities Australia, and Professor for Applied Teaching and Learning Research at the University of Potsdam, Germany. Dirk was a 2012 Fulbright Scholar-in-Residence at the Jeannine Rainbolt College of Education, at the University of Oklahoma, USA. Professor Ifenthaler's research focuses on the intersection of cognitive psychology, educational technology, learning science, data analytics, and computer science. He developed automated and computer-based methodologies for the assessment, analysis, and feedback of graphical and natural language representations, as well as simulation and game environments for teacher education. His research outcomes include numerous co-authored books, book series, book chapters, journal articles, and international conference papers, as well as successful grant funding in Australia, Germany, and USA—see Dirk's website for a full list of scholarly outcomes at www.ifenthaler.info. Professor Ifenthaler is the Editor-in-Chief of the Springer journal Technology, Knowledge and Learning (www.springer.com/10758). Dirk is the Past-President for the AECT Design and Development Division, 2013–2015 Chair for the AERA Special Interest Group Technology, Instruction, Cognition and Learning and Co-Program Chair for the international conference on Cognition and Exploratory Learning in the Digital Age (CELDA).

Zahed Siddique is a Professor of Mechanical Engineering at the University of Oklahoma. His research interests are in areas of product design, product platform design, and engineering education. He is interested in experiential learning, peer-to-peer learning, technology enhanced education, motivation, and game-based learning for engineering. Zahed is the Chair of Design Education Committee (DEC) of American Society of Mechanical Engineers (ASME). He is the faculty advisor of the Sooner Racing Team (FSAE) and coordinator of the Mechanical Engineering Capstone Program.

Farrokh Mistree is the L.A. Comp Chair and Professor in the School of Aerospace and Mechanical Engineering at the University of Oklahoma, Norman, Oklahoma. Farrokh is a Fellow of ASME, an Associate Fellow of AIAA, a Life Member of The Honor Society of Phi Kappa Phi and a Member of ASEE, RINA and SNAME. He was named the ASME Ruth and Joel Spira Outstanding Engineering Design Educator in 2011. In September 2012 he was recognized as a Distinguished Alumnus of the Indian Institute of Technology, Kharagpur, India. In December 2012, he received the Life Time Achievement Award from the International Society for Agile Manufacturing, Lafayette, Louisiana. Farrokh's current research focus is model-based realization of complex systems by managing uncertainty and complexity. The key question he is investigating is what are the principles underlying rapid and robust concept exploration when the analysis models are incomplete and possibly inaccurate? His current education focus is on creating and implementing, in partnership with industry, a curriculum for educating strategic engineers—those who have developed the competencies to create value through the realization of complex engineered systems.

Critical Support Systems to Enhance the Development and Assessment of 21st Century Expertise in Engineering Students

Enrique Palou, Silvia Husted, Gladis Chávez-Torrejón, Zaira Ramírez Apud, Lourdes Gazca, Judith Virginia Gutiérrez Cuba, Nelly Ramírez-Corona and Aurelio López-Malo

Abstract Our goal is to enhance the development of the broad range of so-called 21st century expertise in engineering students by designing critical support systems. Recently our Department generated new curricula for its undergraduate degrees in chemical, food and environmental engineering. These new "integrated and spiral" curricula (that started in fall 2012) include several departmental courses considered chemical, food, and environmental engineering "pillars", which were revamped to enhance the development of 21st century expertise. "Pillar" courses were redesigned taking into account technological advances and recent research on human learning and cognitive processes that underlie expert performances. Using the *Framework for 21st Century Learning,* and guidelines from research on *How People Learn* we: defined the standards for chemical, environmental, and food engineering 21st century expertise; created formative and summative assessments to evaluate student attainment of it; designed instruction activities to promote this expertise; developed professional development opportunities for "pillar" course instructors; and generated corresponding learning environments to foster 21st century expertise in these courses. By means of Tablet PCs and associated technologies high-quality learning environments were created to promote an interactive classroom while integrating multiple formative assessments. Up to date "pillar" courses are improving student understanding of the engineering method, ability to solve practical problems and complete real-world projects while developing 21st century expertise. This chapter discusses results of implementation at selected "pillar" courses, particularly with regards to metacognitive awareness, critical and creative thinking while emphasizing the potential of Tablet PCs and associated technologies to facilitate cognition and learning.

E. Palou (✉) · S. Husted · G. Chávez-Torrejón · Z. Ramírez Apud · L. Gazca ·
J. V. Gutiérrez Cuba
Center for Science, Engineering, and Technology Education, Universidad de las Americas
Puebla, Puebla 72810, Mexico
e-mail: enrique.palou@udlap.mx

S. Husted
e-mail: silvia.hustedrs@udlap.mx

G. Chávez-Torrejón
e-mail: gladis.chaveztn@udlap.mx

© Springer International Publishing Switzerland 2015
X. Ge et al. (eds.), *Emerging Technologies for STEAM Education,*
Educational Communications and Technology: Issues and Innovations,
DOI 10.1007/978-3-319-02573-5_12

Keywords 21st century learning · Creative thinking · Metacognition · Critical thinking · How people learn · Tablet PCs

Introduction

Universidad de las Américas Puebla (UDLAP) established since 2003 the Center for Science, Engineering, and Technology Education (CSETE), which is stimulating new paradigms in science, engineering and technology education research. CSETE is acting as a catalyst to bring together faculty and students who are interested in educational research, to disseminate the results of that research, and to provide professional development opportunities for Mexican and other Ibero-American countries faculty, graduate students, and K-12 instructors. There are several Science, Technology, Engineering, Arts, and Mathematics (STEAM) related projects that are underway at CSETE including the one that is described in this chapter.

A team of several faculty members and graduate students at UDLAP's CSETE has been using mobile technology since 2007 to improve engineering teaching and learning by creating richer learning environments. We have learned a lot about the potential of Tablet PCs and associated technologies to create learning environments that are knowledge-, learner-, community-, and assessment-centered as highlighted by the *How People Learn* (HPL) framework (Bransford, Brown, & Cocking, 2000). The redesign of several undergraduate and graduate courses significantly increased student participation; formative assessment and feedback were more common and rapid; instructors utilized the information gained through real-time formative assessments to tailor instruction to meet student needs (Gazca, Palou, López-Malo, & Garibay, 2009; Gutiérrez Cuba, López-Malo, & Palou, 2011, 2012; Palou et al., 2012). In these courses, particularly important were opportunities to make students' thinking visible and give them chances to revise, as well as opportunities for "what if" thinking.

Z. Ramírez Apud
e-mail: tajaza@hotmail.com

L. Gazca
e-mail: maria.gazca@udlap.mx

J. V. Gutiérrez Cuba
e-mail: judith.gutierrezca@udlap.mx

N. Ramírez-Corona · A. López-Malo
Chemical, Environmental, and Food Engineering, Universidad de las Americas Puebla, Puebla 72810, Mexico
e-mail: nelly.ramirez@udlap.mx

A. López-Malo
e-mail: aurelio.lopezm@udlap.mx

Context

UDLAP is a Mexican private institution of higher learning committed to first-class teaching, public service, research and learning in a wide range of academic disciplines including business administration, the physical and social sciences, engineering, humanities, and the arts. Since 1959, the Commission on Colleges of the Southern Association of Colleges and Schools (SACS) has accredited UDLAP in the United States (Gazca, López-Malo, & Palou, 2012). UDLAP's Chemical, Food, and Environmental Engineering Department offers several graduate programs (accredited as of high quality by the Mexican National Council of Science and Technology) comprising two M.Sc. programs (Food Science and Chemical Engineering) and two Ph.D. programs (Food Science and Science, Engineering, and Technology Education), as well as three undergraduate programs. The Food Engineering undergraduate program is approved by the Institute of Food Technologists (IFT) and accredited by the *Consejo de Acreditación de la Enseñanza de la Ingeniería* (CACEI), which is the peer-accrediting agency of the US ABET in Mexico, the Chemical Engineering undergraduate program is also accredited by CACEI, while the Environmental Engineering is an undergraduate program that just started in fall 2012 (Altamirano, Gazca, López-Malo, & Palou, 2013).

During 2011–2012 UDLAP's Chemical, Food, and Environmental Engineering Department generated new curricula for its undergraduate degrees in Chemical (CE), Food (FE), and Environmental Engineering (EE). These new "integrated and spiral" curricula (Asociación Nacional de Facultades y Escuelas de Ingeniería [ANFEI], 2002, 2007; Litzinger, Lattuca, Hadgrafta, & Newsletter, 2011; National Academy of Engineering [NAE], 2004, 2005; Rascón-Chávez, 2010; Sheppard, Macatangay, Colby, & Sullivan, 2008) includes several departmental courses considered chemical, food, and environmental engineering "pillars", which are designed to enhance the development of 21st century expertise in students from each of the undergraduate degrees (Partnership for 21st Century Skills, 2009a, 2009b, 2009c). Integrative learning comes in many varieties: connecting skills and knowledge from multiple sources and experiences; applying theory to practice in various settings; utilizing diverse and even contradictory points of view; and understanding issues and positions contextually (Huber & Hutchings, 2004). Thus significant knowledge within individual disciplines serves as the foundation in our integrated curricula, but integrative learning goes beyond academic boundaries. Indeed, integrative experiences will occur in "pillar" courses as learners address real-world problems, unscripted and sufficiently broad to require multiple areas of knowledge and multiple modes of inquiry, offering multiple solutions and benefiting from multiple perspectives (Huber & Hutchings, 2004). Our spiral curricula include a sequence of courses, matched closely with the development of students' mathematical sophistication and analytical capabilities and integrated with coursework in the sciences. Students develop a conceptual understanding of engineering basics in "pillar" courses, which stress practical applications of these principles. Unlike the traditional approach, each of the "pillar" courses includes a mix of these topics, presented in a variety

Table 1 Chemical (CE), Food (FE), and Environmental Engineering (EE) "pillar" courses

Course name	Semester	Course type[a]
Introduction to Chemical Engineering (CE) Introduction to Environmental Engineering (EE) Introduction to Food Engineering (FE)	1st	Introductory (*cornerstone*)
Introduction to Chemical, Food, and Environmental Engineering Design (CE, FE, and EE)	2nd	Engineering design (*cornerstone*)
Material balances (CE, FE, and EE)	2nd	Engineering science (*cornerstone*)
Energy balances (CE, FE, and EE) Thermophysical properties laboratory (CE, FE, and EE)	3rd	Engineering science
Modeling and simulation in Chemical, Food, and Environmental Engineering (CE, FE, and EE)	5th	Engineering technology
Statistical control of products and processes (CE, FE, and EE)	6th	Engineering technology
Quality assurance (CE, FE, and EE)	7th	Engineering technology
Chemical plant design (CE) Design of equipment for environmental control (EE) design and development of food products and processes (FE)	8th	Engineering design (*capstone*)

[a] Sheppard et al. (2008)

of disciplinary contexts (Collura, Aliane, Daniels, & Nocito-Gobel, 2004). A solid background is developed by touching key concepts at several points along the spiral in different courses, adding depth and sophistication at each pass. Each "pillar" course also stresses the development of several essential skills, such as problem-solving, oral and written communication, the design process, teamwork, project management, computer analysis methods, laboratory investigation, data analysis and model development. Thus the "pillar" courses serve both as the basis for depth in disciplinary study and as part of the broad multidisciplinary background. The "pillar" courses of these new curricula are presented in Table 1.

Chemical, environmental, and food engineering students have a great opportunity for a multidisciplinary collaborative experience in these "pillar" courses.

Guidelines from Research on *How People Learn*

Chemical, Food, and Environmental Engineering "pillar" courses were designed (or re-designed) taking into account technological advances (Bienkowski et al., 2005; Biswas, 2007; Kowalski, Kowalski, & Hoover, 2007a; Kowalski, Williams, Reed, & Vanides, 2007b; Kowalski et al., 2013a, 2013b; Tront, Eligeti, & Prey, 2006; Twining et al., 2005; Wise, Toto, & Yon Lim, 2006) and recent research on human learning and cognitive processes that underlie expert performances (Bransford et al., 2000; Bransford, Vye, & Bateman, 2002). Thanks to a Hewlett-Packard (HP) *Catalyst Initiative* grant UDLAP received 63 HP Tablet PCs to (re)design "pillar" courses. In particular, we were interested in using Tablet PC technologies to encourage active learning (interactive engagement) and probe student understanding through frequent formative assessments as described in detail elsewhere (Gazca et al., 2009; Gutiérrez Cuba et al., 2011; Palou et al., 2012; Ramirez-Corona, Ramirez Apud, López-Malo, & Palou, 2013).

Using Information About How People Learn

During the past 40 years, research on human learning has exploded. Although we have a long way to go to fully uncover the mysteries of learning, we know a considerable amount about the cognitive processes that underlie expert performances and about strategies for helping people increase their expertise in a variety of areas (Bransford et al., 2002). Several committees organized by the US National Academy of Sciences have summarized this research in reports published by the National Academy Press. A key publication that informs our current discussion is *How People Learn: Brain, Mind, Experience and School* (Bransford et al., 2000).

An organizing structure used in the *How People Learn* volume (hereafter HPL) is the HPL framework. It highlights a set of four overlapping lenses that can be used to analyze any learning situation. In particular, it suggests how HPL learning environments should be developed:

1. *Knowledge centered.* Based on a careful analysis of what students need to know and be able to do when they finish our courses, which would provide them with the foundational knowledge and skills as well as cultivate the attitudes needed for successful transfer.
2. *Learner centered.* Connecting to the strengths, interests, and preconceptions of learners and helping them learn about themselves as learners.
3. *Community centered.* Creating an environment, both within and outside the classroom, where students feel safe to ask questions, learn to use technology to access resources and work collaboratively, and are helped to develop lifelong learning skills.
4. *Assessment centered.* Providing multiple opportunities to make students' thinking visible so they can receive feedback and be given chances to revise.

The HPL framework provides a convenient way to organize a great deal of information about the nature of competent (expert) performance and about ways to help people develop their own competence (Bransford et al., 2002). The framework highlights a set of four overlapping lenses that are useful for analyzing the quality of various learning environments. Balance among the four lenses is particularly important to create high-quality learning environments (Carney, 2005; Gazca et al., 2009).

Design of "Pillar" Courses

A major issue is to help students develop the kinds of connected knowledge, skills, and attitudes that prepare them for effective lifelong learning (Novak, 1998). This involves the need to seriously rethink not only how to help students learn about particular isolated topics but to rethink the organization of entire courses and curricula (Gazca et al., 2009). People who want to improve educational quality often begin with a focus on teaching methods. Questions about teaching strategies are important, but they need to be asked in the context of whom we are teaching and what we want our students to accomplish (Bransford et al., 2002). The reason is that particular types of teaching and learning strategies can be strong or weak depending on our goals for learning and the knowledge and skills that students bring to the learning task (Jenkins, 1978; Schwartz & Bransford, 1998).

A model developed by Jenkins (1978) highlights important constellations of factors that must be simultaneously considered when attempting to think about issues of teaching and learning. The model illustrates that the appropriateness of using particular types of teaching strategies depends on: (a) the nature of the materials to be learned; (b) the nature of the skills, knowledge, and attitudes that learners bring to the situation; and (c) the goals of the learning situation and the assessments used to measure learning relative to these goals. A particular teaching strategy may flourish or perish depending on the overall characteristics of the ecosystem in which it is placed (Bransford et al., 2002). The Jenkins model fits well with a proposal by Wiggins and McTighe (2005). They suggest a "working backwards" strategy for creating high-quality learning experiences. In particular, they recommend that educators: (1) begin with a careful analysis of learning goals; (2) explore how to assess students' progress in achieving these goals; and (3) use the results of steps 1 and 2 to choose and continually evaluate teaching methods (assumptions about steps 1 and 2 are also continually evaluated.) When using a "working backwards" strategy for designing (or redesigning) "pillar" courses, our choice of teaching strategies derived from a careful analysis of learning goals, rather than vice versa (Gazca et al., 2009).

The ability to design engineering undergraduate courses and corresponding high-quality learning environments require that we move beyond procedural strategies and models. We also need to understand the kinds of skills, attitudes, and knowledge structures that support competent performance. Thus, for the redesigning of the "pillar" courses, we "worked backwards" taking into account Jenkins model as well as the HPL framework. Especially important was knowledge of key concepts and models that provide the kinds of connected, organized knowledge structures and accompanying skills and attitudes that can set the stage for future learning (Bransford & Schwartz, 1999). Our (re)designs involved a transformation of studied courses from a lecture-based format to a challenge-based format as previously described (Gazca et al., 2009; Gutiérrez Cuba et al., 2011; Palou et al., 2012). We used the HPL framework as a set of lenses for guiding the redesign of the lessons, development of our challenges but also the overall instruction that surrounded the challenges. Particularly important were opportunities to make students' thinking visible and give them chances to revise (Bransford et al., 2002). We also noted the importance of provided opportunities for "what if" thinking, given variations on the challenge and for new problems that also involved the lesson's concepts. Attempts to help CE, FE, and EE students reflect on their own processes as learners (to be metacognitive) were also emphasized (Ramirez-Corona et al., 2013).

For a thorough discussion of the ways that *How People Learn* can guide the design of environments to support high-quality learning we recommend Bransford et al. (2002), which also provides very specific examples and guidelines based on the HPL framework. Furthermore, it also examines some of the challenges and opportunities for high-quality learning that accompany the use of new technologies. Further, Carney (2005) identified goals and sub-goals of each lens of the HPL framework as well as classroom practices associated with each of them. As many practices can serve multiple goals, she further described their possible relationships.

The Framework for 21st Century Learning

This Framework presents a holistic view of 21st century teaching and learning that combines a discrete focus on 21st century student outcomes (a blending of specific skills, content knowledge, expertise and literacies) with innovative support systems to help students master the multi-dimensional abilities required of them in the 21st century and beyond (Partnership for 21st Century Skills, 2009a). The key elements of 21st century learning are displayed in Fig. 1, which represents both 21st century

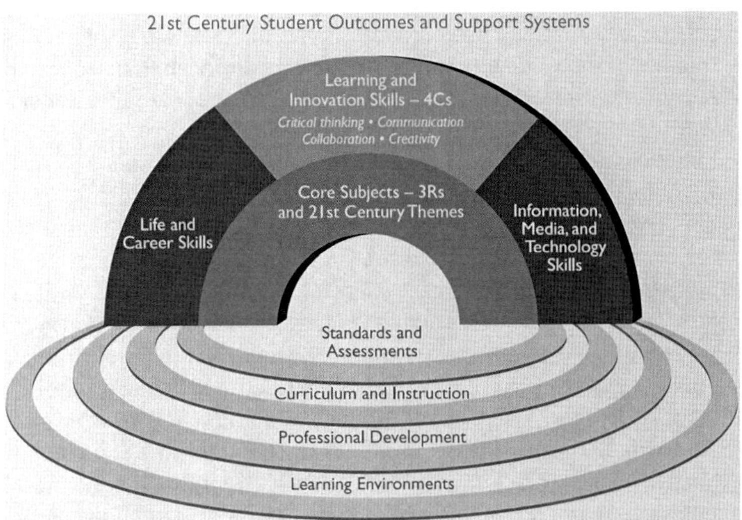

Fig. 1 The framework for 21st century learning. (Adapted from Partnership for 21st Century Skills, 2009a)

student outcomes (as represented by the arches of the rainbow) and 21st century learning support systems (as represented by the pools at the bottom).

While Fig. 1 represents each element distinctly for descriptive purposes, the Partnership for 21st Century Skills (P21) views all the components as fully interconnected in the process of 21st century teaching and learning. The critical systems necessary to ensure 21st century readiness for every student include: (a) 21st century standards, (b) assessments, (c) curriculum, (d) instruction, (e) professional development, and (f) learning environments, which must be aligned to produce a support structure that produces 21st century outcomes for today's students. A detailed description of the elements (outcomes and support systems) of the Framework for 21st Century Learning is available elsewhere (Partnership for 21st Century Skills, 2009a, 2009b, 2009c). UDLAP's Chemical, Food, and Environmental Engineering Department defined the standards for chemical, environmental, and food engineering 21st century expertise; created formative and summative assessments to evaluate student attainment of 21st century expertise; designed instruction activities to promote 21st century expertise; developed professional development opportunities for instructors of the "pillar" courses; and generated corresponding learning environments that promote 21st century expertise.

Standards for chemical, environmental, and food engineering 21st century expertise include: (a) Core Engineering Subjects as proposed by NAE (2004, 2005) ABET (2015), and IFT (2012) in the US, as well as ANFEI (2002, 2007) in Mexico; in addition to (b) 21st Century Themes (such as global awareness, financial, economic, business and entrepreneurial literacy, civic literacy, health literacy, and environmental literacy); (c) Learning and Innovation Skills (such as creativity and innovation, critical thinking and problem solving, and communication and collaboration); (d) Information, Media and Technology Skills (such as information literacy, media literacy, and information, communications and technology literacy); and (e) Life and Career Skills (such as flexibility and adaptability, initiative and self-direction, social and cross-cultural skills, productivity and accountability, leadership and responsibility) as proposed by P21 (2009a, 2009b).

The following section will discuss results of implementation at selected courses (some "pillar") particularly focusing on students' metacognition, critical and creative thinking while emphasizing the potential of Tablet PCs and associated technologies to facilitate cognition and learning. Understanding the 21st century learner and adapting instruction generalizes to all disciplines, but in particular it is important in the STEAM disciplines to facilitate learning that supports students' critical and creative thinking. In our case, development and assessment of metacognitive, critical, and creative thinking skills were the links between the language-liberal arts and Science, Technology, Engineering, and Mathematics (STEM) education. Thus, for us STEAM includes sharing knowledge with communication and language arts "voice", better understanding the past and present cultures and aesthetics through fine arts as well as understanding sociological developments, human nature and ethics via liberal arts.

Results of Implementation at Selected Courses

Capturing Differences of Learning Environments by Means of the VaNTH Observation System

The VaNTH observation system (VOS) is an assessment tool developed to capture qualitative and quantitative classroom observation data from teaching and learning experiences of the bioengineering classroom. VOS is a four-part system that incorporates the elements of HPL framework and uses four recurring methods of collecting classroom data: recording student-teacher interactions, recording student academic engagement, recording narrative notes of classroom events, and rating specific indicators of effective teaching. VOS was developed from the Stallings Observation System, which consisted of three components that registered the presence and absence of over 600 in-class student and teacher behaviors and activities (Cox & Cordray, 2008; Gazca et al., 2009).

Similar to other classroom observation systems, VOS provides information about the types of pedagogy and interactions occurring within a class along with information about levels of student engagement. Unlike previous observation systems, VOS contains a category that explicitly measures the presence of the four HPL framework lenses and the interactions of these lenses within observed courses (Cox & Cordray, 2008). The four components of the VOS include the following: (1) the Classroom Interaction Observation (CIO), sampled real-time, which records student and faculty interactions; (2) a time-sampled Student Engagement Observation (SEO), which notes whether students are engaged or unengaged with academic tasks; (3) qualitative Narrative Notes (NN) on the lesson content, lesson context, extenuating circumstances, and additional information about the classroom; and (4) Global Ratings (GR), which provide summative information about major aspects of the pedagogy underlying the class session (Harris & Cox, 2003). VOS was used to systematically assess HPL framework implementation in "pillar" courses' classrooms as well as in selected "traditional taught" courses to assess studied redesigned classrooms. Further details can be observed in Gazca et al. (2009) and Gazca, Palou, López-Malo, & Garibay (2011).

Introduction to Engineering Design (EI-100) and Food Chemistry (IA-332) were redesigned as previously described while the two "traditional" studied courses were Material Balances (IQ-210) and Biophysics (FS-320). Observers measured differences in classroom experiences resulting from the innovations and redesigned learning environments as well as in IQ-210 and FS-320 as can be seen in Figs. 2 and 3.

By means of VOS' CIO, SEO, and GR components (Harris & Cox, 2003) it was documented that EI-100 and IA-332 redesign significantly ($p < 0.05$) increased student participation (Gazca et al., 2009; Gazca et al., 2011). Using VOS' CIO, NN, and GR components (Harris & Cox, 2003) it was recognized that formative assessments and feedback were more common in the redesigned courses (Gazca et al., 2009; Gutiérrez Cuba et al., 2011).

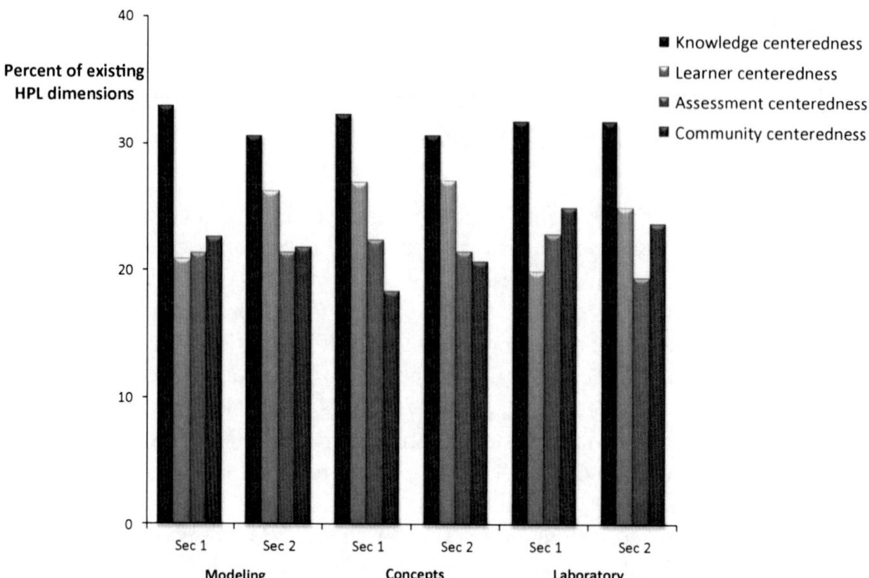

Fig. 2 Percentage of "HPL-ness" observed in the course *Introduction to Engineering Design* (EI-100) three sessions (modeling, concepts, or laboratory) and two sections (Sect. 1 with 40 students or Sect. 2 with 68 students) taught by six different instructors. (Adapted from Gazca et al., 2011)

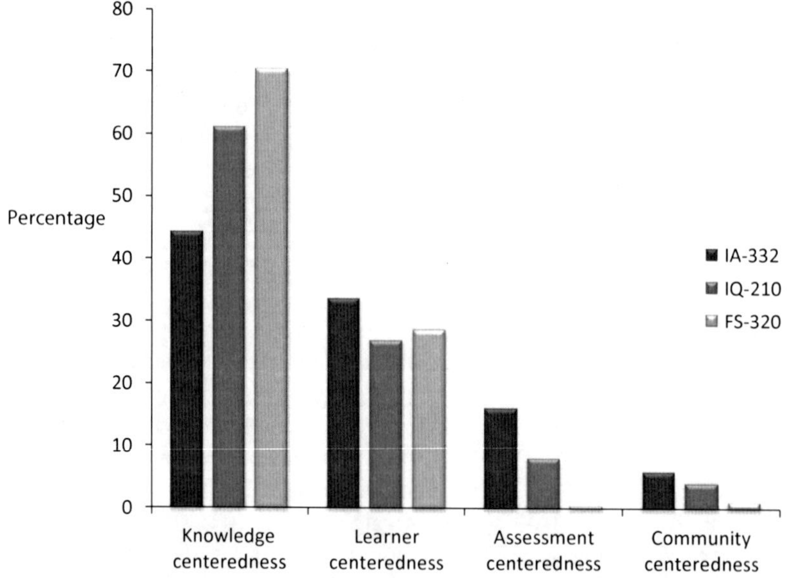

Fig. 3 Percentage of "HPL-ness" observed in *Material Balances* (IQ-210, 21 students), *Biophysics* (FS-320, 24 students), and *Food Chemistry* (IA-332, 23 students) courses taught by three different instructors. (Adapted from Gazca et al., 2011)

Instructors in these redesigned courses utilized the information gained through real-time formative assessment to tailor instruction and meet student needs (Cox & Cordray, 2008; Gazca et al., 2009, 2011; Gutiérrez Cuba et al., 2011; Harris & Cox, 2003). VOS captured important differences among redesigned and "traditional" classroom experiences. These differences may be used to measure levels of "HPLness" of a lesson. Moreover VOS clearly captured differences among instructors' teaching styles. In addition, VOS generated detailed feedback that instructors may use to self-assess (Cox & Cordray, 2008; Gazca et al., 2009, 2011; Gutiérrez Cuba et al., 2011; Harris & Cox, 2003). Student final grades in redesigned courses were higher than those found in "traditional" courses. Further, fewer students failed the course and the percentage of students who stayed in the course until the end was higher in the redesigned courses (Gazca et al., 2009, 2011).

Using Tablet PCs and Associated Technologies to Reveal Student Thinking

As previously described, the HPL framework (Bransford et al., 2000, 2002) was applied to redesign the courses Food Chemistry (IA-332) and Advanced Food Chemistry (IA-530). Our goal was to improve undergraduate and graduate food chemistry teaching and learning by creating high-quality learning environments to promote an interactive classroom while integrating formative assessments into classroom practices by means of Tablet PCs and associated technologies (Gazca et al., 2009; Palou et al., 2012). We utilized *InkSurvey*, a web-based tool to pose open-ended questions to students during class and receive real-time student responses (Kowalski et al., 2007a, 2013a, 2013b). Furthermore, we identified classroom assessment techniques appropriate to the course and adapted them into a Tablet PC/*Classroom Presenter* environment to gauge student learning in real time, provide immediate feedback, and make real-time pedagogical adjustments as needed (Anderson, Anderson, McDowell, & Simon, 2005). The redesign of IA-332 and IA-530 increased student participation and formative assessments while instructors utilized the information gained through real-time formative assessment to tailor instruction to meet student needs (Gutiérrez Cuba et al., 2011, 2012; Kowalski et al., 2007, 2013a, 2013b; Tront et al., 2006).

As an example (further details are available at Gutiérrez Cuba et al., 2011), Table 2 displays the means of grades (out of 10) of undergraduate and graduate students in the three quizzes of studied courses (i.e., Food Chemistry and Advanced Food Chemistry) for 2008, 2009, and 2010 classes. With the use of Tablet PCs and associated technologies (*InkSurvey* and *Classroom Presenter*) during several formative assessments prior to the quiz, students improved their results (2009 and 2010 grades) in these summative assessments (quizzes) with respect to students' grades before course redesign and Tablet PC implementation (2008). Furthermore, in both studied courses, undergraduate and graduate, the formative assessment exercises performed with the Tablet PC and *InkSurvey* had a positive impact on the grades of the summative quizzes (Gutiérrez Cuba et al., 2011).

Table 2 Mean grades of undergraduate and graduate students in course's quizzes for 2008 (before course redesign and Tablet PC implementation), 2009, and 2010 classes (redesigned courses that utilized Tablet PCs and associated technologies). Same teacher taught every one of the classes. (Adapted from Gutiérrez Cuba et al., 2011)

	Year/Students	Quiz 1	Quiz 2	Quiz 3
Undergraduate	2008/25	7.8	7.4	8.9
	2009/23	8.0	8.0	9.8
	2010/10	9.8	7.9	9.3
Graduate	2008/5	7.7	7.5	9.0
	2009/7	8.0	8.0	9.1
	2010/7	9.0	8.0	9.6

Because of the anonymity afforded by Tablet PC technologies, as stated in end-of-course surveys students felt comfortable sharing their ideas with classmates. This situation enabled instructors to assess student understanding frequently during the processes of instruction, problem solving, and peer evaluations to quickly identify the most common difficulties, provide immediate feedback, redirect classroom activities, and/or refine instruction based on feedback received (Gutiérrez Cuba et al., 2011, 2012; Kowalski et al., 2007, 2013a, 2013b; Tront et al., 2006).

Tablet PC associated technologies generated possibilities for self-assessment, making it possible for students to anonymously analyze their own and classmates' results. Another positive result of Tablet PC use was a visible increase in student motivation to participate in class discussions and problem-solving activities mediated through technologies (*InkSurvey* and *Classroom Presenter*) associated with Tablet PCs. Further, the redesigned IA-332 and IA-530 courses enhanced student understanding of the engineering design approach to problem solving as well as students' abilities to solve practical food chemistry problems and complete real world food engineering projects as directly assessed in several other student work products such as problem-based learning projects, assignments, exams, and journals (Gutiérrez Cuba et al., 2011, 2012).

Students' initial conceptions provided the foundation on which more formal understanding of the subject matter was built. Further, frequent formative assessment helped make students' thinking visible to themselves, their peers, and their instructor. Facilitated by Tablet PC technologies, feedback (in both courses) that guided modification/refinement in thinking increased. Additionally, several other important impacts have been evident, particularly on instructor: (1) identifying the most common difficulties in undergraduate and graduate food chemistry courses while providing immediate feedback of both written work products and oral presentations from students; (2) helping students reflect on their own processes as learners; and (3) understanding of how through the use of Tablet PC associated technologies, student thinking can be revealed. Therefore the student learning experience in the classroom can be enhanced resulting in improvements in both instruction and student academic success (Gazca et al., 2009, 2011; Gutiérrez Cuba et al., 2011, 2012; Kowalski et al., 2007, 2013a, 2013b; Palou et al., 2012; Simon, Anderson, Hoyer, & Su, 2004).

Furthermore, in order to examine how graduates students perceived the use of Tablet PCs and associated technologies, we conducted semi-structured interviews with IA-530 graduate students that had completed the course (Gutiérrez Cuba, López-Malo, & Palou, 2012). The analysis indicated a number of themes that consistently appeared within the interview sessions and were addressed by students from different viewpoints. Five overall themes emerged: student participation in class by means of Tablet PCs, impact on learning, potential of Tablet PCs and associated technologies, formative assessments, as well as advantages and disadvantages of using the Tablet PC in IA-530 classroom. Our findings demonstrated that graduate students believed that using Tablet PCs and associated technologies: (a) increased their motivation to participate in class as well as their scores in graded work-products; (b) made the classroom more active and students constantly thinking, thus learning-with-understanding increased; (c) caused the university to implement it into other classes; (d) enabled the teacher provided a great deal of real-time feedback to students that made their thinking visible and gave them chances to revise. Among the disadvantages, students believed that teachers should be fully aware that students will be able to check their e-mails and social networks while using the Tablet PCs (Gutiérrez Cuba et al., 2012).

Assessing Metacognitive Awareness During Problem-Solving

Practicing engineers are hired, retained, and rewarded for solving problems. Usually workplace engineering problems are substantively different from the kinds of problems that engineering students most often solve in the classroom; therefore, learning to solve classroom problems does not necessarily prepare engineering students to solve workplace problems (Jonassen, 2011; Jonassen, Strobel, & Lee, 2006). Therefore, the primary purpose of engineering education should be to engage and support learning to solve problems (Ramirez Apud, Ramirez-Corona, López-Malo, & Palou, 2012). Hence, we designed and implemented several problem-solving learning environments (PSLEs), a term that represents problem-solving instruction in a more open-ended way than problem-based learning (Jonassen, 2011). Problem solving is a schema-based activity (Jonassen, 2010, 2011; Jonassen et al., 2006; Ramirez Apud et al., 2012). That is, in order to solve problems, learners must construct schemas for problems.

Constructing models of problems greatly facilitates schema development. Having constructed a robust schema for different kinds of problems, learners are better able to transfer their problem-solving skills. Learning to solve problems requires practice in solving problems, not learning about problem solving (Jonassen, 2011). PSLEs assume that learners must engage with problems and attempt to construct schemas of problems, learn about their complexity, and mentally wrestle with alternative solutions (Jonassen, 2010, 2011).

Hence, to engage and support students in learning how to solve problems by practicing solving problems (Ramirez Apud et al., 2012) we built PSLEs for two chemical engineering senior concurrent courses entitled Kinetics and Homogeneous Reactor Design and Mass Transfer Unit Operations I. PSLEs were developed by following the design activities proposed by Jonassen (2011):

1. Interacted with the teacher of the studied course to identify and articulate problems relevant to the discipline.
2. Analyzed problems, first by creating a causal model of the problem space.
3. Conducted an activity theory analysis to identify the historical, cultural, experiential factors that affect problem solving on the context chosen (Schraw & Dennison, 1994).
4. Determined what kind of problems were each one of them.
5. Constructed case supports and cognitive scaffolds for each problem type.
6. Constructed each PSLE that included some combination of case components and cognitive strategies.
7. Implemented and assessed the effects of the developed PSLEs.

Problems vary in different ways, so different kinds of problems call on different conceptions and skills. Consequently, learning methods should also vary (Jonassen, 2010, 2011; Jonassen et al., 2006). Based on those differences among problems, different kinds of reaction and separation engineering problems were developed, such as story problems, troubleshooting/diagnosis problems, decision-making problems, and design problems. Comprehensive results are discussed elsewhere (Ramirez Apud et al., 2012; Ramirez-Corona et al., 2013; Reyes Guerrero, Ramirez-Corona, López-Malo, & Palou, 2014).

Metacognition refers to people's abilities to predict their performances on various tasks and to monitor their current levels of mastery and understanding (Bransford et al., 2000).

Flavell (1976, 1979) distinguished two characteristics of metacognition: knowledge of cognition (KC) and regulation of cognition (RC). KC includes knowledge of the skills required by different tasks, strategic knowledge and self-knowledge. RC includes the ability to monitor one's comprehension and to control one's learning activities. There is a considerable amount of evidence that supports the value of a metacognitive approach to instruction (Bransford et al., 2002). It includes an emphasis on learning with understanding and on problem solving, but part of the emphasis is on understanding the cognitive and emotional processes involved in these kinds of activities.

The Metacognitive Awareness Inventory (MAI) designed by Schraw and Dennison (1994) was utilized as a pre- (first day of classes) post- (last day of classes) test. MAI is a 52-item inventory that measures adults' metacognitive awareness. Items are classified into eight subcomponents subsumed under two broader categories, KC and RC. Furthermore, in order to assess metacognitive awareness during problem-solving activities, students had to answer the corresponding problem as well as 2–3 embedded problem-solving prompts (Jonassen, 2011) and 4–6 embedded metacognitive prompts (from MAI, chosen based on the level of complexity of the problem and the type of knowledge and skills required to solve it). A final design challenge was used to simultaneously assess student attainment of learning outcomes for both courses through the synthesis and analysis of the reaction and

Table 3 Comparisons of students' Metacognitive Awareness Inventory (MAI) mean scores regarding MAI prompts' scores (KC: knowledge of cognition and RC: regulation of cognition) to MAI pre-test corresponding items' scores for each studied problem (1: story problem, 2: trouble-shooting/diagnosis problem, 3: decision-making problem) at studied courses (Kinetics and Homogeneous Reactor Design: IQ407 and Mass Transfer Unit Operations I: IQ412). (Adapted from Reyes Guerrero et al. (2014))

			Mean	Standard deviation	$p^a<$
KC	Pre-Test	IQ407	72.04	20.60	0.001
	Problem 1	IQ412	84.73	15.68	0.001
	Problem 2	IQ407	79.37	17.93	0.123
		IQ412	75.27	18.19	0.563
			73.19	19.98	
RC	Pre-Test	IQ407	69.98	21.58	0.001
	Problem 3	IQ412	78.46	15.61	0.001
			82.56	16.26	

[a] By using Mann-Whitney Test

separation stages in a chemical plant. Students were asked to carry out a presentation of their solution methodology and obtained results and conclusions for this challenge. Presentations were videotaped to be further examined (Ramirez-Corona et al., 2013; Reyes Guerrero et al., 2014).

Results for the pre-post MAI exhibit a significant ($p < 0.05$) increase in student metacognitive awareness as can be seen in Table 3. Similar results have been previously reported for a chemical engineering junior course and for a photography class, as well as for professional educators and dental hygiene students (Gassner, 2009; Ramirez-Corona et al., 2013; Stewart, Cooper, & Moulding, 2007).

Male and female participants showed no significant difference ($p > 0.05$) in their knowledge of cognition or regulation of cognition at the end of the semester. Notable progress was also noticed by means of the embedded MAI prompts while solving different kinds of problems (such as story problems, decision-making problems, troubleshooting/diagnosis, and design problems) throughout studied courses, in which students also improved the quality of their embedded problem-solving answers and corresponding partial grades.

Analysis of final presentations allowed us to identify students' abilities to solve complex problems as well as their argumentative and metacognitive skills (Bransford et al., 2000; Flavell, 1976, 1979; Jonassen, 2010, 2011; Jonassen et al., 2006). The vast majority of students attained course learning outcomes at an acceptable level as reported by Ramirez-Corona et al. (2013) and Reyes Guerrero et al. (2014).

Development and Multidimensional Assessment of Critical and Creative Thinking

Everyone thinks; it is our nature to do so (Chávez-Torrejón, Husted, Ramirez-Corona, López-Malo, & Palou, 2014). However, much of our thinking, left to itself, is biased, distorted, partial, uninformed or downright prejudiced. Yet the quality of our life and that of what we produce, make, or build depends precisely on the quality of our thought. Shoddy thinking is costly both in money and in quality of life. Excellence in thought, however, must be systematically cultivated (Holyoak & Morrison, 2005; Paul & Elder, 2008). Critical thinking is the art of analyzing and evaluating thinking with a view to improving it (Paul & Elder, 2008). According to Elder and Paul (2007) whenever we think, we think for a purpose within a point of view based on assumptions leading to implications and consequences. Thus, a well-cultivated critical thinker: (a) raises vital questions and problems, formulating them clearly and precisely; (b) gathers and assesses relevant information, using abstract ideas to interpret it effectively; (c) comes to well-reasoned conclusions and solutions, testing them against relevant criteria and standards; (d) thinks open-mindedly within alternative systems of thought, recognizing and assessing, as need be, their assumptions, implications, and practical consequences; and (e) communicates effectively with others in figuring out solutions to complex problems (Elder & Paul, 2007; Paul & Elder, 2008).

Creative thinking includes the capacity to combine or synthesize existing ideas, images, or expertise in original ways and the experience of thinking, reacting, and working in an imaginative way characterized by a high degree of innovation, divergent thinking, and risk taking (Association of American Colleges and Universities [AACU], 2013). The Confluence Model of Creativity developed by Sternberg and Lubart (1993) is based on the *Investment Theory of Creativity* proposed by the same authors, which suggests that creativity is a decision, the decision of how and when to use one resource or the other is the most important source of individual differences. According to the *Investment Theory of Creativity*, creativity requires a confluence of six distinct but interrelated resources: intellectual skills, knowledge, thinking styles, personality, motivation, and environment (Husted, Gutiérrez Cuba, Ramirez-Corona, López-Malo, & Palou, 2014a). Creative people are ones who are willing and able to metaphorically buy low and sell high in the realm of ideas. Buying low means pursuing ideas that are unknown or out of favor, but that have growth potential. Often, when these ideas are first presented, they encounter resistance. The creative individual persists in the face of this resistance, and eventually sells high, moving on to the next new, or unpopular, idea. In other words, such an individual acquires the creativity habit. Major creative contributions generally begin with undervalued ideas (Sternberg & Lubart, 1993; Sternberg & O' Hara, 2005; Sternberg, Lubart, Kaufman, & Prelz, 2005).

If we are to produce engineers who can solve society's most pressing technological problems, we must provide our students with opportunities to exercise and augment their natural critical and creative abilities and we must create classroom environments that make these exercises effective (Felder, 1982, 1987, 1988). This section will describe in detail how two second-semester cornerstone (and "pillar") courses (Introduction to Chemical, Food, and Environmental Engineering Design, LQI-1031, and Material Balances, LQI-1021) as well as a capstone and "pillar" course (Design and Development of Food Products and Processes, IA-444) are helping UDLAP's Chemical, Food, and Environmental Engineering Department to achieve these objectives. Comprehensive results regarding didactic interventions and corresponding assessments implemented with the purpose of enhancing critical and creative thinking and improving the design processes in selected "pillar" courses as well as courses' alignment to the Confluence Model of Creativity of Sternberg and Lubart (1993) are available elsewhere (Chávez-Torrejón, et al., 2014; Husted et al., 2014a; Husted, Ramirez-Corona, López-Malo, & Palou, 2014b, 2014c).

Assessments of creative and critical thinking were grounded on the *Consensual Assessment Technique* (Amabile, 1982), which is based on the idea that the best measure of creativity regardless of what is being evaluated, is the assessment by experts in that field. Studied courses' major projects were presented to experts that assessed students' critical thinking by means of a specialized rubric (*Critical Thinking Grid*, CTG, Foundation for Critical Thinking, 2013) while their creative thinking was assessed by the *Creative Thinking VALUE Rubric* (CTVR, AACU, 2013; Rhodes, 2010) and a rubric adapted from the *Investment Theory of Creativity* (ITC, Sternberg & Lubart, 1993), which provided a multidimensional assessment of creativity and critical thinking. Instructor, peer-, and self-assessments were also performed throughout LQI-1021, LQI-1031, and IA-444 courses on several assignments (formative) as well as on studied courses' major projects (summative). CTG and ITC performance levels could be from exemplary (value of 4, skilled, marked by excellence in clarity, accuracy, precision, relevance, depth, breadth, logicality, and fairness) to unsatisfactory (value of 1, unskilled and insufficient, marked by imprecision, lack of clarity, superficiality, illogicality, inaccuracy, and unfairness). CTVR performance levels were entitled capstone or exemplar (value of 4), milestones (values of 3 or 2), and benchmark (value of 1). Evaluators were further encouraged to assign a value of zero if work did not meet benchmark level performance.

Mean values from CTG rubric assessment of LQI-1031 (second semester cornerstone course) two major projects were 2.78 ± 0.58 for *purposes* (meaning that in average, students demonstrated an understanding of the assignment's purpose), 2.77 ± 0.77 for *key questions, problems, or issues* (students defined the issue; identified the core issues, but may not fully explored their depth and breadth), 2.85 ± 0.47 for *information* (students gathered sufficient, credible, and relevant information, included some information from opposing views, and distinguish between information and inferences drawn from it), 2.67 ± 0.74 for *interpretations and inferences* (students followed some evidence to conclusions, but inferences are more often than not unclear, illogical, inconsistent, and/or superficial), 2.23 ± 0.69 for *assumptions* (students are failing to identify assumptions, or failing to explain them, or the assumptions identified are irrelevant, not clearly stated, and/or invalid), 2.58 ± 0.67 for *concepts* (students identified some key concepts, but use of concepts was superficial and inaccurate at times), and 2.53 ± 0.59 for *implications, and practical consequences* (meaning that in average, students are having trouble identifying significant implications and consequences and/or identifying improbable implications). The vast majority of students attained LQI-1031 projects' expected critical thinking outcomes between the level of *competent, effective, accurate and clear, but lacks the exemplary depth, precision, and insight* and the level of *inconsistent, inef-*

fective thinking, showing a lack of consistent competence: often unclear, imprecise, inaccurate, and superficial (Elder & Paul, 2007; Paul & Elder, 2008). Therefore, it is suggested to further integrate critical thinking in subsequent courses in order to foster its development in our Chemical, Food, and Environmental Engineering students (Chávez-Torrejón et al., 2014).

Mean values from CTVR rubric assessment for two major projects from LQI-1031 were 3.10 for *Acquiring Competencies* (attaining strategies and skills within a particular domain), 3.10 for *Taking Risks* (may include personal risk, fear of embarrassment or rejection, or risk of failure in successfully completing assignment, i.e. going beyond original parameters of assignment, introducing new materials and forms, tackling controversial topics, advocating unpopular ideas or solutions), 3.30 for *Solving Problems* (developing a logical, consistent plan to solve the problem, recognizing consequences of solution and articulating reason for choosing proposed solution), 2.60 for *Embracing Contradictions* (integrating alternate, divergent, or contradictory perspectives or ideas), 2.50 for *Innovative Thinking* (novelty or uniqueness of idea, claim, question, form, etc.), and 3.20 for *Connecting*, *Synthesizing*, and *Transforming* (transforming ideas or solutions into entirely new forms). While mean values from ITC rubric assessment of two major projects from the same course (LQI-1031) were 3.00 for *creative performance*, 3.44 for *motivation* that incorporates level of commitment, project pride, and interest in task, 3.00 for *intellectual styles* that includes indicators such as autonomy and rules, 3.25 for *creative personality* with indicators such as tolerance for ambiguity, risk taking, will, and perseverance, 3.00 for *knowledge of domain* that comprises application of formal and informal knowledge, 3.33 for *intellectual processes* which includes indicators such as sensitivity, problem identification, ideation, ability to recognize ideas that have potential to be valued, as well as ability to sell your ideas effectively and persuade of its value, and 2.38 for the *creative product* itself, which includes its originality, quality, importance, and feasibility that in this case are the two designed products for corresponding LQI-1031 two major course projects. The vast majority of the LQI-1031 teams were able to attain projects' expected outcomes at an intermediate level (AACU, 2013; Rhodes, 2010; Sternberg & Lubart, 1993). Therefore, it is suggested to further integrate creativity in subsequent pillar courses in order to foster meaningful development of students' creative thinking. Furthermore, reflections integrated in the two projects' design binders, suggest that these projects allowed students to strengthen their learning and understanding of key concepts regarding course learning outcomes, expand their notion of the engineering design processes and link this knowledge to real life examples (Husted et al., 2014a).

Material Balances (LQI-1021) is an introductory (second semester) course that was taught in a traditional format, "lecture-homework-exam", but nowadays constitutes a "pillar" course for Chemical, Food, and Environmental Engineering undergraduate programs. As many courses in engineering science, the subject content is usually presented as abstract knowledge, where the attained knowledge is conditioned to the styles of learning and intelligence possessed by each student, factors that make it impossible to maintain a consistent teaching pace (Husted et al., 2014b). In the proposed new learning environment, a change on the traditional format of teaching is introduced through several active-creative experiences, where the main goal is that students reach the level of knowledge required to solve material balances while strengthening their cognitive flexibility. Thus, achieving a level of fluency allows them to perform various representations of a material balance and explain them to an expert audience. Students were able to build concrete examples of a material balance in an everyday situation (preparing pancakes; home-produced recycled paper; fruit juice extraction; cocktail making; sweet potato candy—*camote*—production; homemade cheese, pineapple jam, and gummy bears; lemonade making; preparing *dulce de leche*, and so on) and represent them in many ways (physically, verbally, symbolically, and by means of a multimedia presentation). Mean values from ITC rubric assessment of LQI-1021 final projects were 3.13 for *creative performance*, 3.80 for *knowledge of domain* (application of formal and informal knowledge), 3.31 for *intellectual style* (includes indicators such as autonomy and rules), 3.28 for *motivation* (level of commitment, project pride, and interest in task), 3.02 for *intellectual processes* (which includes indicators such as sensitivity, problem identification, ideation, ability to recognize ideas that have potential to be valued, as well as ability to sell your ideas effectively and persuade of its value), and 2.90 for *creative personality* (with indicators such as tolerance for ambiguity, risk taking, will, and perseverance). In this course an additional *Fluency Rubric* was developed, which was divided into four modules that correspond to each project deliverable (dossier, poster, video, and oral presentation). Assessment results (Husted et al., 2014b) demonstrate that LQI-1021 students achieved an average score of 3.6/4.0 in the generating ideas aspect; 90 % of students were able to undertake an ideation process, participating with several proposals for the team project. This assessment includes sensitivity to problems in context and decision-making; every team reached a consensual agreement on the mass balance process for their final project. The average score obtained in the figural representation was 3.5/4.0. Regarding flowchart development students obtained a mean grade of 3.3/4.0, although in some cases students did not identify in which process step the mass was lost; therefore, they were not able to represent it on their diagrams. Most teams (70 %) were able to perform a proper symbolic representation of their selected process. However, 13 % of the class population failed to explain the reasons why in some cases there exists a "loss of mass"; therefore, they had to make inferences and adjust numerical fractions in order to perform the required calculations. 90 % of the class population was able to define the constitutive equations for their mass balance process; even so their numerical solutions were scored with a mean of 2.8/4.0. According to the experts' assessments, students successfully described the problem definition and solution and the group average score was 3.8/4.0. Only 30 % of the teams were ranked as *sufficient* while 70 % were scored as *excellent* (Husted et al., 2014b).

Mean values from CTVR rubric assessment of IA-444 (food engineering capstone course) final projects were 2.35 for *Acquiring Competencies*, 2.42 for *Taking Risks*, 2.44 for *Solving Problems*, 2.44 for *Embracing Contradictions*, 2.40 for *Innovative Thinking*, and 2.24 for *Connecting, Synthesizing,* and *Transforming* (Husted et al., 2014c). Therefore, senior food engineering students' creative thinking was at an intermediate level in both the capacity to combine or synthesize existing ideas or expertise in original ways and the experience of thinking, reacting, and working in an imaginative way (AACU, 2013; Rhodes, 2010; Sternberg & Lubart, 1993). In general, scores around 2 (milestones lower level of performance) were assigned for four of the team projects, for team 5 higher scores were assigned (milestones higher level of performance). None of the invited experts believed that food products and corresponding presentations of team projects did not meet the minimal expectations (Husted et al., 2014c).

Final Remarks

The Introduction to Engineering Design course has undergone many changes since its inception, the most important of which have sought to orient the course towards the *How People Learn* (HPL) framework (in the case of EI-100 course) and then adapting it to Chemical, Food, and Environmental Engineering programs using the *Framework for 21st Century Learning* (for the course LQI-1031). VaNTH Observation System (VOS) enabled us to determine that it is in fact a course designed according to the HPL framework. Furthermore, each of the course sessions engaged students in learning environments that were knowledge-, learner-, assessment-, and community-centered. Use of the Classroom Interaction Observation instrument of VOS, also enabled us to carry out observations related to the use of the Tablet PCs as a learning tool in this course, identifying important differences among sessions and the facilitators who taught the course. As clearly displayed in Figs. 2 and 3, it is clear that the differences among the different groups basically depend on the facilitator. The knowledge and experience of him/her with Tablet PCs and especially with the HPL framework are indispensable prerequisites for the course to be HPL-centered, and they are also determining factors in order for students to achieve satisfactory learning outcomes. This makes the need all the greater for facilitators and first-year students to be trained on the HPL framework. Facilitators need to be very familiar with the framework, its use and assessment, while students need a period of time to become familiar with the new framework before they can become successful with it. Another important result has been the timely feedback we have been able to provide to every facilitator who taught a VOS-studied course since 2008. This feedback has enabled them to know what their strengths and weaknesses are in their use of the HPL framework, so that they can improve in future courses.

By means of Tablet PCs and associated technologies, we were able to create high-quality learning environments that promote an interactive classroom, integrating multiple formative assessments into classroom practices. Therefore, "pillar" courses have increased active student participation, peer- and team-interactions, and feedback processes since instructors are utilizing the information gained through real-time formative assessment to tailor instruction to meet student needs. These "pillar" courses also utilize active, collaborative and cooperative learning strategies.

The studied problem solving learning environments approach helped almost every student, regardless of its gender or academic strength. In general, students that achieved high scores in the Metacognitive Awareness Inventory pre-test obtained minor gains in metacognitive awareness scores in their post-tests, while students who achieved lower scores in the pre-test obtained larger gains in metacognitive awareness scores in their post-tests.

The results achieved by students in the studied "pillar" courses demonstrate that assessment of critical thinking and creativity are not easy tasks. The applied rubrics allowed us to evaluate not only the final product of a critical thinking or creative process, but several important aspects during this critical and creative processes. Assessed rubrics allowed the identification of several opportunity areas to improve the studied engineering cornerstone and capstone courses. With sights set on this, additional didactic interventions are needed to further enhance critical and creative thinking, make the design processes more efficient, as well as overall improve the critical and creative thinking experiences for students in these studied courses.

The *Framework for 21st Century Learning* was extremely helpful, allowing us to holistically: (a) define the standards for chemical, environmental, and food engineering 21st century expertise; (b) create formative and summative assessments to evaluate student attainment of it; (c) design instruction activities to promote this expertise; (d) develop professional development opportunities for "pillar" course instructors; and (e) generate corresponding learning environments that foster 21st century expertise in these courses.

Acknowledgements We acknowledge financial support from HEWLETT-PACKARD (HP) through the HP Catalyst Grant Initiative for the project "Critical Support Systems to Enhance the Development of 21st Century Expertise in Engineering Students: Using Tablet PCs and Associated Technologies, the *Framework for 21st Century Learning*, and Guidelines from Research on *How People Learn*". Author Chávez-Torrejón gratefully acknowledges financial support for her PhD studies from *Universidad de las Américas Puebla*. Author Husted gratefully acknowledges financial support for her PhD studies from *Programa de Mejoramiento del Profesorado* (PROMEP) of the Mexican Ministry of Public Education (SEP) and *Universidad Autónoma de Ciudad Juárez*. Authors Ramírez Apud and Gazca acknowledge financial support for their PhD studies from the National Council for Science and Technology of Mexico (CONACyT) and *Universidad de las Américas Puebla*. Author Gutiérrez Cuba gratefully acknowledges a postdoctoral fellowship from CONACyT.

References

ABET. (2015). Criteria for Accrediting Engineering Programs Effective for Reviews During the 2015-2016 Accreditation Cycle. Engineering Accreditation Commission. ABET. http://www.abet.org/accreditation/accreditation-criteria/criteria-for-accrediting-engineering-programs-2015-2016. Accessed 24 June 2015.

Altamirano, E., Gazca, L., López-Malo, A., & Palou, E. (2013). Direct and indirect assessment of Universidad de las Américas Puebla's food engineering program outcomes. Proceedings of the 2013 American Society for Engineering Education Annual Conference and Exposition. http://www.asee.org/search/proceedings. Accessed 24 June 2015.

Amabile, T. M. (1982). Social psychology of creativity: A consensual assessment technique. *Journal of Personality and Social Psychology, 43*(5), 997–1013.

Anderson, R., Anderson, R., McDowell, L., & Simon, B. (2005). Use of classroom presenter in engineering courses. Proceedings of the 35th Frontiers in Education Conference. http://fie-conference.org. Accessed 24 June 2015.

Asociación Nacional de Facultades y Escuelas de Ingeniería. (2002). *La formación de ingenieros para el siglo XXI. Planeación prospectiva y estratégica*. México: Asociación Nacional de Facultades y Escuelas de Ingeniería.

Asociación Nacional de Facultades y Escuelas de Ingeniería. (2007). *Ingeniería México 2030: Escenarios de Futuro*. México: Asociación Nacional de Facultades y Escuelas de Ingeniería.

Association of American Colleges and Universities. (2013). AACU value rubrics. Association of American Colleges and Universities. http://www.aacu.org/value/rubrics/index_p.cfm?CFID=2 7703138&CFTOKEN=51989935. Accessed 24 June 2015.

Bienkowski, M. A., Haertel, G., Yamaguchi, R., Molina, A., Adamson, F., & Peck-Theis, L. (2005). *Singapore Tablet PC program study. Executive summary*. Menlo Park: SRI Center for Technology in Learning.

Biswas, S. (2007). Teaching courses with Tablet PC: experience and student feedback. Proceedings of the 2007 American Society for Engineering Education Annual Conference and Exposition. http://www.asee.org/search/proceedings. Accessed 24 June 2015.

Bransford, J. D., & Schwartz, D. (1999). Rethinking transfer: A simple proposal with multiple implications. *Review of Research in Education, 24*, 61–100.

Bransford, J. D., Brown, A. L., & Cocking, R. R. (2000). *How people learn. brain, mind, experience and school. expanded edition*. Washington, D. C.: National Academies Press.

Bransford, J. D., Vye, N., & Bateman, H. (2002). Creating high-quality learning environments: Guidelines from research on how people learn. In P. Albjerg Graham & N. G. Stacey (Eds.), *The knowledge economy and postsecondary education: Report of a workshop* (pp. 159–198). Washington, D. C.: National Academies Press.

Carney, K. (2005). *Toward a definition of HPL-ness. Center for the study of learning, instruction, and teacher* development. Chicago: University of Illinois.

Chávez-Torrejón, G., Husted, S., Ramirez-Corona, N., López-Malo, A., & Palou, E. (2014). Fostering the development of critical thinking in an introduction to chemical process engineering design course. Proceedings of the 2014 American Society for Engineering Education Annual Conference and Exposition. http://www.asee.org/search/proceedings. Accessed 24 June 2015.

Collura, M. A., Aliane, B., Daniels, S., & Nocito-Gobel, J. (2004). Development of a multidisciplinary engineering foundation spiral. Proceedings of the 2004 American Society for Engineering Education Annual Conference and Exposition. http://www.asee.org/search/proceedings. Accessed 24 June 2015.

Cox, M. F., & Cordray, D. S. (2008). Assessing pedagogy in bioengineering classrooms: Quantifying elements of the 'how people learn' model using the VaNTH observation system (VOS). *Journal of Engineering Education, 97*(4), 413–431.

Elder, L., & Paul, R. (2007). *The thinker's guide to analytical thinking*. Tomales: Foundation for Critical Thinking Press.

Felder, R. M. (1982). *Does engineering education have anything to do with either one? Toward a systems approach to training engineers*. Raleigh: North Carolina State University. http://www.ncsu.edu/felder-public/Papers/RJR-Monograph.pdf. Accessed 24 June 2015.

Felder, R. M. (1987). On creating creative engineers. *Engineering Education, 77*(4), 222–227.

Felder, R. M. (1988). Creativity in engineering education. *Chemical Engineering Education, 22*(3), 120–125.

Flavell, J. (1976). Metacognitive aspects of problem-solving. In L. B. Resnick (Ed.), *The nature of intelligence* (pp. 231–236). Hillsdale: Lawrence Erlbaum.

Flavell, J. (1979). Metacognition and cognitive monitoring: A new area of cognitive developmental inquiry. *American Psychologist, 34*(10), 906–911.

Foundation for Critical Thinking. (2013). *Critical thinking grid*. Tomales: Foundation for Critical Thinking Press.

Gassner, L. (2009). *Developing metacognitive awareness: A modified model of a PBL-tutorial*. Unpublished Thesis for the Bachelor of Odontology in Oral Health. Sweden: Malmö University.

Gazca, L., Palou, E., López-Malo, A., & Garibay, J. M. (2009). Capturing differences of engineering design learning environments by means of VaNTH observation system. Proceedings of the 2009 American Society for Engineering Education Annual Conference and Exposition. http://www.asee.org/search/proceedings. Accessed 24 June 2015.

Gazca, L., Palou, E., López-Malo, A., & Garibay, J. M. (2011). Analysis of the implementation of the how people learn framework through direct classroom observation in selected food engineering courses. Proceedings of the 2011 American Society for Engineering Education Annual Conference and Exposition. http://www.asee.org/search/proceedings. Accessed 24 June 2015.

Gazca, L., López-Malo, A., & Palou, E. (2012). Curricular mapping and indirect assessment of Universidad de las Américas Puebla's engineering school outcomes. Proceedings of the 2012 American Society for Engineering Education Annual Conference and Exposition. http://www.asee.org/search/proceedings. Accessed 24 June 2015.

Gutiérrez Cuba, J. V., López-Malo, A., & Palou, E. (2011). Using tablet PCs and associated technologies to reveal undergraduate and graduate student thinking. Proceedings of the 2011 American Society for Engineering Education Annual Conference and Exposition. http://www.asee.org/search/proceedings. Accessed 24 June 2015.

Gutiérrez Cuba, J. V., López-Malo, A., & Palou, E. (2012). Graduate student perspectives on using tablet PCs and associated technologies. Proceedings of the 2012 American Society for Engineering Education Annual Conference and Exposition. http://www.asee.org/search/proceedings. Accessed 24 June 2015.

Harris, A. H., & Cox, M. F. (2003). Developing an observation system to capture instructional differences in engineering classrooms. *Journal of Engineering Education, 92*(4), 329–336.

Holyoak, K. J., & Morrison, R. G. (Eds.). (2005). *The Cambridge handbook of thinking and reasoning*. New York: Cambridge University Press.

Huber, M. T., & Hutchings, P. (2004). *Integrative learning: Mapping the terrain*. Washington, D. C.: AAC&U and The Carnegie Foundation for the Advancement of Teaching.

Husted, S., Gutiérrez Cuba, J. V., Ramirez-Corona, N., López-Malo, A., & Palou, E. (2014a). Multidimensional assessment of creativity in an introduction to engineering design course. Proceedings of the 2014 American Society for Engineering Education Annual Conference and Exposition. http://www.asee.org/search/proceedings. Accessed 24 June 2015.

Husted, S., Ramirez-Corona, N., López-Malo, A., & Palou, E. (2014b). A creative experience for chemical, food, and environmental engineering students in a material balances course. Proceedings of the 2014 American Society for Engineering Education Annual Conference and Exposition. http://www.asee.org/search/proceedings. Accessed 24 June 2015.

Husted, S., Ramirez-Corona, N., López-Malo, A., & Palou, E. (2014c). Creativity and its assessment in a design and development of food products and processes course. Proceedings of the 2014 American Society for Engineering Education Annual Conference and Exposition. http://www.asee.org/search/proceedings. Accessed 24 June 2015.

IFT. (2012). Resource Guide for Approval and Re-Approval of Undergraduate Food Science Programs. Institute of Food Technologists. http://www.ift.org/~/media/Knowledge%20Center/Learn%20Food%20Science/Become%20a%20Food%20Scientist/Resources/ResourceGuide_UndergradFoodScience.pdf. Accessed 24 June 2015.

Jenkins, J. J. (1978). Four points to remember: A tetrahedral model of memory experiments. In L. S. Cermak & F. I. M. Craik (Eds.), *Levels of processing and human memory* (pp. 429–446). Hillsdale: Lawrence Erlbaum.

Jonassen, D. H. (2010). Assembling and analyzing the building blocks of problem-based learning environments. In K. H. Silber & W. R. Foshay (Eds.), *Handbook of improving performance in the workplace, volume one: Instructional design and training delivery* (pp. 361–394). Hoboken: Wileys.

Jonassen, D. H. (2011). *Learning to solve problems: A handbook for designing problem-solving learning environments*. New York: Routledge.

Jonassen, D. H., Strobel, J., & Lee, C. B. (2006). Everyday problem solving in engineering: Lessons for engineering educators. *Journal of Engineering Education, 95*(2), 1–14.

Kowalski, F., Kowalski, S., & Hoover, E. (2007a). Using InkSurvey: A free web-based tool for open-ended questioning to promote active learning and real-time formative assessment of tablet PC-equipped engineering students. Proceedings of the 2007 American Society for Engineering Education Annual Conference and Exposition. http://www.asee.org/search/proceedings. Accessed 24 June 2015.

Kowalski, F., Williams, J., Reed, R., & Vanides, J. (2007b). Transforming teaching and learning using tablet PCs. a panel discussion using tablet PCs. Proceedings of the 2007 American Society for Engineering Education Annual Conference and Exposition. http://www.asee.org/search/proceedings. Accessed 24 June 2015.

Kowalski, F., Kowalski, S., Colling, T., Gutierrez Cuba, J. V., Gardner, T., Greivel, G., Palou, E., & Ruskell, T. (2013a). Using InkSurvey with pen-enabled mobile devices for real-time formative assessment: I. Applications in diverse educational environments. Proceedings of the Workshop on the impact of pen and touch technology on education. http://arxiv.org/abs/1308.3727. Accessed 24 June 2015.

Kowalski, F., Kowalski, S., Colling, T., Gutierrez Cuba, J. V., Gardner, T., Greivel, G., Palou, E., & Ruskell, T. (2013b). Using InkSurvey with pen-enabled mobile devices for real-time formative assessment: II. Indications of effectiveness in diverse educational environments. Proceedings of the Workshop on the Impact of Pen and Touch Technology on Education. http://arxiv.org/abs/1308.3729. Accessed 24 June 2015.

Litzinger, T. A., Lattuca, L. R., Hadgrafta, R. G., & Newstetter, W. C. (2011). Engineering education and the development of expertise. *Journal of Engineering Education, 100*(1), 123–150.

National Academy of Engineering. (2004). *The engineer of 2020: Visions of engineering in the new century*. Washington, D. C.: National Academies Press.

National Academy of Engineering. (2005). *Educating the engineer of 2020. Adapting engineering education to the new century*. Washington, D. C.: National Academies Press.

Novak, J. D. (1998). *Learning, creating, and using knowledge*. Hillsdale: Lawrence Erlbaum.

Palou, E., Gazca, L., Díaz García, J. A., Rojas Lobato, J. A., Guerrero Ojeda, L. G., Tamborero Arnal, J. F., Jiménez Munguía, M. T., López-Malo, A., & Garibay, J. M. (2012). High-quality learning environments for engineering design: Using tablet PCs and guidelines from research on how people learn. *International Journal of Food Studies, 1*, 1–16.

Partnership for 21st Century Skills. (2009a). Framework for 21st century learning. http://www.p21.org/index.php?option=com_content&task=view&id=254&Itemid=119. Accessed 24 June 2015.

Partnership for 21st Century Skills. (2009b). P21 framework definitions. http://www.p21.org/documents/P21_Framework_Definitions.pdf. Accessed 24 June 2015.

Partnership for 21st Century Skills. (2009c). The MILE guide. http://www.p21.org/documents/MILE_Guide_091101.pdf. Accessed 24 June 2015.

Paul, R., & Elder, L. (2008). *The miniature guide to critical thinking. Concepts and tools*. Tomales: Foundation for Critical Thinking Press.

Ramirez Apud, Z., Ramirez-Corona, N., López-Malo, A., & Palou, E. (2012). Implementing problem-solving learning environments in a kinetics and homogeneous reactor design course. Proceedings of the 2012 American Society for Engineering Education Annual Conference and Exposition. http://www.asee.org/search/proceedings. Accessed 24 June 2015.

Ramirez-Corona, N., Ramirez Apud, Z., López-Malo, A., & Palou, E. (2013). Assessing metacognitive awareness during problem-solving in a kinetics and homogeneous reactor design course. Proceedings of the 2013 American Society for Engineering Education Annual Conference and Exposition. http://www.asee.org/search/proceedings. Accessed 24 June 2015.

Rascón-Chávez, O. A. (2010). *Estado del Arte y Prospectiva de la Educación en Ingeniería en México*. México: Academia. de Ingeniería.

Reyes Guerrero, S., Ramirez-Corona, N., López-Malo, A., & Palou, E. (2014). Assessing metacognition during problem-solving in two senior concurrent courses. Proceedings of the 2014 American Society for Engineering Education Annual Conference and Exposition. http://www.asee.org/search/proceedings. Accessed 24 June 2015.

Rhodes, T. (Ed.). (2010). *Assessing outcomes and improving achievement: Tips and tools for using rubrics*. Washington, D. C.: Association of American Colleges and Universities.

Schraw, G., & Dennison, R. S. (1994). Assessing metacognitive awareness. *Contemporary Educational Psychology, 19,* 460–475.

Schwartz, D. L., & Bransford, J. D. (1998). A time for telling. *Cognition and Instruction, 16*(4), 475–522.

Sheppard, S. D., Macatangay, K., Colby, A., & Sullivan, W. M. (2008). *Educating engineers: Designing for the future of the field*. San Francisco: Jossey-Bass.

Simon, B., Anderson, R., Hoyer, C., & Su, J. (2004). Preliminary experiences with a tablet PC based system to support active learning in computer science courses. Proceedings of the 9th Annual Conference on Innovation and Technology in Computer Science Education Leeds, UK: ITICSE'04.

Sternberg, R. J., & Lubart, T. I. (1993). Creative giftedness: A multivariate approach investment. *Gifted Child Quarterly, 37*(1), 7–15.

Sternberg, R. J., & O' Hara, L. (2005). Creatividad e inteligencia. *Cuadernos de Información y Comunicación, 10,* 113–149.

Sternberg, R. J., Lubart, T. I., Kaufman, J. C., & Prelz, J. E. (2005). Creativity. In K. J. Holyoak & R. G. Morrison (Eds.), *The Cambridge handbook of thinking and reasoning* (pp. 351–369). New York: Cambridge University Press.

Stewart, P. W., Cooper. S. S., & Moulding, L. R. (2007). Metacognitive development in professional educators. *The Researcher, 21*(1), 32–40.

Tront, J. G., Eligeti, V., & Prey, J. (2006). Classroom presentations using tablet PCs and Write-On. *Proceedings of the 36th Frontiers in Education Conference*. http://fie-conference.org. Accessed 24 June 2015.

Twining, P., Evans, D., Cook, D., Ralston, J., Selwood, I., Jones, A., Underwood, J., Dillon, G., & Scanlon, E. (2005). *Tablet PCs in schools. Case study report*. London: British Educational Communications and Technology Agency.

Wiggins, G., & McTighe, J. (2005). *Understanding by design, expanded* (2nd ed.). Alexandria: Association for Supervision and Curriculum Development.

Wise, J. C., Toto, R., & Yon Lim, K. (2006). Introducing tablet PCs: Initial results from the classroom. *Proceedings of the 36th Frontiers in Education Conference*. http://fie-conference.org. Accessed 24 June 2015.

Enrique Palou is Professor and Past-Chair, Chemical, Food, and Environmental Engineering Department, and director of the Center for Science, Engineering, and Technology Education at Universidad de las Américas Puebla in Mexico. He teaches engineering, food science, and education related courses; has been awarded University-wide awards for teaching excellence six times. Professor Palou has authored one book, 28 book chapters and more than 150 scientific publications. He has presented 330 papers at international meetings. Dr. Palou has been PI or Co-PI in over 45 research projects (national and international funding) for more than US\$ 4.5 million and has participated in several consulting projects for the food industry. The National Research System of Mexico elected Dr. Palou as National Researcher since 1998, and nowadays is at the highest possible level. He was elected member of the Mexican National Academy of Engineering in 2000 and to the Mexican National Academy of Sciences in 2012. His research interests include emerging technologies for food processing, predictive microbiology, natural antimicrobials, creating effective learning environments, using Tablet PCs and associated technologies to enhance the development of 21st century expertise in engineering students, and building rigorous research capacity in science, engineering and technology education.

Silvia Husted recently finished her Science, Engineering, and Technology Education PhD studies at Universidad de las Américas Puebla. Her dissertation focuses on the development and assessment of creative thinking in engineering. Silvia's areas of interest include cognitive learning processes, creativity, educational technology, and designing effective learning environments. Dr. Husted holds a Masters degree in Holistic Design by Universidad Autónoma de Ciudad Juárez

(UACJ) and a BA in Graphic Design from the same university with a major in Technology and Development of Web Applications by UACJ's Instituto de Ingeniería y Tecnología. She is a professor at UACJ, as member of the Technology and Design Academies, she teaches courses in the Graphic Design and Industrial Design undergraduate programs, as well as in a Master's program in Creative Processes for Design.

Gladis Chávez-Torrejón is currently a Science, Engineering, and Technology Education PhD student at Universidad de las Américas Puebla (UDLAP). Her dissertation focuses on the development and assessment of critical thinking in engineering. Gladis' areas of interest include learning processes, critical thinking, and assessment. Mrs. Chávez-Torrejón holds Bachelor and Masters degrees in Psychology. She is instructional supervision coordinator of Distance Learning at UDLAP, where she previously worked at Registrar Processes and Student Incorporation.

Zaira Ramírez Apud (Benemérita Universidad Autónoma de Puebla) is currently a Professor at the Biology School of Benemérita Universidad Autónoma de Puebla (BUAP). She did her undergraduate studies in Biology at BUAP, her Master studies in Ecosystem Management at Universidad Autónoma de Baja California, and holds a PhD in Science, Engineering, and Technology Education from Universidad de las Américas Puebla. Her dissertation focused on the development and assessment of metacognition in engineering students. Dr. Ramírez Apud teaching experience includes ethics and development of complex thinking skills related courses. Her research interests include faculty development, outcomes assessment, and creating effective learning environments, as well as environmental education. She has several publications related to the development of complex thinking skills as well as problem-solving processes.

Lourdes Gazca has a BA in Education with a specialization in Teaching Mathematics from Universidad de las Américas Puebla (UDLAP) and a Masters in Business Administration with specialization in Educational Institutions from the same university. She holds a PhD in Science, Engineering, and Technology Education from UDLAP. Her dissertation validated the VaNTH Observation System in Mexico and demonstrated the usefulness of the How People Learn framework to create effective learning environments. Currently, she teaches undergraduate and graduate courses at UDLAP, Universidad Anáhuac Puebla, and Universidad Iberoamericana Puebla. Her research interests include active and collaborative learning, designing effective learning environments, competency-based curriculum and its assessment. She has participated in numerous conferences. For many years she has been working on the development of teachers in different states of Mexico.

Judith Virginia Gutiérrez Cuba is currently a Curriculum Designer and Teacher in a private university in Puebla. Previously she worked as Instructional Supervisor at Universidad de las Américas Puebla and Department Chair of Distance Learning in a governmental institution. She holds a PhD in Science, Engineering, and Technology Education from Universidad de las Américas Puebla. Her dissertation focused on using Tablet PCs and associated technologies to reveal engineering undergraduate and graduate students' thinking. Her research interests include curriculum design, assessment, on-line education, and educational technology. Dr. Gutiérrez Cuba has been teacher, tutor and designer of on-line courses in several private universities.

Nelly Ramírez-Corona is currently a Full Time Professor of Chemical Engineering at Chemical, Environmental, and Food Engineering Department, Universidad de las Américas, Puebla. Her teaching experience is in the area of Process Dynamics and Control, Kinetics, Catalysis and Reactor Design. She did her undergraduate studies in Chemical Engineering at Universidad Autónoma de Tlaxcala, and her Master and Doctoral studies at Instituto Tecnológico de Celaya. Her research interests are in the field of Process Systems Engineering, and include the analysis and design of thermally coupled and alternative distillation configurations, the design of non-ideal distillation systems and the synthesis, optimization and control of chemical processes with recycle streams; as well as creating effective learning environments and using Tablet PCs and associated technologies to enhance the development of 21st century expertise in engineering students.

Aurelio López-Malo is Professor in the Department of Chemical, Food, and Environmental Engineering at Universidad de las Américas Puebla. Dr. López-Malo is co-author of the book Minimally Processed Fruits and Vegetables, editor of two books, has authored over 30 book chapters and more than 150 scientific publications in high-impact international journals, is member of the Journal of Food Protection Editorial Board. Dr. López-Malo received his PhD in Chemistry in 2000 from Universidad de Buenos Aires in Argentina, a Masters in Food Engineering in 1995 from Universidad de las Américas Puebla, and he graduated as a Food Engineer from the same institution in 1983. He belongs to the National Research System of Mexico as a National Researcher Level III. He is Member of the Institute of Food Technologists (IFT), the International Association for Food Protection (IAFP), and the American Society for Engineering Education (ASEE). Dr. López-Malo has been PI or Co-PI in over 40 research projects (national and international funding) for more than US$ 4.5 million and has participated in many consulting projects for the food industry. His research interests include Natural Antimicrobials, Predictive Microbiology, Emerging Technologies for Food Processing, Minimally Processed Fruits, and K-16 Science and Engineering Education.

Part V
Arts

The Language Arts as Foundational for Science, Technology, Engineering, Art, and Mathematics

Lawrence Baines

Abstract To what extent are the language arts relevant, useful, and self-sustaining in an era of rapid technological and scientific innovation? Historically, the language arts have been influenced by three curricular models—competency-based instruction, the Heritage Curriculum, and the process approach. The suitability of these curricular models for the future, the myriad ways that the language arts support and extend innovation, and the unique attributes of 21st century literacies are discussed.

Keywords Technology · English · Language arts · Curriculum · Standards · STEM · Liberal arts

The Language Arts as Foundational

As an undergraduate at the Massachusetts Institute of Technology (M.I.T.), the Nobel-Prize winning physicist Richard Feynman raged against the university's requirement that students take courses in English and the Humanities. "I was interested in science. I was no good at anything else" (Feynman 2006, p. 43). Although Feynman claimed that he had no interest in the language arts, he was a voracious reader. Over the course of his life, he authored books and articles, gave hundreds of lectures, participated in think tanks, wrote about art, and argued endlessly over scientific theories. If anything, Feynman's career provides convincing evidence that the language arts–reading, writing, thinking, and speaking—are integral to the fields of Science, Technology, Engineering, and Mathematics (STEM).

Indeed, the National Research Council (2011) estimates that about half of the time spent by scientists and engineers at work is spent on reading and writing. It is no accident that many of the world's most renowned scientists also happen to be highly accomplished writers. Authors on the *New York Times* bestseller lists routinely include scientists and mathematicians, such as Brian Greene (string theory), Stephen Hawking (mathematics and astronomy), Michio Kaku (physics), Oliver Sacks (psychiatry), Richard Dawkins (biologist), and Atul Gawande (medicine).

L. Baines (✉)
The University of Oklahoma, Norman, USA
e-mail: lbaines@ou.edu

© Springer International Publishing Switzerland 2015

X. Ge et al. (eds.), *Emerging Technologies for STEAM Education,*
Educational Communications and Technology: Issues and Innovations,
DOI 10.1007/978-3-319-02573-5_13

Scientific and mathematical theories, by their very nature, must be articulated coherently and clearly so that they can be evaluated and modified. A scientist who lacks the ability to translate mental constructs into words and symbols likely dooms them to oblivion. Science progresses by determining the precise veracity of new theories; not by accepting fuzzy hunches and inchoate instincts. What is the scientific method if not a vehicle for divining the truth? As Schallert (1987) writes:

> We live alone inside our skin, with our thoughts, wishes, and feelings coursing through the shimmering mass of neural matter locked inside our skulls. When we formulate messages that we wish to express or actions that we need others to perform, we often choose to fashion our thoughts into language. The texts we produce act as road maps or recipes that others like us can use to reconstruct what they believe we intended. (p. 65)

To appease the humanities and to acknowledge the importance of the arts and creativity, reformers have urged a change from a curricular emphasis on STEM to one based upon STEAM (Doss, 2013). The language arts certainly exist as part of the arts (the A in STEAM), but they are more than that. The language arts provide the very foundation upon which knowledge in STEM is created.

Conceptions of the Language Arts

In the book *What is English?*, Elbow (1990) sets out to define the domain of the language arts classroom, but fails, concluding that the field resists categorization. If, as Elbow claims, the language arts are not about "the ingestion of a list or a body of information," but instead about "the making of meaning and the reflecting back on this process of meaning making" (p. 18) then their malleability seems particularly well-suited to STEAM and the continual drive to make sense of the world.

According to Mandel (1980) there exist three models of the language arts curriculum: competency-based, heritage, and process (Baines & Farrell, 2002). Most contemporary standardized testing assumes a competencies approach. What a Certified Public Accountant, lawyer, nurse, or teacher needs to know is decided upon, then an assessment is devised to evaluate the extent to which knowledge has been mastered. A cut-off point is set so that everyone who scores above the cut-off point is considered to have mastered the competencies and everyone who scores below the cut-off point is considered to have fallen short of mastering the competencies.

Among the three approaches to the curriculum, the competency-based approach has become dominant. Today, every state in the nation administers competency tests and 70% of American students attend high schools that require exit exams (Center for Education Policy, 2012). Some states in the United States, such as New Hampshire, are even attempting to move towards a purely competency-based system of instruction for K-12 education, without regard to a student's chronological age (Gewertz, 2012). A competency-based model for higher education has been proposed for college-level courses as well, and in fact, has been adopted by a few, online, for-profit institutions (Kamenetz, 2013).

Critics of competency-based programs (Thomas, 2012; Stoddard, 2010) typically note that tests do not handle complexity well, nor do they consider the attitudes, aptitudes, or motivations of the students, themselves. These are substantial criticisms as computers continue to take on more and more rote tasks, leaving humans, at least for now, to handle the more nuanced and complex decision-making. Competency-based instruction is wholly concerned with the curricular objective—not the student, yet the student is the most important variable in any situation involving learning (Slavin, 1987).

The Heritage Curriculum is perhaps best represented by the work of former literary critic cum education reformer, E. D. Hirsch, who turned an article published in 1983 in *American Scholar* entitled "Cultural Literacy" into an influential, multimillion dollar foundation (The Core Knowledge Foundation), a series of books (*What Every ___ Grader Should Know*), and a lucrative consulting business. The rationale behind the Heritage Curriculum is that the great works of literature build identity and create a common heritage. As Krystal (2014), noted, "The canon formalized modern literature as a select body of imaginative writings that could stand up to the Greek and Latin texts. Although exclusionary by nature, it was originally intended to impart a sense of unity; critics hoped that a tradition of great writers would help create a national literature" (p. 91).

The problem with the Heritage Curriculum is in deciding which books and whose heritage will be represented and to what extent these books and representations are relevant to all readers (Kohn, 2004). A second challenge of the Heritage Curriculum is the difficulty of keeping the canon current. Literature is cumulative, so with each new classic, the canon is enlarged, ad infinitum. In *The Western Canon* (1984), Bloom suggests a "modest" reading list of over 800 books, which would take the average reader about 20 years to complete.

The Common Core

In many ways, the new national curriculum in the United States, the Common Core Curriculum, merges aspects of competency-based instruction and the Heritage Curriculum. Common Core exams are purposefully designed to be competency-based, as students who fail to demonstrate mastery by attaining the minimum cut-off score on exams will face consequences—no promotion to the next grade, no graduation from high school, no driver's license, no chance for college.

Although the Common Core carefully avoided naming specific literary works in its initial launch, the now infamous Appendix B names and cites literary works as exemplars of the kinds of texts that would be appropriate (Common Core Standards Appendix B, 2014). While the titles of literary works in Appendix B are supposedly only exemplars, they have become, de facto, the New Literary Canon for students in many schools.

Consider the following standard for students in grades 11–12:

CCSS.ELA-Literacy.RL.11-12.9 Demonstrate knowledge of eighteenth-, nineteenth- and early-twentieth-century foundational works of American literature, including how two or more texts from the same period treat similar themes or topics. (Common Core English Language Arts Standards, 2014)

If a teacher ever wonders what might constitute a foundational work of nineteenth century American literature, the answer likely can be found in Appendix B.

Although the case for continuing the study of canonical works is explicit in the Common Core (Shakespeare, mythology, and canonical literature are repeatedly mentioned), there is no way around the fact that fewer literary works can be studied over the high school years. The mantra for the Common Core is *fewer, clearer, and higher* (Common Core Standards Initiative Standards-Setting Criteria, 2014), and the curriculum recommends moving to a preponderance of nonfiction, 70% of all reading, by grade 12 (Jago, 2013).

An examination of the types of questions on sample Common Core assessments reveals an emphasis on the careful reading of challenging canonical works. Consider the following two questions from Oregon's version of the Common Core test for students in grades 9–10 (Oregon Common Core State Standards, 2014):

> Students analyze how the character of Odysseus from Homer's Odyssey—a "man of twists and turns"—reflects conflicting motivations through his interactions with other characters in the epic poem. They articulate how his conflicting loyalties during his long and complicated journey home from the Trojan War both advance the plot of Homer's epic and develop themes. [RL.9–10.3]

> Students analyze how artistic representations of Ramses II (the pharaoh who reigned during the time of Moses) vary, basing their analysis on what is emphasized or absent in different treatments of the pharaoh in works of art (e.g., images in the British Museum) and in Percy Bysshe Shelley's poem "Ozymandias." [RL.9–10.7]

The best training for getting high scores on such questions would be a return to New Criticism and perusing canonical works in search of the *objective correlative*. As coined by T. S. Eliot, the objective correlative is the meaning that must be reached through scrupulous analysis of a text and nothing but the text. According to Eliot (1921), the author must create "a set of objects, a situation, a chain of events which shall be the formula of that particular emotion; such that when the external facts, which must terminate in sensory experience, are given, the emotion is immediately evoked." In other words, if the author writes effectively, then no wrong interpretation is possible—if, and this is a crucial if, the reader is astute enough to grasp the right meaning.

The kind of close reading favored by the Common Core implies a quick and fervent return to New Criticism—not that some teachers ever left it. To be sure, studies of how literature gets taught (Applebee, 1993; Applebee & Squire, 1966; Stotsky, 2010) have always found that literary study has largely remained teacher-centered, analytical, and focused on great works and right interpretations.

The Process Approach

Advocates of the process approach to the English curriculum are less interested in charting competencies and reading specific canonical works than helping students learn techniques that will help guide them through school and through life. For process-oriented teachers, it is wrong to force reading lists and predetermined competencies upon students who have no investment or interest in them.

Consider the student who is already competent on the first day of school. For such a student, a class devoted to building the competency that he/she already holds would be worthless. Similarly, just because Harold Bloom once praised a literary work as great art does not mean an adolescent will find it revelatory. A literary work is worthwhile only to the extent that it speaks to its reader. Moffett (1965) wrote:

> We must give students an emotional mandate to play the symbolic scale, to find subjects and shape them, to invent ways to act upon others, and to discover their own voice. (p. 248)

Of the three approaches to curriculum, the process approach alone permits the student to have a say in what is to be learned. A student's interests, background, abilities, ambitions, and personality are inconsequential to competency-based instruction and to the Heritage Curriculum.

Because of the difficulty of establishing preset benchmarks and formulating uniform assessments for a fluctuating, individualistic curriculum, the process model has never gained much traction in public schools, where accountability has become a do-or-die affair for more than three decades. To keep students and teachers tethered to standards, most states have legislated that student test scores must be tracked over time. In this way, uniformity and standardization consistently win out over initiatives that advocate for the development of creativity and the "soft" objectives associated with enhancing the welfare of the child.

Yet, when one considers the increasing complexity of the world, the range of talent among students, and the universe of possibilities for the future, the process model would seem more appropriate for a STEAM-age than the other two models, which offer fixed curricula and assume a predetermined right answer for every question.

Consider some of the rudimentary expectations of citizenship in a country like the United States. The knowledge needed to pay taxes, vote, earn money, remain healthy, think logically, make wise choices, and improve one's quality of life cannot be gleaned from a standardized test, nor can they be wrought from close analysis of great literature. For process-oriented teachers, the goal is not assessing the extent to which a student can identify the attributes of canonized authors or reciting passages from great works. The goal is for students to become independent, savvy, deep thinkers who speak with eloquence and panache.

The process approach also presumes that not all students in a language arts class will major in English in college or become professional writers. Rather than prescribe what is to be learned and how it is to be learned, the process approach allows students to develop skills in accordance with their interests and future career aspirations.

Thus, the process approach would appear to be the most versatile, practical way forward for the language arts, especially in light of the sociological, technological, and scientific changes anticipated over the next 100 years. However, the forces favoring an expansion of competency-based learning and the heritage curriculum are formidable. Just because an approach to the curriculum is illogical and inappropriate does not preclude it from becoming dominant in American public education (Spring, 2010).

The Technolocially-Enhanced Language Arts

As early as 1917 (Dench), film was heralded as a potential replacement for texts as a medium worthy of study. About the transformative power of film, Hoban (1942) wrote, "Motion pictures have all the vital ability to influence and improve education that the printing press had five hundred years ago" (p. 4).

In a cutting-edge article in 1931, Robinson declared that radio would alter the basic structure of schools. "Radio…would carry more genius to the common child than he has ever had or ever possibly could have; that it is the greatest system for training teachers that we know; and all together I think it is justified even in a technical sense as a medium for instruction in public education" (p. 91).

In 1937, the president of the National Council of Teachers of English (NCTE) Holland Roberts advocated that television become an integral part of the language arts curriculum because "English teachers who do not use this new medium in their teaching will be swept into the dust bin of the past" (Radner, 1960, p. 11).

In 1961, when behavioral psychology was in its heyday and B. F. Skinner was one of the most celebrated scientists in the world, programmed learning seemed like a brilliant solution to all that ailed traditional schooling. About machine learning, Foltz wrote, "Programed learning… could very well aid in the amelioration of some of the deplorable conditions in our educational system, to say nothing of feeding the hunger for learning in emergent nations" (p. 66).

Even the overhead projector had a brief run as the "technology that would change everything." Writing in 1965, Schultz proclaimed, "There is no limit on imagination. Thus there is no limitation on how you can use transparencies and overhead projection to communicate effectively with your class. Just as science is opening new vistas for mankind, overhead projection is opening new doors for teaching" (p. 31).

Of course, the early stages of the Internet prompted a flurry of prognostications. In the debut issue of the magazine *Wired*, Perelman (1993) wrote, "In the new economy, where mindcraft replaces handicraft as the main form of work, HL makes obsolete the teaching, testing, and failure on which academic credentialism rests" (p. 71).

More recently, comics have been heralded as effective tools for teaching the language arts. Bitz (2004) found that comics helped students, especially English Language Learners, realize a "noticeable improvement in writing." By using comics, "mechanical errors were fixed, story structures were tightened, and character voices were honed" (Binz, 2004, p. 585).

Undoubtedly, innovation, particularly in the form of new tools for learning, can be exciting and transformative, but too often the tools are mistaken for the messages that they deliver. As media guru Marshall McLuhan (1967) cleverly noted during the height of his fame in his book, *The Medium is the Massage,* our technologies only carry the meaning; they do not constitute it.

Richard Clark, director of the Center for Cognitive Technology at the University of Southern California states, "The media are mere vehicles that deliver instruction but do not influence student achievement any more than the truck that delivers our groceries causes changes in nutrition" (2001, p. 2).

The point is that the language arts have always integrated technological innovations as they have emerged. Rather than replace the language arts, technological innovation gives students and teachers ever more tools with which to create and reflect upon meaning (Partnership for 21st Century Skills, 2014).

New Tools

The Executive Committee of the National Council of Teachers of English updated its definition of "21st century literacies" in February, 2013 (NCTE, 2014).

> Literacy has always been a collection of cultural and communicative practices shared among members of particular groups. As society and technology change, so does literacy. Because technology has increased the intensity and complexity of literate environments, the 21st century demands that a literate person possess a wide range of abilities and competencies, many literacies. These literacies are multiple, dynamic, and malleable. As in the past, they are inextricably linked with particular histories, life possibilities, and social trajectories of individuals and groups.

These 21st century literacies are critical to conceptions of the curriculum and expectations for student performance. In two meta-analyses of the teaching of composition, Graham et al. (2007, 2012) found that students who wrote using computers scored higher overall on writing assessments than students who wrote by hand. However, higher scores were not attributable to the delivery system (the computer vs. writing by hand), but rather by the bundle of "extras" that could not be replicated in the "writing by hand" environment—having access to an online dictionary and thesaurus, having experience with revision using word processing programs, and having access to software targeted specifically to struggling writers.

Although the writing assessment administered by the National Assessment of Educational Progress (National Center for Education Statistics, 2012) prohibits the use of any books or other materials during students' timed writing tests (the limit is usually around 25 min), students who type their compositions on the computer rather than handwrite are free to use the computer's online thesaurus/dictionary. As a result, students who have extended experiences with writing on computers and who are used to utilizing online dictionaries are poised to perform better on timed NAEP writing tests than students who have not had much experience writing on a computer.

Relles and Tierney, (2013) found that administering writing tests on computers dramatically disadvantages poor and minority children who may lack access to the latest technological tools. They write:

> The data suggest students who are underprepared according to traditional writing criteria face additional barriers to academic success because of low computer skills. The implications are twofold. First, under preparedness may be systemic across discourses. Second, today's remedial writers may be challenged by a kind of literacy double jeopardy that is unique to the 21st century. (p. 497)

In 2011, the NAEP began administering all its writing tests for 8th and 12th graders using computers. In 2019, the NAEP will begin administering the writing test for 4th graders on the computer. To gain a genuine understanding of student performance on writing, it will be necessary to monitor not only the achievement gap between students, but also the technology gap between students, both at school and at home.

The ability to offer technologically-enhanced educational experiences to students depends upon the relative funding for a particular school as well as the abilities and experiences of the teacher in the classroom. For schools that can acquire top-notch technology and keep teachers employed who know how to use it, rich possibilities abound. Three recent, favorable technological applications in the language arts include:

- Using video games and multimedia as tools for teaching writing (Gerber & Price, 2011; Heaven, 2014; Proske, Roscoe & McNamara, 2014),
- Using multisensory stimuli to enhance the quality of reading comprehension (Baines, 2008, 2013; Dymock & Nicholson, 2010; Laitusis, 2010),
- Using multimedia to teach listening and speaking skills (Fisher & Frey, 2014; Nguyet & Mai, 2012; Skouge, Rao & Boisvert, 2007).

Of course, technology is constantly evolving, so techniques that might help engage students in learning the language arts now might have limited appeal in the future. Curricular initiatives based upon the use of the radio or the transparency machine, for example, are no longer considered cutting edge. On the other hand, emerging technologies such as 3-dimensional printing, enhanced reality (through virtual supplements), and artificial intelligence (AI) hold great promise for the language arts.

Conclusion

In 1930, in an essay entitled "Economic Possibilities for our Grandchildren" economist John Keynes wrote, "We are being afflicted with a new disease of which some readers may not yet have heard the name, but of which they will hear a great deal in the years to come–namely, technological unemployment. This means unemployment due to our discovery of means of economising the use of labour outrunning the pace at which we can find new uses for labour" (p. XXX)

Unfortunately, technological unemployment has become an all-too-familiar phenomenon in many areas of the world, with countries, such as Greece, Spain, South Africa, and Yemen presently sporting jobless rates among young adults as high as 50%. In the United States, bankrupt Detroit, with its declining population and shuttered factories, recently posted an overall unemployment rate of 25 % (Detroit Free Press, 2014).

In an exacting study on the future of employment, Frey and Osborne (2013) estimate the probability of computerization for 702 occupations in the near future. They write,

> While computerization has been historically confined to routine tasks involving explicit rule-based activities, algorithms for big data are now rapidly entering domains reliant upon pattern recognition and can readily substitute for labour in a wide range of non-routine cognitive tasks. In addition, advanced robots are gaining enhanced senses and dexterity, allowing them to perform a broader scope of manual tasks. This is likely to change the nature of work across industries and occupations. (p. 44)

Some jobs with the highest probability of technological unemployment include: property title examiners, mathematical technicians, insurance underwriters, freight agents, library technicians, insurance claims clerks, bank tellers, and loan officers, all with 98 % or more probability of displacement. Among the jobs with the lowest probability of technological unemployment are: social workers, surgeons, medical researchers, psychologists, teachers, school administrators, and clergy, all with less than 1 % probability of being replaced.

An obvious difference between the 99 % group and the 1 % group is that reading, writing, thinking, and communicating with others are integral to the jobs in the 1 % group. In the 99 % group, literacy skills may be useful, but they are non-essential.

The language arts are foundational in the sense that they provide the supporting structure upon which learning in STEM is built. For example, a person who wants to become a doctor must be able to research, to think, to read critically, and to communicate with clarity because the very lives of patients depend on the ability to do so. The foundational skills of the language arts are essential, not only to doctors, but to all jobs in the 1 % group.

The OECD (Organization of Economic Cooperation and Development) has spent a great deal of effort and money advocating that countries enrich the quality of the educational experiences of children. Through hundreds of publications and vast repositories of *big data* (see www.oecd.org), the OECD presents a convincing case that an inextricable link exists between the quality of education and a country's economic future. According to the OECD (2012), to be successful in the decades ahead, children must become increasingly sophisticated and effective readers—of not only books and print materials—but of all texts, including information available online:

> Technological innovations have a profound effect on the types of skills that are demanded in today's labour markets and the types of jobs that have the greatest potential for growth. Most of these jobs now require some familiarity with, if not mastery of, navigating through digital material where readers determine the structure of what they read rather than follow the pre- established order of text as presented in a book. (p. 1)

A study of the practices of business leaders concurs that high levels of literacy will be required of most future workers (National Commission on Writing, 2004). In a survey of must-have skills for prospective employees, CEOs emphasized that proficiency, not only in reading, but also in writing, is absolutely essential. The survey found that:

- 80 percent or more of salaried employees have some responsibility for writing
- Writing is almost a universal professional skill required in service industries
- More than half of the companies surveyed say that they frequently or almost always take writing into consideration when hiring employees
- Even hourly employees (lower paid workers) often have some writing responsibilities

In the United Kingdom, a study by Kotzee and Johnston (2011) found that "the quality of students' writing seriously affects their chances in the job market" (p. 45). The desirability of reading and writing for prospective employees has been confirmed by many studies in a host of countries across the globe (Casale, 2011; Gatti, Grazia Mereu, Tagliaferro, & European Centre for the Development of Vocational Training, 2000; Jama, Dugdale, & National Literacy Trust, 2012; Rivera-Batiz, 1990; Yang & Sun, 2012).

Even John Keynes (1930), sage of the Golden Age of Capitalism, seems to give teachers of the language arts a nod of recognition when he writes:

> We shall honour those who can teach us how to pluck the hour and the day virtuously and well, the delightful people who are capable of taking direct enjoyment in things, the lilies of the field who toil not, neither do they spin.

The language arts, which undergird knowledge in STEM, offer a hedge against technological unemployment and a reprieve from a life of misery and insignificance. If any field can demonstrate how to pluck an hour virtuously and how to savor the unexpurgated world, it is the language arts.

References

Applebee, A. (1993). *Literature study in the secondary school*. Urbana: NCTE.

Applebee, R., & Squire, J. (1966). National study of high school english programs: A record of english teaching today. *English Journal, 55*(3), 273–290.

Baines, L. (2008). *Teacher's guide to multisensory learning*. Washington, D. C.: ASCD.

Baines, L. (2013). *Teaching challenging texts*. New York: Rowman & Littlefield.

Baines, L., & Farrell, E. (2002). The Tao of instructional models. In J. Flood, D. Lapp, J. Jensen & J. Squire (Eds.), *Handbook of research on teaching the english language arts* (pp. 74–86). Mahwah: Lawrence Erlbaum.

Binz, M. (2004). The comic book project: Forging alternative pathways to literacy. *Journal of Adolesent & Adult Literacy, 47*(7), 574–588.

Bloom, H. (1984). *The western Canon*. New York: Penguin.

Casale, D. (2011). English language proficiency and earning in a developing country. *The Journal of Socio-Economics, 40*(4), 385–393.

Center for Education Policy. (2012). *State high school exit exams: A policy in transition*. Washington, D. C.: Center on Education Policy.

Clark, R. (2001). *Learning with media*. Charlotte: Information Age.

Common Core English Language Arts Standards (2014). The Common Core. http://www.corestandards.org/ELA-Literacy.

Common Core Standards Appendix, B. (2014). The common core. http://www.corestandards.org/assets/Appendix_B.pdf.

Common Core Standards Initiative Standards-Setting Criteria. (2014). The common core. http://www.corestandards.org/assets/Criteria.pdf.

Dench, E. (1917). *Motion picture education.* Cincinnati: Standard Publishing Company.

Detroit Free Press. (2014). Raw data: Detroit's unemployment rate over the last decade. http://www.freep.com/article/20130721/OPINION05/307210033/Raw-Data-Detroit-s-unemployment-rate-over-last-decade.

Doss, H. (2013). The innovation curriculum: Stem, steam, or sea? Forbes. http://www.forbes.com/sites/henrydoss/2013/09/17/the-innovation-curriculum-stem-steam-or-sea/.

Dymock, S., & Nicholson, T. (2010). High 5! Strategies to enhance comprehension of expository text. *Reading Teacher, 64*(3), 166–178.

Elbow, P. (1990). *What is English?* New York: Modern Language Association.

Eliot, T. S. (1921). Hamlet and his problems. In *The sacred wood: Essays on poetry and criticism.* New York: Alfred A. Knopf. http://www.bartleby.com/200/sw9.html.

Feynman, R. (2006). *Classic Feynman.* New York: W. W. Norton.

Fisher, D., & Frey, N. (2014). Speaking and listening in content area learning. *Reading Teacher, 68*(1), 64–69.

Foltz, C. (1961). *The world of teaching machines.* Washington, D.C.: Electronic Teaching Laboratories.

Frey, C., & Osborne, M. (2013). The future of employment: How susceptible are jobs to comperisation? http://www.oxfordmartin.ox.ac.uk/downloads/academic/The_Future_of_Employment.pdf.

Gatti, M., Grazia Mereu, M., Tagliaferro, C., & European Centre for the Development of Vocational Training, T. (2000). *Changing occupational profiles in the hotel industry: Case studies in France, Italy and Spain.* Synthesis Report. Thesaloniki. Greece: European Centre for the Development of Vocational Training.

Gerber, H., & Price, D. (2011). Twenty- First- century adolescents, writing, and new media: Meeting the challenge with game controllers and laptops. *English Journal, 101*(2), 68–73.

Gewertz, C. (2012). N.H. schools focus on competency. *Education Week, 31*(20), 1.

Graham, S., & Perin, D. (2007). A meta-analysis of writing instruction for adolescent students. *Journal of Educational Psychology, 99*(3), 445–476.

Graham, S., McKeown, D., Kiuhara, S., & Harris, K. (2012). A meta-analysis of writing instruction for students in the elementary grades. *Journal of Educational Psychology, 104*(4), 879–896.

Heaven, D. (2014). Story is where the action is. *New Scientist, 222*(2970), 22–23.

Hirsch, E. (1983). Cultural literacy. *American Scholar, 52,* 159–169.

Hoban, C. (1942). *Focus on learning: Motion pictures in the school.* Washington, D.C.: American Council on Education.

Jago, C. (2013, January 10). What english classes should like in the common core era. Washington Post. http://www.washingtonpost.com/blogs/answer-sheet/wp/2013/01/10/what-english-classes-should-look-like-in-common-core-era/.

Jama, D., Dugdale, G., & National Literacy Trust. (2012). *Literacy: State of the nation–a picture of literacy in the UK today.* London: National Literacy Trust.

Kamenetz, A. (3. November 2013). Are you competent? Prove it. *New York Times,* p. ED 26.

Keynes, J. (1963, c1930). *Essays in persuasion* (pp. 358–373). New York: W.W. Norton. http://www.aspeninstitute.org/sites/default/files/content/upload/Intro_Session1.pdf.

Kohn, A. (2004). *What does it mean to be well-educated?* New York: Beacon Press.

Kotzee, B., & Johnston, R. (2011). Can't string a sentence together? *UK Employers' Views of Graduates' Writing Skills. Industry And Higher Education, 25*(1), 45–52.

Krystal, A. (2014). What is literature. *Harpers, 328*(1966), 89–94.

Laitusis, C. (2010). Examining the impact of audio presentation on tests of reading comprehension. *Applied Measurement In Education, 23*(2), 153–167.

Mandel, B. (1980). *Three language arts curriculum models: Pre- kindergarten through college.* Urbana: NCTE.

McLuhan, M. (1967). *The medium is the massage.* New York: Penguin.

Moffett, J. (1965). I, you, and it. *College Composition and Communication, 16*(5), 243–248.

National Center for Education Statistics. (2012). *The nation's report card: Writing 2011*. Washington, D.C.: Institute of Education Sciences.

National Commission on Writing. (2004). *Writing: A ticket to work… or a ticket out*. Washington, D. C: College Board.

National Council of Teachers of English. (2014). The NCTE definition of 21st century literacies. http://www.ncte.org/positions/statements/21stcentdefinition.

National Research Council. (2011). *Successful k-12 STEM education: Identfying effewctive approaches in science, technology, engineering, and mathematics*. Washington D. C.: The National Academies.

Nguyet, N., & Mai, L. (2012). Teaching conversational strategies through video clips. *Language Education in Asia, 3*(1), 32–49.

Oregon Common Core State Standards. (2014). Oregon common core state standards for English language arts & literacy in history/social studies, science, and technical subjects grades 9–10. http://www.ode.state.or.us/wma/teachlearn/commoncore/elaappendixb-9-10.pdf.

Organization of Economic Cooperation and Development. (2012). PISA in focus 12. Paris: OECD. http://www.oecd.org/pisa/pisaproducts/pisainfocus/49442737.pdf.

Partnership for 21st Century Skills. (2014). Framework for 21st century learning. http://www.p21.org/our-work/p21-framework.

Perelman, L. (1993). School's out. *Wired, 1,* 72.

Proske, A., Roscoe, R., & McNamara, D. (2014). Game-based practice versus traditional practice in computer-based writing strategy training: Effects on motivation and achievement. *Educational Technology Research & Development, 62*(5), 481–505.

Radner, S. (1960). *Fifty years of english teaching: A historical analysis of the presidential addresses of NCTE*. Champaign: NCTE.

Relles, S., & Tierney, W. (2013). Understanding the writing habits of tomorrow's students: Technology and college readiness. *The Journal of Higher Education, 84*(4), 477–505.

Rivera-Batiz, F. (1990). English language proficiency and the economic progress of immigrants. *Economics Letters, 34*(3), 295–300.

Robinson, J. (1931). Broadcasting to the schools of a city. In L. Tyson (Ed.), *Radio and education* (pp. 91–92). Chicago: University of Chicago Press.

Schallert, D. (1987). Thought and language, content and structure in language communication. In J. Squire (Ed.), *The dynamics of language learning* (pp. 65–79). Urbana: National Council of Teachers of English.

Schultz, M. (1965). *The teacher and the overhead projector*. Englewood Cliffs: Prentice-Hall.

Skouge, J., Rao, K., & Boisvert, P. (2007). Promoting early literacy for diverse learners using audio and video technology. *Early Childhood Education Journal, 35*(1), 5–11.

Slavin, R. (1987). Mastery learning reconsidered. *Journal of Educational Research, 57*(2), 175–213.

Spring, J. (2010). *The American school, a global context: From the puritans to the Obama administration*. New York: McGraw Hill.

Stoddard, L. (2010). *Educating for human greatness*. Sarasota: Peppertree Press.

Stotsky, S. (2010). Literary study in grades 9, 10, and 11: A national survey. Forum: A publication of the association of literary scholars, critics, and writers, 4. http://www.alscw.org/publications/forum/forum_4.pdf.

Thomas, P. (2012). *De-testing and de-grading students: Authentic alternatives to accountability and standardization*. New York: Peter Lang.

Yang, W., & Sun, Y. (2012). The use of cohesive devices in argumentative writing by Chinese EFL learners at different proficiency levels. *Linguistics & Education, 23*(1), 31–48.

Lawrence Baines is Associate Dean of Research and Graduate Studies in the Jeannine Rainbolt College of Education at The University of Oklahoma. His latest books are Project-Based Writing in Science (Sense Publishers, 2014) and Teaching Challenging Texts (Rowman & Littlefield, 2013).

Putting the "H" in STEAM: Paradigms for Modern Liberal Arts Education

Armanda L. Lewis

Abstract This chapter seeks to connect current debates about the value of traditional liberal arts education to emerging trends in the learning sciences that promote metacognition, active learning, and other 21st century skills. This paper proposes that STEAM (Science, Technology, Engineering, Arts, and Mathematics), an emerging K-12 approach that infuses the arts within STEM fields, has enormous potential to infuse the liberal arts with design thinking, collaboration, creative computing, and innovation while maintaining the level of deep reflection and critical thinking associated with humanist inquiry. While STEAM has yet to reach higher education in the same way that it has K-12 grades, it is argued that the trends in K-12 foreshadow coming trends in higher education. STEAM within higher education looks at movements that address interactivity, innovation, and inquiry in the form of interactive media design studios, makerspaces, and digital humanities initiatives. This chapter will examine artifacts produced thus far and propose further empirical research studies within higher education to advance what we know about emerging technology-enhanced learning environments and their role in disciplinary knowledge formation. A secondary goal is to create a stronger dialog between K-12 research and higher education trends that have their roots in pre-college initiatives.

Keywords Humanities · Liberal arts · Creative computing · Maker

Introduction

Current debates in higher education consider the types of educational experiences regarded as valuable for future professional success and well-being. On one hand, the pragmatic side of vocational and professional preparation is contrasted with the cultural aspects of a liberal arts education, a broad form of educational preparation that exposes students to traditional bodies of knowledge within the arts, humanities, and sciences (The Carnegie Foundation, 2010). On the other hand, there is a

A. L. Lewis (✉)
New York University, New York, USA
e-mail: al861@nyu.edu

© Springer International Publishing Switzerland 2015
X. Ge et al. (eds.), *Emerging Technologies for STEAM Education,*
Educational Communications and Technology: Issues and Innovations,
DOI 10.1007/978-3-319-02573-5_14

disciplinary divide within liberal arts education, with STEM- (Science, Technology, Engineering, & Math) related degrees associated with job creation and humanistic degrees regarded as essential for civic and moral preparation (Koblik & Graubaud, 2000; Pascarella et al., 2005). As evidenced by increased funding streams, rhetorical buzz, and curricular innovation, trends have emphasized STEM initiatives, positing that these fields hold greater potential for future professional success and cost benefit of an expensive degree (Selingo, 2013). As a result, humanistic disciplines have needed to re-articulate how they prepare students to thrive post-graduation.

The present focus is on STEAM (Science, Technology, Engineering, Arts, & Math) – an emerging approach that infuses the arts and design within STEM fields – within liberal arts education. STEAM initiatives found in liberal arts environments uniquely infuse humanist inquiry with STEM-related inquiry and technological know-how. Instead of STEAM paradigms that position arts and humanities as enhancements to core STEM knowledge, the liberal arts paradigms examined here will explore the ways in which the humanities, informed by STEM principles, can prepare students for the creative problem solving, collaboration, and computational thinking associated with 21st century digital literacy. The overarching aim of this review is to examine liberal arts STEAM curricula from a learning sciences perspective, argue for its potential to reconceive humanist education, and distill core cognitive, neural, and socio-cultural benefits of effective STEAM education. In doing so, this chapter will offer an overview of the movement in higher education, with an emphasis on the humanities, articulate cognitive and other types of development best supported by liberal arts, and analyze cases of innovative curricula. Important to note is that mention of liberal arts in the present chapter emphasizes humanities knowledge within liberal arts context.

Humanistic Education Within the Liberal Arts

Understanding the humanities within liberal arts education and ways that scholars and practitioners have viewed undergraduate education in response to broader socio-economic and pedagogical changes is necessary to contextualize STEAM initiatives within those spaces. A liberal arts curriculum historically has featured general knowledge deemed necessary and valuable to civic life, followed by specialization. The focus is on inquiry and self-motivated inquiry and deep understanding within a community of peers. Recent attempts to position liberal arts in modern times have either provided a defense for a threatened but valued form of lifelong preparation (Chopp, Frost, & Weiss, 2014; Newfield, 2009; Woodward, 2009) or argued for alternatives to traditional liberal arts education due to fundamental changes in societal needs (Davidson, 2008; Szeman, 2003; Thomas & Seely Brown, 2011).

Nussbaum (1997) traces the dual conception of liberal arts education to its Classical origins, with representations shifting from tradition-steeped instruction for the elite to a focus on timeless skills that prepare all to contribute to society. This manifests itself currently as an opposition between examples of socio-cognitive development, and technical and vocational training that prepares students for jobs and long-term financial security. Knowledge associated with liberal arts education, such as critical thinking, moral character, problem solving, and the ability for lifelong learning, are more difficult to quantify and often demonstrate themselves over time (Goldberg, 1971). The humanities form the foundation for this "cultivation of the whole human being for the functions of citizenship and life generally", and can even be thought of as the essence of general education (Nussbaum, (1997, p. 9).

STEM fields are less threatened within the liberal arts due to the privileging of the scientific model of research, the overt linkage between quantitative disciplines and job opportunities, and the increase in scientists as public intellectuals (Miller, 2012). Humanistic fields, however, are facing an unprecedented mandate to justify their existence—What is it that humanists do? What does humanistic knowledge impart? How can this knowledge be explicitly tied to job skills? Why can't the humanities be more like the sciences? Scholars defend the humanities as uniquely capable of promoting the capacity to reason analytically, the understanding of different perspectives or circumstances, and the use of imaginative problem solving. Critics, though, point to employment statistics or concentrate on how to infuse scientific methods and principles into the humanities (Pinker, 2013; Slingerland, 2008).

In *The Value of the Humanities*, Small (2014) writes that humanistic knowledge is of value precisely because it is not necessarily practical, and must be understood and valued contextually, with an emphasis on dialectic meaning-making. This recalls Bruner's (1991) thesis that solely cognitive models of the mind are lacking in nature since they fail to grasp the complexity and dynamic processes occurring between mind and society. In *The Marketplace of Ideas*, Menand (2010) calls for a re-articulation of the value of a liberal arts education on its own terms. Arguing that a broad humanist preparation encourages complex inquiry and creative problem solving, he seeks to address current rhetoric highlighting the vulnerable or impractical nature of liberal arts in the technological age. Additionally, by connecting the socio-cognitive benefits of such an education to those skills deemed necessary to succeed in modern society, Menand counters theorists that emphasize the need for liberal arts to incorporate scientific rigor, adopt social scientific methods, or become a marginal discipline in the face of more practical fields. In a more pragmatic manner, Chopp (2014) uses U.S. Treasury Department data to argue that many employers seek skills that the humanities already encourage, namely critical thinking, an understanding of diversity, and creativity.

Measuring Humanist Knowledge

While the many supporters and critics of humanistic knowledge within the liberal arts pose logical, philosophically-driven arguments, there is a dearth of empirical studies that report the changes in cognitive and socio-cultural knowledge that happen while engaging in humanistic through and inquiry. Traditionally, theorists have concentrated on how STEM disciplines can support non-scientific thinking. The studies that have attempted to measure the outcomes of humanistic knowledge within liberal arts education are few, but yield interesting results. Earlier self-report studies reported overall learning gains (Hayek & Kuh, 1998), increases in personal development (American Association of State Colleges and Universities, 1976), and greater levels of engagement in educational activities (Pascarella & Terenzini, 1998) by selective liberal arts students when compared with self-reports from students at other types of institutions.

The Center of Inquiry in the Liberal Arts (Pascarella et al., 2005) conducted a more comprehensive Wabash National Study of Liberal Arts Education, a multi-institutional longitudinal study examining good liberal arts practices, institutional ethos, impacts of liberal arts on intellectual and personal growth, and long-term effects of liberal arts education. Utilizing multiple instruments, the study provides some support for supporters of liberal arts education. Utilizing the Critical Thinking Test of Collegiate Assessment off Academic Proficiency and the Need for Cognition Scale and Positive Attitude toward Literacy Activities Scale to measure effective reasoning/problem solving and inclination for life-long learning, respectively, researchers reported statistically significant increases in reading comprehension, critical thinking, writing, openness to diversity and challenge, and intrinsic motivation (learning for self-understanding). Pascarella and Blaich (2013) expanded on results to develop deep learning scales to measure students' experiences with higher-order learning, integrative learning, and reflective learning; results indicate that deep learning experiences contribute to a significant degree the 4-year critical thinking gain, even after controlling for confounding influences and direct exposure to clear and organized instruction. These results hold when compared to those of research universities and regional institutions. Despite gains in these themes traditionally associated with liberal arts education, the same study reported significant decreases in math and science knowledge over the 4 years and when compared with students at other institutional types of institutions. What is vital is a way to integrate STEM and arts/humanities knowledge so that the existence of multiple domains does not adversely affect learning.

The Emergence of STEAM

STEAM, a largely K-12 initiative conceived to bridge the interdisciplinarity, creativity, and innovation found in both art and science, has garnered support from governmental and educational advocates (Ghanbari, 2014; U.S. Congress, 2011; Yakman, 2008). Duncan (2010) called for an integration of arts and humanities into STEM education for what he terms a "well-rounded curriculum. It is the making of connections, conveyed by a rich core curriculum, which ultimately empowers students to develop convictions and reach their full academic and social potential" (p. 1). With STEAM-dedicated conferences and a journal (STEAMConnect's AS-CEND Conference, Northeastern Illinois University's Annual Conference, among others; *The STEAM Journal*), there are increasing examples of STEAM as a theory of STEM education seen through the lens of 21st century skills, which champions learning/innovation (critical thinking, creativity, collaboration), digital literacy (information and media understanding), and career skills (flexibility, leadership, cross-cultural skills) (Trilling & Fadel, 2009). From a pedagogical perspective, curricula lean heavily on constructivist principles, with an abundance of maker movements, project-based assignments, and collaborative, inquiry-based design experiments. Scholars see the arts as infusing inventiveness and adaptability into the analytical and computational thinking associated with being a scientist. The STEM to STEAM initiative (stemtosteam.org), developed at the Rhode Island School of Design (RISD), highlights such ideas in its official description:

> STEAM represents the economic progress and breakthrough innovation that comes from adding art and design to STEM (Science, Technology, Engineering and Math) education and research…To realize this potential, scientists, artists and designers must develop new ways of working together and new modes of research and education. This will keep America at the forefront of innovation, ensuring our sustained global leadership and cultural prosperity in the 21st century". (RISD Office of Government Relations, 2013, p. 1)

Paralleling the overall trend in higher education to emphasize the vocational benefits of education, STEAM rhetoric stresses skills that lend themselves to professional success, which translates to the ability to gain employment, increase job opportunities, and address the current focus on entrepreneurship (Fredette, 2013; National Research Council, 2007). Published research is growing, but there are three noticeable absences. One is that existing STEAM research is largely focused on K-12 education, with few overt discussions of STEAM within the higher education sector. Another is that studies tend to look at the role of the aesthetic arts rather than the humanities. Lastly, research has examined the approach's creative and economic potentials (Eger, 2013; Henriksen, 2014; Maeda, 2013) rather than probe the latest learning evidence about the cognitive, neural, and socio-cultural development that occurs in learners engaging in STEAM activities. Subsequent sections will look at such learning that happens in college age students.

The Rise of STEAM in the Liberal Arts

While one can point to dozens upon dozens of formal and informal STEAM initiatives at the K-12 level, extant higher education examples remain few, though there has been an increasing call for curricular re-design to address 21st century skills preparation. Chopp (2014) proposes the curricular concept of knowledge design, which will be helpful in integrating current learning research. Knowledge design is "aimed at placing creativity and agility at the heart of learning and scholarship by embracing new learning platforms and recognizing the power of visualization and the remixing of knowledge" (19). The idea behind knowledge design corresponds with more active, student-centered, participatory learning techniques encouraged in the learning sciences, and the interdisciplinary and playful nature of the STEAM movement (Soloway, Guzdial, & Hay, 1994). It also parallels closely with rhetoric championing design thinking in teaching and learning (Kafai & Harel, 1991), the importance of cognitive acquisition and participation (Greeno, Collins, & Resnick, 1996; Sfard, 1998), and the integration of multiple media and modes in social, context-based learning environments (Brown, Collins, & Duguid, 1989; Jewitt & Kress, 2003).

Subsequent sections will highlight three types of STEAM initiatives within traditional liberal arts education that leverage interactivity, innovation, and inquiry: the interactive media, maker, and digital humanities programs. Specifically, the types of interrelated knowledge promoted by these programs include the development of complex cognitive processes (computational and systems thinking knowledge, transfer), socio-cultural capabilities (collaboration, multicultural growth, multimedia and multimodal communication), and know-how associated with entrepreneurship (adaptability and innovation). In contrast to K-12 STEAM movements that focus on using visual and other artistic forms to make sense of scientific fields, liberal arts movements that are STEAM-like leverage technologies and scientific methodologies to explore humanistic knowledge. The following examines Sarah Lawrence College's Games, Interactivity, and Playable Media concentration, various makerspaces, and Hamilton College's Digital Humanities Initiative.

Understanding the Humanities Through STEAM

The purpose of this section is to address ways that STEAM initiatives cultivate certain types of knowledge and learning within the liberal arts. Support is provided by recent findings from cognitive science, neuroscience, and psychology that highlight the improvement of mental models, socio-cultural learning, and relational thinking. The aim is to articulate cognitive and other types of development best supported by liberal arts, and how knowledge cultivated by humanist study enhances skills in STEM disciplines to create a well-rounded STEAM initiative. Traditionally, theorists have concentrated on how STEM disciplines are best supported by inquiry-based learning, project-based learning, and constructivist techniques. What does current research in the learning sciences have to say about learning with respect to maker, interactive media, and digital humanities programs?

All three areas, ideally, maximize project-based learning, collaboration, inquiry-based learning, deep learning and concept formation through artifact production. Through the act of production, the learner is in constant dialog with the subject matter and misconceptions are revealed and refined over time. STEAM naturally allows for these ideas that encourage multiple and iterative approaches to problem-solving within a complex learning environment (Bruner, 1991; Jonassen & Land, 1999; Spector, 2011). One reason that STEAM environments have such potential is that they maximize cognitive disequilibrium, a process of disruption in mental state due to error or surprise, and ideally reconciliation of that discrepancy through learning (D'Mello, Lehman, Pekrun, & Graesser (2014); Rescorla, 1988). Another rationale for supporting STEAM environments within liberal arts is creativity, which has been shown to enhance learning experiences for and is in line with 21st century skills (Csikszentmihalyi, 1997). While very little mention has been made specifically of STEAM as an approach within higher education, the following lessons in interactivity, inquiry, and innovation demonstrate that STEAM initiatives are already observable.

Lessons in Interactivity and Creative Computing: The Multimedia Design Studio

Interactive media programs that blend the arts and sciences are not new, as evidenced by long-time programs at MIT (Media Lab), NYU (Interactive Telecommunications Program), RISD (Digital + Media Program), and Carnegie Mellon (Digital Media Program) that take a playful and interdisciplinary approach to addressing and designing for real-world issues. What makes these and similar programs innovative is a resistance of disciplinary isolation and an acknowledgement that memorization of facts and rote procedural training is insufficient for future success (von Glaserfeld, 1989).

In various analyses of the types of learning that occur in multimedia design spaces, researchers (Ito et al., 2010; Knobel & Lankshear, 2010) identify collaboration, and creativity as key ingredients for productive media arts practices, gauged in these cases by the level of collaborative creativity and personal expression evident in final designs. In the liberal arts context, the multimedia design studio not only addresses issues of personal identity formation and expression, but is essential for core and emerging humanist knowledge to form.

Sarah Lawrence College, for example, has the newly formed Games, Interactivity, and Playable Media program, whose official aim is "to foster technical and digital literacy in the arts. Designed for experimentation, this initiative helps students establish digital proficiency while supporting the exploration of a wide range of new media forms and technologies... Students are encouraged to coordinate these project-based investigations of the digital throughout their studies in the humanities, including literature, philosophy, politics, sociology, theatre, and writing" (Sarah Lawrence College, n. d.). Unpacking this statement reveals a focus on literacies and more abstract competencies, rather than specific skills. The acquisition of knowledge and perspectives that span media and modes come together in open and project-based learning environments that are connected with increases in student agency over their own learning and creative problem-solving capabilities (Birchfield et al., 2008). The program also adopts rhetoric current in K-12 education that stresses learner-driven knowledge discovery; students must connect the general competencies associated with physical computing, multimedia production, or programming, and apply them to their own fields of interest. This requires the construction of learner ecologies (Barron, 2004), in which learners construct complex cognitive, social, and technological support strategies around specific topics of interest.

Sample courses, which could all be characterized as STEAM, include Introduction to Creative Computing, cross-listed with computer science, Kinetic Sculpture with Arduino and Playable Media for Mobile Devices, both cross-listed with visual arts, and New Media Literacies, cross-listed with literature. What is noticeable is the amount of required disciplinary crossover to meet the courses' learning goals and objectives. For the creative computing course, novice programmers complete weekly assignments that build into a set of practices that can be harnessed to complete a final project. The focus, in the spirit of Brennan and Resnick (2012), is on the development of computational concepts (ex. recursion), practices (ex. debugging and mashups), and perspectives (ex. points of view about the environment). Traditional computer science encourages logic and optimization, and the arts and humanities introduce the idea of messiness, viewpoints, and heuristics vital in real-world situations. Likewise, the two visual arts courses require artifacts designed for specific scenarios, and leverage current theories of play and embodiment that promote engagement and applicability (Csikszentmihalyi, 1997; Vygotsky, 1978). The new media course also requires a final multi-media project that situates humanist inquiry within real-world technological phenomena. One point in common with these courses is a recognition that "designing a learning environment begins with identifying what is to be learned and, reciprocally, the real world situations in which the activity occurs" (Barab & Duffy, 2000, p. 48). Another is the incremental nature of knowledge building, a scaffold technique that supports novices' knowledge construction.

At the New York City College of Technology-CUNY, a cursory analysis of students' work from emerging media courses indicates students' ability to refine concepts over the course of a semester, pull from different disciplines to accomplish a goal, and position themselves as practicing professionals. These indicate that learners are seeing themselves as members of a knowledge-based community and can articulate their roles as emerging experts of that knowledge (Bransford, Brown, & Cocking, 2000; Brown et al., 1989).

Lessons in Innovation: The rise of Makerspaces

Makerspaces, also called hacker spaces or innovation labs, broadly include constructionist, interdisciplinary fabrication environments in which learners explore a concept through the embodied exercise of creating a physical object. A growing focus on the learning that happens in maker spaces reflects an abundance of research in comparison with similar studies for multimedia design studios or digital humanities spaces. Maker initiatives, which happen in makerspaces, form part of the STEAM movement since design are necessary for the creation of a usable object. Constructionism encompasses constructivist tenets, with the added emphasis on active cognitive processing and making sense of a topic through the manipulation and construction of physical and virtual objects (Churchill & Hedberg, 2008; Kafai, 2006; Papert, 1980). The process is frequently iterative and collaborative, and involves the learner creating an alpha version, reflecting on its utility and appropriateness, and then refining further versions until the initial problem is addressed satisfactorily. Kafai and Resnick (1996) provides evidence of the various learning supported by constructionist environments, including creating linkages between discrete but related mental representations, socio-cultural-cognitive growth occurring through collective interests, and reflective cognition encouraged by iterative processes.

While constructionism more generally focuses on the creation of knowledge through any type of "object to think with", maker initiatives focus more on the types of learning supported through physical manipulation and construction of artifacts. Spanning the areas of physical computing, wearables and crafts, engineering, and multimedia production, maker initiatives are often associated with DIY movements that promote agency, creativity, and resourcefulness. Recent research (Bequette et al., 2013; Buechley, Peppler, Eisenberg & Kafai, 2013; Kafai & Peppler, 2014; Peppler & Glosson, 2013) looks holistically at the negotiation and production of knowledge in these makerspaces. Blikstein (2014) chronicles an activity where students used 3D printing techniques to build monuments for female historical figures. Challenges include issues with workflow and division of labor, but positives included an integrated interdisciplinary experience. While the end goal was the development of monuments embodying historical knowledge and highlighting absences, a secondary accomplishment was the integration of mathematical and engineering knowledge. Successful STEAM initiatives showcase a seamless and logical integration of different disciplinary knowledge to accomplish a goal.

Several of these studies examine different e-textile makerspaces that blend engineering and crafts within a project-based learning environment. Norris (2014) provides evidence that the act of designing artifacts influences and is influenced by students' valuing of self, supporting socio-cultural theories of learning that posit that the successful construction of physical artifacts affects judgment about one's own capability and sense of self (Ackerman, 2004; Kafai & Harel, 1991). Peppler (2013) also supports e-textiles for identity formation, arguing that e-textiles "are 'coded' for girls, encouraging them to engage in computing by engaging their creative interests" (p. 40). She goes on to connect participation in e-textile construction to cognitive growth, specifically an increase in knowledge about the properties of electronic circuits. A paired-samples t-test revealed a statistically significantly higher on posttests evaluating students' ability to produce a working circuit, as well as significantly higher knowledge about current flow, polarity, and connectivity.

The work being accomplished in the emerging multimodal learner analytics space yields promise for understanding maker spaces in psychological and even neural terms. From a psychological perspective, the project-based learning occurring in such spaces encourage metacognition around discrete intuitions about a topic. diSessa (2004; 2006) has written extensively about the misconceptions of novice learners around particular scientific topics. In the knowledge in pieces framework, diSessa theorizes that the learner's body of knowledge undergoes a series of conceptual changes as separate elements composing that knowledge are continuously connected and reconnected to make sense of a phenomena. In studies their digital fabrication spaces, Blikstein (2014) and Worsley and Blikstein (2013) present initial results for "automated multimodal analysis of student expertise while they engage in building tasks" (Worsley & Blikstein, 2013, p. 94). Using object manipulation and gesture data analysis, automated models that successfully predict the level of expertise indicate the importance of coordinated, two-handed object manipulation. This coincides with neuroscience research that identifies two-handed interactions to be an essential part of successful and creative problem-solving since generating an idea and appropriate idea selection are key (Hoppe, 1988). Two-handedness is reflected through biometric readings that report brain activity in regions in both hemispheres, which as a collective have been associated with concept expansion and creative problem solving generation (Abraham, 2014; Abraham et al., 2012; Fink, Benedek, Grabner, Staudt, & Neubauer, 2007). Humanist inquiry is associated with grappling with different ways of viewing complex issues that have no inherent solution, and we would argue that maker activities make this cognitive exercise embodied. By necessity, makerspace projects, with an emphasis on fabrication and tangibles, would require this type of coordinated embodiment that could develop over time given properly scaffolded learning opportunities.

Some notable makerspaces at large institutions, including the Invention Studio at Georgia Tech, are characterized as startup and innovation incubators that evoke current higher education trends that promote entrepreneurship and invention. Within liberal arts colleges, one key difference is that the focus of the makerspace is often on the acquisition of knowledge, specifically the process by which information is acquired and understood on the learners' own terms. The technology is similar between spaces, with microcontrollers, programmable software and interfaces, 3D printers, and more available. Wheaton College's Whale Lab is termed a "making/fabrication space meets interdisciplinary research lab", while Davidson College's Campus Maker/Innovation Space seeks "to invigorate intellectual inquiry and collaboration across conventional academic boundaries", and the University of Mary Washington's ThinkLab, a lab space that introduces emerging technologies to the community and aggregates pedagogical innovation harnessing those technologies. Rhetorically, these examples encourage interdisciplinary discovery, disciplinary knowledge building over professional end goals, and a community of practice around making.

At Thinklab, blog entries from the freshman seminar, Makerbots and Mashups, chronicle a series of micro-failures, common in the design world. In one assignment, teams of two create sets of chess pieces and write posts highlighting the "what went wrong" aspects of going from conception to implementation, to iterative refinement. Students demonstrate an articulate awareness as they reflect on actions taken. Other assignments include deconstructing a t-shirt and making some new wearable, and a final project integrating the technologies. In "Final Project Fail!", one student remarks "I originally wanted to make an octopus plush toy with LED lights on its tentacles. Well, after spending four class periods sewing and cutting, the LED lights did not light up… I have decided I am going to sew a couple LED lights on the octopus's head. Making the octopus's head was hard because I did not know how to sew a circle, so I stuffed fluff in a piece of cloth and used string to tie the end. I will have to somehow figure out how to sew the head onto the tentacles. This is going to be a challenge!" (Jessicahwu, 2013). In this case, the learner lists numerous challenges, but perseveres to come up with a final product. This artifact has morphed from the original specifications, but demonstrates the learner's level of creativity to come up with solutions to those specifications that she was unable to address. During this process, she is gathering a set of schema and problem-solving approaches that she can leverage in the future.

In this vain, another student adds, "There was certainly a lot of error involved on my part during the course. In a very non-scientific way, I would just quickly try different things until something worked. This applies to 3D printing, seeing how different sensors react to various things, etc. It was frustrating at times, but I eventually just accepted that I would probably have to try a few different approaches every time for almost anything I did" (Brett2016, 2012). This cognitive strategy of informed tinkering, of attempting strategies until the best one is revealed works towards what we know about how novices progress towards expertise (Bransford et al., 2000). In addition to encouraging schema development, maker learning opportunities promote collaboration. One student blogs that "collaborating with fellow students played a huge role in creating my projects" (Wboadurg, 2012), and goes on to describe the process of finding peers for collective design sessions or for assistance.

These quotes represent the more obvious advantages of this type of hands-on seminar, including the encouragement of collaboration and creativity, embodied interactions with design concepts, and exposure to emerging tools. Despite these pluses, there are several areas of improvement. There is no indication that the skills learned in the freshman year are integrated into the curricula of subsequent years. The assignments leaned heavily on those that would be most appropriate for the visual arts, without considering rich opportunities for disciplinary engagement like tying activities to issues in literature, political science, and biology. Maker experiences will make liberal arts education richer only if they are tied to core disciplinary issues.

Lessons in Inquiry: The Digital Humanities

STEAM has the potential to infuse within liberal arts education rich opportunities for interactivity and innovation that mesh with the socio-economic pressures about professional preparation and learning trends promoting 21st century skills. Recalling the core knowledge and skills typically associated with the humanities, deep inquiry and critical thinking are at the top. The humanities have evolved throughout history. Most recently, the humanities have grown to incorporate new tools and methods that reflect, in part, the enormous quantity of humanistic work and exegesis and the growth of digital tools. The digital humanities as term has multiple meanings (Gold, 2012), but generally refers to the use of digital and computational tools to make sense of and glean patterns from humanist data that ranges in medium.

Hamilton College has pioneered a humanist model for supporting teaching and research initiatives through the Digital Humanities Initiative (DHi), described as "a collaboratory… where new media and computing technologies are used to promote humanities-based teaching, research, and scholarship across the liberal arts" (Hamilton College, n. d). Based on the principle of the atelier, DHi offers more general skills training, but within the framework of specific projects. Participants are given phased support, with the idea that, over time, faculty will have more agency and can play more active roles in the learning and development process. This approach has several implications. In keeping with good instructional technology practices, the emphasis is kept on the research in question, and technologies are only a means to addressing that research. This means that uses of technologies are situational and grounded. In keeping with current theories of learning (Bruner, 1991), faculty are provided scaffolded learning experiences with technology so that knowledge construction is incremental and manageable. Another is based on active learning principles, and the notion that humanist knowledge can be practical through the use of technology.

The digital humanities as STEAM movement highlights the innovative, iterative, and multi-method nature of modern humanist research. DHi accomplishes this resource-wise through configured physical space (technology-enhanced on-site spaces), and through communication technologies that create a digital network of scholars and information.

An essential aspect about the digital humanities as STEAM movement is the incorporation of scientific training and methods into humanist inquiry. Large-scale collaboration has long been a requisite for the advancement of scientific knowledge, while the humanities have developed largely through specialized collaborations. Recently, as evidenced by DHi and other initiatives, humanists scholars have embraced collaboration and the progress that can occur only through joint inquiry. Another parallel to scientific training is inquiry-based learning, in which students take an active role in developing hypotheses and experiments. In the humanities, this takes that form co-directed projects between faculty and students, shown to increase student interest and understanding of complex topics. Yet another is the use of quantitative methods as a way to manage large amounts of data.

Future Directions

This chapter has sought to connect current debates about the value of traditional liberal arts education to emerging trends in the learning sciences that promote metacognition, active learning, and other 21st century skills. Within K-12 spaces, researchers are beginning to produce empirical evidence that STEAM offer learning opportunities around design thinking, creativity, and innovation, while maintaining the deep cognition and reflection associated with humanist inquiry. While STEAM has yet to reach higher education in the same way that it has K-12, previous discussion has demonstrated the existence of conceptually similar initiatives that address interaction, innovation, and inquiry in novel ways than traditional liberal arts training. Reflecting pre-college STEAM initiatives that allow building, mashing up, or geeking out, higher education versions expand the field with unique visions of interactive and computational media design, digital humanities, and makerspaces.

Table 1 STEAM paradigms in modern liberal arts education

STEAM paradigm	Liberal arts STEAM type	Liberal arts example	Traditional humanist knowledge	Other forms of knowledge
Inquiry	Digital humanities: the intersection of humanities and computing to reveal patterns and new forms of knowledge	Hamilton college's digital humanities initiative	Critical thinking and humanistic analytic skills; metacognition; perspectival thinking; reading comprehension; textual analysis and writing	Computational thinking; design thinking; quantitative analysis skills; reductionist perspectives; visualization
Interactivity	Interactive and computational media: the integration of visual arts techniques, digital film production, and creative computing for a designed, real-world experience	Sarah Lawrence college's games, interactivity, and playable media program	Editing; ethical and moral understanding; heuristics; metacognition; perspectival thinking; synthesizing capabilities	Debugging; iterative design thinking; optimization; play; situated cognition; visualization and mashups
Innovation	Makerspaces: interdisciplinary fabrication environments where learners undertake projects in an iterative fashion	Campus maker/innovation space at Davidson college; ThinkLab at University of Mary Washington; and the Whale Lab at Wheaton college	Civil character; metacognition; perspectival thinking; synthesizing capabilities	Embodied learning; iterative design thinking; play; situated cognition

Table 1 summarizes the three principal STEAM liberal arts paradigms of inquiry, interactivity, and innovation. While the interactivity represented in interactive and computational media studios is observed at the younger levels, liberal arts versions make overt connections between STEM and humanist knowledge and themes, and promote active learning and reflection. The three makerspaces examined are less conceptually tied to specific disciplinary knowledge, perhaps due to the newness of the concept of open and atelier-style learning environments within the wider college community. Much potential remains, though, for creating maker learning opportunities that require students to confront and negotiate domain knowledge. Digital humanities efforts integrate most logically with traditional humanist inquiry, and are in the best position to transform the discipline from within.

For all three paradigms, there remain few overt linkages to learning sciences research, specifically empirical evidence of conceptual change, the impact of the socio-cultural on domain knowledge acquisition within these interactive learning environments, and detailed content analysis of learner artifacts. This paper has attempted to lay the foundation for additional inquiry into constructivist learning environments within higher education, and present the ways in which these environments connect themselves discursively to broader discussions about the value of liberal arts education to promote various kinds of knowledge and skills. One future strand of research would be to explore the ways in which K-12 teachers trained in STEAM methods are preparing future generations who will expect and perhaps demand embodied, creative solving problem solving learning experiences in their curricula.

References

Abraham, A. (2014). Creative thinking as orchestrated by semiotic vs. cognitive control brain networks. *Frontiers in Human Neuroscience, 8*(95), 1–6.

Abraham, A., Pieritz, K., Thybusch, K., Rutter, B., Kröger, S., & Schweckendiek, J., et al. (2012). Creativity and the brain: Uncovering the neural signature of conceptual expansion. *Neuropsychologia, 50*(8), 1906–1917.

Ackerman, E. (2004). Constructing knowledge and transforming the world. In M. Tokoro & L. Steels (Eds.), *A learning zone of one's own: Sharing representations and flow in collaborative learning environments* (pp. 15–37). Amsterdam: IOS Press.

American Association of State Colleges and Universities. (1976). *Value-centered education and moral commitment*. Washington, D. C.: American Association of State Colleges and Universities.

Barab, S. A., & Duffy, T. D. (2000). From practice fields to communities of practice. In D. Jonassen & S. M. Land (Eds.), *Theoretical foundations of learning environments* (pp. 25–56). Mahwah: Lawrence Erlbaum Associates.

Barron, B. (2004). Learning ecologies for technological fluency: Gender and experience differences. *Journal of Educational Computing Research, 31*(1), 1–36.

Bequette, M., Brah, L., Fields, D. A., Halverson, E., Kafai, Y., Litts, B., Owens, T., Peppler, K., Santo, R., & Sheridan, K. (June 2013). *The MAKE movement and connections to the CSCL community*. Panel at the 10th International Conference of Computer Supported Collaborative Learning (CSCL 2013). Madison, WI.

Birchfield, D., Thornburg, H., Megowan-Romanowicz, M. C., Hatton, S., Mechtley, B., Dolgov, I., & Burleson, W. (2008). Embodiment, multimodality, and composition: Convergent themes across HCI and education for mixed-reality learning environments. *Advances in Human-Computer Interaction, 2008*. Article, 874563, 1–19.

Blikstein, P. (2014). Digital fabrication and 'making' in education: The democratization of invention. In J. Walter-Herrmann & C. Büching (Eds.), *FabLabs: Of machines, makers and inventors* (pp. 1–21). Bielefeld: Transcript Publishers.

Bransford, J. D., Brown, A. L., & Cocking, R. R. (2000). *How people learn*. Washington, D. C.: National Academy Press.

Brennan, K., & Resnick, M. (2012). *New frameworks for studying and assessing the development of computational thinking*. Paper presented at the 2012 Annual Meeting of the American Educational Research Association (Vancouver, Canada April 13–17).

Brett2016 (15. December 2012). Final reflection post [Blog post]. http://umwthinklab.com/2012/12/15/final-reflection-post-3/. Accessed 21 March 2014.

Brown, J. S., Collins, A., & Duguid, P. (1989). Situated cognition and the culture of learning. *Educational Researcher, 18*, 32–42.

Bruner, J. (1991). *Acts of meaning*. Cambridge: Harvard University Press.

Buechley, L., Peppler, K., Eisenberg, M., & Kafai, Y. (2013). *Textile messages: Dispatches from the world for e-textiles and education*. New York: Peter Lang.

Carnegie Foundation for the Advancement of Teaching. (2010). The 2010 Carnegie classification: Methodology [PDF file]. http://classifications.carnegiefoundation.org/downloads/2010classifications_logic.pdf. Accessed 15 March 2014.

Chopp, R. (2014). Remaking, renewing, reimagining: The liberal arts college takes advantage of change. In R. Chopp, S. Frost, & D. H. Weiss (Eds.), *Remaking college: Innovation and the liberal arts* (pp. 13–24). Baltimore: The Johns Hopkins University Press.

Chopp, R., Frost, S. & Weiss, D.H. (Eds.). (2014). *Remaking college: Innovation and the liberal arts*. Baltimore: The Johns Hopkins University Press.

Churchill, D., & Hedberg, J. (2008). Learning objects, learning tasks and handhelds. In L. Lockyer, S. Bennett, S. Agostinho, & B. Harper (Eds.), *Handbook of research on learning design and learning objects: Issues, applications and technologies* (pp. 451–469). Hershey: Information Science Reference.

Csikszentmihalyi, M. (1997). *Creativity: Flow and the psychology of discovery and invention*. New York: HarperCollins Publishers, Inc.

Davidson, C. (2008). Humanities 2.0: Promise, perils, predictions. *PMLA, 123*(3), 707–717.

D'Mello, S., Lehman, B., Pekrun, R., & Graesser, A. (2014). Confusion can be beneficial for learning. *Learning and instruction, 29,* 153–170.

diSessa, A. A. (2004). Metarepresentation: Native competence and targets for instruction. *Cognition and Instruction, 22*(3), 293–331.

diSessa, A. A. (2006). A history of conceptual change research. In R. K. Sawyer (Ed.), *The Cambridge handbook of the learning sciences* (pp. 265–281). Cambridge: Cambridge University Press.

Duncan, A. (2010). The well-rounded curriculum [Press Release]. http://www2.ed.gov/news/speeches/2010/04/04092010.html. Accessed 1 April 2014.

Eger, J. (2013). STEAM…now! *The STEAM Journal, 1*(1): Article 8. http://scholarship.claremont.edu/steam/vol1/iss1/8/. Accessed 15 March 2014.

Fink, A., Benedek, M., Grabner, R. H., Staudt, B., & Neubauer, A. C. (2007). Creativity meets neuroscience: Experimental tasks for the neuroscientific study of creative thinking, *Methods, 42*(1), 68–76.

Fredette, M. (2013). Full STEAM ahead. *Transforming Education Through Technology, The Journal, 40*(10), 35–38.

Ghanbari, S. (2014). STEAM: The wave of the future embedded in ideals of the past. *The STEAM Journal, 1*(2), Article 27. http://scholarship.claremont.edu/steam/vol1/iss2/27/. Accessed 15 March 2014.

Gold, M. K. (Ed.). (2012). *Debates in the digital humanities*. Minneapolis: University of Minnesota Press.

Goldberg, M. H. (1971). *Design in liberal learning*. San Francisco: Jossey-Bass.

Greeno, J. G., Collins, A. M., & Resnick, L. B. (1996). Cognition and learning. In D. C. Berliner & R. C. Calfee (Eds.), *Handbook of educational psychology* (pp. 15–46). New York: Macmillan Library Reference USA.

Hamilton College. (n. d.). Mission statement [Web page]. http://www.dhinitiative.org/about/mission. Accessed 1 March 2014.

Hayek, J., & Kuh, G. (November 1998). *The capacity for life-long learning of college seniors in the mid-1980s to the mid-1990s*. Miami, FL: Paper presented at the annual meeting of the Association for the Study of Higher Education.

Henriksen, D. (2014). Full STEAM ahead: Creativity in excellent STEM teaching Practices. *The STEAM Journal, 1*(2), Article 15. http://scholarship.claremont.edu/steam/vol1/iss2/15/. Accessed 2 March 2014.

Hoppe, K. D. (1988). Hemispheric specialization and creativity. *The Psychiatric Clinics of North America, 11*(3), 303–315.

Ito, M., Baumer, S., Bittanti, M., Boyd, D., Cody, R., Herr-Stephenson, B., Horst, H. A., Lange, P. G., Mahendran, D., Martínez, K. Z., Pascoe, C. J., Perkel, D., Robinson, L., Sims, C., & Tripp, L. (2010). *Hanging out, messing around, and geeking out: Kids living and learning with new media*. Cambridge: The MIT Press.

Jessicahwu. (18. April 2013). Final project fail! [Blog post]. http://umwthinklab.com/2013/04/18/final-project-fail/. Accessed 14 Feb 2014.

Jewitt, C., & Kress, G. R. (2003). *Multimodal literacy*. New York: Peter Lang Publishers.

Jonassen, D., & Land, S. M. (Eds.).(1999), *Theoretical foundations of learning environments*. Mahwah: Lawrence Erlbaum Associates.

Kafai, Y. B. (2006). Constructionism. In R. K. Sawyer (Ed.), *The Cambridge handbook of the learning sciences* (pp. 35–46). Cambridge: Cambridge University Press.

Kafai, Y., & Harel, I. (1991). Learning through design and teaching: Exploring social and collaborative aspects of constructionism. In I. Harel & Y. Kafai (Eds.), *Constructionism* (pp. 85–106). Norwood: Ablex.

Kafai, Y. B., & Peppler, K. A. (2014). Transparency reconsidered: Creative, critical, and connected making with E-textiles. In M. Ratto & M. Boler (Eds.), *DIY citizenship: Critical making and social media*. Cambridge: MIT Press.

Kafai, Y. B., & Resnick, M. (Eds.). (1996). *Constructionism in practice: Designing thinking, and learning in a digital world*. Mahwah: Lawrence Erlbaum.

Knobel, M., & Lankshear, C. (2010). *DIY media: Creating, sharing and learning with new technologies*. New York: Peter Lang.

Koblik, S., & Graubaud, S. (Eds.). (2000). *Distinctively American: The residential liberal arts colleges*. New Brunswick: Transaction Publishers.

Maeda, J. (2013). STEM + Art = STEAM. *The STEAM Journal, 1*(1), Article 34. http://scholarship.claremont.edu/steam/vol1/iss1/34/. Accessed 26 Jan 2014.

Menand, L. (2010). *The marketplace of ideas: Reform and resistance in the American university*. New York: W.W. Norton.

Miller, T. (2012). *Blow up the humanities*. Philadelphia: Temple University Press.

National Research Council. (2007). *Rising above the gathering storm: Energizing and employing America for a brighter economic future*. Washington, D. C.: The National Academies Press.

Newfield, C. (2009). Ending the budget wars: Funding the humanities during a crisis in higher education. *Profession*, 270–284.

Norris, A. (2014). Make-her-spaces as hybrid places: Designing and resisting self constructions in Urban classrooms. *Equity & Excellence in Education, 47*(1), 63–77.

Nussbaum, M. (1997). *Cultivating humanity: A classical defense of reform in liberal education*. Cambridge: Harvard University Press.

Oxtoby, D. W. (2014). Breaking barriers and building bridges in teaching. In R. Chopp, S. Frost, & D. H. Weiss (Eds.), *Remaking college: Innovation and the liberal arts* (pp. 77–84). Baltimore: The Johns Hopkins University Press.

Papert, S. (1980). *Mindstorms: Children, Computers, and Powerful Ideas*. New York: Basic Books.

Pascarella, E.T. & Blaich, C. (2013). Lessons from the Wabash National Study of Liberal Arts Education. Change: *The Magazine of Higher Learning, 45*(2), 6–15.

Pascarella, E. T., & Terenzini, P. (1998). Studying college students in the 21st century: Meeting new challenges. *Review of Higher Education, 21*(2), 151–165.

Pascarella, E. T., Wolniak, G. C., Seifert, T. A. D., Cruce, T. M., & Blaich, C. F. (2005). Liberal arts colleges and liberal arts education: New evidence on impacts. *ASHE Higher Education Report, 31*(3), 1–148.

Peppler, K. (2013). STEAM-powered computing education: Using E-textiles to integrate the arts and STEM. *Computer, 46*(9), 38–43.

Peppler, K., & Glosson, D. (2013). Learning about circuitry with E-textiles in after-school settings. In M. Knobel & C. Lankshear (Eds.), *The New Literacies Reader*. New York: Peter Lang Publishing.

Pinker, S. (6 August 2013,). Science is not your enemy: An impassioned plea to neglected novelists, embattled professors, and tenure-less historians. *The New Republic*. http://www.newrepublic.com/article/114127/science-not-enemy-humanities. Accessed 17 Feb 2014.

Rescorla, R.A. (1988). Pavlovian conditioning. It's not what you think it is. *American Psychologist, 43*(3), 151–160.

RISD Office of Government Relations. (2013). STEAM by US region [PDF file]. http://stemtosteam.org/wp-content/uploads/2013/07/STEAM-by-US-region.pdf. Accessed 1 March 2014.

Sarah Lawrence College. (n. d.). Games and interactive media [Webpage]. http://www.slc.edu/undergraduate/clusters/games-interactive-media/. Accessed 11 Nov 2013.

Selingo, J. (2013). *College (Un)Bound: The future of higher education and what it means to students*. New York: New Harvest.

Sfard, A. (1998). On two metaphors for learning and the dangers of choosing just one. *Educational Researcher, 27*(2), 4–13.

Slingerland, E. (2008). *What science offers the humanities: Integrating body and culture*. Cambridge: Cambridge University Press.

Small, H. H. (2014). *The value of the humanities*. Oxford: Oxford University Press.

Soloway, E., Guzdial, M., & Hay, K. (1994). Learner-centered design: The challenge for HCI in the 21st century. *Interactions, 1*(22), 36–48.

Spector, J. M. (2011). Learnign to solve problems in the digital age: Introduction. In D. Ifenthaler, I. P. Kinshuk, D. G. Sampson, & J. M. Spector (Eds.), *Multiple perspectives on problem solving and learning in the digital age* (pp. 1–8). New York: Springer.

Szeman, I. (2003). Culture and globalization, or, the humanities in ruins. *CR: The New Centennial Review, 3*(2), 91–115.

Thomas, D., & Seely Brown, J. (2011). *A new culture of learning: Cultivating the imagination in a world of constant change*. Lexington: CreateSpace.

Trilling, B., & Fadel, C. (2009). *21st century skills: Learning for life in our times*. San Francisco: Jossey-Bass.

U. S. Congress. (2011). 12th Congress, 1st Session. H. Res. 319 [PDF file]. http://www.gpo.gov/fdsys/pkg/BILLS-112hres319ih/pdf/BILLS-112hres319ih.pdf. Accessed 1 Nov 2013

von Glasersfeld, E. (1989). Cognition, construction of knowledge, and teaching. *Synthese, 80,* 121–140.

Vygotsky, L. S. (1978). *Mind in society*. Cambridge: Harvard University Press.

Wboadurg. (14. December 2012). My thoughts on the semester [Blog post]. http://umwthinklab.com/2012/12/14/my-thoughts-on-the-semester/. Accessed 12 Feb 2014.

Woodward, K. (2009). The future of the humanities—in the present and in the public. *Daedelus, 138*(1), 110–123.

Worsley, M., & Blikstein, P. (2013). *Towards the development of multimodal action based assessment*. Proceedings of the Third International Conference on Learning Analytics and Knowledge (LAK '13), Dan Suthers & Katrien Verbert (Eds.). ACM, New York, NY, USA, 94–101.

Yakman, G. (2008). STΣ@M Education: An overview of creating a model of integrative education [PDF file]. Unpublished. http://www.steamedu.com/2088_PATT_Publication.pdf. Accessed 14 Jan 2014.

Armanda L. Lewis currently serves as the Director of Educational Technology for NYU's Faculty of Arts & Science, where she provides leadership and planning for the effective and strategic use of emerging technologies and supports a wide range of educational technology projects to promote increased interactivity, global awareness, and creativity. She holds a doctorate in literature and is currently completing a Ph.D. in educational technology, specializing in technology-enhanced language acquisition, design patterns, and learning analytics.

Reconceptualizing Liberal Education in the 21st Century

The Role of Emerging Technologies and STEAM Fields in Liberal Education

Aytac Gogus

Abstract This chapter reviews the essential learning outcomes that students develop through a 21st century liberal education, along with principal themes in the literature about higher education in the 21st century. This chapter shows examples of high impact liberal education practices in both European and American colleges and universities. This chapter also discusses the role of emerging technologies and STEAM (Science, Technology, Engineering, Arts, and Mathematics) fields in liberal education. Questions to be addressed include the following: What kind of liberal education curriculum and learning environment can better prepare university students for success in the 21st century workplace? Why is liberal education necessary? What is the role of emerging technologies to meet the liberal education learning outcomes? Principle themes in the literature and implications of liberal education are discussed.

Keywords Liberal education · College liberal arts curriculum · Learning outcomes · STEAM · MOOC · Mobile technologies

A Brief Review of Liberal Education

The word liberal is derived from liber that means free in Latin. Antiquity roots of liberal education go back thousands years. In the ancient world, liberal meant reserved to free citizens, as opposed to slaves and ordinary people (Burns, 2002). The term liberal arts refers to specific subjects in a curriculum while liberal education implies an educational philosophy, coming down from the ancient civilizations, and then, refers to "a common course of study in recognized academic areas, designed to develop in its learners the intellectual capacities needed to perform society's most valued roles" (Burns, 2002, p. 4). Liberal education is a philosophy of education

A. Gogus (✉)
Okan University, Istanbul, Turkey
e-mail: aytacgogus@gmail.com

© Springer International Publishing Switzerland 2015
X. Ge et al. (eds.), *Emerging Technologies for STEAM Education,*
Educational Communications and Technology: Issues and Innovations,
DOI 10.1007/978-3-319-02573-5_15

that empowers individuals, liberates the mind, cultivates judgment, and fosters personal and intellectual growth and social responsibility. Liberal education liberates free minds from inherited ignorance and allows a free person to discover and reflect what is real and what truly exists (Guerra, 2013).

A philosophical attention to liberal education raises "the question of the connection between how we learn and how we live" (Roth, 2013, p. 104). Roth (2013) discusses on how a tradition of liberal education is related to professional, personal and political lives:

> The mission of universities focused on liberal learning should be, in Richard Rorty's words, "to incite doubt and stimulate imagination, thereby challenging the prevailing consensus." Through doubt, imagination and hard work, students "realize they can reshape themselves" and their society ...The free inquiry and experimentation of a reflexive, pragmatic education help us to think for ourselves, take responsibility for our beliefs and actions, and be better acquainted with own desires and our own hopes. (Roth, 2013, p. 104)

The idea of liberal education is attractive since liberal education has the potential to cancel impassive habits of mind, producing global citizens who think and produce solutions to problems of today's world and creating a critical public culture, through an emphasis on analytical thinking, argumentation, and active participation in debate about problems of today's world (Nussbaum, 2004). Nussbaum (2004) states that "a liberal arts college or university that helps young people learn to speak in their own voices and to respect the voices of others will have done a great deal to produce thoughtful and potentially creative world citizens (p. 45)." Liberal education in colleges and universities allows teaching the virtues of critical analysis and respectful debates about deliberative democracy that is seriously needed for each country in creating a world community to work together for solutions of urgent problems (Nussbaum, 2004).

College Liberal Arts Curriculum and Liberal Education Approach

The seven liberal arts, that are grammar, rhetoric, logic, arithmetic, geometry, music, and astronomy, established by the Roman Empire in the 13th century, functioned as a common curriculum, a one-size-fits-all educational experience (Burns, 2002). To the seven liberal arts, the Renaissance humanists added history and physical exercises in the 15th century. In the 18th and 19th centuries, a liberal curriculum referred to preparing a young person for success and leadership in society, business, or government. Also, a liberal curriculum was made to develop an understanding of the shared culture, common concepts, values, traditions and an understanding of the other cultures to facilitate communication and mutual confidence among those of that culture (Adler, 1988). The liberal education in the 20th century referred to liberal arts colleges or larger institutions to study arts and science disciplines and general education in the initial years of college. However, the Association of American Colleges and Universities (AAC&U) points out that the liberal education in the 21st century referred to all schools, community colleges, colleges, and universities, as well as across all fields of study by emphasizing the essential learning outcomes across the entire educational continuum—from school through college—at progressively higher levels of achievement (AAC&U, 2007, p. 18).

Liberal education incorporates multiple disciplines and ways of knowing in combination with the specific study domain for professional development. AAC&U's notion of the practical liberal arts is that well-rounded and integrated learning in the arts, humanities, social sciences, natural sciences, and professional studies prepares students for contemporary problems (Shinn, 2012). AAC&U defines a liberal arts college as "a particular type of institution—often small, often residential—that facilitates close interaction between faculty and students, and whose curriculum is grounded in the liberal arts disciplines" (AAC&U, 2011, p. 3). AAC&U emphasizes a new paradigm of liberal education that provides both disciplinary depth and a multidisciplinary, holistic, and integrative approach to the complex local and global challenges (Shinn, 2012). AAC&U defines liberal education as below:

> Liberal education is an approach to learning that empowers individuals and prepares them to deal with complexity, diversity, and change. It provides students with broad knowledge of the wider world (e.g. science, culture, and society) as well as in-depth study in a specific area of interest. A liberal education helps students develop a sense of social responsibility, as well as strong and transferable intellectual and practical skills such as communication, analytical and problem-solving skills, and a demonstrated ability to apply knowledge and skills in real-world settings. (AAC&U, 2011, p. 3)

Liberal education guides students in how to use critical thinking and ethical judgments to concrete problems in the real world (Williams, Zdravkovich, & Engleberg, 2002). AAC&U's Report of the Greater Expectations National Panel (2002) states that, "liberal education has the capacity to develop mental agility, as well as intellectual power; a deep understanding of world's variety, as well as knowledge of Western culture; ethical action in service of the individual and society as well as critical judgment" (p. 24). Liberal education aims to prepare students to think more constructively about global issues.

Benefits of Liberal Education

Students in liberal education ask many common questions like why students should take the general education classes in order to graduate; why someone who wants to be an engineer, a sociologist or a manager should study subjects that are not directly related to their study domain; why someone should study any courses that are not used in the selected major or the job that students want to be trained? In order to be able to answer these questions, the benefits of a liberal education should be understood. Liberal education supports students learning how to think and learning how to learn. Harris (2010) summarizes some benefits of a liberal education as below:

1. *Learning how to think*

   1. Liberal education supports students to develop strength of mind and an ordered intellect. The mind needs exercise to be able to grasp ideas, do intellectual work, develop the habits of attention and concentration, the habit of organized thinking and of rational analysis, develop the ability to follow arguments and the ability to distinguish the important concepts, and grasp the knowledge of organized solutions, of hierarchical procedures, and of rational sequences that can be applied to any effort to perform better in any job (Harris, 2010; Williams et al., 2002).

   2. Liberal education supports students to develop the ability to think independently. From liberal education, students gain the diverse body of knowledge together with the tools of examination and analysis that enable to develop opinions, attitudes, values, and beliefs, based not upon the authority of anybody and not upon ignorance, or prejudice, but upon students' own examination and evaluation of argument and evidence. Diverse studies allow students to see the relations between ideas and philosophies. Also, these studies allow to develop the ability to think independently, in the face of pressures, misrepresentation, and overemphasized truths by politicians, advertisers, and others who have an agenda for a half-educated public (Harris, 2010; Shinn, 2012).

   3. Liberal education supports students to understand the world. A wide ranging education, covering multi-disciplines, allows understanding a phenomena through knowledge of a wide range of events, philosophies, and procedures. While a mind educated in only one discipline can overwhelm with a simple phenomenon, a mind educated in multi-disciplines can understand many phenomenon with a general knowledge of multiple disciplines (Harris, 2010; Riordan, 2005; Shinn, 2012).

2. *Learning how to learn*

   1. Liberal education supports students to develop the skill of learning and organizing ideas and thus enables students to understand new material more easily, to learn faster and more thoroughly and permanently (Harris, 2010).

   2. Liberal education supports students to develop good learning habits that allow students to learn new information easier and faster since the brain remembers how a person learned the previous information and develops new pathways to transfer the new information from short-term memory into long-term memory by finding a relevant schema to attach the new information (Harris, 2010). The good learning habits can be transferred from one subject to another since the brain remembers the pathways (Harris, 2010; Shinn, 2012).

   3. Liberal education provides students a general knowledge in the first year course so that students can learn new subjects by one of the most common methods of learning, analogy. The mind created its own analogies by making connections between old and new knowledge; therefore, the liberal education creates an improvement of perception and understanding (Harris, 2010; AAC&U, 2002).

4. Liberal education supports students to enhance creativity. The mind uses stored knowledge, and a wide range of knowledge supports the producing of new ideas, solutions, and better understanding (Harris, 2010; Williams et al., 2002).

The Essential Learning Outcomes that Students Develop Through a 21st Century Liberal Education

A liberal education in the 21st century allows students developing complex and transferable skills and abilities to be able to deal with complex problems, to be innovative and creative in their workplaces or study areas, and to be responsible citizens in a globally engaged democracy. Being prepared to understand complex problems, developing a global perspective on the diversity of human experience, and taking action in changing demands in a knowledge-intensive economy are vital for today's college students (VT, 2013).

AAC&U (2007) describes the essential learning outcomes, which students develop through a 21st century liberal education, in the report *College Learning for the New Global*:

"Students should prepare for 21st century challenges by gaining:

- Knowledge of human cultures and the physical and natural world through study in the sciences and mathematics, social sciences, humanities, histories, languages, and the arts
- Intellectual and practical skills, including
    - Inquiry and analysis
    - Critical and creative thinking
    - Written and oral communication
    - Quantitative literacy
    - Information literacy
    - Teamwork and problem solving
- Personal and social responsibility, including
    - Civic knowledge and engagement—local and global
    - Intercultural knowledge and competence
    - Ethical reasoning and action
    - Foundations and skills for lifelong learning
- Integrative and applied learning, including
    - Synthesis and advanced accomplishment across general and specialized studies" (p. 3).

AAC&U's project *Greater Expectations: A New Vision for Learning as a Nation Goes to* College ((2002) is a national panel report from the work of representatives of many colleges, universities, high schools, and businesses. The Greater Expectations project allows meetings in which teams from institutions committed to excellence in undergraduate education came together to learn from one another and to plan initiatives in efforts to promote student learning (Riordan, 2005). In the Greater Expectations Report, liberal education refers to certain learning outcomes. Liberal education in the twenty-first century expresses any study to communicate affectively, work cooperatively, and behave ethically (Fong, 2004). Liberal education also promotes students to think knowledgeably, insightfully, critically, and responsibly (Fong, 2004). The operative concern is how any subject or professional program can be taught liberally. Main concerns of higher education institutes include a lack of professional knowledge base, a lack of payment, and issues of accessibility (Fong, 2004).

Colleges require for students to develop basic knowledge, skills and attitudes as part of their core curriculum. These attributes are: communication, analysis, problem solving, value in decision making, social interaction, developing a global perspective, effective citizenship, aesthetic engagement (Riordan, 2005). Riordan (2005) states that:

> Most faculties have been educated as specialists in particular disciplines, of course, so the question of how the abilities students will need in the 21st century relate to those disciplines is critical. I think of "disciplines" as habits of mind and heart, ways of thinking, and methodological perspectives that inform and enhance the way one approaches the variety of challenges, issues, and opportunities we face as human beings. (p. 54).

Since liberal education curriculum refers to general education including study of natural sciences, mathematics, social sciences, histories, languages, arts, and basis of engineering, liberal education curriculum and STEAM (Science, Technology, Engineering, Arts, and Mathematics) fields have intersections and provide a multidisciplinary approach to important contemporary problems and intellectual engagement.

A Review of Liberal Education Learning Outcomes from American and European Colleges and Universities

Liberal education courses at Harvard University are presented in a general education program by aiming to meet four key criteria: (1) foster judgment, (2) develop creativity, (3) construct the communicative skills, and (4) emphasize fundamental principles, intellectual frameworks, and criteria of assessment (Domínguez, 2004).

Liberal education courses at Brown University introduce students to the many ways of thinking and of approaching knowledge that comprise a liberal education and seek to (BU, 2013):

- Expose and critique the diverse historical and cultural forces that shape the construction of knowledge in all disciplines
- Teach the arts of critical reflection: questioning thoughtfully, listening openly, and speaking cogently about differing points of view
- Develop responsible citizens by examining the ways that power and privilege affect human lives and providing pathways to meaningful change

Brown University summarizes liberal learning goals for undergraduates (BU, 2013):

- Work on your speaking and writing
- Understand differences among cultures
- Evaluate human behavior
- Learn what it means to study the past
- Experience scientific inquiry
- Develop a facility with symbolic languages
- Expand your reading skills
- Enhance your aesthetic sensibility
- Embrace diversity
- Collaborate fully
- Apply what you have learned

As an example of a liberal education curriculum, Virginia Tech, the Curriculum for Liberal Education (CLE) aims to "foster and develop intellectual curiosity and critical thinking, strong analytic, communication, quantitative, and information literacy skills, the capacity for collaboration and creative problem solving, the ability to synthesize and transfer knowledge, intercultural knowledge and understanding, and ethical reasoning and action" (VT, 2013). The AAC&U's essential learning outcomes are used by American colleges and universities as a guiding vision and national benchmarks for college learning and liberal education in the 21st century.

In Europe, the European Qualifications Framework (EQF) is used as a translation device to make national qualifications at all levels of education, from preschool to doctoral degrees across Europe in order to promote learners' mobility between countries, facilitate their lifelong learning, and obtain a common reference framework (EQF, 2006). Learning outcomes for higher education level includes three areas (EQF, 2006):

- Knowledge—Advanced knowledge of a field of work or study, involving a critical understanding of theories and principles.
- Skills—Advanced skills, demonstrating mastery and innovation, required to solve complex and unpredictable problems in a specialized field of work or study.
- Competencies—Manage complex technical or professional activities or projects, taking responsibility for decision making in unpredictable work or study contexts; take responsibility for managing professional development of individuals and groups.

By using a described framework, each university and college develops their own students learning outcomes. The EQF has common themes for students learning outcomes such as developing skills in (EQF, 2006):

- Written and oral communication
- Scientific and quantitative reasoning
- Critical analysis and logical thinking
- Analysis and integration of concepts
- Ways to identify, access, retrieve, and apply relevant information.

The EQF has common themes for students learning outcomes that match the intellectual and practical skills of AAC&U's essential learning outcomes for liberal education. Although learning outcomes in any types of higher education emphasize on intellectual and practical skills as 21st century skills, liberal education learning outcomes focus more on developing a multidisciplinary, holistic, and integrative approach to the complex local and global challenges. The essential learning outcomes, which students develop through a 21st century liberal education, emphasize on liberal education courses to allow students to develop "knowledge of human cultures and the physical and natural world through study in the sciences, mathematics, social sciences, humanities, histories, languages, and the arts" (AAC&U, 2007). As a result, AAC&U's essential learning outcomes are superior guides that should be used in all liberal education colleges and universities in all countries, because the essential learning outcomes represent the basis of a liberal education besides representing the 21st century skills.

Suggestions for Liberal Education Curriculum

According to Williams et al. (2002), America's liberal education universities and colleges offer a core curriculum designed to develop a liberal mode of thinking that is essential to good citizenship, lifelong learning and professional development. However, America's liberal education universities and colleges curriculum emphasizes a wide review of knowledge, basic principles and abstractions rather than programs intended to prepare students for vocations with marketable skills (Williams et al., 2002). These authors suggest the following criteria for assessing the efficacy of liberal education curriculum (Williams et al., 2002):

1. Intellectually challenging curriculum: Do students learn how to engage in research, reasoning and creative inquiry, and how to apply critical thinking skills?
2. Learning-centered programs and courses: Can students demonstrate learning through a variety of active and collaborative teaching applications?
3. Socially responsible and culturally relevant curriculum: Do students develop an understanding of the needs and perspective of other cultures?
4. Practical curriculum: Do students develop the ability to connect theories and principles to practical wisdom and action?
5. Purposeful curriculum for responsibilities in a diverse society: Are all students personally empowered and informed by learning?
6. Accessibility of the liberal education: Is liberal education inclusive and available to all students?

Being educated in a single discipline does not allow developing liberal education qualities and also global learning qualities that include a balance of knowledge, such as world geography and history, skills like the ability to read and understand international news sources, attitudes like an interest in other cultures and a sense of responsibility for our shared planet (Summit, 2013). However, liberal education programs have a concern about the amount of time available in a general education program besides a certain degree program requirements. A balanced curriculum is necessary to cover the essential liberal learning outcomes besides covering learning outcomes of a single discipline.

Demands for Liberally Educated Employees

There is a demand for liberally educated employees who have capacity to think critically, communicate clearly, and solve complex problems. Liberally educated employees should be engaged and informed citizens who have higher levels of learning, knowledge, and intellectual and interpersonal skills to deal with complex cross-cultural interactions and to drive innovations (Hart Research Associates, 2013). According to the employers survey reports (AAC&U, 2013), employers recognize the importance of providing a liberal education in colleges and universities, and emphasize students' intellectual and practical skills on the following areas:

- Critical thinking and analytical reasoning (82% more emphasis)
- Complex problem solving and analysis (81% more emphasis)
- Written and oral communication (80% more emphasis)
- The application of knowledge and skills in real-world settings (78% more emphasis)
- The location, organization, and evaluation of information from multiple sources (72% more emphasis)
- Innovation and creativity (71% more emphasis).

Employers are highly focused on innovation for the success of their companies and expect their employees to solve complex problems that require a broader skill set than in the past.

AAC&U (2013) suggests that college education should help students to develop these capabilities and students should be able to apply liberal learning outcomes to complex problems and real-world settings. Employers state that the following practices help students' succeed beyond graduation (AAC&U, 2013):

- Develop research questions in their field and evidence-based analyses (83%)
- Complete a project prior to graduation that demonstrates their acquired knowledge and skills (79%)
- Complete an internship or community-based field project (78%)
- Develop the skills to conduct research collaboratively (74%)
- Acquire hands-on or direct experience with the methods of science (69%)
- Work through ethical issues and debates to form their own judgments about the issues at stake (66%)

AAC&U (2013) suggests that the following priorities should be considered for future plans and policies in higher education:

- Higher achievement standards in K-12 education to be able to prepare students to college
- Increased access to higher education through financial aid, social and academic support
- Increased graduation rates in higher education by developing of key learning outcomes
- Tracking of results of the quality and actual achievement of key learning outcomes.

Employers indicate that they prioritize critical thinking, communication, and complex problem-solving skills over a job candidate's major field of study when making hiring decisions. The liberal education approach helps students meet employers' required skills. A college or university education should provide both broad knowledge in STEAM areas of study as well as knowledge in a specific major and a field of interest.

Role Of Emerging Technologies and Steam Fields in Liberal Education

Traditional science training provides a solid foundation of facts and basic science technique, but rarely examines how to foster scientists' creativity, cross-disciplinary problem identification and solving skills (Madden et al., 2013). Liberal education approach allows having a multidisciplinary program to foster creative thinking by combining studies in STEAM fields. The development of STEAM curriculum that allows creating innovations in modern science and technology is necessary. In a world with greater population, global interconnection, technological advancement, and large-scale problems, STEAM curriculum can address the complex problems that require sophisticated problem solving skills and innovative solutions (Madden et al., 2013). In recent years, the higher education curriculum is changed to maximize the integration of emerging technologies in order to link higher education more closely to employers' expectations and to meet the students' needs after graduation (Bridges, 2000). There are computing demands on the higher education curriculum, such as the deconstruction of the subject, the modularization of the curriculum, the cross-curricular key skills, the learning through experience, the learning about outside the academy, the potential of web-based learning, and the reaffirmation of the subject as the academic and organizational identity (Bridges, 2000). STEAM curriculum should deal with these demands of the higher education.

Accessing to a web-based curriculum and reusable learning objects are the most obvious effects of the new technologies in higher education. Bridges (2000) summarizes the most obvious effects of the new technologies on the channels of learning which it makes available on its geographical reach and on the flexibility provided by the asynchronous character of learning as below:

- There are huge data on the web, sophisticated search engines, and accelerated delivery systems accessible to anyone with a PC. The emerging technologies provide the transmission of knowledge and support its distillation, analysis, ordering and manipulation. Due to the lack of quality control of the Web materials, students need to read the available materials critically and to assess their reliability for themselves.
- Images and sounds become much more readily and speedily accessible on the web as multimedia resources that allow the presentation of the work.
- Learner-centered multi-layered, multimedia, multi-dimensional learning environment have the power to construct individualized learning and support constructivist approach to learning. The technology allows interactions between learners, scholars and researchers without any institutional, social and national boundary. Thus, being in a community of learners extends opportunities for collaborations in the construction of knowledge.

STEAM curriculum should take advantages of the new technologies on the channels of learning and consider benefiting from learner-centered multi-layered, multimedia, multi-dimensional learning environment in higher education.

The Role of Technology in Liberal Education

The use of emerging technologies is essential to be successful in life. Therefore, understanding of the emerging technologies and developing technical skills are essential parts of liberal education outcomes. Many fundamental courses in science, mathematics, engineering, arts and history rely on modern technologies to promote students' conceptual understanding, problem solving and critical thinking skills.

Bowen (2012) argues that there is a little evidence showing liberal education work. In Academically Adrift, Arum and Roksa (2011) state that of 2300 students at 24 American colleges, 45% of students showed no significant improvement in students' critical thinking, complex reasoning, and writing skills during the first year and half of college. Also, a majority of seniors showed moderate improvement in thinking skills, academic motivation, and openness to diversity (Blaich & Wise, 2011). Bowen (2012) suggests using emerging technologies effectively to improve liberal education core skills, such as critical thinking, complex reasoning, and writing. Effective integrating of emerging technologies requires an understanding of the interplay between content knowledge, pedagogical knowledge, and technological knowledge by engaging students to reach learning outcomes. The use of emerging technologies alters the availability of knowledge and the content delivery and the nature of the classroom (Bowen, 2002).

Widely available mobile technologies motivate college students to collaborate through searching, assessing and sharing knowledge. Students who grow up with mobile technologies are conditioned to think and create collaboratively since students readily access information and having opportunities to apply their knowledge

(Rossing, 2012). Mobile technologies can promote liberal education outcomes if the faculty and instructional designers guide students on integrating mobile technologies into learning activities. Rossing (2012) emphasizes that "the incorporation of mobile technology in higher education appears to be both inevitable and beneficial, so proponents of liberal education should actively and prudently direct it" (p. 70). Students without technological skills become part of professional disadvantages, such as reduced cultural and civic participation and limited problem solving capacity. Therefore, developing technical skills is important for graduates, but it would be a mistake to allow technological skills to constitute the central focus of liberal education (AAC&U, 2007; Rossing, 2012). Rossing (2012) underline that instead of skills associated with specific technologies, students need to develop adaptable performance skills and critical thinking skills for the use of emerging technologies and for job readiness.

Changes in the global higher education landscape include emerged technologies like social platforms that allow informal online social learning and Open Educational Resources (OER) that allows self-directed education (Gore, 2013). In the book entitled, *Teaching Naked: How Moving Technology out of Your College Classroom Will Improve Student Learning,* Jose Antonio Bowen (2012) defines a college classroom as a flat screen. Bowen (2012) emphasizes communicating with and engaging the students by using tools that students are familiar with. For example, the use of Learning Management Systems, asynchronous and synchronous communication and collaboration technologies, and social networking tools. Bowen (2012) acknowledges the useful quality of the material on the web such as Khan Academy, EdX, Open Courseware, and iTunes. Bowen (2012) suggests students to access the material outside of contact time by engaging in active learning activities such as doing problem-based learning, peer instruction, and interactive discussion. If the content is not available, the instructor can record audio or video lectures by using the Echo360's Personal Capture software and post it online to allow the students to watch it prior to attending the face-to-face lecture (Bowen, 2012).

Reconceptualizing Liberal Education Curriculum for Accessibility

Accessibility and capability to introduce creativity in teaching and learning practices are fundamental characteristics in higher education recently (Ahrache, Badir, Tabaa, & Medouri, 2013). The emergence of the Internet allowed the astonishing evolution in online educational content. The introduction of open content license for such content generates new means of elaborating and delivering teaching resources and techniques (Ahrache et al. 2013). A new concept, Massive Open Online Courses (MOOCs), is a rapid change for education in the last years. MOOCs take advantage of web technologies to offer free online education to everybody in the world. MOOC is denoted as Massive (registration is not capped), Open (widely available, open and free registration), Online (no face-to-face attendance); and

Course (the concept of a pedagogically designed learning journey) (Gore, 2013). A MOOC system is consisted of five main elements that are instructors, learners, topic, material, and context (Ahrache et al. 2013). The objective of the MOOCs platforms are to provide an elastic learning environment for a community of learners where everyone contributes by information and perspectives besides those provided by the instructor. A MOOC platform incorporates videos of different sources and links to online resources, extra study materials and forums. A MOOC platform also offers widened access to quality educational materials and courses supported by legendary professors from prestigious universities. For example, Sebastian Thrun and Peter Norvig from Stanford University presented a free, online course through a MOOC platform in 2012 (Gore, 2013). The course, Introduction to Artificial Intelligence, has not only attracted interest in academia, but also over 160,000 learners worldwide. This heralded it as the first true MOOC (Gore, 2013; Mehaffy 2012). Access and availability are the most important features of a MOOC course.

Opposite to entirely online education, blended courses have advantages of both online education and in-person, campus-based teaching and learning. A national nonprofit blended learning course model, called Global Challenges, offer partly or fully online courses that can be adopted as a turnkey course or customized to fit a wide range of pedagogical forms and needs (Summit, 2013). Global Challenges systems have a course shell that consist of several elements like sample syllabus, learning objectives, lesson modules, quizzes or exams, assignments, discussion forums, assessment tools, student guide, *New York Times* electronic daily edition and digital archives, teaching toolkit, and an online archive of readings, slides, videos and links. All of these are available through public sites or pre-loaded onto the Epsilen learning management system (Summit, 2013). Collaboration is a driving philosophy of the Global Challenges project to enable faculty to expand their disciplinary reach while also introducing students to global perspectives and resources (Summit, 2013). The course of Global Challenges project is called a Massive, Collaboratively Designed Course (MCDC) (Summit, 2013). Global Challenges offers a new approach to liberal learning by engaging both students and faculty into global teaching and learning activities.

The globally educated students should gain experiences and skills in comparing different cultures and systems, and also in dealing with relationships between the local and the global (Stearns, 2010). The 21st century students' global knowledge and understanding are vital and should not be limited to meet with liberal education outcomes. Demands of students for course platforms and systems should be considered by liberal education curriculum designer.

Implications of Liberal Education

The demand for what has variously been identified as transferable skills, cross-curricular skills, core skills and key skills, became a driving force on higher education curriculum change in the next century (Bridges, 2000). Bridges (2000) believes that the development of skills is a diversion from a student's main studies, and that the potential list of skills becomes so long that it is self-defeating. Therefore, Bridges (2000) suggests that four skills are key to the future success of graduates with whatever they intend to do in later life. These four are communication skills, numeracy, the use of information technology, and learning how to learn.

Rene V. Arcilla (2007) states the big question of liberal education:

> For the last few decades, our societies have been challenging liberal educators in turn to explain why and how their practices remain pertinent to a swiftly changing, endlessly modernizing world. Many such educators have themselves joined the ranks of the doubting and contributed to sharpening and disseminating this criticism. Leaving aside the strains these changes have also put on K–12 and vocational and professional educations, could alteration in the social conditions of liberal education be presaging the latter's extinction? (Arcilla, 2007, p. 15).

The issues about the liberal education colleges and universities include curriculum and assessment debates, faculty development opportunities, effective utilization of technology, and budget uncertainties (Williams et al., 2002). The principal themes in the literature about higher education in the 21st century (Skolnik, 1998) can be summarized as below:

- Pressure for institutional and employee survival
- Economizing faculty time while maintaining quality education
- Pervasive measurements of learning outcomes versus effective measurements
- Transition from a teaching (instruction) paradigm to a learning paradigm;
- Extensive use of information technologies
- Learning networks versus social networks
- Consumer-centrism vs. student- and learning-centrism.

According to Bridges (2000), the agenda of the change of the traditional university curriculum considers:

- The development of more generic capacities like critical thinking and problem solving according to employers' expectation from a graduate employee
- The improvement of the interpersonal dimensions of working in an academic as well as an employment context. For example, team work, oral and written communication, presentational skills, and the development of personal confidence in social situations
- The way businesses function and how knowledge can be applied in these settings. Also, the inclusion of work experience as part of undergraduate programs
- The establishment of basic skills such as numeracy, writing skills, and the use of information technology.

The rationale of the change of the traditional university curriculum is derived significantly from the needs of the national economy by employers, rather than an idea of a liberal education (Bridges, 2000). As Williams et al. (2002) state, access to liberal education is vital for everybody in the world:

> Liberal education must be vibrant and speak to the challenge of living while continuing to honor the past. Students must engage the great problems of the present and future. Liberal education is needed now and for all. (p. 38)

Liberal education is a significant effort in the 21st century to support students to develop fundamental cognitive skills. Thus, students can be prepared to think more constructively about global issues and use liberal qualities to adopt technological and scientific developments.

References

AAC&U. (2002). *Greater expectations: A new vision for learning as a nation goes to college.* Washington, D. C.: Association of American Colleges and Universities (AAC & U).

AAC&U. (2007). *College learning for the new global century.* Washington, D. C.: Association of American Colleges and Universities (AAC & U).

AAC&U. (2011). *LEAP vision for learning: Outcomes, practices, impact, and employers' views.* Washington, D. C.: Association of American Colleges and Universities (AAC & U).

Adler, M. (1988). *Reforming education: The opening of the American mind. Edited by Geraldine Van Doren.* New York: Macmillan.

Ahrache, El. S. I., Badir, H., Tabaa, Y., & Medouri, A. (2013). Massive open online courses: A new dawn for higher education? *International Journal on Computer Science and Engineering, 5*(5), 323–327.

Arcilla, R. V. (2007). The question of liberal education. *Liberal Education,* Spring 2007.

Arum, R., & Roksa, J. (2011). *Academically adrift: Limited learning on college campuses.* Chicago: University of Chicago Press.

Blaich, C., & Wise, K. (2011). *From gathering to using assessment results.* NILOA Occasional. Paper, 8.

Bowen, J. A. (2012). *Teaching naked: How moving technology out of your college classroom will improve student learning.* San Francisco: A Wiley Imprint.

Bridges, D. (2000). Back to the future: the higher education curriculum in the 21st century. *Cambridge Journal of Education, 30*(1), 37–55.

BU (2013). Brown University (BU) liberal learning goals. http://www.brown.edu/Administration/Registrar/concentrationforms/LiberalLearningGoals.pdf. Accessed 14 March 2014.

Burns, G. (2002). *Liberal education at Franklin Pierce.* Fall: Franklin Pierce University.

Domínguez, J. I. (2004). Liberal education at Harvard in this new century. http://isites.harvard.edu/fs/docs/icb.topic733185.files/Dominguez.pdf. Accessed 14 March 2014.

EQF. (2006). *The European qualifications framework (EQF): A new way to understand qualifications across Europe.* European Commission. – IP/06/1148 05/09/2006.

Fong, B. (2004). Liberal education in the 21st century. *Liberal Education,* Winter 2004.

Gore, H. (2013). *Massive Open Online Courses (MOOCs) and their impact on academic library services: Exploring the issues and challenges.* Bucks: The Open University.

Guerra, M. (2013). *The place of liberal education in contemporary higher education.* Symposium: Higher Education and The Challenges of Reform. Soc, 50, 251–256.

Harris, R. (2010). On the purpose of a liberal arts education. http://www.virtualsalt.com/libarted.htm. Accessed 14 March 2014.

Hart Research Associates. (2013). *It takes more than a major: Employer priorities for college learning and student success.* Washington, D. C.: Association of American Colleges and Universities (AAC & U).

Madden, M. E., Baxter, M., Beauchamp, H., Bouchard, K., Habermas, D., Huff, M., Ladd, B., Pearon, J., & Plague, G. (2013). Rethinking STEM education: An interdisciplinary STEAM curriculum. *Procedia Computer Science, 20,* 541–546.

Mehaffy, G. L. (2012). Challenge and change. *Educause Review, 45*(5), 25–42.

Nussbaum, M. (2004). Liberal education and global community. *Liberal Education,* Winter 2004.

QAA. (2008). *The framework for higher education qualifications in England, Wales and Northern Ireland (FHEQ).* The Quality Assurance Agency (QAA) for Higher Education 2008, UK.

Riordan, T. (2005). Education for the 21st century: Teaching, learning, and assessment. *Change: The Magazine of Higher Learning, 37*(1), 52–56.

Rossing, J. P. (2012). Mobile technology and liberal education. *Liberal Education,* Winter 2012, p. 70.

Roth, M. (2013). An anti-traditional tradition: The American idea of liberal education. *Social Sciences in China, 34*(2), 96–104.

Shinn, L. D. (2012). Liberal education in the age of the unthinkable. *Change: The Magazine of Higher Learning, 44*(4), 15–21.

Skolnik, M. L. (1998). Higher Education in the 21st century. Perspectives on an emerging body of literature. *Futures, 30*(7), 635–650.

Stearns, P. (2010). Global education and liberal education. *Liberal Education,* Summer 2010.

Summit, J. (2013). Global citizenship demands new approaches to teaching and learning: AASCU's global challenges initiative. *Change: The Magazine of Higher Learning, 45*(6), 51–57.

VT. (2013). *Curriculum for liberal education: A guide for students, advisors & faculty.* Virginia Tech (VT), 2013–2014.

Williams, R. A., Zdravkovich, V., & Engleberg, I. (2002). *Liberal education. Why now? Why for all?* (pp. 34–41). Fall: Liberal Education.

Aytac Gogus is Associate Professor at Educational Science Department of Faculty of Education at Okan University since March 2015. Dr. Gogus has been a visiting research scholar in the Department of Curriculum & Instruction of the Judith Herb College of Education at University of Toledo between July 2014 and January 2015. Dr. Gogus has worked at the Center for Individual and Academic Development at Sabancı University between September 2007 and February 2015. Dr. Gogus was promoted to Associate Professorship degree in Educational Science by Interunity Board in Turkey on January 25, 2014. She received her Ph.D. in Instructional Design, Development, and Evaluation (IDD&E) at Syracuse University in May 2006 and was a postdoctoral fellow in IDD&E until May 2017. She received her first Master's in Mathematics from the Middle East Technical University and her second Master's degree in IDD&E in May 2001. She worked as a course writer and instructional designer on designing and developing college level online mathematics courses for McGraw Hill Higher Education Online between October 2005 and May 2007. She has teaching experiences in higher education for 15 years and in K-12 setting for 4 years. In her research projects, Dr. Gogus took advantages of her interdisciplinary background, research and teaching experiences and studied on many educational research studies for 15 years. She has 60 publications and presentations.

Predicting the Future: Altering the Course of Future Liberal Arts Curriculum Through an Examination of the Discipline and the Addition of STEAM Elements

Michael Marmon

Abstract Liberal arts education as an academic discipline has a rich and illustrious history in the Western world. The skills that are bestowed upon its graduates are numerous and include enhanced critical thinking, ability to research and conduct analyses. However, there is the perception held by some in America that liberal arts curriculum is not a worthwhile endeavor for students from an economics perspective and funding would be better spent on other academic disciplines. These criticisms raise the question as to what role should liberal arts education should assume in the twenty-first century. The answer to this question is to alter the aforementioned perception regarding liberal arts education through the supplementation of science, technology, engineering, arts and mathematics (STEAM) elements into liberal arts curriculum. The assertion made is that addition of STEAM will prepare liberal arts graduates with the skills required for a twenty-first century knowledge based economy.

Keywords Liberal arts · Post-Secondary education · Curriculum · STEAM

Introduction—Liberal Arts Education Conceptualized

There is a widely held belief that a liberal arts education is not one of the starting points on the pathway to financial stability. Degrees in the liberal arts discipline such as Anthropology, Sociology or Psychology are considered to be "irrelevant" or lesser than programs that are from more respected fields and are less likely to provide the bearer of a liberal arts degree with financial stability upon their completion. Such positions are rather simplistic and do not reflect the rigor associated with the type of degree programs falling under an all-encompassing term such as liberal arts nor does it reflect the "flexibility, creativity, critical thinking, and strong communication skills" present in these programs (Christ, 2012).

M. Marmon (✉)
University of North Texas, Denton, USA
e-mail: mcmarmon@gmail.com

© Springer International Publishing Switzerland 2015

X. Ge et al. (eds.), *Emerging Technologies for STEAM Education,*
Educational Communications and Technology: Issues and Innovations,
DOI 10.1007/978-3-319-02573-5_16

The attitudes held regarding a liberal arts education in the United States is one of perceptions, both positive and negative. Positively speaking, a liberal arts education is said to provide a graduate with a myriad of career choices and an enhanced comprehension of how the world functions through the acquisition of such knowledge (Sigurdson, n.d.). As mentioned earlier, the contrarian position regarding the subject simply emphasizes the lack of prospects available to graduates based off of their academic major choices (Barlow, 2011). Regardless of the position held, the evidence provided by both is anecdotal and enhancements through the addition of rigorous elements to this curriculum would only improve the opinions held of a liberal arts education.

Certainly, improvements can be made to alter the perceptions held regarding liberal arts education in the United States through the selection and implementation of STEAM principles at the university level. STEAM, also known as Science, Technology, Engineering, Arts and Mathematics would provide a liberal arts major with an added dimension from a skills perspective that would assist in erasing any negative notion or connotation associated with a liberal arts education. To better understand the benefits that STEAM might hold for a college level education, it is best to provide a theoretical context through an examination of the concept of liberal arts education, STEAM and the outcomes associated with the integration of the latter into the former.

Liberal Arts—A Contentious Debate of Perceptions

As liberal arts education entered the twenty-first century, it began to manifest itself as a curriculum that sought to be diverse in the information presented in these courses as well as their structure. Specifically, a modern liberal arts curriculum from a conceptual perspective is broad in the selection of courses that cover a variety of subjects while focusing in-depth on a major field of study (What is a 21st Century, 2013). This approach has maintained the link between modern liberal arts education and the curriculum of its predecessors from decades past. Alan Ryan muses, "liberal education opens a conversation between ourselves and the immortal dead, gives us voices at our shoulders asking us to think again" (Greene & Greene, 2010, p. 13).

Ryan's position highlights one of the many virtues of a liberal arts education; it is a connection to the past that acts as context to the present (philosophically and historically), which in turn endows a greater understanding of the world, as they know it. Of course, those who view education in black and white terms would view this particular philosophical underpinning to a liberal arts education as a detriment. Opponents of liberal arts education contend that this academic discipline is not prudent and should be the proverbial butt of jokes because of the previously mentioned criticism that highlights the lack of economic prospects (i.e. Obtaining employment after graduation) for those graduating from said programs (Kiley, 2013). These same critics are incapable of seeing the forests for the trees on the matter as some advocate the complete revocation of funds for liberal arts programs mainly because of the content present for academic programs such as these (Kiley, 2013).

The debate regarding liberal arts education is based more on perceptions held on a spectrum rather than the actual content being delivered from instructor to participating student. Carol Schneider (2004) asserts that liberal arts education in the United States is a commodity to be prized as it fulfills the illustrious tenets of "democratic freedom, scientific progress and excellence" (p. 6). To achieve these educational tenets, liberal arts curriculum designers have placed much importance on research and analysis through the cultivation of oral and written communication skills (Jones, 2012). By combining a foundational academic curriculum composed from a variety of different disciplines with these research and communication skills results in graduates that have a greater comprehension of not only academia but society as well.

The other end of the spectrum seeks to assess higher education from a perspective that is not academic in nature and could best be described as a perception based on the concept of value. There is a disagreement with regards to "value" semantically as those supporting modern liberal arts education find its value within its concept of scholarship and learning for the sake of learning as its own reward. There is the opposite opinion of those who feel such lofty intentions carry little practical value in today's society. The argument being made against a liberal arts education today is one based on the perception of usefulness, with the prevailing opinion that these particular educational programs have lost said benefits to individuals possessing a liberal arts degree (Noddings, 2013). Specifically, individuals who share this belief feel that the argument centers around the need to be ready for the world that resides outside the confines of a college campus.

Barrow, Brock and Rouse (2013) explain that readiness assumes the form of skills deemed "critical to succeed in a realm such as business" (p. 4). The overall perceived lack of appreciation or understanding of value is a simplification that is perhaps tied to the critic's philosophical or political beliefs. In particular, conservatives view liberal arts education differently as their connection to the past is traditionally more rigid than the open approach found with those who support the liberal arts (Surber, 2010). Ultimately, this perception as it relates to value or purpose leads these individuals to not understand either and leads them to champion a curriculum that focuses on a specific discipline or more specifically, the set of skills that will be obtained upon graduation.

Modern liberal arts education in the United States seeks to provide a student with a diverse and foundational exposure to a multitude of different subjects that result in a wide knowledge on a range of subjects. The intent upon completing a liberal arts degree is that the student will have a skill set that is based on research and critical thinking skills. These skills have resulted in the creation of opposing perceptions of modern liberal arts education as some view these skills as essential and others who fail to see the value. The issue that arises with criticizing liberal arts programs on the basis of value economically (i.e., availability of jobs upon graduation, annual salary, etc.), or the lack of business related skills, is that these beliefs are based on personal sentiment not empirical fact.

Much like the criticisms levied at liberal arts education from the perspective of sentiment, the proponents cannot dismiss such opponents as wrong because of a difference of opinions on the subject. Simply ignoring the issue or continuing the debate fails to address the negative perceptions of liberal arts education held and these dissenting positions necessitate a reflection on how to improve this curriculum. Through the supplementing of a STEAM related curriculum to existing liberal arts education, it is possible to alter the perceptions mentioned earlier through an introspection of the content, which could be utilized to remedy any perceived deficiencies associated with these programs.

Science, Technology, Engineering, Arts and Mathematics—Skills Necessary for the Twenty-First Century

Liberal arts education at the post-secondary level in the United States receives a lot of criticism on the basis that the curriculum being delivered is neither relevant nor practical to the individuals receiving this instruction. Opponents feel that liberal arts graduates are at a competitive disadvantage compared to those graduating from more specialized degree programs. Bender (2013) argues that despite its connection to the past, it is possible to recapture the essence of liberal arts education and also adapt the curriculum to reflect current trends in education. Bender highlights the seemingly perpetual flexibility of liberal arts from an instructional perspective through the assertion that the programs are adaptable through the implementation of new or innovative curriculum elements. One such implementation is the addition of focused instructional components based on Science, Technology, Engineering, Arts and Mathematics elements to existing liberal arts programs. This would hypothetically strengthen the curriculum from a rigor perspective and which in turn would also remedy the issues that are the root cause of the aforementioned negative perceptions held towards these programs.

STEAM or Science, Technology, Engineering, Arts and Mathematics represents a paradigm shift in America education from kindergarten to the completion of a college degree as it supplements curriculum in such a way that it would alter the clearly defined boundaries of academic disciplines. From a conceptual perspective, STEAM represents an enhancement of the traditional STEM concept of "innovation and economic growth" through the use of science, technology, engineering and mathematics approaches and an implication of the importance of the arts into these disciplines (Should, 2013). Education curriculum with a focus on STEAM is said to be preparing students for a world founded upon the notion of an "innovation economy" (Fantauzzacoffin, Rogers, & Bolter, 2012, p. 4). This concept is predicated on the importance of creative and innovative endeavors as well as ingenuity resultant from the shift from an economy that produces raw goods to one dependent on information (Sawyer, 2006).

This shift from a society that is economically based on the production of physical materials to an information economy, highlights the importance to possess a specific set of skills to be successful. Such a shift in the economic landscape returns the discussion back to the perceptions of a liberal arts education and the viability for graduates from these programs to be successful in a society based on an abstract commodity such as information. These perceptions further highlight the need to examine the possibilities offered by STEAM careers. The United States Department of Labor recognizes the aforementioned shift and acknowledges the dramatic lack of workers for this type of economy. Specifically, the Department of Labor asserts that these "knowledge workers" are essential to the continued competitiveness economically and sustained expansion of the United States in this realm (The STEM, 2007).

The fields that are considered to be STEAM related according to the Department of Commerce range from the computer sciences and engineering to the physical and life sciences but the arts as well (STEM, 2011). The crux of the perception regarding the value of a STEAM career stems from the lack of qualified individuals with STEAM related skills and the perception that the industries that would best utilize these skills are going through a period of growth. A recent report noted based off of current data, explained that the rate of creating college graduates with STEAM related skills must raise roughly to "one-third" the amount of graduates from the year prior every year for the next ten to fulfill the perceived needs for the United States workforce (Morella & Kurtzleben, 2013). The argument that is being framed regarding science, technology, engineering, art and mathematics in this country is founded on the belief that the nation is lacking in individuals with the skills that STEAM is said to provide. Assessments of future labor levels such as these tend to focus on the dearth of individuals in these fields but fail to highlight the skills required by graduates to obtain employment in these positions.

An advisory council for science and technology to the President stated that 1 million STEAM graduates would be needed to fill vacant technology positions in the coming 10 years (Boscia, 2013). Boscia's comment exemplifies the narrow focus on the potential job prospects in STEAM fields and further necessitates a re-framing of the discussion from a job forecast position to an examination of the essential skills required to fulfill these vacancies. The rationale for altering the central focus of a debate on a national level encourages a greater understanding of what programs an individual should complete academically to obtain jobs that are STEAM centric. Moreover, the proverbial first step in changing from a fulfillment of vacancies mindset to a philosophy determined to cultivate essential STEAM skill sets creates the necessary awareness of the subject.

Exposure and conceptual understanding of STEAM on a national level is required to not only understand the role and value of STEAM in present/future America but education by extension as well. To gain exposure on matter, a reframing of public awareness on the subject has begun to take shape in the House of Representatives. Specifically, House Resolution 51 seeks to add arts and design into federal programs focused on science, technology, engineering and mathematics as these concepts are essential to "innovation and economic growth for the United States" (H.Res.51, 2013, para. 1). At first glance, the modification of May's title as STEM awareness month to STEAM awareness month might be inconsequential to the average American citizen. However, such an action taken by Congress demonstrates that the United States government places an intrinsic value for the arts and design in today's twenty-first century economy. Furthermore, government interest extends past changes that might be dismissed as superficial with the creation of a caucus dedicated specifically to STEAM and has a core principle of pursuing "policy changes that will encourage educators to integrate arts, broadly defined, with traditional science" (Reps. Bonamici, 2013).

How does one measure the acceptance of STEAM within the contemporary American landscape? The answer is relatively apparent as funding provides a tangible means by which to observe something as abstract as the acceptance of this academic concept. Of course, funding must be placed within an understandable context as STEM currently receives 3 billion dollars from the federal government each year (Preparing, 2013). It is true that STEAM does not currently enjoy the levels of federal funds afforded to STEM but this disparity in funding will be reversed as STEAM concepts continue to evolve. As it stands currently, there are numerous programs that offer funds for STEAM related programs in substantial amounts. For instance, the Department of Education currently has a program offering over 1 million dollars to elementary schools that seek to "combine math and science with the arts" (Chen & Cheers, 2012, para. 6). Moreover, the funding provided by the Department of Education is not all of the opportunities available to educators, as the President's Committee on the Arts and Humanities has numerous grants available to institutions that have developed programs that are STEAM centric (PCAH, n.d.). These opportunities might pale in comparison to the current funding levels for STEM but they do give the indication that growth in this area will continue as STEAM integrates itself into new academic disciplines, such as liberal arts.

As it stands currently, the perceived deficiency of liberal arts education is predicated on inherently subjective notions, such as personal perception related to the limited positive impact for both the economy and the bearer of said degree is rather simplistic. Regardless of the validity or lack thereof behind such sentiment, these criticisms have yielded a golden opportunity to re-evaluate liberal arts education as it currently appears in American institutions of higher learning. If the administrators within these programs review their degree structures and curriculum critically, it is possible to alter these perceptions through the supplementation of STEAM principles into courses and programs being offered to students. After all, it is evident that while the argument against liberal arts is misguided and by extension, relatively specious, these contentions can be resolved through the inclusion of skills offered by STEAM curriculum that results in a positive benefit to both the individual pursuing post-secondary degrees in liberal arts and the nation as a whole.

Changing Perceptions of Liberal Art Programs with Science, Technology, Engineering, Arts and Mathematics

The widely held perception of the relevance of liberal arts education in the United States is that the degree programs falling under this umbrella should not be pursued, as the return on investment from an economic standpoint is low. The reaction by proponents has always been a response that highlights the joys and necessities of lifelong learning by the students completing these degree programs. The issue that arises with maintaining the position for lifelong scholarship is that it falls on the deaf ears of its opponents, especially with those who control government funding for post-secondary institutions in the age of reducing budgets across a multitude of state and federally funded agencies. This leads to the logical conclusion that the negative perceptions about the lack rigor and economic value regarding liberal arts as an educational commodity be remedied with the inclusion of STEAM elements to such programs and curriculum. The benefits of such a move would result in the conferring of liberal arts degrees to individuals with skills deemed important and essential through investigations conducted by the federal government but even the critics of these programs as well.

To properly integrate STEAM elements into all facets of a liberal arts degree: the department itself, the programs inherent to the department and finally, the curriculum to compose classes themselves, several aspects need to occur prior to altering or implementing these components at the aforementioned levels of a liberal arts program. Most importantly, a college administration must not only "buy into" the concepts, but also understand the return on investment that STEAM would provide to their institution if they follow this course of action. The administrators for both the institution and these academic programs would quickly realize the benefit of a STEAM education from a funding perspective that also illustrates their comprehension of societal and governmental trends towards an emphasis on STEAM.

The level of government interest in STEAM fields, especially within the realm of higher education is to the benefit of both the institution and the student with an interest in STEAM concepts attending the university or college since it minimizes the institution's financial risk for implementing a STEAM curriculum while exposing students to external funding opportunities to assist in paying for their education.

Re-Structuring of Core Liberal Arts Curriculum

As the cost for implementing STEAM components into the structure of a liberal arts institution or department is arguably minimal because of the opportunities afforded by the federal government, the question inexorably turns to how to implement said structures into this curriculum. Klein and Balmer (2007) offer a theoretical foundation for why a re-structuring must occur within the core curriculum of liberal arts programs as there is an isolation of concepts between courses in STEAM fields and those in liberal arts. The approach for developing a liberal arts curriculum that utilizes STEAM components must realize that learning is an activity that is inherently social, where individual ideas are developed, conveyed and acted upon intellectually in a group setting and should not remain limited because of where they originate (Narum, 2013). Narum is essentially emphasizing that cross-disciplinary ideas should not be kept or limited to their department of origin.

Breaking down the prevailing barriers between departments would be the logical starting point for creating a liberal arts education that could be considered STEAM centered or place an emphasis with teaching its students these concepts. Qayoumi (2011), President of California State University, offers the perspective for how a research university should approach the creation of STEAM centered liberal arts programs through an institutional commitment to both sets of ideas and principle through the discussion between various entities ("academic leaders, planners, administrators and even students") on the subject. Qayoumi's approach at his specific institution is the most pragmatic. It is inclusionary in that it seeks to provide understanding for the need to include STEAM components into liberal arts education through continued discussion with the primary stakeholders. This establishes a sense of acceptance for said improvements based on feelings of implied mutual consent between the institution's administration and its faculty on the matter rather than perpetuating negative sentiment that this decision was made by a despotic administrator forcing these changes upon them. Moreover, these discussions will assist in the blurring of the boundaries between academic departments that have been traditionally separated in the past by discipline or subject.

For liberal arts education to increase its relevance in the twenty-first century, its faculty must extend the olive branch to departments dedicated to science, technology, engineering and mathematics to not only aid in the acceptance of the proposed changes but also how to integrate them. Specifically, the liberal arts departments should not only view the members of the STEAM department as "allies" but as vessels of knowledge that can assist in understanding these concepts in the context of curriculum and "the ways it can enhance teaching and learning" in their own department (Pannapacker, 2013). The creation of interdepartmental relationships between liberal arts programs and those within the fields of science, technology, engineering, arts and mathematics are essential as those individuals would be the resource necessary for properly understanding the content and provide ideas for how to integrate them into the curriculum or degree program in such a way that maintains the intellectual integrity of the original course or academic structure.

The intellectual key to creating liberal arts courses that contain STEAM components is the understanding how these elements fit within the structure of the course. The shape that integrated STEAM elements would assume within this educational structure would be assignments or projects, which seek to utilize these elements and numerous examples of such a usage. In particular, the uses of STEAM in liberal arts courses is limited to the imagination of the instructor or the instructional designer, which assumes that these components could utilized in a variety of contexts regardless of the subject. One such example of using STEAM in a liberal arts field is the implementation of material science and textiles in arts or theater courses to create such artifacts as "build interactive garments, sculptures, and other textile-based interactive artifacts" (Peppler, 2013, p. 39). Peppler (2013) explains that these assignments seek to enhance the aesthetics of the artifact with electronic designs, this approach places an emphasis on the creative side of the process of using electronics to enhance an artistic project. Peppler's example of mixing material science with the arts is only one of many possible applications of STEAM components in a liberal arts curriculum resulting in the transmission of STEAM concepts to students in a non-STEAM setting. Most importantly, it gives these students the ability to both creatively and critically deconstruct these STEAM concepts through the understanding of them within the confines of liberal arts curriculum to resolve a defined objective.

The highlighted example is but one use of STEAM concepts in the realm of a liberal arts course. The approach for the instructor would be the emphasis of discovery of interests that pertain to STEAM fields and to utilize them in the creation of projects for their course. This method of inclusion enables the student to take ownership for the implementation of STEAM skills that interest them. For example, a student in an arts course has an assignment might pursue the usage of technological concepts such as web design or the development of a multimedia project to describe the history of renaissance art in Europe. Assignments such as these create an overlap between STEAM concepts and liberal arts that is developed in a constructivist fashion. In addition, examples such as these not only provide the student with useful skills (web development and multimedia communication), but it makes the student receptive to ideas and concepts that they might not be exposed to otherwise because of the traditional approach to liberal arts curriculum.

From a more high-level approach to re-designing liberal arts programs would be to alter the structure of a degree program to include STEAM courses as a possible area of specialization or as selected minor required for completion of a degree. SUNY Potsdam offers a unique approach to STEAM through its offering of a student-initiated program focused on a mixture of STEAM courses (Science and the arts) with defined course purposes of focusing on Limnology and Energy Analysis (Madden et al., 2013). This program is relatively unique as it allows for the student to develop their own course structure and would be made possible through the participation between departments with different academic focuses. Its strength lies not in the knowledge transferred but rather how that knowledge is utilized. The program includes elements that seek to take this knowledge and apply it to the resolution of "thematic problems, such as global overpopulation or water shortages" (Madden et al., 2013, p. 544). The proposed STEAM centric program at SUNY Potsdam highlights the approach for creating such a program within liberal arts program as a joint venture between departments providing students with a means for utilizing their acquired knowledge as well as allowing students to select courses that relate to their interests. Most importantly, the model being offered by SUNY Potsdam is the one that should be followed and that results in the creation of joint programs designed by the faculty from both STEAM and liberal arts programs.

Much of the commentary today regarding higher education focuses on the criticisms of a liberal arts degree. It is said that these degrees lack value in the type of economy that the United States is migrating towards and lack the relevance from the perspective of course content or objectives as well. The debate has even been restructured as pitting STEAM versus liberal arts, a position which inherently places importance on one field over the other and ultimately, widens the schism between these departments beyond their intellectual concepts. The faculty and administrators within STEAM departments and their liberal arts counterparts should not be operated in academic isolation, rather, they should be encouraged to find common ground and share ideas regarding content, instructional styles or best practices.

Enhancing Liberal Arts Education with STEAM

This chapter has discussed the positive impact that STEAM could have upon liberal arts education from a variety of perspectives. Yet, a discussion of practical applications of STEAM curriculum into a liberal arts context is required to fully understand how this positive impact will manifest itself. The chief reasoning for integrating STEAM activities into liberal arts curriculum is that these activities "focuses on creativity and trans-disciplinary thinking" through the "exploration and connections made between art, music, mathematics, science, and more" (Henriksen, 2014, p. 2). The utilization of STEAM activities in a classroom setting carries positive learning outcomes through the beliefs held by a student's feeling that "using their hands" results in a better understanding of the information being presented (Ghanbari, 2014, p. 1). This usage of STEAM elements in liberal arts courses could be considered more effective because of their interactive components.

While the effectiveness of these STEAM activities is quite exciting, the focus must turn to the types of activities that could be considered STEAM centric. One example is the use of augmented reality (AR) technology being utilized in the context of music education and the simplification of complex information, such as "notations, guitar tablature and diagrams" that require repetition for the participant to remember effectively (Keebler, Wiltshire, Smith, Fiore, & Bedwell, 2014, p. 172). Augmented reality systems could enhance the learning experience of students in a music instruction courses for guitars and present information about the instruments as well as how to play them. Liarokapis (2005) conceptualized an augmented reality system to learn the guitar through the usage of "three dimensional models, sounds and textual augmentations" (p. 5) to instruct individuals on the basic elements of guitars from non-traditional method. The work conducted by Motokawa and Saito (2006) complements the position of Liarokapis as AR allows the user to use a display to showcase a "visual guide" over the real guitar that shows such information as "a model manual form for where to hold the strings" (p. 243).

The inclusion of STEAM related activities into traditional liberal arts courses could discussed at length as there are nearly endless variations that leverage the elements of science, technology, engineering, arts and mathematics as a method for instruction. In the end, the focus should not be on the STEAM activities themselves. The emphasis should be on how the activities enhance the liberal arts curriculum as a whole and also how these activities ease the costs associated with transferring information. The defining takeaway from the augmented reality example is that the technology provides a new context by which to shape the learning experience. It also highlights that the design of these sorts of activities by the student themselves could increase their understanding of the information present in the course. That is what makes STEAM instructional components inherently interesting. The emphasis on developing elements to facilitate learning can assume any form and results in the creation of a "creative and artistically infused experience for teaching and learning" (Henriksen, 2014, p. 1). Most importantly, the utilization of these elements in liberal arts courses implies that STEAM would further enhance the creative thought that is borne from a liberal arts instruction.

The Future of Liberal Arts Education

The future of liberal arts education will be one that is linked to the educational principles of science, technology, engineering, arts and mathematics (STEAM) through the inclusion of the arts component. The risk for pursuing such a path for the institution and the liberal arts programs themselves is relatively low. The prospect of additional funding through the aforementioned government channels to assist in improving the quality of STEAM education should be considered enticing and would greatly improve the likelihood of altering liberal arts content at these institutions. The changes suggested, if pursued would cause the essence of a traditional liberal arts program to change minimally, if anything, STEAM would provide another angle through which to view the world. Thus, pursuing educational initiatives such as these would improve the educational quality of these programs through the exposure to concepts and ideas that they might not have experienced otherwise. Most importantly, the purpose of a liberal arts education is meant to prepare the graduate with the skills necessary to navigate the career environment that awaits them. If we as educators are to prepare liberal arts graduates for the future, we must emphasize the inclusion of STEAM in our curriculums if they are to be competitive in a job market that is based on innovative uses of technology.

Admittedly, this future of liberal arts education is a logical path to be taken by university and program administrators as it illustrates the need for flexibility in the type of content being delivered to students. The focus of the economy has changed from an emphasis on the manufacturing of raw materials and goods to one that is technological/informational in nature. The transition to an information or knowledge-based economy requires that the academic programs bestowing these degrees must change their emphasis. Specifically, the knowledge required for understanding the economic situation or reality faced by its graduating students must change as well. Furthermore, from a conceptual or theoretical context, liberal education has went relatively unchanged since its creation and the integration of STEAM elements into the required curriculum will not only change the composition of these degree programs but it will also seek to ensure that the programs remain true to the spirit of a liberal arts program.

Conclusion

A liberal arts education is a unique experience designed to provide the graduate with an experience that is both foundational and multi-disciplinary, where the graduating student leaves the confines of these programs endowed with enhanced critical thinking and research skill sets. Unfortunately, the issue that perpetually haunts college majors of this type is a series of perceptions built upon the question of the applicability of such degrees in a twenty-first century based knowledge economy. Perceptions such as these fail to fully understand the value of a liberal arts education in the United States because of the broad spectrum of content being taught to students either virtually or in traditional classroom settings.

The arguments against funding for liberal arts programs in America or the perception of the content being irrelevant because of its lack of specialized focus is both simplistic and relatively specious. If the theoretical framework for a liberal arts education dates back to Ancient Greece, perhaps today is the time to re-evaluate the structure and core curriculum of liberal arts education as it currently appears in American institutions of higher education. After all, individuals living in the innovation economy of the twenty-first century require the ability to analyze, integrate and apply what they know to new challenges and contexts (Daynard, Ondrechen, Ambrose, & Poiger, 2013). These skills are a natural byproduct of a liberal arts education and are cultivated in these programs. It is these skills that should be emphasized when determining the liberal arts course of the future as they provide context to restructure these degrees from liberal arts programs so that they fit within this future context.

Much has been said about the re-conceptualization of liberal arts education from the basis of negative perceptions held by its detractors and the response that should be taken is to establish a well-rounded liberal arts education as a desired degree to possess in an ever-changing economic environment. In the end, the debate is not one that should not be questioning of which field of study is superior to the other. It should be about how elements of several can be used to enhance the viability of its "rival." Science, technology, engineering, arts and mathematics or STEAM integrated into liberal arts programs and curriculum hypothetically should result in the credence necessary to be received as a valued degree while maintaining its aura of lifelong learning. Liberal arts education is by all accounts adaptable considering the longevity of existence and the addition of STEAM to it will not dilute the ideals inherent to these degrees.

To better understand the Liberal Arts education of the future requires an examination of the past from a theoretical and conceptual perspective. Through understanding of the theoretical underpinnings of the past, it is possible to determine the course that is required for the future through an accentuation of specific skills (critically thinking, research and analysis etc.) honed while obtaining these degrees. As part of a knowledge or innovation economy, STEAM principles and concepts built into liberal arts education endows the users with the science and technology skills necessary to be highly sought after individuals with a diverse and deep collection of skills. While the negative perceptions are quick to ignore the essential skills these degree programs provide, such criticisms should not be ignored but rather examined and utilized to determine how to evolve the curriculum or program structure to consider the social/economic realities that individuals will enter once they graduate.

References

Barlow, R. (2011). Liberal arts vs. career majors: What's an education for? Boston University. http://www.bu.edu/today/2011/liberal-arts-vs-career-majors-what%E2%80%99s-an-education-for/. Accessed 19 Feb. 2014.

Barrow, L., Brock, T., & Rouse, C. E. (2013). Postsecondary education in the United States: Introducing the issue. *The Future of Children, 23*(1), 3–16.

Bender, T. (2013). Liberal arts, civic life, and the practicality question. *The Journal of General Education, 62*(2–3), 112–119.

Bonamici and Schock Lead 28 House Members in Support of STEM to STEAM—Founders of Congressional STEAM Caucus Seek Improvements to America COMPETES. (2013). Welcome to Representative Suzanne Bonamici. http://bonamici.house.gov/press-release/bonamici-and-schock-lead-28-house-members-support-stem-steam-founders-congressional. Accessed 15 March 2014.

Boscia, T. (2013). Serious about STEM. *Human Ecology, 41*(2), 8–11.

Chen, K., & Cheers, I. (2012). STEAM ahead: Merging arts and science education. http://www.pbs.org/newshour/rundown/the-movement-to-put-arts-into-stem-education/. Accessed 2 Dec. 2014.

Christ, C. (2012). Myth: A liberal arts education is becoming irrelevant. American council on education. http://www.acenet.edu/the-presidency/columns-and-features/Pages/Myth-A-Liberal-Arts-Education-Is-Becoming-Irrelevant.aspx. Accessed 14 March 2014.

Daynard, R. A., Ondrechen, M. J., Ambrose, S., & Poiger, U. (2013). *Liberal education at Northeastern: Strengthening the NU Core*. Faculty Senate Documents and Reports. Paper 10.

Fantauzzacoffin, J., Rogers, J. D., & Bolter, J. D. (2012). *From STEAM research to education: An integrated art and engineering course at Georgia Tech*. In Integrated STEM Education Conference (ISEC), 2012 IEEE 2nd (pp. 1–4). IEEE.

Ghanbari, S. (2014) STEAM: The wave of the future embedded in ideals of the past. The STEAM Journal, *1*(2) Article 27. doi: 10.5642/steam.20140102.27. http://scholarship.claremont.edu/steam/vol1/iss2/27.

Greene, H., & Greene, M. W. (2010). *The hidden Ivies: 50 top colleges—from Amherst to Williams—That rival the Ivy League*. HarperCollins. New York, NY.

Henriksen, D. (2014). Full STEAM ahead: Creativity in excellent STEM teaching practices. The STEAM Journal, 1(2) Article 15. doi: 10.5642/steam. 20140102.15. http://scholarship.claremont.edu/steam/vol1/iss2/15.

H.R. 51-113th Congress. (2013). Expressing the sense of the House of Representatives that adding art and design into federal programs that target the Science, Technology, Engineering, and Mathematics (STEM) fields encourages innovation and Economic growth in the United States (H.Res.51)." Congressional Record 113 (Feb 04, 2013). https://www.congress.gov/bill/113th-congress/house-resolution/51/text.

Jones, G. (2012, November 16). The Liberal Arts as a Practical Education: Helping Students make Connections between Liberal Arts Majors and Future Employment. https://www.nyu.edu/frn/publications/new.faces.new.expectations/Jones.html. Accessed 26 June 2015.

Keebler, J. R., Wiltshire, T. J., Smith, D. C., Fiore, S. M., & Bedwell, J. S. (2014). Shifting the paradigm of music instruction: Implications of embodiment stemming from an augmented reality guitar learning system. *Frontiers in Psychology, 5,* 471. doi:10.3389/fpsyg.2014.00471.

Kiley, K. (2013). North Carolina governor joins chorus of Republicans critical of liberal arts. Inside higher education. http://www.insidehighered.com/news/2013/01/30/north-carolina-governor-joins-chorus-republicans-critical-liberal-arts. Accessed 15 March 2014.

Klein, J. D., & Balmer, R. (2007). Engineering, liberal arts, and technological literacy in higher education. Technology and society magazine. *IEEE, 26*(4), 23–28.

Liarokapis, F. (2005). *Augmented reality scenarios for guitar learning.* In Proceedings of the 3rd International Conference on Eurographics UK Theory and Practice of Computer Graphics, pp. 163–170, Canterbury, UK.

Madden, M. E., Baxter, M., Beauchamp, H., Bouchard, K., Habermas, D., Huff, M., & Plague, G. (2013). Rethinking STEM Education: An Interdisciplinary STEAM Curriculum. *Procedia Computer Science, 20,* 541–546.

Morella, M., & Kurtzleben, D. (2013). The state of STEM. U.S. *News Digital Weekly, 5*(26), 11.

Motokawa, Y., & Saito, H. (2006). *Support system for guitar playing using augmented reality display.* In Mixed and Augmented Reality. ISMAR 2006. IEEE/ACM International Symposium on (pp. 243–244). IEEE.

Narum, J. L. (2013). The theory and practice of transforming undergraduate STEM education: Reflections from the PKAL Experience. *Liberal Education, 99*(1). https://www.aacu.org/publications-research/periodicals/theory-and-practice-transforming-undergraduate-stem-education.

Noddings, N. (2013). Renewing the spirit of the liberal arts. *The Journal of General Education, 62*(2), 77–83.

Pannapacker, W. (2013). Stop calling it 'digital humanities' and 9 other strategies to help liberal-arts colleges join the movement. The chronicle of higher education. http://chronicle.com/article/Stop-Calling-It-Digital/137325/. Accessed 15 March 2014.

PCAH announces new grants to stimulate inclusion of the arts with math and science. President's committee on the arts and the humanities. President's committee on the arts and the humanities. (n.d.). http://www.pcah.gov/news/pcah-announces-new-grants-stimulate-inclusion-arts-math-and-science. Accessed 2 Dec. 2014.

Peppler, K. (2013). STEAM-powered computing education: Using E-textiles to integrate the arts and STEM. *Computer, 46*(9), 38–43.

Preparing a 21st century workforce science, technology, engineering, and mathematics (STEM) education in the 2013 Budget. (2013). White House gov. http://www.whitehouse.gov/sites/default/files/microsites/ostp/fy2013rd_stem.pdf. Accessed 18 Feb 2014.

Qayoumi, M. (2011). President's column: Next steps for STEM at CSUEB. California State University—East Bay. https://www20.csueastbay.edu/news/2011/03/presidents-friends-view-031411.html. Accessed 29 March 2014.

Sawyer, R. K. (2006). Educating for innovation. *Thinking Skills and Creativity, 1*(1), 41–48.

Schneider, C. G. (2004). Practicing liberal education: Formative themes in the reinvention of liberal learning. *Liberal Education, 90*(2), 6–11.

Should STEM Become STEAM? (2013). *District Administration, 49*(2), 22. http://www.districtadministration.com/article/should-stem-become-steam. Accessed 26 June 2015.

Sigurdson, R. (n.d.). Why study liberal arts?. University of Northern Iowa. http://www.uni.edu/reineke/whystudyla.htm. Accessed 14 March 2014.

STEM: Good Jobs Now and for the Future. (2011). United States department of commerce. http://www.esa.doc.gov/reports/stem-good-jobs-now-and-future. Accessed 18 Feb 2014.

Surber, J. (2010). Well, naturally we're liberal. The chronicle of higher education. http://chronicle.com/article/Well-Naturally-Were-Liberal/63870/. Accessed 15 March 2014.

The STEM Workforce Challenge: The Role of the Public Workforce System in a National Solution for a Competitive Science, Technology, Engineering, and Mathematics (STEM) Workforce. (2007). United States department of labor. http://www.doleta.gov/youth_services/pdf/. Accessed 28 Feb 2013.

What is a 21st Century Liberal Education?. (2013). Association of American colleges and universities. https://www.aacu.org/leap/what_is_liberal_education.cfm. Accessed 15 March 2014.

Michael Marmon comes from an academic background that places much of an emphasis on technology from societal and political perspectives. His undergraduate work focused on these concepts through the acquisition of degrees in film and political science. He later fleshed out these concepts by acquiring a degree in information resources and library science. He considers himself a "lifelong" learning and is currently pursuing a PhD in Learning Technologies from the University of North Texas.

Part VI
Mathematics

The 21st Century Mathematics Curriculum: A Technology Enhanced Experience

David A. Coffland and Ying Xie

Abstract Technology has the potential to impact the content of the mathematics curriculum in secondary schools as well as the methods used to teach it. Although the United States mathematics curriculum has undergone contentious shifts of emphasis over the last half century, there are points of agreement on what needs to be learned by secondary students. However, current mathematics curricula often result in three separations in students' understanding and uses of mathematics. The first separation is the artificial distance between school and students' "real-life" mathematical experiences. The placement of related mathematical concepts into different courses is the second separation. The third separation is the lack of mathematic applications in other curricular subjects. This chapter focuses on the 21st Century Skills, students' problem posing, and technology integration as vehicles to change classroom mathematics to reconcile these separations. Together, these tools enable mathematics educators to re-conceptualize the mathematics classroom as a place where students learn mathematics by exploring the uses of mathematics across all of the subjects in STEAM education.

Keywords Secondary mathematics · Technology · 21st century skills · Problem posing · Mobile technology

Introduction

How Did We Get Here? A Brief History

Any attempt to describe a new mathematics curriculum must give some consideration to the reforms attempted over the last 60 years in the United States. These

D. A. Coffland (✉)
Idaho State University, Pocatello, USA
e-mail: coffdavi@isu.edu

Y. Xie
Northern Illinois University, DeKalb, USA
e-mail: yxie@niu.edu

© Springer International Publishing Switzerland 2015
X. Ge et al. (eds.), *Emerging Technologies for STEAM Education,*
Educational Communications and Technology: Issues and Innovations,
DOI 10.1007/978-3-319-02573-5_17

curricula can be seen as alternating shifts in emphasis between conceptual understanding and computational or symbolic manipulation skills.

Following the launch of Sputnik and the subsequent passage of the Elementary and Secondary Education Act, the curricular reforms known as New Math were developed in the 1960s (Usiskin, 2010). With its inclusion of topics such as set theory and instruction based upon formal thinking strategies of professional mathematicians, New Math was confusing to teachers and parents alike (Schoenfeld, 2007). Its increased emphasis on conceptual understanding also took some time away from traditional drill and practice activities. This led to a counter-movement that pushed for a back-to-basics curriculum. The back-to-basics movement of the 1970s sought to re-establish the centrality of computational and symbolic manipulation skills that were perceived as underemphasized in the New Math (Schoenfeld, 2007).

The back-to-basics curriculum left many students without the deep conceptual understanding of mathematics necessary to solve a wide variety of problems (Schoenfeld, 2004). Additionally, reports such as *Everybody Counts* (NRC, 1989) stated that the mathematics curriculum acted as a filter, causing the loss of "half the students from mathematics every year" (p. 7) and even higher mathematics requirements only "hold some students in class temporarily" (p. 7).

To address these issues, the National Council of Teachers of Mathematics published the *Curriculum and Evaluation Standards for School Mathematics* in 1989. The Standards detailed a curricular emphasis on problem solving with a firm base in conceptual understanding (NCTM, 1989). While not eliminating the need for computational or symbolic manipulation practice, a late addition to the document listed such practice as an item to receive decreased emphasis in the new curriculum (Schoenfeld, 2004).

It was this de-emphasis that led to another counter movement and the subsequent "Math Wars" at the turn of the century. More fully described by Schoenfeld (2004), the Math Wars became political arguments rather than scholarly debates, complete with websites providing instructions on how to lobby school boards and legislatures. From this, two camps emerged: reformists and traditionalists. It also led to an apparent dichotomy that there were only two, mutually exclusive ways to teach mathematics.

In the last decade, it has been pointed out that the apparent dichotomy was over-stated (Boaler, 2008b) and the two curricula have major points of agreement (Schoenfeld, 2004). Daro as cited by Schoenfeld (2004) provided a partial list of commonalities between traditional and reform curricula:

Add, subtract, multiply, and divide single digit numbers automatically and accurately;
Add, subtract, multiply, and divide integers, decimals, and fractions accurately, efficiently, and flexibly without calculators;
Understand the mathematics they study and use;
Use the mathematics they know to solve problems with calculators and computers;
Be fluent with the symbolic language of algebra and understand how to use the basic laws of algebra when solving mathematics problems;
Explain and justify their reasoning and understand the reasoning of others;
Reason with increasing rigor and mathematical maturity as they advance through the curriculum. (p. 282)

Although there are still disagreements between the reformists and traditionalists (Schoenfeld, 2006), these points can serve as the beginning of what a re-conceptualized curriculum might look like. The key point of agreement between traditionalists and reformists is that the current situation in mathematics education is unacceptable and changes need to be made. This can be seen in the fact that although roughly 2 million American students enter Kindergarten each year, only 839 doctorates in mathematics were awarded to U.S. citizens or permanent residents in 2012 (NSF, 2013). This indicates that those 839 doctorate recipients were the survivors of a Darwinian process that de-selected over 99.95% of students from achieving the highest possible education in mathematics. In contrast, 5870 U.S. citizens or permanent residents earned doctoral degrees in biology or biomedical sciences during 2012 (NSF, 2013).

In this context, another curricular movement began in 2009 that resulted in the development of the Common Core State Standards (CCSS). Begun in that year by a coalition of governors and state education leaders, the CCSS attempts to provide a set "of consistent, real-world learning goals" (Common Core State Standards Initiative, 2014, para. 1). As of late 2014, 43 states and the District of Columbia had adopted these standards.

In mathematics education, the CCSS call for focus, coherence, and rigor (CCSSI, 2014). Focus is defined as spending greater time and effort on fewer topics rather than merely surveying a larger number of topics. Coherence is the connection of mathematical concepts across grade and topic boundaries. A coherent curriculum must be "connected across grades so that students can build new understanding onto foundations built in previous years" (para. 5). Rigor is defined to be students' "deep, authentic command" (para. 7) of conceptual understanding, procedural skills and fluency, and application.

The Present Day: What's Lacking?

The mathematics curriculum in the United States, circa 2010, had a number of problems. Figure 1 shows the top-down character of curriculum implementation.

As indicated in Fig. 1, the curriculum is often presented to the teacher through the medium of textbooks and ancillary materials. Willoughby (2010) stated that textbooks are driven by market forces to be homogenous in content and focus on easily evaluated skills. Further, the textbook publishers' financial considerations cause the books to be written to common standards of high population states. The variety of sources of content leads to texts, and subsequently classes that attempt to cover material rather than attain a connected understanding of mathematics (Wiggins & McTighe, 2005; Willoughby, 2010). There are a number of issues with such a curriculum structure. Three of these problems can be identified as "separations" of school mathematics from important aspects of mathematical learning and use.

The first separation is that school mathematics remained disconnected from real life. The NCTM, in *Principles and Standards for School Mathematics* (2000),

Fig. 1 Top-down structure of current curricular implementation

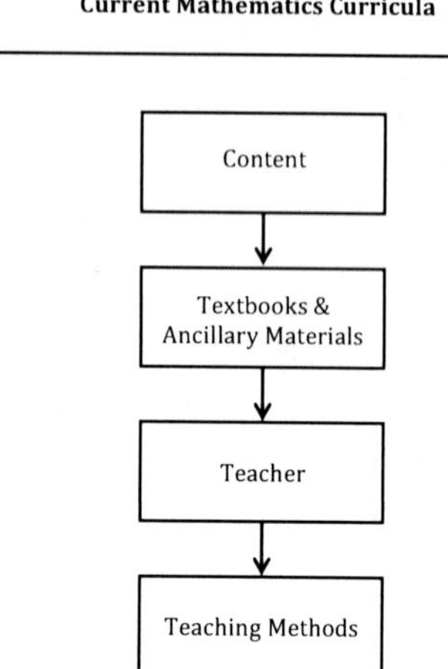

reaffirmed the need for mathematics in life and the workplace; however, nearly a decade later, Boaler (2008a) could still state:

> There are two versions of math in the lives of many Americans: the strange and boring subject that they encountered in classrooms and an interesting set of ideas that is the math of the world, and is curiously different and surprisingly engaging. (p. 5)

The second separation is that each course in school mathematics is often disconnected from other courses in the mathematics curriculum. Related topics are often placed in different courses, separated by years, teachers, and even physical distance and thus separated in the students' minds. Wiggins and McTighe (2005) provided an example of students being able to find the hypotenuse of a right triangle with legs of six and eight, but not being able to calculate the distance between the points (3, -5) and (-5, 1). This was attributed to the distance formula and Pythagorean theorem being separated into Algebra and Geometry courses without sufficient linkage between the two presentations of the same problem. This separation has sometimes been made due to curricula authors' determination of what "big picture" mathematical ideas should be included in the texts (Cuoco, Benson, Kerins, Sword, & Wareman, 2010).

The third separation is that school mathematics is divorced from other subjects in the secondary curriculum. The NRC (1989) noted that students needed to understand mathematical ideas in order to apply them to topics in science and technology. The NCTM Principles and Standards for School Mathematics (2000) echoed the idea that mathematics is needed in a technological society. Usiskin (2010) pointed out that although pure mathematics has its place in the curriculum, mathematics is in the school curriculum "because of its applications" (p. 29); however, he went on to note that math curricula "differ significantly on the relative importance to pure and applied mathematics" (p. 29). The very notion of pure mathematics in the K-12 curriculum, while perhaps necessary for higher-level mathematics learning, illustrates the separation between mathematics education and other subjects.

Preceding and somewhat paralleling the development of the CCSS, the Partnership for 21st Century Skills was created to start a national conversation between educators, policy-makers, and business leaders. Developed around student outcomes and support systems, the Framework for 21st Century Learning provides a set of curricular connections with life and career skills.

The 21st Century framework consists of student outcomes and a set of support systems (Partnership for 21st Century Skills, 2014). The outcomes are further divided into skills and themes. The 21st Century themes consist of the core curriculum topics (English, world languages, arts, mathematics, economics, science, geography, history, government and civics) as well as five interdisciplinary topics (global awareness; financial, business, & entrepreneurial literacy; civic literacy, health literacy, and environmental literacy).

The 21st Century skills represent a collection of abilities that impact all aspects of education and life. The Learning and Innovation skills address abilities such as creativity, problem solving, and communication that will benefit students in both their education and their career. The Information, Media, and Information, Communication, & Technology Literacies address learners' abilities to use technology to access information efficiently and effectively. The Life and Career Skills focus on the characteristics and traits that will make students capable of handling changing responsibilities in their personal and professional lives.

Taken as a whole, the 21st Century themes and skills apply to a wide variety of subjects in the secondary curriculum and provide connections to students' future lives and careers. With mathematics as the vehicle for enhancing students' capabilities in areas such as media literacy, information literacy, financial, and entrepreneurial literacy, a connection to students' real lives, both present and future, can be made. In this way, the 21st Century skills represent a possible solution to the first separation problem, that school mathematics is disconnected from students' real lives.

Our Recommendations for the Re-Conceptualization

In order to address the three separations within the secondary mathematics curriculum, a re-conceptualization of the mathematics curriculum is needed. However, a reconceptualization does not imply the last 25 years of curriculum reform should be ignored. Key among the ideas is the understanding that the mathematics curriculum is not a set of textbooks or activities but extends to the knowledge, skills, and dispositions that students acquire from their school mathematics experience.

In 1989, the NRC published *Everybody Counts* calling for national standards and the NCTM (1989) published their *Curriculum and Evaluation Standards for School Mathematics*. These two publications provided the impetus for the standards movement in mathematics. The NCTM (2000) revised and updated their standards in *Principles and Standards for School Mathematics*. In this text, the standards were divided into content and process standards—the former concerned with what students should learn and the latter addressed "ways of acquiring and using content knowledge" (p. 29). The process standards were reflective of Cuoco, Goldenberg, and Mark's (1996) Habits of Mind as both a curricular principle and a set of desired outcomes.

The National Research Council (2001) built upon these ideas and published a set of five strands that mathematics curricula should strive to achieve. They are:

> Conceptual understanding—comprehension of mathematical concepts, operations, and relations
> Procedural fluency—skill in carrying out procedures flexibly, accurately, efficiently, and appropriately
> Strategic competence—ability to formulate, represent, and solve mathematical problems
> Adaptive reasoning—capacity for logical thought, reflection, explanation, and justification
> Productive disposition—habitual inclination to see mathematics as sensible, useful and worthwhile, coupled with a belief in diligence and one's own efficacy. (p. 5)

These strands provide a set of the goals for the mathematics curriculum.

The Common Core State Standards (CCSSI, 2009) followed this trend as the standards addressed the content of the mathematics curriculum and the mathematical processes. The processes were built upon the NCTM's (2000) process standards and the NRC's (2001) strands in order to "describe varieties of expertise that mathematics educators at all levels should seek to develop in their students" (CCSSI, 2014, para. 1).

Rather than replace these ideas, we seek to build upon them through emphasis and addition. We propose to emphasize two aspects of mathematics instruction. These are the use of student-driven problem posing and the full integration of technology into mathematics education.

The problem-posing emphasis grows out of the NRC's (2001) strategic competency strand, specifically the ability to formulate problems. In this case, the ability to formulate problems is defined as the student's capacity to take a real-life situation and ask questions that may lead to mathematical answers. It becomes the responsibility of the teacher to guide students in the process of asking questions then identify or develop appropriate problems on the mathematical topic.

The phrase "full integration of technology" is used here to mean the application of hardware and software tools in an appropriate and seamless manner. Technology, in the form of desktop, laptop, or tablet computers should provide the tools necessary to explore today's lesson topic, provide conceptual understanding, optimize skill attainment, evaluate students' attempts at solutions, and provide the teacher with a full set of instructional and management tools.

These recommendations follow from the various incarnations of the mathematics curriculum and the disagreements over it during the last 50 years. In reports and reform documents spanning the turn of the century, both the NCTM (1980, 1989, 2000) and the NRC (1989, 2001) have called for an increased emphasis on problem solving. The Strategic Competence strand from *Adding it Up* (NRC, 2001) specifies that students should have the "ability to formulate, represent, and solve mathematical problems" (p. 5). Yet texts have often been designed to be as similar as possible to previous versions of the materials for commercial reasons (Willoughby, 2010). We recommend a more dramatic shift in the structure of the curriculum, increasing the emphasis on problem posing using the 21st Century themes and skills as a rich source of topics. The curriculum should be revised so that students explore topics such as financial, information, or media literacy to ask questions that lead to mathematical problem posing. Then students can apply technology to represent and solve those problems.

When reformers have attempted to add more concept-based activities to the mathematics curriculum, traditionalists have raised concerns that needed skills in computation and symbolic manipulation will deteriorate, possibly to the point that students will be incapable of finding solutions (Schoenfeld, 2007). We accept as axiomatic that students learn and develop skills at different rates. Therefore, we envision a curriculum that is fully integrated with technology to provide support for both conceptual understanding and the individualized practice on necessary computation and symbolic manipulation skills in an efficient manner. For such a curriculum to work in practice, it must also make available a suite of instructional and management tools for the teacher to successfully implement the individualized technology applications. By using technology in this way, we argue that the focus goal of the Common Core State Standards can be attained (CCSSI, 2009). In the following sections, this re-conceptualization of the curriculum will be described in greater detail.

The 21st Century Math Curriculum

The Re-Conceptualized Curriculum

As discussed earlier, the current math curriculum suffers from unnecessary and even obstructive separations from students' real life experience, among different subject areas within math, and other subject areas identified from the 21st century themes and skills. We envision *connection* as the main focus of a new math curriculum that we call the 21st Century Math Curriculum (21st CMC). Within this new curriculum, a math class is a place with teachers and students asking questions, posing problems, and seeking answers. The questions will urge students to make connections among today's lesson, previous life experiences, and contents from other subjects to achieve a deeper understanding of the uses of mathematics across topics. The 21st CMC will have the following three characteristics: (1) connecting mathematics course content with real life, embodying and stressing the messiness of real life); (2) connecting between related topics within mathematics, enabling and encouraging learning progression; (3) connecting math to other subjects in the curriculum, emphasizing an interdisciplinary approach. These are seen in Fig. 2.

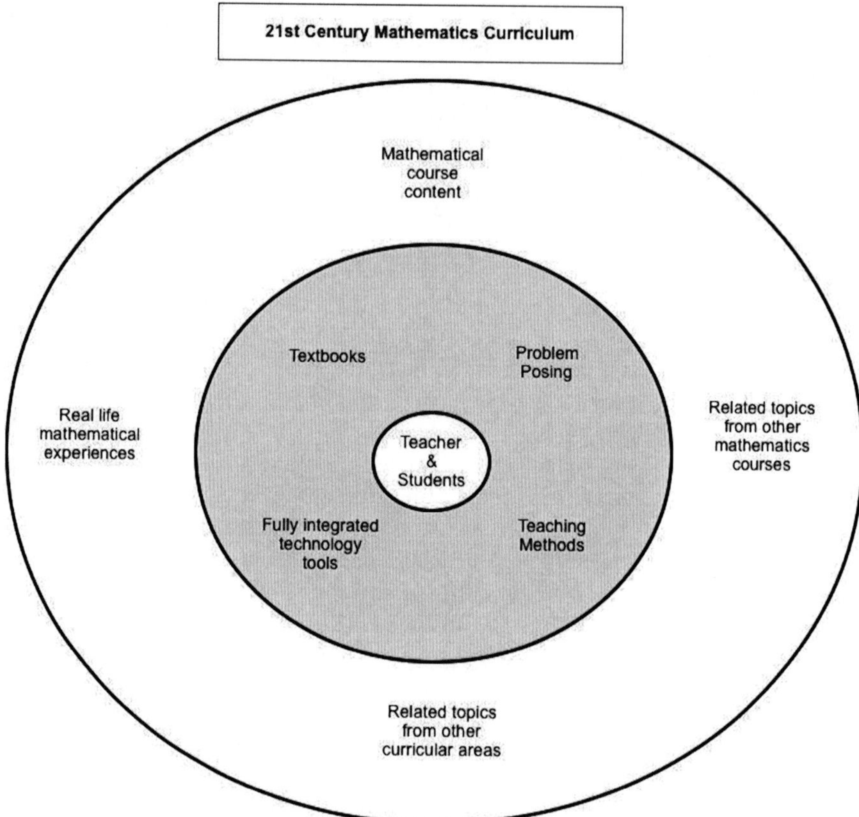

Fig. 2 The integrated structure of the 21st Century mathematics curriculum

In contrast with school mathematics curricula that lack the personal and social aspects children enjoy (Wijers, Jonker, & Kerstens, 2008), a number of previous research studies indicated that human daily lives in non-school contexts are rich of math problems and reasoning (Cole, 1996; Lave, 1988; Pea & Martin, 2010; Saxe, 1988). Esmonde et al. (2013) argued that to reform mathematics classrooms, teachers should encourage students to mathematize problems they encountered in their daily lives in model-building projects in an effort to foster mathematical inquiry and discourse. Mathematical problem-solving and problem formulation has long been recognized as the focus of mathematic reform (Kilpatrick, 1987). Silver (2013) noted that problem posing has become "a focus in the field" (p. 157). In addition to calls for using problem-posing activities to promote students' problem-solving skills, we propose that problem posing can serve as a vehicle for connecting school math with real life, sub-domains within math curriculum, and math with other subjects, as called for by the 21st century themes and skills. A problem-posing approach aligns with Jonassen's (1999) statement that "Students learn domain content in order to solve the problem, rather than solving the problem as an application of learning" (p. 218).

Problem-Posing

Since Silver (1994) identified students' problem posing as an area of interest in mathematics education, an increasing number of educators and researchers have advocated the integration of problem posing into math curriculum (e.g., Cai, 2005; Ellerton, 1986; Silver & Cai, 1996). Research studies about problem posing also sprouted. Problem posing was found to promote students' problem-solving skills, augment their attitudes toward math, improve the development of mathematical thinking, and enhance creativity (Cai & Cifarelli, 2005; English, 1998; Silver, 1994, 1997). Although problem posing is closely related to problem solving, it could bring mathematical learning to a higher level. English (2009) recognized a limitation of problem solving, especially traditional word problems, "While not denying the importance of these types of problems in the curriculum, they do not adequately address the mathematical knowledge, processes, representational fluency, and communication skills that our students need for the 21st century" (p. 352). In response, Bonotto (2013) maintained, "the problem-posing process represents one of the forms of authentic mathematical inquiry, which, if suitably implemented in classroom activities, could move well beyond the limitations of word problems...." (p. 38).

Recent research has started to show the benefit of merging students' real life experiences with their classroom learning. For example, Bonotto (2013) introduced a number of cultural artifacts and examined fifth-grade students' problem posing based on these artifacts including menus, coupons, or informational pamphlets. In the first experiment, the author found that students were able to pose problems that used information from the artifacts and in some cases, added information in their problems. Following up with a second experiment using a theme park brochure, other fifth grade students were asked to create as many solvable problems as possible. The students created a large number of problems that were mathematically relevant and solvable even with the relative paucity of language in the brochure. The author recommended using problem posing to "foster flexible thinking, enhance students' problem-solving skills, and prepare students to cope with natural situations they will have to face out of school" (p. 53). In Bonotto's study, pieces of real-life situations were brought into the math classroom. In a similar light, we propose problem posing to be used in a much larger scale and to a much larger extent in the new curriculum.

Applications

In our envisioned 21st CMC, every unit starts with authentic questions and problem posing activities based on Brown and Walter's "What-if?" And "What-if-not?" strategies (2005), students will be placed in the center of a realistic and stimulating context that many researchers called for. Starting math classes with problem-posing activities involving real-life situations allows students to see the natural connections between math and other domains required by the 21st century skills.

Math Connected to Real Life

Advocates (e.g., Gravemeijer, 1994) of Realistic Mathematics Education stressed that math learning in school should involve problem situations experientially real to students. Yet, little success was achieved toward building meaningful connections between students' lives in and out of school (Goldman & Booker, 2009). Middle school mathematics seems to emphasize students' development of procedural efficiency (Civil, 2002). McDermott and Webber (1998) petitioned for math moments "to overlap systematically with the lives of children" (p. 323). Students should be encouraged to capture their real-life mathematical phenomena and bring them to the classroom for problem conceptualization and solution. This approach could not only help them to view informal occurrences through a mathematical lens but better engage them in problem-posing and -solving activities in a contextualized manner. In the long run, such activities could cultivate students' mathematical habits of mind in order to make connections between mathematical ideas and contexts outside classrooms.

Besides having the students capture and conceptualize mathematical problems from their everyday experiences, realistic situations for problem solving can also be introduced by the teacher. For instance, a class in the Algebra II curriculum can start with questions initiated by the teacher, such as, "How much money will I need to save in order to retire?" or "What will be the average price of a car in 10 years?" In order to answer these questions, students will find that they need to use exponential equations, a topic that already exists in the current content of the curriculum. Students can model the growth of realistic exponential growth situations using spreadsheets and an iterative process. They can move from their iterative model and inductive reasoning to a single equation and satisfy themselves that it is appropriate through deductive logic. In this way, exponential growth and decay concepts found in this unit can be integrated with the 21st Century financial literacy goal of *knowing how to make appropriate personal economic choices*. Compound interest is a starting point that can lead to present and future values, inflation, time value of money, and mortgage amortizations. Using real-life questions in this way will address the Information Literacy skills of *Accessing information efficiently and effectively* and *Use information accurately and effectively for the issue or problem at hand*.

Math Connected to Other Math Courses

Similarly, connections can and should be made between different courses' content in the secondary math curriculum. Problem posing can serve as a connection for these learning progressions across grade levels. The content matter provides the opportunity to teach students, over the entire course of their secondary mathematics career, how to ask questions, pose problems, seek answers, and increase their mathematical knowledge.

An example of a posed question for one such sequence, across a variety of secondary classes, is "What can we know about triangles?" Over the course of the curriculum, students have the opportunity to address this question several times, on increasingly deeper levels. During each re-visitation of the original problem, students should pose more detailed and specific questions to attempt to answer.

Prior to middle school, the Common Core Standard 5.G.3 (CCSSI, 2009) asks fifth grade students to classify two-dimensional figures according to their properties. For triangles, this requires that students analyze the lines and angles of triangles and sort them by types of angles or how many sides of equal length are present. To meet this standard, students should be given the opportunity to explore triangles that they find or create. Discussions of student's exploration should lead to more questions such as:

1. Can triangles have one, two, or three right angles?
2. Can triangles have one, two, or three obtuse angles?
3. Can triangles have one, two, or three acute angles?
4. Are equiangular and equilateral triangles the same shape?
5. Can isosceles triangles ever be right triangles? Scalene triangles? Equilateral triangles? Obtuse triangles? Acute triangles?
6. Is there a pattern between the number of equal sides and the number of equal angles in a triangle?
7. Is there a pattern in the lengths of the sides of triangles?

Some of these questions will be answered yes or no while others may evade a firm answer. The curricular materials available to teachers should indicate which have firm answers for students of this age and which lead to explorations in secondary school (such as #6) or college (such as #1–2). After the fifth grade students participate in a triangle-based, problem-posing unit, they can partially answer their first question: What can we know about triangles? They should be aware that some knowledge about triangles is still to come in the curriculum.

In seventh grade, students can revisit the question of "What can we know about triangles?" The CCS Standard 7.G.2 requires students to construct triangles from three measures of angles or sides and determine if the given conditions result in one, multiple, or no triangles. Questions such as "Can exactly one triangle be built from a given set of information?" and "Do certain combinations of angles or lengths even result in triangles?" can be asked and answered by students.

By eighth grade, CCS Standard 8.G.7 requires students to apply the Pythagorean theorem to determine missing side lengths in right triangles. This is yet another step, albeit, only for a special case, along the path of increasing what students can know or find about triangles.

During high school, students have multiple opportunities to refine their understanding of triangles. They can pose problems about triangles such as, "What do we need to know to determine if two triangles are identical?" or "What is the minimum we need to be given to determine a triangle completely?" To answer these, students will use theorems to prove triangles congruent or apply the Laws of Sines and Cosines to solve triangles. The Pythagorean theorem will make another appearance in the form of trigonometric identities. However, rather than being an exercise in arbitrary symbolic manipulation, the identities become answers to the question "What can we show is true based upon our prior knowledge of triangles?"

Math Connected to Other Subjects

Problem situations can be designed to incorporate content from various domains identified by the 21st century themes and skills to allow the students to see the natural connection among these subject domains. For example, topics from health literacy can be integrated into a new mathematics curriculum, specifically probability and statistics. Each time a new strain of the flu is reported, how worried should students be that they might contract the illness? When a news report states there is an increase in traffic accidents in the week after the change to daylight savings time, what is the actual level of danger? And how does the increased risk compare to other behaviors? By collecting information from multiple sources, students can calculate a range of probabilities for events while attaining the Information Literacy standard via its *Evaluate information critically and competently* and *Manage the flow of information from a wide variety of sources* tasks. This topic can connect to health education as students learn what health or sanitary practices can reduce the risks they have calculated.

Another example of a cross-curricular connection is to examine the statistics and mathematics behind polling and elections. The mathematical result of the statistics that underlie the collection of data for pre-election polls is dependent on the sampling and data collection procedures. Additionally, a study of poll results combined with states' electoral votes can provide insight into how political candidates present themselves to different constituencies in different parts of the country or state. This connects to the Civic Literacy tasks of *Participating effectively in civic life through knowing how to stay informed and understanding governmental processes* and *Exercising the rights and obligations of citizenship at local, state, national and global levels.*

Statistics can also provide a connection to Media Literacy and the task of *Examine how individuals interpret messages differently, how values and points of view are included or excluded, and how media can influence beliefs and behaviors.* Many of the common statistics discussed or displayed in media may have different meanings to the general public and mathematicians. Examples of this include convenience samples, distorted graphs, the meaning of correlations, and the definition of the term "statistical significance." A new curriculum should provide students with the knowledge necessary to determine when the information presented is accurate and appropriate.

When mathematics is connected to other curricular areas, it is important that arts and language arts not be omitted as non-mathematical. The Communication and Collaboration tasks of *Articulate thoughts and ideas effectively using oral, written and nonverbal communication skills in a variety of forms and contexts* and *Use communication for a range of purposes (e.g. to inform, instruct, motivate and persuade)* provide opportunities for connections to these subjects. While geometry has always had a connection to visual arts though shape and perspective, a connection between music and trigonometry is found when examining the frequencies of musical notes and how modeling different notes using sine or cosine functions. Additionally, a critical component of any mathematical or statistical argument is to place the finding into an understandable context. By explaining, in clear, logical, and precise language the meaning of mathematics or statistics, the student can apply lessons learned in language arts and speech (rhetoric) to the field of mathematics.

In summary, within such a math curriculum starting with big questions from real-life situations or other applicable disciplines, students will likely move beyond the "spectator" attitude we usually see in current math classrooms (Hollenbeck, Wray, & Fey, 2010). As Weber, Inglis, and Mejia-Ramos (2014) pointed out, "People are more likely to continue learning and using mathematics if they learn it with understanding and see its beauty and the possibility of applying it to matters that interest them...." (p. 83).

Technology Tools

As pointed out at the beginning of this chapter, changes to the mathematics curriculum have failed to have a lasting impact. This should be expected since the modern mathematics curriculum has evolved over decades and there is resistance to changing it (Schoenfeld, 2004). As Schoenfeld pointed out, there are parts of society that resist any changes to mathematics teaching that might de-emphasize traditional skills (e.g. computation, symbolic manipulation etc.). Yet, since both reformers and traditionalists in the "Math Wars" have areas of agreement in what mathematics should be taught, perhaps a more appropriate question to consider is "How will technology enhance the learning of the 21st CMC?"

Technology Use for Math Learning

A variety of technology tools have been widely used in and out of math classrooms. In a recent review of educational technology applications for enhancing mathematics achievement in K-12 classrooms (Cheung & Slavin, 2013), educational technologies, overall, produced a positive but modest effect on mathematical achievement. The technologies that were introduced into mathematical curriculums generally fell into one of the three categories: Computer-Managed Learning (CML), Comprehensive Models and Supplemental CAI Technology. Supplemental CAI programs referred to programs that provide additional instruction to supplement traditional classroom instruction, including *Jostens, PLATO,* and *Larson Pre-Algebra.*

Computer-managed learning systems, similar to learning management systems, use computers to assess students' mathematics levels, assign mathematics materials at appropriate levels, score tests on this material, and chart students' progress, such as *Accelerated Math*. Comprehensive models combine computer-assisted instruction with non-computer activities (such as teacher-led instruction and cooperative learning), including *Cognitive Tutor* and *I Can Learn*. Among all three types of educational technology, supplemental CAI programs produced the largest effect on students' mathematical achievement (with an effect size of $+0.18$). Other types of technologies, including computer-management learning (CML) and comprehensive programs had little effect on math learning. This review also found a negative trend over a 3-decade span with the mean effect sizes for studies in the 80s, 90s, and after 2000 as $+0.23$, $+0.15$, and $+0.12$ respectively.

From this review (Cheung & Slavin, 2013), it is clear that the most effective technologies implemented in math classes are supplemental in nature so that the curriculum stayed the same. Moreover, the effect of the technologies had been marginal. Although the findings for this meta-analysis study could be disappointing, we still believe that technology tools can facilitate the implementation of the 21st CMC and in turn gradually improve students' math learning experiences and outcome. Mobile technologies, in particular, have the capability to carry out this mission.

Using Mobile Technology for the 21st CMC

Because of the unique affordances including permanence, accessibility, immediacy and portability, mobile technologies could be uniquely qualified for bringing mathematical problem situations student encounter off campus into the formal learning environment. Research on mobile practices of youth aged 13–17 shows that taking photos and videos with mobile devices is the second most popular activity after texting (Lenhart, Ling, Campbell, & Purcell, 2010). The unique features of mobile devices, such as permanence and portability allow students to collect pieces of their valued contexts with them. Researchers, such as White, Booker, Carter Ching, and Martin (2012), view students' out-of-school experiences with mathematics as a presently "untapped" arena for developing their mathematical skills. They advocate the use of handheld devices for mathematical learning by (a) making the personal mathematical and (b) making mathematics personal. Mobile technology allows for students to capture their real problem-solving situations by means of pictures, audio, and videos. In this way, problem posing from students' real life situations presents itself as having the potential to address the separation of mathematics and real life in our envisioned 21st CMC.

Besides allowing students to pull pieces of their everyday life into math classrooms for problem posing, mobile technologies can also help students to make connections about content they learned in various classes. Mobile devices are becoming increasingly popular among school students. According to the survey conducted by Harris Interactive on behalf of Pearson, 42 % middle school students own at least one mobile device including smartphones and/or tablets and another 25 % intend to purchase one in the near future (within the next 6 months) (Harris Interactive, 2013). Compared to desktop and laptop computers, such devices are cheaper and more light-weight so that students could easily carry them from one class to another. In order to facilitate a seamless association of content among different classes, cross-curricular apps could be developed to allow students to capture problems from one class, and solve the problems in another. An example might include the finding of a line of best fit in mathematics for a set of biology data examining mold growth in different levels of relative humidity. An engineering example would be the use of trigonometric functions to find the loads on a triangular roofing truss.

Mobile and similar handheld devices in classrooms designed according to the 21st CMC can load e-textbooks and run apps developed to support student concept attainment and skill development. Relative to computers and their associated software, these apps are more readily available to students both in and out of the classroom. Hence, a new, more powerful kind of e-textbook should be designed and developed to turn the envisioned math curriculum into reality. Mobile technology allows for a mathematics e-book to become a dynamic tool rather than a static presentation of skills and concepts. Dynamic demonstrations of concepts, access to expert advice on problem solving methods, immediate feedback on practice problems, and dynamic concept exploration are just some of the possibilities. Fey, Hollenbeck, and Wray (2010) recognized that one most valuable contribution of computing technologies to mathematics is "in promoting multiple representations of data and relationships and connections or topics from different strands of the discipline." (p. 273). These authors also envisioned embedding these functions into an electronic textbook. Across the range of computing technologies, e-textbooks should be equipped with sophisticated search engines, virtual manipulatives, dynamic graphing, and calculation tools. In the earlier example about exponential equations, students would be able model present and future values, inflation, time value of money, and mortgage amortizations by using a spreadsheet or graphing application immediately available via the e-textbook. Further, data such as yearly inflation rates could be downloaded from web sites directly hyperlinked in the text. The 21st CMC inevitably requires drastic changes from the textbook publishers and the design of such textbooks requires the collaboration of experts from all relevant disciplines.

Many mathematics classrooms have access to technology such as graphing calculators and desktop computers projected onto interactive whiteboards. Both types of hardware allow students to interact with mathematics content, yet both have advantages and disadvantages. Graphing calculators are a useful exploration and computation tool often found in the hands of all students in a classroom. However, they currently lack the ability to serve as flexible teaching tools—showing videos, running multiple programs, and sharing content simply and efficiently. A desktop machine connected to a projector is an excellent demonstration tool but an entire class cannot use a single computer. Tablet computers or similar mobile devices offer the possibility of achieving the best of both graphing calculator and desktop machines. A single app can turn a tablet into a graphing calculator. They are flexible tools able to run a variety of applications. Tablets have communication tools—text and video messaging, email, and wireless data networking—available for sharing of information between teachers and students. They can also display content through the projectors already in classrooms. With a lower cost than desktop or portable computers, they may become ubiquitous within schools.

A cautionary note about mobile devices is that although such devices are increasingly used in STEM classrooms (Scanlon, Jones, & Waycott, 2005), research studies are still in infancy. For example, Seppälä and Alamäki (2003) and Cortez et al. (2004) used mobile devices for communication only. A few studies have examined the effect of using mobile devices to deliver the content (Franklin & Peng, 2008) or practice the skills related to a content area (e.g. Klopfer, Yoon, & Perry, 2005; O'Malley et al., 2013; Pelton & Pelton, 2012). More sophisticated uses of mobile devices included functioning as a learning portal (Norris & Soloway, 2013; Thibodeaux, 2013) and augmenting geo-sensing reality (Huang, Lin, & Cheng, 2010; Maldonado & Pea, 2013; Wijers et al., 2008). These attempts produced varying degrees of success in these experiments. Findings associating the use of mobile technologies with academic achievement were rare. A few studies found mobile technologies and modified pedagogy helped students master some important skills, such as self-directed learning (Klopfer et al., 2005), collaborative learning, and spontaneous reaction (Norris, Soloway, Tan, & Looi, 2013). More studies are needed about the use of mobile technologies for students to connect math learning with real life, other math courses and other subject areas.

Moving Forward

Looking to the future, many of the ideas and tools needed for the 21st Century Mathematics Curriculum have already been envisioned. Others still need to be developed for classroom use. We recommend the development of these tools be aimed at mobile devices as their platform. Mobile devices are more likely than any other platform to follow the students from class to class and into their lives outside of school. We make four specific recommendations:

- Technology needs to be developed to meet the goals outlined in this chapter. Specific needs are for apps that allow exploration of mathematics concepts in all strands of the curriculum, including problem posing and problem solving. Further, a common standard that allows these apps to share student data must be developed.
- Publishers of textbooks need to differentiate their e-texts from paper versions. This should be done by adding the features discussed in this chapter. By making the electronic versions of the texts more useful to teachers and students, the demand for e-texts will be increased.
- Secondary mathematics teachers need to add more problem-posing activities into their lessons—both as an introduction to the need to learn the content and as a means to problem-solving achievement.
- The 21st Century Skills need to become embedded within the mathematics curriculum as a bridge to other subject areas as well as to students' real lives.

When these tools for mobile devices are available and fully integrated into the classroom, it is our belief that the three separation problems of school mathematics will be eliminated.

References

Boaler, J. (2008a). *What's math got to do with it? Helping children learn to love their least favorite subject—and why it's important for America.* New York: Penguin.

Boaler, J. (2008b). When politics took the place of inquiry: A response to the National Mathematics Advisory Panel's review of instructional practices. *Educational Researcher, 37,* 588–594.

Bonotto, C. (2103). Artifacts as sources for problem-posing activities. *Educational Studies in Mathematics, 83,* 37–55.

Brown, S. I., & Walter, M. I. (2005). *The art of problem posing* (3rd ed.). New York: Routledge.

Cai, J. (2005). U.S. and Chinese teachers' knowing, evaluating, and constructing representations in mathematics instruction. *Mathematical Thinking and Learning: An International Journal, 7*(2), 135–169.

Cai, J., & Cifarelli, V. (2005). Exploring mathematical exploration: How do two college students formulate and solve their own mathematical problems? *Focus on Learning Problems in Mathematics, 27*(3), 43–72.

Cheung, A. C., & Slavin, R. E. (2013). The effectiveness of educational technology applications for enhancing mathematics achievement in K-12 classrooms: A meta-analysis. *Educational Research Review, 9,* 88–113.

Civil, M. (2002). *Everyday mathematics, mathematicians' mathematics, and school mathematics: Can we bring them together? Journal for Research in Mathematics Education Monograph, 11,* 40–62. (Reston: NCTM).

Cole, M. (1996). *Cultural psychology: A once and future discipline.* Cambridge: Harvard University Press.

Common Core State Standards Initiative. (2009). *Common core state standards for mathematics.* Washington, D. C.: Common Core State Standards Initiative.

Common Core State Standards Initiative. (2014). Development process. http://www.corestandards.org/other-resources/key-shifts-in-mathematics/.

Cortez, C., Nussbaum, M., Santelices, R., Rodríguez, P., Zurita, G., Correa, M., & Cautivo, R. (2004). Teaching science with mobile computer supported collaborative learning (MCSCL). Proceedings in Wireless and Mobile Technologies in Education. pp. 67–74. IEEE.

Cuoco, A., Goldenberg, E. P., & Mark, J. (1996). Habits of mind: An organizing principle for mathematics education. *Journal of Mathematical Behavior, 15,* 375–402.

Cuoco, A., Benson, J., Kerins, B., Sword, S., & Wareman, K. (2010). Mathematics applied to curriculum development: Lessons learned on the job. In B. J. Reys, R. E. Reys, & R. Rubenstein (Eds.), *Mathematics curriculum: Issues, trends, and future directions* (pp. 265–276). Reston: National Council of Teachers of Mathematics.

Ellerton, N. F. (1986). Children's made-up mathematics problems—A new perspective on talented mathematicians. *Educational Studies in Mathematics, 17*(3), 261–271.

English, L. D. (1998). Children's problem posing within formal and informal contexts. *Journal for Research in Mathematics Education, 29*(1), 83–106.

English, L. D. (2009). The changing realities of classroom mathematical problem solving. In L. Verschaffel, B. Greer, W. Van Dooren, & S. Mukhopadhyay (Eds.), *Words and worlds: Modelling verbal descriptions of situations* (pp. 351–362). Rotterdam: Sense Publishers.

Esmonde, I., Blair, K. P., Goldman, S., Martin, L., Jimenez, O., & Pea, R. (2013). Math I am: What we learn from stories that people tell about math in their lives. In B. Bevan, P. Bell, R. Stevens, & A. Razfar (Eds.), *LOST opportunities: Learning in out of school time* (pp. 7–27). Netherlands: Springer.

Fey, J. T., Hollenbeck, R. M., & Wray, J. A. (2010). Technology and the mathematics curriculum. In B. J. Reys, R. E. Reys, & R. Rubenstein (Eds.), *Mathematics curriculum: Issues, trends, and future directions* (pp. 41–49). Reston: National Council of Teachers of Mathematics.

Franklin, T., & Peng, L. W. (2008). Mobile math: Math educators and students engage in mobile learning. *Journal of Computing in Higher Education, 20*(2), 69–80.

Goldman, S., & Booker, A. (2009). Making math a definition of the situation: Families as sites for mathematical practices. *Anthropology & Education Quarterly, 40*(3), 369–387.

Gravemeijer, K. P. E. (1994). *Developing realistic mathematics education*. CDbeta press.

Harris Interactive. (2013). New study reveals U.S. students believe strongly that mobile devices will improve education. Pearson News Releases. http://www.pearsoned.com/new-study-reveals-u-s-students-believe-strongly-that-mobile-devices-will-improve-education/#.Uyn-skl6jIZI.

Hollenbeck, R. M., Wray, J. A., & Fey, J. T. (2010). Technology and the teaching of mathematics. In B. J. Reys, R. E. Reys, & R. Rubenstein (Eds.), *Mathematics curriculum: Issues, trends, and future directions* (pp. 265–276). Reston: National Council of Teachers of Mathematics.

Huang, Y. M., Lin, Y. T., & Cheng, S. C. (2010). Effectiveness of a mobile plant learning system in a science curriculum in Taiwanese elementary education. *Computers & Education, 54*(1), 47–58.

Jonassen, D. H. (1999). Designing constructivist learning environments. In C. Reigeluth (Ed.), *Instructional-design theories and models: A new paradigm of instructional theory* (Vol. II, pp. 215–239). Mahwah: Lawrence Erlbaum Associates.

Kilpatrick, J. (1987). Problem formulating: Where do good problems come from? In A. Scheonfeld (Ed.), *Cognitive science and mathematics education* (pp. 123–147). Hillsdale: Lawrence Erlbaum Associates.

Klopfer, E., Yoon. S., & Perry, J. (2005). Using palm technology in participatory simulations of complex systems: A new take on ubiquitous and accessible mobile computing. *Journal of Science Education and Technology, 14*(3), 287–295.

Lave, J. (1988). *Cognition in practice: Mind, mathematics and culture in everyday life*. Cambridge: Cambridge University Press.

Lenhart, A., Ling, R., Campbell, S., & Purcell. K. (2010). *Tee/IS and mobile phones*. Washington, D. C.: Pew Internet and American Life Project.

Maldonado, H., & Pea, R. D. (2013). From the pilot to the classroom: Scaling science inquiry activities for mobile collaboratories. To be presented at the Integrating Mobiles into Math and Science Learning Environments Symposium. 2013 Annual meeting of the American Educational Research Association (AERA), San Francisco.

McDermott, R., & Webber, V. (1998). When is math or science? In J. G. Greeno & S. Goldman (Eds.), *Thinking practices in mathematics and science learning* (pp. 321–340). Mahwah: Erlbaum.

National Council of Teachers of Mathematics. (1980). *Agenda for action: Recommendations for school mathematics of the 1980s*. Reston: National Council of Teachers of Mathematics.

National Council of Teachers of Mathematics. (1989). *Curriculum and evaluation standards for school mathematics*. Reston: National Council of Teachers of Mathematics.

National Council of Teachers of Mathematics. (2000). *Principles and standards for school mathematics*. Reston: National Council of Teachers of Mathematics.

National Research Council. (1989). *Everybody counts: A report to the nation on the future of mathematics education*. Washington, D. C.: National Academy Press.

National Research Council. (2001). *Adding it up: Helping children learn mathematics*. Washington, D. C.: National Academy Press.

National Science Foundation. (2013). Doctorate recipients from U. S. universities. http://www.nsf.gov/statistics.sed/2012/pdf/tab18.pdf.

Norris, C., & Soloway, E. (2013). We collaborate mobile learning platform: Using mobile technologies as an Essential tool for all the time, everywhere collaborative learning. Presentation at 2013 AERA Annual Meeting.

Norris, C., Soloway, E., Tan, C., & Looi, C. (2013). Inquiry pedagogy and smartphones: Enabling a change in school culture. *Educational Technology, 53*(4), 33–40.

O'Malley, P., Jenkins, S., Wesley, B., Donehower, C., Rabuck, D., & Lewis, M. E. B. (2013). Effectiveness of using iPads to build math fluency. Online Submission.

Partnership for 21st Century Skills. (2014). Framework for 21st century learning. http://www.p21.org/our-work/p21-framework.

Pea, R. D., & Martin, L. (2010). Values that occasion and guide mathematics in the family. In K. O'Connor & W. R. Penuel (Eds.), *Learning research as a human science: National society for the study of education yearbooks* (Vol. 109, no. 1, pp. 34–52). New York: Teachers College Press.

Pelton, F., & Pelton, T. (2012). Sharing strategies with teachers: iPods in math class. In Society for information technology & teacher education international conference (Vol. 2012, No. 1, pp. 4363–4366).

Saxe, G. B. (1988). Candy selling and mathematics learning. *Educational Researcher, 17*(6), 14–21.

Scanlon, E., Jones, A. C., & Waycott, J. (2005). Mobile technologies: Prospects for their use in learning in informal science settings. *Journal of Interactive Media in Education, 2005*(2), 17.

Schoenfeld, A. (2004). The math wars. *Educational Policy, 1,* 253–286.

Schoenfeld, A. (2006). What doesn't work: The challenge and failure of the what works Clearinghouse to conduct meaningful reviews of studies of mathematics curricula. *Educational Researcher, 35*(2), 13–21.

Schoenfeld, A. (2007). Problem solving in the United States, 1970–2008: Research and theory, practice and politics. *ZDM Mathematics Education, 39,* 537–551.

Seppälä, P., & Alamäki, H. (2003). Mobile learning in teacher training. *Journal of Computer Assisted Learning, 19*(3), 330–335.

Silver, E. (1994). On mathematical problem posing. *For the Learning of Mathematics, 14*(1), 19–28.

Silver, E. A. (1997). Fostering creativity through instruction rich in mathematical problem solving and problem posing. *Zentralblatt für Didaktik der Mathematik, 29*(3), 75–80.

Silver, E. (2013). Problem-posing research in mathematics education: Looking back, looking around, and looking ahead. *Educational Studies in Mathematics, 83,* 157–162.

Silver, E., & Cai, J. (1996). An analysis of arithmetic problem posing by middle school students. *Journal for Research in Mathematics Education, 27,* 521–539.

Thibodeaux, J. (2013). A comparison over time between high school math outcomes in the implementation of iPad pilot courses (Master Thesis).

Usiskin, Z. (2010). The current state of the school mathematics curriculum. In B. J. Reys, R. E. Reys, & R. Rubenstein (Eds.), *Mathematics curriculum: Issues, trends, and future directions* (pp. 25–40). Reston: National Council of Teachers of Mathematics.

Weber, I., & Mejia-Ramos J. P. (2014). How mathematicians obtain conviction: Implications for mathematics instruction and research on epistemic cognition. *Educational Psychologist, 49*(1), 36–58.

White, T., Booker, A., Carter Ching, C., & Martin, L. (2012). Integrating digital and mathematical practices across contexts: A manifesto for mobile learning. *International Journal of Learning and Media, 3*(3), 7–13.

Wiggins, G., & McTighe, J. (2005). *Understanding by design.* Upper Saddle River: Pearson.

Wijers, M., Jonker, V., & Kerstens, K. (2008). MobileMath: The phone, the game and the math. In Proceedings of the European Conference on Game Based Learning, Barcelona (pp. 507–516).

Willoughby, S. (2010). Reflections on five decades of curriculum controversies. In B. J. Reys, R. E. Reys, & R. Rubenstein (Eds.), *Mathematics curriculum: Issues, trends, and future directions* (pp. 77–85). Reston: National Council of Teachers of Mathematics.

David A. Coffland is an Associate Professor of Instructional Technology at Idaho State University. He started his educational career as a high school mathematics teacher before moving to higher education in 2000. His research interest focuses on the integration of technology to improve mathematics learning and teaching.

Ying Xie is an Assistant Professor at Northern Illinois University. She earned her Ph.D. in Instructional Systems from Penn State University. Her current research focuses on the integration of emerging technologies and creation of cognitive tools to promote reflective thinking, higher-order learning, and knowledge construction.

Can K-12 Math Teachers Train Students to Make Valid Logical Reasoning?

A Question Affecting 21st Century Skills

Hong Liu, Maria Ludu and Douglas Holton

Abstract Valid logic is the mortar that binds all building blocks of critical thinking and analytical thinking. It is the common factor and foundation of three 21st century cognitive skills—critical thinking, analytical thinking and problem solving. According to the Common Core Standards of K-12 mathematics in the United States, proposition and basic first order predicate logic is embedded as a small topic in geometry courses. However, its applications crosscut almost all topics in STEAM (Sciences, Technology, Engineering, Arts and Mathematics) subjects. We inspected how logic is expected to be taught according to the USA K-12 Common Core State Standards and compared with the Singapore curriculum. We found that the difference is not about what should be taught, but how it is taught. The question of this chapter is: How can our K-12 teachers effectively teach logic lessons so that our students can use basic logic to connect concepts and recognize typical logical fallacies? We argued that the answer to that question affects the 21st century skills of the workforce. We hope that our analysis may shed light on the difficult problem in reforming math education and promoting 21st century skills in the workforce.

Keywords Logical reasoning · Critical thinking · Problem solving · Analytical thinking · K-12 Common core state standards · Deep learning

H. Liu (✉) · M. Ludu · D. Holton
Embry-Riddle Aeronautical University, Daytona Beach, FL, USA
e-mail: liuho@erau.edu

M. Ludu
e-mail: ludua@erau.edu

D. Holton
e-mail: douglas.holton@erau.edu

© Springer International Publishing Switzerland 2015
X. Ge et al. (eds.), *Emerging Technologies for STEAM Education,*
Educational Communications and Technology: Issues and Innovations,
DOI 10.1007/978-3-319-02573-5_18

Introduction

Formal logic is a mathematical subject that studies the forms and complexity of symbolic computations based on symbolic constructs, inference rules and tautologies. We use the term Informal Logic or Logical Reasoning to refer to the broader applications of formal logic such as inductive and deductive reasoning that are used in scientific methods as well as abductive reasoning as an inference to the best explanation (but not necessarily valid) in everyday language. Valid logical reasoning patterns can be symbolically expressed as tautologies (Truth), and logic fallacies are contradictions (False) in formal logic. Hence, formal logic provides the theoretic framework for valid logical reasoning. There is not a clear line between where informal logic ends and formal logic begins. The two only differ in their forms of expression and contexts of application.

Mathematics is based on logical reasoning (Bakó, 2002). In our calculus courses, we observed that an increasing number of first year college students could not identify the logical connections between the examples and counter-examples used for explaining concepts and theorems. Instead, they only focused on checking the calculations of the examples without paying attention to the purposes of the examples (Epp, 1987; Liu & Raghavan, 2009; Raghavan Sena, Bethelmy & Liu, 2008). Consequently, their learning is limited to algorithmic mimicking and demonstrates little understanding. Many of them did not know which one among the inverse, converse, and contrapositive of an if-then conditional statement is equivalent to the conditional statement (Epp, 2003; Hawthorne & Rasmussen, 2014). This deficiency in logical reasoning can seriously restrict students' critical thinking and analytical thinking ability. If college graduates fail to understand deductive reasoning logic, we cannot expect them to comprehend complex mathematical deductions, write correct branching statements for their programs, or draw sound conclusions from scientific experiments.

According to the Common Core State Standards (CCSS) of USA K-12 curricula (CCSSO, 2010; Charles A. Dana Center, 2014), only one chapter of basic formal logic topics is covered in a Geometry course. There is no indication that the content is mandatory to high school students. Logic education only constitutes in a small component of K-12 education, but its applications crosscut almost all subjects, as it a foundation of critical and analytical thinking. We will argue that it is one of the most critical components in K-12 education based on the Common Core State Standards and the general education of college curricula for improving competences in 21st century skills.

The authors realize that the question in our title is too fundamental, and the scope of the problem is too great for us to provide any convincing answers. Though we will provide some technical recommendations, we do not think that our recommendations can be silver bullets to help solve the macroscopic problem. In the following five sections, we divide the question in the title into the following five questions: Section "Why does logic education matter to 21st century skills?", why does logic education matter to 21st century skills? Section "What is broken in k-12 logic education?", what is broken in logic education? Section "Why is logic education challenging to both students and teachers?", why is logic education challenging to both students and teachers? Section "What logic topics should be taught?", what logic topics should be taught in K-12 schools according to standards in the U.S. and other developed countries such as Singapore? Section "How can we use emerging technology to promote logic education?", how can we use emerging technologies to promote logic education? We hope that our analysis can help the US K-12 educational policy makers recognize the urgency of promoting fundamental logical reasoning education. We also recommend using emerging technologies to effectively train K-12 mathematics teachers and K-12 students in making sound logic deductions.

Why Does Logic Education Matter to 21st Century Skills?

21st cognitive skills include critical thinking, analytical thinking and problem solving (Finegold & Notabartolo, 2011). Logical reasoning is a common factor and foundation of these three skills. We will examine two dichotomous roles logical reasoning plays—the rigorous logical thinking that is a necessary ingredient to judicious decision making, and the logical fallacies that may lead to poor decisions. We will present examples to demonstrate that logical reasoning crosscuts almost all topics in STEAM (Science, Technology, Engineering, Arts and Mathematics). Difficulties with logical reasoning skills make it harder for students to adapt to the emerging technologies and keep pace of the changes with necessary skills for the 21st century.

Rational Thinking, Critical Thinking, and Analytical Thinking

Rational thinking, critical thinking, and analytical thinking are three concepts that are sometimes confused with one another and with logical reasoning. We would like to clarify these terms before we explain why we are investigating STEAM education issues from a logical reasoning point of view.

Formal logic is a branch in mathematics, and logical reasoning is taught in mathematics, sciences, and philosophy (Devlin, 2000). Rational thinking, on the other hand, is a concept in psychology (Kahneman, 2011). Someone who is acting irrationally might be considered emotional. Rigorous mathematics education can train students to be logical, but not necessarily rational. A math genius may make irrational decisions frequently based on unchecked emotions. On that other hand, psychological consulting services can help their clients to be rational about some incidents, but not necessarily make them logical. Thus, this chapter focuses on logical thinking, not rational thinking.

There are some confusing overlaps between critical thinking and analytical thinking, as well. While critical thinking involves dialogical short-term mental processing, analytical thinking is a problem solving skill that takes a more systematic research approach. Critical thinking needs to be sensitive to where the facts end and opinions start. Analytical thinking is derived from mathematical analysis and defined as the abstract separation of a whole into its constituent parts in order to study the parts and their relations. The difference between critical thinking and analytical thinking is that the former is based on qualitative mental models, and the latter is based on quantitative mathematical models (Warner, 2014). For example, when a Boy Scout troop discusses strategies to win a competition in a national camporee, the boys need to use critical thinking skills to debate the pros and cons of all recommended strategies. The boys may need to lay out possible competition scenarios, strategies and counter strategies (if, and then) based on their previous experiences and the possible logical sequences of activities. When the camporee organizers propose the schedule and charge of the events, they need to use analytical thinking to conduct basic statistical analysis so that the event may start with sufficient participants and ends with a balanced budget.

We can rank the relationships among logical reasoning, critical thinking, and analytical thinking according to the levels of complexity and the intensity of the mental effort involved. The dependent relationship of the three types of thinking is in reverse order: Sound critical thinking depends on valid logical reasoning, and rigorous analytical thinking depends on sound critical thinking. Critical thinking is not only the ability to reason logically but the ability to find relevant material in memory and deploy attention when needed. Analytical thinking further demands a problem solver or decision maker to have the ability to decompose complex problem to its constituent components, to find the causality of components, and to evaluate the available options based on observed data and processed information.

The "Mortar" Role of Logic in Learning, Problem Solving, and Decision-Making

In his book on *Object-Process Methodology*, Dori (2002) defined the informatics hierarchy from the bottom to the top as follows: data, information, knowledge, understanding, expertise, wisdom, and ingenuity. Dori's definitions of informatics hierarchy will be useful for us to measure the depth and complexity of education materials and testing problems. It can be used to assess learning from the perspective of the complexity and depth of content (Pirnay-Dummer, 2010; Spector, 2010). Such an assessment compensates the assessment of learning based on Bloom's taxonomy of learning, which focuses only on the learning depth of the learner, but neglects the informatics complexity of the content to be learned. The first two levels of informatics require only memorization, and a computer program can save and process the low levels of informatics. It primarily depends on human intelligence to organize and digest knowledge. To gain knowledge, a learner has to invoke logical thinking activities to identify the logic relationship of the information entities in order to absorb, assimilate, process, and analyse information. Understanding and expertise are an exclusive human mental capacity. The critical thinking activities must be invoked to build a mental model (Johnson-Laird, 1983) so that it can reveal the deep cause and effect chains of the problem under concern, and this revelation can be used to predict future events. Learning is to seek understanding. A mental model is a sense-making framework that recognizes the qualitative relationship among constituents such as data, events, cause and effects. One is called as an expert in a domain if one has understood relevant constituent knowledge in the domain and is capable of applying analytical thinking skills to solve new problems in the domain using good judgment and making smart decisions. In this process, it typically requires an expert to build mathematical models that reflect the quantitative relationship of the essential components (de Jong & Van Joolingen, 2008; Spector, 2010). The models can be evaluated and validated based on an understanding of previously solved problems in the domain and used to provide the justifiable solutions, judgments and decisions. Knowledge, understanding, and expertise are three levels of informatics hierarchy that are ranked by the depth and breadth of the informatics structures.

Roughly speaking, logical reasoning can transform information to knowledge; critical thinking can transform knowledge to understanding, and analytical thinking can transforms understanding to expertise. Though such strict matches are impossible in reality due to the ambiguity and context sensitive nature of the terms, the rough matches help us to clearly illustrate the integral role of logical reasoning. In a metaphorical manner, let us map data and information to bricks and concrete blocks; knowledge, understanding and expertise to walls, rooms, and houses; and *logic as mortar*. We can imagine that logical reasoning is binding bricks or blocks to a wall; critical thinking is joining walls to rooms; and analytical thinking is connecting rooms to a house. We use logical reasoning, critical thinking and analytical thinking to learn, to make decisions and to solve problems. Both sound critical thinking and analytical thinking are based on valid logical reasoning. In conclusion, valid logical reasoning is a necessary condition for students to learn how to make judicious decisions and solve problems.

Logic and its Interdependent Relationship to STEAM

Gries and Shneider (1994) described logic as *the glue* in the preface of their book *A Logical Approach to Discrete Math*:

> Logic is the glue that binds together methods of reasoning, in all domains. The traditional proof methods—for example, proof by assumption, contradiction, mutual implication, and induction—have their basis in formal logic. Thus, whether proofs are to be presented formally or informally, a study of logic can provide understanding.

Galileo Galilee called mathematics the language of science. In his book *The Assayer* (1623), he described mathematics as follows:

> Philosophy is written in this grand book, the universe which stands continually open to our gaze. But the book cannot be understood unless one first learns to comprehend the language and read the letters in which it is composed. It is written in the language of mathematics, and its characters are triangles, circles and other geometric figures without which it is humanly impossible to understand a single word of it; without these, one wanders about in a dark labyrinth.

Two attributes of mathematics make it the language of science and distinguish it from other natural languages: (1) it is based on valid logical inferences and (2) its symbols and the interpretations of its symbols must be unambiguous. Making sound logical inferences is the foundation of Mathematics and Sciences. Engineering and Technologies are the disciplinary fields that apply sciences and mathematics to solve industrial and business problems. Logical reasoning, as the foundation of mathematics and sciences, is also the foundation of Engineering and Technology.

In medieval universities, the seven liberal arts of classical antiquity consisted of the lower level *trivium*: Grammar, Logic, and Rhetoric, which in turn were the foundation for the upper level *quadrivium*: Arithmetic, Geometry, Music and Astronomy. In modern universities, liberal arts education refers to certain areas of literature, languages, art history, music history, philosophy, history, mathematics, psychology, and science. Hence, either in terms of medieval universities or modern universities, logic is not an only interdependent component of liberal arts education, but also an essential foundation of liberal arts education.

Based on the definitions of medieval and modern liberal arts education, we will argue that logical reasoning is also a crucial element in traditional Arts subjects. In Joseph (2002), Sister Miriam Joseph thus described the Trivium of classical antiquity:

> Grammar is the art of inventing symbols and combining them to express thought; logic is the art of thinking; and rhetoric [is] the art of communicating thought from one mind to another; the adaptation of language to circumstance….Grammar is concerned with the thing as-it-is-symbolized, Logic is concerned with the thing as-it-is-known, and Rhetoric is concerned with the thing as-it-is-communicated.

Euclid of Alexandria is often referred to as the "Father of Geometry." Roughly 2400 years ago, he wrote Elements, a collection of 13 books containing information about algebra, number theory, perspective conics, geometry and logic. Euclid's work on logic reasoning impacted not only all mathematicians and scientists, but also many great politicians and artists. (Nicolay & Hay, 2015). One of America's greatest leaders, President Abraham Lincoln, once stated:

> In the course of my law reading I constantly came upon the word "demonstrate". I thought at first that I understood its meaning, but soon became satisfied that I did not. I said to myself, 'What do I do when I demonstrate more than when I reason or prove? How does demonstration differ from any other proof?' I consulted Webster's Dictionary. They told of 'certain proof,' 'proof beyond the possibility of doubt;' but I could form no idea of what sort of proof that was. I thought a great many things were proved beyond the possibility of doubt, without recourse to any such extraordinary process of reasoning as I understood 'demonstration' to be. I consulted all the dictionaries and books of reference I could find, but with no better results. You might as well have defined blue to a blind man. At last I said, 'Lincoln, you never can make a lawyer if you do not understand what demonstrate means;' and I left my situation in Springfield, went home to my father's house, and stayed there till I could give any proposition in the six books of Euclid at sight. I then found out what 'demonstrate' means, and went back to my law studies.

In his biography of Lincoln, his law partner Billy Herndon tells how late at night Lincoln would lie on the floor studying Euclidean geometry by lamplight. Lincoln's logical speeches and some of his phrases such as "dedicated to the proposition" in the Gettysburg address are accredited to his understanding of the *Elements*.

Grammar, Logic and Rhetoric are three necessary interdependent components of effective communication and all subjects of Arts depend on effective communication, which consequently depends on sound logical reasoning. In the beginning of the article "The History of Mental Models," Johnson-Laird (2005) quoted from C.S. Peirce about deduction:

> Deduction is that the mode of reasoning which examines the state of things asserted in the premises, forms a diagram of that state of things, perceives in the parts of the diagram relations not explicitly mentioned in the premises, satisfies itself by mental experiments upon the diagram that these relations would always subsist, or at least would do so in a certain proportion of cases, and conclusion their necessary, or probably, truth. (C.S. Peirce, 1931–1958, 1.66)

The definition of (logical) deduction given by C.S. Peirce pointed out the crucial function of logical deduction—to make inferences in our thinking and reasoning. A valid logical inference makes a valid conclusion from the premises, and invalid logic inference makes an invalid conclusion from the premises. If college students cannot distinguish valid logical inferences, or if they maintain logical fallacies, they are building their academics on sinking sands because *Logic*, unlike any other subject, crosscuts all subjects in STEAM education.

Logic Education and 21st Century Skills

Critical thinking, analytical thinking, and problem solving abilities are important 21st century skills (Finegold & Notabartolo, 2011). Partnership for 21st century Skills (www.p21.org) defined Learning and Innovation Skills in terms of Critical Thinking, Communication, Collaboration, and Creation. Additionally, the first set of skills listed by the ETS CPPI (Collegiate Personal Potential Index) are Critical Thinking and Problem Solving. The second item is to test the ability to form opinions based on logic and facts, (i.e. logical reasoning ability).

We argue that logical reasoning is a *common factor and core foundation* of critical thinking, analytical thinking, and problem solving skills. Improving logical reasoning education at the middle school level may thus help improve K-12 math education and 21st century skills. Though we look at the issues from different levels of granularity and perspectives, we will argue that focusing on this core competency has the following benefits:

1. One may measure and compare the logical reasoning abilities of students in different countries based on existent data.
2. Logical reasoning is a relatively small component such that we can propose a feasible plan to improve it.
3. We can assess the long-term performance on STEM topics between a control group of students and a group of students who have taken intensive and effective logic education.

Students may have difficulty with critical thinking and analytical thinking because they are not free from the troubles of the fundamental logical thinking. Hence, instead of focusing on critical thinking and analytical thinking directly as others have done (Finegold & Notabartolo, 2011), we focus on foundational instructions in logical reasoning to improve STEAM education and prepare students for 21st century skills.

What is Broken in K-12 Logic Education?

We begin with a literature review of difficulties people have with logical reasoning tasks. Then we will present our results of testing a logic task (Wason Selection) in four calculus classes. Lastly, we will use an example to demonstrate the chain effect of invalid logic education in calculus.

Literature Review

Deductive logic appears deceptively simple if we look at it in a nutshell (Guha, 2014). The two mathematics forms in Formal Language are: Modus Ponens ($p \rightarrow q$, p; $\therefore$ q) and Modus Tolens ($p \rightarrow q$, $\sim q$; $\therefore$ $\sim p$). Few people admit that they have any problems about the two forms of deduction. However, the British psychologist P. N. Johnson-Laird put it in 1975: "It has become a truism that whatever formal logic may be, it is not a model of how people make inferences." (p. 7.) A common estimate is that under 5% of people use "correct" logic spontaneously (Epp, 1986; Johnson-Laird, 1975). Epp (1986) observed that very few of her students have an intuitive feel for the equivance begween a statement and its contrapositive or realized the converse of a true statement could be false. Futhermore, Epp (2003) and Bakó (2002) observed that many students of pure mathematics could not write proofs properly. It is mainly because they failed to see the logical moves that underlie the steps of a mathematical proof (Guha, 2014).

Martin and Harel, (1989) asked 39 prospective elementary teachers to judge the mathematical correctness of inductive and deductive verification statements. 52% of the tested students accepted incorrect deductive arguments as valid for unfamiliar statements, and more than 33% of the students did not understand why a counterexample may satisfy the conditions of a conjecture but violate the conclusion. 18% believed that only one counterexample is not sufficient to disprove a statement. Martin and Harel found that people consider a proof as "what convinces me." (pp. 41–42).

Senk (1985) tested 1520 students on proof writing in geometry classes. Her conclusion was that only 30% of the students taking geometry courses that teach proof were able to reach a 75% mastery level in proof writing. Brumfield (1973) tested 52 students that had taken accelerated geometry course in the previous year and have been placed in an AP Calculus course. 81% did not attempt to write a proof, and less than 10% were correct in writing a proof. The conclusion of the testing was that even students in advanced courses get insufficient meaningful mathematics out of the traditional proof-oriented geometry course. Driscoll (1983) concluded that students needed to be properly instructed to understand the nature of proof, and how it is different from common (everyday) argumentation.

Wason Selection Task to College Students

The Wason Selection Task (http://www.philosophyexperiments.com/wason/) tests the correct application of conditional statements (e.g. the equivalence of contrapositive statements). Wason's original research in 1966 indicated that not even 10% of subjects found the correct solution in this task. This result was replicated in Evans, Newstead and Byrne (1993).

The first author gave an abstract version and an intuitive version of the Wason Selection Test to four calculus classes that have 112 students. Both versions are based on the same conditional statements and a participant can get correct answers if he or she can identify the original statement into its equivalent contrapostive statement. The abstract version is to check if the four cards follow a rule given as a conditional statement. When this abstract version was given, only seven students found the correct answer. The intuitive version is to check two people or two photo IDs if the law about legal drinking age is followed. Almost everybody got it correctly. The testing result confirmed the discovery in Wason (1966) and Evans et al. (1993) that less than 10% of students could find the correct answer. When the same test was given to the college juniors and senior in an upper level elective class in Mathematical Modelling and Simulation (Liu & Raghavan, 2009), five out of 16 of them answered the abstract version correctly. The test confirms what Johnson-laird claimed that "correct" logic is often not spontaneously used (Johnson-Laird, 1975; Epp, 1986). Scientists and philosophies can make mistakes sometimes when giving hasty answers without pen and paper (Kahneman, 2011).

Chain Effect of Invalid Logic Deduction in Calculus

The example given below illustrates the chain effects of invalid abductive logical reasoning. Similar observations about the college students' confusion between necessary and sufficient conditions can be found in Epp (1986). After students learned the concepts of infinite sequences and series, convergence and divergence, they were taught a theorem as follows:

Theorem :

(Statement A) : *If a series* $\sum_{n=1}^{\infty} a_n -$ *is convergent*

then,(Statement B) : $\lim_{n \to \infty} a_n = 0.$

The theorem says that the statement B is necessary for the statement A. Students learned Statement B1 is a True Statement as an instance of B.

$$Statement\ B1 : \lim_{n \to \infty} 1/n = 0.$$

Now, we polled the classes for the question whether the Statement A1 must be true.

$$Statement\ A1 : \sum_{n=1}^{\infty} 1/n\ (called\ harmonic\ series)\ is\ convergent.$$

Unfortunately, the majority of our students agreed that the Statement A1 must be true. They believed that the theorems above can deduce the conclusion that the harmonic series must be convergent, which is not correct. This is a very typical case of misunderstanding where students are confused between a conditional statement and its converse statement. We know that if our students are insensitive to the difference of sufficient conditions and necessary conditions of theorems, confused about the converse, inverse and contrapositive statements, it will be very hard to explain to them about the logical connections of theorems and concepts even when we give them many examples and counterexamples. This leads to a chain effect: if students fail to recognize the difference between deductive and abductive logic inferences, a valid logical inference and a logical fallacy, they cannot even understand basic calculus knowledge about the relationship between convergent sequences and series.

Abductive reasoning is a form of logical inference that goes from an observation to a hypothesis that accounts for the observation, ideally seeking to find the simplest and most likely explanation. In abductive reasoning, unlike in deductive reasoning, the premise is necessary, but probably insufficient to entail the conclusion. That is to say the conclusion is not guaranteed from the premise. One can understand abductive reasoning as *"inference to the best explanation."* In summary, students who made the wrong conclusion applied the invalid *abductive* logical reasoning. The mistake can be more clearly illustrated by the following simplified statements and everyday example.

Major Premise: If A is true, then B is true.
Minor Premise: A1 is an instance of A, B1 is an instance of B, and B1 is true.
Conclusion: A1 is true.
A: It is raining in a local community,
B: The lawns in the community are wet
Theorem: If A is true, then B is true.
B1: My lawn is wet, (B1 is an instance of B)
A1: It is raining outside my house (A1 is an instance of A).

Contrary to a previous logically equivalent math problem, most students could realize that *my lawn can be wet (B1) because my sprinkling system is on.* A1 (*it is raining*) is just one of the many valid explanations of B1 *(My lawn is wet)* and A1 is not necessary true even the statement B1 is true.

Why is Logic Education Challenging to Both Students and Teachers?

In this section, we review why logic education is challenging to K-12 students and teachers. Next, we take a hard look at the status quo implementation of logic education in the United States, and why most people do not develop valid logical thinking naturally. Finally, we scrutinize the negative feedback system of logic education in USA.

Challenges in Teaching Proofs in Geometry

Two Dutch educators, Dina van Hiele-Geldof and Pierre van Hiele, claimed that their students performed poorly in secondary geometry, which focuses on deductive reasoning and proof, because students did not develop the required high level logical thinking during the elementary grades (Mason, 2014). They developed a model, known as the van Hiele levels, that identifies the "levels of thinking" and suggested the five recurring instructional "phases":

1. Level 0 "Visualization": the learners should be able to visual recognize the shapes by their appearance as a whole
2. Level 1 "Analysis": the learners should be able to analyse and describe the geometrical shapes by using their properties
3. Level 2 "Abstraction": the learners start using deductive reasoning to answer to the question "why...", by making logical connections and understanding the relationships between the properties
4. Level 3 "Deduction": the learners should be able to combine simple proofs to form a system of formal proof. This is the level of understanding the Euclidian geometry.
5. Level 4 "Rigor": the learners are able to work with abstract geometric systems. This is the level of understanding the Non-Euclidian geometry.

The van Hiele levels have five properties: Fixed sequence, Adjacency, Distinction, Separation, and Attainment. Van Hiele believed that the property of separation was one of the main reasons for failure in geometry. A teacher who is reasoning at one level cannot be understood by a student reasoning a lower level. Even if the teacher believes that they are expressing themselves clearly and logically, the teacher may not understand how the student is reasoning, and the learner-teacher connection is not established.

Why Doesn't Valid Logical Reasoning Come Naturally?

In the book *Thinking Fast and Thinking Slow* (2011), the renowned psychologist and Nobel laureate Daniel Kahneman defined two types of thinking systems as follows: "System I operated automatically and quickly, with little or no effort and no sense of voluntary control. System II allocated attention to the effortful mental activities that demand it, including complex computations. The operations of system II are often associated with the subjective experiences of agency, choices and concentration (p. 18.)". System I includes some components used for everyday reasoning such as associative priming based on resemblance and continuity in time and space. Rational thinking that includes slow and deep logical reasoning is part of System II. A statement such as "since the lawn is wet, it must have rained" is the type of abductive inference System I might make based on everyday experiences and patterns of the converse type: "if it rained, then the lawn is wet." However, the first statement is not valid logically. The lawn can be wet because the sprinkler was on. A student who has been effectively taught basic logic can be vigilant to the possible falsehood of a converse of a valid entailment statement. This abductive logic example is a typical example of System I thinking, using the wrong logic based on the logic converse association.

It is clear that it takes the effort of the System II thinking to identify the logic mistakes of abductive reasoning. As Kahneman emphasized in this book, our System II is a lazy system and it does not automatically work unless we identify the need to invoke the system. Most mathematical problems, especially the math courses above college algebra, require system II thinking to gain understanding. However, too many students get used to the easy learning style such as simply checking calculations between steps, remembering formulas, and mimicking procedures, with little to no conceptual understanding. An important question for us is: can we make our students respond to our teaching and queries with more "surprise" in classes and cultivate them to ask more "why" questions? The students who are trained to observe everything under a logical reasoning lens will certainly ask why frequently.

Negative Feedback Loop Discourages Logic Learning

Several factors may discourage the effective teaching and learning of logical thinking skills in K-12 schools and universities:

1. Many students and many teachers cannot identify typical logical fallacies.
2. Treating student feedback as a customer satisfaction score discourages teachers from teaching topics that are more difficult and require more logical thinking effort on the part of students.
3. Teachers have to "teach to the test," and the tests may not adequately assess logical thinking and other critical reasoning skills.

A negative feedback system develops in which the poorer a student is in logical reasoning, the more likely he or she will choose subjects that require little logical reasoning to succeed in the courses. The more students are poor in logical reasoning in a school, the more likely the teachers in the school will teach shallow knowledge that has little challenges in logical reasoning.

When students take a calculus course with deficiency in algebra (e.g. do not know how to solve quadratic equations), they may eventually catch the missing knowledge in calculus course. However, it is not likely that they can automatically catch their logical fallacies in an upper level course that requires sophisticated logical reasoning. The ability to conduct logical reasoning in daily life reflects the competences of the person. This ability is deep rooted in one's thinking habit. It has to be cultivated gradually in school, in family, and in other learning environments.

What Logic Topics Should be Taught?

In this section, we will inspect the logic education components of several curricula based on the USA Common Core State Standards (CCSS) and the Core Plus Mathematics of CCSS, and then compare the topics with those in Singapore curricula. Based on the inspection of CCSS and Singapore curricula, we will make some suggestions.

Logic Education Based on the Common Core Standards in USA

The High School Integrated Model Course Sequence Alignment to Core-Plus Mathematics by Achieve, Inc. (CPMP, 2008) described the objectives covered in section C of Fundamentals of Logic as follows:

> This relatively short unit formalizes the vocabulary and methods of reasoning that form the foundation for logical arguments in mathematics. Examples should be taken from numeric and algebraic branches of mathematics as well as from everyday reasoning and argument. While this unit emphasizes the application of reasoning in a broad spectrum of contexts, the following unit will mainly apply logical thinking to geometric contexts.

These two logic education objectives of CPMP, 2008, their corresponding learning outcomes and covered course units are given in table 1:

Core Plus Mathematic of CCSS (CPM CCSS, 2011) provides the main page references in Core-Plus Mathematics Courses 1–3 and Course 4: Preparation for Calculus for each of the CCSS mathematical content standard. The CMP CCSS, 2011 emphasizes that the students should be capable of reasoning abstractly and quantitatively, constructing viable arguments and critiquing the reasoning of others.

Table 1 CPMP, 2008, course units covers the logic education objectives

Objectives	Learning outcomes	Course units
Use mathematical notation, terminology, syntax, and logic; use and interpret the vocabulary of logic to describe statements and the relationship between statements	Identify and give examples of definitions, conjectures, theorems, proofs, and counterexamples	Course 2 unit 3 and course 3 units 1 and 3
	Describe logical statements using such terms as assumption, hypothesis, conclusion, converse, and contrapositive	Course 3 units 1 and unit 3
	Recognize syllogisms, tautologies, and circular reasoning and use them to assess the validity of an argument, is not addressed	*Not addressed*
Make, test, and confirm or refute conjectures using a variety of methods	Distinguish between inductive and deductive reasoning; explain and illustrate the importance of generalization in mathematics	Course 3 unit 1
	Construct simple logical arguments and proofs; determine simple counterexamples	Course 3 units 1 & 3, course 2 unit 3
	Demonstrate through example or explanation how indirect reasoning can be used to establish a claim	Course 3 unit 1
	Recognize and avoid flawed reasoning; recognize flaws or gaps in the reasoning used to support an argument	Course 3 unit 1

Comparison with Singapore Curriculum

We compare how logic topics are taught in Singapore and several states in the United States. The PISA test of Reading, Mathematics, and Science Literacy (Fisher, 2010) showed the U.S. now ranks 25th in math, 17th in science, and 14th in reading, while Shanghai China ranks number one, and Singapore ranks number two in all three categories (also see Carnoy & Rothstein, 2013).

The Singapore curriculum aligns with US standards but has different teaching methods (Singapore Academy, 2011). In the US Curriculum, a large number of math concepts are covered and revisited each year. In this way, the students that did not acquire mastery in a concept would have the chance to understand the topic in the next year. Unfortunately, this creates differences in the level of understanding of a concept, and in the same grade level there are students which do not fully internalize the concepts and see this spiralling process only as a repetition and do not sense the full complexity of it. By contrast, the Singapore Math Curriculum covers a less number of concepts each year, but allocates a greater amount of time per each concept to be taught. They are taught to an increasing depth and give students the possibility to reach mastery before introducing new concepts.

Barry Garelick described some other unique features of Singapore Math in the *San Diego Jewish Journal* (2011) as follows:

> … the books (referring to Singapore textbooks) are noticeably short on explicit narrative instruction. The books provide pictures and worked out examples and excellent problems; the topics are ordered in a logical sequence so that material mastered in the various lessons builds upon itself and is used to advance to more complex applications. But what is assumed in Singapore is that teachers know how to teach the material—the teacher's manuals contain very little guidance. Singapore's strength is the logical consistency of the development of mathematical concepts. And much to the chagrin of educators who may have learned differently, mastery of number facts and arithmetic procedures is part and parcel to conceptual understanding.

Besides the math curricula in Singapore, we also compared the math curricula of P. R. China with that of the United States. There are no significant differences about which logical reasoning topics are included in the curricula and textbooks among the three countries. However, we found that whenever it is proper to apply, the Chinese textbooks include mathematics proofs in both lessons and homework exercises. We checked the sample test problems from some Singapore schools as well as Chinese schools and found that their tests emphasize mathematics proofs far more than those in the United States. But for the most part, *the differences between the three countries are not about what should be taught, but how it is taught.*

We propose to start logic education in early grades and insert small logic education modules for middle school (Bakó, 2002). Similar to the Singapore curriculum, each module takes about 2–3 weeks and offers adequate drills and exercises to assure deep learning. We need to increase mathematical proof exercises in homework and add more weight of mathematical proofs in math exams. In addition, logic should be taught by a combination of intuitively visual expressions and rigorous formal expressions.

Critical Topics for Logical Reasoning Education

Geometry provides a rich context for the early development of mathematical thinking. It builds up the thinking process progressively: starting with lower order thinking processes, such as identifying the shapes, and advancing to higher level thinking processes, such as investigating properties of shapes and then solving geometric problems and creating patterns. In addition to the relevant topics of logic education included in K-12 Common Cores above and State standard in appendix 1–4, we would like to recommend and emphasize the following three components as mandatory:

1. Learn how to justify each step of deduction either in algebra and geometry and give plenty of exercises that apply deductive reasoning, for example, direct and indirect (proof by contradiction) proves in Euclidean Geometry and algebra (Agile Mind, 2011; Moore, 1994; Gift of Logic, http://www.giftoflogic.com/faq.html)
2. Identify logical fallacies (https://en.wikipedia.org/wiki/List_of_fallacies).
3. Learn abductive reasoning in a basic statistics context (http://en.wikipedia.org/w/index.php?title=Abductive_reasoning&oldid=636486476).

Critical School Years for Logical Reasoning Education

A critical transition in a child's cognitive development occurs during the middle school years. According to Piaget's four stages of cognitive development, children at age 11 or 12 enter the fourth and final stage of cognitive development, called the formal operational stage. Children at pre-adolescence age from 7 to 11 are at the third stage of cognitive development called concrete operational stages. At the third stage, children mostly use inductive reasoning, drawing general conclusions from personal experiences and specific facts, adolescents become capable of deductive reasoning, in which they draw specific conclusions from abstract concepts using logic. This capability results from their capacity to think hypothetically. Children at the third stage are able to incorporate inductive reasoning, but struggle with deductive reasoning, which involves using a generalized principle in order to try to predict the outcome of an event. During the final stage at middle school years, children show significant growth in their ability to think abstractly, use advanced reasoning skills, make hypotheses and inferences, and draw logical conclusions. Ideally, the middle school years provide educators with great opportunities to foster good logical thinking and mathematical practices.

How can we Use Emerging Technology to Promote Logic Education?

Logical thinking crosscuts all disciplinary fields in STEAM. Applying rigorous logical reasoning to prove mathematics theorems, draw scientific conclusions, and make sound arguments in debate is one of most important 21st century skills for future American workforce. We argued in Section "What logic topics should be taught?" that the middle school years are the critical time for foster the children in sound logic education. In this section, we will focus on the training of both middle school mathematics teachers as well as middle school students directly. We selected the following three tasks as our top list to promote logical reasoning education.

1. Develop innovative training materials for formal logic education and mathematics proofs, including high tech virtual classroom simulations to train pre-service and in-service K-12 math teachers.
2. Design different logic training games for middle school boys and girls that are not only attractive to them according to their gender differences, but also seamlessly synergize visual intuitiveness and mathematics rigor to foster logical thinking. For example, design games that analyse and using one given concept in its algebraic form, geometric (visual) form, application form, etc. Exposing the player to different angles towards the same concept builds connectivity.
3. Offer short-term summer workshops and online training to help K-12 teachers and students improve their logical reasoning skills.

Many colleagues in K-12 education research or practice have probably been working on those tasks for years or decades. Our perspective of the following discussion is how emerging technology can be used to make the teachers' training more effective and students' learning more engaged.

Use Education Technology to Offer Easily Accessible Logic Courses for Middle School Teachers

The quality of teacher training will be crucial to the success of the teaching logical reasoning to achieve new CCSS in math. If we cannot assure that our math teachers are well trained in logical reasoning and mathematics proofs, it will be in vain to promote logical reasoning education for the students in K-12 schools. As we argued in the section above, middle school years are the most critical time to properly train the students in logical thinking, and the training for middle school mathematics teachers is paramount. However, three conditions are necessary to make the training or retraining of middle school math teachers successful: (1) Grants and other resource for covering the cost of the training including the stipends to teachers; (2) Training materials in formal logic and mathematics proofs that have been proven effective and feasible; (3) Facility and proven education technology to be used to train and test the readiness of the teachers to teach real middle school students.

It requires an interdisciplinary team of mathematicians, cognitive scientists, experts in pedagogy and teacher education to work together to develop quality training materials and offer effective training programs to middle school teachers. Federal and state government grants (NSF, NIH, HHMI, etc.) are the primary sources of funding to support these types of projects. Those grants have attracted many college teachers in to collaborate with K-12 teachers to train new K-12 teachers and provide summer STEAM workshops for K-12 students. The sponsored projects have already made noticeable impacts to motivate college bounded students, especially minority students to make STEAM career choices. We observed that the government grants helped to make abundant STEAM education materials, mostly online multimedia materials freely available to K-12 teachers. Unfortunately, those materials are underused because there is inadequate training and incentive for K-12 teachers to use them.

Design and Develop Attractive Games for Middle School Boys and Girls to Foster Logical thinking

We all know that computer games are popular with the post-millennial generation. Most children in this generation have learned how to play computer games before they learned how to write. The testing results from two different versions of Wason Selection Tasks (one concrete version and the other abstract version) indicate that we can effectively teach logical reasoning by offering intuitive examples to help students understand equivalent abstract examples. Visual animations in video games can scaffold learning to abstract mathematics ideas if the game is properly designed. If the education content can mix seamlessly with the entertainment, the game can both attract the children and learn valuable knowledge.

There are so many different games to attract the different age groups of boys and girls. An interesting research problem is to find how many effective educational games were designed for middle school geometry and algebra and how much (if any) content was targeted at formal or informal logic education. We divide the education games into two basic categories in terms of the targeted users: the first category is for unsupervised learning that targets massive independent student users; and the second category is supervised learning that targets primarily to trained instructors besides students. We found that most of logical educational games of the first category are bipolarized: one subtype is the game oriented websites that have the fun of games but lack of rigorous educational contents; the other subtype is education-oriented websites that have the rigorous educational lessons, but are short of the attraction of real games. The contents of game-oriented websites (http://www.mathsisfun.com/ and www.learninggamesforkids.com) are mostly puzzles. On the contrary, the contents of the education-oriented websites (https://www.brainpop.com/ and www.shmmoop.com) include formal lessons for logical reasoning and proofs. Those websites use some funny animations and stories relevant to middle school kids to attract their attention. This approach, unfortunately, has only limited success to attract students like real games. The problem of the second category of educational games is their limited accessibility due to the instructional costs. For example, the SUCCEED workshops of Shodor (www.shodor.org) provide K-12 students the opportunities to investigate forensics and scientific computing through logical reasoning and discovery. The program emphasizes hands on investigations and agent-based simulations (Agentsheets and NetLogo). GUTS (code.org/curriculum/mss), another computer science education program provides logic training lessons to middle kids by using the agent-based programming platform StarLoGo (http://education.mit.edu/projects/starlogo-tng). The learning environment of peers, the context of intuitive applications and the timely feedback of these programs contribute to the success of engaged learning.

It is much more challenging and expensive to design and develop effective education games for unsupervised student users than those for trained instructors. The former requires the collaboration of mathematicians, cognitive scientists, experts in pedagogy and teacher education, computer programmers and software engineering. However, the impact of the former is much broader than that of the latter in terms of the number of users. A successful education game of the first category can potentially help millions of middle school children to use deductive correct logic correctly. We cannot understate its impact to STEAM education.

Offer Problem-Based Learning Summer Programs and After School Programs to Foster Logical Thinking

Educational technologies and online and blended courses have started to transform the paradigm of education in both colleges and K-12 schools (New Media Consortium, 2014). The Florida Virtual School has become an attractive option for K-12 students to take their favourite subjects online. Now, K-12 students can access thousands of video tutorials for their math and science courses through websites such as the Khan Academy. At the current stage of educational technology, we do not think that most of middle school children can gain valuable education from online material without adult supervision.

Parents play a paramount role in their children's education, and they should be the owners of their own children's education. If parents cannot schedule time to serve as tutors or hire tutors, there are plenty of free or inexpensive after school academic enrichment programs to help children. Other education technologies such as adaptive learning environments, intelligent tutoring programs, etc. can be used to reduce the cost of personalized learning. Courtney (2014) predicted that intelligent computer aided education systems can make personalized education available to more and more students in the next 10 years.

Many prestigious research universities offer summer academic enrichment programs (see Duke TIP Talent Search, http://tip.duke.edu/) to talented K-12 students. Those summer programs provide excellent problem-based learning opportunities for the participants. Many of them provide effective logical reasoning training under fun application context. Unfortunately, those programs are very selective based on the applicants' academic competence and only small percentage of families can afford. We hope more regional universities, liberal arts colleges, and community colleges offer similar problem-based summer programs with focus on logical reasoning education to middle school children in their local communities. In order to provide equal learning opportunities, those summer programs should apply for government grants to subsidize partial or total tuition so that children from low income families can participate. The United States has about 5000 colleges. If most of those colleges will contribute their spare facilities and faculties to offer summer academic camps, the collective impact to US K-12 education, especially CCSS, is immeasurable.

In the summer of 2013, Dr. Andrei Ludu and the first author offered a summer SeaPerch underwater robotics camp to 22 commuting middle school kids. Computer Animation and hands-on experiments were used to illustrate how Archimedes used physics principles and logic to discover the crown mystery. The kids first learned *if the crown is made of pure gold, then its volume should the same as the original gold bar that the king gave.* They understood that the same amount of water should flow out when the gold bar and crown were submerged into two equal-sized vessels full of water. The students got a sense of eureka when they saw that the crown expelled more water out of the vessel. They instantly identified the contrapositive logic claim. *Since the volumes of the crown and gold bar are not equal, the crown is not made of pure gold.*

Conclusion

In summary, this book chapter analysed the relationship between logical reasoning, critical thinking and analytical thinking. We argued that the soundness of upper level critical thinking and analytical thinking depends on valid logical reasoning. To address the problem of logic education deficiencies, we investigated the issue from a microscopic level based on our first-hand observations in our own math classes. In order to find feasible remedies, we also compared how logic is taught in the K-12 math curricula of other countries, especially Asian countries such as Singapore and P.R. China. We found that the difference is not about what logical reasoning topics should be taught, but how those topics are taught. Our observation is that inadequate logical reasoning education is at the root of unsatisfactory overall USA K-12 mathematics education. The question in our title is fundamental and the scope of the problem is nationwide. It is beyond the scope of this book chapter and our ability to provide any convincing answers to the questions that we brought forth. We hope that our analysis may shed light on the difficult problem in reforming American math education and promoting 21st century skills in the American workforce.

Acknowledgements The authors would like to thank Dr. Michael Spector at University of North Texas for our casual conversation about logic education and its impact to American math education inspired us to write this book chapter.

References

Bakó, M. (October 2002). Why we need to teach logic and how can we teach it? *International Journal for Mathematics Teaching and Learning,* (ISSN 1473-0111.). http://www.cimt.plymouth.ac.uk/journal/bakom.pdf. Accessed March 2015.

Brumfield, C. (1973). Conventional approaches using synthetic Euclidean geometry. In K. B. Henderson (Ed.), *Geometry in the mathematics curriculum: 1973 Yearbook* (pp. 95–115). Reston: National Council of Teachers of Mathematics.

Carnoy, M., & Rothstein, R. (2013). *What do international tests really show about U. S. student performance?* http://www.epi.org/publication/us-student-performance-testing/. Accessed March 2015.

CCSSO (Council of Chief State School Officers), & the National Governors Association Center. (2010). Common core state standards initiative: Preparing American's students for college and career. Washington, D. C. http://www.corestandards.org/Math/. Accessed March 2015.

CCSS. (2011). Common Core State Standards. http://www.corestandards.org/.

Charles A. Dana Center. (2014). CCSS resource. http://ccsstoolbox.agilemind.com/resources_samples.html. Accessed March 2015.

CPMP. (2008). Second Edition of Core-Plus Mathematics Parent Resource. http://wmich.edu/cpmp/parentresource2/mathcontent.html.

Courtney, T., Kerstin Carlson, Le F., & Andrea, B. (n.d.). United States Institute of Research, Are Personalized Learning Environments the Next Wave of K-12 Education Reform? http://www.air.org/resource/.

De Jong, T., & Van Joolingen, W. R. (2008). Model-facilitated learning. In J. M. Spector, M. D. Merrill, J. van Merriënboer, & M. P. Driscoll (Eds.), *Handbook of research on educational communications and technology* (3rd ed., pp. 454–465). Florence: Taylor & Francis e-Library.

Devlin, K. (2000). *The math gene, how mathematical thinking evolved and why numbers are liking gossip.* Great Britain: Weidenfeld & Nicolson.

Dori, D. (2002). *Object-process methodology, a holistic system paradigm.* Berlin: Springer-Verlag.

Driscoll, M. J. (1983). *Research within reach: Elementary school mathematics and reading.* St. Luis: CEMREL, Inc.

Epp, S. S. (2003). The role of logic in teaching proof. *American Mathematical Monthly,* 110(10), 886–899.

Epp, S. S. (1987). The logic of teaching calculus. In R. G. Douglas (Ed.), *Toward a lean and lively calculus* (pp. 41 -60). Washington, D. C.: Mathematical Association of America.

Evans, J., Newstead, S. E., & Byrne, R. M. J. (1993). *Human reasoning: The psychology of deduction.* New York: Psychology Press (ISBN 978-0-86377-313-6).

Finegold, D., & Notabartolo, A. S. (2011). 21st competencies and impact. http://www.hewlett.org/uploads/21st_Century_Competencies_Impact.pdf. Accessed March 2015.

Fisher, J. (2010). ABC news, China debuts top international education ranking. http://abcnews.go.com/Politics/china-debuts-top-international-education-rankings/story?id=12336108. Accessed March 2015.

Gries, D., & Shneider, F. B. (1994). *A logical approach to discrete math.* New York: Springer.

Guha, N. (2014). Teaching logic: Cracking the hard nut. http://www.redalyc.org/pdf/1794/179430480009.pdf. Accessed March 2015.

Hawthorne, V., & Rasmussen, C. (2014). A framework for characterizing students' thinking about logical statements and truth tables. *International Journal of Mathematical Education in Science and Technology, 46*(3), 1–17.

Johnson-Laird, P. N. (1975). Models of deduction. http://mentalmodels.princeton.edu/papers/1975models-of-ded.pdf. Accessed March 2015.

Johnson-Laird, P. N. (1983). *Mental models: Tiwards a cognative science of language, inference, and consciousness*. Cambridge: Cambridge University Press.

Johnson-Laird, P. N. (2005). The history of mental models. http://mentalmodels.princeton.edu/papers/2005HistoryMentalModels.pdf. Accessed March 2015.

Kahneman, D. (2011). *Thinking fast and slow*. New York: Farrar, Straus and Giroux.

Knuth, E. J. (2002). Second school mathematics teachers' conception of proof. *Journal for Research in Mathematics Education, 33*(5), 379–405.

Liu, H., & Raghavan, J. (2009). A mathematical modeling module with system engineering approach for teaching undergraduate students to conquer complexity, The Proceedings of Conference ICCS 09, Part II. *LNCS, 5545,* 93–102.

Martin, W. G., & Harel, G. (1989). Proof frames of preservice elementary teachers. *Journal for Research in Mathematics Education, 20,* 41–51.

Mason, M. (2014). Van Hiele model, http://en.wikipedia.org/wiki/Van_Hiele_model. Accessed March 2015.

Miriam, J. (2002). The trivium: The liberal arts of logic, grammar, and rhetoric. http://clinister.com/the-trivium-the-sister-miriam.html. Accessed March 2015.

Moore, R. C. (1994). Making the transition to formal proof. *Educational Studies in Mathematics, 27*(3), 221–237.

New Media Consortium. (2014). *New horizon report–K-12 education review*. http://redarchive.nmc.org/publications/2014-horizon-report-higher-ed.

Nicolay, J. G., & Hay, J. (2015). Lincoln's Cooper Institute speech, and other political events of 1859–1860. *Century Illustrated Monthly Magazine, 34*(1887), 509–34. http://ebooks.library.cornell.edu/cgi/t/text/pageviewer-idx?c=cent;cc=cent;rgn=full%20text;idno=cent0034-4;didno=cent0034-4;view=image;seq=0519;node=cent0034-4%3 A4. Accessed March 2015.

Pirnay-Dummer, P., Ifenthaler, D., & Spector, J. M. (2010). Highly integrated model assessment technology and tools. *Educational Technology Research & Development, 58*(1), 3–18.

Raghavan, J., Sena, L., Bethelmy, D., & Liu, H. (2008). Problem solving experience through light-dose computational mathematical modules for Engineering students, the proceedings of the 2008 ASEE Annual Conference.

Recio, A. M., & Godino, J. D. (2001). Institutional and personal meanings of mathematical proof. *Educational Studies in Mathematics, 48,* 83–99. (Kluwer Academic Publishers).

San Diego Jewish Journal. (2012). Singapore style. http://sdjewishjournal.com/site/3193/math-singapore-style/. Accessed March 2015.

Scope and Sequence for Primary Mathematics. (2008). http://www.singaporemath.com/Default.asp?gclid=CNqY47jb270CFUoV7Aod4B8AEA. Accessed March 2015.

Senk, S. (1985). How well do students write geometry proofs?. *Mathematics Teacher, 78*(6), 448–456.

Singapore Academy. (2011) http://www.schoolsthatcan.org/index.php/2011/12/30/singapore-math-with-vinny-dotoli-of-the-harlem-academy/.

Spector, M. (2010). Assessing progress of learning in complex domains. The 11th International Conference on Education Research: New Educational Paradigm for Learning and Instruction.

Stylianides, A. J., & Stylianides, G. J. (2009). Proof constructions and evaluations. *Educational Studies in Mathematics, 72,* 237–253. http://www.math.ksu.edu/~bennett/onlinehw/qcenter/stylianides.pdf. Accessed March 2015.

Tanenbaum, C., Carlson Le Floch, K., & Boyle, A. (2013). United States Institute of Research, are personalized learning environments the next wave of K-12 education reform? http://www.air.org/resource/are-personalized-learning-environments-next-wave-K-12-education-reform.

Warner, J. (2014). http://blog.readytomanage.com/how-is-critical-thinking-different-from-analytical-or-lateral-thinking/. Accessed March 2015.

Wason, P. C. (1966). Reasoning. In B. M. Foss (Ed.), *New horizons in psychology*, 19. Harmondsworth: Penguin.

Hong Liu is an associate professor in mathematics and computing at Embry-Riddle Aeronautical University. He taught undergraduate and graduate courses in mathematics, computer sciences, and software engineering. His research interest includes partial differential equations, software engineering, data mining, and computational science education. He served as the supervisor of software development team at Lab of Advanced Instrumentation Research 2003–2006 and led the team developing and delivering three real-rime embedded software packages to Thomas Jefferson Nuclear Accelerate Facility Lab. He serves as the adviser of the SIAM student chapter at Embry-Riddle and mentors a team of student researchers in SIAM chapter to build a fleet of autonomous underwater vehicle called Eco-Dolphins. He taught summer workshops on SeaPerch underwater robotics to middle school students. Hong Liu has involved STEM education projects and served as the PI of an NSF TUES grant. He is a father of a grown up son and teenage girl.

Maria Ludu graduated from Bucharest University, College of Physics, in 1983, Section of Nuclear Physics for Reactors with the thesis "Effect of gamma irradiation on semiconductors". From 1983 to 1988 she worked in chemical industry in nondestructive testing labs. In 1986 she moved to research at the Institute of Nuclear Physics working for the CAMDU Romanian-Canadian company in designing the nuclear power plant in Cernavoda Romania. In 1988 she moved to education and she taught high school physics and mathematics in Bucharest, Romania. In 1998 Maria and her family moved to Louisiana, where Maria continued her teaching career as mathematics high school teacher, then as Math Coordinator in Baton Rouge Louisiana. In 2009 she graduated from Louisiana State University with a Master's in Science, with thesis "Rate of change with applications in physics problems". Starting 2009 she taught college physics at Northwestern State University, where they published the Physics Lab Manual designed for NSU. Maria and her husband, Andrei moved to Daytona Beach in 2011. At present she enjoys teaching mathematics at Embry-Riddle Aeronautical University.

Douglas Holton is the Associate Director of the Center for Teaching and Learning Excellence (CTLE) at ERAU and formerly an Assistant Professor of Instructional Technology and Learning Sciences at Utah State University. As part of the CTLE, Dr. Holton has consulted with faculty on their use of evidence-based teaching practices and technologies and has conducted workshops and developed resources for enhancing teaching and learning. Dr. Holton's research background in STEM education has involved developing educational software and assessment instruments and conducting research on topics related to conceptual change and educational technology.

Modeling for Dynamic Mathematics

Toward Technology-Integrated Aesthetic Experiences in School Mathematics

Lingguo Bu and Markus Hohenwarter

Abstract Dynamic mathematics learning technologies support a modelcentered approach to mathematics teaching and learning, which enhances students' and teachers' mathematical experience in the STEM disciplines toward mathematical understanding and aesthetic feelings. This chapter first reviews the theoretical foundation of model-centered learning and instruction and then elaborates a modelcentered prospective on the teaching and learning of middle and high school mathematics, integrating emerging dynamic and interactive mathematical learning technologies (e.g., GeoGebra) and drawing illustrative cases from recent mathematics teacher development projects and classroom experiments. Specific mathematical topics are discussed to showcase the transformative nature of dynamic mathematics in supporting sense-making and enriching classroom discussions. Using mathematical modeling and didactical modeling as a primary theme, this chapter illustrates the generative power of emerging digital technologies in addressing new standards for mathematical practices. Modeling not only provides a pathway toward mathematical understanding and self-assessment, but also allows students to experience the aesthetic dimension of mathematical inquiry in the broad context of STEAM education.

Keywords Dynamic learning technology · Mathematical modeling · Didactical modeling · Mathematical practice · Mathematical understanding·Mathematical aesthetics

L. Bu (✉)
Southern Illinois University, Carbondale, USA
e-mail: lgbu@siu.edu

M. Hohenwarter
Johannes Kepler University, Linz, Austria
e-mail: markus.hohenwarter@jku.at

© Springer International Publishing Switzerland 2015
X. Ge et al. (eds.), *Emerging Technologies for STEAM Education,*
Educational Communications and Technology: Issues and Innovations,
DOI 10.1007/978-3-319-02573-5_19

Introduction

Emerging mathematics learning technologies challenge traditional views and practices of mathematics education and provide opportunities to transform the teaching and learning of mathematics in accordance with new standards, addressing both the intellectual and the aesthetic aspects of mathematical experiences. Let's consider a case in prospective teacher education for a glimpse of the dynamic interactions between mathematical exploration and new digital technologies. Matt (pseudonym) is a second-year prospective teacher in elementary teacher education. When requested to explain the mathematical processes behind an everyday optical phenomenon involving geometric reflection, he responded using a sketch and verbal descriptions (Fig. 1). Matt explained the sketch in front of his classmates: There is light in the environment, which shines on Mary and her yo-yo. The yo-yo reflects the light, at some angles, to the mirror which then reflects it into Mary's eyes. He further explained how the eyes perceive the incoming light through its rods and cones and send messages to the brain. Matt was not alone. A survey of his classmates' work showed much similarity across their responses, which are mathematically incomplete but contain significant ideas about the problem situation. In a traditional set-

Fig. 1 A prospective teacher's initial response to a real-world problem

ting, however, Matt's ingenuous response would have been quickly corrected by the instructor using standard solutions from a textbook. Decades of research in mathematics education has clearly shown the detrimental effects of product-oriented mathematics instruction and the crying need to balance the processes and products of mathematical problem solving or, in other words, to emphasize the interplay between procedural and conceptual mathematical knowledge (cf. National Council of Teachers of Mathematics [NCTM], 2000; National Research Council [NRC], 1989, 2001, 2005; Silver, 1986; Silver, Mesa, Morris, Star, & Benken, 2009).

Through cognitive lenses, however, we find a rich variety of illuminating ideas in Matt's responses. First, he had a sketchy knowledge of the behavior of light rays, including its wave nature and its reflection. Second, he recognized that there were multiple light rays in the environment participating in the process of multiple reflections. Third, he seemed to know the mirror image was the outcome of brain perceptions. In short, Matt's sketch and explanation gave us a snapshot of his initial *mental model* of the problem situation and how he used the mental model to represent and reason about the problem. Indeed, what Matt presented is his mental model, which, on the one hand, captures the basic structure of the problem situation as he saw it at that moment, and on the other hand, allows him to simulate the dynamic processes and formulate his explanation, albeit incomplete (Johnson-Laird, 1983; Norman, 1983; Seel, 2003, 2014). Mental model, as a theoretical construct for understanding human reasoning, has gained recognition in education as a way to accept, analyze, and build upon students' prior knowledge such as preconceptions and misconceptions.

If we recognize the meaningfulness of Matt's mental model, what might be the next step to intervene with his existing model of the problem and bring about conceptual changes and enhancements? Using a model-based approach, we could engage Matt and his classmates to take advantage of the new learning technologies to construct a dynamic model of their internal ones and to further debug and alter their dynamic models as a way to solve the problem and foster the development of a mathematically complete and robust mental model (Jonassen, 2006; Milrad, Spector, & Davidsen, 2003). The modeling process, as expected, is not straight forward. It is full of twists and turns, both cognitively and technologically, where Matt was learning progressively about the problem space, his own conceptions, his classmates' diverse perspectives, the technological utilities, and the mathematical simplicity of the problem as well as its complexity, ultimately reaching an insightful understanding (see Fig. 2).

Didactically, the resulting dynamic model serves to situate a range of mathematical ideas in a context that provides a conceptual framework for mathematical meaning. After critique and modification, the dynamic model amounts to a shared conceptual model (Norman, 1983; Seel & Blumschein, 2009) as a learning goal or a new starting point for further problem inquiry. A model-based approach to a routine problem has thus addressed all the core learning principles recommended by the National Research Council (NRC) (2005), including students' preconceptions, integration of mathematical facts within a conceptual framework, and metacognition.

Mathematics has generally been considered difficult by school students, including elementary and middle school teachers. When given a real-world problem, they

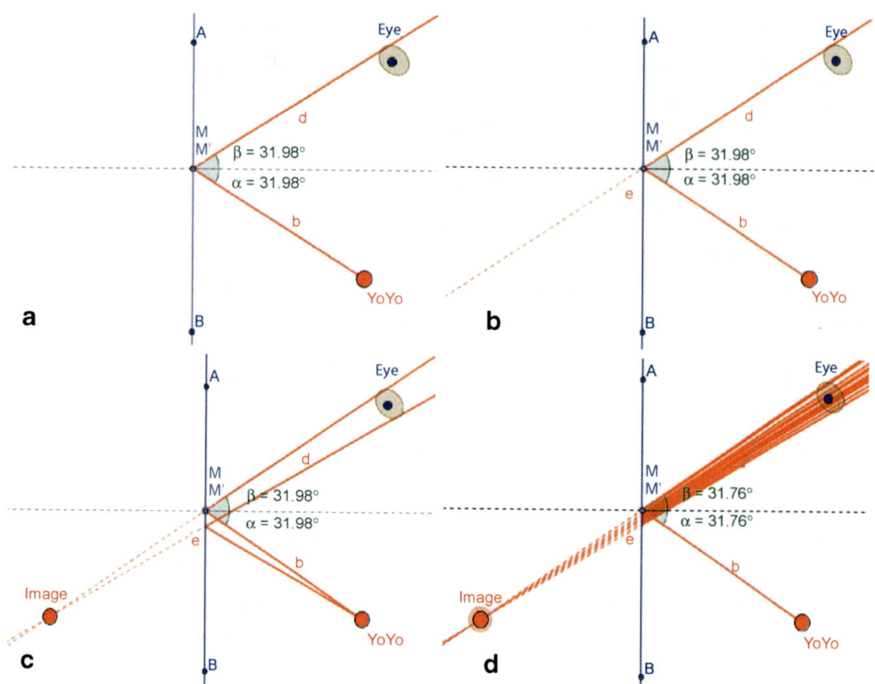

Fig. 2 A progression of dynamic models of the mirror reflection problem

tend to ask for a formula. When a formula is given, they tend to use it for the wrong purposes. There is plenty of evidence that the formula is merely memorized as a mnemonic or recited by many students as an abstract object without a conceptual framework to enable its meaning making. Among various reasons, research in the past three decades has pointed to the striking lack of generative conceptual models on the part of students who struggle with school mathematics (Perkins, 1986; Ryan & Williams, 2007; Schwartz, 2007; Silver, 1986). Meaning, in general, arises from a network of mathematical ideas or a conceptual model, which embodies the dynamic connections among related concepts and operations in one's mathematical experience.

Modeling, however, is a demanding endeavor requiring both cognitive and technological resources. Traditionally, it is accessible only to students who are mathematically experienced, thus empowering them on a healthy cycle of mathematical achievements. Unfortunately, those who struggle with the mathematical concepts are frequently asked to repeat the same meaningless practice without addressing the underlying models. In *Everybody Counts: A Report to the Nation on the Future of Mathematics Education*, the National Research Council (1989) emphatically pointed out, "Repetition rarely works; more often than not, it simply reinforces previous failure." (p. 13). The 21st century, however, has ushered in a growing collection of mathematics learning technologies, including both open-source and commercial environments on both computers and mobile devices. These new learning technologies have, on an unprecedented scale, changed the representational infrastructure of mathematics teaching and learning as well as professional mathematical practices (diSessa, 2007; Kaput & Schorr, 2008; Kaput, Hegedus & Lesh, 2007). Being rich in representation resources and intrinsically interactive and dynamic, they have also challenged the very nature of mathematical practices and mathematics teaching, calling for a reconceptualization of both traditional and applied mathematics and promising a democratic access to genuinely powerful mathematics (Kaput & Schorr, 2008; Kaput et al., 2007). Modeling, whether as a mathematical practice or a didactical means to foster mathematical understanding, has become an affordable and worthwhile endeavor in mathematics teaching and learning. In what follows, we present an overview of the emergent mathematics learning technologies, the theoretical foundation of model-centered learning, and further illustrate feasible model-based teaching-learning progressions in our effort to reconceptualize school mathematics for understanding.

Understanding, Modeling, and Dynamic Learning Technologies

Understanding and Mental Models

Understanding has been the single most resounding voice in the ongoing mathematics education reform across both school mathematics and mathematics teacher preparation and professional development (Council of Chief State School Officers [CCSSO], 2010; Darling-Hammond et al., 2008; NCTM, 2000). In *Principles and Standards for School Mathematics* (NCTM, 2000), there are 928 instances of the term *understand* or *understanding* across its 419 pages. Similarly, in the *Common Core State Standards for Mathematics* (CCSSO, 2010), there are 260 instances through its 93 pages where the term *understand* or *understanding* is used to describe expectations of students' mathematical performance. But what constitutes mathematical understanding? NCTM (2000) characterizes mathematical understanding as the integration of a student's procedural and conceptual knowledge in a way that empowers him or her to make connections among diverse representations and also feel competent in problem solving, reasoning, and communication. The Common Core State Standards for Mathematics (CCSSO, 2010) follows the same line of criteria for mathematical understanding, placing emphasis on students' awareness of the connections across conceptual origins, procedural skills, and applications as well as their ability to justify mathematical ideas in a way appropriate to their mathematical maturity.

Mathematical understanding, as characterized by NCTM (2000) and CCSSO (2010) in their influential standards, is in fact grounded in cognitive research about the nature of human learning and positioned to redress the alarming lack of understanding among large numbers of school students, particularly in mathematics (NRC, 1989, 2000, 2001, 2005, 2010). Since the early 1980s, research in cognitive sciences has given prominence to mental models as a theoretical construct to make sense of human reasoning (Johnson-Laird, 1983; Norman, 1983; Seel, 2005, 2008, 2014). When faced with a novel problem situation, humans instinctively construct a mental model to represent its perceived structure and simulate its dynamics for reasoning and decision-making (Perkins, 1986; Spector, 2009). Such mental models may be either consistent with or incompatible with a domain-specific conceptual model. From the viewpoint of mental models, we see mathematical misconceptions or mistakes as intelligent, albeit frequently incomplete or even wrong, constructions, which ought to be valued and utilized as existing resources or as points of entry and engagement in subsequent instructional interventions, however incorrect as they are with respect to the instructional goals (Ryan & Williams, 2007; Vygotsky, 1997). In spite of different nuances in its definition, mental model, as an underlying construct to approach human understanding is cited by numerous researchers to analyze cases of understanding or the lack thereof in various disciplines (Battista, 2008; Bruner, 1991; Ifenthaler & Seel, 2010; Jonassen, 2011; Merrill, 2000; Minsky, 2006; Nickerson, 1985; Perkins, 1993, 2009; Resnick & Ford, 1981; Spector, 2008).

Modeling for Understanding

Why has school mathematics been taught in so many classes in a model-less and accordingly meaningless way? Before addressing the question, we invite our readers to think about the following problem and, better yet, try it with a group of school students or prospective teachers. *Markus followed a certain route from Kansas City to St. Louis Airport. His car averaged 60 miles per hours (mph) on his trip to St. Louis Airport. It averaged 40 mph on the way back to Kansas City because of the bad weather conditions. What was the average speed for his round trip?* How would you respond to the problem? How would your students respond to the problem and why? The vast majority of students, including prospective teachers who have not seen the problem before, would instinctively carry out $(60 + 40) \div 2 = 50$, feeling somehow confident about their answer, "It must be correct; what else?"

Indeed, it is an intelligent response, building upon an existing schema about the formula for arithmetic average: $m = (a + b) \div 2$. However, the formula does not capture the structure or the processes of the problem situation, leading to an innocent mistake. As a matter of fact, that formula is *meaningless* in this specific context; its meaning can be traced back to its mathematical origins. There are countless examples in school mathematics, where formulas or theorems take the misleading role of an object, which, if not grounded in the intended conceptual framework, tends to have a life of its own and causes learning difficulties. As another example from school geometry, consider the area of a triangle, which is typically given in a textbook as $A = (1/2)bh$ without a complete picture about the rationale or the problem space, mathematically and cognitively. Why does one multiply the base by the height and then by one-half? Which side is the base? What does the height mean? Used as an instrument, the formula can get the right answer in most, if not all, typical cases but will eventually lead to conceptual mistakes in a non-standard problem situation (see Fig. 3).

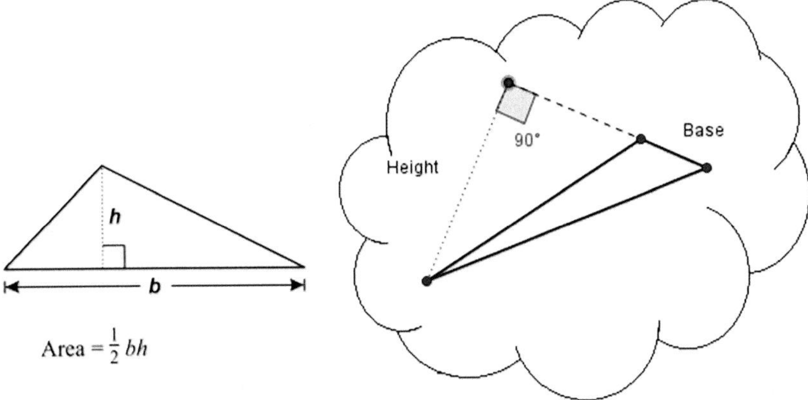

Fig. 3 A formula does not capture the mathematical or cognitive complexity

Not surprisingly, many students and mathematics teachers tend to attach mathematical understanding to such instrumental use of rules and formulas and fail to construct a relational foundation for such formalism (Skemp, 1976, 2006). In his famous reflection about mathematics teaching, Skemp reflected on his own experience and remarked, "I used to think that math teachers were all teaching the same subject, some doing it better than others. I now believe *there are two effectively different subjects being taught under the same name 'mathematics'*" (1976, 2006, p. 91). Skemp's two subjects refer to instrumental mathematics, where understanding is attached to the instrumental use of mathematics, and relational mathematics, where understanding is grounded in mathematical relations in a conceptual framework.

A mathematical idea is thus grounded in an intricate relational network between its simplistic surface structure and its complex underlying processes. Gravemeijer (1994, 2008), from the theoretical perspective of Realistic Mathematics Education (Freudenthal, 1978; Streefland, 1991; Treffers, 1987), calls for increased attention to the historical and contextual origins of mathematical concepts and a modeling approach to connecting the abstract knowledge of teachers and the experiential knowledge of students. By situating mathematical development in real-world or realistic contexts, students can progressively construct a *model of* the problem situation and further reconceptualize it as *a model for* the targeted mathematical concept (Gravemeijer, 2008; Gravemeijer, Cobb, Bowers, & Whitenack, 2000; Gravemeijer & van Galen, 2003).

In fact, modeling is nothing new in the teaching and learning of mathematics with many connotations in practice. On the one hand, mathematical modeling is frequently a goal of itself in mathematical practices where mathematicians construct, test, prove, and extend purposeful mathematical representations of a real-world situation as a way to solve the problem or generate new knowledge (Mooney & Swift, 1999). Pollak (2003), after reviewing the history of the teaching of modeling, concludes, "modeling is one aspect of mathematics that *all* students can share throughout their schooling and that can unify the school mathematics experience" (p. 668). From a curricular point of view, Pollak (2003) further points out that "a curriculum that emphasizes modeling can perhaps keep students together through most, if not all, of their elementary and secondary school mathematics education" (pp. 668–669). On the other hand, modeling is increasingly employed as a didactical tool to situate, motivate, animate, or analyze the development of mathematical ideas (Freudenthal, 1983; Goldin, 2007; Gravemeijer, 1994; Schwartz, 2007; Van den Heuvel-Panhuizen, 2003; Zbiek & Conner, 2006). Recent development has shed light on the mutually mediating connections between modeling, mental models, and affect in learning and instruction. As students engage in modeling activities, either explanatory or exploratory, they also construct a model of themselves, as an intrinsic component of their mental models, with respect to the modeling activity (Goldin, 2007; Ifenthaler & Seel, 2011; Seel, 2014).

Modeling with Technology: GeoGebra

Modeling is essentially a cultural process supported and constrained by the cultural tools available, including language, semiotic systems, and technologies. The traditional tools, such as paper and pencils, have until recently given prominence to verbal descriptions, abstract notations, and static and inert imagery in mathematics teaching and learning (Moreno-Armella, Hegedus, & Kaput, 2008), leaving much of mathematical understanding to the imagination and reflection of the learners. Subsequently, the advent of hand-held calculators and personal computers in the last three decades of the 20th century took over the tedious computations and graphing in school mathematics, contributing further to the perplexing nature of school mathematics. Calculators and computers, however, are not solely to blame for the lack of understanding in mathematics instruction. They may have just exposed the limitations of traditional mathematics teaching, which has largely focused on the instrumental aspects of mathematics (Fey, 2006; Skemp, 1978). Fey (2006), in reviewing three decades of empirical research on the benefits and risks of technology use in mathematics education, concludes that there is consistent finding that "thoughtful use of such tools tends to enhance student understanding and problem-solving ability, with no significant diminution of learning traditional computational skills" (p. 350). Technology changes the very nature of school mathematics and the methods of mathematic teaching (NCTM, 2000).

The 21st century ushered in another round of technological innovations in mathematics teaching and learning—the next generation of hand-held calculators and dynamic and interactive mathematics learning environments (DIMLE) such as TI-*n*spire™, Geometer's Sketchpad™, Cabri™, and open-source environments like GeoGebra™ (Martinovic & Karadag, 2012). Grounded in decades of empirical research and theorizing in mathematical cognition, these 21st-century technologies pride themselves on dynamically linked multiple representations, interactivity, computation and programming tools, modeling and simulation utilities, assessment tools, computer algebra systems (CAS), and user customizable tools. Most of the DIMLEs have a consistent user interface across diverse hardware and software platforms, offering web accessibility and mobile apps. The rapid growth of these

DIMLEs has proven, to a large extent, the transformative evolution of the representational infrastructure from traditional static media to new dynamic and interactive media in school mathematics, affording widespread access to powerful mathematics (Hegedus & Moreno-Armella, 2009; Kaput & Thompson, 1994; Kaput, Noss, & Hoyles, 2002; Kaput et al., 2007). The time has arrived for the mathematics education community to reconceptualize mathematics teaching and learning in accordance with the ongoing cultural needs and the affordances of the new DIMLE systems. Modeling with technology promises to be a strategic fit between the current cultural trends in Science, Technology, Engineering, and Mathematics (STEM) Education and the diverse representational infrastructure in mathematics education as an effort to promote mathematical understanding.

While all the DIMLE systems are worthwhile in theory development and classroom deployment, we choose to review the features of open-source GeoGebra (www.geogebra.org), in part because of our own experiences in research and classroom teaching, as a case study to discuss the implications of a model-based approach to mathematics teaching and learning. GeoGebra was initiated by Markus Hohenwarter and first released in 2002 at www.geogebra.org, featuring an integrated environment of dynamic algebraic and geometric objects and tools. In its subsequent development, GeoGebra has been supported by a dedicated international team, who, in response to feedbacks of the international users across all levels of mathematics and mathematics education, has continuously extended GeoGebra's mathematical coverage and functionality (Hohenwarter & Preiner, 2007). By November 2014, GeoGebra, in its version 5.0.44, has four interlinked views—algebra, spreadsheet, CAS, and 2-D and 3-D geometries in addition to a variety of web-friendly exporting tools. A growing number of researchers and teachers in mathematics education have taken interest in GeoGebra in mathematics education and explored its practical and theoretical implications (Bu & Schoen, 2011). Not surprisingly, GeoGebra, along with other similar DIMLEs, has not made mathematics easier; rather it has brought meaning to the center stage of mathematics education and fundamentally changed the nature of traditional mathematical tasks. It has been gradually contributing to the realization of futuristic visions for a new era of mathematics teaching and learning, which includes modeling and simulations (Kaput et al., 2007; Schwartz, 2007), worldwide connectivity, dynamic and interactive representations, experimental school mathematics (Borwein & Devlin, 2009), co-actions between tools and learners (Moreno-Armella & Hegedus, 2009), partnerships in learning (Jonassen, 1996; Salomon, Perkins, & Globerson, 1991), systematic exploration of representational conversions (Duval, 2006), synergy between mathematical content and technology (diSessa, 2007), and generative designs (Stroup, Ares, & Hurford, 2005; Stroup, Ares, Hurford, & Lesh, 2007).

Among the numerous examples, we consider the construction of an ellipse—a planar locus of all the points with a constant sum of distances to two other points called the foci. Using two pins, a string, and a pen, one could easily construct an example (Fig. 4), leaving the problem space to further mathematical analysis and one's imagination. Within a dynamic DIMLE such as GeoGebra, however, the ellipse task assumes a new character both cognitively and technologically. If one point of the ellipse is given, how could we construct all the other points of the

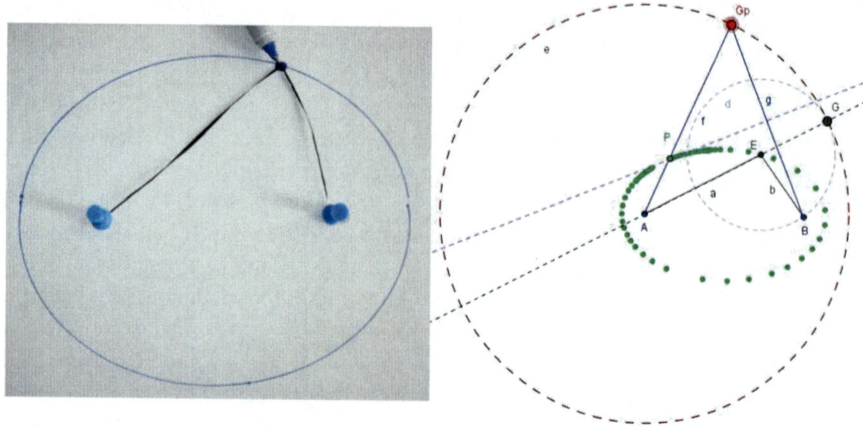

Fig. 4 Dynamic technology changes the very nature of a mathematical task

curve? How could we fix the sum of the two distances? The construction task thus becomes mathematically challenging and immensely interesting, embedding quite a few geometric concepts such as circles and perpendicular line bisectors (Fig. 4). Almost necessarily, students are going to make mistakes in the construction process while getting acquainted with both the cognitive demands of the task and the supports and constraints of the DIMLE environment. Most probably, they are going to discover alternative pathways toward the construction using the DIMLE tools. The constructed ellipse, because of its dynamic and interactive nature, becomes a mathematical *toy* with a personal affective attachment, which students can manipulate for systematic exploration. The endpoint of a construction naturally becomes a new starting point, generating more questions and answers for exploration and reflection. So what is an ellipse? A verbal description of all the qualifying points or a visual object that has an oval shape or a dynamic life-like mathematical object that plays out according to the specific context? Or perhaps it comprises all of the above. Indeed, a robust understanding of the mathematical idea of an ellipse resides in the process of dynamically coordinating these different semiotic representations (Duval, 2006; Sfard, 1991).

Modeling for Mathematical Aesthetic Experience

Mathematics is beautiful. Those who have managed to experience the appealing and motivating order and power of mathematics would not hesitate telling their audience about their personal feelings about mathematics. Indeed, one of the primary goals of mathematics education, especially in the schools, is to engage students in a way so that they could appreciate the power and beauty of mathematical thinking (Dreyfus & Eisenberg, 1986; Sinclair, 2006). In this regard, however, we have collectively failed miserably (Dreyfus & Eisenberg, 1986). To a large portion of school children as well as adults, mathematics remains quite the opposite of beauty and power, causing insurmountable anxiety and fear (Ashcraft, 2002; Gresham, 2007; Tobias, 1993). While the causes of math anxiety are not well understood, some traditional teaching styles could have played a role in perpetuating students' anxiety about mathematics (Ashcraft, 2002). Mathematical aesthetics, though hard to define in everyday language, has always been a concern of mathematics educators. Dreyfus and Eisenberg (1986) contended that mathematical aesthetics was "terribly amiss in the mathematics curriculum" and that was "a tremendous mistake" (p. 9). After almost 30 years, NCTM president Linda Gojak (2014), in her reflection on 25 years of standards-based mathematics education, reiterated the same concern and called on the mathematics education community to teach for an aesthetic appreciation of mathematics:

> As mathematics educators, … we should not just teach mathematics, we should teach a love of mathematics. Knowing the content of some mathematics is a trivial achievement. Being inclined to see the beauty in mathematics and to go on doing mathematics are great achievements. (para. 14)

We agree with Gojak about teaching for a love of mathematics, which could well be the single most generative factor in mathematics learning. With the diverse technologies at hand, it is indeed trivial to solve traditional mathematical problems, even complicated ones involving logarithms, trigonometry, and systems of equations. Free tools such as wolframalpha™ and Android™- or iOS™-based Myscript Calculator™ can not only provide immediate answers but also use multiple representations or even allow finger-drawn script input or voice recognition. Without any doubt, more advanced and convenient technologies are under development, which will further trivialize the algorithmic aspects of school mathematics. With tedious procedures taken over by technologies, we may eventually have an opportunity or be compelled to reconsider the aesthetic aspects of mathematics, which have been neglected for too long. Surrounded by powerful computers and mobile devices, we are reminded once more of G. H. Hardy (1940/1967), who wrote in *A Mathematician's Apology* about a mathematician's work:

> A mathematician, like a painter or a poet, is a maker of patterns. If his patterns are more permanent than theirs, it is because they are made with ideas. A painter makes patterns with shapes and colours, a poet with words…. The mathematician's patterns, like the painter's or the poet's, must be beautiful; the ideas, like the colours or the words, must fit together in a harmonious way. Beauty is the first test: there is no permanent place in the world for ugly mathematics…. It may be very hard to define mathematical beauty, but that is just as true of beauty of any kind—we may not know quite what we mean by a beautiful poem, but that does not prevent us from recognizing one when we read it. (1967, pp. 84–85)

Research in cognitive sciences in the 21st century sheds fresh light on Hardy's reflection and the critical significance of feelings, emotions, and whole-mindedness in human cognition (Groff, 2013; Johnson, 2007; Minsky, 2006). There is growing evidence from cognitive sciences, mathematicians, and child educators that STEM education benefits from a penetrating component of arts or aesthetics in what can be labeled as STEAM education. Mathematical aesthetics is generally conceived to be the characteristics of one's meaningful mathematical experience, including

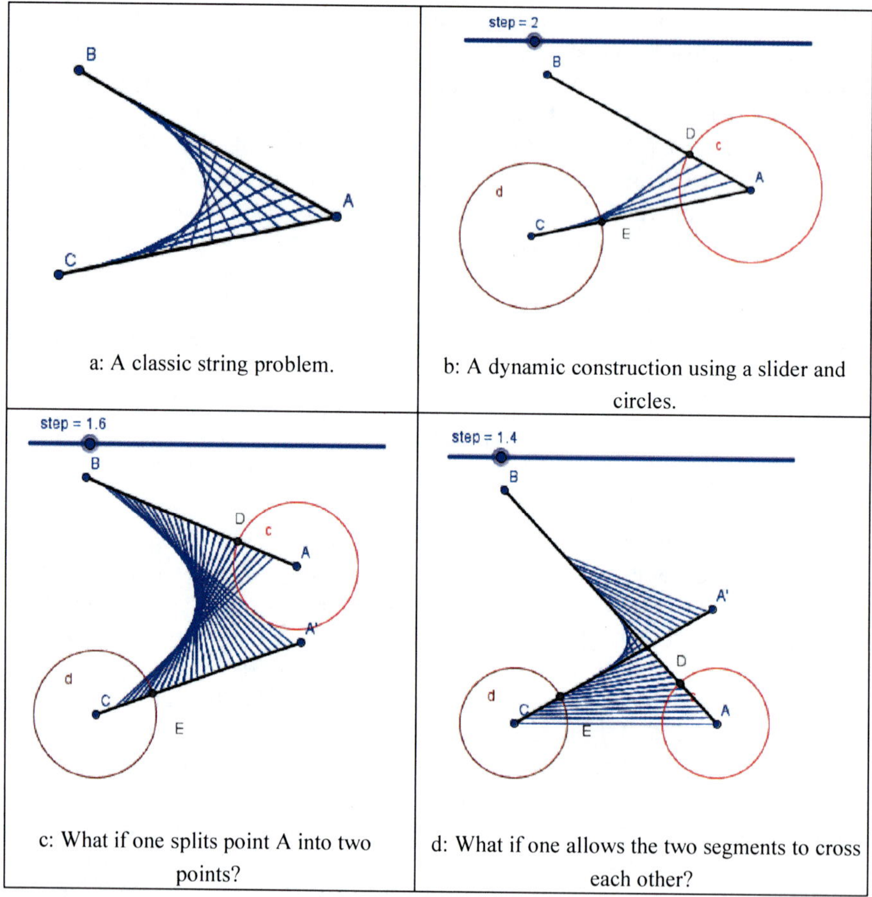

a: A classic string problem.

b: A dynamic construction using a slider and circles.

c: What if one splits point A into two points?

d: What if one allows the two segments to cross each other?

Fig. 5 A dynamic model of the string problem and its aesthetic appeal

simplicity, conciseness, clarity, elegance, pattern, order, and beauty, all of which have a personal touch as well as a historical dimension in the system of mathematics ideas.

About the pedagogical implications of mathematical aesthetics, Sinclair (2006) identified three roles—motivational, evaluative, and generative — in mathematics teaching and learning. As an example, Sinclair referred to the rhythmic approach of Somervell (1906/1975) and the string-parabola problem (Fig. 5a) for its mathematical appeal and expressive power. In a modeling environment such as GeoGebra, the problem becomes more intellectually appealing and visually expressive, further allowing one to pose explorative questions. How does one model the progressive unfolding of the lines while coordinating the two endpoints? What if one changes the density of the lines? What if one splits the common point into two points? What if one allows the two initial lines to intersect each other? While the dynamic process cannot be presented on paper, Fig. 5 captures a few snapshots of the intriguing simulation. A seemingly intractable problem assumes a new life and a visual appeal in the process of modeling and simulations. It makes one wonder about the problem, the underlying structure, and other possibilities. There are in fact a rich variety of classic problems in mathematics which, with strategic instructional planning, afford generative aesthetic experiences for students (Dreyfus & Eisenberg, 1986; Sinclair, Pimm, & Higginson, 2006).

Beyond intellectual and visual appeal, mathematics learning is full of motivating discontinuities and surprises (Freudenthal, 1978; Polya, 1981). These unexpected surprises may cognitively counteract the unavoidable anxiety associated with genuine problem solving, which requires the construction of a context-specific mental model on the part of the problem solver (Seel, 2014). Again, there are numerous classic problem situations that provide cognitive surprises to students of mathematics. However, few students have the perseverance to sustain such mathematical exploration over a long period of time in order to experience the surprises before giving up their effort. New DIMLE systems like GeoGebra provide the tools for students to model mathematics from either real-world situations or existing mathematical ideas to seek insight and surprises.

Figure 6 represents a dynamic approach to the classic problem which involves inscribing a square within an arbitrary triangle (Polya, 1945/2004; Schoenfeld, 1985). The problem is not only a classic example of strategic problem solving but also comes with an elegant surprise. Initially it may be intractable. When one relaxes the conditions by allowing a fourth point to be free (Fig. 6b), the solution gradually takes shape, since the free point seems to be travelling on a line (Fig. 6c). The linear conjecture suggests a final solution (Fig. 6d), which could be dynamically explored and tested in GeoGebra (Fig. 6e). After exploring the problem place, one is convinced to a large extent that the free point may indeed follow a line. A proof, at the appropriate level, thus follows, revealing more mathematical insight into the original problem (Fig. 6g). Aha, what a surprise!

The solution in Fig. 6 is indeed simple and beautiful, after one eventually comes to understand the deep structure of the problem. It also makes one wonder if there are other alternative solutions. Those who come to understand and excel in mathematics at any level could readily give a few examples. Under a modeling perspective, those problems become potentially accessible to all students of mathematics using the tools of GeoGebra. In mathematical practices, such surprises come as a result of deep reflection and frequently multiple iterations of problem solving and exploration (Dreyfus & Eisenberg, 1986). However, they have profound aesthetic implications and may indeed become an integral part of a conceptually sound mental model. About the aesthetic power of surprises in education, Eisner (2002) contends:

> Surprise is itself a source of satisfaction. Familiarity and routine may provide security, but not much in the way of delight. Surprise is one of the rewards of work in the arts. In addition, it is from surprise that we are most likely to learn something. What is learned can then become a part of the individual's repertoire, and once it is a part of that repertoire, new and more complex problems can be generated and successfully addressed. (pp. 7–8)

In summary, there exists a general consensus about the pedagogical power of mathematical aesthetics among mathematicians, educators, and cognitive scientists. In

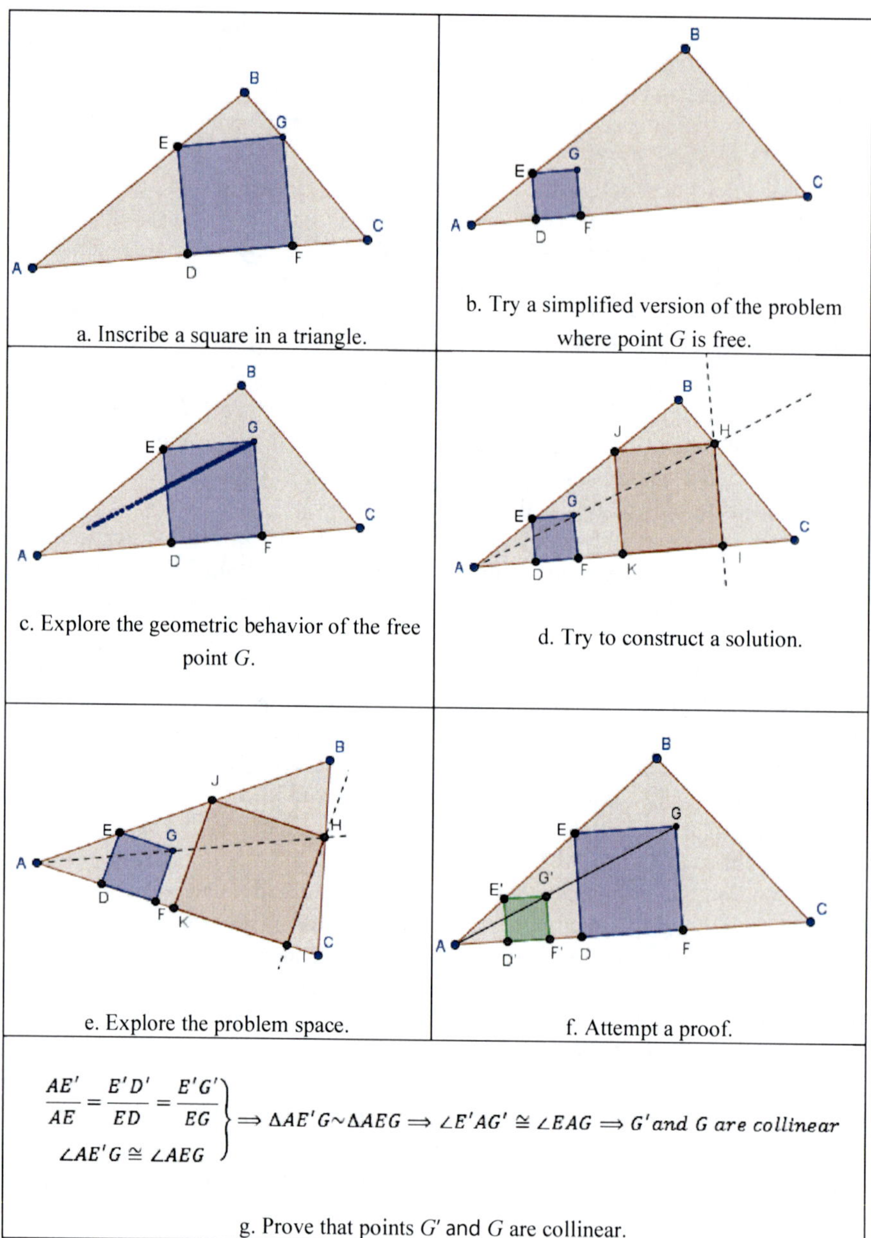

$$\left.\begin{array}{l} \dfrac{AE'}{AE} = \dfrac{E'D'}{ED} = \dfrac{E'G'}{EG} \\[2mm] \angle AE'G \cong \angle AEG \end{array}\right\} \Rightarrow \Delta AE'G \sim \Delta AEG \Rightarrow \angle E'AG' \cong \angle EAG \Rightarrow G' \text{ and } G \text{ are collinear}$$

g. Prove that points G' and G are collinear.

Fig. 6 Inscribing a square in a triangle: a beautiful surprise

reality, mathematical aesthetics may well be an essential characteristic of mathematical understanding, which builds on students' long-term meaningful experience with mathematics and sustains their mathematical curiosity. Modeling with DIMLE technologies provides a theoretically sound and pedagogically rich environment for students to experience genuine mathematics. Again, we would like to quote Eisner (2002) who reminds us that "[i]deas, whether in the abstract forms we call mathematics or in the qualitative forms we call the visual arts, can be beautiful entities, but for them to be experienced as beautiful requires an attentive and constructive mind" (p. 207).

Model-Centered Learning for Dynamic Mathematics

Dynamic mathematics has for long been a vision or a dream of pioneering mathematics educators, who are committed to bringing meaningful and powerful mathematics to all students through a synergy of flexible representations, interactive communication technologies, and social networking (diSessa, 2007; Kaput, 1992; Kaput et al., 2007; Stroup et al., 2005). In a sense, dynamic mathematics is what has been cherished by mathematicians and mathematics educators as well as students who understand mathematics (e.g., Freudenthal, 1973; Lesh & Doerr, 2003; Polya, 1981). The advent of DIMLE technologies has finally given democratic access to the life of a mathematical idea, which, in addition to their abstract symbolism and static images, has a host of dynamic processes that define its identity and meaningfulness. The notion of dynamic mathematics is a synthesis of learning and instructional theories, mathematics, and computational technologies, especially object-oriented programming (Booch, 1994). In essence, it is a social, cultural, and historical development, whose profound influences are still unfolding, leading to both hopes and uncertainties. Among other alternative DIMLEs, GeoGebra stands out. The fact that GeoGebra, in early 2014, has more than 20 million active users across the world, half of whom being adolescents, is educationally significant. There is little doubt that dynamic mathematics is here to stay and will continue to challenge traditional views of school mathematics and the ways of mathematics teaching. We have no other choices but strive to reconceptualize school mathematics and mathematics teaching (cf. Kelly, 2003).

As dynamic mathematics takes shape through commercial and open-source endeavours, research communities in instructional sciences and mathematics education have renewed their interest in modeling as an effort to go beyond constructivist perspectives on mathematics teaching and learning and further integrate diverse views on mathematics problem solving and inquiry (Doerr & Pratt, 2008; Lesh & Doerr, 2003; Milrad et al., 2003; Zbiek & Conner, 2006). Modeling involves a variety of mathematical orientations and pedagogical focuses. There are modeling activities that are largely exploratory, allowing students to get acquainted with the targeted mathematical object (Doerr & Pratt, 2008). There are also modeling activities that allow students to express their mathematical thoughts and further diagnose and improve their mathematical understanding. There are modeling activities that start with a real-world problem and ask students to gradually construct a mathematical solution in a process called horizontal mathematization (Treffers, 1987; Van den Heuvel-Panhuizen, 2003). There are modelling activities that build on an existing mathematical idea and allow students to move on to a higher level of understanding in a process called vertical mathematization. In teaching practices, mixed methods are frequently used to support the diversity of student needs in mathematics teaching and learning. A modeling perspective, however, does highlight a systems approach to a mathematical idea, seeking to coordinate both students' (externalized) mental models and the domain-specific conceptual models.

In field practices, teaching dynamic mathematics to mathematics teachers and their students involves several layers of complexities—the mathematics content, the DIMLE system, the socio-mathematical dynamics of the classroom (e.g., Yackel & Cobb, 1996), and the mathematics standards. In terms of instructional design, we are informed by the principles of Model-Facilitated Learning (MFL) (de Jong & van Joolingen, 2008; Milrad et al., 2003). MFL is compatible with the theoretical tenets of Realistic Mathematics Education (Freudenthal, 1983; Streefland, 1991; Treffers, 1987) with specific guidelines for learning in a DIMLE system—managing cognitive complexity and maintaining content transparency. Under MFL, a learning cycle starts with a real-world or realistic problem situation that lends itself to the diverse mathematical representations and modeling utilities. During problem orientation and exploration, technological modules will be called on to manage the cognitive complexity and maintain the mathematical transparency according to the specific needs of the students. Given the intrinsic conflict between complexity and transparency, strategic pairing of mathematical tasks and technology tools is conducted to enable student learning. The ultimate goal of MFL learning is to develop insight, including aesthetic experiences, frequently through iterative cycles and model modifications, into the mathematical structure of the problem.

While the MFL framework informed us about the needs to manage cognitive complexity and maintain mathematical transparency in mathematics teaching in a DIMLE system, we learned through years of field experience about the daunting complexity of a classroom socio-mathematical environment. The integration of a DIMLE system such as GeoGebra brings the socio-mathematical complexity of the classroom to a new level—excitingly complex. The instructor is faced with an enormous variety of misconceptions, incomplete solutions, diversely correct solutions, and many unexpected solutions. It is an exciting mix of challenges and opportunities, calling for strategic management. To coordinate such productive mathematical practices, we find Smith and Stein's (2011) work on the five mathematics teaching practices particularly informative for dynamic mathematics teaching under a model-centered perspective. The instructor needs to "anticipate" likely student responses during the instructional design stage through what could be called a thought experiment. During classroom instruction, the instructor needs to continuously "monitor" students' diverse responses in individual or small-group settings, and "select" a few particular students' artefacts for whole-class discussion, and then "sequence" diverse student responses according to the learning goal, and finally "connect" students' diverse responses to make a case for the focal mathematical idea. It is expected that in a real classroom setting, these five practices will move back and forth or overlap in response to the ongoing activities of the students. Nonetheless, they go hand in hand with the MFL framework. If the MFL framework addresses the cognitive development in mathematics teaching,

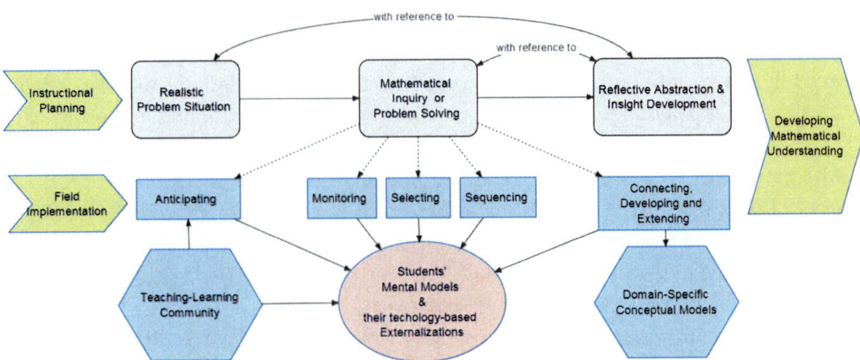

Fig. 7 A framework of model-centered learning for dynamic mathematics

Smith and Stein's (2011) five practices constitute the social fabric that moves the classroom community forward, taking advantage of the existing cognitive resources and achieving a common goal in mathematics learning. Figure 7 is a synthesized framework of model-centered learning for dynamic mathematics.

Teachers' Perceptions About Dynamic Technology

Under the framework of Model-Centered Learning for Dynamic Mathematics, Geo-Gebra was fully integrated into an online professional development course on mathematics problem solving with two cohorts of inservice elementary (K-8) teachers in 2010 and 2012, respectively, in a rural region of the US Midwest. Fifty-three classroom teachers, who were either generalist teachers or mathematics or science specialists, were engaged in 45 hour of intensive mathematical inquiry in the form of modeling and problem solving across a wide range of topics in school mathematics. The instruction was primarily delivered online through a university course management system, which provided instructional videos, interactive instructional modules, discussion forums, and web-exported dynamic GeoGebra worksheets. As expected, GeoGebra was particularly effective and efficient for offering partial or complete dynamic artefacts to support ongoing discussions of the online learning community—among participants and between the instructional team and the teacher participants. Dynamic modeling instilled a new life to otherwise dry and formulaic mathematics and scaffolded and sustained the progress of the learning community within an online environment (cf. Eseryel, Ge, Ifenthaler, & Law, 2011; Ge & Land, 2004). Dynamic modeling did not make the mathematics easier but certainly made it more meaningful. Most teachers, after rounds of frustrations, emotional fluctuations, and pleasant findings, came to appreciate the complexity and intellectual appeal of even the elementary mathematics they had been teaching for years.

Toward the end of their course work, the teacher participants were surveyed on 25 questions about their involvement with modeling and dynamic mathematics along the four dimensions of attitudes, curriculum, mathematical content, and pedagogy (Bu, Mumba, Henson, & Wright, 2013). First, in terms of teachers' attitudes toward dynamic mathematics with GeoGebra, the majority thought of their experience as meaningful and almost all the teachers spread words about GeoGebra within their local community. The vast majority indicated that GeoGebra did not make mathematics more difficult to learn or teach and would continue to use GeoGebra. Second, about the curricular implications of dynamic mathematics, more than half of the teachers felt that GeoGebra challenged their existing conception of mathematics. The vast majority, however, felt that they could adapt instructional materials for teaching dynamic mathematics and that they would face challenges from their students. Most importantly, all the teachers believed that GeoGebra helped their students create their own mathematics ideas. Third, regarding the mathematical content, the majority felt that they relearned some mathematical ideas which would otherwise have been hard to reach and that dynamic mathematics was distinctively different than traditional views of mathematics. Finally, about the pedagogical implications of GeoGebra, the majority felt that GeoGebra helped them make connections among mathematical ideas, reach out to diverse children, rethink about teaching methods, and provide meaningful feedback to students. They also indicated that their students generally like GeoGebra and that they would be willing to learn about dynamic mathematics *with* their students.

Conclusion

The ubiquitous presence of dynamic mathematics learning technologies has pushed mathematical understanding to the forefront of mathematical education practice, research, and development. The human nature of mathematical understanding calls for a holistic perspective on mathematics teaching and learning, integrating a variety of cognitive, social, cultural, aesthetic, and technological resources and innovations. A model-centered approach holds encouraging promises in bringing meaning and understanding into the practices of mathematics education while utilizing powerful dynamic mathematics environments. On the one the hand, we must recognize and tap into the natural power of the human brain-mind for model construction, albeit frequently incomplete or flatly mistaken, and further support students' experience with and construction of conceptually robust and generative mathematical models. On the other hand, we must attend to the emotional and aesthetic dimension of mathematical learning in order to promote student's mathematical ownership and personal feelings about mathematics and its intellectual appeals. There is reason to be optimistic about the future possibilities along both directions, particularly on account of the rapid advances of open-source technologies such as GeoGebra and the converging research findings in cognitive sciences and mathematics education (Eisner, 2002; Groff, 2013; Johnson, 2007; Lesh & Doerr, 2003; Pimm & Sinclair, 2006; Sinclair et al., 2006). Citing specific examples from school mathematics and teacher development, this chapter surveyed the theoretical implications and practical implementations of model-centered learning for mathematics teaching and learning in a technology-rich environment. We conclude that modeling with dynamic technology is a pedagogically powerful approach to mathematics education, which empowers students and their teachers to experience genuine mathematics in the real world and across the STEAM domains, allowing them to construct, diagnose, evaluate, and appreciate mathematical meaning in a thoughtful, emotional, and ultimately aesthetic manner.

Looking into the future, we see an exciting era of mathematics teaching and learning when school students and their teachers come face to face with powerful mathematics far beyond the burdensome memorization of rules, formulas, and theorems. Yet we also feel uncertain about the uncharted territory of technology-infused mathematics teaching and learning. Education, and mathematics education in particular, has been disappointingly slow in responding to the advancement of the digital technologies. Fey (2006) remarked that "if one were to compare syllabi, teaching, and examination in many high school and early college mathematics courses today with those of half a century earlier, there would be remarkable similarities in expectations for student learning and in classroom practices" (p. 348). Indeed, there is a rich variety of teaching tools in today's mathematics classrooms with powerful touch technologies alongside paper-pencils and chalkboards. Frequently we find ourselves with a piece of chalk in the left hand and a digital stylus in the right hand, staging a choreography of the old and the new in teaching and doing mathematics, feeling the tension from both sides. Students are adapting to new representational media at such a high rate that researchers can barely catch up. We simply do not have the luxury of time for a two-year control-treatment experiment before allowing students to have access to the new technologies. Or rather, should we adult educators and researchers adapt to the new technologies in our methodology and philosophy of mathematics education? The same can be said of traditional textbooks, which have struggled to catch up with the dynamic mathematics technologies. As our personal reflection on writing this chapter, we struggled painstakingly to present some dynamic mathematical processes on paper. Interestingly, the GeoGeba community, through its online GeoGebraTube, has launched a GeoGebra Math Book, which seeks to transform the traditional notion of a mathematics textbook into a book of dynamic mathematics. Little research has been conducted about the impact, both curriculum-wise and cognitively, of such dynamic mathematics resources on student learning, teacher development, and assessment. Are there any mathematical ideas that are better explored using traditional tools and media? If so, how do we pair up existing technology tools and mathematical tasks (Doerr & Pratt, 2008)? Furthermore, how do students and mathematics teachers adapt to and evaluate the validity of emerging dynamic mathematical objects across the STEAM disciplines?

Indeed, the mathematics education of school students is at a crossroads. Technically, emerging and pervasive digital technologies have trivialized traditionally valued complex mathematical computations and procedures, leaving little for paper-and-pencil manipulation. Politically, new national and state standards have shifted the curricular focus onto understanding, problem solving skills, and productive dispositions toward mathematical reasoning. A natural tension thus exists between the growing public expectations and the traditional mathematics curricula, calling for innovative instructional designs that suit the changing needs of students and the evolving visions for 21st century mathematics education and quantitative literacy. It is within such a context that we call for the reconceptualization of school mathematics from a model-centered perspective to foster mathematical understanding, promote ownership, and infuse aesthetic experiences into students' mathematical experiences. In light of the enormous complexity of technology, mathematics, and human cognition, we acknowledge the relevancy of the uncertainty principle (Spector, 2000; Streefland & van den Heuvel-Panhuizen, 1998) in dynamic mathematics teaching and learning. Ultimately, mathematics learning, as well as mathematics teaching, is as much as an art as it is a science, where we must remain "flexibly purposive" (Eisner, 2002, p. 205) and make meaningful connection across the STEAM disciplines in our instructional design and ensuing teaching practices. We call on our colleagues and mathematics teachers to contribute to the ongoing technology-integrated reconceptualization of mathematics and mathematics teaching and revitalize the role of mathematics as a driving force in STEAM education.

Acknowledgements The authors would like to thank the anonymous reviewers and editors for their constructive comments and suggestions. The article makes references to findings of a project supported by the Illinois School Board of Education through an MSP Grant (#4963-80-30-039-5400-51). The analyses and views expressed in the article belong to the authors and do not necessarily reflect those of the funding agency.

References

Ashcraft, M. H. (2002). Math anxiety: Personal, educational, and cognitive consequences. *Current Directions in Psychological Science, 11*(5), 181–185.

Battista, M. T. (2008). Development of the shape makers geometry microworld: Design principles and research. In G. W. Blume & M. K. Heid (Eds.), *Research on technology and the teaching and learning of mathematics: Cases and perspectives* (Vol. 2, pp. 131–156). Charlotte: Information Age Publishing.

Booch, G. (1994). *Object-oriented analysis and design with applications* (2nd ed.). Menlo Park: Addison-Wesley.

Borwein, J., & Devlin, K. (2009). *The computer as crucible: An introduction to experimental mathematics.* Wellesley: A K Peters.

Bruner, J. (1991). The narrative construction of reality. *Critical Inquiry, 18,* 1–21.

Bu, L., & Schoen, R. (Eds.). (2011). *Model-centered learning: Pathways to mathematical understanding using geogebra.* Rotterdam: Sense Publishers.

Bu, L., Mumba, F., Henson, H., & Wright, M. (2013). Geogebra in professional development: The experience of rural inservice elementary (k-8) teachers. *Mevlana International Journal of Education, 3*(3), 64–76.

Council of Chief State School Officers. (2010). *Common core state standards for mathematics.* Washington, D. C.: National Governors Association Center for Best Practices, Council of Chief State School Officers. http://www.corestandards.org/math. Accessed 14 Oct 2011.

Darling-Hammond, L., Barron, B., Pearson, P. D., Schoenfeld, A. H., Stage, E. K., Zimmerman, T. D., et al. (2008). *Powerful learning: What we know about teaching for understanding.* San Francisco: Jossey-Bass.

de Jong, T., & van Joolingen, W. R. (2008). Model-facilitated learning. In J. M. Spector, M. D. Merrill, J. van Merriënboer, & M. P. Driscoll (Eds.), *Handbook of research on educational communications and technology* (3rd ed., pp. 457–468). New York: Lawrence Erlbaum Associates.

diSessa, A. A. (2007). Systemics of learning for a revised pedagogical agenda. In R. A. Lesh, E. Hamilton, & J. J. Kaput (Eds.), *Foundations for the future in mathematics education* (pp. 245–261). Mahwah: Lawrence Erlbaum Associates.

Doerr, H. M., & Pratt, D. (2008). The learning of mathematics and mathematical modeling. In M. K. Heid & G. W. Blume (Eds.), *Research on technology and the teaching and learning of mathematics: Research syntheses* (Vol. 1, pp. 259–285). Charlotte: Information Age Publishing.

Dreyfus, T., & Eisenberg, T. (1986). On the aesthetics of mathematical thought. *For the Learning of Mathematics, 6*(1), 2–10.

Duval, R. (2006). A cognitive analysis of problems of comprehension in a learning of mathematics. *Educational Studies in Mathematics, 61,* 103–131.

Eisner, E. W. (2002). *The arts and the creation of mind.* New Haven: Yale University Press.

Eseryel, D., Ge, X., Ifenthaler, D., & Law, V. (2011). Dyanmic modeling as a cognitive regulation scaffold for developing complex problem solving skills in an educational massively multiplayer online game environment. *Journal of Educational Computing Research, 45*(3), 265–286.

Fey, J. T. (2006). Connecting technology and school mathematics: A review of the didactical challenge of symbolic calculators: Turning a computational device into a mathematical instrument. *Journal for Research in Mathematics Education, 36,* 348–352.

Freudenthal, H. (1973). *Mathematics as an educational task.* Dordrecht: D. Reidel Publishing.

Freudenthal, H. (1978). *Weeding and sowing: Preface to a science of mathematics education.* Dordrecht: D. Reidel Publishing.

Freudenthal, H. (1983). *Didactical phenomenology of mathematical structures.* New York: Kluwer Academic Publishers.

Ge, X., & Land, S. M. (2004). A conceptual framework for scaffolding ill-structured problem-solving processes using questions prompts and peer interactios. *Educational Technology Research and Development, 52*(2), 5–22.

Gojak, L. M. (2014). A reflection on 25 years in mathematics education. http://www.nctm.org/about/content.aspx?id=41883. Accessed 14 April 2014.

Goldin, G. (2007). Aspects of affect and mathematical modeling processes. In R. A. Lesh, E. Hamilton, & J. J. Kaput (Eds.), *Foundations for the future in mathematics education* (pp. 281–299). Mahwah: Lawrence Erlbaum Associates.

Gravemeijer, K. (1994). Educational development and developmental research in mathematics education. *Journal for Research in Mathematics Education, 25,* 443–471.

Gravemeijer, K. (2008). Learning mathematics: The problem of learning abstract knowledge. In J. M. Spector, M. D. Merrill, J. van Merriënboer, & M. P. Driscoll (Eds.), *Handbook of research on educational communications and technology* (3rd ed., pp. 545–549). New York: Lawrence Erlbaum Associates.

Gravemeijer, K., & van Galen, F. (2003). Facts and algorithms as products of students' own mathematical activity. In J. Kilpatrick, W. G. Martin, & D. Schifter (Eds.), *A research companion to principles and standards for school mathematics* (pp. 114–122). Reston: National Council of Teachers of Mathematics.

Gravemeijer, K., Cobb, P., Bowers, J., & Whitenack, J. (2000). Symbolizing, modeling, and instructional design. In P. Cobb, E. Yackel, & K. McClain (Eds.), *Symbolizing and communicating in mathematics classrooms: Perspectives on discourse, tools, and instructional design* (pp. 225–273). Mahwah: Lawrence Erlbaum Associates.

Gresham, G. (2007). A study of mathematics anxiety in pre-service teachers. *Early Childhood Education Journal, 35*(2), 181–188.

Groff, J. (2013). Expanding our "frames" of mind for education and the arts. *Harvard Educational Review, 83*(1), 15–39.

Hardy, G. H. (1940/1967). *A mathematician's apology.* London: Cambridge University Press. (Original work published 1940).

Hegedus, S. J., & Moreno-Armella, L. (2009). Introduction: The transformative nature of "Dynamic" Educational technology. *Zentralblatt für Didaktik der Mathematik, 41,* 397–398.

Hohenwarter, M., & Preiner, J. (2007). Dynamic mathematics with geogebra. *Journal of Online Mathematics and Its Applications,* 7. http://mathdl.maa.org/mathDL/4/?pa=content&sa=view Document&nodeId=1448. Accessed 1 May 2010.

Ifenthaler, D., & Seel, N. M. (2010). *From model-based to schema-based reasoning: Looking ofr the magic number x.* Paper presented at the 2010 American Educational Research Association.

Ifenthaler, D., & Seel, N. M. (2011). A longitudinal perspective on inductive reasoning tasks. Illuminating the probability of change. *Learning and Instruction, 21*(4), 538–549.

Johnson, M. (2007). *The meaning of the body: Aesthetics of human understanding.* Chicago: University of Chicago Press.

Johnson-Laird, P. N. (1983). *Mental models: Toward a cognitive science of language, inference, and consciousness.* Cambridge: Harvard University Press.

Jonassen, D. H. (1996). *Computers in the classroom: Mindtools for critical thinking.* Englewood Cliffs: Prentice Hall.

Jonassen, D. H. (2006). *Modeling with technology: Mindtools for conceptual change* (3rd ed.). Upper Saddle River: Pearson.

Jonassen, D. H. (2011). *Learning to solve problems: A handbook for designing problem-solving environments.* New York: Routledge.

Kaput, J. (1992). Technology and mathematics education. In D. A. Grouws (Ed.), *Handbook of research on mathematics teaching and learning* (pp. 515–556). New York: Macmillan.

Kaput, J., & Schorr, R. (2008). Changing representational infrastructures changes most everything: The case of simcalc, algebra, and calculus. In G. W. Blume & M. K. Heid (Eds.), *Research on technology and the teaching and learning of mathematics: Cases and perspectives* (Vol. 2, pp. 211–253). Charlotte: Information Age Publishing.

Kaput, J., & Thompson, P. W. (1994). Technology in mathematics education research: The first 25 years in the jrme. *Journal for Research in Mathematics Education, 25,* 676–684.

Kaput, J., Noss, R., & Hoyles, C. (2002). Developing new notations for a learnable mathematics in the computational era. In L. D. English (Ed.), *Handbook of international research in mathematics education* (pp. 51–75). Mahwah: Lawrence and Erlbaum Associates.

Kaput, J., Hegedus, S., & Lesh, R. (2007). Technology becoming infrastructural in mathematics education. In R. A. Lesh, E. Hamilton, & J. Kaput (Eds.), *Foundations for the future in mathematics education* (pp. 173–191). Mahwah: Lawrence Erlbaum Associates.

Kelly, B. (2003). The emergence of technology in mathematics education. In G. M. A. Stanic & J. Kilpatrick (Eds.), *A history of school mathematics* (Vol. 2, pp. 1037–1081). Reston: National Council of Teachers of Mathematics.

Lesh, R., & Doerr, H. M. (Eds.). (2003). *Beyond constructivism: Models and modeling perspectives on mathematics problem solving, learning, and teaching.* Mahwah: Lawrence Erlbaum Associates.

Martinovic, D., & Karadag, Z. (2012). Dynamic and interactive mathematics learning environments: The case of teaching the limit concept. *Teaching Mathematics and its Applications, 31*(1), 41–48.

Merrill, M. D. (2000). Knowledge objects and mental models. *The instructional use of learning objects: Online version.*

Milrad, M., Spector, J. M., & Davidsen, P. I. (2003). Model facilitated learning. In S. Naidu (Ed.), *Learning and teaching with technology: Principles and practices* (pp. 13–27). London: Kogan Page.

Minsky, M. (2006). *The emotion machine: Commonsense thinking, artificial intelligence, and the future of the human mind.* New York: Simon & Schuster.

Mooney, D. D., & Swift, R. J. (1999). *A course in mathematical modeling.* Washington, D. C.: Mathemaitcal Association of America.

Moreno-Armella, L., & Hegedus, S. (2009). Co-action with digital technologies. *ZDM, 41,* 505–519.

Moreno-Armella, L., Hegedus, S. J., & Kaput, J. J. (2008). From static to dynamic mathematics: Historical and representational perspectives. *Educational Studies in Mathematics, 68,* 99–111.

National Council of Teachers of Mathematics. (2000). *Principles and standards for school mathematics*. Reston: Author.

National Research Council. (1989). *Everybody counts: A report to the nation on the future of mathematics education*. Washington, D. C.: National Academy of Sciences.

National Research Council. (2000). *How people learn: Brain, mind, experience, and school (expanded edition)*: Committee on Developments in the Science of Learning. Washington, D. C.: National Academies Press.

National Research Council. (2001). Adding it up: Helping children learn mathematics. In J. Kilpatrick, J. Swafford, & B. Findell (Eds.), *Mathematics learning study committee, center for education, division of behavioral and social sciences and education*. Washington, D. C.: National Academy Press.

National Research Council. (2005). *How students learn: Mathematics in the classroom*. Washington, D. C.: National Academies Press. (Committee on how people learn, a targeted report for teachers, M.S. Donovan and J.D. Bransford, Editors. Division of behavioral and social sciences and education).

National Research Council. (2010). Preparing teachers: Building evidence for sound policy. Committee on the study of teacher preparation programs in the United States, Center for Education. Division of behavioral and social sciences and education. Washington, D. C.: National Academies Press.

Nickerson, R. S. (1985). Understanding understanding. *American Journal of Education, 93*, 201–239.

Norman, D. A. (1983). Some observations on mental models. In D. Gentner & A. L. Stevens (Eds.), *Mental models* (pp. 7–14). Hillsdale: Lawrence Erlbaum Associates.

Perkins, D. N. (1986). *Knowledge as design*. Hillsdale: Lawrence Erlbaum Associates.

Perkins, D. N. (1993). Teaching for understanding. *American Educator, 17*(3), 8, 28–35.

Perkins, D. N. (2009). *Making learning whole: How seven principles of teaching can transform education*. San Francisco: Jossey-Bass.

Pimm, D., & Sinclair, N. (2006). Aesthetics and the 'mathematical mind'. In N. Sinclair, D. Pimm, & W. Higginson (Eds.), *Mathematics and the aesthetic: New approaches to an ancient affinity* (pp. 223–254). New York: Springer.

Pollak, H. O. (2003). A history of the teaching of modeling. In G. M. A. Stanic & J. Kilpatrick (Eds.), *A history of school mathematics* (Vol. 1, pp. 647–671). Reston: National Council of Teachers of Mathematics.

Polya, G. (1945/2004). *How to solve it: A new aspect of mathematical method* (2nd ed.). Princeton: Princeton University Press.

Polya, G. (1981). *Mathematical discovery: On understanding, learning, and teaching problem solving* (Combined ed.). New York: Wiley.

Resnick, L. B., & Ford, W. W. (1981). *The psychology of mathematics for instruction*. Hillsdale: Lawrence Erlbaum Associates.

Ryan, J., & Williams, J. (2007). *Children's mathematics 4–15: Learning from errors and misconceptions*. New York: Open University Press.

Salomon, G., Perkins, D. N., & Globerson, T. (1991). Partners in cognition: Extending human intelligence with intelligent technologies. *Educational Researcher, 20*(3), 2–9.

Schoenfeld, A. H. (1985). *Mathematical problem solving*. Orlando: Academic Press.

Schwartz, J. L. (2007). Models, simulations, and exploratory environments: A tentative taxonomy. In R. A. Lesh, E. Hamilton, & J. J. Kaput (Eds.), *Foundations for the future in mathematics education* (pp. 161–171). Mahwah: Lawrence Erlbaum Associates.

Seel, N. M. (2003). Model-centered learning and instruction. *Technology, Instruction, Cognition and Learning, 1*, 59–85.

Seel, N. M. (2005). Designing model-centered learning environments: Hocus-pocus or the focus must strictly be on locus. In J. M. Spector, C. Ohrazda, A. van Schaack, & D. A. Wiley (Eds.), *Innovations in instructional technology: Essays in honor of m. David Merrill* (pp. 65–90). Mahwah: Lawrence Erlbaum Associates.

Seel, N. M. (2008). Empirical perspectives on memory and motivation. In J. M. Spector, M. D. Merrill, J. van Merriënboer, & M. P. Driscoll (Eds.), *Handbook of research on educational communications and technology* (3rd ed., pp. 39–54). New York: Lawrence Erlbaum Associates.

Seel, N. M. (2014). Model-based learning and performance. In J. M. Spector, M. D. Merrill, J. Elen, & M. J. Bishop (Eds.), *Handbook of research on educational communications and technology* (4th ed., pp. 465–484). New York: Springer.

Seel, N. M., & Blumschein, P. (2009). Modeling and simulation in learning and instruction: A theoretical perspective. In P. Blumschein, W. Hung, D. Jonassen, & J. Strobel (Eds.), *Model-based approaches to learning: Using systems models and simulations to improve understanding and problem solving in complex domains* (pp. 3–15). Rotterdam: Sense Publishers.

Sfard, A. (1991). On the dual nature of mathematical conceptions: Reflections on processes and objects as different sides of the same coin. *Educational Studies in Mathematics, 22,* 1–36.

Silver, E. A. (1986). Using conceptual and procedural knowledge: A focus on relationships. In J. Hilbert (Ed.), *Conceptual and procedural knowledge: The case of mathematics* (pp. 181–198). Hillsdale: Lawrence Erlbaum Associates.

Silver, E. A., Mesa, V. M., Morris, K. A., Star, J. R., & Benken, B. M. (2009). Teaching mathematics for understanding: An analysis of lessons submitted by teachers seeking nbpts certification. *American Educational Research Journal, 46,* 501–531.

Sinclair, N. (2006). *Mathematics and beauty: Aesthetic approahces to teaching children.* New York: Teachers College Press.

Sinclair, N., Pimm, D., & Higginson, W. (Eds.). (2006). *Mathematics and the aesthetic: New approaches to an ancient affinity.* New York: Springer.

Skemp, R. R. (1978). Relational understanding and instrumental understanding. *Arithmetic Teacher, 26*(3), 9–15.

Skemp, R. R. (2006). Relational understanding and instrumental understanding. *Mathematics Teaching in the Middle School, 12*(2), 88–96. (Original work published in 1976).

Smith, M. S., & Stein, M. K. (2011). *Five practices for orchestrating productive mathematics discussions.* Reston: National Council of Teachers of Mathematics.

Somervell, E. L. (1906/1975). *A rhythmic approach to mathematics.* Reston: National Council of Teachers of Mathematics. (ERIC Document Reproduction Service No. ED108964). Retrieved, June 22, 2009. from ERIC.

Spector, J. M. (2000). Building theory into practice in learning and instruction. In J. M. Spector & T. M. Anderson (Eds.), *Integrated and holistic perspectives on learning, instruction and technology: Understanding complexity* (pp. 79–90). Dordrecht: Kluwer Academic Publishers.

Spector, J. M. (2008). Cognition and learning in the digital age: Promising research and practice. *Computers in Human Behavior, 24*(2), 249–262.

Spector, J. M. (2009). Foreword. In P. Blumschein, W. Hung, D. Jonassen, & J. Strobel (Eds.), *Model-based approaches to learning: Using systems models and simulations to improve understanding and problem solving in complex domains* (pp. ix–x). Rotterdam: Sense Publishers.

Streefland, L. (Ed.). (1991). *Fractions in realistic mathematics education: A paradigm of developmental research.* Dordrecht: Kluwer Academic Publishers.

Streefland, L., & van den Heuvel-Panhuizen, M. (1998). Uncertainty, a metaphor for mathematics education? *The Journal of Mathematical Behavior, 17,* 393–397.

Stroup, W. M., Ares, N. M., & Hurford, A. C. (2005). A dialectic analysis of generativity: Issues of network-supported design in mathematics and science. *Mathematical Thinking and Learning, 7,* 181–206.

Stroup, W. M., Ares, N., Hurford, A. C., & Lesh, R. (2007). Diversity-by-design: The what, why, and how of generativity in next-generation classroom networks. In R. A. Lesh, E. Hamilton, & J. J. Kaput (Eds.), *Foundations for the future in mathematics education* (pp. 367–393). Mahwah: Lawrence Erlbaum Associates.

Tobias, S. (1993). *Overcoming math anxiety (revised and expanded).* New York: W. W. Norton & Company.

Treffers, A. (1987). *Three dimensions: A model of goal and theory description in mathematics instruction–the wiskobas project.* Dordrecht: D. Reidel Publishing Company.

Van den Heuvel-Panhuizen, M. (2003). The didactical use of models in realistic mathematics education: An example from a longitudinal trajectory on percentage. *Educational Studies in Mathematics, 54,* 9–35.

Vygotsky, L. S. (1997). *Educational psychology (R. Silverman, Trans.).* Boca Raton: St. Lucie Press. (Original work published 1926).

Yackel, E., & Cobb, P. (1996). Sociomathematical norms, argumentation, and autonomy in mathematics. *Journal for Research in Mathematics Education, 27,* 458–477.

Zbiek, R., & Conner, A. (2006). Beyond motivation: Exploring mathematical modeling as a context for deepening students' understandings of curricular mathematics. *Educational Studies in Mathematics, 63,* 89–112.

Lingguo Bu is an associate professor of mathematics education in the Department of Curriculum and Instruction at Southern Illinois University Carbondale. He has a rich background in STEM education and has taught undergraduate and graduate courses in foundations of learning and instruction, mathematics, mathematics education, and teacher professional development. He is actively engaged with classroom teachers through state and federally funded mathematics and science partnership grants that seek to build learning communities to promote K-16 student achievement. His research interests include model-centered learning and instruction in mathematics education, problem/project-based learning, emergent dynamic mathematics learning technologies, and interdisciplinary studies that explore the complexity of STEM cognition through the synergy of literacy, mathematics, dynamic technology, and design research.

Markus Hohenwarter is professor of mathematics education at the Johannes Kepler University Linz, Austria since 2010. His main research focus is the use of technology for teaching and learning mathematics. He started the development of the open source dynamic mathematics software GeoGebra in Austria and has been involved in several international teacher professional development projects in Florida, England, Hungary and Austria.

Part VII
Epilogue

Moving Forward with STEAM Education Research

Xun Ge, Dirk Ifenthaler and J. Michael Spector

Abstract In this concluding chapter, the importance of STEAM education in supporting the 21st century skills is again emphasized. We have analyzed three themes that emerged from the chapters included in this book: (1) different perspectives towards STEAM education and the role of Arts, (2) the role of technology in STEAM education, and (3) the pedagogy and curricula development in STEAM education. Based on our literature review and the scholarly work contributed by the authors of this book, we have identified a number of areas that need to be focused on as we move forward with research, development and practice in the broad area of STEAM education. The chapter concludes with a discussion of future directions for research and practice.

Keywords Science, Technology, Engineering, Art, and Mathematics (STEAM) education · 21st century skills · The Arts · The role of technology · Competence-based learning · Well-rounded individuals · Reconceptualizing curricula · STEAM pedagogy

Introduction

With much interest and excitement, we have read, reviewed, and reflected on the previous 19 chapters that are included in this book. We were amazed by the various creative ideas the authors shared, the innovative efforts they made, the multiple

X. Ge (✉)
University of Oklahoma, Norman, USA
e-mail: xge@ou.edu

D. Ifenthaler
University of Mannheim, Mannheim, Germany
e-mail: dirk@ifenthaler.info

Deakin University, Melbourne, Australia

J. M. Spector
University of North Texas, Denton, USA
e-mail: Mike.Spector@unt.edu

© Springer International Publishing Switzerland 2015
X. Ge et al. (eds.), *Emerging Technologies for STEAM Education,*
Educational Communications and Technology: Issues and Innovations,
DOI 10.1007/978-3-319-02573-5_20

perspectives they offered, and the scientific principles they applied to their STEAM projects. We conclude this book with this chapter by presenting our analysis of the themes that emerged from the chapters, as well as our editorial comments for future directions with STEAM research and practice. We hope this chapter will serve to invite further dialogues among the authors and professionals in the larger community of educational research and practice about STEAM education.

Following an introduction, this chapter provides a brief background of the key concepts, including STEM education, STEAM education, 21st century skills, and the relationships among these concepts. Then, three major themes that emerged from the 19 chapters are discussed. The first theme is the different perspectives of STEAM education in relation to the role of the Arts, design disciplines, and the humanities (hereafter referred to more simply as the Arts) and the goals of STEAM education. The second theme is STEAM education and the role educational technology plays in various contexts. The third theme focuses on various pedagogical approaches and models as well as curricula design. After analyzing the main themes generated from the chapters, we discuss the implications for future research, particularly how the research on STEAM education can move forward based on our understanding of the current status of STEAM education.

STEM, STEAM, and Partnership 21st Century Skills

The 21st century is an exciting age for innovations and technology advancement. It is also a challenging time for educators, as well as for those who are concerned with education; the challenge is to ensure that students are ready for an ever-changing world and fully capable of becoming tomorrow's progressive leaders, productive workers, and responsible citizens. In 2002, The Partnership for 21st Century Skills (P21) (http://www.p21.org/) was founded as a coalition bringing together the business community, education leaders, and policymakers to position 21st century readiness at the center of U.S. K-12 education and to kick-start a national conversation on the importance of 21st century skills for all students. In 2006, President Bush announced the American Competitiveness Initiative (http://en.wikipedia.org/wiki/STEM_fields) to address shortfalls in federal government support of educational development and progress at all academic levels in the Science, Technology, Engineering, and Mathematics (STEM) fields and prepare a pipeline of secondary school and college students ready to major in STEM disciplines and choose STEM fields as their future careers.

Since then, the U.S federal government has poured in a lot of funding to support educational research in K-12 education and college education in the STEM disciplines; the same is occurring in many other developed countries. During the same period, a few educational leaders and researchers began exploring how to integrate the Arts into STEM education. For example, the Rhode Island School of Design in Providence (RISD; see http://www.risd.edu/about/STEM_to_STEAM/) has an initiative to include art and design in STEM education. The National Technology Leadership Coalition (see http://www.ntlcoalition.org/) holds an annual summit that since 2012 has had an emphasis on STEAM education. These educators believe that STEAM education will not only facilitate STEM education, but also bring about additional benefits for learners. There have been other movements in the U.S. and other parts of the world to motivate students in STEM disciplines through Arts and Design. Examples can also be found at the University of Minnesota (see https://www.kutztown.edu/academics/visual_arts/arted/PDF/APlaceFor.pdf), at the MC²STEM High School in Cleveland (see http://www.mc2stemhighschool.org/), the University of Virginia's Center for Technology & Teacher Education (see http://curry.virginia.edu/research/labs/engineering-design-initiative), and the European KiiCS (Knowledge Incubation in Innovation and Creation of Science) project (see http://www.kiics.eu/en/). Along with these and other initiatives are the pedagogy and specific strategies for conducting STEAM education.

Those who support the STEAM initiatives recognize a number of perceived values of integrating Arts into the curricula. Particularly, the integration of Arts promotes not only students' cognitive growth, but also emotional and psychomotor growth, strengthens their critical thinking and problem solving, cultivates their creativity and encourages self-expression. As we examine the stated advantages of Arts integration and refer to the 21st century skills, STEAM education seems to make perfect sense. First of all, language and arts are core subjects and 21st century themes (http://www.p21.org/). Secondly, 21st century skills include some essential skills, such as *learning and innovation skills*, which further break down into *creativity* and *innovation*, *critical thinking* and *problem solving*, *communication* and *collaboration*. Therefore, STEAM education seems to be a promising pedagogical approach that may effectively help students to achieve the goals in STEM disciplines while at the same time developing 21st century skills that will prepare them to lead and take on the challenges.

STEAM Education and Role of Arts: Different Perspectives

Several different perspectives about STEAM education have emerged from the chapters of this book: (1) Arts supports learning in STEM domains, (2) Arts cultivates well-rounded individuals, (3) STEAM supports Arts education. In order to understand the first two perspectives, we need to examine the role of Arts and understand their perceived benefits for learners.

Arts Support Learning in STEM Domains

There are different views about the role of the Arts. The first view reflects the utility perspective of Arts, that is, Arts are tools to learn STEM subjects. Sousa and Pilecki (2013) argue that many scientists, mathematicians, and engineers use skills borrowed from the arts as scientific tools. Those skills include observing accurately, perceiving an object in a different form, constructing meaning, expressing one's observations accurately, working effectively with others, thinking spatially, and perceiving kinesthetically.

Sousa and Pilecki also contend that arts develop cognitive growth, such as developing learners' critical thinking, creativity, problem-solving and decision-making skills, as well as communications and collaboration skills. A study suggested that students who played instruments had higher math scores than those who did not (Haley, 2001). Another study indicated that Arts improve long-term retention of content (Rinne, Gregory, Yarmolinskaya, & Hardiman, 2011). Additionally, some other studies demonstrated a strong relationship between music education and academic achievement (e.g., Fitzpatrick, 2006; Johnson & Memmott, 2006).

Arts also seem to promote creativity. Encouraging students to participate in the Arts-related activities can foster spontaneity and self-expression, which lead to creative results (Sousa & Pilecki, 2013). The Arts-related activities are effective ways of introducing children to some basic concepts in science and mathematics. They allow students to work collaboratively and engage in group planning, problem-solving, and decision making. These are some essential 21st century skills.

All these advantages about the Arts suggest appropriate alignments with the 21st century skills and that integrating Arts in STEM can help students to achieve 21st century skills and promote learning in STEM domains. This perspective reflects a focus on competence-based skill development, which is discussed in Chapter "The Language Arts as Foundational for Science, Technology, Engineering, Art, and Mathematics" (Baines) and Chapter "Education, Training, Competencies, Curricula and Technology" (Spector). While indicating that communication is an important 21st century skills, Spector argues that those who can speak clearly naturally migrate to leadership and management positions. In fact, most of the chapters share the competence-based perspective in practicing STEAM education, including Chapter "Active Learning Approaches to Integrating Technology into a Middle School Science Curriculum Based on 21st Century Skills" (Christensen & Knezek) and Chapter "Preparing Students with 21st Century Skills: Integrating Scientific Knowledge, Skills, and Epistemic Beliefs in Middle School Science Curricula" (Gu & Belland), focusing on the competencies that will help students to be successful in their science learning, such as creativity, critical thinking, communication and collaboration. Gu and Belland (Chapter "Preparing Students with 21st Century Skills: Integrating Scientific Knowledge, Skills, and Epistemic Beliefs in Middle School Science Curricula") argue how effective integration of engineering and art design into science curriculum can help to promote middle school students' argumentation abilities in science learning. Chapter "Critical Support Systems to Enhance the Development and Assessment of 21st Century Expertise in Engineering Students" (Palou et al.) imply how Arts help to facilitates learning by supporting students' critical and creative thinking in engineering education.

In the same manner, Gogus (Chapter "Reconceptualizing Liberal Education in the 21st Century the Role of Emerging Technologies and Steam Fields in Liberal Education") maintains that liberal arts lead to competency development and prepare them to deal with complexity, diversity, and change. The author argues that a liberal education helps students develop a sense of social responsibility, as well as strong and transferable intellectual and practical skills such as communication, analytical and problem-solving skills, as well as a demonstrated ability to apply knowledge and skills in real-world settings. Apparently, enhancing Arts in the curriculum enables individuals to develop their competencies needed for their future careers.

Arts Cultivate Well-Rounded Individuals

The second perspective reflects a humanistic view about developing a whole person. This view holds that the Arts provide the very foundation upon which knowledge in STEM is created (see Baines, Chapter "The Language Arts as Foundational for Science, Technology, Engineering, Art, and Mathematics"). However, Spector (Chapter "Education, Training, Competencies, Curricula and Technology") has a slightly different perspective from Baines (Chapter "The Language Arts as Foundational for Science, Technology, Engineering, Art, and Mathematics"), which places an emphasis on striking a balance between individual and societal interests and needs. Spector proposes integrating liberal arts and humanities into STEM education to emphasize the development of abilities associated with esthetics, innovation, and creativity.

According to Sousa and Pilecki, (2013), the Arts provide a higher quality of human experience throughout a person's lifetime. This view also supports 21st century mission to prepare all students for the challenges of work, life, and citizenship today and beyond, as well as ensure ongoing innovation in our economy and the health of our democracy. In fact, developing well-rounded individuals helps to develop the fine qualities and attributes that are needed for STEM disciplines. Liu, Ludu, and Holton (Chapter "Can K-12 Math Teachers Train Students to Make Valid Logical Reasoning? A Question Affecting 21st Century Skills") argue that everyone needs to acquire logic education, which they regard as an essential component of the curriculum that is necessary to develop critical thinking and problem solving skills.

Arts Development Supported by STEAM Education

A totally opposite but interesting perspective is that humanities can be understood through STEAM, and certain types of knowledge and learning within the liberal arts can be cultivated through STEAM. Lewis (Chapter "Putting the "H" in Steam: Paradigms for Modern Liberal Arts Education") argues that STEAM education is an emerging K12 approach that infuses the liberal arts with design thinking, collaboration, creative thinking, and critical thinking associated with humanistic inquiry. She illustrates with examples how the STEAM paradigms, that is, *inquiry, interactivity*, and *innovation* can be incorporated into the liberal arts curriculum to promote metacognition, active learning, and other 21st century skills.

Interestingly, Shen, Liu, and Jiang (Chapter "Reconceptualizing a College Science Learning Experience in the New Digital Era: A Review of Literature") believe that the learning of sciences and arts can mutually support each other. On one hand, the students apply their scientific understanding of light to create artistic products, and on the other hand students use visual aids as a means to communicate their scientific ideas and findings both informatively and aesthetically, which also fuel their creative thinking. Based on these chapters, we contend that when the Arts are strengthened and developed, it will result in nurturing well-rounded individuals with essential qualities, which allow them to develop complex and transferable skills and abilities to deal with complex problems innovatively and creatively.

STEAM Education and the Role of Technology

Technology plays several important roles in STEAM education. First, information literacy, media literacy, and information and communication technology literacy are listed among some of the most important 21st century student outcomes. Therefore, it is a subject area to be studied by students and a skill set to be measured as a learning outcome. Secondly, technology is viewed as a tool to support students' learning and a vehicle for teachers to support their instructional activities as they integrate technology in their instruction. For example, in Biin and Weston's chapter (Chapter "An Indigenous Learning Approach to Computer Science Education 21st Century Skills for Middle and High School Aboriginal Children on British Columbia's West Coast"), technology was a subject area for students to learn computer programming, yet it was also a vehicle for students to learn the values of indigenous language and culture and the appreciation of their natural environment. Milner-Bolotin (Chapter "Technology-Enhanced Teacher Education for 21st Century: Challenges and Possibilities") shares her experience of engaging teacher-candidates in learning how to use technology while engaging in the process of technology integration in their instructions.

In some other chapters, technology is described as tools to carry out or support education in STEAM disciplines. For example, Baines (Chapter "The Language Arts as Foundational for Science, Technology, Engineering, Art, and Mathematics") indicates that technology has always been integrated as a vehicle or tool in teaching language, which is a view shared by many other authors in the book. Grant (Chapter "Using Mobile Devices to Support Formal, Informal and Semi-Formal Learning") summarizes the usefulness of mobile devices as a form of technology in supporting learning and instruction with STEAM disciplines, including creating representations of knowledge, supporting performance and decision-making, and enabling personalized learning.

Moreover, technology is also illustrated as cognitive tools not only to support visualization in science education (e.g., Shen, Jiang, & Liu, Chapter "Reconceptualizing a College Science Learning Experience in the New Digital Era: A Review of Literature") and provide mental modeling in mathematics (e.g., Bu & Hohenwarter,

Chapter "Modeling for Dynamic Mathematics Toward Technology-Integrated Aesthetic Experiences in School Mathematics "), but also to enhance STEAM education by developing students' aesthetic understanding, appreciation, and expression while engaging them in STEM learning activities.

STEAM Education: Pedagogy and Curriculum Development

Some useful instructional strategies, models and tools are identified in support of STEAM education, including visual representation, model-centered learning, community-based learning, and storytelling. In addition, several chapters discuss reconceptualization of STEAM curricula guided by various pedagogical frameworks aligned with Framework for 21st Century Learning (http://www.p21.org/).

Instructional Strategies, Models, and Tools to Support STEAM Education

The contributors of this book used a variety of strategies to scaffold students' cognitive and metacognitive processes in STEAM disciplines while stimulating their interest and engaging them in deep learning. One of the effectives strategies being discussed is visual representation. Visual representation is the representation of knowledge that facilitates information processing, knowledge construction, and problem solving. Shen, Jiang, and Liu (Chapter "Reconceptualizing a College Science Learning Experience in the New Digital Era: A Review of Literature") discuss how computer visualization and simulations support science education. One of the examples is the PhET Interactive Simulation, in which abstract and complex scientific phenomena are visually represented to provide students with specific scenarios and allow the opportunity for them to interact with visual objects. Visual representation not only draws students' attention, but also helps to identify misconceptions and facilitate deeper conceptual understanding.

Further, Castrol-Alonso and his colleagues (Chapter "The Potential of Embodied Cognition to Improve Steam Instructional Dynamic Visualizations") elaborate on the potential of using the embodied system, an emerging technology, to augment or extend the dynamic visualization demonstrated through videos and animations. The embodied dynamic visualization systems can address the issue of transiency, as found in conventional dynamic visualization systems, and improve instruction to support STEAM education through human manipulations and gesture interactions.

Bu and Hohenwarter (Chapter "Modeling for Dynamic Mathematics Toward Technology-Integrated Aesthetic Experiences in School Mathematics") present a model-centered approach to middle and high school mathematics education. This approach not only enhances students' mathematical understanding and self-assessment, but also allows students to experience the aesthetic dimension of mathematical inquiry in the broad context of STEAM education.

Storytelling is another strategy used to support STEAM education. Biin and Weston (Chapter "An Indigenous Learning Approach to Computer Science Education 21st Century Skills for Middle and High School Aboriginal Children on British Columbia's West Coast") developed the ANCESTOR computer program and used digital storytelling as a means to learn computer science while promoting students' interest in computer science for Aboriginal youth and adult learners and fostering their understanding of natural environments. Storytelling was incorporated into the program as a way to bridge the mainstream curriculum. Through working on digital storytelling projects, the secondary school students developed digital literacy, learned about cultural values, and collaborated with peer students to create Indigenized materials and practices for computer science education. In this example, the digital storytelling project became a means to integrate science learning with the Arts.

Reconceptualizing STEAM Curricula

To meet the needs and challenges of the 21st century, a number of authors have reconceptualized and reconstructed curricula in STEAM disciplines following various pedagogical frameworks. For example, Palou and his colleagues (Chapter "Critical Support Systems to Enhance the Development and Assessment of 21st Century Expertise in Engineering Students") reconceptualized their "pillar" courses in food, chemicals, and environmental engineering by creating a student-centered learning environment based on the frameworks of *21st Century Learning* and *How People Learn*, emphasizing metacognitive awareness, critical thinking, and creativity. The *How People Learn* framework consists of four components of a learning environment, which are knowledge-centered, learner-centered, community-centered, and assessment-centered, based on Bransford, Brown, and Cocking's (1999) works (also see http://www.nap.edu/openbook.php?isbn=0309070368). Similarly, Christensen and Knezek (Chapter "Active Learning Approaches to Integrating Technology into a Middle School Science Curriculum Based on 21st Century Skills") propose adopting an active learning framework to positively influence students' academic achievement as well as their attitudes toward science and related fields.

Coffland and Xie (Chapter "The 21st Century Mathematics Curriculum: A Technology Enhanced Experience") reconceptualized a secondary mathematics curriculum to what they call 21st Century Math Curriculum (21st CMC), which (1) embodies and stresses the messiness of real life, (2) enables learning progression, and (3) emphasizes an interdisciplinary approach. The CMC curriculum was designed to connect mathematics course content with real life, connect related topics within mathematics, and connect math to other subjects in the mathematics curriculum.

Ifenthaler, Siddique, and Mistress (Chapter "Designing for Open Innovation: Change of Attitudes, Self-Concept, and Team Dynamics in Engineering Education") presented a case study investigating the effects of a Learning Organization model on engineering students' attitude changes toward engineering, self-confidence, and team dynamics. This new curriculum emphasized the development of personal competencies in a collaborative learning framework and environment. In this model, learning was achieved at three levels: individual learning, team-based learning, and community-based learning. Although many of these curriculum frameworks were designed to support STEM education, they can well be adapted to and integrated with STEAM education.

In light of the Framework for the 21st century skills, the traditional curricula for STEAM no longer meet the current demands of the 21st century. Gogus (Chapter "Reconceptualizing Liberal Education in the 21st Century") argues that the liberal education curriculum needs to focus on *learning how to think* and *learning how to learn*, and we believe that these emphases should also be integrated in the curricula of other disciplines. Although not every chapter explicitly makes a link to the Arts, the authors' effort to integrate the Arts in different disciplines is self-evident in their chapters. Apparently, the curricula are gradually moving away from subject- or content-centered approaches. Instead, increasing emphases have been placed on non-content components, that is, essential competence for 21st century skills, such as metacognitive awareness, affect, self-confidence, self-concept, and team-building. As can be seen from the chapters discussed above, a number of curricula have been re-conceptualized to include knowledge-centered, learner-centered, community-centered, and assessment-centered approach (Bransford et al., 1999; Collins, Brown, & Newman, 1987). These curricula take into consideration both competence development as well as the arts, design and the humanities.

STEAM Education: Moving Forward

Although STEAM education is not a novel concept, it has been reexamined in recent years in the context of promoting 21st century skills and the digital age of technology-rich learning environments. The research in this area has been somewhat limited. We have found many assumptions but a lack of empirical studies in the research reported herein and elsewhere. There is not a lot of empirical research to support any of the themes associated with STEAM education, and much territory remains to be explored and charted. We need more empirical evidence to support assumptions and hypotheses if systematic and sustained progress in learning and instruction is expected. Based on our literature review and the scholarly work contributed by the authors of this book, we have identified a number of areas that need to be focused on as we move forward with research, development and practice in the broad area of STEAM education.

First of all, we need more research and empirical evidence to help us understand the architecture of cognition and the relationships between the Arts and various STEM domain areas (Anderson, 1983). Particularly, we need to draw upon the research evidence from cognitive psychology, educational technology, instructional design and neuroscience to help us understand the interrelationships in language ability, Arts education, and the progressive development of knowledge and ability in science, mathematics, and engineering. We hope that research in these areas, especially in neuroscience concerning how the human brain works in various learning and performance situations, will help to explain or confirm assumptions people have about the mutual benefits of learning Arts and STEM and provide insight to how critical thinking, creative problem-solving, innovation are developed over time. Empirical evidence will also help to inform not only educators and researchers, but also policymakers, administrators, curriculum developers, and instructional designers about the importance of Arts and integration of Arts in school curricula.

A couple of chapters in this book (e.g., Chapter "Reconceptualizing a College Science Learning Experience in the New Digital Era: A Review of Literature" and Chapter "The Potential of Embodied Cognition to Improve Steam Instructional Dynamic Visualizations") discuss the use of visualization tools or providing dynamic modeling to facilitate students' articulation, argumentation, problem representation, and communication, as means to develop students' scientific understanding and reasoning, as well as critical thinking and problem solving in other areas. We need to continue this line of research in the context of STEAM education, tapping the potential of technology as cognitive tools to support the development of 21st century skills, for the purpose of either competence-based education or humanity education. Jonassen and Carr (2000) categorized cognitive tools into various types to support multiple knowledge representations, such as visualization tools, dynamic modeling tools, semantic organization tools, and socially shared cognitive tools. Our research needs to continue to examine the impact of these various *mindtools* on STEAM education, for example, the cognitive and metacognitive functions of each type of tools, and in what ways, under what conditions, and during which learning processes each tool provides support for knowledge representation, argumentation, problem solving, and metacognitive processes (Camilla & Cooper, 2014).

We also need various types of research, including quantitative studies, qualitative studies, design-based research, and program evaluation to investigate and evaluate the impact of various STEAM education curricula and learning environments, as well as the effectiveness of instructional approaches and strategies (Merrill, 2013). It is also desirable to conduct longitudinal studies to gain an in-depth understanding of the impact of STEAM education on students' 21st century skill development, such as measuring learners' mental models at different times in their learning experiences and job careers (Ifenthaler, 2014; Ifenthaler & Seel, 2011, 2013).

Furthermore, either for the purpose of understanding the impact of STEAM education on students' competence acquirement and skill development, or examining students' attitude and affect in becoming well-rounded individuals, either short-term or long-term, we cannot go without conducting research in developing and validating effective instruments. We need to have strong, robust and validated measurements to assess students' cognitive and metacognitive gains in order to understand the effects of STEAM education (Ifenthaler, Pirnay-Dummer, & Seel, 2010).

As an educational research community, we need to continue to use research-based evidence to inform policymakers and administrators about the importance of STEAM education to prepare all students for the challenges of work, life, and citizenship in the 21st century and beyond. Additionally, we need to continue the dialogue about how to strike a balance between competence-based education and well-rounded education, as well as how to develop and implement STEAM curriculum that reflects that balance. As implied by 21st century skills, education is not all about pursuing economic benefits and job careers, but also to grow future leaders, responsible citizens, and innovative creators of the society. In order to help our students to achieve the goals laid out in the 21st century skills, we need to move away from the test-driven curricula and promote 21st century learning through STEAM education.

Conclusion

This book consists of a great collection of scholarly works or practice from the fields illustrating the current state of STEAM education practice and research. We have learned a lot from the multiple perspectives, various experiences, and research findings contributed by the authors in the process of editing this volume. We realize that even though people use the term "STEAM," their interpretations, perspectives, and intentions can be different. Regardless, contributors share common goals and aspirations of helping students reach 21st century skills through STEAM education. Throughout this book, we can see that educational researchers and practitioners have been making efforts to research STEAM education, design and develop STEAM curricula, and integrate technology to support STEAM learning environments. Meanwhile, we also notice that there is a lack of empirical research in STEAM education, and there are more assumptions than empirically-tested theories and scientific evidence in this book. Thus, we have identified the areas that need to be worked on as we move forward. We understand that we need to work not only with educators and researchers, but also policymakers, administrators, curriculum developers, and instructional designers if we want to promote STEAM education and affect changes focusing on 21st century skills. It takes effort and time for the change to take effect. We hope this book serves to start the conversation on STEAM education toward that effort.

References

Anderson, J. R. (1983). *The architecture of cognition*. Cambridge: Harvard University Press.
Bransford, J. D., Brown, A. L., & Cocking, R. R. (Eds.). (1999). *How people learn: Brain, mind, experience and school*. Washington, D. C.: National Academy Press.
Camilla, F., & Cooper, M. (2014). An introduction and guide to evaluation of visualization techniques through user studies. In W. Huang (Ed.), *Handbook of human centric visualization* (pp. 285–313). New York: Springer.
Collins, A., Brown, J. S., & Newman, S. E. (1987). *Cognitive apprenticeship: Teaching the craft of reading, writing and mathematics* [Technical Report No. 403]. Cambridge: BBN Laboratories.

Fitzpatrick, K. R. (2006). The effect of instrumental music participation and socioeconomic status on Ohio fourth-, sixth-, and ninth-grade proficiency test performance. *Journal of Research in Music Education, 54*(1), 73–84.

Haley, J. A. (2001). The relationship between instrumental music instruction and academic achievement in fourth grade students. Retrieved from ProQuest Digital Dissertations. (AAT 3026550).

Ifenthaler, D. (2014). Toward automated computer-based visualization and assessment of team-based performance. *Journal of Educational Psychology, 106*(3), 651–665. doi:10.1037/a0035505.

Ifenthaler, D., & Seel, N. M. (2011). A longitudinal perspective on inductive reasoning tasks. Illuminating the probability of change. *Learning and Instruction, 21*(4), 538–549. doi:10.1016/j.learninstruc.2010.08.004.

Ifenthaler, D., & Seel, N. M. (2013). Model-based reasoning. *Computers & Education, 64*, 131–142. doi:10.1016/j.compedu.2012.11.014.

Ifenthaler, D., Pirnay-Dummer, P., & Seel, N. M. (Eds.). (2010). *Computer-based diagnostics and systematic analysis of knowledge*. New York: Springer.

Johnson, C. M., & Memmott, J. E. (2006). Examination of relationships between participation in school music programs of differing quality and standardized test results. *Journal of Research in Music Education, 54*(4), 293.

Jonassen, D. H., & Carr, C. S. (2000). Mindtools: Affording multiple knowledge representations for learning. In S. P. Lajoie (Ed.), *Computers as cognitive tools: No more walls* (Vol. 2, pp. 165–196). Mahwah: Lawrence Erlbaum Associates.

Merrill, M. D. (2013). First principles of instruction: Identifying and designing effective, efficient and engaging instruction. San Francisco: Wiley.

Rinne, L., Gregory, E., Yarmolinskaya, J., & Hardiman, M. (2011). Why arts integration improves long-term retention of content. *Mind, Brain, and Education, 5*(2), 89–96. doi:10.1111/j.1751-228X.2011.01114.x.

Sousa, D. A., & Pilecki, T. (2013). *From STEM to STEAM: Using brain-compatible strategies to integrate the arts*. Thousand Oaks: Corwin Press.

Xun Ge is Professor of Instructional Psychology and Technology and Chair of the Department of Educational Psychology, Jeannine Rainbolt College of Education, the University of Oklahoma. She holds a Ph.D. in Instructional Systems from the Pennsylvania State University. Dr. Ge's primary research interest involves scaffolding students' complex and ill-structured problem solving and self-regulated learning through designing instructional scaffolds, cognitive tools, learning technologies, and open learning environments (including virtual learning community, game-based learning, inquiry-based learning, and problem- based learning). Over the past years, her scholarly works has evolved to link cognition to motivation. Dr. Ge is also interested in studying the impact and assessment of game-based learning in supporting complex, ill-structured problem solving. Dr. Ge has extensive research experience in STEM education, and she has collaborated with scholars from diverse disciplines around the world. Dr. Ge's research has been published in a co-edited book published by Springer, multiple book chapters in some highly regarded books, and numerous articles in many leading journals of the field, not to mention many other conference proceeding papers. Dr. Ge has been recognized for three prestigious awards she has received—*2012 Outstanding Journal Article, 2004 Outstanding Journal Article,* and *2003 Young Scholar Award granted* by *Educational Technology Research & Development* and the American Educational Communications and Technology.

Dirk Ifenthaler is Professor for Instructional Design and Technology at the University of Mannheim, Germany as well as an Adjunct Professor at Deakin University, Melbourne, Australia. His previous roles include Professor and Director, Centre for Research in Digital Learning at Deakin University, Australia, Manager of Applied Research and Learning Analytics at Open Universities Australia, and Professor for Applied Teaching and Learning Research at the University of Potsdam, Germany. Dirk was a 2012 Fulbright Scholar-in-Residence at the Jeannine Rainbolt College of Education, at the University of Oklahoma, USA. Professor Ifenthaler's research focuses on the intersection of cognitive psychology, educational technology, learning science, data analytics, and computer science. He developed automated and computer-based methodologies for the assessment, analysis, and feedback of graphical and natural language representations, as well as simulation and game environments for teacher education. His research outcomes include numerous co-authored books, book series, book chapters, journal articles, and international conference papers, as well as successful grant funding in Australia, Germany, and USA—see Dirk's website for a full list of scholarly outcomes at www.ifenthaler.info. Professor Ifenthaler is the Editor-in-Chief of the Springer journal *Technology, Knowledge and Learning* (www.springer.com/10758). Dirk is the Past-President for the AECT Design and Development Division, 2013–2015 Chair for the AERA Special Interest Group Technology, Instruction, Cognition and Learning and Co-Program Chair for the international conference on Cognition and Exploratory Learning in the Digital Age (CELDA).

J. Michael Spector is a Professor of Learning Technologies at the University of North Texas. Previously he was a Professor of Educational Psychology and Instructional Technology at the Learning and Performance Support Laboratory at the University of Georgia, Associate Director of the Learning Systems Institute at Florida State University, and Chair of Instructional Design, Development and Evaluation at Syracuse University. Prior to that, he was Director of the Educational Information Science and Technology Research Program at the University of Bergen, and the Senior Scientist for Instructional Systems Research at Armstrong Laboratory. He earned a Ph.D. in Philosophy from The University of Texas at Austin. His research focuses on intelligent support for instructional design, assessing learning in complex domains, and technology integration in education. Dr. Spector served on the International Board of Standards for Training, Performance and Instruction (*ibstpi*). He is a Past-President of the Association for Educational and Communications Technology and a Past-Chair of the Technology, Instruction, Cognition and Learning Special Interest Group of AERA. He is editor of *Educational Technology Research & Development* and edited the third and fourth editions of the *Handbook of Research on Educational Communications and Technology*, as well as the *Encyclopedia of Educational Technology*.

Author Index

Subject Index

© Springer International Publishing Switzerland 2015

409

X. Ge et al. (eds.), *Emerging Technologies for STEAM Education,*
Educational Communications and Technology: Issues and Innovations,
DOI 10.1007/978-3-319-02573-5